THE ENCYCLOPEDIA OF POLITICS AND RELIGION

THE ENCYCLOPEDIA OF POLITICS AND RELIGION

Robert Wuthnow, *Editor in Chief*

VOLUME II

Congressional Quarterly Inc.
Washington, D.C.

1414 22nd Street, N.W., Washington, D.C. 20037

Published in the United Kingdom by Routledge
11 New Fetter Lane, London EC4P 4EE

Book design and production by Kachergis Book Design,
Pittsboro, North Carolina

Printed and bound in the United States of America

The paper used in this publication meets the minimum requirements of the American National Standard for Information Sciences—Permanence of Paper for Printed Library Materials, ANSI Z39.48-1984.

LIBRARY OF CONGRESS CATALOGING-IN-PUBLICATION DATA
Encyclopedia of politics and religion / Robert Wuthnow,
editor in chief.
p. cm.
Includes bibliographical references (p.) and indexes.
ISBN 1-56802-164-X (set : alk. paper).
ISBN 1-56802-162-3 (v. 1 : alk. paper).
ISBN 1-56802-163-1 (v. 2 : alk. paper)
1. Religion and politics—Encyclopedias. I. Wuthnow, Robert.
BL65.P7E53 1998
322'.1'03—dc21 98-29879

About the Editors

EDITOR IN CHIEF

ROBERT WUTHNOW is the Gerhard R. Andlinger Professor of Social Sciences, director of the Center for the Study of American Religion, and professor of sociology at Princeton University. He received a Ph.D. from the University of California, Berkeley. He is the author or editor of many articles and books, including *God and Mammon in America; Christianity in the 21st Century: Reflections on the Challenges Ahead,* winner of the 1994 Critics Choice Book Award in Contemporary Issues from *Christianity Today* magazine; *Acts of Compassion: Caring for Others and Helping Ourselves,* nominated for the Pulitzer Prize and the National Book Award; and *Communities of Discourse: Ideology and Social Structure in the Reformation, the Enlightenment, and European Socialism,* winner of the 1990 Distinguished Book Award from the Society for the Scientific Study of Religion.

EDITORIAL BOARD

JAMES A. BECKFORD is professor of sociology at the University of Warwick. He received a Ph.D. from the University of Reading. He is a former president of the Association for the Sociology of Religion, president-elect of the International Society for the Sociology of Religion, and the author of several articles, book chapters, and books, including *Secularization, Rationalism and Sectarianism, Religion and Advanced Industrial Society,* and *The Changing Face of Religion* (with Thomas Luckmann).

L. CARL BROWN is the Garrett Professor in Foreign Affairs Emeritus at Princeton University. He received a Ph.D. from Harvard University. A former president of the Middle East Studies Association, he is the author or editor of many publications, including *Imperial Legacy: The Ottoman Imprint on the Balkans and the Middle East, The Modernization of the Ottoman Empire and Its Afro-Asian Successors* (with Cyril E. Black), and *Centerstage: American Diplomacy since World War II.*

KAREN E. FIELDS is professor in the Department of Religion and Classics at the University of Rochester and institute associate at the Frederick Douglass Institute for African and African-American Studies. She received a Ph.D. from Brandeis University. She is the author of several articles, reviews, and books, including *Revival and Rebellion in Colonial Africa,* a translation of Emile Durkheim's *Les Formes élémentaires de la vie religieuse,* and *Lemon Swamp and Other Places: A Carolina Memoir* (with Mamie Garvin Fields).

CHARLES F. KEYES is professor in the Department of Anthropology at the University of Washington and director of the Northwest Regional Consortium for Southeast Asian Studies. He received a Ph.D. from Cornell University. He has published numerous articles, reviews, and books, including *Asian Visions of Authority: Religion and the Modern States of East and Southeast Asia* (with Helen Hardacre and Laurel Kendall), *Southeast Asian Studies in the Balance: Reflections from America* (with Charles Hirschman and Karl Hutterer), and *Reshaping Local Worlds: Rural Education and Cultural Change in Southeast Asia.*

DANIEL H. LEVINE is professor in the Department of Political Science at the University of Michigan. He received a Ph.D. from Yale University. He is the author of *Constructing Culture and Power in Latin America* and *Popular Voices in Latin American Catholicism (Voces Populares en el Catolicismo Latinoamericano),* as well as several articles, book chapters, and reviews.

LAMIN SANNEH is the D. Willis James Professor of Missions and World Christianity and a professor of history at Yale University. He received a Ph.D. from the University of London. He is an editor-at-large of *The Christian Century* and has written several articles and books, including *The Crown and the Turban: Muslims and West African Pluralism, Encountering the West: Christianity and the Global Cultural Process: The African Dimension,* and *West African Christianity: The Religious Impact.*

KENNETH D. WALD is professor in the Department of Political Science at the University of Florida. He received a Ph.D. from Washington University. Among his many articles, reviews, and books are *Private Lives, Public Conflicts: Battles over Gay Rights in American Communities* (with James W. Button and Barbara A. Rienzo), *Religion and Politics in the United States,* and *Crosses on the Ballot: Patterns of British Voter Alignment Since 1885.*

Contents

VOLUME I

VOLUME II

List of Appendix Materials

Documents on Politics and Religion

Selected Readings

Reference Materials

List of Appendix Materials

Documents on Politics and Religion

Selected Readings

Reference Materials

K

Kenya

In the British colony of Kenya, East Africa, Mau Mau, a secret anticolonial movement, emerged after World War II, reflecting both the political frustration of mass nationalism in a white settler colony and religious transition within an African people. Originating in the Kikuyu tribe, Mau Mau called not only for the expulsion of the British from Kenya but also for a return to ancient African customs.

While Mau Mau did not drive the British out of Kenya, it did make white supremacy untenable. The British had to allow Africans a greater share in colonial power as a condition for isolating and then suppressing Mau Mau. More bleakly, the movement's narrow character suggested that broad-based nationalism, such as that likely to sustain liberal governance, was not always a natural successor to colonial rule.

The movement's African opponents apparently coined the name Mau Mau, onomatopoeia for "greedy eaters" and a comment on the fees its activists charged for swearing in new recruits, often forcibly. The movement called itself, among other things, "land and freedom," an ambiguous statement of purpose. The promised land was that farmed since before 1914 by British settlers. But reallocation of the land was open to question—whether by political patronage or by the labor right won by the African families who had worked on the land for two generations. Freedom was equally contradictory. Leaders wanted power. Members aspired to the private achievement of morally responsible adulthood. This presupposed land of one's own on which to labor independently, to honor God and the ancestors, and to provide for a posterity. Mau Mau adhered to a peasant rather than a nationalist ideology.

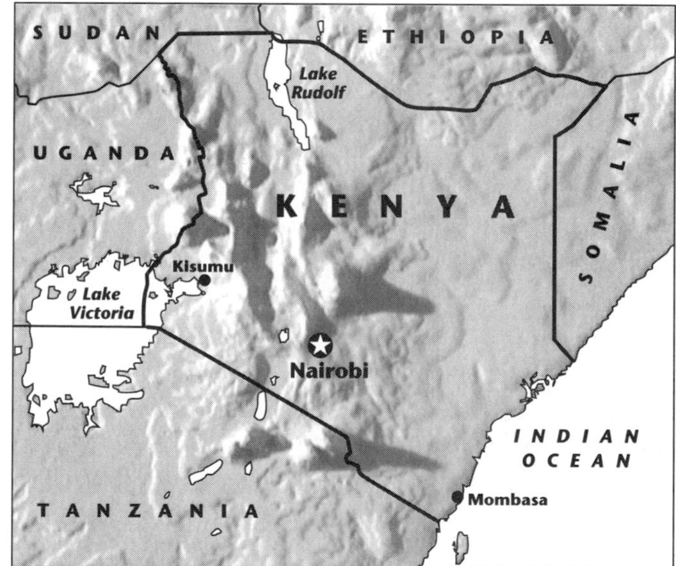

In 1952 the British, fearing a Mau Mau–led uprising, declared a state of emergency in Kenya. In the ensuing guerrilla war Mau Mau killed two thousand people, almost all of them Africans, and lost six times that number of its own. Eighty thousand people, 10 percent of them women, were detained, subject to proof of moral rehabilitation as a condition of release. The British took four years to win the war (the state of emergency was lifted in 1960); the decisive blow was to break the guerrillas' supply train, often their mothers and sisters, by concentrating the affected population into strategic villages.

Indeed, it was Mau Mau's resilience that forced the British government, against convention, to intervene in local colonial politics. The emergency cost £55 million, a burden the British treasury shared with the colonial government. Moreover, British regiments reinforced African troops. London told Kenya's sixty thousand whites that it, in effect, could no longer afford their dominance; they must gamble on African nationalism instead. But until independence in 1963 the British tried to mold that nationalism, to distance the new state from any Mau Mau legacy. Most whites and many Africans still considered Mau Mau to be a reactionary tribal antithesis to a modern national consciousness.

Political and Social Dynamics

Mau Mau developed within the Kikuyu, Kenya's largest ethnic group. Although the movement gained few adherents from Kenya's other African peoples, it was scarcely "tribal," even if it also called itself "Gikuyu and Muumbi," the Kikuyu Abraham and Sarah. Rather, Mau Mau divided the Kikuyu, and when the British armed Mau Mau's internal resistance, the equally anticolonial "loyalists," the emergency turned into a Kikuyu civil war. But internecine murder also reflected the moral impact of new social divisions between propertied and landless, literate and illiterate, junior official and unskilled laborer. While precolonial Africa had never been egalitarian save in nationalist myth, these new inequalities were more troubling because they were more intimate when experienced within ethnic groups than among them.

The Kikuyu suffered these divisions more deeply than other groups. Thus when open agitation failed to dent white supremacy, they alone took up the covert, potentially violent alternative. For the Kikuyu, more than for the other tribes, militant nationalism jostled with potentially treasonable factionalism. The latter could be quashed only by strong, arguably illicit, means, not by debate. Colonial rule had pulled Kikuyu apart with its normal combination of threat and opportunity but to an unusual degree. Many had lost land not only to white settlers but also to their neighbors and had nothing to sell but cheap labor. The literates exercised clerical power over others; the propertied exploited urban food and housing markets. All had equal, but opposite, causes for political action: despair or ambition. Such divisions first stimulated but then crippled Mau Mau, possibly more effectively than British arms.

The movement's rural, land-owning leaders perhaps never intended violence; they limited their followers to male household heads whose domestic prosperity proved their public seriousness. But other Mau Mau emerged among the landless laborers on white farms and in the slums of the Kenyan capital, Nairobi. In many localities the edge of discontent was sharpened by young men already disciplined in the use of force, war veterans who had returned from North Africa and Southeast Asia. These popular Mau Mau, in turn, enrolled unmarried men and even women in the movement—people who in peasant ideology ought not to be entrusted with authority. Ultimately, the several wings came together in competition rather than under central control in their shared need for loyal secrecy in the face of internal opposition and, beginning in 1950, the British ban on Mau Mau.

Religious Domain

What made Mau Mau notorious at the time of its ascendancy and an interpretive challenge now was its alleged depravity. This characteristic was not just a figment of colonial propaganda; Mau Mau's opponents, black and white, were repelled by its seemingly demonic drive.

Many observers on both sides saw the emergency as a war of religion. The British generally believed in their civilizing mission: Africa needed them. Their Christian heritage and Africa's thirst for progress were their joint title to rule. In the late nineteenth century the Victorian navy had brought British power to East Africa's shores in a crusade against slave exports to the Islamic world. And the British empire recently had stood alone against Nazi racism. Moreover, it continued to liberate peoples from blind tradition while communism was enslaving others to an idolatrous atheism. The British governor regularly addressed Kenya's Anglican church synod in the words of a believer. Missionaries saw colonial rule, for all its selfish faults, as the appointed protector of their evangelistic calling. Christianity, they believed, promised hope to Africans whose lives were otherwise terrorized by malevolent spirits from which their high god was too remote to protect them.

Given this sense of purpose, many whites thought Mau Mau must be anti-Christian; indeed, Africans did not so much resent colonialism as fall into a psychical derangement at their inability to meet the personal demands of Christian civilization. But not all whites thought alike. Officials stuck to a political explanation: that self-interested leaders, suspected Mau Mau leader Jomo Kenyatta at their head, had goaded the inherited inertia of African poverty into utopian demands on progressive British vigor. Settlers tended to blame a savage superstition.

Missionaries saw a war of the gods, situating Mau Mau within a local Christian teleology. It was the second challenge to the young Kikuyu churches; the first crisis had struck in 1929 when some missions banned the practice of clitoridectomy among Christians. Presbyterians had led the attack, Anglicans equivocated, and Catholics abstained in an issue they thought inessential to faith. To Kikuyu women as well as men the surgery was crucial to the initiation rite that raised a girl into a woman, fit for married authority. Whites thought it mutilated womanhood and made childbirth dangerous. Mau Mau seemed determined to revert to such barbarism.

Kikuyu Christians had split after 1929. Some founded independent churches and schools in the belief that enlightenment should not belittle culture. The rump of the European missions soon more than regained their numbers and continued to grow into African churches. A decade later they were fired by the East African "revival" movement, which converted many from conformity to faith. Revival challenged mission authority with the priesthood of all "saved" believers. Yet it brought not schism but brotherhood, emptying white priests of pride and Africans of resentment. In missionary eyes this Christian promise of racial harmony posed a direct threat to the ethnic nationalism of the independent schools. Leading the counterattack was Mau Mau, a revival of traditional belief in Christian clothes. Its hymns were blasphemous parodies, substituting Jomo Kenyatta for Jesus Christ (Jesu Kristo). A bishop thought it the devil's work, "the 'black mass' of Kikuyuism." It was this drama of redemption in danger that threw the missions into the work of rehabilitation behind the detention camps' wire.

For others among Kenya's whites, no more religious than other modern Europeans, Mau Mau's real horror was its oaths of initiation, sworn on soil, vegetable matter, and the blood of goats. The seemingly bestial nature of the oaths was held to turn Mau Mau members into Kikuyu outcasts, murderous fanatics, held together by black magic.

The Kikuyu knew their political and legal oaths were dangerous, but the oaths made Mau Mau effective. They insulated the morality of mutual human commitment, under the rational judgment of God, from the human envy transmitted by sorcery. But the legitimacy or risk of the oaths depended on the authority of whoever administrated them in relation to his guardianship of the land on which they were sworn. In 1952 many Kikuyu elders felt that too many Mau Mau recruiters were swearing in members with whom they shared no close land affinity. But the elders also acknowledged that the great evil of colonial rule might justify otherwise doubtful measures. Kikuyu worried about their oaths with more knowledge than whites. Some Mau Mau oaths—those rumored to involve human blood and therefore sorcery—were certainly beyond the pale.

But did Mau Mau threaten the young Kikuyu Christians? There is no simple answer. Only 15 percent of Kikuyu were thought to be Christian at the time. Of those, 90 percent of Protestant church members fell away and took the goat oath, a betrayal of Christ's sacrifice. The Protestant missionaries saw the emergency as a time of martyrdom and erected a memorial church to the scores of Christians who died for their faith. Those who died were mostly revivalists who rejected the oath. But they also were suspect to the British because they refused to bear arms, protected as they were by "the blood of the Lamb." Conversely, some of the staunchest "loyalists" were traditional believers. On the other side, some guerrilla leaders took their Bibles into the forests and deplored the faith that rival leaders placed in traditional prophets. Most Kikuyu, on both sides of the war and on neither, lived in multifaith households. If it was a war of religion, both sides were to some extent at war with themselves. Indeed, there is evidence that concern for the peace of local clan land, where the peace had not already been destroyed by long histories of dispute, demanded religious toleration. When independent churches were closed at the outset of the emergency, their congregations were, with few exceptions, taken in by the local mission churches; they reseparated relatively easily when the emergency ended.

Mau Mau was a political project that emerged at a particular moment in religious transition. The demand for loyalty at a time of danger raised urgent questions about moral courage and its obverse, the evil that corrupts unity of purpose. It appears that in the 1950s most Kikuyu felt they had to protect themselves, in the oath, against the sorcery that land rivalry and political jealousy still used as a tool. Their "High God," whether traditional or Christian, was impotently above the operation of such evil forces unless Christ had come into their life through revival.

But today Kenyans apparently believe God to be more powerful than forty years ago. Fifteen percent of Kikuyu were Christian in 1952; ten years later 60 percent claimed to be; in 1972 three-quarters. Other agricultural people of Kenya call themselves more completely Christian. As Christian symbols have become more universal and the Christian faith has become perhaps too political, evil has come to be associated not with sorcery but with the devil. Mau Mau came at an earlier stage in this widening of religious consciousness; the Kikuyu need for peace may well have accelerated it. Political unity otherwise faced too narrow an insistence that authority lay with senior landowners of the clan and where their watchful ancestors slept.

See also *Africa, Christian; African independent churches; African traditional religions; Anglicanism; Catholicism, Roman; Colonialism; Ethnicity; Witchcraft.*

John M. Lonsdale

BIBLIOGRAPHY

Barnett, Donald L., and Karari Njama. *Mau Mau from Within: Autobiography and Analysis of Kenya's Peasant Revolt.* London: McGibbon and Kee, 1966.

Berman, Bruce B., and John M. Lonsdale. *Unhappy Valley: Conflict in Kenya and Africa.* London: James Currey; Athens: Ohio University Press, 1992.

Kanogo, Tabitha. *Squatters and the Roots of Mau Mau.* London: James Currey; Athens: Ohio University Press, 1987.

Kershaw, Greet. *Mau Mau from Below.* Oxford: James Currey; Athens: Ohio University Press, 1997.

Maloba, Wunyabari O. *Mau Mau and Kenya: An Analysis of a Peasant Revolt.* Bloomington: Indiana University Press, 1993.

Rosberg, Carl G., and John Nottingham. *The Myth of "Mau Mau": Nationalism in Kenya.* New York: Praeger; London: Pall Mall Press, 1966.

Smoker, Dorothy W., ed. *Ambushed by Love: God's Triumph in Kenya's Terror.* Fort Washington, Pa.: Christian Literature Crusade, 1994.

Throup, David W. *Economic and Social Origins of Mau Mau.* London: James Currey; Athens: Ohio University Press, 1987.

Khomeini, Ruholla Musavi

Shiʿite Muslim clergyman who led the Iranian revolution, in 1978–1979, that toppled the monarchy and led to the establishment of Iran as an Islamic state. Some Iranians believed that Khomeini (1902–1989) was the *imam,* or incarnation of the salvational leader in Shiʿite doctrine who would establish justice on Earth.

Khomeini was the son and grandson of clergymen. His father was murdered when he was five months old, and his mother died when he was sixteen. After distinguishing himself at the mosque-university of Qum, south of Tehran, where he began study in 1921, he graduated from the highest level of seminary studies. This achievement entitled him to issue authoritative opinions in matters of Islamic law, and he became a *mujtahid,* a rank near the top of the religious hierarchy.

For twenty years Khomeini devoted himself to the study and teaching of ethics and theosophy, a blend of mysticism and philosophy. The modernizing policies of the monarch, Reza Shah Pahlavi, however, had alienated the clergy. In 1941 Britain and the Soviet Union forced the shah to abdicate on grounds that he harbored pro-German sympathies. At the time of the shah's abdication, Khomeini wrote a political work, *Revealing the Secrets,* that condemned the regime's commitment to Westernization and secularization. In this book he demanded that rulers consult with the Islamic jurists and argued that Iran's problems—autocratic rule, corruption, economic inequality, and social injustice—were due mainly to the failure of its governments to abide by this practice. In taking this line, Khomeini implied that he would support secular rule if the government ruled with justice.

Khomeini then reverted to his earlier apolitical preoccupation with Islamic ethics and theosophy, and little is known about his political beliefs until 1962. Undoubtedly, he came under the sway of Sayyid Muhammad Husayn Burujirdi, Qum's outstanding leader from 1947 until his death in 1962. Burujirdi admonished the clergy to stay out of politics, advice that Khomeini appears to have taken.

Activism and Exile

In 1962 Khomeini, now referred to as Ayatollah ("sign of God"), again took up the cudgels to attack the policies of the ruling monarch, Muhammad Reza Pahlavi, the son of Reza Shah. Khomeini's protests were centered on the shah's reform measures, known as the "White Revolution," which included land reform and enfranchisement of women. The shah's regime depicted Khomeini's opposition to this program, and that of the Iranian clergy in general, as reactionary. The rhetoric, however, ignored the fact that for many clergymen, and indeed for many in the secular opposition, the White Revolution did not aim at true reform of the country's ills but instead was a patent effort by the shah and his supporters to augment their political and economic power.

Khomeini bluntly challenged the shah in a series of dramatic speeches that led to his arrest on several occasions and nearly to his execution. Ultimately, caution prevailed and the shah backed off because Khomeini by then had advanced to the highest clerical rank—*marja'-i taqlid* ("source of imitation"). Faced with the prospect of widespread social unrest that his martyrdom surely would have caused, the government expelled Khomeini from Iran in October 1964. He settled in Najaf, south of Iraq's capital, Baghdad, and the burial site of the first Shi'ite *imam*.

This period of exile was a critical factor in the downfall of the shah. Khomeini was able to draw on his position as one of Shi'ite Islam's most powerful leaders and his presence in the holiest Shi'ite city to mobilize increasing popular protest against the shah. His message during the time of his exile, which lasted until 1979, was that the shah's government was corrupt, that Iranian rulers had enriched themselves at the expense of the Iranian people, and that the country's pro-Americanism had converted it into a client state of a Western power that was intent on undermining Islam.

As broad-based social protest mounted in Iran, Khomeini continued to denounce the Pahlavi state. He wrote a series of lectures on the authority of the jurist in Islamic society, which were published as a book. In this work, *Islamic Government* (1971), Khomeini insisted that Islamic teachings demanded the fusion of religion and politics. Condemning all ideas and actions that contravened this position, he boldly argued for direct rule by the clergy in contemporary Islamic society. His interpretation of a tenet of Shi'i law known as "the mandate of the jurist" *(wilayat al-faqih)* was a departure from established doctrine. The mainstream interpretation of this doctrine held that the jurist could exercise only certain custodial prerogatives pertaining to the welfare of the disadvantaged—such as managing the affairs of minors, widows, and the mentally and physically impaired. Khomeini, however, sought to convert this principle into an entitlement empowering Muslim jurists to exercise substantive executive authority. Abandoning his earlier willingness to accept enlightened secular rule, he maintained that Islam and secular rule were incompatible.

Ruholla Musavi Khomeini

The Iranian Revolution

The spark that ignited the revolution was a newspaper editorial in January 1978, written by the minister of information, that attacked Khomeini in personal terms. This attack brought immediate protests, starting a chain of events that lasted through the year. Faced with massive numbers of protesters, the shah fled from Iran in January 1979. Khomeini, then in Paris, returned to Tehran on February 1. He established his regime ten days later when the shah's government collapsed.

Khomeini appeared to many as a salvationist leader and accordingly exemplified many of the qualities attributed to charismatic leaders by the German sociologist Max Weber (1864–1920). With strong popular support, he moved swiftly to implement his ideas about Islamic government, brooking little questioning of the Shi'i order that he and his supporters established. His ideas were inscribed into a new constitution, adopted in December 1979. (The preamble refers to Khomeini by name on five occasions.) Khomeini believed that the immediate implementation of Islamic law would provide the dynamic to resolve Iran's pressing social problems.

Khomeini favored radical redistribution of wealth in society, but, realizing that many clergymen did not agree with him, he never fully and unambiguously threw his authority behind this position. Some of the major issues of the revolution thus remained unresolved at the time of his death in 1989. Among these were land reform and the role of the state in the economy. The major foreign policy issues were a confrontation with the United States over seizure of hostages in the U.S. Embassy in 1979 and a border war with Iraq (1980–1988). Relations with the West continue to be strained, though there are signs of improvement.

There is little doubt that Khomeini was the most popular leader in modern Iranian history. Probably his most memorable achievement was to force a reconsideration of the relationship between the religious and temporal spheres in Shi'ite Islam. It remains to be seen whether his forceful merging of these two spheres under clerical rule will prevail as the Iranian revolution moves into its second generation.

See also *Censorship; Fundamentalism; Iran; Islam; Jihad; Weber, Max.*

Shahrough Akhavi

BIBLIOGRAPHY

Arjomand, Said. *The Turban for the Crown.* New York: Oxford University Press, 1988.

Dabashi, Hamid. "Ayatollah Khomeini: The Theologian of Discontent." In *Theology of Discontent: The Ideological Foundation of the Islamic Revolution in Iran,* edited by Hamid Dabashi. New York: New York University Press, 1993.

Fischer, Michael M. J. *Iran: From Religious Dispute to Revolution.* Cambridge: Harvard University Press, 1980.

Khomeini, Ruholla Musavi. *Islam and Revolution: Writings and Declarations of Imam Khomeini.* Translated and edited by Hamid Algar. Berkeley, Calif.: Mizan Press, 1981.

Moin, Baqer. *Khomeini: Sign of God.* London: I. B. Tauris, 1994.

Mottahedeh, Roy P. *"Wilayat al-Faqih."* In vol. 4 of *Encyclopaedia of the Modern Islamic World.* New York: Oxford University Press, 1995.

King, Martin Luther, Jr.

Clergyman and the leader of the American civil rights movement. King (1929–1968) was one of the most important reformers of the twentieth century. Born in Atlanta, Georgia, he was educated at Morehouse College and at Boston University, where he received his Ph.D. and developed his theological views. After a short time spent as pastor of the Dexter Avenue Baptist Church in Montgomery, Alabama, King took up the struggle for the political and social equality of African Americans in the United States.

King's career can be divided into two major periods: the first begins with the bus boycott in Montgomery in 1955 and ends with the march from Selma, Alabama, to Montgomery in 1965. The second period starts with the Selma march and ends with King's assassination in Memphis, Tennessee, in 1968. The early period is shaped primarily by efforts to achieve basic citizenship rights for black Americans. During this phase, with the success of the Montgomery boycott in 1955, the formation of the Southern Christian Leadership Conference in 1957, and the passage of the Civil Rights Act of 1964 and the Voting Rights Act of 1965, King emerged as one of the leading moral voices of the nation. This period also marked the most successful stage of the civil rights movement in that King along with his allies brought about the beginning of the end of Jim Crow, that is, legally sanctioned discrimination against blacks.

The second phase of King's life consisted of volatile transformations in the ideological scope of King's vision and the movement he represented. Within a short span of three months after the Selma march, King began to articulate his vision of radical democracy—focusing primarily on the poor and the powerless—as well as voice an uncharacteristic pessimism about America's moral will to confront the evil of racism and economic oppression. In spite of these shifts, King's vision for and faith in America remained.

The Influence of the Black Church

King's vision and activism were nurtured in the black church, an institution that called forth a black public and provided vocabularies for political argument. The suffering servant, a grace-centered piety, a concern with human fallibility, rituals of conversion, a preoccupation with evil, are all part of black religious life and, consequently, tools in black political life. King's message used these tools and gave voice to the duality at the center of the black religious imagination: sentiments grounded in a dialectic between spirituality and radical secularism, and relief and protest. For King, hard distinctions between one's commitment to the Gospel and one's activism against evil in the world made little sense. All Christians are called to enact the Gospel in their day-to-day lives.

King, like Mahatma Gandhi, believed in the transforma-

Martin Luther King Jr.

tive power of suffering. King argued that knowledge of God was spread to the unbelieving Gentile through the suffering servant, whose suffering was not due to something that he had done but was vicarious and redemptive; those unbelievers would be redeemed by seeing that the suffering servant was innocent and they would thus become conscious of themselves. His wounds would heal the nation.

King likened the struggle for civil rights, then, as one for the soul of America. Racism and poverty were evils that threatened the nation. King's message was one of a turning back to the country's ideals—a recognition of crisis and national decline. But in this crisis he saw possibility. Dangers and opportunities, he believed, which can spell either salvation or doom, reside in every crisis.

The Later Years

Still, the events of the later sixties disturbed him. Racial uprisings exploded in 1965 and consumed the nation for the next three years; the Vietnam War divided America, and his own opposition to the war divided the traditional civil rights leadership, particularly the alliance with white liberals. King increasingly was aware that America was on the verge of destruction, and he felt more strongly than ever a prophetic duty to warn America. But by late 1965 Americans were not so willing to listen to King's social prophecy.

In spite of the success of the civil rights movement, America was still poisoned by racism, a sickness, King noted, as native to the soil as "pine trees, sagebrush and buffalo grass." Besides, the price of change up to this moment had been cheap, King warned, for the cost of desegregating southern rest rooms and lunch counters was very little and required no redistribution of wealth. But the sickness of the nation's soul required structural change. King continued to believe that the spirit of democracy would overcome the evil of racism and economic exploitation. But a genuine transformation had to occur: America had to be born again. This could be achieved only if the nation began to confront its sins honestly.

King spent the last years of his life speaking for and organizing among the poor, the powerless, and the racially downtrodden; his last days were spent among striking black garbage workers. Although many failed to heed his message of love and the power of suffering, King's words remain a part of the nation's political and moral conscience.

See also *African American experience; Civil rights movement; Gandhi, Mohandas Karamchand.*

Eddie S. Glaude Jr.

BIBLIOGRAPHY

Branch, Taylor. *Parting the Waters: America in the King Years, 1954–1963.* New York: Simon and Schuster, 1988.

Garrow, David. *Bearing the Cross: Martin Luther King Jr. and the Southern Christian Leadership Conference, 1955–1968.* New York: Morrow, 1986.

King, Martin Luther. *Stride toward Freedom: A Leader of His People Tells the Montgomery Story.* New York: Harper and Row, 1958.

———. *Where Do We Go from Here: Chaos or Community.* New York: Harper and Row, 1968.

Lewis, David L. *King: A Critical Biography.* New York: Praeger, 1971.

Korea

Korea, a peninsula bordered by China to the north, the Yellow Sea to the west, and the Sea of Japan to the east, has a varied and sometimes contentious religious life. The Strait of Tsushima separates Korea from the Japanese islands of Kyushu and Honshu. Since 1945 the Korean nation has been divided into two separate and mutually hostile polities, the Democratic People's Republic of Korea in the north (North Korea) and the Republic of Korea in the south (South Korea). Historically, Korean religious life was an amalgam of Confucian, Buddhist, and indigenous popular and shamanic traditions. This mixture persists in South Korea today along with Protestant Christianity, Catholicism, indigenous "new religions," and a small Muslim community. The North Korean constitution guarantees freedom of religion, but fragmentary information suggests that religion is ideologically discouraged and there are strong deterrents to religious practice.

Religion and the Confucian State

The premodern Korean state was the moral arbiter of social and ritual life, defining good and wholesome customs as those which, by Confucian measure, fostered the morality and well-being of the people. Korean Neo-Confucians, like their Chinese cousins, saw themselves as restoring the moral order of a lost golden age by establishing proper hierarchical relationships and maintaining social order by encouraging proper behavior, etiquette, and ritual. In the fifteenth century reforming officials in the service of the newly established Choson dynasty (1392–1910) broke the political and economic power of the Buddhist clergy by confiscating monastery lands and banning monks from the capital city. Confucian rituals of the life cycle and commemorations of the dead were to replace Buddhist, shamanic, and popular practices. Shamans were denounced as potential charlatans whose public dancing and bawdy play provoked immorality.

In modern times, during South Korea's three decades of rapid economic development (1960–1990), one heard echoes of the old Confucian state's prerogative as the moral arbiter of custom in policies aimed at reforming weddings, funerals, ancestor veneration, and sixty-first birthday celebrations observing the completion of a full cycle of life. The government's utilitarian insistence on economies of time and money was seen as fostering wholesome customs and a harmonious moral climate.

Although over the course of the Choson dynasty Confucian ethical premises became ubiquitous "Korean values," the Confucian transformation cannot be understood as a religious "conversion" in the Christian or Islamic sense. Buddhist monks and shamans continued to provide a variety of religious services to bring good fortune to the living and aid to the dead. Women, who were responsible for the health, harmony, and prosperity of their households, represented their families' interests at Buddhist temples and shaman shrines.

Korea's foremost Confucian association has recently declared itself to be a "religion." Social conservatives rally round the banner of "Confucianism" in their campaign to preserve the ban on marriages between persons of the same surname hailing from the same lineage. This incest taboo extends to tens of thousands of people. Establishing a Confucian religion may be politically expedient in a polity that recognizes the interests of organized Christians and Buddhists, but it ignores older Korean notions of Confucianism and Buddhism as broadly available "teachings" (*kyo*) rather than mutually exclusive "churches" in the Western sense.

Heterodoxy and Syncretism

In dynastic times, millennial visions and other practices that seemed to violate the premises of Confucian morality implied treason against the state. Early Korean Catholics, practicing in secret, were hunted down and executed in a series of persecutions culminating in 1866. Particularly incendiary were reports that Catholics had destroyed their family ancestor tablets, thus violating the fundamental obligation of sons to honor their fathers and grandfathers across generations of living and dead. In the late nineteenth century, Tonghak, "Eastern Learning," a millennial movement proclaiming the equality of all human beings, became the nucleus of the largest peasant insurrection in Korean history, a reaction against corrupt officialdom and foreign influence.

Officially recognized today, some three hundred to four hundred new religions in South Korea range from tiny sects to large, well-established faiths. Ch'ondogyo, descended from Tonghak, boasts six hundred thousand followers. The Unification Church, a Christian-influenced religion founded in 1954 by Sun Myung Moon (1920–), gained considerable notoriety outside Korea in the 1970s for its zealous missionizing, spectacular dabbling in overseas real estate, and alleged ties to the dictatorial regime of Park Chung Hee (1917–1979). Church adherents, contemptuously called "Moonies," were more visible on the streets of New York and Tokyo than within Korea itself. In recent years Chungsan'gyo, a synthesis of East Asian thought, has gained popularity on university campuses. Many new religions include a strong element of Korean nationalism.

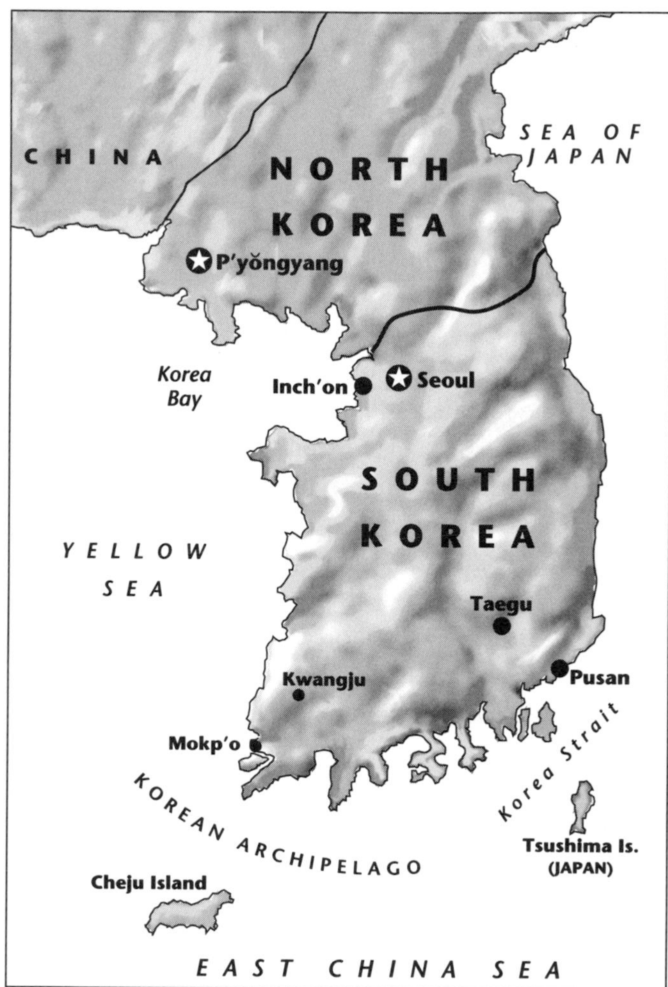

Christianity and the Modern Transformation

Korea's collision with the Western powers and its colonization by the Japanese empire (1910–1945) prompted the emergence of a new class of intellectuals who faulted Korea's traditions—in their judgment, conservative and unenlightened—for the country's weakness and humiliation. Protestant missionaries, mindful of how Catholics, operating in secret, had provoked the state's retribution, entered Korea in the 1890s with official permission, bringing Western-style schools and hospitals, the institutional accoutrements of modernity. Many early Korean progressives marked their rejection of the Korean past by becoming Christians. Because the missionaries were not of the same nation or race as the colonizers, the Christian community gave early nationalists a space where they could define themselves against both a failed tradition and the colonial presence that had supplanted it.

Protestant Christianity claims at least a third of all religiously active Koreans, and Korean missionaries are active abroad. Korean Christians see themselves as having a unique mission to proselytize Christianity within Asia as an Asian church that has weathered the historical tribulations of colonial oppression, national division, civil war, and rapid industrialization.

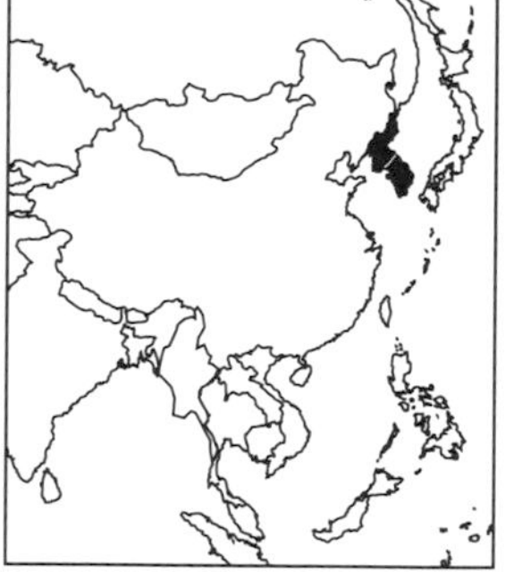

Refugees from the once well established Christian communities in North Korea have been a strong voice for political conservatism and anticommunism since 1945. At the other side of the political spectrum, beginning in the 1970s, liberal Protestants and Catholics became active in challenging the human rights abuses of the Park regime. Church activists addressed the plight of industrial workers and marginalized farmers. Many social activists became adherents of Minjung theology (the theology of the masses), which spoke of the historic suffering of the Korean people and saw shamanic rituals as a means of articulating and expelling grievances (*han*).

Shamans Reviled and Revived

From the end of the nineteenth century, the perceived need to eradicate "superstition" was a tenet of modernity throughout East Asia. Suppressing shamans—as practitioners of bogus medicine and irrational belief—was no less a priority for early Korean nationalists than for their Japanese colonizers. Ironically, this history of suppression by the Japanese is invoked today in revivalist public performances of shaman rituals to enhance their luster as national traditions. In contrast, aging shamans recall that in a newly independent Korea they were routinely harassed by the police. In the 1970s, in the name of national development, the Park regime initiated "antisuperstition" campaigns that were reminiscent of earlier Japanese colonial efforts.

A countertradition, initiated by folklorists during the colonial period, regarded shamans and their rituals as survivals of an ancient cult that predated foreign-derived Buddhist and Confucian influences. In the 1970s, even as the government cracked down on shamans, folklorists under the auspices of the Ministry of Culture and Information zealously recorded their songs and preserved their rituals in the face of industrial transformation. By the 1980s some shamans were subsidized by the government as "national treasures," exemplars of "intangible cultural properties" and icons of Korean identity. Dissidents, influenced by Minjung theology, appropriated the form of shamanic rituals into a theater of protest, where the grievances of the regime's victims could be articulated from beyond the grave.

Despite this romanticization, shamans are subject to a variety of harassments in their day-to-day practice. Noise ordinances curtail their work. Christian neighbors complain to the police. Sacred sites fall victim to urban renewal schemes. Some members of this community suggest that because they lack the clout of an organized "religion," they are unable to defend their own legitimate interests.

Religion in Korea Today

In contemporary South Korea, religious concerns sometimes color political perceptions, but usually as a defensive rather than an aggressive assertion of religious interests. In 1987, when Kim Young Sam ran for president as an opposition candidate, the ruling party is said to have encouraged the laity's fear that Kim, a Christian, would curtail the activities of Buddhist monasteries. When a series of disasters followed Kim's 1992 election, he found it necessary to counter rumors that he had removed an important Buddhist image from the presidential residence. The Christian community, citing historical memories of coerced worship at Shinto shrines during Japan's colonial occupation, has successfully opposed the establishment of national rituals honoring the mythical founder of the Korean nation, Tan'gun. Other religious idioms have been more easily claimed as national heritage: Buddhist temples, Confucian shrines, theatrical performances by shamans designated as national treasures, and the symbology of protest theater. Organized "religion," a relatively recent concept in Korea, asserts itself in a social field where a great many sacred sites and practices are simultaneously reinscribed as expressions of national culture. Contradictions are inevitable.

See also *Christianity in Asia; Confucianism; Unification Church.*

Laurel Kendall

BIBLIOGRAPHY

Clark, Donald N. *Christianity in Modern Korea.* New York: University Press of America for the Asia Society, 1986.

Deuchler, Martina. *The Confucian Transformation of Korea: A Study of Society and Ideology.* Harvard-Yenching Institute Monograph Series, no. 36. Cambridge: Harvard University, Council on East Asian Studies, 1992.

Eckert, Carter J., et al. *Korea Old and New: A History.* Seoul: Ilchokak for the Korea Institute, Harvard University, 1990.

Kendall, Laurel. "A Rite of Modernization and Its Postmodern Discontents: Of Weddings, Bureaucrats, and Morality in the Republic of Korea." In *Asian Visions of Authority: Religion and the Modern States of East and Southeast Asia,* edited by C. F. Keyes, Laurel Kendall, and Helen Hardacre. Honolulu: University of Hawaii Press, 1994.

Kim, Kwang-ok. "Rituals of Resistance: The Manipulation of Shamanism in Contemporary Korea." In *Asian Visions of Authority: Religion and the Modern States of East and Southeast Asia,* edited by C. F. Keyes, Laurel Kendall, and Helen Hardacre. Honolulu: University of Hawaii Press, 1994.

Korea Foundation. *Korean Cultural Heritage.* Vol. 2, *Thought and Religion.* Seoul: Korea Foundation, 1996.

Kurds

The Kurds are an ancient people who inhabit a large area in western Iran, northeastern Iraq, and southeastern Turkey. Significant populations also reside in Armenia, Azerbaijan, and Syria. They are generally believed to number about 3.5 million to 4 million in Iraq, 7 million to 8 million in Iran, and 14 million to 16 million in Turkey.

Many theories exist concerning the origins of the Kurds.

One claim stipulates that the Kurds are Indo-Europeans, primarily of Mede and Iranian origins. An alternate theory suggests that they originate from the Caucasus and are related to the Armenians and Georgians. It is believed that their original language resembled that of the Georgians but changed with Iranian and Armenian influence and later on with Aramaic and Arabic.

The Kurds, like most people of the area, are a racial mixture, owing to migrations, invasions, and domination by various groups such as Arabs, Armenians, Assyrians, Chaldeans, Greeks, Kassites, Persians, and Turks. From ancient records we get a picture of a proud and tough people, unresponsive to foreign authority. The Kurds remain a distinct and separate people, perhaps attributable to the remoteness and inaccessibility of their rugged mountainous territory and to their self-sufficient economy, which made communication difficult and reduced the need for contact with outsiders. The Kurds have never possessed an independent political entity. Yet many of the factors that helped to preserve the Kurds' identity have also helped to divide them. In addition, the Kurds in later years were principally divided among three countries—Turkey, Iran, and Iraq. The variety of spoken dialects impeded communication; even in Iraqi Kurdistan the Kurds speak several dialects, varying with the region.

The majority of the Kurds are Sunni Muslims of the Shafiʿi school of law, although there are Shiʿites and heterodox groups such as Ahl al-Haqq (the people of divine truth) and the Yazidis, two syncretistic sects with pre-Islamic influences. Sufi orders such as the Naqshbandiyya and Qadiriyya came to play an important role in Kurdish society.

After World War I Kurdish aspirations for independence were boosted by the Treaty of Sèvres, which recognized the rights of Kurds and Armenians to achieve autonomy and independence provided that the majority of the people sought independence and proved themselves capable of governing. Kurdish hopes were dashed in 1923 by the emergence of Mustafa Kemal (later called Atatürk) as the first president of the Republic of Turkey and by the signing of the Treaty of Lausanne, which dropped any reference to the Kurds by name. Atatürk's abolition of the sultanate-caliphate and his emphasis on secular and Turkish nationalism were anathema to most Kurds.

The Kurds have made attempts at dialogue with national governments of the countries they inhabit, with international bodies, and within the Kurdish community itself. They have also traveled the road of violent struggle. The Kurds have not, however, presented a unified community with an organized program for action but instead one that has been torn apart by the contact of feudalism, tribalism, religion, and ideology with urbanization, modernization, and other upheavals. The other parties of the dialogue, including Britain, France, Russia, and the United States, gave the Kurds little more than verbal and often transitory support. Considering Kurdish uprisings little more than tribal insurgencies, which they were until the 1930s and 1940s, these countries determined their policies toward the Kurds in the light of their own best interests at the moment.

Turkey

Following World War I, the Kurds waged several unsuccessful revolts and uprisings in Turkey. Turkish nationalists, preoccupied with warding off public fears of the country's dismemberment along ethnic and religious lines, pursued policies inimical to Kurdish nationalism. For many years they insisted that the Kurds were only "mountain Turks." Atatürk's attempts to ban the use of Kurdish and to secularize Turkey ran into stiff opposition. Many uprisings occurring in 1925 and 1929 were brutally crushed, resulting in the displacement of a million Kurds and the enactment of martial law.

During the 1960s and early 1980s the restrictions on the Kurds were toughened, leading to new questions about their status, despite some liberalization in Turkish political life. In 1978 a tough and violent Marxist Kurdish Workers Party (PKK) was established and in 1984 it launched a guerrilla war, which has not yet ended. More than 30,000 people have died, mostly Kurds. And more than 3,500 villages and towns in the southeast have been depopulated, leading to the displacement of about 2.5 million to 3 million Kurds.

During the Persian Gulf War in 1991, Turkey slightly modified its hardline position on the Kurds. The law banning the use of Kurdish was repealed, but in reality it remains in effect for publishing, education, and official documents. The PKK expanded its influence into the protected Kurdish zone in northern Iraq after the Gulf War, leading Turkey to intervene militarily with limited success. The repressive Turkish policies increased sympathy for the PKK, which emerged as the most powerful Kurdish movement in Turkey.

Iran

The Kurdish situation in Iran was slightly better than in

Turkey. Several tribal uprisings occurred in the 1920s and 1930s as Reza Shah Pahlavi (1877–1944) sought to weaken the autonomous power of the tribal forces. Kurdish nationalist activity emerged in the 1940s and reached a new level following the entry of the Soviets into northern Iran, where they supported the establishment of the pro-Soviet republic of Azerbaijan.

The Kurdish Democratic Party (KDP) also established the autonomous republic of Mahabad within Azerbaijan. It received military support from Mustafa Barzani, the leader of the Iraqi Kurds. In 1947, Iran, with Western help, reassumed authority and suppressed Kurdish nationalism. Following Mahabad's fall, the shah suppressed all nationalist activities. The shah's conflict with Iraq following the overthrow of the Iraqi monarchy by Abdul Karim Qasim in 1958 led the countries to support each other's dissidents, including the Kurds. The Iranian KDP received support from Iraq until the signing of the Algiers agreement in 1975 between Iran and Iraq. During the Islamic revolution in 1978–1979, Kurdish nationalists mobilized mass support for Kurdish autonomy. Because of the Kurdish Sunni majority, the new regime's Shi'ite orientation served to increase the support. Guerrilla warfare ensued, but the Kurds steadily lost ground and finally moved their bases from inside Iranian Kurdistan to near and inside Iraqi territory.

Iraq

The history of Iraq and the Iraqi Kurds offers an excellent example of the post–World War I period of new divisions, confused boundaries, increased nationalism and new ideologies, and foreign interference. External powers edged the Iraqi Kurds toward autonomy and then suddenly changed policies. Tribal uprisings were encouraged or discouraged, depending on the extent to which they served the political interests of colonial powers and neighboring countries.

Several tribal uprisings erupted in Iraq in the 1920s and 1930s, but most did not begin to take nationalist tones until the 1940s. These uprisings were also quelled and Barzani, the leader of the last uprising, ended up in exile in the Soviet Union. After the 1958 revolution, Qasim, who had become premier of Iraq, allowed Barzani to return. Qasim's policy of wooing the Kurds and his advocacy of Arab-Kurdish partnerships alienated the pan-Arabists without giving satisfaction to Kurdish demands. The growing influence and military independence of Barzani's forces aroused Qasim's suspicions, and when Barzani refused to heed the government's orders, Qasim took a tough stand and accused Kurdish leaders of harboring reactionary and secessionist motives. Barzani established control in the most rugged mountain areas near the borders with Turkey and Iran and waged a tough guerrilla campaign against the government. The rebellion continued on and off with interrupted periods of cease-fires and negotiations until 1968.

When the pan-Arab Ba'th Party returned to power in 1968, its leaders quickly realized they could not afford a continuous preoccupation with the Kurdish problem. Negotiations between Barzani and Saddam Husayn, the vice president of the ruling Revolutionary Council, culminated in a dramatic agreement on March 11, 1970. This agreement brought recognition of the Kurdish identity and admission that the Iraqi people consist of two main nationalities, Arab and Kurdish. Autonomy was promised to the Kurds within four years in those areas where they formed a majority. The Kurdish language was given official status, and Kurds were to be taken into the government according to their numbers in the population. The 1974 Autonomy Law placed internal security, defense, oil, and foreign affairs in the hands of the central government. The law made it clear that the Iraqi government considered the "Kurdistan area" and its people an indivisible part of Iraq.

Disagreements soon arose, however, and distrust replaced early cooperation. By mid-1972, Barzani's forces received pledges of covert assistance from Iran, Israel, and the United States. Intermittent negotiations were conducted but to no avail.

Encouraged by promises of foreign assistance and suspicious of Ba'athist goals following two attempts on his life, Barzani escalated his demands. He insisted that oil-rich Kirkuk be included in the Kurdish area and that the Kurds have the authority to maintain their own forces and establish contacts with foreign powers. In March 1974, when the negotiations failed, the government unilaterally implemented the agreement of March 11, 1970, retaining control of Kurdish areas.

Heavy fighting ensued in the spring, summer, and fall. The Iraqi armed forces, better trained and equipped than the Kurdish irregulars, were able to make costly but steady advances against Barzani's men, leading to increased tensions between Iraq and Iran. The increasing gravity of the situation led to new mediation efforts, and an agreement was reached in Algiers on March 6, 1975. The agreement resulted in gains for both sides. For Iran it meant that Iraq accepted Iranian demands that the Shatt al Arab boundary between the two countries run along the thalweg line and that Iraq end its support for opponents of the shah. For Iraq it signified an early end to the costly Kurdish rebellion and tiny land gains. Both sides avoided a costly conflict that would have disrupted oil production.

The Iraqi government followed a policy that combined severity with leniency in dealing with the Kurds. It implemented major economic development programs designed to transform the economic structure of the Kurdish areas and to improve the living standards. At the same time, it began to implement tough security measures in which thousands of Kurds were deported and resettled in other areas of Iraq, leading to the creation of a strategic border zone stretching from six to twelve miles along the border of Turkey and Iran. As a result of growing opposition to this policy by some of the regime's Kurdish supporters, and because some Kurdish groups began to take up arms against the regime, the government modified this policy. Kurdish guerrilla activity, however, remained isolated and ineffective until the Iran-Iraq war in 1980.

The Kurdish opposition's collaboration with Iran during the war led to a brutal policy of repression and to the destruction of numerous villages and towns near the border. Unsuccessful negotiations took place between the regime and the Kurdish leaders Mas'ud Barzani of the KDP and Jalal Talibani of the Patriotic Union of Kurdistan (PUK). In 1988 Iranian and Kurdish forces accused Iraq of using chemical weapons leading to the death of many Kurdish civilians in the town of Halabjah. After the Gulf War of 1991 the Kurds rose up in the wake of the Iraqi defeat. Kurdish guerrillas, bolstered by the desertion of Kurdish tribal forces who had sided with the government in the past but believed that the regime was on its last legs, occupied all of Iraqi Kurdistan as well as cities such as Kirkuk. Within weeks, however, government forces had defeated the rebels. More than a million Kurds fled toward Iran and Turkey, leading the Western allies to intervene militarily and to establish a safe haven zone for the Kurds.

The establishment under U.S. and British protection of a Kurdish government evenly divided between Barzani and Talibani led to major confrontations over turf and money. External manipulations by Ankara, Baghdad, Tehran, and Washington further complicated the situation. For fear of their own Kurds, neither Iran nor Turkey was interested in seeing an independent Kurdish state. Fighting erupted in 1994 and 1996. In 1996 Barzani sought Baghdad's support against Talibani, who was backed by Tehran, and expelled him from the Kurdish zone's capital of Arbil. Both the KDP and the PUK have since pursued an autonomy agreement with Baghdad, although it is unclear how and what kind of agreement could be reached under the present fluid regional environment.

See also *Atatürk, Kemal; Iran; Iraq; Islam; Turkey.*

Edmund Ghareeb

BIBLIOGRAPHY

Ghareeb, Edmund. *The Kurdish Question in Iraq.* Syracuse: Syracuse University Press, 1981.

Ghassemlou, A. R., et al. *People without a Country: The Kurds in Kurdistan.* London: Zed Press, 1980.

Gunter, Michael. *The Kurds and the Future of Turkey.* New York: St. Martin's Press, 1997.

Khadduri, Majid. *Republican Iraq.* London: Oxford University Press, 1969.

Khadduri, Majid, and Edmund Ghareeb. *War in the Gulf: The Iraq-Kuwait Conflict and Its Implications.* New York: Oxford University Press, 1997.

McDowell, David. *The Kurds: A Nation Denied.* London: Minority Rights Publishers, 1992.

L

Latin America

Latin America is the collective term for the nations of Middle and South America and the Caribbean, in most of which Romance languages are spoken. The area has been the lively scene of interaction between religion and politics since the Spanish (1492) and Portuguese (1500) conquests. Under royal patronage *(patronato real),* the Roman Catholic Church was subordinate to the state. Church officials, priests, and influential laity lobbied colonial administrators for allocation of land and other resources and argued over many general or local issues. During the first century of colonial rule, clerics were exceptionally active in politics, attempting to influence government administrators as they established colonial policies. Bishops and priests stood for or against government practices, carrying prolonged appeals to Spain to legal bodies there or to the king. Bartolomé de Las Casas, Anton de Montecinos, and many others defended indigenous rights heroically.

The church's economic base was royal gifts, especially large tracts of land. This land and royal grants received for building churches and schools and for charity work enabled the church to become a ubiquitous presence in city and countryside. Through centuries of service, it gained the strong loyalty of the poor. The church offered both consolation and celebrations of birth, coming of age, and death. Sunday Mass and feast days were used to teach doctrine and church discipline, contributing to popular piety and political conservatism. Peasants and the native peoples, though, maintained a strong measure of independent religiosity either in popular religion—a mixture of orthodox beliefs and spiritism—or in Native American religion.

Independence and Liberalism

A small but highly visible sector of priests—Miguel Hidalgo and José María Morelos in Mexico, for example—led independence movements in the early nineteenth century. After independence was won from Spain in the 1820s, union of church and state continued under national patronage, resisted by the Vatican but favored by Latin American clerics. In some countries the church had somewhat weak protectors in conservative political parties. But in others the church greatly increased its land holdings through gifts and had an influential voice in public affairs.

Political opponents made church property and the church's public voice well focused targets. Nineteenth-century European liberalism intensified Latin American anticlericalism, which became official government policy in some new nations. Decades of intense conflict over the public role of the church and its land holdings ensued. By the 1920s the church, as in Mexico and Guatemala, found itself greatly reduced. Governments there closed most church schools, expelled foreign (mostly Spanish) priests, forbade corporate ownership of lands or church buildings, and took away political rights, such as voting, from clergy.

Throughout Latin America the church began the twentieth century in a weakened position with a thin supply of clergy but few challengers. At this stage the church had little political influence, maintaining itself through informal ties of churchmen with governing elite members. The church

UNITED STATES OF AMERICA
GULF OF MEXICO
MEXICO
Mexico City
BAHAMAS IS.
TURKS & CAICOS ISLANDS
Havana
CUBA
DOMINICAN REPUBLIC
HAITI
Port-au-Prince
Santo Domingo
San Juan
VIRGIN IS.
PUERTO RICO
CAYMAN ISLANDS
GREATER ANTILLES
JAMAICA
Kingston
CARIBBEAN SEA
LESSER ANTILLES
ATLANTIC OCEAN
BELIZE
Belmopan
HONDURAS
GUATEMALA
Guatemala City
Tegucigalpa
San Salvador
NICARAGUA
Managua
EL SALVADOR
COSTA RICA
San Jose
Panama City
PANAMA
Gulf of Panama
TRINIDAD & TOBAGO
Caracas
VENEZUELA
GUYANA
Georgetown
Paramaribo
SURINAM
Cayenne
FRENCH GUIANA
Bogotá
COLOMBIA
PACIFIC OCEAN
Amazon
Quito
ECUADOR
BRAZIL
PERU
Lima
La Paz
BOLIVIA
Brasília
Rio de Janeiro
PARAGUAY
Asunción
PACIFIC OCEAN
CHILE
ARGENTINA
URUGUAY
Buenos Aires
Montevideo
ATLANTIC OCEAN
Santiago
FALKLAND/MALVINAS ISLANDS
Strait of Magellan
South Georgia
Cape Horn
SCOTIA SEA

did not support itself through regular personal contributions, as churches did in the United States and Canada.

As intellectual challenges of Marxism and religious challenges of Protestantism loomed in the early twentieth century, both the Vatican and some Latin American church leaders responded, fostering lay movements. These groups, especially Catholic Action, became the basis of a small progressive church movement in Brazil, Chile, and, to a lesser degree, elsewhere. The writings and visits of French Catholic intellectuals, especially Jacques Maritain, Louis-Joseph Lebret, and Emmanuel Mounier, encouraged Latin American Catholic intellectuals to view democracy favorably and economy critically. Influential Latin American thinkers included clerics like Henrique Vaz in Brazil and Manuel Larraín in Chile and lay people like Brazil's Alceu Amaroso Lima. Maritain's integral humanism, which emphasizes a person's contribution to culture and society as part of one's Christian vocation, influenced the ideologies of Christian Democratic parties and the social revolutionary thought of a small Catholic left.

After World War II ended in 1945, the Vatican recruited European and North American missionaries, made crucial appointments of progressive bishops, and fostered the regional bishops conference (Council of Latin American Bishops) and national bishops conferences. Greatly increasing the number of priests and sisters in Latin America, missionaries brought the church's increased presence to remote areas and city neighborhoods and reinforced a Catholic reform movement.

The church was changing from a medieval Christendom model of political activity within a Christian state to one of Neo-Christendom, almost exclusively committed to Catholic schools, labor unions, and periodicals within a secular state. The bishops, as in Chile, often saw themselves as remaining above partisan politics.

Christian Democratic political parties became important, especially in Chile, El Salvador, Guatemala, and Venezuela. Prominent Christian Democratic presidents included Eduardo Frei Montalva of Chile (1964–1970), Rafael Caldera in his first Venezuelan presidency (1969–1974), and José Napoleón Duarte (1980–1982 and 1984–1988) in El Salvador. These parties began as moderate alternatives to the political and economic conservatism of the Catholicism of the sixteenth to nineteenth centuries. They emphasized religious values but became virtually indistinct from other center-right parties, favoring welfare or reform versions of capitalism.

Religion and Social Reform

Latin American intellectuals provided important statements about religion and social reform. Important beyond his native Peru, Víctor Raúl Haya de la Torre advocated a blending of popular Catholicism and social reform. Another influential Peruvian, Marxist José Carlos Mariátegui, saw religion as a source for social revolution, inspiring a later generation of Catholic intellectuals and activists. Both European and Latin American intellectual influences would converge in Paulo Freire's *Pedagogy of the Oppressed* (1973), a comprehensive revolutionary view of training ordinary men and women to assume political roles.

Latin American bishops, theologians, and lay leaders became world leaders in applying the teachings of the Second Vatican Council (1962–1965), with its focus on the church's openness to the world and concern for the poor. Beginning at their Second General Conference (1968) at Medellín, Colombia, the bishops devised a statement that was at the same time this-worldly and biblical. They envisaged a continent with grave social inequalities and a sinful church. This vision involved a change from an other-worldly, fiesta-bound institution to one that enjoined Catholics at all levels to work for justice and peace. Within this view, the church set about internal reforms and viewed itself as a servant building up civil society. Progressive church leaders emphasized theology of liberation, small Bible-study groups (base Christian communities), and preferential treatment of the poor. Gustavo Gutiérrez's *Theology of Liberation* (1973) provided the widely read early statement of liberation theology.

These changes occurred as military regimes began taking over most governments of the region (1964–1990). The church thus came into conflict with repressive military practices, especially massive violations of human rights. As virtually the only institution that the military could not disband or control, the church became the voice of the voiceless, except in Argentina where Catholic progressive leaders were few. The most prominent of Catholic groups were the Vicariates of Solidarity in various Chilean regions. Tiny Catholic radical groups were soon done away with by military and paramilitary forces. Rightist death squads murdered hundreds of human rights and social justice advocates, such as Salvadoran archbishop Oscar Romero, who was shot by an assassin in 1980. The Nobel Peace Prize went to two Catholic lay activists for human rights work, Adolfo Pérez Esquivel of Argentina (1980) and Rigoberta Menchú Tum of Guatemala (1992).

The progressive emphases alienated some traditional Catholics and left many others unsatisfied. These ideological divisions intensified debates within the church and formation or reinforcement of countertrends. Spiritualizing emphases like the Catholic Charismatic Renewal or associations of clergy and laity like Opus Dei, Legionnaires of Christ, and Sodalitium Christianae Vitae served to counter what were regarded as excessively activist, even superficially Marxist, tendencies. In the 1970s the Latin American Bishops Conference itself became a conservative target. Archbishop Alfonso López Trujillo became secretary general of the organization and in 1978 was elected its president. Despite increasing conservative influence, Latin American bishops at their Third General Conference (1979) at Puebla, Mexico, reinforced Medellín's progressive policies and further emphasized work for the poor.

Conservative influences became increasingly evident in the 1980s. The experiences of John Paul II (who became pope in 1978), a Polish citizen under Nazi and then Communist rule, were thought to have contributed to his forceful efforts to curb Latin American progressive tendencies. John Paul's appointments of conservative bishops, while still a minority in many countries, allowed them to join with centrists to slow the progressive trends in national and Latin American bishops conferences and seminary faculties, call into question liberation theologians' writings, and emphasize spiritual rather than political aspects of biblical messages in education and worship.

The Church and Democracy

The church was instrumental in turning Latin American societies from military rule to democratically elected governments in the 1980s and 1990s. In a few countries where strong political party systems function well, as in Chile, the church sought a less public role. But through most of the region, the church has been highly critical of fraudulent elections (Mexico and Guatemala), failure of governments to meet the health and educational needs of the lower classes, and corruption in government. The church's criticism of the debt burden and free market capitalism, called neoliberalism in Latin America, has been strong. Many Catholic groups, such as the influential Jesuit order through its regional superiors, issued widely circulated critiques of the current economic system and called on governments to moderate the effects of widespread poverty.

Human rights organizing, begun by many religious groups to counter abuses under the military, expanded throughout Latin America. The movement's first political demand after military rule was settling accounts with torturers by establishing truth commissions. Civilian governments, responding to these pressures, achieved varying degrees of success in establishing public records of the dead and disappeared. But truth commissions either failed to name oppressors, or governments pardoned all but a few of the officers held accountable, claiming the need for reconciliation to maintain public peace.

Human rights advocates turned to challenging government abuses of human rights; more fundamentally, they sought to strengthen citizen action and hold governments to a rule of law as the foundation of the new democracies. They obtained new constitutional articles defining the rights of children and lobbied for the observance of law at the municipal and national levels. Transnational networks within churches and Pope John Paul II, whose most consistent message in his many trips to Latin America has been the protection of human rights, reinforced these efforts.

Personal Belief and Local Action

Religion and politics have often become closely connected at the personal and grassroots levels. Differing kinds of religious conversions or personal religious orientations have led some people to political activism, while other believers, exposed to the same religious messages, continue to view their religion as private or exclusively otherworldly. Many Latin Americans are reconstructing popular cultures toward a more politically active force, using religious—especially biblical—messages to do so.

In El Salvador and Guatemala's civil wars, for example, Catholics made sense of political violence in theological terms, portraying suffering and death by political repressors as martyrdom. In many countries, inspired by liberation theology, small groups of men and women meet in largely self-governing small groups, seeking commitment to follow a biblical message with political implications. Ordinary men and women debate political issues, weigh options, and seek pragmatic solutions. Small congregations of evangelical Protestants are also conditioning participants to speak out, act on their own behalves, and cooperate. In doing so, they promote democratization.

These grassroots Christian activists and worshipers have

joined in the political process to improve their neighborhoods. They have also promoted national causes. Base community members served as the backbone of the Brazilian Autoworkers Union and its offspring, the Labor Party, electing members to regional and national political offices. Sectors of the church furnish large numbers for the Movement for the Landless, the largest Brazilian movement of the late 1990s. They are encouraged in this effort by the Brazilian bishops, who have sponsored a three-year (1997–1999) national program in human rights education.

Protestants, presumed quiescent because there are fewer of them, are becoming politically active in new ways. They have used existing parties or created their own to express their political demands. Protestants now number some forty million in Latin America, half of them in Brazil. The fastest growing segment have been Pentecostals, some 75–90 percent of the Protestant population in many countries. (By far the largest number of Latin American Protestants belong to groups that have been Latin American for decades and are not invaders from North America.) With a critical political mass and growing middle-class status, Protestants are demanding more equal benefits from the state. Leaders include Benedicta da Silva, a prominent Pentecostal senator in Brazil.

Other Faiths and the State

Church and state separated in Brazil in 1890, to the ultimate benefit of the church. Church and state have separated in other countries over the years. But both Pentecostals and the religiously nonaffiliated are exerting pressures on lawmakers to remove some vestiges of Catholic privilege that still exist in law, such as special mention of Catholicism in national constitutions and the teaching of Catholic doctrine and morality in public schools.

The Latin American Catholic Church absorbed little of the ecumenical spirit of Vatican II. Most national bishops conferences have been reluctant to cede religious equality to groups who are presumed to be rending the cultural unity of their countries. And Catholic bishops and lay supporters have carried on contentiously in the public forum about the aggressive tactics of Pentecostals, Mormons, Jehovah's Witnesses, and other groups. In 1995, for example, a Brazilian pastor of the rapidly expanding Universal Church of God repeatedly kicked a statue of Mary, the mother of Jesus, during a televised sermon. This act was recognized as excessive but expressive of some churches' strong preaching against Catholic practices. With each side viewing the other's demands as morally unacceptable, political action by Protestants and Catholics represents what observers believe is an appropriate response within a democratic context.

As Afro-Brazilian religions, which mix elements of Christian and African traditional religions and emphasize spirits as having influence over the events of human life, gained public acceptance, these too entered politics. Afro-Brazilian religions were largely perceived as quiescent politically until the 1950s. By then Umbanda, a Brazilian new religion, had been gaining strength in numbers. Attacks by the Brazilian bishops and the Catholic Electoral League on Afro religions in the 1950s overcame the reluctance of leaders to engage in politics, which the religions founders had prohibited. Umbandists mobilized politically to achieve religious freedom, bringing greater unification of members and of enormously varied tendencies within the Umbanda movement. Rather than form their own political party, many Umbandists joined in a religious interest group and supported those politicians who would help to defend their interests. Other Afro-Brazilian religious groups comprise so many social characteristics in varying combinations that no generalizations regarding their contributions to Brazilian politics were possible in the 1990s.

For indigenous peoples the Guatemalan and Bolivian bishops and the bishops in Chiapas, Mexico, have promoted indigenous interests, acted as mediators in the Central American and Chiapan peace processes, and supported the emergence of new political forces. Church centers—especially in Peru, Bolivia, and southern Mexico—have fostered indigenous cultural awareness and political activism. Víctor Hugo Cardenas Conde, who was elected Bolivia's first indigenous vice president in 1993, grew politically through church sponsorship of Aymara cultural centers.

The Latin American Catholic Church is enjoying a religious revival, with increased church attendance, growing numbers of seminarians and sisters, and enhanced lay participation. This resurgence occurs side by side with the efflorescence of Pentecostalism, Afro-Brazilian, and indigenous religions. Changes within the church—especially liberation theology, small communities, and support for democracy—have greatly influenced churches in other regions, especially the Philippines, Korea, and Africa. The new politics of religion in Latin America will include battles over religious pluralism as well as struggles for human rights protection and building civil society.

See also *Anticlericalism; Base communities; CELAM; Christian democracy; Human rights; Liberation theology; Maritain, Jacques; Romero, Oscar A.* See also specific countries.

Edward L. Cleary

BIBLIOGRAPHY

Berryman, Phillip. *The Religious Roots of Rebellion: Christians in Central American Revolutions.* Maryknoll, N.Y.: Orbis Books, 1982.

Cleary, Edward L. *The Struggle for Human Rights in Latin America.* Westport, Conn.: Praeger, 1997.

Cleary, Edward L., and Hannah Stewart-Gambino, eds. *Conflict and Competition: The Latin American Church in a Changing Environment.* Boulder, Colo.: Lynne Rienner, 1992.

———. *Power, Politics, and Pentecostals in Latin America.* Boulder, Colo.: Westview Press, 1997.

Dussel, Enrique. *The Church in Latin America, 1492–1992.* Maryknoll, N.Y.: Orbis Books, 1992.

Garrard-Burnett, Virginia, and David Stoll, eds. *Rethinking Protestantism in Latin America.* Philadelphia: Temple University Press, 1993.

Ireland, Rowan. *Kingdoms Come: Religion and Politics in Brazil.* Pittsburgh: University of Pittsburgh Press, 1991.

Levine, Daniel H. *Popular Voices in Latin America Catholicism.* Princeton: Princeton University Press, 1992.

Mainwaring, Scott, and Alexander Wilde, eds. *The Progressive Church in Latin America.* Notre Dame, Ind.: University of Notre Dame Press, 1989.

Mecham, J. Lloyd. *Church and State in Latin America.* 2d ed. Chapel Hill: University of North Carolina Press, 1966.

Latter-day Saints, Church of Jesus Christ of

A dynamic movement that began as a Protestant sect, the Church of Jesus Christ of Latter-day Saints, also known as the Mormon Church, has become an international denomination and is the fastest growing religious group in the world. The church originated from a vision reportedly received in 1820 by fourteen-year-old Joseph Smith, who lived in Palmyra, New York. God and Jesus Christ appeared to him, announcing that the Christian churches of the day were all false and commissioning him to begin a new, authentic line of prophets. In 1827 Smith claimed that an angel named Moroni appeared to him and revealed lost golden tablets that told a fantastic story of Christianity's forgotten history in pre-Columbian North America.

By 1829 Smith had translated and published the Book of Mormon, based on these tablets, which supposedly had been written by a prophet named Mormon. These new scriptures revealed that Jesus had appeared in the New World and established his church. Church members regard the Book of Mormon as a second Testament of Jesus in addition to the Bible. Members of the Church of Jesus Christ of Latter-day Saints, which was founded in 1830 in Fayette, New York, thus became nicknamed Mormons by nonmembers who knew them only by their reliance on the new scriptures.

Persecution

There have been two fundamental sources of the Mormon Church's (and members') political activism. The first are the church's postmillennial doctrines: as latter-day stewards of God's kingdom on earth, Mormons must amass political and economic resources in order to preserve a temporal foundation from which Jesus will rule when he ultimately returns to earth. The second was the church's obvious, sometimes desperate, search for self-defense and survival. Many early church leaders' efforts to influence levels of regional, state, and even federal government were pursued to thwart persecution from non-Mormons and to promote the welfare of Mormon communities.

From the point of view of nineteenth-century non-Mormons, the movement constituted a potential voting bloc in local elections as its members migrated to new communities and across states and, because the church was in some ways viewed as a theocracy, followed instructions from church leaders on how and for whom to vote. In addition, Mormon missionaries were active in Europe and produced a stream of converts immigrating to the United States that fed the nativist prejudices of the time. The arrival of European converts increased to such an extent that the church began to discourage them from relocating. Nativism and fear of a European invasion worked against the early church much as Irish immigration in pre–Civil War America fed concerns that there was a Vatican conspiracy to flood the nation with Catholics who would take over the national government.

As both Mormon and non-Mormon historians have documented, the church's swelling membership rolls, and its potential for economic and political influence, fueled much of the hostility against it. And, full of millennial exuberance, some belligerent Mormon leaders at times avowed themselves to be above the laws of the land; at other times, state officials who ought to have been more sensitive to religious liberties than they were proclaimed the Mormons outlaws.

The Temple of the Church of Jesus Christ of Latter-day Saints, in Kensington, Maryland, near Washington, D.C.

The emerging Mormon sect was distinctly delegitimized and stigmatized by its opponents. Joseph Smith was reputed to possess mesmerizing control over his followers. His opponents, suggesting that his religious movement was merely a con game to enrich himself, referred to him as the "Profit Smith."

Mormons often ran for local offices where they formed a considerable portion of certain local populations, and in the 1844 national presidential campaign Joseph Smith ran for president. Smith had been critical of President Martin Van Buren, and it is likely that he was reluctant to throw his considerable following behind any mainline party candidate. (In fact, at its height, the Mormon city of Nauvoo, Illinois, in the early 1840s was second in size only to Chicago.) Thus Smith offered himself as a presidential candidate, intending to introduce his prophetic, theocratic plans to the nation after the election. None of these events eased tensions between Mormons and non-Mormon citizens.

A non-Mormon newspaper criticized Smith for his political ambitions, personal wealth, and rumors of polygamy in the church. Smith allegedly had his followers sack the newspaper office. He and his brother Hyrum later were arrested and held in the Carthage, Illinois, jail, where they were held for trial for conspiracy. Pistols were smuggled into their cell, a lynch mob came for them, and a gunfight ensued in which both Smith brothers were killed.

The Mormons encountered constant friction during the nineteenth century. Some of this strain was rooted in the debate over polygamy (or, more accurately, polygyny—the taking of more than one wife), which was illegal in the United

States. Plural marriage was denounced by the clergy of other denominations, in newspapers, and by politicians in Congress.

The Move to Utah

In 1847 Smith's successor, Brigham Young, led the Mormons to the relative isolation of northern Mexico, to an area that would pass to U.S. possession under the terms of the treaty of Guadalupe Hidalgo that, in 1848, ended the war with Mexico. Mormons—who were among the religious, political, and economic leaders in the territory—sought statehood. In 1850 the U.S. Congress established the area as the Utah Territory.

Washington-appointed territorial governors became increasingly frustrated with trying to control a region in which church leaders made virtually all important decisions and granted permissions sometimes contrary to federal law. There was violence between Mormon and non-Mormon immigrants. In 1857 rumors of a possible rebellion spread, and an army of 1,800 federal troops was dispatched to support the region's non-Mormon governor in what the Mormons still remember as the Utah war. Responding to what they saw as an invasion with guerrilla tactics, the Mormons blocked or fortified mountain passes, sabotaged bridges, interrupted the troop supply trains, poisoned wells, and so on. No major pitched battles were fought, but the presence of the U.S. military had an enormous effect on creating solidarity in the Mormon subculture.

In 1879 George Reynolds, a polygamist and secretary to Brigham Young, tested the constitutional limits of freedom of religion as granted under the First Amendment. The U.S. Supreme Court rejected Mormon claims (in *Reynolds v. United States)* that polygamy was protected as a religious belief. Reynolds was convicted, and his prison term was upheld, setting a major precedent in the U.S. courts.

Five times during the late nineteenth century the Mormons applied for statehood and were turned down by Congress. Typical of non-Mormon reactions was the Edmunds-Tucker Act of 1887, which was intended to disenfranchise the church and redistribute its assets away from church control. In 1890 the Mormon Church effectively banned polygamy, and in 1896 Utah was admitted to the Union.

Mormons and Mainstream Politics

Controversy arose in 1898, when Brigham H. Roberts, an admitted polygynist, won a congressional race in Utah. The House of Representatives refused to seat him. Reed Smoot was elected to the Senate as a Republican in 1902. Like Roberts, his seat was challenged because some anti-Mormons suspected the church still approved of polygyny. Three years of investigative hearings elapsed before Smoot was installed as a Utah senator. Church leaders used the public hearings to parade their own public relations exhibits of morality before the national media, and Smoot went on to a distinguished thirty-year career in the Senate. He was certainly not the last Mormon representative to be elected, but he was the last to experience open prejudice against his religion.

Mormons are commonly perceived as a conservative Christian church and are often identified with Protestant fundamentalists because of their opposition to abortion and birth control. Individual Mormons have become integrated into mainstream politics as public officials (albeit frequently in a conservative mode). There is no evidence, however, that they or rank-and-file members are disproportionately right wing, radical, or in other respects odd. Nationally prominent Mormon politicians and political advisers have included Ezra Taft Benson (secretary of agriculture under President Dwight D. Eisenhower in the 1950s and later himself president of the church); U.S. senators Frank E. Moss, Orrin Hatch, and Jake Garn; and Air Force general Brent Scowcroft, who served as military adviser to Presidents Ronald Reagan and George Bush.

At times the church has been able to mobilize its members to discourage legislation with which it disapproves, such as the proposed Equal Rights Amendment of the late 1970s, in states as disparate as Utah, Nevada, and Florida. The Mormon leadership was also successful during the early 1980s in preventing placement of an underground missile defense system in Utah. Nevertheless, overall the church stresses patriotism and loyalty to the U.S. Constitution. Just as the Church of Jesus Christ of Latter-day Saints has evolved from a persecuted radical sect into a respected, less controversial denomination, so has its political thrust become mainstream.

See also *Cults; Nativism; Theocracy.*

Anson Shupe

BIBLIOGRAPHY

Alexander, Thomas G. *Mormonism in Transition: A History of the Latter-day Saints, 1890–1930.* Urbana: University of Illinois Press, 1986.

Arrington, Leonard J., and Davis Bitton. *The Mormon Experience: A History of the Latter-day Saints.* New York: Vintage Books, 1980.

Brodie, Fawn M. *No Man Knows My History: The Life of Joseph Smith.* 2d ed. New York: Knopf, 1986.
Heinerman, John, and Anson Shupe. *The Mormon Corporate Empire.* Boston: Beacon Press, 1985.
Hill, Marvin E. *Quest for Refuge: The Mormon Flight from American Pluralism.* Salt Lake City: Signature Books, 1989.
Mauss, Armand L. *The Angel and the Beehive: The Mormon Struggle with Assimilation.* Urbana: University of Illinois Press, 1994.
Shipps, Jan. *Mormonism: The Story of a New Religious Tradition.* Urbana: University of Illinois Press, 1985.

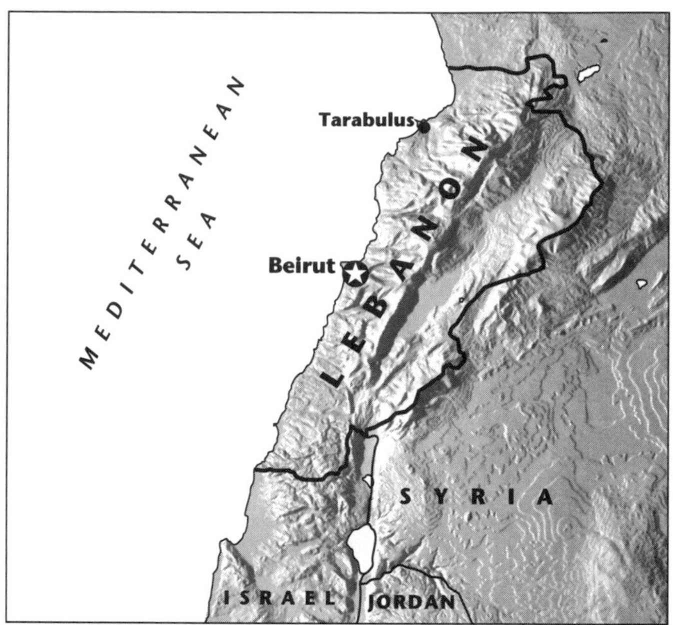

Lebanon

Lebanon is an Arab country in Southwest Asia that borders the Mediterranean Sea. The modern state of Lebanon owes its borders to the French; after World War I the League of Nations awarded France a mandate over Syria and Lebanon. In contrast to Syria, where the mandate was received with hostility, France enjoyed long-standing allies in Lebanon, in particular among the Maronite Catholics. By early 1920, only months after the mandate began, the French high commissioner in Beirut declared the establishment of Great Lebanon. Lebanon's mountains and valleys have been historically a refuge for minorities, including the Druze, Shi'i Muslims, the Greek Catholics and Greek Orthodox, and the Uniate Christian Maronites. In creating Greater Lebanon the state now included the major coastal cities of Tripoli, Beirut, Sidon, and Tyre, as well as the Biqa valley, all historically part of Syria. This enlargement was fateful because it profoundly complicated an already intricate confessional system of religious affiliation by which power and privilege are shared. The civil war that erupted in 1975 stemmed significantly from the demographic time bomb that had been ticking since the creation of Greater Lebanon.

After Independence

Lebanon won its independence in 1943, and the outline of its political system was contained in an unwritten National Pact that defined the terms of the bargain for sharing power. Precise population figures for Lebanon's sects are impossible to find—the data are politically explosive. In fact, the last census was conducted in 1932 under French supervision, and those results are highly suspect. Nonetheless, at independence, the presumption was that the Maronites were the largest community, followed by the Sunni and Shi'i Muslims, and that the Christians overall (encompassing thirteen sects, including three Armenian ones) outnumbered Muslims by a ratio of six to five. Following the logic of numerical strength, the Maronites, Sunnis, and Shi'is were awarded the top political offices—the positions of president, prime minister, and parliamentary speaker, respectively—and major positions were allocated to the other sects as well, including all of the top positions in the civil service and the military.

Religious institutions are autonomous in Lebanon so that questions of personal status such as marriage, divorce, birth, and death are the exclusive preserve of the Maronite patriarchy, the Supreme Islamic Shi'i Council, and parallel institutions. A corollary to the inescapable importance of confessional identity in Lebanon is the fact that patronage is deeply embedded in Lebanese society. Thus the power brokers in modern Lebanon are political bosses (or *za'ims*) who wield enormous influence, even though they only occasionally hold formal political office. These members of the political elite frequently rotate through the ministries, enjoying the spoils of office before making room for a rival.

Lebanon has a strong parliamentary tradition, and the elections for parliament are conducted through an intricate system of multiconfessional lists. Voters cast multiple votes for as many as two dozen candidates, depending on the size of their district. The innovation of the Lebanese electoral system is that seats are allocated by confession, but regardless of the voter's identity, he or she casts a ballot for every vacant seat. Thus, in a district where Maronites, Druze, and Shi'is are all allocated seats, every eligible voter has the right to decide which Maronite, Druze, or Shi'i candidates they prefer. This phenomenon of crossover voting is intended to foster alliances across confessional lines and reduce interconfessional tensions, since all candidates will strive to build attractive multiconfessional blocs to lure voters. For the first three decades of its history, the political system worked more or less as planned, and by the late 1960s the political ingenuity of the Lebanese was often praised as a model for other heterogeneous societies.

Unfortunately, the political system proved to be quite inflexible. Despite the fact that the numerical dominance of the Christians was called into doubt by the 1960s, few serious steps were taken to make room for new faces in the political system. This shortcoming was especially obvious in the case of the Shi'i community, which traditionally lived in southern Lebanon and the Biqa valley, both regions appended to Lebanon in 1920 by the French. The Shi'i Muslims, who have had the highest birthrate in modern Lebanon by far, were on the political and economic periphery until they began to find an assertive voice in the 1960s and 1970s. In this same period Palestinian guerrilla groups also began to develop a strong armed presence in Lebanon, and they found many allies among the politically disinherited Shi'i youths who were crowding into the engorged suburbs of Beirut, as well as Lebanon's other cities.

Civil War

To a significant degree, the Lebanese civil war (1975–1990) was fought to determine the fate of the political status quo. The prime beneficiaries of the existing system were the Maronites, and their opponents sought to dramatically reform the political system. The war was not strictly a struggle between Christians on the one hand and Muslims on the other. Many Greek Orthodox supported the predominantly Muslim Lebanese National Movement that was aligned with the Palestinian resistance movement, and the Armenians, who are all Christians, maintained a studied neutrality throughout.

Despite horrendous fighting in 1975 and 1976, the civil war was stalemated, largely because of Syria's intervention in 1976. When Israel invaded in 1982, with the intention of ensuring the victory of Maronite allies, there was momentary elation among the war-weary Lebanese, but Maronite supremacy would prove impossible to sustain in the face of challenges from the country's other communities. Without question, the most profound threat to Maronite privilege was posed by the Shi'i community. The Shi'is were politicized by several developments, including the Islamic revolution in Iran in 1979; the charismatic leadership of an Iranian cleric with Lebanese roots, Musa al-Sadr; and the continuing Israeli occupation of southern Lebanon, from which the Shi'is have suffered disproportionately.

There is no majority community in Lebanon; even the Shi'is comprise no more than a third of the population. Although the Muslims now account for at least 60 percent of the population, no single confessional group can dominate the political system. This fact of political life is reflected in the Ta'if accord of 1989, the blueprint for ending the civil war. The Ta'if agreement was carried out in 1990, with a hard push by the Syrians and a wink from the United States. The accord effectively retains the confessional system but reshuffles political privileges between the sects. The parliament is now split fifty-fifty between Christians and Muslims. The prerogatives of the Maronite president have been reduced by the power of the Sunni prime minister, and the Shi'i speaker of the parliament has been enhanced. Arguably, the civil war proved that each of the major communities possesses a veto on the attempt of any single community to dominate Lebanese politics. It is significant that the most notable rivalry at century's end is not between Christians and Muslims, but between Sunni and Shi'i Muslims, each striving to check the other's ambitions.

In the difficult circumstances of the 1990s, when economic recovery in Lebanon was thwarted by the slow peacemaking in the Arab-Israeli conflict, the Lebanese faced a revival of patronage and confessional politics, and secular parties fared poorly. An attempt to permit civil marriage in 1998 aroused the opposition of many of the country's religious institutions and demonstrated that however much individual Lebanese might yearn to be free of their confessional cages, the keys are still in the hands of those who play by the rules of confessional politics.

See also *Catholicism, Roman; Druze; Islam; Orthodoxy, Greek; Syria.*

Augustus Richard Norton

BIBLIOGRAPHY

Collings, Deirdre, ed. *Peace for Lebanon? From War to Reconstruction.* Boulder and London: Lynne Rienner Publishers, 1994.

Hudson, Michael C. *The Precarious Republic: Political Modernization in Lebanon.* New York: Random House, 1968.
Johnson, Michael. *Class and Client in Beirut: The Sunni Muslim Community and the Lebanese States, 1840–1985.* London and Atlantic Highlands, N.J.: Ithaca Press, 1986.
Khalaf, Samir. *Lebanon's Predicament.* New York: Columbia University Press, 1987.
Norton, Augustus Richard. *Amal and the Shi'a: Struggle for the Soul of Lebanon.* Austin: University of Texas Press, 1987.
Picard, Elizabeth. *Lebanon: A Shattered Country.* New York and London: Holmes & Meier, 1996.
Salabi, Kamal S. *A House of Many Mansions: The History of Lebanon Reconsidered.* Berkeley and Los Angeles: University of California Press, 1988.

Liberalism

Liberalism is a philosophy, movement, or even a cast of mind basically concerned with the importance of personal freedom and social improvement. One of the major political ideologies of the modern world, its status is paradoxical. The collapse of state socialism in Eastern Europe in the early 1990s, and to some degree in China, has led some to think that all are liberals now, yet some intellectuals have proclaimed the death of liberalism in the face of philosophical uncertainty about whether such an ideology can any longer be confidently endorsed.

Political ideologies share a number of important characteristics. They provide an interpretation of the (political) world that adherents find useful in explaining or understanding power: its origin, legitimacy, distribution, and deployment. More particularly, political ideologies rest on some view of human nature that underpins that interpretation. For example, conservative thinkers often want to insist on human imperfectibility, on necessarily limited expectations of social harmony, progress, or freedom from criminal activity, from the presence of the rogue. Liberals have, however, been more optimistic about the possibilities of intellectual, moral, and social improvement. At root, the dispute concerns the malleability of human nature in relation to social institutions.

Political ideologies persist through time in the sense that individuals separated temporally, and often in location, see themselves as part of an enduring current of ideas that has sufficient continuity and coherence to persist. But precisely because political ideologies interpret the political realm, they are subject to modification and development in the light of the practical world they seek to understand. For example, liberalism has had to take into account events like the English, American, and French Revolutions and developments like the spread of democracy, the profound social changes wrought by capitalism, or, more generally, industrial society. From this point of view, no political ideology can ever be frozen: what it seeks to interpret changes, and the world of the late-twentieth-century liberal is very different from the world of the seventeenth-century liberal with whom, nevertheless, the modern liberal would wish to claim an affinity.

All political ideologies, moreover, help to guide action. They claim not only to help to interpret the world but also to provide an orientation to the evaluation of change. Since political ideologies are complexes of (at least) value commitments, broad philosophical ideas—cosmologies, epistemologies, ontologies—and policy prescriptions, they suggest to adherents what political activity is desirable, and, therefore, what, if anything, is to be done. Hence in considering liberalism, for example, the ideas of philosophers like nineteenth-century British economist John Stuart Mill and the political practice of liberal politicians like William Ewart Gladstone, four-time prime minister of Great Britain (1868–1874, 1880–1885, 1886, and 1892–1894), are both relevant.

What Constitutes Liberalism?

These widely recognized characteristics of political ideologies lead to equally widely recognized, and intractable, problems in identifying with any precision the content of a political ideology. If we suppose that there is some essential core to liberalism, for example, we presuppose the existence of something called *liberalism* before we attempt to identify its essence. But how shall we identify that liberalism independently of adherence to particular values? If we try to derive its content from the positions of thinkers and political actors who called themselves liberals, there are a number of obvious problems. We seem to make a fetish of the word: people could be liberals even if they did not so describe themselves. We suppose that self-identification is a reliable guide: could we not deny the description liberal to someone who thought he or she was? And we face the dilemma resulting from the combination of continuity and change: seventeenth-century English philosopher John Locke and nineteenth-century philosopher Thomas Hill Green are both regarded as liberals, but their political philosophies are very different because the worlds they lived in, sought to understand and to change were very different. In discussing liberalism (or any other political ideology) we are relying on some sort of consensual view of the development of political ideas and practice, which is always vulnerable to the challenges already mentioned.

Naturally, parallel points to those made in this discussion of political ideologies could be made about other systems of ideas or practices that provide an orientation to the world, and a sphere of action within it—such as particular religious adherence and membership of a church—so there may be dispute about which persons' beliefs and practices are to be included within some particular designation. That issue arises especially in a changing world that has to be reinterpreted in the light of new challenges to individual and collective activity.

Historians have confronted this problem in discussing liberal Anglican politics and liberal Catholicism. But these examples are also instances in which the political and the religious were intertwined in trying to answer the question of what is to be done in the light of social conditions. Liberal politics in England in the nineteenth century involved shifting coalitions of liberal Anglicans, evangelicals, nonconformists, and Whigs confronting issues like the slave trade, religious toleration, elementary education, and the extension of the franchise. These issues illustrate liberalism's concern with liberty, its uncertain response to egalitarian ideas and democratic aspirations, and its ameliorative ambitions. Members of quite different churches could share what might be called a liberal outlook, without necessarily embracing full-blown political liberalism.

Liberal Catholicism in France, associated particularly with early-nineteenth-century philosopher Félicité Robert de Lamennais, was a reaction to the Bourbon regime that had been restored after the French Revolution (1789–1799). Lamennais turned against the restored Bourbons and sought to identify the cause of Catholicism with the cause of liberty. The program of the liberal Catholics embraced many of the particular classic freedoms of liberalism: freedoms of conscience, association, publication, and the distancing or separation of the church from the state. Scholars have been particularly interested in the relation between Lamennais's ideas and the work of the French nineteenth-century political thinker Alexis de Tocqueville.

Liberty

Most would see the primary commitment of liberalism as consisting in a celebration of the value of liberty itself. In his essay *On Liberty* (1859), John Stuart Mill began with a brief review of the threats to liberty that he thought had been confronted in the past—the pretensions of the state and the pretensions of the church. Liberty in the face of the claims of monarchs or other claimants to state power, and liberty from the demands of theological authority, had, he thought, been largely won—even if both were to be jealously guarded. But a new threat had arisen: the threat to individual liberty, and to the development of individuality, as a result of what was to become known as mass society. Like Tocqueville, Mill feared the tyranny of public opinion, the stultifying effect on individuality imposed by the need to conform—the emergence of an enervated mediocrity of persons lacking strength of character or concern with self-culture.

Other challenges to individual freedom have been of concern to liberals: the power of economic classes or corporations and the power of those who control information and the media are notable examples. It would be a mistake to suppose that all those, even liberals, who celebrated liberty had the same conception of that value. Indeed, this point is hotly contested between those who suppose that true liberals must endorse a conception of freedom as absence of interference and those who allow that it may be liberal to be concerned about the freedom to do something or become something. Poverty, for example, may be an impediment to freedom and thus raises the question of the relationship between liberty and equality in liberal thought.

Liberalism has long been identified with a desire to demarcate the public from the private. As Mill recognized, the historical priority had been the liberation of the individual from an overbearing state. The ideas that liberty consists in the absence of interference, and that the task is to define the proper scope of public power while reserving a sphere of private life not subject to political regulation, are corollaries. This concern with the separation of the public from the private holds not only for liberalism's adherents but also for its critics, who have alleged that support for the distinction, as understood by liberals, neglects and disguises power relationships that impinge on liberty in ways liberals themselves should worry about—notably gender and familial relations. This controversy is of course closely related to that about the liberal conception of freedom.

Liberal political thought has acknowledged the necessity of the state but at the same time has been wary of it. Unlike anarchists, liberals have not thought that a harmonious social existence would be possible in the absence of that state, but unlike authoritarians like English philosopher and political theorist Thomas Hobbes (1588–1679), they have wanted to place limits on state power—a thought aptly captured by Locke's anti-Hobbesian remark that men fearful of polecats would not make arrangements to be devoured by lions. The state is necessary, but its very power makes it dangerous. It is this view that animates the liberal desire to separate the public from the private, a desire which has issued in a number of constitutional and policy prescriptions.

The most fundamental of these prescriptions is of course that political power should be constitutionally regulated, or, to take Locke once again, that political power had to be restrained to pursue only its proper purposes. The notions of a division of powers, or a balancing interpenetration between branches of government, the use of a constitutional court, the promulgation of a set of fundamental rights, a tenderness toward private property or more generally the market, a hostility to established religion, a commitment to the rule of law rather than of men—these are the typical devices chosen to restrain the power of the state while accepting its necessity. Although the sort of state power to which liberals originally objected may have been monarchical, the liberal is not comforted by the thought that the public-private divide is being breached by a democratically elected government.

Democracy

The notion that liberalism is in some sense a dominating political ideology rests on the alleged ubiquity of the acceptance that a free market is the most efficient and liberty-respecting method to provide for material needs and wants, and perhaps also for economic growth, and the apparent irresistibility of claims to self-government or democracy in some form. But there is much more to liberalism than a commitment to the so-called free market, even when combined with some sort of representative government, and any (necessarily subjective) assessment of the number of political regimes in the world that are liberal democracies would still return the answer that they are a minority.

The existence of a market rather than a command economy or a heavily state-directed scheme of economic provision, coupled with the use of the ballot box, is compatible with great illiberalism with respect to recognition of rights to free speech, to association, to religious observance and so on. Some recent modes of governance, like those of U.S. president Ronald Reagan and British prime minister Margaret Thatcher, have appeared to combine neoclassical commitments to unleashing market forces with conservative commitments in other policy arenas.

What is meant by liberal democracy? Popular self-government may be seen as a restraint on state power: elections provide a mechanism by which citizens impose limits on the uses to which governments put their coercive power and their authority. Yet popular self-government appears dangerous. It licenses the rule of a majority that may not be tender of liberal commitments—for example, to freedom of speech, association, and movement—and it may be used to legitimize interference with property and the market in ways the liberal finds destructive.

The liberal assessment of democracy has been made more complex by the association of democratic programs with utilitarianism (the doctrine that the ethical value of conduct is determined by the utility of its results). Classical utilitarianism, associated with English philosopher, economist, and jurist Jeremy Bentham (1748–1832) and the philosophical radicals, came to endorse representative government as a mechanism to harness the pursuit of self-interest by rulers. But classical utilitarianism also supposes that the purpose of government is to promote the greatest happiness, and, despite Bentham's own view that all coercion is undesirable and legitimate only if outweighed by a contribution to the greatest happiness that would be impossible in its absence, such a conception of the purpose of government places no principled limit on the scope of its activities.

Hence some have seen Benthamism as a deviation from the true doctrine of liberalism, which, it is claimed, generates such limits from a prior commitment to the value of individual liberty, a value only contingently and instrumentally connected to the Benthamite metric of happiness. Although Mill self-evidently proclaimed the value of liberty, as well as the desirability of representative government, his success in reconciling the two is still debated. And some of the moves he made in that reconciliation—such as rejecting the secret ballot and allowing plural votes to certain classes of citizen—sit uneasily with the modern egalitarian understanding of democracy. More generally, many classical liberals of Mill's time—like James Fitzjames Stephen, Matthew Arnold, and Henry Maine—were dismayed by what they saw as the emergent tyranny of democracy in practical politics.

The term *liberal democracy* is used to describe a political system in which liberal and democratic commitments are combined, but this may be a tension-filled combination.

More particularly, in approaching the development of liberalism, we have to take account of its hesitant response to egalitarian ideas. Liberalism and libertarianism have both been associated with doctrines of natural rights. Such doctrines assert that all persons, whenever born, enjoy certain rights in virtue of being persons. In theological form, these could be seen as either God-given or necessary corollaries of duties to God. In secular form, they could be seen either as logical preconditions of any rights-talk, as in the twentieth-century British jurisprudent H. L. A. Hart's view that if there are any moral rights at all the right to equal freedom must be among them, or simply asserted as the foundation of subsequent argument, as in the American philosopher Robert Nozick's libertarianism, contained in his book *Anarchy, State, and Utopia* (1974).

Rights—Natural and Equal

The natural rights theories of the seventeenth and eighteenth centuries were usually radical, rationalist, and individualist. But they were also juristic in the sense that asserting that every individual has the same rights does not entail a commitment to any equal outcomes, for example in the distribution of resources. Equal rights, whether natural or positive, are compatible with great inequality of actual conditions. The liberal emphasis on the importance of rights has been criticized from both left and right. Radicals, famously nineteenth-century German political philosopher Karl Marx, complained that declarations of rights were a device that gave a false universality to the state, leaving the actual conditions of capitalist society—exploitation and alienation in various forms—untouched. Conservatives, like the eighteenth-century British statesman Edmund Burke, complained that the abstract rationalism of such doctrines neglected the way in which rights were rooted in the historical development of particular communities. The liberal defense to such charges has been that the practice of rights provides not only a vital defense of freedom but also a method for developing social cohesion. The question has become whether the most philosophically sophisticated defenses of modern liberalism are too egalitarian, or not egalitarian enough, and whether they are too individualistic, or not individualistic enough.

The problem of egalitarianism arises because of the work of the philosopher John Rawls, whose two books—*A Theory of Justice* (1971) and *Political Liberalism* (1993)—have provided the rich arguments to which others have responded. Rawls took justice to be the fundamental virtue of a political system and explored how individuals might be thought to contract for the content of principles of justice that would regulate a political society, conceived as a scheme of social cooperation. He concluded that individuals would want to ensure a system of equal basic liberties but would be prepared to accept inequalities if they were attached to positions in society available to all under equality of opportunity and if those inequalities were to the benefit of the worst-off group in society. This last requirement—the difference principle—has attracted enormous attention. It has been seen as too egalitarian by those who think that Rawls has an over-extended view of the nature of social cooperation in relation to the claims of the individual. It has been seen as insufficiently egalitarian by those who want to pursue further Rawls's thought that individual talent is the result of morally arbitrary luck, to be discounted in the distributive systems of a just society. Hence liberal egalitarians have been discussing the relationship between equality of resources and equality of welfare, or of the opportunity for welfare.

The assertion has been made that modern liberalism is infected with individualistic commitments that neglect important truths about the sources of identity of people and that further neglect the important value of community and culture to the nature of social cooperation and individual well-being. Rawls's scheme is alleged to rely on the notion that individuals can have a commitment to some procedural conception of what is right in the absence of a substantive conception of what is good, and that there is some deep incoherence in this approach. The conflict is usually presented as concerning individualism and communitarianism; sometimes, as liberalism and communitarianism (the view that identity is rooted in community and that communities are desirable social formations).

Who Defines the Good?

Neutralist liberals (of whom Rawls is one) hold that the state should be neutral about conceptions of the good. The nature of the good life is not to be settled for citizens: rather, they are to be provided with an agreed framework in which they can explore, work out, and revise their own conceptions. Private individuals are to be allowed the space—through a scheme of rights and so on—to settle for themselves what is the good life for them, and the nature of social cooperation requires that they do this within a publicly endorsed frame of action. In similar vein, the contemporary British political theorist Brian Barry has argued that matters of religious belief and sexual orientation are so important to individuals and, at least in the case of religion, matters of such epistemological uncertainty that the state must be impartial and that more generally it must be impartial between individuals' conceptions of the good. It is to regulate their interaction through a contractually conceived notion of impartiality and principles dealing with avoiding harm to others.

Liberal perfectionists, however, claim that we should be concerned more directly with persons' well-being, and such a concern involves discrimination between the conceptions of the good individuals happen to have. Sometimes autonomy is presented as one of the most important elements of that well-being, although neutralists maintain that "autonomy" is simply one conception of the good.

These arguments are new versions, or perhaps new sites, of older problems within liberalism. Why should equal liberty be a foundational principle? What does equal liberty require? The detailed explanation of institutions compatible with, or required by, some principle of equal liberty has varied greatly. Hugo Grotius, a seventeenth-century Dutch humanist; John Locke; and Samuel Pufendorf, an eighteenth-century German jurist and historian, each began from an interpretation of the Bible, and in particular of Genesis. They believed that it provided them with a guide to God's intentions and a reason to develop a scheme of natural rights. God's gift to Adam they took to be a gift to all men, so that there was no natural political authority and no natural private property. Both were human institutions in need of explanation and justification, for all were born free and equal. The explanation of the difference between natural equality and the political inequalities of their own world they found in a social contract, since for all three consent was the foundation of political society. Whereas for Pufendorf and Grotius consent was also a sufficient explanation of the origin of private property, Locke tried to show how private property could legitimately have arisen (that is, without violating natural rights) by the expenditure of individual labor. He thought that he had thereby produced a possible justification of the unequal private property distribution of his own day; it remains controversial how equally he wished political rights to be distributed.

It is not controversial, however, that Locke's doctrine was based on natural rights, conferred on men as logical accompaniment to their duties to God, duties themselves consistently specified, in his view, by reason and revelation. Natural rights have certain features: in particular, they are rights that all persons are thought to possess, irrespective of time and place, of when are where they are born. All persons are God's workmanship, for Locke. Some modern liberalisms maintain the commitment to a principle of equal freedom, or of equal concern and respect, but not couching that commitment in the language of natural rights. But others, particularly of a more libertarian hue, have continued to use that discourse and to specify the requirements of the social recognition of the natural rights to one's body, or self-ownership. They have variously concluded that all have an equal right to natural resources, or to an unconditional universal basic income, or to the fruits of their talents. These writers have been trying to take into account advanced capitalism, a very different economic and social world from the one in which Locke lived, but there is a clear intellectual inheritance as well.

The Secularization of Liberalism

Although Locke's theory depends crucially on its theological underpinning, modern liberalism has a highly secular stamp. There is nothing peculiar to liberalism in this general movement of secularization of thought. But we might see in the modern concern with developing a political theory that can be exhibited as neutral or impartial between competing conceptions of the good both an epistemological and a doctrinal connection with earlier liberalism.

Locke himself was concerned about the value of toleration, about the state's openness—in terms of membership or rights—to those with a variety of religious views, and with the associated question of the limits of observance that could be required of citizens. It is noteworthy, however, that he did not wish to extend toleration to Catholics or to atheists. The first he excluded because he was troubled by the possible conflict of loyalties to domestic political society and to the pope. Atheists he excluded because he thought they lacked any substantial foundation on which they could take an oath. And Locke, of course, took part in practical politics associated with the Earl of Shaftsbury and opposition first to the future King James's claim to the throne and later to his occupation of it because of his Catholic sympathies.

Later declarations of rights included the right to freedom of worship and the claim that the state should be uninterested in the religion of particular citizens. In England, it was the nineteenth-century liberals who repealed the Test Acts, which required candidates for public office to meet certain religious criteria, and the Corporation Act, which required religious conformity from members of municipal corporations (1828) and provided for Catholic emancipation (1829). This practical toleration has been described as the chief cause of the liberal Anglican Whigs. But republican liberty is not exhausted by the negative idea of noninterference; in American thought, it was associated with the sovereignty of the people and an attempt to harness virtue to the pursuit of public affairs. Ideas of so-called ancient liberty, the freedom to participate in the joint determination of common affairs, remained part of the intellectual background.

The very notion of toleration seems to have an element of a willingness not to persecute or coerce those with whom one nevertheless disagrees or whose practices are found objectionable, and in this sense it links closely to the modern impartialist liberal formulation that the state should be neutral between conceptions of the good. Although the liberal concern with toleration was no doubt primarily a question of religious toleration, it has in that way become more generalized. In addition, participatory political rights are a special case of the right to be taken into account in any hypothetical contract for justice. More generally, the public becomes associated with the procedural issues, and the private, with substantive concerns.

There is, further, an epistemological link to be explored, and one which helps to explain the apparent paradox that, although some celebrate the alleged spread of adherence to (selected) liberal values, others are announcing the death of liberalism. This link is made through the association between liberalism and hopes for improvement. Liberalism has certainly had ameliorative ambitions, whether the emphasis be the rule of law, economic growth through market institutions, or prospects for moral improvement. Locke can be seen objecting to the power of a Hobbesian sovereign; Scottish economist Adam Smith (1723–1790), to the defects of a mercantilist or physiocratic state policy toward economic activity; the French *philosophes* of the Enlightenment, to the pernicious consequences of lack of freedom of speech and publication for the growth of scientific knowledge and improvements in social behavior. In this way, the ameliorative ambition has been associated with a rationalist, scientific cast of mind, often in the claim that improvements in scientific knowledge would be the basis for improving the human condition.

For the Betterment of Humankind

This limited optimism has of course never gone unchallenged by opponents, such as the conservative Burke and the French Catholic reactionary Joseph de Maistre (1753– 1821). The search for reliable knowledge must involve deep skepticism toward ideas whose claim on our reason is limited to their being asserted by those in authority. Locke famously pursued that argument, and the rejection of innate ideas, in his *Essay Concerning Human Understanding* (1690), generally regarded as a crucial contribution to the self-confidence of Enlightenment thinkers. The scope for improvement was severely circumscribed for those who accepted the doctrine of original sin, but rational skepticism toward that doctrine, the rejection of authoritatively determined dogma, the rejection of innate ideas, were in complex ways interconnected.

Some of these complexities are well illustrated by the fate of so-called Catholic Modernism in the last decade of the nineteenth century and the early twentieth century. Conscientious people confronted the tension between modern science and traditional Catholic teaching. They hoped that the church could be revitalized by greater accommodation with modern conditions, either through revision of doctrine or through social changes, or both. The movement was condemned, but it has been suggested that the condemnation only postponed confronting the underlying issues.

The hope for improvement contained within liberalism was also for many a call actually to improve conditions. And this call could have a source outside merely secular considerations. For example, the complex political alliance that finally legislated in England against slavery had as major figures men like William Wilberforce (1759–1833), an evangelical English reformer, and his like-minded friends in the Clapham Sect. They interested themselves in hospitals, prison conditions, and the penal system. More generally, they felt a deep obligation to God to use their talents wisely. Others, like the English philanthropist Thomas Foxwell Buxton (1786–1845), thought his politics, and more particularly his abolitionism, followed from his religious beliefs.

Modern liberalism retains its ameliorative ambitions and is replete with references to what rational or reasonable individuals would or should accede to. In that way, it retains its commitment to reasonable assent as the touchstone of legitimacy. What is justified is what rational individuals assent to—or would assent to. It also treats reason as a potentially interpersonal bond in diverse societies: whatever our own conception of the good, we can agree on a framework of political institutions or justice or the rule of law.

It is just this component of liberalism's heritage that has led to the charge that liberalism is dead, and it is in just these areas that liberals have faced problems with the empirical diversity of modern society. For the claim has been that these commitments—to rational assent as a test of legitimacy and to the power of reason to unite those with diverse commitments—are themselves unrealistic in the practical world and philosophically unsupported. The search for publicly justifiable principles will be fruitless.

Multiculturalism and Neutrality

The difficulties liberalism encounters in practice may be illustrated by the question of religious education and of multiculturalism more generally. Even if we allow the neutralist claim, that the state should be impartial between conceptions of the good, we have to accept that religious persons place great importance not only on their own freedom of worship and religious observance but also on the transmission of their beliefs and the necessary background to understanding them. The question then arises, what should a state that conscientiously adopted the neutralist perspective actually do in the provision of education?

Many states have adopted the view that education for children is compulsory—on some combination of arguments from autonomy, well-being, social inclusion, collective economic prosperity—and they have buttressed the compulsory character of education by state provision or state support for its provision. It has been hotly debated as to whether the state should provide education for all without regard to religious belief, leaving that to voluntary provision, or whether it should provide funds to support schools with their own religious affiliations, whatever they might be, or whether it should provide funds only for such religiously affiliated schools if they did not make particular religious observance a condition of acceptance of prospective pupils.

Even though the historical debate was not informed by the present-day concept of neutrality, a contemporary liberal has a dilemma as to which policy best expresses a neutralist commitment. There is also often a practical tension between the (historically grounded) liberal reaction to community or culture on the grounds that these may well be inhibiting to freedom in one of its many forms and the realization that association with both may play an important part in the provision of individual well-being, social cohesion, and the pursuit of a conception of the good.

The title of British philosopher Alasdair MacIntyre's book *Whose Justice? Which Rationality?* (1988) already conveys the skepticism it elaborates. The optimism of liberalism is misplaced. There is more than one rationality, more than one justice, because these ideas exist within particular social settings, and there is no overarching community or society of rational political deliberators who share something in common that transcends their substantive differences. This critique complements the more specific charge that liberal individualism is ontologically unsound, relying on an insupportable picture of a person divorced from a social setting that gives meaning to his conception of himself. Both deny the vision of the individual they attribute to prominent liberal doctrines, although the one gives primacy to culture, and the other, to community in grounding their complaints. Many believe that globalization, the spread of market relations, will, at least in the short to medium term, produce all sorts of nationalist and protectionist political reactions that liberalism, with its cosmopolitan aspirations, will regret.

See also *Communitarianism; Conservatism; Enlightenment; Globalization; Individualism; Justice, Social; Pluralism.*

Andrew Reeve

BIBLIOGRAPHY

Arblaster, Anthony. *The Rise and Decline of Western Liberalism.* Oxford: Blackwell, 1984.

Bellamy, Richard. *Liberalism and Modern Society.* Pittsburgh: Pennsylvania State University Press, 1992.

Brent, Richard. *Liberal Anglican Politics: Whiggery, Religion, and Reform, 1830–1841.* Oxford: Clarendon Press, 1987.

Gray, John. *Liberalism.* Milton Keynes: Open University Press, 1986.

Manning, D. J. *Liberalism.* London: J. M. Dent, 1976.

Mulhall, Stephen, and Adam Swift. *Liberals and Communitarians.* 2d ed. Oxford: Blackwell, 1996.

Vidler, Alec R. *The Church in an Age of Revolution.* Rev. ed. Harmondsworth: Penguin, 1971.

Liberation theology

Liberation theology emerged in Latin America in the late 1960s as part of a general effort in Roman Catholicism to rethink the role religion should play in society and politics and to rework religious and political structures to make room for participation by the poor and powerless. The writers and thinkers who created liberation theology constitute a distinct generation in the Latin American church. Highly educated (often in Europe) and with experience far beyond the norm for ecclesiastical careers, these young men began holding seminars, writing and publishing, advising movements, forming leaders, and, after a while, entering into contact with one another. These interchanges were reinforced by local and regional initiatives that joined elements from the churches with professionals, activists, and organizers in pursuit of common goals: medical students and doctors worked with local clergy and community leaders to promote health committees; educators joined together in alternative schools; cooperatives formed as communities called on clergy for assistance; and clergy helped communities find new sources of aid.

The first major book to put a name to the movement, *A Theology of Liberation* by Gustavo Gutiérrez, was published in 1973, capping a long period of writing and reflection. Since that time, writers like Gutiérrez, Leonardo Boff, Juan Luis Segundo, Jon Sobrino, and others have advanced a concern with historical change, insisted on the necessity and primacy of action to promote justice, and underscored the importance of everyday experience as a source of religiously valid values. From these foundations, liberation theology has spurred and legitimized organizational innovation and undergirded a notable clerical populism throughout the region that has sent sympathetic priests, sisters, and pastoral agents "to the people." Their notion of religious service embraces values of solidarity and shared experience and identifies strongly with people whose lives are deformed by oppressive structures.

Commitment to the poor has several dimensions: to side with the poor, to listen and learn lessons from the poor, to be present among the poor. This commitment goes beyond charity or serving as agent, representative, or voice for the poor. All of that is valid, to be sure, but the core goal is to change unjust structures and in this way to remove the need for charity, spokesmen, agents, or others to serve as voices for the voiceless. The commitment is socially specific: not to the poor in spirit but rather to the materially poor. The social expression and cultural meaning of poverty vary enormously over time and across countries, but poor people everywhere lack power and face a constant struggle with scarcities: of money and resources, of health, of opportunities.

By the mid-1960s economic and political transformations were producing new kinds of poor people in Latin America. In contrast to their mostly peasant ancestors, poor people were by then likely to be more physically mobile, to have access to communications media, and even to be literate. They were more available for organization, more capable of organizing themselves. In these circumstances, the message of liberation theology (with its characteristic stress on justice and activism in the pursuit of justice) resonated strongly.

A Political Theology

The political resonance of liberation theology takes many and varied forms. The new legitimacy of prophetic roles, such as denouncing injustice and working for change, made its way into church documents critical of economic inequality and political injustice. Theologians helped draft influential church statements on politics and public policy. Liberationist insistence on going to the people spurred efforts to promote organization among the poor. Extensive networks of groups were established: base communities (small groups originally formed for religious study), peasant and urban unions, cooperatives, neighborhood associations, self-help groups, and communal kitchens, as well as centers for research and publication. Church-sponsored institutions provided these groups with shelter, protection, and invaluable human and material resources. Such institutions have been particularly active in human rights groups, peasant unions, and urban subsistence groups.

Central to the innovative character and impact of liberation theology was a radical shift in religion's view of itself and the world. The axiomatic and deductive logic long central to Catholic tradition—in which established principles set out in official doctrine by authoritative spokesmen are applied to delimited circumstances by groups under tight control—was challenged by something much more inductive and messy. Experience, above all the experience of the poor, became a source of new and religiously valid insight. In the effort to understand this experience—to make sense of why Latin American societies were the way they were—liberationist thinkers drew heavily on the new Marxist sociology being created about this time in Latin America. Concepts of class, exploitation, and dependence began to appear in religious discourse. Working with notions of class, and using a sociological understanding of the world, meant that generalities about the common good, charity, avoidance of violence, and promotion of peace yielded precedence to powerful and specific critiques of injustice.

Practical consequences soon followed. Initial encounters with Marxist theory were reinforced and carried forward by alliances forged from the ground up between Catholic and Marxist groups from Chile and Peru to Central America and Brazil. Looking at their own societies, this generation saw unjust social structures marked by inequalities of class and power and held together by force. The turn to sociology meant that the moral vocabulary of religion—the words and symbols used to make sense of the world—now found expression in explicit social references. It is one thing to talk about the common good; it is quite another to point to specific issues of land, wages, and inequality, naming time and place. Insisting on the social specifics of poverty put liberationists and those who espoused their ideas at the heart of conflicts. Central among these conflicts were the civil wars in Central America and resistance to arbitrary government and military rule throughout the continent. Activists were also deeply involved in the organization of peasant movements and urban neighborhood groups and in promoting and defending human rights throughout the region.

Liberation theology has changed considerably in tone and emphasis in the more than three decades since its ideas first began to find expression—and a ready audience—in Latin America. In the early years considerable stress was placed on the primacy of politics and political action as necessary tools for rebuilding unjust and unequal societies along lines more in accord with God's love for the poor. There was much enthusiasm for socialism, a disposition for confrontation with established powers, and a belief that once the people became fully aware of their situation, large-scale change would soon follow. Consciousness raising was the order of the day.

The New Face of Liberation

The collapse of socialism, the defeat of the Sandinista revolution in Nicaragua in 1990, and the failure of many groups in which liberationists placed their hopes have combined to prompt a new look at incremental change and political democracy. For some time theologians have also been slowly shifting their agendas away from class and politics to new issues such as developing a distinctively liberationist spirituality; exploring the teachings of historical precursors such as Bartolomé de Las Casas, the sixteenth-century bishop famous as the defender of the Indians; and crafting a liberationist understanding of ecological issues.

Early work on the social effect of liberation theology drew more from writings by theologians and activists than from direct study of groups or group members themselves. The cultural and political potential of groups was highlighted, their egalitarian quality was underscored, and their unity and common purpose were exalted. The weight of evidence now available on liberationist grassroots organization (base communities, cooperatives, neighborhood associations, mothers' clubs, and subsistence organizations of all kinds) paints quite a different portrait. Most members of liberationist groups come not from the poorest of the poor but rather from lower-middle-class and stable working-class populations, including peasants with some land. In any event, the orientations of any given group cannot be predicted from the socioeconomic attributes of its members. Group purpose owes more to the efforts of pastoral agents and activists and the particular views they try to put into action. Most clerical agents are recruited from religious orders, which gives them more freedom of action within the church than that of typical parish priests. Both agents and members of groups are overwhelmingly female. Most groups are less ambitious, more localized, less explicitly political, and much more conventionally religious than originally supposed.

The predominantly female membership of groups enriches but also limits their goals. They are enriched because women have tangible needs rooted in daily life. Moreover, because church organizations are culturally sanctioned vehicles for women, they help to draw hitherto silent voices into public spaces. But objectives are also limited because the same cultural predispositions that make members suspicious of politics (as "dirty," as "men's work") undermine efforts to move beyond the local level. To be sure, the fact that people—here poor women—think and move within constraints does not mean that they do not think or move at all. The experience of communal kitchens and subsistence organizations, or of human rights campaigns linked with liberation theology and run by women, are important examples.

Liberation theology's early impact was magnified by a factor of surprise. That change should arise in the Catholic Church took many observers unawares. Wedded to theories of secularization, scholars had little room in their analytical schemes for vigorous moves by religious groups to reclaim the public stage, much less in the name of change. Elites and activists were also taken by surprise and challenged by the energetic surge of the new ideas and groups that religion began to push and pull onto the public scene. Liberation theology drew strength by combining the power of religious speech with the legitimacy of religious institutions and the space for action that they marked out. New issues were placed before the public eye and on the agendas of governments and major institutions.

Liberationists played a critical role in writing the documents produced at the 1968 Second General Conference of Latin American Bishops in Medellín, Colombia, as well as the countless pastoral letters and other communications in which bishops' conferences and individual prelates set out an agenda critical of the "established disorder." Working within the institutional structure has obvious advantages but also carries costs. Activists are open to a range of pressures and are vulnerable to loss of cover as sympathetic bishops retire and supportive religious orders change their positions. But for the most part these negative results came later. In the movement's early days working within the institutional structure of the churches clearly empowered liberationists, giving them access to important material and symbolic resources.

Problems and Prospects

In recent years notices of the decay and death of liberation theology have abounded. Reading the signs of contemporary events, scholars and journalists have joined religious and political activists in writing obituaries for liberation theology as a vision of faith and action able to inspire and sustain change. Sustained opposition from the Vatican, the fall of socialism in Europe, the defeat of the Sandinista regime in Nicaragua, and the growth of evangelical Protestantism among groups that liberationists had seen as their core constituency have reinforced a sense that the promise of liberation theology is at best played out, at worst, an illusion that never was. Although some write in mourning and others with evident satisfaction, there is broad agreement that the creative force of liberation theology is spent, its promise unlikely ever to be fulfilled.

Some authors have noted problems in the very project of liberation theology as originally formulated. Excessive dependence on images and categories of social class, for example, led many to misread the character of popular identities and self-perceived needs. This created unwitting gaps between liberationist activists and the very people for whom they claimed to speak. An inadequate appreciation of the problems involved in any move to long-term political action further weakened movements and made them vulnerable to defection and betrayal. Other writers note that liberationists never managed to break with the hierarchical tradition and position of the Catholic Church. Notable differences remained between those who "went to the people" and the people themselves.

Despite these difficulties, it is too early to write obituaries for liberation theology. It is more useful rather to specify its long-term impact on religion, on politics, and on the relation between the two. A clear distinction should be drawn between the resonance of ideas and the fate of specific movements or alliances. Liberationist ideas have clearly entered the mainstream of both religion and politics. Issues like human rights, accountability, and the legitimacy of active participation by ordinary people have been put on the agendas of crucial institutions and attracted national and world attention.

Liberation theology has undergirded a practical theory of rights grounded in presumptions of equality and access. Movements have fared less well, and many have foundered on a deadly combination of repressive violence (above all in Central America), the gap between radical visions of activists and the more modest goals most members espouse, and, finally, on the impact of democracy itself. The return of civilian rule and political democracy opened new channels for activism and led to splits as members divided among available alternatives. The practical legacy of liberationist movements will depend on whether the generation that came to maturity in liberationist movements remains activist, and in what specific ways.

See also *Base communities; Human rights; Jesuits; Justice, Social; Latin America.*

Daniel H. Levine

BIBLIOGRAPHY

Berryman, Phillip. *Liberation Theology.* New York: Pantheon, 1989.

Boff, Leonardo. *Ecclesiogenesis.* Maryknoll, N.Y.: Orbis, 1986.

———. *Ecology and Liberation.* Maryknoll, N.Y.: Orbis, 1995.

———. *Jesus Christ Liberator.* Maryknoll, N.Y.: Orbis, 1978.

Gutiérrez, Gustavo. *Las Casas: In Search of the Poor of Jesus Christ.* Maryknoll, N.Y.: Orbis, 1992.

———. *The Power of the Poor in History.* Maryknoll, N.Y.: Orbis, 1983.

———. *A Theology of Liberation: History, Politics, and Salvation.* Maryknoll: Orbis, 1973.

———. *We Drink from Our Own Wells.* Maryknoll, N.Y.: Orbis, 1985.

McGovern, Arthur. *Liberation Theology and Its Critics.* Maryknoll, N.Y.: Orbis, 1989.

Smith, Christian. *The Emergence of Liberation Theology.* Chicago: University of Chicago Press, 1993.

Libya

Libya, or the Socialist Libyan Arab People's Jamahiriya (state of the masses), is the fourth largest Arab country in size, with a land mass of about 1.8 million square kilometers. About 90 percent of the country is desert; less than 2 percent is arable land. Libya's approximately five million people rely on imports for more than 65 percent of their food, although attempts have been made to increase the domestic supply. The people of Libya are predominantly Arab, and nearly all are Muslim.

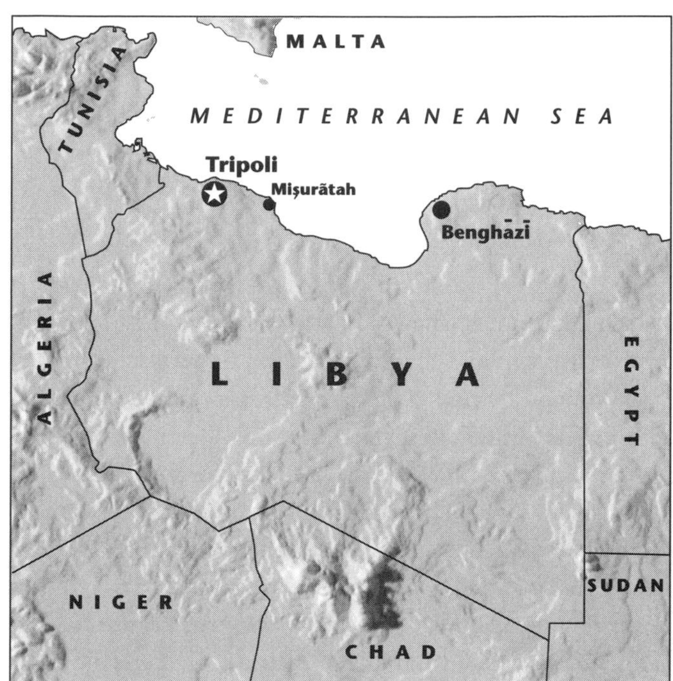

Historical Background

Until its independence in 1951, Libya, composed of the regions of Tripoli, Cyrenaica, and Fezzan, was not a separate country and was frequently controlled by foreigners, although full control was often limited to the coastal regions. Libya's culture and history have been greatly affected by migrations of Semitic peoples, who easily integrated with the local people. These migrants were the Phoenicians (about 900 B.C.) and the Arab Muslims, who started their invasions in A.D. 643 and, as the first invaders to control the interior, gave the country its religious and cultural foundations.

Greeks, Romans, Egyptians, Vandals, and Byzantines conquered Libya before various Arab dynasties from Egypt, Hejaz Iraq, Syria, and Tunisia. In 1510 Spanish forces briefly occupied Tripoli and other parts of Libya and then handed the area to the crusading Knights of Malta, who were expelled by the Ottomans in 1554. The Ottomans maintained loose control over Libya, and in 1714 the Ottoman governor Ahmad al-Qaramanli declared his autonomy. He established a hereditary dynasty that lasted until 1835 under ostensible Ottoman or Arab rule. Prior to the reestablishment of direct Ottoman rule in 1835, a civil war occurred as a result of oppression by the Qaramanlis and a financial crisis brought about by American and European successes against the piratical activities of the Qaramanlis in the Mediterranean.

The Ottomans were able to regain control except in Cyrenaica, which had come under the control of Shaykh Muhammad bin Ali al-Sanusi, an Algerian religious reformer. In 1843 al-Sanusi had begun to establish the first of 150 Sufi religious *zawiyas* (lodges) as part of his new Sufi brotherhood, the Sanusiya. Al-Sanusi sought a return to Islamic orthodoxy and the revitalization of Islam in North Africa. The *zawiyas* helped to settle tribal disputes and became centers of trade and agriculture. After al-Sanusi's death in 1859, his son moved to Al-Kufra oasis and transformed the order into a religious military organization, which became the actual authority in much of Libya and in large areas of Chad and Sudan.

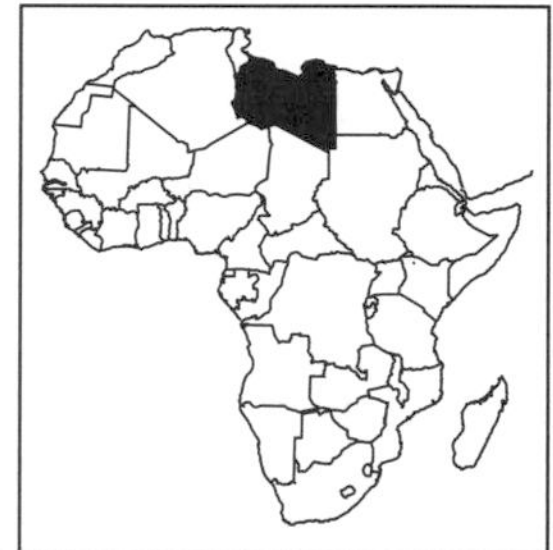

Following an invasion by Italy in 1911, the Sanusiya movement led the fierce popular resistance to Italian control over Tripoli and Cyrenaica. The Italians were persuaded to reduce their presence and to grant the Libyans a limited autonomy under al-Sanusi's grandson, Idris. When Benito Mussolini became prime minister of Italy in 1922, a more brutal policy was pursued against the Libyans. Al-Sanusi went into exile in Egypt and was replaced by an Italian governor. Under the leadership of Shaykh Omar al-Mukhtar, resistance was carried on for nine years until al-Mukhtar was captured and executed. In 1934 Italy reunited the whole country under its control, and by 1939 Libya was incorporated into Italy.

During World War II al-Sanusi allied himself with the British and fought against the Axis powers of Germany and Italy. After the war Cyrenaica and Tripoli were occupied by the British and Fezzan by the French. After long debates the United Nations voted in 1949 to give the country two years to prepare for independence. On December 24, 1951, the independent United Libyan Kingdom was established under Idris al-Sanusi. Libya became a loosely federated state with a weak central government. In 1953–1954 an impoverished Libya signed treaties allowing Britain and the United States to establish military bases in return for economic aid. Libya also joined the Arab League and the United Nations in 1953 but remained neutral on most issues.

Qaddafi's Regime

The discovery of oil in 1959 was a mixed blessing that led to many dramatic changes. The sudden economic boom, the mismanagement and corruption of some powerful elements of the ruling elite, and the growing urbanization contributed to radicalization of the society. The Arab-Israeli conflict and Western support for Israel aroused pan-Arabist feeling; in particular, the war between Arabs and Israel that took place in June 1967 greatly exacerbated the internal climate. In 1969 a group of young officers led by Muammar al-Qaddafi overthrew the monarchy in Libya. After the coup, Qaddafi nationalized foreign banks, confiscated Italian colonists' property, moved against oil companies to demand higher prices, and closed U.S. and British military bases.

Qaddafi pursued a unique blend of Arab nationalism and Islam. Early on he adopted *shari'a* (Islamic law). Despite his mistrust of the orthodox *ulama* (learned men) and of the Sanusi brotherhood, he saw Islam as a progressive force. In 1973 Qaddafi proclaimed his cultural revolution, which he saw as an alternative to "materialistic capitalism and atheistic communism." He surrendered all of his official titles to become the revolutionary regime's leader in 1974. As the regime became even more radicalized, he dissolved the ruling revolutionary council and established a system of direct democracy in an attempt to create a popular base and to eliminate the increasing opposition. In 1977 Libya was declared the Socialist Libyan Arab People's Jamahiriya, and popular sovereignty was declared.

The new system was based on basic popular congresses to which all Libyans belonged on the basis of professional affiliations such as unions, syndicates, or residential areas. The 2,150 local popular congresses were to discuss all policy issues, foreign and domestic, and elect delegates to the General People's Congress. In 1977 the People's Congress, the equivalent of a parliament, elected a general secretary, or prime minister, and other secretaries (ministers). A General Popular Committee was set up as an administrative organ that implemented the decisions of the People's Congress. The system, which was intended to favor direct popular democracy, banned political parties and special interest groups, which allegedly undermined the common interest of the society. The cumbersome nature of the system, however, and the constant individual commitment it required made it difficult to operate. This difficulty led Qaddafi to establish revolutionary committees responsible to him. He also called for the decrease in the number of professional soldiers and for an increase in the number of trained and armed members of the revolutionary committees, most of whom were young loyal activists. The revolutionary committees were given a unique role in defending the regime and pursuing its opponents, particularly as reports of coup attempts increased. Qaddafi reportedly escaped an attempt on his life in 1984.

The regime benefited greatly from the rise in oil prices and from nationalization in 1973. Major development programs were launched, and foreign workers were brought into the country to aid in this effort. Free education, health care, and other social services were provided to the public. The regime passed legislation affirming equality between men and women and established wage parity for male and female workers and new rights for women in marriage and divorce. Although opposition to the regime began to surface as early as 1975, the opposition remained fragmented and ineffective, operating mainly from outside the country while the regime retained the support of the lower classes.

Foreign Policy

Libya under Qaddafi pursued a foreign policy linking Islam, Arab nationalism, and socialism. Libya's unwavering support for the Palestinian cause became a major component of its foreign policy, leading to direct confrontations with Israel, the United States, other Arab countries, and even the Palestine Liberation Organization. The regime's failure to attain its declared objective of Arab unity resulted in a shift in emphasis to the Maghrib and Africa. In 1989 Libya joined the Maghrib Arab Union of Algeria, Morocco, Tunisia, and Mauritania and made efforts to curb and oppose American, French, Israeli, and white South African political and military activities in Africa. It supported revolutionary governments in Angola, Burkina Faso, Ethiopia, Ghana, Mozambique, and Zimbabwe. It also supported revolutionary movements such as the *Polisario* in the Sahara, the Irish Republican Army, Muslim guerrillas in the Philippines, the National Liberation Front (Frolinat) in Chad, and the African National Congress (ANC) in South Africa.

These policies led to friction with the United States. Initially the United States did not oppose the new regime because it was viewed as anti-Soviet and reformist. Libya's support for the Palestinians and other revolutionary groups, considered terrorists by Washington, soured ties and led to many confrontations, including minor air and sea battles in 1986.

On April 15, 1986, after levying charges that Libyan agents were behind an attack on a Berlin nightclub that killed three people and wounded two hundred, some of whom were U.S. citizens, the United States launched attacks against Libyan military complexes and a port. Qaddafi's residence was also bombed, leading to the death of seventy people, including his adopted daughter. Allegations that Libya was implicated in the bombings of Pan American flight 103 over Lockerbie, Scotland, in 1988 and a French UTA flight over Niger in 1989 led the United Nations Security Council to impose sanctions on Libya and to demand a surrender for trial of the accused intelligence agents. In 1996 the United States accused Libya of developing chemical weapons and imposed unilateral sanctions against Libya and Iran.

The decline in oil prices in the mid-1980s led Qaddafi's regime to focus on domestic affairs. The regime also began to diversify the economy to lessen dependence on oil and to encourage agricultural cooperatives and family-run enterprises. It also improved relations with its neighbors and began to open its frontiers with them. Nevertheless, the sanctions contributed to the country's economic difficulties. Inflation increased, passing 100 percent in 1995, and continued to rise. Oil production declined and the great investment projects of the early 1970s were showing limited results. The level of social services was reduced, as were foreign imports and salaries. Meanwhile the mainly Islamic opposition increased its activities and in 1993 attempted a coup. Despite these threats, the regime remains firmly entrenched and benefits from huge oil reserves, which are estimated to last fifty years at the current production level.

See also *Qaddafi, Muammar al-*.

Edmund Ghareeb

BIBLIOGRAPHY

Cooley, John. *Libyan Sandstorm.* New York: Holt, Rinehart and Winston, 1982.

Evans-Pritchard, E. E. *The Sanusi of Cyrenaica.* Oxford: Clarendon Press, 1949.

Khadduri, Majid. *Modern Libya: A Study in Political Development.* Baltimore: Johns Hopkins University Press, 1963.

Mark, Clyde. *Libya: A CRS Issue Brief.* Washington, D.C.: Library of Congress, 1997.

Simons, Geoff. *Libya: The Struggle for Survival.* New York: St. Martin's Press, 1996.

Liturgy

Most societies engage in certain actions on public occasions to define, renew, defend, purify, and restore their vitality. Liturgy, from a Greek term that means the "work of the people," refers to such occasions, perhaps observed with sacrifice or dances. Whereas the notion of liturgy may have specifically Greek origins, public rituals have been the primary institution by which a wide range of groups, communities, and societies have ensured that their members—the living and the dead, the young and the old, men and women—experience themselves as connected with and fully present to one another. In this article *liturgy* will refer to those rituals that appear to constitute social order: in some cases the liturgy is the only constitution.

This use of the term may seem strange to contemporary citizens who may be accustomed to thinking of liturgies as something uniquely religious, of particular churches rather than of entire societies. Even in their modern, denominational form, however, one can still detect the fundamentally political nature of such liturgies, as laws are given, infractions confessed, forgiveness given, creeds stated, and allegiance to a king sworn by faithful followers. Liturgies are intensely political precisely because they charter and define a social system. More specifically, these rituals serve to transform the young into adults, purify the community, ward off alien influences, avert disaster, or restore a past imagined to have been compelling, authoritative, and pristine.

Transformation Rituals

What might be called rituals of transformation create the appearance of a social order in which all are present in an approved manner: the young properly disciplined, equipped, and attired and the old or deceased properly honored and assuaged. Thus the coming of age into adulthood, getting married, and dying are dramatized in public rituals not only to ensure the successful passage of the individual from one stage in life to the next but to ensure the continuity of the society from one generation to the next. In these rites of transformation, the self is forged, whether through initiation into adulthood, into marriage, or finally into the company of the ancestors. Further, rites of initiation are obviously political in that they may determine when an individual will be seen to have the right to hold property, take on adult roles, acquire a spouse, or assume an honored position in the company of the departed.

When rituals of transformation fail to present adequate numbers of the young for adult status, social movements will arise that dramatize the demands of the youth on the larger society. For instance, youth movements during the 1960s in American society and in other Western nations dramatized the unwillingness of the youth to make commitments and sacrifices to the family or to the nation-state. Conversely, when rites of transformation fail, one can expect new attempts to ritualize the demands of the larger society on the young. During the Nazi regime in Germany in the 1930s and 1940s, the young were recruited, disciplined, placed in uniform, and assigned public roles in ways that dramatized the capacity of the society to renew itself through the transformation of the nation's youth. An example from the mid-1990s in American society is the mass rituals of "Promise Keepers": Christian men who are mobilized to renew their commitments to the support and nurturance of their families.

Demands for sacrifice and commitment from the young are often justified by claims that the social order itself transcends time. In return for the sacrifice of their animal spirits and youthful longings, the young are given a place in a "timeless" social order. Such sacrifices, however, can be painful, and rituals of initiation must therefore provide an adequate and legitimate outlet for the anger and aggression that they generate. The baptismal liturgy in Christianity, for instance, requires not only the "death" of the individual's former self but militant service in the war against evil in the world.

Many liturgies thus enable a society to transcend the passage of time by linking one generation to another, but only at some cost to the individual. The individual may be asked not only to give up youthful longings but to delay fulfilling aspirations for autonomy, satisfaction, and recognition. It is therefore necessary for rituals of transformation to redirect the individual's anger toward targets outside the community. For instance, the prehistoric hunt may have been ritualized as a means of redirecting the anger of the young away from the older generation; youthful violence might also be redirected toward consumption or toward the members of other communities and societies. Rituals of transformation thus are not only critical in maintaining the continuity of a society over time but in protecting a social system from the force of intergenerational conflict.

Rituals of Aversion

Societies tend to be endangered not only when the ties between generations are threatened but when the boundaries with other societies are weakened. For instance, natural disasters, invading armies or peoples, novel ideas and ways of life, foreign currencies, and newly imported microbes can place a society in *imminent* danger. What might be called rituals of aversion are therefore employed to mobilize the loyalty and commitment of a people to meet such threats. In many Christian churches the litany, in which the congregation and clergy recite prayers of supplication, traditionally has been performed as a public ritual to avert a wide range of social ills and disturbances. An analogy might be the practice, recalled during the Jewish feast of the Passover, of smearing blood on the doorway of the household—a rite believed to have averted the threat of a plague from the people of Israel during the time of their captivity in Egypt. In times of crisis or impending conflict, there is a danger that friends and allies will inadvertently endanger one another in moments of confusion and panic. Thus military rites may distinguish allies from combatants, just as fascist liturgies required supporters of the Nazi regime to identify themselves with insignia and gestures of assent. Such rituals may be thought of as "buying time" for a society by averting a threat from its environment or by mobilizing a people to meet extraordinary danger.

A society may also be endangered when it loses control over its members' friendships and affections, devotion and loyalty. The more that individuals find inspiration and authority in alien sources, the less likely will they be to honor with commitment and sacrifice the claims of their own societies. Even when a society's boundaries are relatively secure, the society may become less cohesive as its members import alien ideas or adopt novel customs. Some may be seeking unconventional or foreign sources of wisdom and thus become host to outside influences; others may become more actively and intentionally subversive. Colonies are prime examples of societies that are vulnerable to such influences, but so is any society that is open to foreign investment and exchange, that is bound to other societies by a common currency, or that is susceptible to the appeals of alien ideas and music or to foreign political institutions and religious beliefs.

In societies that formally separate religious institutions from the state, moreover, religion may influence politics in ways that appear to be intrusive or illegitimate. For instance, the inauguration of a Roman Catholic mayor at a eucharistic liturgy performed by a Catholic bishop might arouse the fears of urban Protestants that Catholics would have undue influence in the local government. Indeed, ritual is often used precisely for the political purpose of enabling one ethnic or interest group to lay claims to social status and to legitimate political authority at the expense of another group. Attempts in England to revise the Book of Common Prayer in recent decades became intensely political in part because they undermined or enhanced the status of particular constituencies. For instance, some argued that the Book of Common Prayer, before revision, united all social classes in an elevated form of language that otherwise would have been the exclusive cultural possession of the upper social strata. The language of the revisions, it was felt, cut that cultural tie in a self-conscious appeal to a speech devoid of multiple and ambiguous meanings and thus allegedly more accessible to those, particularly in the middle class, still outside the church. The implicit constitution of the nation, not only of the church, was at issue.

Purification or Scapegoating

Societies faced with the intrusion of outside influences may respond with rituals of purification in which certain members of the society are chosen to bear the stigma of perceived pollution by outside influences; the practice is sometimes referred to as *scapegoating.* Under Adolf Hitler, Jews were marked with the Star of David, a symbol of Judaism, to distinguish them as the bearers of pollution to Nazi Germany. In some societies, individuals are regularly singled out to engage in ritualized acts of defilement, before being purified and made suitable for returning to their roles in everyday life. Rituals of purification for returning warriors are a case in point, as are certain rituals involving women in acts of caring for the remains of the dead.

When a society believes itself to be in *immanent* danger, however, more stringent rites of purification may call for the actual sacrifice of victims chosen as symbols of pollution: the poor, infirm, deviant, disruptive, or diseased. Such individuals may be exorcised, expelled, or killed for the sake of the renewal of the community through purification. The Christian observance of the Lord's Supper, or the Eucharist, commemorates an event of public scapegoating; it also provides for the purification of the worshippers through the death of Jesus. The worshippers believe that this sacramental meal removes from them the stain of their past failures and transgressions; it washes away their sins. When a society is unable to purify itself in such a fashion, the blame for societal failure and for transgressions against the law is often placed on those least able to defend themselves. The political nature of these liturgies is evident when they fail to restore a society's confidence in its own purity. In these circumstances, social movements are likely to politicize demands for purity by attacking minorities and aliens.

Liturgies of Restoration

When a society is vulnerable to threats from outside as well as from within, more dramatic and effective rituals are called for: rituals that are believed to restore the virtues and authority of an earlier period of relative purity and vigor. Religious rituals that proclaim the advent of the Second Coming of Jesus, for instance, foreshadow the return of divine rule over earthly kingdoms. Similarly, Native American Ghost Dances celebrate the return of ancestral presence and power to a people threatened with extinction. These rituals might be called liturgies of restoration. At times, an inauguration of a ruler may be believed to restore ancient dominions. The pope's coronation of Charlemagne, king of the Franks, as Holy Roman emperor in 800, for instance, was believed to restore the Roman Empire.

In a complex, modern society public liturgies may evoke the recovery of the nation's previous glory, the return of its dispersed people, and the reestablishment of its traditional boundaries; mass liturgies in the fascist movement in Germany and Italy during the 1930s are recent examples. Conversely, private rituals of restoration have been performed by ethnic groups that are suppressed by a dominant majority. Such rites have been instrumental in maintaining the integrity and hope of groups denied autonomy by the larger society; the liturgies of Jews forced into assimilation or hiding are a case in point. It is worth noting that liturgical changes in the Roman Catholic and Anglican Churches have been resisted by communicants who perform the older rites in the hope of a restoration of traditional standards and beliefs.

The political aspects of religious liturgy thus become manifest under certain conditions: enhanced conflict between genders and generations; danger to the community or society from external sources; danger to the cohesion of the community from internal sources; and a weakening of both the boundaries and the cohesion of the social system.

See also *Religious organization.*

Richard K. Fenn

BIBLIOGRAPHY

Bloch, Maurice. *Prey into Hunter: The Politics of Religious Experience.* Cambridge: Cambridge University Press, 1992.

———, and Jonathan Parry, eds. *Death and the Regeneration of Life.* Cambridge: Cambridge University Press, 1982.

Burkert, Walter, Rene Girard, and Jonathan Z. Smith. *Violent Origins: Ritual Killing and Cultural Formation,* edited by Robert G. Hamerton-Kelly. Stanford, Calif.: Stanford University Press, 1987.

Kertzer, David I. *Ritual, Politics, and Power.* New Haven and London: Yale University Press, 1988.

Lincoln, Bruce, ed. *Religion, Rebellion, and Revolution: An Interdisciplinary and Cross-cultural Collection of Essays.* New York: St. Martin's, 1985.

O'Keefe, Daniel Lawrence. *Stolen Lightning: The Social Theory of Magic.* New York: Vintage Books, 1983.

Parkin, David, ed. *The Anthropology of Evil.* Oxford: Blackwell, 1986.

Wilson, Bryan. *Magic and the Millennium.* Heinemann Educational Books, 1973.

Lobbying, Religious

Religious lobbying occurs when people of faith organize groups to petition their governments. Across the world, churches, synagogues, denominations, and other religious organizations work to shape politics and policy. In contrast to private religion, which affects individuals only, religious lobbying is a collective phenomenon involving explicitly religious groups and institutions in politics.

Influence in the United States

Organized religion has actively influenced politics throughout the history of the U.S. Republic. Early in the nineteenth century, religious groups waged spirited battles over a range of issues, including Sunday mail delivery, foreign policy, lotteries, dueling, and the removal of Native Americans from the eastern United States. Later in the same century the controversy over slavery drew much of its inspiration and strength from religious groups. So intense and divisive was the issue that some churches split into northern and southern wings. In the twentieth century the Prohibition movement was, in essence, a religious struggle. Religious groups also influenced the debate over other issues such as child welfare, women's suffrage, and the progressive and populist responses to industrial capitalism.

Until the twentieth century U.S. religious lobbying was primarily ad hoc. Few religious communities had an organized presence in Washington, D.C., or in state capitals. The Prohibition movement marked a turning point at which organized religion became more active. During that fight the Methodist Church established an office on Capitol Hill. In the next few decades several denominations and other religious organizations followed suit. By the 1950s there were approximately 16 religious lobbying organizations in Washington—a number that had increased to approximately 100 by the late 1990s.

During the 1960s many religious communities established new lobbying offices in response to confrontations over civil rights and the Vietnam War. Most of the new religious lobbies advocated liberal positions. They sought to change civil rights laws and challenge U.S. Vietnam War policy. At crucial moments religious lobbying seemed to make a difference. Hubert Humphrey, who served as Senate majority leader during the passage of the 1964 Civil Rights Act, contended that the influence of organized religion was crucial to the passage of major civil rights legislation.

Although it is difficult to generalize, lobbyists for Jewish, Catholic, and mainline Protestant traditions often shared a liberal position on many issues other than civil rights. Lobbyists for these religious communities generally favored reduced levels of defense spending, increased levels of foreign aid, and more government assistance to the poor. Occasionally members disagreed with the liberalism of religious lobbyists who represented them. Most often, critics charged that lobbyists for mainline Protestant denominations—the Protestant churches that have historically defined the mainstream of American culture—do not represent their members. For example, most members of the Episcopal, Presbyterian, Methodist, and Lutheran Churches identified themselves as members of the Republican Party and voted for Republican candidates, yet their lobbyists advocated a liberal agenda. But public-opinion data showing member attitudes on specific issues, not partisan identity, revealed a mix of agreement and disagreement between the positions of lobbyists and their members.

In the late 1970s many conservative religious lobbies emerged. Forming a crucial part of a broader conservative movement, religious conservatives formed political organizations in response to a host of shocks, including the Supreme Court's controversial 1973 ruling about abortion, *Roe v. Wade,* which declared unconstitutional all but the least restrictive state statutes regulating abortion. That decision epitomized a growing perception among religious conservatives that the morality of government was eroding. In response, a number of new organizations thundered onto the political stage with concerns about abortion, school prayer, education, gay rights, and family values.

The leading organization, headed by Jerry Falwell, was the Moral Majority. Several other groups joined Falwell's to form a coalition that received much media attention and appeared formidable. In 1980 Christian conservative organizations claimed credit for electing a new Republican majority in the Senate and a conservative Republican president, Ronald Reagan. During the 1980s they lobbied Congress and the president to adopt policies advancing a conservative social agenda. They exerted some influence on individual lawmakers and on the nature of the public debate, but their principal concerns fell far short of final passage. Despite feverish lobbying efforts, legislation making abortion illegal and establishing official school prayer failed to pass. Some political analysts and conservative activists concluded that the Republicans in government favored economic issues over the social issues religious conservatives supported.

The 1980s culminated with both the termination of several leading Christian conservative organizations, including the Moral Majority, and the failed presidential campaign of Pat Robertson, a televangelist and leader of the Christian right. On the heels of these defeats, Robertson formed the Christian Coalition, which emerged as the leading Christian conservative organization of the 1990s. This organization gave a different face to Christian conservative lobbying. Grassroots efforts were more sophisticated and extensive than the conservative religious lobbying of the previous decades. The organization also deemphasized explicitly religious language and changed its policy focus to be more inclusive. For example, efforts to pass a constitutional amendment banning virtually all abortions were changed to a limited goal of banning so-called partial birth abortions. The Christian Coalition also lobbied for the Contract with America, the platform of the Republicans in Congress who gained the majority in the election of 1994. This alliance with Republican insiders led the Christian Coalition to add economic issues—such as tax cuts and a balanced budget amendment—to a policy agenda previously limited to social issues.

Much religious lobbying is difficult to categorize as liberal or conservative, and religious alliances have changed often. The Prohibition movement was more a Protestant than a Catholic cause. And Roman Catholic opposition to legalized abortion and support for parochial schools did not engender much backing from Jewish and mainline Protestant lobbies. Later in the twentieth century Roman Catholic and Protestant lobbyists did not typically join in Jewish advocacy of foreign aid to Israel.

Occasionally, religious lobbyists transcend their political and religious differences to form a common coalition. In 1993 a diverse coalition of religious lobbyists—Jewish, Catholic, mainline and evangelical Protestant, and Muslim—joined together to support the Religious Freedom Restoration Act. Religious advocates claimed the legislation was necessary because a 1990 Supreme Court decision, *Employment Division v. Smith,* granted to the government an excessive capacity to restrict religious liberty. The act was designed to restore safeguards against government action that had been in place before the Supreme Court decision. With the broad support of the religious community, the bill passed by a wide margin. It was later overturned by the U.S. Supreme Court in *City of Boerne v. Flores* (1997).

Tactics

To achieve their policy goals, religious lobbyists, like all lobbyists, choose from two broad categories of tactics: insider or outsider lobbying. Outsider lobbying involves urging grassroots members and the broader public to petition their government to change its policies. Letter-writing campaigns, protests, and media outreach are common outsider tactics. Using insider strategies, lobbyists develop a relationship with elected officials. The relationship is cultivated in a variety of formal and informal settings in which lobbyists gain access to government officials to discuss public policy concerns.

Religious lobbyists practice both sorts of tactics, but U.S. religious lobbyists use outsider tactics most frequently. Rather than crafting legislative details, religious lobbyists are more likely to advocate general legislative goals. They do this in part because most religious lobbies are resource-poor organizations with a tax status that precludes them from making the campaign contributions often necessary for insider access. The American emphasis on the separation of church and state also can delegitimize the insider status of religious activists, so many religious lobbyists remain outsiders in the midst of Washington politics. And many religious lobbyists believe insider politics promotes compromises in public policy that are sometimes deemed breaches of faith. Viewing insider politics as a potential threat to the integrity of their faith, religious lobbyists abstain from this form of lobbying more than do their secular counterparts.

Securing their insider status, most secular lobbyists have previous government experience and form what scholars have termed a revolving door between government positions and lobbying work. Religious lobbyists have not been a part of this movement. In the 1980s, 50–75 percent of all lobbyists—but less that 10 percent of religious lobbyists—had former government experience. Religious lobbying organizations could solicit former government officials to serve as their lobbyists, but they have preferred instead to hire lobbyists from within their organizations. This practice further limits their insider contacts in government.

Obviously, there are exceptions to this outsider style of lobbying. Many religious lobbyists have enjoyed exceptional insider access that allowed them to influence legislation. Some lobbyists gained this access because they possessed valuable information. For example, many religious lobbyists have contacts with international missionaries and others who can offer valuable assessments of foreign countries. During the 1980s Thomas P. "Tip" O'Neill, then Speaker of the House, is reported to have consulted religious communities working in Central America for information relevant to foreign policy toward that region. In other situations, religious lobbyists have used insider and outsider tactics in tandem. They have used the active support of a unified constituency to gain access to lawmakers.

In the 1990s Ralph Reed, former executive director of the Christian Coalition, used focus groups and opinion polls to choose a package of issues with broad public support. He sought both to generate increased grassroots pressure on Congress and to strengthen insider relationships with congressional leaders, primarily Republicans. Deliberately echoing the Republicans in Congress, he termed the Christian Coalition's agenda a Contract with the American Family. Although it is difficult to measure the influence of any lobby, religious or otherwise, the 1996 Christian Coalition scorecard of congressional votes showed that 26 of 100 senators scored a perfect 100, and an additional 16 received scores greater than 75.

Religious lobbies in the United States are potentially powerful because of the breadth of their membership. At the end of the twentieth century approximately two-thirds of American citizens claimed membership in a religious organization, compared with one-fifth who belong to a labor union or work in business. Yet people join most religious organizations for nonpolitical reasons; lobbying, then, is often a small part of many organizations' missions. Typically, only a modest portion of organized religion's resources is devoted to lobbying. Yet some issues spark intense religious involvement. As a result, organized religion's political influence varies. Sometimes the religious voice is faint; at other times it transforms the republic.

Outside the United States

Religious lobbying is shaped by the structure of government, the legal status of religion, and religion's role in a given society. In the United States the constitutional separation of powers enables groups to lobby several institutions of government, including Congress, the executive branch, the courts, and the government bureaucracy. This system of multiple access leads to the increased prevalence of all lobbyists—including religious lobbyists.

In contrast, most European governments feature parliamentary democracy and proportional representation, which usually give parties more power than interest groups. In a proportional system any organized interest—whether a majority or a minority—can form a political party and gain representation in parliament in proportion to its presence in the voting population. Not surprisingly, proportional systems have spawned multiparty systems and explicitly religious parties such as the Christian Democrats across Europe. In Holland, for example, three Christian Democratic parties dominated Dutch politics until the 1960s. More recently, religious parties have declined in Europe, but they remain an important place for religious interests to gain representation.

Outside Europe a similar pattern prevails in parliamentary democracies. In Israel, eighteen small religious parties coexist with the Labor and Likud Parties. Some research indicates an increase in the number of autonomous interest groups. For example the Gush Emunim, formed in 1973, independently lobbied the government to change its policy of Israeli settlement in Palestine-occupied territories. Most religious interests, however, aligned themselves with one of the major or minor parties.

Most parliamentary systems do not separate powers in government. This arrangement largely restricts lobbyists' access to the ruling party (or coalition of parties) in the executive branch and the parliament. Compounding the problem for lobbyists, many European countries feature a system of corporatist intermediation; in economic policy the government confers official recognition on business and labor in-

Ralph Reed, former executive director of the Christian Coalition, and U.S. Speaker of the House Newt Gingrich greet supporters at the coalition's 1995 annual conference. Widely regarded as the leading Christian lobbying organization in the United States in the 1990s, the Christian Coalition used sophisticated lobbying techniques to seek public support for its conservative agenda.

terests to formulate public policies. Because labor and business lobbyists are granted a privileged status, noneconomic interests such as religion are often limited. Yet government sometimes consults churches on issues such as education. The public funding of church schools across Europe is surely the result of active lobbying by organized religion.

Whether a government is corporatist or not, religious lobbying is less prevalent in countries outside the United States, but it occurs nevertheless. In Great Britain the Church of England is officially established by the state and occasionally lobbies government. In 1986, for example, the Church of England joined with a number of unions to defeat a government bill designed to extend trading opportunities on Sundays. In Italy and Ireland the Roman Catholic Church has lobbied on issues of abortion and divorce laws. In South Korea some church leaders have advocated food aid for famine victims in North Korea.

Throughout American and world history, religious lobbyists have advocated a diversity of causes. Some scholars and activists have contested the legitimacy of religious lobbying; they contend that religious faith affects the individual but not the government. Yet many religious traditions insist that religion is concerned with morality and justice, which inescapably leads to politics. When religious citizens and organizations translate their faith into a concern about politics, they lobby their governments. Throughout history, lobbying has been an important way for religious citizens to organize and express the political implications of their faith.

See also *Abolitionism; Abortion; Christian democracy; Civil rights movement; Education; Environmentalism; Fundamentalism; Gush Emunim; Justice, Social; Nongovernmental organizations; Temperance movements.*

Daniel J. B. Hofrenning

BIBLIOGRAPHY

Adams, James Luther. *The Growing Church Lobby in Washington.* Grand Rapids, Mich.: Eerdmans, 1970.

Drezon-Tepler, Marcia. *Interest Groups and Political Change in Israel.* Albany: State University of New York Press, 1990.

Ebersole, Luke. *Church Lobbying in the Nation's Capital.* New York: Macmillan, 1953.

Findlay, James F. *Church People in the Struggle: The National Council of Churches and the Black Freedom Movement, 1950–1970.* New York: Oxford University Press, 1993.

Hertzke, Allen D. *Representing God in Washington: The Role of Religious Lobbies in the American Polity.* Knoxville: University of Tennessee Press, 1988.

Hofrenning, Daniel J. B. *In Washington but Not of It: The Prophetic Politics of Religious Lobbyists.* Philadelphia: Temple University Press, 1995.

Moen, Matthew. *The Christian Right and Congress.* Tuscaloosa: University of Alabama Press, 1989.

———. *The Transformation of the Christian Right.* Tuscaloosa: University of Alabama Press, 1992.

Weber, Paul, and W. Landis Jones. *U.S. Religious Interest Groups: Institutional Profiles.* Westport, Conn.: Greenwood Press, 1994.

Low Countries

Belgium and the Netherlands, both constitutional monarchies in Western Europe bordering the North Sea, are known as the Low Countries. *Pillarization,* a term that describes the division of society on the basis of religion or ideology, has been institutionalized in each of these countries. Elements of pillarization also exist in Austria, Germany, Italy, and Switzerland.

Both Belgium and the Netherlands have Roman Catholic pillars. The Netherlands also has Protestant and Socialist pillars, and Belgium has Socialist and Liberal pillars. Pillars are organizational complexes that strive toward self-sufficiency (autarky). The more services a pillar provides, the more self-sufficient it is. Pillars promote social exclusiveness and an in-group mentality.

In Belgium the Catholic pillar is the most self-sufficient: it provides almost all services from the cradle to the grave. Catholic institutions embrace most schools (from kindergarten to university), hospitals, old people's homes, youth movements, cultural associations, sport clubs, newspapers, magazines, book clubs, and libraries. The Catholic pillar also has a health insurance fund, a trade union, and banks. But a pillar is institutionalized only if this network is intertwined with a political channel—in Belgium, for example, the Christian People's Party. The political party represents the Catholic network in the political arena, ensures that no legislation is adopted that is to its detriment, and seeks to promote favorable legislative actions.

By the 1950s comprehensive pillars had been consolidated in the Netherlands and Belgium. They had emerged during the last decades of the nineteenth century to insulate Catholics from an increasingly secularized world, to liberate the lower classes (the Socialist pillar), and, in the Netherlands, to emancipate and insulate the Protestant lower classes. Thus pillarization was also partly an acclimatization of the churches to the modern world: protection through adaptation.

In the 1960s pillars in the Netherlands had begun to totter. Christian parties lost voters, and Protestant and Catholic

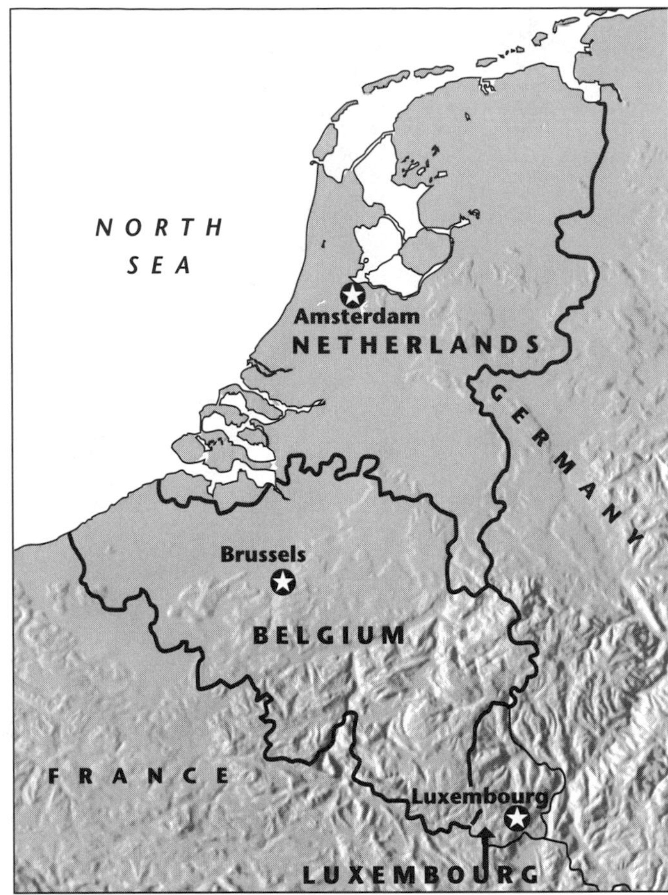

parties merged in a new party, the Christian Democratic Appeal. National and local federations and mergers of Catholic, Protestant, and neutral organizations were also registered. Catholic newspapers abandoned their religious signature, and Protestant and Catholic radio and television stations lost large numbers of members. Professionalization of services, a shortage of funds, and legal regulations in education and health also contributed to weakening the system of pillarization.

In Belgium, secularization and related trends did not break up the pillars. Beginning at the end of the 1960s, debates about whether the Catholic community should continue providing pillarized services and questions about the character of a Catholic organization resulted in a new legitimization of the pillar: sociocultural Christianity. The core values of this new collective consciousness are the right to erect one's own network of organizations based on freedom of assembly and choice; private enterprise; subsidiarity; and economic efficiency. These values also include articulation of a Christian identity in evangelical values: a humane approach toward people receiving services, the community spirit of Christian institutions, stewardship, local authority, spiritual welfare, and self-development. This "sacred canopy" is symbolized by a *C,* which refers more and more to Christian (that is, evangelical) rather than Catholic because Catholic is considered to be limited and to have a restricted appeal. The more economically oriented organizations of the pillar recommend themselves as bastions of freedom of assembly and choice, while the sociocultural organizations appeal mainly to so-called Christian values. It might be argued that these values are not uniquely Christian, even in their particular combination, but anchoring them in the Gospel and referring to God and Christ confers on them a sacred foundation.

Secularization of the two societies has produced different results. Depillarization continues in the Netherlands, but in Belgium, Catholic legitimization has expanded into a broader Christian one. The absence of Protestant and neutral organizations, and the antagonism between the existing pillars in Belgium, precludes mergers and the creation of federations. To continue its appeal to a population becoming less integrated, the Catholic Church saw universalization of its values as the only solution—an innovation that was particularly successful in consolidating and extending the power base of the Christian pillar.

See also *Europe, Western; Religious organization.*

Karel Dobbelaere

BIBLIOGRAPHY

Billiet, Jaak B. "Political Parties and Democratic Organizations in Flanders." In *Private Groups and Public Life: Social Participation, Voluntary Associations, and Political Involvement in Representative Democracies,* edited by Jan W. van Deth. New York and London: Routledge, 1997.

Coleman, John A. *The Evolution of Dutch Catholicism, 1958–1974.* Berkeley: University of California Press, 1979.

Dobbelaere, Karel, "Secularization, Pillarization, and Religious Change in the Low Countries." In *World Catholicism in Transition,* edited by Thomas M. Gannon. New York and London: Macmillan, 1988.

Lutheranism

The largest of the religious movements issuing from the Protestant Reformation of the sixteenth century, Lutheranism had its historic stronghold in Germany and Scandinavia. In the nineteenth century Lutheran missionary movements helped spread this version of Western Christianity to Asia, Africa, and Latin America, but after Europe, North America is home to most Lutherans. More than eight million adherents live in the United States alone.

Martin Luther

Lutherans see their movement as an element of reform within Catholic Christianity. Their founders, they believe, attempted to retain the features that Martin Luther and his coworkers considered to be "evangelical," which means centered not in church laws but in the gospel of grace. Yet their churches everywhere had to adapt to the varieties of political orders in which they found themselves. So it is difficult to speak of only one Lutheran Church or approach to politics.

Obedience to Authority

Luther (1483–1546), a German Augustinian monk and professor of Old Testament scriptures, more than anyone else shaped the movement. He tried to steer a course between the authoritarianism he had seen in the Roman Catholic Church and the Holy Roman Empire, on the one hand, and the anarchy he feared during the Peasants' War of 1525, on the other. Reacting against the latter, he and his followers tended to side with authority. A favorite Scripture was the word of Paul the Apostle in Romans 13, which commanded all beings to be subject to the "powers that be" because they were ordained of God.

While determining an attitude toward public politics, the Lutherans also had to revise the internal politics of the church. Since Catholic bishops would not ordain the Lutheran-minded clergy or were repudiated by such clergy, most of the German principalities saw their prince serving as bishop. In Scandinavia different circumstances prevailed. Thus, in Sweden the church was governed by bishops in the "apostolic succession" (the belief that church authority comes from the apostles through an unbroken succession of bishops) on the order of those in the Church of England after the break with Rome. But in both places, ties between church and state were intimate and entangling, with the "state" or civil authorities dominating. In effect, the generally obedient church became a kind of department of the state, and the clergy were often lower-level civil servants.

It has been difficult for Lutherans through the centuries to mount criticism of authority or to engage in revolt or revolution. Thus, in the American colonies Lutheran leadership tended to invoke the "obedience to authority" theme when the American Revolution broke out in 1776. Many Lutherans prayed for the English monarchy, their "powers that be," until the colonies asserted independence. Thereupon, considering the colonial leaders to be their authority, most of them lined up with the revolutionary forces.

The Two Kingdoms, the Two Hands of God

Lutherans did not obey authority unambiguously and certainly seldom out of motives designed to satisfy leaders of the state. They did so on the basis of their reading of the Bible and ancient interpreters such as Saint Augustine. In the line of thinking that they found congenial, there was to be a sharp separation between "two kingdoms," two "realms," and the activities of the two "hands of God." God was sovereign in both, of course; there were no limits to the activity of the Lord of history.

In the church, however, God ruled with righteousness and grace. In that realm, sinners experienced forgiveness. In the state, God ruled with law. The same citizens as believers had to work to keep the two realms separate, although they lived in and should serve through both. For Lutherans, unlike many of their Calvinist contemporaries, whether or not a ruler was a Christian was a secondary question. God could rule justly through unbelieving but just leaders. Nor did Lutherans believe that their obedience to earthly authority or participation in citizen life was helping to "bring in the Kingdom" (that is, to realize God's purpose in a new ordering of society). They served in the political order as part of their calling, their vocation. Serving well did not make them righteous before God.

The righteousness that availed before God was instead a gift that came with faith in Jesus Christ. On that basis, believers were to make their faith turn active in love, but the state was not necessarily a privileged instrument for that. Some Lutherans have understood the notion that there are "two kingdoms," a secular realm and a spiritual realm, as representing a simple dualism, a radical polarity, and have put all their energies into the spiritual realm. But their doing so is a misreading of Lutheran understandings of political life.

In the United States

Most Lutherans in Europe lived in what was left of the Holy Roman Empire in Germany, where scores of princes had relatively strong local authority, or under monarchs in Scandinavia. Therefore life in a republic, as in the United States, was a new experience, but one that they found congenial. Most of them stress the need for the church to promote morality in politics and to inform that morality with religion, which means that the first task of the church in the civil order is to produce good citizens. Through the years, however, Lutheran bodies, like many others, have made political statements and worked to stimulate some kinds of group expressions of Christianity in the political realm. Seldom have American Lutherans been in the forefront of the more radical movements such as abolition; in fact, Lutherans who lived in the Confederate states tended to support the Confederacy on the ground that it was their legitimate government and that they must obey it. At the same time, they have not followed many other Christians in forming political movements whose aim is to promote America as a Christian nation, nor have they insisted that their rulers be Lutheran or Christian of any sort. Lutherans have often served in political office on local and national levels alike. They have tended to be intensely patriotic. Those of German descent were regarded with suspicion during World War I, even though their loyalties were clearly with the United States. That suspicion led many to abandon vestiges of Old World identifications and interests.

Resistance to Authority

It would be misleading to portray Lutherans as simply passive. There are in Lutheran teachings resources for resisting arbitrary authority. Lutherans like to quote biblical verses that remind believers that they should obey God rather than men. In Hitler's Germany, although the majority went along with the regime or were relatively passive, there were significant forms of resistance. Thus Martin Niemoeller, who preached in a church where Lutheran and Reformed approaches were fused, was critical of the Nazi regime and was sent to a concentration camp for it. The young Lutheran theologian Dietrich Bonhoeffer (1906–1945) felt impelled by conscience not to obey authority and to work actively for the overthrow of Hitler, work for which he paid with his life near the end of World War II. In Scandinavia, Norway's Lutheran bishop Eivind Berggrav stood out as a resister, and the Lutheran cleric-playwright Kaj Munk was killed by the Nazis in Denmark, where the churches did better than elsewhere at speaking up for Jews.

Around the world in the late twentieth century, Lutherans became more active than they had been in the past in opposition to regimes they found to be oppressive. While by no means a majority church in South Africa, Lutheranism produced critics of apartheid—such as Bishop Manas Buthelezi, Dean T. A. Farisani, who was tortured, and the lay preacher Tshifhiwa Muofhe—and identified with reform movements. In El Salvador many associated with and sometimes led resistance movements against corrupt governments; Bishop Medardo Ernesto Gómez Soto provided such leadership, and Pastor David Ernesto Fernandez Espino was tortured and murdered in 1984. Such activity on the part of Lutherans was based on the principle of obeying God rather than men and also followed some root ideas of Luther himself, who declared, for instance, that in conscience one could not kill in a war one believed to be unjust.

One aspect of Lutheranism that often receives attention in politics has been its contribution to individualism. Although Lutherans receive the Gospel in community, they stress personal appropriation of it and personal freedom.

Surrounding Politics

While Lutherans in republics may use their denominational agencies in attempts to change political situations—for example, during the civil rights movement—and to have their quota of task forces and quasi-lobbies, they tend to put their energies into less overt and less formal political engagements. It is sometimes said of Lutheranism that it is less a "justice" church than a "mercy" church.

As part of their calling, their vocation, Lutherans are expected to be active in the secular realm as well as the spiritual, most of them working there through voluntary associations and organizations. They have founded hospitals, homes for orphans and the aged, and immigrant relief agencies wherever they went. They have not excelled at the task of addressing the structural ills of society. They do have, however, a good reputation for participating in endeavors that are not directly political but that will help alter conditions and policies. Thus many Lutherans engage in works of charity through Lutheran agencies or use their faith to address human need through secular organizations.

Lutheranism has been a majority voice in much of Germany and Scandinavia but a minority and not a shaping voice on the American scene. American religion-in-politics was of the Calvinist-Puritan and Anglican sort until late in the eighteenth century, when the religion of reason and science in the Enlightenment influenced the founding of the nation. Then, in the middle of the nineteenth century, significant numbers of Catholics came to the United States. Most of them believed in the transformation of society through religious political action. The Lutherans made their way alongside these other movements, less sure that they could turn the secular realm into the spiritual Kingdom of God or alter the structures of society, but sure that they were to serve God by being exemplary citizens no matter what the external situation.

See also *Bonhoeffer, Dietrich; Germany; Individualism; Protestantism; Reformation; Scandinavia; South Africa; State churches.*

Martin E. Marty

BIBLIOGRAPHY

Altman, Walter. *Luther and Liberation: A Latin American Perspective.* Minneapolis: Augsburg Fortress, 1972.

Bachmann, E. Theodore, and Mercia Brenne Bachmann. *Lutheran Churches in the World: A Handbook.* Minneapolis: Augsburg Fortress, 1989.

Bodensieck, Julius. *The Encyclopedia of the Lutheran Church.* Minneapolis: Augsburg Fortress, 1963.

Edwards, Mark. *Luther's Last Battles: Politics and Polemics, 1531–1546.* Ithaca, N.Y.: Cornell University Press, 1983.

Forell, George W. "Luther's Conception of 'Natural Orders.'" *Lutheran Church Quarterly* 18 (1945): 166.

Hertz, Karl H., ed. *Two Kingdoms and One World: A Sourcebook in Christian Social Ethics.* Minneapolis: Augsburg Fortress, 1976.

Nelson, E. Clifford. *Lutherans in North America.* Minneapolis: Augsburg Fortress, 1975.

Schwartz, Hans. *True Faith in the True God: An Introduction to Luther's Life and Thought.* Minneapolis: Augsburg Fortress, 1996, esp. Chapter 6.

M

Madison, James

A key architect of the U.S. Constitution of 1787 and one of the most significant American figures in the history of the relationship between politics and religion. Madison (1751–1835), who was born in Virginia and educated at Princeton, was a co-author of the influential *Federalist Papers,* a series of commentaries on the Constitution aimed at building support for its ratification, and the major author of the U.S. Bill of Rights (1789). He served as secretary of state under President Thomas Jefferson and then was twice elected president himself, in 1808 and 1812.

Madison's views on church and state, articulated in the "Memorial and Remonstrance against Religious Assessments" (1785), paved the way for the passage of Jefferson's bill for religious liberty in Virginia in 1786. Madison held this bill to be "the strongest legal barrier that could be erected against the Connection of Church and State so fatal to the liberty of both." The views expressed in the "Memorial and Remonstrance" have been enormously influential, particularly as they found expression in the language of the First Amendment to the Constitution: "Congress shall make no law respecting an establishment of religion, or prohibiting the free exercise thereof."

James Madison

As a political philosopher, Madison had an ethical vision of religious liberty that went far beyond mere toleration and called for strict separation of church and state. As a political realist, he had an empirical vision that saw the multiplicity and diversity of religious groups as contributing to religious freedom and to religious and political health. He was, moreover, able to extend this pluralistic insight creatively to politics in general. Indeed, this pluralistic insight constitutes a cardinal premise of his creative political theory of the "extensive republic," a federal republic composed of individual states and capable of reconciling liberty and large geographic size. As a wise practitioner of politics, Madison had a prudential vision that enabled him to work skillfully toward his goals of national strength, republican governance, and individual freedom in a manner that set a splendid standard for American public life.

Madison's ethical vision clearly advanced the cause of religious, political, and cultural freedom. He sought to enhance the integrity, vitality, and health of both religion and the state and of the public life that they sometimes share. His empirical understanding highlighted the value of pluralism and strengthened the operation of a democratic and constitutional system in both the religious and political spheres. Madison's prudential skills established a standard of civility crucial to fruitful dialogue on the religious, political, and cultural issues that continue to agitate society.

The political philosophy articulated by Madison is highly relevant today. Religious liberty and a wise separation of church and state continue to make great sense in preserving the integrity, vitality, and health of both the spiritual and secular domains. Madison's commitment to the value of a multiplicity and diversity of religious and other interests continues to serve as a safeguard against the dangers of religious, political, or economic monopoly. His commitment to civility (reflecting his insistence that religious issues be approached with "forbearance, love, and charity") is crucial for dealing with the inevitable tensions in religion and public life.

Madison's political philosophy presents no barrier to religion's legitimate efforts to nourish American public life. His legacy encourages citizens to address the challenging question of how religion can do so without the adverse consequences of troublesome religious action in public life or troublesome governmental action affecting religious life.

See also *Constitution, U.S.; Jefferson, Thomas; Pluralism; Separation of church and state; documents section.*

Neal Riemer

BIBLIOGRAPHY

Alley, Robert S., ed. *James Madison on Religious Liberty.* Buffalo, N.Y.: Prometheus Books, 1985.

Brant, Irving. *James Madison.* 6 vols. Indianapolis, Ind.: Bobbs-Merrill, 1941–1961.

Lugo, Luis E., ed. *Religion, Public Life, and the American Polity.* Knoxville: University of Tennessee Press, 1994.

Riemer, Neal. *James Madison: Creating the American Constitution.* Washington, D.C.: Congressional Quarterly, 1986.

Rutland, Robert A. *James Madison: The Founding Father.* New York: Macmillan, 1987.

Mahdi

Mahdi is the title of the God-guided leader in Islamic traditions who will fill the world with justice—in Arabic, "the guided one." In the turmoil that occurred during the first century of Islamic history, opposition to the emerging caliphate sometimes took the form of messianic revolts, and the title of mahdi came to be associated with this revolutionary tradition. The earliest figure to be identified as a mahdi was Muhammad ibn al-Hanafiyyah, in 686.

As Shiʿi Muslim theology developed, the idea of the return of the rightful leader (the *imam*), who was in concealment, became identified with the anticipated mahdi. As a result, the concept of mahdi was associated with Shiʿi revolutions. From the Fatamid dynasty in the tenth century and the Safavids in the sixteenth to the Iranian revolution in the 1970s, the hope of a mahdist restoration has been a significant part of Shiʿi political awareness.

Among Sunni Muslims the idea of mahdi was more prevalent in popular religion than in mainstream theology. In times of turmoil, however, mahdist movements developed throughout the Sunni world. The founder of the Mawhhid (Almohad) dynasty in North Africa, Ibn Tumart (died 1130), assumed the title of mahdi. There were mahdist movements in India, including that of Muhammad of Jaunpur in the sixteenth century.

In the modern era, perhaps the most famous Sunni mahdi, Muhammad Ahmad, raised a revolution in Sudan at the end of the nineteenth century and established a state that lasted almost two decades. Mahdist revolts against European imperialists took place in many areas, including Algeria late in the nineteenth century and Nigeria in the twentieth. In the second half of the twentieth century, there were few explicitly mahdist movements, but mahdist-style anticipation continues to be significant in defining the nature of leadership and sociopolitical expectations throughout the Muslim world.

See also *Islam.*

John O. Voll

Malaysia

Malaysia, a multiethnic and multireligious country, is located in Southeast Asia on the South China Sea. Malays, who

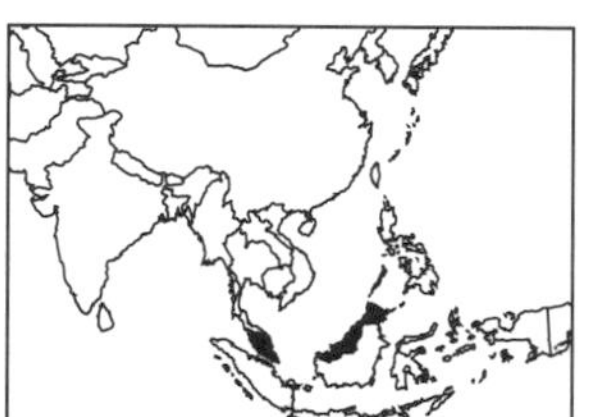

are Muslims, constitute about 50 percent of the country's population of twenty million, and they are the dominant political and cultural force. Ethnic Chinese (35 percent), ethnic Indians (11 percent), and small indigenous groups (2 percent), all of whom are non-Muslims, constitute the remainder of the population.

Because the Malays are themselves divided politically, the support of the Chinese or the Indians is critical to any Malay faction, not only in ensuring its survival as the dominant political force but also for the continued political dominance of the Malays in general. Therefore Malay dominance has always been a negotiated one, which explains why interethnic and interreligious coalition parties, whether as an opposition group or as the ruling party, have dominated democratic electoral politics in Malaysia since the end of World War II.

Religion has become the ethnic identifier in Malaysia. It is certainly the case for the Malays; by default, it is also true for the non-Malays, who are perceived by both the government and the public as first of all non-Muslims and then as Christians, Buddhists, Hindus, and others.

Although the powerful cultural influences of Buddhism and Hinduism affected the inhabitants of the Malay world, it was Islam, brought by Arab and Indian merchants and Chinese traders from the fourteenth century onward, that came to dominate the spiritual and material world of peoples of the region living under a number of feudal Malay rulers.

Islam became the source of legitimacy for the Malay rulers, and the complex of hierarchical institutions within the ambit of feudal power and authority became Islamicized, too, but often spiced with local, pre-Islamic cultural flavors. Although Islam and Malay identity fused during this era, many Hindu and pre-Hindu cultural practices, collectively referred to and embraced as customs, were still observed by both the ruler and his people. Malayness had two central pillars: Islam as the religious and universal one, and Malay customs as the local, moral one.

Colonial Rule

In the eighteenth century the British colonized Malaysia, introducing a clear distinction between religion and the state through a civil administration and a legal system different from the Islamic and customary legal system and courts. To colonize millions of hectares of virgin tropical forest and turn them into rubber, oil-palm, and coffee plantations, the British brought in thousands of indentured laborers from India and China, changing the makeup of Malaysian society forever.

Separation of religion and state and ethnic pluralism became major political issues throughout the 1930s, during the Second World War, and until the early postwar period, articulated as ethnic-based and religious-oriented nationalist movements. The Malay nationalist movement was fragmented, but the factions within were united on the role of Islam as the definer of Malay identity and as one of the three pillars—along with the Malay language and Malay ruler—of the imagined Malay nation. Chinese immigrants were divided over the issue of homeland. Some considered Malaya their home, but many still looked to China.

The Japanese occupation (1941–1945) transformed ethnic and religious politics in Malaysia into an open and eventually violent conflict. A faction within the Malay nationalist movement welcomed the Japanese and worked with them, but the rest supported the anti-Japanese movement led by the British. Because the Japanese had massacred thousands of Chinese and buried them in mass graves in Malaysia, the Chinese were anti-Japanese and supported British efforts to regain control of Malaysia.

When the Japanese surrendered in 1945, ethnic violence broke out in many places and continued for about two weeks. It was mainly between Malays, especially those who were perceived as collaborating with the Japanese, and the Chinese from the radical group within the anti-Japanese movement. Hundreds were killed on both sides, children and adults. Although the Chinese attack was both ethnically and ideologically motivated, the Malays pointed to Islamic and pre-Islamic cult practices to defend their actions. A series of open, if minor, ethnic conflicts followed.

The British tried to contain this ethnic hostility by attempting to establish a unitary state through the Malayan Union project, in which feudalism was to be abolished and equal citizenship granted for all. The union failed, and in 1948 a federation-style government was reinstalled, consisting of the rulers and their provincial states and forming the Federation of Malaya (later Malaysia).

The Federation

The somewhat problematic federation structure of governance still survives. Through the constitution, it institutionalized a multiethnic and multireligious political system that left society in a state of stable tension. In May 1969 open ethnic conflict broke out mainly in Malaysia's capital city, Kuala Lumpur, mainly between Malays and Chinese.

The aftermath of the 1969 incident brought about the long-term, state-initiated pro-Malay affirmative action policy called the New Economic Policy of 1971–1990. It also led to Islamic resurgence, especially among Malay Muslim youth, which has affected not only the non-Muslim non-Malays but the Malay-dominated state itself.

In the 1990s Malayness was not only about redressing perceived socioeconomic imbalances and injustices but also about ethnicity, language, custom, provincial identity, and culture, with Islam as the essential ingredient. Moderate, state-defined Malayness is not uncontested, however. The Pan-Malaysian Islamic Party, the main Islamic party in Malaysia that has controlled the province of Kelantan for decades, remains the alternative definer of Malayness. Islam appeals to Muslims of all classes and background, making it almost impossible to identify which particular ideological interpretation, voice, or personality dominates.

Islam has become more visible in Malaysia than ever before. The proliferation of Muslim financial institutions, medical centers, counseling and social work services, tourist agencies, and supermarkets and clothing, furniture, food, and confectioneries have expanded the exercise of Islam from one that is largely spiritual, abstract, and symbolic to one that is highly profiled and materialistic.

With increased emphasis on Malay and Islamic identity and consciousness in economic and public life, the relationship between the Malay Muslims and the non-Malay non-Muslims has become more strained than ever, thus challenging the idea of Malaysia as a united nation. Most religious and ethnic minorities have chosen to stay in Malaysia, taking advantage of the booming Malaysian economy.

Shamsul A. B.

BIBLIOGRAPHY

Fatimi, S. Q. *Islam Comes to Malaysia.* Singapore: Malaysian Sociological Research Institute, 1963.

Lee, Raymond, and Susan Ackerman. *Sacred Tensions: Modernity and Religious Transformation in Malaysia.* Columbia: University of South Carolina Press, 1997.

Mutalib, Hussein. *Islam and Ethnicity in Malay Politics.* Singapore: Oxford University Press, 1990.

Muzaffar, Chandra. *Islamic Resurgence in Malaysia.* Kuala Lumpur: Fajar Bakti, 1987.

Roff, William. *The Origin of Malay Nationalism.* New Haven: Yale University Press, 1967.

Yegar, Moshe. *Islam and Islamic Institutions in British Malaya: Policies and Implementation.* Jerusalem: Magnes Press, Hebrew University, 1979.

Zainah, Anwar. *Islamic Revivalism in Malaysia: Dakwah among Students.* Kuala Lumpur: Pelanduk, 1987.

Maritain, Jacques

One of the twentieth century's most influential Roman Catholic scholars. Maritain (1882–1973) was best known for his contributions to the theory and practice of democracy, as well as to the articulation of the United Nations Universal Declaration of Human Rights and the charter of UNESCO (United Nations Educational, Scientific, and Cultural Organization) after World War II.

Born into a famous liberal Protestant family, Maritain converted to Catholicism in 1906 after studying the work of French philosopher Henri Bergson in Paris. Later, he taught at several major universities, among them the Institut Catholique in Paris (1914–1939), the Pontifical Institute of Mediaeval Studies in Toronto (1933–1945), and, in the United States, Princeton University (1948–1960) and (from time to time) the University of Notre Dame, site of the Jacques Maritain Center since 1958. Author of more than sixty books, Maritain also found time to serve as the ambassador from France to the Vatican (1945–1948). Returning to France in 1961, he entered the congregation of the Little Brothers of Jesus in Toulouse in 1970.

Maritain dug new foundations in Catholic social thought for the principles of democracy and thus supplied the practical rationale on which the Christian Democratic parties of Europe and Latin America were built in the years following World War II. At the core of his political thought was the Bergsonian insight that democracy not only is compatible with Christianity but also represents a flowering of Christianity's deepest understandings of the human "person"—a term to which Maritain gave special meaning. Correlatively, Maritain distinguished between "individual" and "person"—a dog or a cat may be an individual, but not a person, and the rights of the person have a transcendent source beyond the power of the state.

Maritain saw democracy as the political order most in keeping with Jewish and Christian beliefs because of its respect for the dignity and freedom of each human being, as well as for the radical human equality ("under God") embodied in it. This understanding, while biblically grounded, had not until Maritain found full official expression in the teachings of the Catholic Church, which had been battered by nineteenth-century European experience into excessive wariness about the abuses to which liberal theories are prey. The constituent principles of the democratic idea—the dignity of the person, the transcendent origin of human rights ("endowed by their Creator"), the sharp distinction between society and state, the importance of prudence—find unity, Maritain argued, both in the laws of human nature and in the laws of Jewish and Christian faith. In this he nearly echoed American statesman Thomas Jefferson's appeal to "the laws of nature and nature's God" (Declaration of Independence, 1776). And, indeed, Maritain self-consciously located many of his positive inspirations on this subject in the

Jacques Maritain

American experience, which he took to be the joint fruit of the Bible and practical reason. Without the restraining force of moral laws and religious beliefs, democracy would, Maritain believed (as did early American leaders George Washington, John Adams, and others), be vulnerable to many corruptions by materialism and vagrant public opinion.

For Maritain, "pure" democracies—unchecked in their liberation of unconstrained human whimsy—were prey to various diseases, and a tyranny of the majority could be as evil as that of the solitary despot. True democracy must be ordered democracy based on constitutions with at least three basic characteristics: they must be formed through the consent of the governed; they must protect the dignity and rights of the person; and they must arise from a long educational process that weans citizens from the habits of dictatorship, corrupt nationalism, and mental and spiritual sloth. Maritain's democracy was, then, a limited government, rooted firmly in the soil of the sound habits appropriate to ordered liberty and enlivened by vibrant civic associations.

At the same time, Maritain stressed that it would be a mistake to confuse secular and sacred realms—to mix the things of Caesar and the things of God. Christian faith cannot be made subservient to democracy, nor can democracy claim to be the only form of regime required by Christian belief. While seeing the democratic impulse as the temporal manifestation of the Gospel in the political order, Maritain recognized that democratic principles, traditions, and institutions were first promoted in history by many non-Christians, even anti-Christians.

Maritain's democratic theory influenced the Christian world profoundly (Christian Democratic parties, for example, usually include other Christian communities along with Catholics), and his work was pivotal in such philosophical-political currents as "personalism" and "communitarianism," as is suggested by the title of his influential book *The Person and the Common Good* (1947). The "reconstruction of the social order" advocated by the Christian Democratic parties of both Europe and Latin America rejected nostalgia for the old pre-democratic Christendom, seeking instead to promote human rights that are both lay and pluralist in character.

Maritain was invited to participate in the international discussions that led to the founding in 1946 of UNESCO and the drafting of the UN's Universal Declaration of Human Rights in 1948. Maritain emphasized that practical decisions about practical cooperation often can be reached, even when participants have irreconcilable differences about why and on what principles. His practical wisdom was of considerable benefit in philosophical discussions in pluralistic settings, notably in the 1945 founding of the United Nations. This practical wisdom was buttressed by a formidable theoretical edifice, including highly influential work in the theory of knowledge, metaphysics, natural law, and the new discipline he helped to launch, Christian philosophy—a philosophy not based on faith but concerned with philosophical questions stimulated by faith.

See also *Christian democracy; Communitarianism; Human rights.*

Michael Novak

BIBLIOGRAPHY

Doering, Bernard. *Jacques Maritain and the French Catholic Intellectuals.* South Bend, Ind.: University of Notre Dame Press, 1983.

Evans, J. W. *Jacques Maritain: The Man and His Achievement.* Kansas City, Mo.: Sheed and Ward, 1963.

Knasas, John F. X., ed. *Jacques Maritain and His Metaphysics.* Mishawaka, Ind.: American Maritain Association, 1988.

McInerny, Ralph. *Art and Prudence: Studies in the Thought of Jacques Maritain.* Notre Dame, Ind.: University of Notre Dame Press, 1994.

Royal, Robert, ed. *Jacques Maritain and the Jews.* South Bend, Ind.: University of Notre Dame Press, 1994.

Martyrdom

In its purest form, martyrdom is a voluntary, conscious, and altruistic readiness to suffer and offer one's life for a cause. The Christian martyr seeks certain death. Islamic tradition gives first place to a soldier dying in a holy war, or *jihad,* who aimed to defeat an adversary without, necessarily, losing his own life. Jewish tradition assigns the honor not only to those who affirm the faith against threat, but to victims such as those of the Holocaust, who were not given the choice.

Historical Examples

The literature on martyrs and martyrdom includes historical and biographical records of the acts of those who have, altruistically, offered their lives to demonstrate their commitment to their culture or society. It also includes memorials by opponents, describing them as foolhardy, misguided, traitors, terrorists, or heretics. Martyrologies, paeans to martyrs and martyrdom, often declaimed during religious services, embed the events in a cosmic, covenantal drama. Theologies of martyrdom prescribe appropriate occasions for the sacrificial act. Otherworldly rewards await the martyr. The martyr and the martyr's society may hope for redemption from the evil forces that imposed the suffering and death. Sometimes they simply hope for vengeance upon their opponents and upon the opponents' real or symbolic descendants.

Although much of this literature individualizes the martyr, martyrdom is a religio-political act of conflict between social groups. Typically, the weaker of the antagonists produces martyrs. The group may offer training for confronting the legal process and remaining firm under torture and in the face of execution. The social promotion of martyrdom is illustrated by the "Exhortation to Martyrdom" (c. 235) of Origen, one of the fathers of the church. Each of the antagonists strives to control the meaning of the event. Thus Ignatius of Antioch, condemned to fight beasts in 107, asked his friends not to try to save him and so rob him of the crown of immortality.

Historically, martyrdom did not emerge until culture was differentiated from, and achieved a measure of autonomy from, social structure, when ideas came to function as symbols around which a society could mobilize. In Western society, the death of Socrates (399 B.C.E.), described in Plato's *Phaedo,* is an early example of a martyrdom that defended ideas. The Maccabean martyrs, such as the aged Eleazar and the seven sons of Hannah, are described in the Second and Fourth Books of the Maccabees. Origen cites these examples as worthy of emulation by Christians.

Aqiva ben Yosef, a Palestinian, is reported in rabbinic literature to have supported the Bar Kokhba revolt of Jews against the Romans in Palestine and to have been publicly executed by the Romans in 135 C.E. for violating the Roman edict against teaching the Torah. Husayn ibn Ali Abi Talib, grandson of the prophet Muhammad, was slain in 680 C.E. at Karbala, Iraq, after losing a rebellion against Caliph Yazid. His memory, along with that of his brother, Hasan, has become central in Shiʿite Islamic observance.

Early Christian martyrs include Justin Martyr, executed in the second century under Marcus Aurelius after a court condemned him and a woman, Charita, for subversive activities, and Saint Sebastian, pierced by arrows during the persecution of Christians by the Romans at the end of the third century. The martyrs of Lyon, executed in 177, included many women. Jan Hus, burned at Prague in 1415, is prominent among the martyrs of the Protestant Reformation. Michael Servetus and the Augustinians Heinrich Vos and Johannes Esch in Brussels were Protestant martyrs executed in 1553 following papal trials. Contemporary political martyrdoms often occur within a religio-political context. An example is Archbishop Oscar Romero, slain in 1980 for his opposition to the El Salvadoran government's repression of peasant rebels.

Martyrs are acclaimed by the authors of martyrologies. An example from the fourth century is Eusebius's *Ecclesiastical History* and the *Martyrdom of Justin and His Companions.* In the mid-sixteenth century John Foxe wrote of the papal oppression of English Protestants in *Acts and Monuments.* Artistic representations of the passion of Al-Husayn ibn Mansur al-Hallaj, executed in 922 for an alleged claim to divinity, has a long history in Persia. Martyrologies not only detail the martyrdoms but, along with legal sources, tell of rewards associated with the act. Islamic tradition has it that the Angel of Mercy conducts the martyr to Paradise, where he enters through a special door and is graced with Allah's special favor.

Martyrs may be accredited by organized systems, as in the Roman Catholic beatification process. Jewish and Islamic attribution tends to be less formal. A respected scholar may designate a person as a martyr. Popularly acclaimed martyrs emerge to satisfy the needs of local populations. Medieval popular martyrs include Saint Robert, the martyred boy of Bury St. Edmunds (1190), and little Hugh of Lincoln, whose death was blamed on Jews, who were then driven from England. Joan of Arc, burned in 1431, was not canonized until 1920 as part of the reconciliation of the Vatican and France after World War I. The French Ultramontanists, Roman Catholics north of the Alps, finding what appeared to be vials of blood with bodies in Roman catacombs, believed they had identified martyrs and precipitated a nineteenth-century investigation that ultimately raised doubts about their authenticity. Scholars have revealed that Joseph Goebbels, Hitler's minister for propaganda, fabricated a martyr called Horst Wessel, supposedly an early Nazi reportedly slain by leftists.

Martyrs in Societal Context

The types of martyrs produced, or the likelihood of producing a martyr at all, depend on the degree of political independence and state of internal authority of a society. A crescive society, one that is weak but on the rise, produces martyrs like those of early Christianity. Ideology assumes priority over individual physical survival and so affirms the priority of culture over nature, law and civilization over biological self-interest. An independent and self-determining society produces frontline soldier martyrs, like the missionary martyrs of Christianity or the Muslim *shahid* ("witness," the meaning of the Greek term for *martyr*). In a decaying society, the "martyrs" are victims, dying against their wish and will. A defeated society may produce "antimartyrs," who die in the service of the adversary society. Their own society perceives them as "collaborators."

Sometimes, when the martyrdom has a significant societal context, it is associated with suicide. Suicide, even at the threat of the enemy, is prohibited in the Jewish, Christian, and Islamic traditions. The defenders of Masada against the Romans in 73 C.E. as recounted by Josephus, a Jewish historian and military leader, chose suicide over enslavement. These suicides raise questions about the resistors' knowledge of the law or whether all the defenders were Jewish. Augustine considered suicide a form of murder, and later church councils excluded suicides from a eucharistic funeral. The morality of suicide was no issue in Socrates' Athens. When the Chinese Sung dynastic administration was defeated by the Mongols in the thirteenth century, tens of thousands committed suicide, responding to a loss of social meaning and a way to assert a final personal honor when their world collapsed.

The positive impact of martyrdom on a minority community is due in part to its formulation as a sacrificial act. The martyr is the sacrificial "lamb" and draws the representatives of those in power (military, judiciary, police) into performing the "priestly" role of sacrificial officiant. Since the martyr is doing what God has directed, the opponent is seduced into the martyr's faith. This is precisely the interpretation that in 1096 led some of the Jews of the Rhineland to slay their own wives and children and themselves, despite the prohibition on suicide, in preference to allowing the "unclean" Crusaders to perform their "priestly" role. Conceived as a sacrifice, the martyr, through a baptism of blood, is purified of sin and, while awaiting execution, may even have the power to grant absolution from sin. Through his relics, in the Catholic system, for example, he may be called upon to intercede for the sins of others. Martyrdom may unify a minority by establishing charismatic authority. The rational organizational arrangements for opposing the enemy are energized by martyrdom. The sacrificial act converts economic and political conflict into sacred conflict and so drives it toward the pursuit of goals at any cost. The rationally legitimated authority system is converted into a charismatically legitimated system through the act of martyrdom. The martyr, filled with the Holy Spirit, is conceived not to be spared suffering, and, indeed, the state of mind of the martyr, sustained by deep faith and the support of his community, may account for the beatific appearance of the martyr in art.

The struggle over meaning is reflected in the struggle between a public and a secluded venue for the event. The martyr prefers public execution. Typically, those in power resist slaying the martyr, trying to persuade him or her to recant. When these efforts fail, they rationalize the act as a criminal prosecution and prefer to execute the sentence in secrecy. The event lives in the history of the martyr's society more than it does in the history of the then dominant society. Sometimes the aim is to control the minority through fear. As such, the public burning of heretics in Spain during the Inquisition, for example, was more a form of internal social control, since those burnt were converts, Jews and Moors who had already accepted Catholicism.

Although martyrdom usually does not involve immediate violence against the adversary, it is a political act that deals a moral and thus psychological blow. The martyrdom accompanying the Islamic *jihad,* in contrast, does involve a blow to the enemy. Martyrdom, in this way, seeks to reduce the political authority of the opponent to ineffectiveness by challenging the sacred basis of the adversary's authority. Martyrdom may also strengthen the will of the adversary to repress the minority and so may politicize the relationship between the groups.

The martyr serves as a model for lesser martyrdoms, sacrifices on the part of the faithful. Virginity and celibacy have been thought of in this way in Christianity. Minor martyrdom in Islam includes any act "in the way of Allah."

Martyrs in crescive and self-determining societies may form cells of zealots within the wider society. The members of these cells train one another for the ordeal, a rehearsal for martyrdom, and sustain one another through it. Martyrologies play a part in this training as they do in promoting minor martyrdoms among the wider social group. These martyrs tend to be societal leaders and recruited from the nobility; they therefore tend to be males.

Communities try to control their martyrs as they do military zealots lest, in their enthusiasm, they precipitate a rebellion that the community is ill-prepared to support, as happened in the Bar Kokhba revolt of Judaeans against the Romans. The community sets rules defining the occasions for martyrdom. Thus Jews and Muslims are commanded to give their lives for only three things: to avoid murdering another person, to avoid incestuous relations, and to avoid worshiping strange deities in public. In Islam, to seek martyrdom is prohibited and is viewed as similar to suicide. The medieval Jewish philosopher Maimonides sought to restrict the occasions for martyrdom on the ground that a martyr condemns all his potential descendants to nonbeing. He recommended, where possible, dissimulation, a practice not unlike the Islamic *taqiyya.* Saint Augustine objected to the rush to martyrdom, and Saint Clement of Alexandria said one should not choose martyrdom unless called by God.

The dominant group has an arsenal of weapons against martyrdom. It may attempt, on the one hand, to prevent martyrdom by co-opting potential martyrs, assimilating them into the dominant society and providing them with honorable positions. This approach backfires when the minority attacks the assimilationists, as in the Maccabean assault in 165 B.C.E. on the Seleucid rulers who would hellenize Jews. On the other hand, the group in power may savagely repress the minority by slaying more than it can recruit. This killing may be delegated to specialists within the dominant society, as in the use of special SS units in the concentration camps of Nazi Germany. The dominant society wins the propaganda war if it succeeds in branding the martyrs as criminals or terrorists. The greatest weapon of the modern state against martyrdom is to make it appear meaningless and obsolete.

Samuel Z. Klausner

BIBLIOGRAPHY

Frend, W. H. C. *Martyrdom and Persecution in the Early Church.* Oxford: Blackwell, 1965.

Katz, Jacob. "Martyrdom in the Middle Ages and in 1648–49." In *Yitzhak F. Baer: Jubilee Volume,* edited by S. W. Baron, Ben Zion Dinur, Solomon Ettinger, and Israel Halpern. Jerusalem: Historical Society of Israel, 1960 (Hebrew).

Klausner, Samuel Z. "Martyrdom." In *The Encyclopedia of Religion,* edited by Mircea Eliade. New York: Macmillan, 1987.

Kolb, Robert. *For All the Saints: Changing Perceptions of Martyrdom and Sainthood in the Lutheran Reformation.* Macon, Ga.: Mercer University Press, 1987.

Peterson, Anna L. *Martyrdom and the Politics of Religion: Progressive Catholicism in El Salvador's Civil War.* Albany: State University of New York Press, 1997.

Riddle, Donald W. *The Martyrs: A Study in Social Control.* Chicago: University of Chicago Press, 1931.

Weiner, Eugene, and Anita Weiner. *The Martyr's Conviction: A Sociological Analysis.* Atlanta, Ga.: Scholar's Press, 1990.

Wood, Diana, ed. *Martyrs and Martyrologies.* Oxford: Blackwell, 1993.

Karl Marx

Marxism

Marxism is the diverse theoretical tradition derived from the writings of Karl Marx (1818–1883), which protests economic exploitation and envisions a society of equality and solidarity. In perhaps the most well known passage of the Marxist corpus, Marx branded religion "the opium of the people" and declared that the "criticism of religion is the premise of all criticism." And yet in the very same essay, titled "Contribution to the Critique of Hegel's Philosophy of Right," Marx also makes clear that he does not consider religion itself to be the source of human misery and alienation—in its material-economic, political, social, and relational forms—but rather considers religion a symptom of a larger alienation with its roots in the historical distortions of human economic activity. Moreover, in other writings both Marx and Friedrich Engels (1820–1895) go to some pains to counsel against the political suppression of religion, on both theoretical and political-strategic grounds, as a focus on religion was viewed as a distraction from the more fundamental and immediate concern with the material-economic and political bases of exploitation.

Marx on Religion

Marx's treatment of religion must be understood within the larger context of his historical-materialist theory of society and social change. For Marx, reality is completely delimited to *this* world of human practical activity and social relations, bounded by material nature and society in its historically concrete forms. All other manifestations of apparent social reality, including religion and religious sentiment, are conditioned by the larger historical movement of material, economic forces. In other words, the fundamental human condition of alienation is rooted in economic factors, specifically in capitalist forces and relations of production as manifested in the private ownership of property and the domination of the owners of capital over laborers. These economic structures of society form society's "base," which determine the existence and concrete forms of the other aspects of social life. In sum, Marx believed that capitalism's inherent contradictions—for example, an economic logic predicated on the extreme concentration of capital, the overproduction of manufactured goods, the increasing immiseration of the working classes—and immanent crisis would force the final historical stage of class struggle, as the dialectical logic embedded in history's progression (in other words, the structurally inherent and historically recurring revolutionary reconciliation of competing material forces and interest, accompanying technological advancements) compels oppressed people to the realization of their oppression, and thus their historic mission of human liberation. Marx considered religion to be a distortion of reality but also truly derivative of the larger movement of history. Therefore, Marx saw no need to rid the world of religion, since religious alienation would be swept away with the system's more fundamental contradiction in material production.

However, even with a more nuanced appreciation of Marx's position on the subject, it would be a distortion not to recognize his fundamental antipathy toward religion, and toward Christianity in particular. Marx's understanding of the inevitably alienating form and effect of religion comes largely from German philosopher Ludwig Feuerbach (1804–1872), who claimed that the essence of Christianity is the alienation of human qualities and capacities from human beings, by projecting these—in an idealized form—onto a transcendent and distant divinity. Religion ultimately must place the destiny of humanity outside human control; but Christianity, Marx argued, was especially pernicious in further preaching an ethic of cowardly submission. Marx thus maintained that religion has no function in society other than to veil the irrationalities of the prevailing system of production; and in the capitalist system, he saw the radical individualism of Protestantism as the perfect complement to the bourgeois system of anonymous commodity exchange.

For Feuerbach, the purpose of the critique of religion is to reclaim for humanity the qualities, capacities, and virtues he thought were fraudulently projected onto God. And while Marx accepted Feuerbach's view of religious alienation, he also believed that atheism per se, which merely negates and reverses the claims of theism, could not provide human liberation. In sum, rather than being backward looking, seeking purpose and meaning in the negation of God, the achievement of socialism would allow—indeed, would require—humanity to be forward looking and self-defining.

History of Marxist Theory

Although more complex than widely acknowledged, a general disdain for religion nevertheless permeates the history of Marxist theory since Marx, and particularly within the experience of socialist states. Before the October Revolution of 1917 which brought his party to power, for example, Vladimir Ilyich Lenin (1870–1924) acceded to Marx and Engels's counsel against the active suppression of religion and religious belief, though perhaps more for considerations of tactics than theoretical consistency or conviction. Lenin himself wrote that, although the Communist Party could not be neutral on the matter of religion as a matter of principle, he did not want to ban or expel believers from the party or make atheism part of its official platform. For Lenin, the struggle against capitalism required unity and was thus more immediate and central than were the fine points of the place of religion. Upon the successful overthrow of the tsarist regime, however, the party came to perceive religion as a considerable constraint upon its ability to establish legitimacy and order. In this context, Nikolai Bukharin (1888–1938), among other party members, took a strong theoretical and policy stand against religion, arguing that it must be opposed actively. In the repression of religion, theoretical pretense was pushed to the side as political expediency became its own reason for the systematic persecution of Christians and religious minorities. Over time, the habituation of antireligious state interventions inured into a central tenet of the political rule of socialism in the Soviet Union, its East European satellites, China, and Cuba.

Beginning in the 1960s, however, overtures from both sides of the Christian-Marxist divide began to break down decades of entrenched ideological chauvinism and animosity, opening a dialogue between intellectual elements of the two traditions. A relaxing of East-West tensions at this time and especially a movement toward "de-Stalinization" in many communist countries were important for the dialogue, as was the more open attitude of mainline Western churches, as exemplified in Catholicism's liberalization process under the aegis of Vatican II, in which the church sought to be more sensitive and responsive to the needs and concerns of laypersons. Participants on each side were compelled to consider whether they perhaps did not have more in common than their initial prejudices allowed. Still, some observers of the dialogue questioned the commitment of participants to anything beyond intellectual comparisons of Christian and Marxist traditions; nor, it has been argued, did either side demonstrate an interest in widening the geographic scope of the encounter to areas in which one or the other party did not have some self-serving interest. In any case, the dialogue was short-lived, as the Soviet invasion of Czechoslovakia in

1968 to squelch a liberalization program made further encounters all but impossible.

Liberation Theology Movement

Outside of this largely European process, a different, more practically based dialogue began to materialize in the non-Western nations as committed Christians participated in postcolonial liberation movements which drew upon Marxist insights and inspiration. Especially important in this regard was the emergence of the liberation theology movement in Latin America in the 1970s and 1980s, which held that the church had a role to play in fighting for economic and social justice. Christian activists would play an integral role in the successful deposal of the Somoza dictatorship in Nicaragua and in other revolutionary movements. The liberation theology movement was also fundamental in the grassroots resistance to bureaucratic-authoritarian rule that played a significant role in the region's subsequent transitions to democracy.

Although its role in revolution has proven captivating to the leftist imagination, liberation theology's most interesting work, arguably, has occurred in the more mundane settings of the base ecclesial communities (popularly based, residential-communal, and participatory intentional religious organizations), in which low-level clerics and lay pastoral workers have been working with the poor toward social justice. Inspired by the early Marx of the *Theses on Feuerbach,* theologians like Gustavo Gutiérrez stressed praxis—a theory of action, required to mediate between Marx's grand structural analyses and a strategy of revolutionary social change—over theory in attempting to reformulate theology for the needs of Latin American realities, and specifically the needs of those left in the wake of economic development policies favoring the interests of the capital-owning classes.

This emphasis on praxis places liberation theology alongside dependency theory and radical Brazilian educator Paulo Freire's "pedagogy of the oppressed" (a methodology of popular consciousness raising and organizing) as part of the common genesis of a wider movement in Latin America which American political scientist Steven Leonard has called "critical theories in practice." Freire's earliest work in adult literacy training in Brazil was largely sponsored by and conducted with agencies of the Catholic Church; and while his pedagogical insights into the fundamental need for psychological—as opposed to simply political and economic—liberation predate this cooperation, his theoretical writings were influenced by the character of lay pastoral work that had been practiced for some years prior to this formal cooperation. As well, dependency theory, the historical-structural analysis of economic and political bases of contemporary Latin American society's developmental distortions, gave theology its object of concern and the analytical tools to rethink religious practice; and in turn, Freire's pedagogical theory, particularly its method of popular consciousness raising, has been a constitutive element for both liberation theology's pastoral work with the poor as well as the basis for a new way of thinking about theological activity.

Just as Freire did not so much invent "conscientization" as articulate its practice in a theoretically grounded system, liberation theology does not so much invent the social mission of the committed Christian intellectual and the "preferential option for the poor" as articulate in a more meaningful and useful way its presence in the lives of Christian activists like Freire himself. Developing a praxical theology first entails the recognition that social reality is characterized by the struggle between opposing and unequal forces, and thus one is forced to take sides within this struggle. Gutiérrez and other liberation theologians held that no theoretical explanation of the world, including religion, can be innocent of its social effect and position within its larger historical context; thus to fully understand what is at stake is to, at the same moment, commit oneself to changing the oppressive reality one perceives. And in this, Latin American critical theories come full circle, as one would expect from a truly praxical theoretical system.

The emphasis on praxis and the active commitment to human emancipation from systemic forms of oppression draw liberally from Marx. In both form and content, however, these Latin American traditions may perhaps owe a more direct debt to the Marxism of Antonio Gramsci (1891–1937), the Italian politician and theorist who is perhaps most responsible for recovering and reinvesting the centrality of the concept of "praxis" in Marxist thought. Many of Marx's and Engels's accounts—and especially Marxist accounts since Marx—of the relationship between base and superstructure have suffered from an inattention to praxis.

Gramsci saw the prevailing economic reductionism of his Marxist contemporaries to be an inadequate basis for explaining contemporary society, and the potential bases for social change, particularly for his own society in pre-World War II Italy. He argued that the traditional Marxist view of power, which sees the state as the "instrument of the ruling class," could not adequately account for the real balance of forces and nature of state power in advanced capitalist societies and therefore could not serve as a sound basis for political strategy. In parts of the Marxist corpus, Marx himself conceded occasional instances of the "relative autonomy" and effectiveness of the state and other superstructural forces in taking the leading role in society. Gramsci takes this point much further, however, arguing that the only way to destroy the remnants of the *ancien regime* and to maintain working-class power as already developed was to engage people in building a new social order from the ground up. This revolution was to be premised not only on an alliance between workers and peasants but between both these and traditional intellectuals. But in contrast to the Leninist notion of a vanguard of committed party members, Gramsci's call was for more of a true partnership, arguing that the building of a new social order would require the development and active participation of "organic intellectuals," leaders coming from within the ranks of the oppressed classes.

Although Gramsci saw religion in general, and the Catholic Church in particular, serving an ideological function within modern capitalism, he was unwilling to dismiss religion *a priori* as a force beholden to power and property. Indeed, for Gramsci, the early church provided a model of intellectual action for the party to follow in spearheading a movement against modern advanced industrial capitalism, while the institutionalized church, serving the interests of property, offered instructive warnings against the dangers of revolutionary ossification. In other words, whereas Marx allowed merely for occasional instances of noneconomic structures taking a leading role in the direction of society, Gramsci not only allows for religious action independent of economic motivation and cause, but he also leaves open the question as to whether religion's effect is positive or negative in moving toward a more liberated society.

In the specific case of Christianity, Gramsci does not dismiss its potential role in a popularly based struggle of liberation. To achieve their goal of social transformation, radical activists must take seriously the need to develop a compelling explanation of the world, which like religion entails a motive cause to practical action; and for Gramsci the history of the church reveals that the only efficacious means of developing a compelling explanation is to develop and extend a concrete and meaningful relationship with the people, so as to encourage and help the people develop their own organic intellectuals in a truly cooperative effort to initiate and extend an anticapitalist movement. Under these circumstances, a philosophical system becomes, in Marx's phrase, "a material force" which can alter the "common sense" of an age; if socialist activists did not endeavor to make this active connection to the people, Marxism and the cause of socialist emancipation would atrophy into its own ideological self-justification of power.

Gramsci's analysis recognizes that the ideas, beliefs, norms, and values that infuse societal institutions and the state do not reflect economic class interests in a simple manner, which in turn suggests that the realm of ideology is an additional arena of struggle. Ideology organizes action through the ways in which it is embodied in social relations, institutions, and practices, thereby informing all individual and collective activities. And thus to the extent that a progressive alliance can be successful in altering fundamental attitudes and behavioral dispositions, they may bring about a new way of acting in the world. In this, Gramsci's opening to a revolutionary praxis among the people goes a long way toward establishing a commitment to emancipation centrally based on the active and democratic participation of a self-conscious people.

Freire and liberation theologians, however, take this insight even further when they argue that the basis of collective human liberation is within—and indeed can only be within—the praxis of the oppressed themselves. Liberation theology and Freirian pedagogy rest upon a utopian moment (in other words, a point of initial concern and internal justification of theoretical and political activity), envisioning a world wholly unlike the one the oppressed encounter today; and in the precise sense, so does Marx and Engels's critical theory. The utopian moment of Marx and Engels rests upon a grand scheme of historical material movement, correlations of forces both national and international, and the withering of the state and other manifestations derivative of the capitalist mode of production. By way of contrast, Freire and liberation theologians seek more ordinary utopian moments, everyday revolutions founded upon the dynamic rhythm between theory and practice in the lives of newly self-aware and committed individuals. It is premised on the development of a popular critical edge, embodied in the reflections of self-conscious agents and practical activity aimed at changing the conditions of oppression that people face in their daily lives. Thus at the turn of the twenty-first century, one is faced with the paradox that the Marxist praxis of revolution is developing—if it is developing at all—most clearly not within the ranks of Western socialist parties or labor unions but rather in the work of committed Christians and the poor in the developing world.

See also *Base communities; Cuba; Liberation theology; Revolutions; Russia.*

Gerard Huiskamp and Christian Smith

BIBLIOGRAPHY

Cox, Harvey. "The Marxist-Christian Dialogue: What Next?" In *Marxism and Christianity,* edited by Herbert Aptheker. New York: Humanities Press, 1968.

Freire, Paulo. *Pedagogy of the Oppressed.* New York: Continuum, 1993.

Gramsci, Antonio. *Selections from the Prison Notebooks.* Edited and translated by Quintin Hoare and Geoffrey Nowell Smith. New York: International Publishers, 1971.

Gutiérrez, Gustavo. *A Theology of Liberation.* Maryknoll: Orbis Books, 1973.

Leonard, Stephen T. *Critical Theory in Political Practice.* Princeton: Princeton University Press, 1990.

Marx, Karl, and Friedrich Engels. *On Religion.* New York: Schocken, 1964.

Smith, Christian. *The Emergence of Liberation Theology: Radical Religion and Social Movement Theory.* Chicago: University of Chicago Press, 1991.

Tucker, Robert, ed. *The Marx-Engels Reader.* New York: Norton, 1978.

Maryknoll

The Catholic Foreign Mission Society of America (Maryknoll) is a Roman Catholic association that was established in 1911. Both the Maryknoll Fathers and Brothers, made up of priests and brothers, and the Maryknoll Sisters, a group of nuns, were founded in 1912. A separate organization for lay missioners, the Maryknoll Association of the Faithful, was created in the 1990s. The estate purchased in Ossining, New York, as the mission's headquarters was first called Mary's Knoll because the founders were devotees of the Virgin Mary. It eventually became Maryknoll, and the mission itself is known by that name.

Maryknoll was long a moderately conservative Catholic organization, with missions concentrated in the East. With the rise of communism in China, the Maryknollers came to be viewed as informants for the U.S. government, and missionaries were imprisoned, tortured, and finally expelled in 1950, after the communists proclaimed the People's Republic in 1949.

After 1950 Maryknoll missions were established in several Asian, African, and Latin American countries. More than any other, their work in Latin America—where they became associated first with left-wing politics and later with liberation theologies—pushed Maryknoll to the center of a U.S. political controversy between conservatives and the left. In 1967 Maryknoll missioners Sister Miriam Peter and Fathers Thomas and Arthur Melville were accused of involvement with guerrillas fighting the Guatemalan government and were expelled from Guatemala.

At least since 1973, when Orbis Books, Maryknoll's publishing house, published Gustavo Gutiérrez's *Theology of Liberation,* Orbis has been the main U.S. channel for publication of Asian, African, Latin American, and other works on liberation theologies. In certain political and religious circles in the Americas, Orbis reinforced the image of Maryknoll as a "leftist" religious venture, eliciting harassment from authoritarian governments in Latin America.

The 1980s saw tensions escalating within Maryknoll, and between Maryknoll and both the papacy and U.S. administrations, especially over Central America. Several Maryknoll missioners became involved in lobbying the U.S. Congress and working to change public opinion about U.S. Central American policies, which supported right-wing dictatorships against what many saw as leftist insurgencies. Maryknoll's Justice and Peace Office in Washington, D.C., was the focal point of such efforts and of Maryknoll support for the sanctuary movement (which offered asylum to refugees of Latin American conflicts) and of antimilitary initiatives.

In 1980 U.S.-trained Salvadoran military personnel raped and assassinated Maryknoll sisters Maura Clarke and Ita Ford, Ursuline sister Dorothy Kazel, and lay volunteer Jean Donovan, all Roman Catholic missionaries from the United States. This tragedy focused the attention of the U.S. public on the violence in Central America and on U.S. policies in the region.

In Nicaragua the 1979 Sandinista revolution ended almost fifty years of rule by the Somoza family and put a leftist government in power. When Maryknoll father Miguel D'Escoto accepted the post of secretary of state in the Nicaraguan government, the Vatican unsuccessfully pressured Maryknoll to expel him and then suspended him from ecclesiastical functions in 1985.

In the late 1980s and 1990s increased pressures from the Vatican, a shift to democratically elected governments in Central America, the election of a more liberal U.S. administration, and changes in Maryknoll's own politics strengthened Maryknoll's moderately conservative majority somewhat. These changes also sobered its vocal progressive faction, who nonetheless still have an important voice in the organization.

See also *Central America; Latin America; Liberation theology; Missionaries; Sanctuary; Vatican.*

Otto Maduro

BIBLIOGRAPHY

Berryman, Phillip. *Stubborn Hope: Religion, Politics, and Revolution in Central America.* Maryknoll, N.Y.: Orbis Books/New Press, 1994.

Gutiérrez, Gustavo. *A Theology of Liberation.* Maryknoll, N.Y.: Orbis Books, 1973.

Lernoux, Penny. *Hearts on Fire: The Story of the Maryknoll Sisters.* Maryknoll, N.Y.: Orbis Books, 1993.

Wiest, Jean-Paul. *Maryknoll in China: A History, 1918–1955.* Armonk, N.Y.: M. E. Sharpe, 1988.

Masons

See *Freemasonry*

Mau Mau

See *Kenya*

Mawdudi, Sayyid Abu al-Ala

Pakistani Islamic thinker, political activist, and founder of the Islamic Party. Sayyid Abu al-Ala Mawdudi (1903–1979), whose writings helped to shape the ideology of the contemporary Islamic revival, left an indelible mark on Pakistani politics.

Born in India, Mawdudi was educated in both the traditional Islamic and the modern education systems, but he was, first and foremost, self-taught—a fact that had much to do with the eclecticism and creativeness of his thinking. While still in his teens, Mawdudi embarked on a career in journalism and became active in nationalist politics led by the Indian National Congress Party. He would, however, soon reject Indian nationalism, which he viewed as a vehicle for Hindu hegemony.

His preoccupation with safeguarding Muslim interests and restoring Islam to power in India directed his attention to the cultural struggle with the West. Mawdudi was among the first Islamic thinkers to encourage Muslims to turn away from all Western ideas and institutions and to look to Islam to empower themselves and create an ideal sociopolitical order. This turn to Islam went hand in hand with a reinterpretation of the teachings, function, and meaning of the faith in order to relate individual and social experiences to lasting questions and concerns about freedom, justice, good, evil, and salvation. Mawdudi sought to create viable and logical linkages between piety and politics, statecraft and religious life—in short, to convert Islam into an ideology.

Beginning in 1932, Mawdudi outlined his ideological vision in a systematic fashion in numerous books, articles, and lectures. He called on Muslims to return to the pristine faith but he was not an atavist, for he also sought to modernize Islamic thought and society. He denounced traditional institutions and practices and engaged the modern world, appropriated its values and institutions, and incorporated them into his vision of an Islamic order. His approach was in effect one of "Islamizing modernity."

Politics was integral to this ideological formulation. The cultural struggles that animated Mawdudi's thinking all occurred in the political arena and were deeply influenced by the larger political battles of his time. The centrality of politics to his enterprise is reflected in the importance he attached to the creation of an Islamic state that was to be the culmination of the Muslim struggle and was to serve as the perfect sociopolitical order and the repository of and protector of Islamic values.

The systematic mixing of religion with politics in Mawdudi's works occurred in tandem with streamlining the Islamic faith, redefining its core concepts and symbols, as well as introducing new terms, which since have become the staple of the Islamic discourse: *Islamic state, Islamic ideology,* and *Islamic revolution.* All this allowed Mawdudi to institute a political reading of Islam in which faith became ideology and religious works became social action. Mawdudi's prolific writings spread these ideas across the Muslim world, deeply influencing contemporary Islamic ideology from Sudan to Sumatra.

In 1941 Mawdudi founded the Jama'at-i Islami (Islamic Party), which he headed until 1972. The Jama'at has been the most visible and active Islamic party in Pakistan since the country's creation in 1947. Through it, Mawdudi was able to frame the central questions before state leaders at critical junctures in the country's history, thereby deeply influencing the national political discourse and conceptions of Pakistani identity and their relation to Islam. Mawdudi and the Jama'at popularized the demand for an Islamic constitution, compelled Pakistan to commit itself to Islamization, and instituted a place for Islam in national politics. They also were instrumental in creating an Islamic constituency in Pakistan by relating Islamic concerns to the politics and worldview of the youth, salaried middle classes, and upwardly mobile professionals. Thus, although the Jama'at has never been in a position to capture power in Pakistan, it has succeeded in influencing state policy and public culture. In the process it has instituted a distinct pattern of religiopolitical behavior and organization in society and politics.

See also *Islam; Pakistan.*

Seyyed Vali Reza Nasr

BIBLIOGRAPHY

Adams, Charles J. "The Ideology of Mawlana Mawdudi." In *South Asian Politics and Religion,* edited by Donald E. Smith. Princeton: Princeton University Press, 1966.

———. "Mawdudi and the Islamic State." In *Voices of Resurgent Islam,* edited by John L. Esposito. New York: Oxford University Press, 1983.

Ahmad, Mumtaz. "Islamic Fundamentalism in South Asia: The Jamaat-i-Islami and the Tablighi Jamaat." In *Fundamentalisms Observed,* edited by Martin E. Marty and R. Scott Appleby. Chicago: University of Chicago Press, 1991.

McDonough, Sheila. *Muslim Ethics and Modernity: A Comparative Study of the Ethical Thought of Sayyid Ahmad Khan and Mawlana Mawdudi.* Waterloo, Ont.: Wilfred Laurier University Press, 1984.

Nasr, Seyyed Vali Reza. *Mawdudi and the Making of Islamic Revivalism.* New York: Oxford University Press, 1996.

Mecca

Mecca, a city midway down the western coast of Arabia and forty-five miles inland from the Red Sea port of Jidda, is the holiest place of Islam. Its sanctity stretches far back into antiquity, to Abraham and even Adam according to Muslims. Mecca possessed a spring but little else, and yet it had a shrine—the stone-built Ka'ba—and a sacred compound *(haram)* when the prophet Muhammad was born there about 570. The Ka'ba and other nearby shrines attracted pilgrims to worship and trade there to the benefit of the ruling Arab tribe of the Quraysh, who used their capital to build up a modest commercial network in Arabia.

Muhammad preached his message of submission to God *(islam)* in his native Mecca for ten years. A few were converted, but the opposition of most of his fellow Quraysh drove him from the town in 622, a date that marks the beginning of the Muslim era. Medina, an oasis 275 miles to the north, offered him refuge in the hope that the Meccan holy man might arbitrate their escalating social problems. But Muhammad pursued his own goal of spreading Islam, and by 630 he was so successful that Mecca capitulated to its banished son, though he himself continued to reside in Medina until his death in 632.

Muhammad's first four successors, the Rightly Guided Caliphs, chose to do likewise, and Medina remained the capital of the rapidly expanding Muslim community until 661, when a new dynasty moved the seat of power to Damascus, and later to Baghdad and elsewhere. Although Mecca remained Islam's premier holy city—every Muslim is obliged to make pilgrimage *(hajj)* there at least once in a lifetime—it was a political and commercial backwater sustained by pious endowments and the income from its only business, the care and feeding of the thousands of Muslims—eventually many thousands—who came there as *hajjis* on the fixed days of the pilgrimage month or as pious visitors the year round.

Whatever remote caliph or sultan claimed sovereignty over it, Mecca was under the immediate control of local Arab aristocrats, the sharifs, claiming direct descent from the Prophet. Its location was sufficiently remote from competing authority that the sharif of Mecca invariably took the princely share of the holy city's dues on pilgrims and merchants. The world could not be held entirely at bay, however. The Crusaders had designs on Mecca from the north in the twelfth century, and the Portuguese mounted a southern invasion of the Red Sea in the sixteenth. As the Portuguese threat waned, it was Indian Muslims and then Indonesians who came to Mecca across the Indian Ocean, particularly as steam replaced sail in the nineteenth century. By late in that century Mecca had become a city with a varied Arab, Asian, and African population.

The long Ottoman sovereignty over the holy city (1517–1916) was tenuous at best, but in the first years of the twentieth century Turkish reformers attempted to rein Mecca into their newly centralized government structure. The sharif Husayn (1853–1931) resisted, and thus was born a ten-

Muslims regard the Kaʿba, the cubic stone structure within Mecca's Grand Mosque, as the holiest place on earth.

sion that the British exploited as soon as Turkey entered the First World War on the side of Germany. Husayn, whose religious credentials as ruler and guardian of the Twin Harams made him an attractive candidate for leading the Arabs in a revolt against their Ottoman sovereigns, negotiated with the British for leadership in a broad, postwar independent Arab domain. Neither the leadership nor the domain materialized, but in June 1916 an Arab insurrection against Ottoman sovereignty was proclaimed in Mecca, and the Arab revolt was under way.

From the eighteenth century Mecca had a politically and religiously aggressive neighbor in the Wahhabi-allied house of Saʿud in the Najd. In 1806 the Wahhabis occupied Mecca and Medina, only to be driven out within a few years by an Egyptian expeditionary force. The Wahhabis withdrew, but they did not disappear. They regrouped under Abdul Aziz ibn Saʿud (1880–1953), and by the outbreak of World War I the Saudis too were British clients. After the war Husayn ruled from Mecca an impoverished and marginalized Kingdom of the Hijaz whose dissolution was, increasingly and obviously, the Saudi objective. British conciliation held the Saudis temporarily at bay, but by 1926 the British neither could nor would prevent the inevitable, and the Saudis once again occupied Mecca and Medina. The sharifate was abolished, and both Husayn and his son and successor Ali ended their days far from Mecca. The Saudis purified the holy cities religiously as well as politically, and Mecca would likely have remained an overextended and underfinanced pilgrimage town except for the flow of enormous sums of oil money into the Saudi economy. A prodigious enlargement of the Meccan sanctuary and the improvement of pilgrimage facilities from housing to sanitation were undertaken and completed in 1955.

With the prestige of guardianship of the Twin Harams came the inevitable responsibility for maintaining both the security and the freedom of the annual pilgrimage. The Saudis had their enemies in Islam, and the *hajj* was an inviting time to provoke the house of Saʿud and, since the *hajj* was now televised in its entirely, to flaunt opposition to the regime before the eyes of the entire Muslim world. In November 1979 the kingdom's own fundamentalist dissidents seized the Haram and were dislodged only with force and the scandal of spilled Muslim blood in Islam's holiest place.

That same year the Ayatollah Ruholla Khomeini led an Islamic revolution in Iran, and thereafter the new Shiʿite Islamic republic used Mecca and its *hajj* as a world stage for demonstrating, through placards and slogans, its disdain for the house of Sa'ud. Once again, in July 1987, there was violence in the Haram. The Iranians called for an international Muslim trusteeship over the holy places. The Saudis further tightened security and severely limited the number of pilgrims permitted entry from Iran. Tensions are ongoing.

See also *Islam; Muhammad; Sacred places.*

F. E. Peters

BIBLIOGRAPHY

Baker, Randall. *King Husain and the Kingdom of the Hejaz.* New York: Oleander Press, 1979.

Burton, Richard F. *A Personal Narrative of a Pilgrimage to al-Madina and Meccah.* Reprint. New York: Dover, 1964.

Peters, F. E. *The Hajj: The Muslim Pilgrimage to Mecca and the Holy Places.* Princeton: Princeton University Press, 1994.

———. *Mecca. A Literary History of the Muslim Holy Land.* Princeton: Princeton University Press, 1994.

Medicine

Medicine—the science and art of diagnosing, treating, and preventing disease—has often been tied to beliefs about religion and the supernatural. In North America, religion and medicine have been joined together both in Native American healing traditions and through a long history of Christian engagement with medical practice and its moral implications.

Among the cultures of North America, the relationship between religion and medicine has been close, clear, and, for the most part, uncontested. The diverse native peoples of North America shared a fundamental belief that both sickness and health could be attributed to the action of a supernatural agent. English colonists also understood sickness and health to have a supernatural source. The omnipotent God of the Puritan universe distributed the curse of sickness and the blessing of health in a manner, and for reasons, that humans were not expected to understand. The unpredictability of illness and the constancy of death reminded Christians of their powerlessness before God and prompted them to look inward for signs of their own sinfulness.

Colonial America

When they were ill, Native Americans turned to medicine men and shamans, who healed by calling on supernatural powers. Religion and healing were not joined in quite the same way in the English settlements, but there were among the Puritan divines preacher-physicians who offered medical care and advice to their parishioners. The Puritan ministers viewed this union of religion and medicine—what clergyman and writer Cotton Mather (1663–1728) famously referred to as the "angelical conjunction"—as an ideal way to fulfill their pastoral duty to their flocks. By tending to the physical needs of their parishioners, ministers were able to offer spiritual support and guidance at a critical juncture in the Christian life and practical support to communities that did not have access to the services of a trained physician. By collecting fees for their medical services, many of these preacher-physicians also were able to supplement the often meager compensation their churches offered.

By the middle of the eighteenth century, ministry and medicine had become two distinct professions in the English colonies. Even then, however, the clergy did not retire from the sick room altogether. Indeed, one of the most popular medical self-help manuals available to colonial families was written by one of the most famous clergymen of the century—John Wesley (1703–1791), an English theologian who founded Methodism. Wesley's *Primitive Physick,* first published in 1747, went through more than two dozen American editions. Like others of its time, Wesley's manual combined general advice on the ingredients of good health with specific recipes for herbal remedies and other treatments for common illnesses.

The relationship between religion and medicine took a different form in the French and Spanish New World settlements, which were predominately Roman Catholic, but the appropriateness of their union went unchallenged there as well. In fact, although the Catholic Church discouraged the clergy from studying medicine formally and explicitly prohibited priests from practicing surgery, it accepted and in many cases formally sanctioned medical practice by priests on the mission field and in areas underserved by trained physicians. The New World colonies met both criteria. The Spanish settlements were mission territories with few physicians and surgeons, and there was urgent need for clergy to provide medical aid and operate hospitals in these areas. The French settlements were better served by trained physicians and surgeons, but Catholic priests and women in religious orders still operated hospitals and served as apothecaries.

Just as prominent Protestant clergymen like Cotton Mather and John Wesley published works on medicine,

Catholic clergy wrote what came to be known as pastoral medicine manuals. Appearing in Europe in the eighteenth century and in the United States by the mid-nineteenth century, these manuals were written specifically for clergy. Primarily concerned with emergencies, they equipped priests to offer first aid to victims of accidents or in response to the sudden onset of serious illness. Reflecting the Catholic Church's emphasis on the sacraments as the pathway to eternal life, the manuals also instructed priests on how to intervene in childbirth (even to the extent of performing a caesarean section), detect the signs of imminent death, and distinguish between actual death and a comatose state. In childbirth the goal was to save the infant's life or, if that was not possible, to ensure that it received the sacrament of baptism before its death. For the dying, the aim was to ensure the patient received the church's last rites. This sacrament was of no use to someone whose earthly life had ended, but it was essential to the eternal life of an individual approaching death.

Pre–Civil War Years

With the birth of the American Republic came new developments in the relationship between religion and medicine. Inspired by the language of freedom and the celebration of the individual that were so central to the culture of the years before the Civil War (1861–1865), Americans in the 1830s and 1840s began to turn away from both established religion and the medical establishment. Indeed, rejection of traditional treatments and the will to experiment were equally strong in both medicine and religion. Unconvinced that traditional therapeutics were the sole hope of the sick, Americans experimented with botanical medicine, the healing properties of water and, in the form of homeopathic medicine, a new, more moderate approach to the use of drugs. These years were also the time of what has been called the democratization of American Christianity, a period in which new forms of Protestant Christianity emerged to capture the minds, hearts, and souls of Americans.

One denomination formed out of the religious fervor of the antebellum years became, quite literally, a religion of health. The Seventh-day Adventist Church, officially organized in 1863, had its roots in the millennial expectations that arose among some Christian groups in the 1830s and 1840s. The acknowledged prophet of the church, Ellen Gould White (1827–1915), began to receive divine revelations about Christ's Second Coming in the 1840s, and by the 1860s she was receiving revelations about health and medicine as well. The health message White proclaimed was similar to the prescriptions of many secular health reformers of the period, focusing as it did on a particular dietary regimen. Understood as a divine command, and reinforced by White's personal charisma, the Adventist health message won many adherents in the second half of the nineteenth century. One notable convert was physician John Harvey Kellogg (1852–1943) who, with White, opened a large sanitarium in Battle Creek, Michigan, that was organized around the church's health principles. White and Kellogg parted ways in 1907, but each left an enduring legacy. Kellogg developed the cornflakes cereal that continues to bear his family's name, and White moved her church more formally into medicine by founding additional sanitariums and organizing groups of medical missionaries.

Another healing tradition was also taking root in America in the 1800s. Mind-cure, or mental healing, was inspired by mesmerism, a French export that arrived in the United States in the 1830s. Both a science and a philosophy and a precursor of hypnotism in modern psychotherapy, mesmerism received an enthusiastic reception from the Americans who filled public lecture halls to witness its demonstration. One of its early American public practitioners, Phineas Parkhurst Quimby (1802–1866), went on to develop his own science of mental healing, which he used to restore to health hundreds, perhaps even thousands, of clients throughout the 1850s and early 1860s. One of these clients was Mary Baker Eddy (1821–1910), who later practiced her own science of healing, which she named Christian Science. Although Eddy later denied any connection between the divinely inspired text of her 1875 book *Science and Health* and the methods and unpublished writings of her former healer, a number of Quimby's other clients eagerly sought to carry on his legacy. The New Thought movement that grew out of their efforts was more a philosophy than an approach to healing, but its influence can be detected in both the holistic health movement and the New Age religions of the second half of the twentieth century.

Religious Origins of the Private Hospital System

Seventh-day Adventism and Christian Science represent the union of religion and medicine in one institutional form, the religious denomination, but even more significant was the union of the two in the institutional form of the private hospital. Support for private hospitals emerged in the

1830s and 1840s as a solution to the obvious inadequacies—and dangers—of the public almshouses on which the ailing poor were forced to rely. The principle of Christian charity was central to the founding of these institutions, but so, too, was a clear distinction between the "deserving poor" and those who "deserved" their poverty. It was both unjust and counter to the interests of the community, civic leaders often argued, for "honest working people" to be forced to lie beside "drunks and prostitutes" simply because illness or injury had left them dependent on public relief. The private hospital redressed this injustice and served the community by healing workers valuable to the local economy and saving them from the "moral contamination" of the almshouses.

Concern for the moral life of the community and hope for the conversion of the unchurched provided the impetus for the founding of many private hospitals in the nineteenth century, regardless of whether or not they maintained an explicit religious affiliation. Many hospitals were founded by churches or religious groups, however, and of these a high proportion were Roman Catholic. Every sectarian hospital had a mission to care for its own, but most also sought to reach beyond their immediate faith communities. They did so in the interest of fiscal health—to broaden their bases of paying patients—as well as in the interest of evangelism.

With the rise of scientific medicine at the turn of the twentieth century, however, the culture of most of these hospitals began to change. In most cases, church leaders ceded control, in fact or by law, to physicians, surgeons, and trained hospital administrators. The Catholic Church and the Seventh-day Adventist Church, unlikely bedfellows, were the exceptions to this trend. Both have fought to maintain the religious identity of their institutions while also conforming to the standards of modern medicine. And they have succeeded. For more than a century, the Catholic Church has been the largest private, not-for-profit provider of hospital care in the nation, and in recent years the Adventist system, though smaller than the Catholic, has become one of the nation's five largest not-for-profit health care systems.

Both religious denominations and private hospitals founded in the nineteenth century gave the union of religion and medicine in America a material reality it had not had before, but they also opened it up to new scrutiny. For example, as private hospitals proliferated, taking on an ever greater proportion of the burden of caring for the poor, they began to turn to local and state governments for subsidies and reimbursement payments. Government officials often agreed to these requests, reasoning that it was less costly to pay private hospitals for the care of the poor than it was for municipalities to operate their own charity hospitals. Still, tight government budgets and, not infrequently, anti-Catholic sentiment sometimes led to legislative debates and battles over the constitutionality of public aid to sectarian hospitals.

Pointing to the founding principle of the separation of church and state, opponents of sectarian aid charged that the work of a religious hospital was inherently evangelical and thus should not be supported by public funds. Although states debated most of these cases, one battle reached the U.S. Supreme Court. Resolving a challenge to the appropriation of federal funds to support construction of a charity unit at a Catholic hospital in Washington, D.C., the Supreme Court ruled in *Bradfield v. Roberts* (1899) that the fact that religious sisters managed the hospital was "wholly immaterial" to the case. The justices asserted clearly that church-related institutions providing public services were entitled to public funds. But *Bradfield v. Roberts* did not end the debate over sectarian aid. States continued to enact their own laws prohibiting grants to religious institutions, and other legal challenges were mounted.

Religion, Medicine, and the Law

The growth of the Christian Science Church also raised new questions about religion and medicine. In 1879 Mary Baker Eddy founded the Church of Christ, Scientist, and in 1881 she organized the Massachusetts Metaphysical College to train students in the professional use of Christian Science healing methods. The death in 1888 of a patient under the care of one of Eddy's former students, however, led to formal charges against the practitioner and a media indictment of Eddy and her college. The practitioner was acquitted, but the trial raised questions about the training and legal status of Christian Science healers that continue to be debated more than a century later.

In the 1980s and 1990s a number of Christian Scientists were charged with child abuse, negligence, or manslaughter in the deaths of their children. In each case, the parents entrusted their sick children to Christian Science practitioners who relied solely on prayer to guide the children into the mental state that would restore them to health. In most cases, charges were reduced, and in the well-publicized case of David and Ginger Twitchell, whose two-and-a-half-year-old son Robyn died of a perforated bowel, the Boston couple's

1993 conviction was overturned. But the deaths of these children prompted several states to repeal the religious exemption laws based on the First Amendment clause providing for the free exercise of religion, which had shielded parents and practitioners from prosecution. Most states retained their religious exemption statutes, however, and legal scholars and medical ethicists continue to debate whether a parent's right to religious freedom outweighs the state's obligation to protect children.

Ironically, however, even as decisions to reject modern medicine and embrace spiritual healing have been the source of controversy, changes in science and society have created a more pronounced role for religion in medicine. Recent developments in medical research and technology, changing sexual mores, and a more vigorous assertion of individual rights have generated new demands and raised new questions that have unavoidable implications for religious belief and practice. From the controversy over abortion rights and the conflict over right-to-die legislation, to the uneasy acceptance of new reproductive technologies and the categorical rejection of human cloning, Americans have signaled their unwillingness to leave matters of life and death to science or the courts.

Underlying the public response to these issues is a belief that life is precious and precarious, a fragile gift to be handled with care. Different communities might disagree over the origin of the gift and the rules governing its use, but they share an appreciation of its mysteries. These fundamental beliefs about the value and meaning of life create a place for religion in the worlds of medicine and politics.

See also *Abortion; Christian Science; Constitution, U.S.; Separation of church and state; Seventh-day Adventism.*

Kathleen M. Joyce

BIBLIOGRAPHY

Meyer, Donald B. *The Positive Thinkers: Popular Religious Psychology from Mary Baker Eddy to Norman Vincent Peale and Ronald Reagan.* Rev. ed. Middleton, Conn.: Wesleyan University Press, 1988.

Numbers, Ronald L. *Prophetess of Health: Ellen G. White and the Origins of Seventh-day Adventist Health Reform.* Rev. ed. Knoxville: University of Tennessee Press, 1992.

———, ed. *Medicine in the New World: New Spain, New France, and New England.* Knoxville: University of Tennessee Press, 1987.

Numbers, Ronald L., and Darrel W. Amundsen, eds. *Caring and Curing: Health and Medicine in the Western Religious Traditions.* New York: Macmillan, 1986.

Rosenberg, Charles E. *The Care of Strangers: The Rise of America's Hospital System.* New York: Basic Books, 1987.

Rothman, David J. *Strangers at the Bedside: A History of How Law and Bioethics Transformed Medical Decision Making.* New York: Basic Books, 1991.

Vogel, Virgil J. *American Indian Medicine.* Norman: University of Oklahoma Press, 1990.

Watson, Patricia A. *The Angelical Conjunction: The Preacher-Physicians of Colonial New England.* Knoxville: University of Tennessee Press, 1991.

Mennonites

See *Anabaptists*

Merton, Thomas

One of the pivotal religious figures of the twentieth century. Merton (1915–1968) was born in France. His first significant religious experience came in Rome when he was seventeen. Deeply moved by mosaic icons in the city's most ancient churches, he became aware of Christ not simply as a figure of history but as a living presence.

Merton found mentors in two of his professors at Columbia University in New York: the poet Mark Van Doren and the Thomist philosopher Daniel Walsh. Van Doren, he recalled, made students produce their own explicit ideas. Walsh saw Roman Catholic philosophy in its wholeness.

French philosopher and historian Étienne Gilson's study, *The Spirit of Medieval Christianity,* helped Merton overcome his anti-Catholic prejudices, as did a biography of the poet and Jesuit priest Gerard Manley Hopkins (1844–1889). In November 1938, after several months of instruction, he was received into the Catholic Church. In 1939 he received a master's degree in English from Columbia and took a teaching position at St. Bonaventure's College.

Merton followed the widening war in Europe closely, and his struggle with how he ought to respond to war gave birth to his novel, *My Argument With the Gestapo* (written in 1940 but not published until 1968). He would say that knowing what was going on made it seem desperately important to be voluntarily poor.

In the spring of 1941 Merton went on retreat to the Abbey of Our Lady of Gethsemani, a Trappist monastery in rural Kentucky, where he found monks living a silent and austere life that had not changed in centuries. After intense

Thomas Merton

soul searching, Merton returned to the abbey three days after the United States entered the Second World War and began his monastic life. Six years later he took lifetime vows.

Published in 1948, his autobiography, *The Seven Storey Mountain,* became a bestseller and has been translated into many languages. In the next twenty years he wrote more than sixty books on monastic life, prayer, the lives of saints, religious themes in literature, contemplative practice in other religious traditions, race relations, war, and social injustice. Collections of poetry and photographs, extracts from his journals, and collections of his letters have also been published.

His outspoken opposition to war and his association with such groups as the Catholic Worker (a pacifist movement founded by American reformer and journalist Dorothy Day) and the Fellowship of Reconciliation (an interfaith pacifist group) caused controversy. Some critics accused him of being naive about the communist threat.

In 1963 the head of his religious order forbade publication of a book he had tentatively titled *Peace in the Post-Christian Era.* For a time, Merton was ordered not to publish anything relating to war. Merton's writings on war and peace are credited with influencing the Second Vatican Council's final document, *Constitution on the Church in the Modern World,* which supported conscientious objectors and flatly condemned any form of warfare that destroys whole areas and their populations.

In his final years Merton was also noted for his contact with and writings about contemplative figures and traditions in other religions. On a pilgrimage in Asia in 1968, he met with the Dalai Lama. Soon after that encounter, Merton died of accidental electrocution while attending a Benedictine and Trappist monastic conference near Bangkok, Thailand.

See also *Dalai Lama; Day, Dorothy; Pacifism; Vatican Council, Second; Violence; War.*

Jim Forest

BIBLIOGRAPHY

Forest, Jim. *Living with Wisdom: A Biography of Thomas Merton.* Maryknoll, N.Y.: Orbis Books, 1991.

Merton, Thomas. *Run to the Mountain: The Journals of Thomas Merton.* Vol. 1, 1939–1941. Edited by Patrick Hart. San Francisco: HarperCollins, 1995.

———. *The Seven Storey Mountain.* New York: Harcourt Brace, 1948.

———. *A Thomas Merton Reader.* Edited by Thomas P. McDonnell. New York: Image Books, 1989.

Methodism

Methodism began as a revivalist movement in the Church of England in the eighteenth century and has spread throughout the world. The life, thought, and activities of its English founder, Anglican clergyman John Wesley (1703–1791), have had widespread political repercussions.

Even at the end of the twentieth century traces of his influence and of the Methodist movement that he organized could be found in some of the attitudes of U.S. First Lady Hillary Rodham Clinton; Margaret Thatcher, Britain's longest-serving twentieth-century prime minister; David Lange, Labour prime minister of New Zealand in the 1980s; and Agostinho Neto, president of the Marxist-Leninist government of Angola, who rebelled against the teaching of his Methodist minister father.

John Wesley

The decisive event in the spiritual pilgrimage of John Wesley occurred in 1738, after his failure as an Anglican missionary in Georgia in the American colonies. This intensely personal spiritual experience led to the conviction that salvation, the new birth, was offered to all, and the social and political consequences were to affirm the individual and her or his intrinsic worth and encourage a belief that spiritual perfection, often secularized as improvement, was possible for all in this life. Wesley's use of lay preachers and women class leaders gave previously excluded groups leadership experience. Noting the movement's lack of hierarchy, U.S. president Theodore Roosevelt once said the Methodist audiences were typically American, though historian Sydney Ahlstrom disputes the claim that Methodism was a democratic theology. He is right in pointing to the Methodist insistence that all are sinners and to the church's opposition to Enlightenment humanism, but the social consequences of the belief in divine grace as available for all led to a practice of social inclusion that encouraged political activism.

Wesley was brought up in the English high church tradition that found its political expression in the church and king—loyalties of the Tory Party as opposed to Whig liberalism. Politics did not greatly interest Wesley, which in the days of restricted franchise, rotten boroughs, and corrupt electioneering he saw as the hobby of an aristocratic elite. Strongly influenced by the German pietism he encountered on his journey to Georgia, he taught what he called social holiness, which led him to set up a school for poor children, a free medical dispensary, and a loan society and to fight resolutely against slavery. Wesley's sermon "On the Use of Money" contained the core of his economic teaching, which was to gain all you can, save all you can, and give all you can.

Yet as Wesley ruefully lamented, the social consequences were to move his followers from being mainly poor outcasts into being thrifty and respectable. Once respectability had been reached, the quest for social status began, which in England usually meant the social lure of the established Church of England.

Methodism and Revolution

Wesley urged his English followers to be loyal to the crown and the constitution, but he ordained preachers for the rebel colonies in America—albeit reluctantly—when the bishop of London refused. The War of Independence provided the opportunity for Methodism to take the place in America of an Episcopal church that appeared to be the religious branch of the British state.

In the early years of the Republic, Methodism expanded more quickly than any other denomination as its circuit riders took the gospel of free grace out to the ever-expanding frontier. Revivalism, partly a response to harsh conditions, caught fire in both England and America at the turn of the century, 1790–1820, and brought a huge influx of ill-disciplined new members. Wesleyan leaders in Britain were anxious not to attract the attention of national political leaders lest the church be perceived as a subversive political threat and have harsh repressive measures taken against it. For this reason they opposed the introduction of camp meetings, huge open-air preaching, praying, and singing affairs that sometimes went on throughout the day and night and had been enormously successful in America. When two laymen, Hugh Bourne and William Clowes, both ardent enthusiasts, went ahead in 1806 at Mow Cop, a hill on the Cheshire-Staffordshire border, they were expelled and decided to set up their own sect, which was called Primitive Methodism.

Historians differ on the social and political effects of early Methodism. According to French scholar Elie Halévy,

Methodism could take credit for saving England from revolution, but the Marxist E. P. Thompson thought that Methodism was part of the false consciousness that prevented the emergence of true class consciousness and so stifled revolution. E. J. Hobsbawm has questioned whether there was the numerical strength to lead a successful political mass movement. Two facts seem indisputable. The Wesleyan Conference (a body consisting, at the time, entirely of ministers, with complete control of denominational policy) leadership was totally loyal to the state and opposed to social unrest and colonial rebellion. Both in England and America, however, the Methodist societies shared and were receptive to the cries of the oppressed and downtrodden.

Methodism in the United States

The American Revolution caused a major crisis for Methodism, and it was with difficulty that the American leader, Francis Asbury (1745–1816), prevented an open breach with Wesley. After American independence, at Christmas 1784 a legally constituted conference at Baltimore with Wesley's blessing and with Asbury as first bishop launched the Methodist Episcopal Church. Methodism grew swiftly in America and in the first half of the nineteenth century became the largest of the denominations.

But in becoming American it moved away from Wesley's social teaching in some crucial areas. The best known circuit-rider and leader in the West, Peter Cartwright (1785–1872), gave his warm political support to Thomas Jefferson and then to Andrew Jackson. The most explosive issue was race. Black members in New York and Philadelphia withdrew in protest to set up their own societies, some of which in 1816 became the African Methodist Episcopal Church, and others the African Methodist Episcopal Zion Church, in 1820. Today, both these denominations have more than a million members each.

In 1844 the parent body split into North and South churches over whether bishops should hold bondsmen. A Methodist Southerner, Thomas Crowder, forecast in 1844 that if a bishop was dismissed for owning slaves it was a sign of the larger conflict to come. Bishop Matthew Simpson was a personal friend of President Abraham Lincoln, and 450 ministers of the African Methodist Episcopal North volunteered for chaplain-type work with the Union (Northern) army.

After the American Civil War (1861–1865) black ministers took major roles in the Reconstruction era. A former slave, Henry Turner of the African Methodist Episcopal Church was the first black chaplain to the Union army and became a member of the South Carolina legislature. In 1874 he was one of the first to call for a return to Africa, a cause he championed as bishop. The Methodist Episcopal Church South helped its black members establish an independent black church in 1870, the Colored Methodist Episcopal Church (renamed the Christian Methodist Episcopal Church in 1954).

It took almost a century for the Methodist Episcopal Church to be reunited in 1939. In a further union in 1968 with the German-speaking United Brethren the eleven-million-member United Methodist Church was created. Since 1964 the United Methodists have taken a lead in affirmative action by electing more black bishops than any other mainline denomination (the first was Robert E. Jones in 1916) and appointing them without regard to the racial profile of their area.

After the Civil War northern Methodists and the black Methodist denominations voted overwhelmingly Republican, which was seen as the party of morality. That perception changed when President Franklin Delano Roosevelt's New Deal administration after 1932 gradually won support from Methodists for a second term in office in 1936 and brought a majority of Methodists behind the Democratic Party. This support was no longer deep enough to prevent a majority of Methodists voting for Republican Ronald Reagan in 1980, although the 40 percent who supported Democrat Jimmy Carter in the same election was more than the support given by members of any other mainline Protestant denomination.

In 1908 a Federation for Social Service was set up by northern Methodists, including the liberal-minded Social Gospel professor, Harry F. Ward. In 1916 the Methodists were the first to open an office in Washington, D.C., to bring pressure on Congress and the executive branch as part of their temperance campaign, which contributed to the introduction of Prohibition in 1920. It was the Methodist Women's Division that in 1948 appointed a lobbyist in Washington to push social issues that went beyond alcohol abuse. Today the United Methodist Building on Capitol Hill provides offices for the mainline churches that work together to stimulate local lobbying of members of Congress.

After World War II the Methodist viewpoint was articulated at the highest political level by Bishop G. Bromley Oxnam, who was transferred to Washington to take advantage of his long friendship with John Foster Dulles, President Dwight D. Eisenhower's secretary of state. Dulles and Oxnam shared a deep suspicion of the Soviet Union and a conviction that Christianity was the only ideology to combat atheistic communism. Oxnam had regular meetings with Dulles throughout the secretary's period in office and used them not only to reinforce the cold war mentality but also to criticize the State Department's policy conclusions that had led to support of right-wing dictatorships and refusal to recognize the People's Republic of China.

The Methodists were the first in 1965 to oppose President Lyndon Johnson's escalation of bombing in Vietnam. Three Methodist bishops were part of a delegation to Secretary of Defense Robert McNamara to urge a negotiated peace. The Methodist Board of Social Concerns called for an American withdrawal from Vietnam in 1967 and the next year voted $100,000 to its antiwar campaign. A spokesman for the group said it was the first time a church had tried directly to influence foreign policy. In the opinion of the Methodist ethical theologian Paul Ramsay, churches are rightly concerned with the direction of national life but are not competent to deal with specifics of policy. To criticism that Methodist spokespersons did not speak for the membership, Elliott Corbert, Methodist chief lobbyist, has replied that although there can be a gap of several years in their thinking, the membership usually catches up with the leadership when it has had time to assimilate situations and weigh moral dilemmas.

Nevertheless, a survey conducted for the United Methodists in 1980 showed wide differences: 96 percent of national staff and 92 percent of bishops supported the right to abortion, but only 58 percent of lay chairpersons did so. It seemed that Methodists shared the dilemma of all the mainline churches in having a liberal establishment but only moderate laity. In the Methodist case this divide was pushed to the breaking point in 1980 when David Jessup, a political activist, who was to be backed by the American Enterprise Institute, a conservative Washington think tank, complained that his children had been given appeals for funds for Marxist causes in a United Methodist Sunday School in Maryland. The ensuing uproar distracted the denomination for some years until it was left to Bishop William Cannon at the 1984 Methodist general conference to place social action in a Wesleyan perspective.

In recent years the United Methodists have become worried by their lack of appeal to young people. Membership is declining and aging, which inhibits innovation. At the 1996 Methodist general conference Hillary Rodham Clinton spoke about the importance of work among children. The big rift, however, was over the gay and lesbian issue in which the conference voted to maintain its traditional discipline. Yet there are highly successful United Methodist churches, such as the downtown Glide in San Francisco, that welcome people from a variety of backgrounds, races, and orientations.

Methodism in Britain

In England Methodist preachers were strong supporters of the North in the American Civil War, even in Lancashire, where the cotton famine brought many mills to a standstill and led to workers being laid off. Working-class local (or lay) preachers were receptive to the arguments of reformers and advocates of better conditions for working people. Many Methodists were instrumental in setting up trades unions, especially the Agricultural Workers Union and the Miners Union. Experience with trades unions paved the way for Methodist involvement in national politics when the vote was extended to working men in 1885. But many second-generation Methodists had been upwardly mobile socially and had become factory owners who resisted state limits on their employees' hours of work.

In the late nineteenth century the religious-political alignment in Britain was clear-cut. William Gladstone's accession to the leadership of the Liberal Party in 1868, with a program of high moral fervor that included disestablishing the Anglican Church in Ireland, brought him overwhelming but not unanimous support from Methodists. The first Methodist to enter the British cabinet was Henry Fowler, a Wesleyan minister's son, invited by Gladstone in 1893. Though always dwarfed by the Church of England, the Methodists were the largest of the Free Churches and their political influence was considerable in the years between 1885 and 1914. Under the leadership of Hugh Price Hughes, a determined attempt was made in the 1890s to shake off the sectarian image and move into the mainstream of national life. Unfortunately the issues on which Methodists were most vocal were minority moral issues such as alcohol and gambling, and after World War I the relaxation of public attitudes and collapse of the Liberals as articulators of the national moral conscience made it difficult to influence national legislation.

The emergence of the Labour Party as the main alternative to the Conservatives diminished Methodist influence. Although Morgan Phillips, the party's general secretary, once observed that Labour owes more to Methodism than to Marx, there were other strands in the Labour movement. The first Methodist to be a Labour cabinet minister was Arthur Henderson, a Methodist lay preacher, in 1923, and there have always been Methodists in Labour governments. In 1965 Labour Prime Minister Harold Wilson made leading Methodist minister, Christian Socialist, and pacifist Donald Soper a life peer. The religious service held on the Sunday before the Labour party's annual conference was always held in a Methodist church until 1997, when Prime Minister Tony Blair's New Labour broke with the tradition.

In the postwar years many anti-Labour Methodists went into the Conservative Party, including the future foreign secretary Selwyn Lloyd and future prime minister Margaret Thatcher.

The British Methodist conference has always been alert to sociopolitical issues and in the 1980s was often highly critical of the Thatcher government, especially in 1989 when Dr. John Vincent of the Sheffield Inner City Ecumenical Mission was president. During this period the conference launched Mission Alongside the Poor to fund initiatives in urban priority areas. Because there were large numbers of black Methodists, the conference suggested in 1989 that if Labour did not select a black candidate for a parliamentary by-election in inner London, a mainly Methodist group would nominate one. Today British Methodists are to be found as members of Parliament in all three main parties, but conference rhetoric is usually center-left.

Methodism and Missionaries

For Methodists on both sides of the Atlantic the missionary movement provided an important outlet for women to use their leadership and fundraising abilities. In the American South, for example, women become involved in social and missionary work.

Missions were a form of cultural imperialism that sometimes slipped over into support for territorial control. American Methodists backed their Methodist president William McKinley in 1898 in the wars over Cuba and the Philippines, and the British Wesleyan leadership supported the British army in the war with the Boers that secured South Africa for the British Empire, though many Primitive Methodists sympathized with the Boer farmers.

Missionary outreach has taken Methodism to Africa, Europe, Asia, and the Pacific. Although usually representing a minority tradition, Methodist individuals have often had significant political responsibilities. The Methodist bishop Abel Muzorewa was briefly prime minister of Zimbabwe-Rhodesia in the transition to independence, and a Methodist minister, Canaan Banana, became the first president of Zimbabwe (1980–1987).

David Lange, influenced as a student in London in the 1960s by the Rev. Donald Soper, became Labour prime minister of New Zealand in 1984 and began to carry out his election promise to create a nuclear-free zone in the Pacific. His government refused port entry to a nuclear-armed American aircraft carrier. This was popular in New Zealand but isolated the country from the governments of its main allies, the United States, the United Kingdom, and Australia. In 1985 Soper traveled to New Zealand to support Lange's policy, and on June 4, 1987, the nuclear-free stand was written into law. The government's economic cutbacks caused hardship for the poor and were opposed by the main churches. Lange resigned in 1989.

The Kingdom of Tonga, an island in the Pacific with 119,000 inhabitants, is the only country in the world with a Methodist majority. Under the constitution the king is head of the Free Wesleyan Church. This did not, however, stifle successful criticism by church leaders in 1987 of a royal princess made to permit dumping of hazardous wastes from the United States in the islands.

The inhabitants of the Fiji Islands are divided between indigenous Melanesians, who are almost all Methodists, and the descendants of indentured Tamil laborers, Hindus and Muslims, brought by the British between 1879 and 1916 to cut sugar cane. Commerce and the professions came to be dominated by Indians, causing resentment among the Melanesians. Election results in 1987 were seen as a challenge to social control of the Melanesian chiefs, and a successful military coup was organized by Colonel Sitireni Rabuka in support of traditional values, strict Sabbatarianism, and fundamentalist piety. The coup leaders were all Methodists but their actions split the denomination, provoked litigation, and suspended the country's constitution.

Today Methodists claim a world family of about twenty million members, although many are now part of national churches in union with other denominations, a trend that started in South India in 1947 but now includes former Methodists in North India, Australia, Canada, Japan, France, Belgium, Spain, and elsewhere. A towering figure in the world ecumenical movement was John R. Mott (1865–1955), who was awarded the Nobel Peace Prize in 1946. The World Methodist Council provides a focus for those who treasure the Wesleyan tradition in church life and thought and awards an annual Methodist Peace Prize.

Methodism has always been an activist creed that values hard work and self-discipline. It believes that opportunities should be available for all and has founded schools and colleges. Methodists are generally social optimists who believe that legislation is necessary to protect the weak and right wrong. In 1998 the Methodist Church was the only one of the main Irish denominations to support opening the Good Friday agreement between Nationalists and Unionists to bring peace to Northern Ireland.

See also *Abolitionism; African American experience; Anglicanism; Missionaries; Revivalism; Social Gospel; Temperance movement.*

Stuart Mews

BIBLIOGRAPHY

Bartels, F. L. *The Roots of Ghana Methodism.* Cambridge: Cambridge University Press, 1965.

Bucke, E. S., ed. *The History of American Methodism.* 3 vols. Nashville, Tenn.: Abingdon Press, 1964.

Campbell, James T. *Songs of Zion: The African Methodist Episcopal Church in the United States and South Africa.* Chapel Hill: University of North Carolina Press, 1998.

Davies, R. E., A. R. George, and E. G. Rupp. *A History of the Methodist Church in Great Britain.* 4 vols. London: Epworth Press, 1965, 1978, 1983, 1988.

Hempton, David. *Methodism and Politics in British Society, 1750–1850.* London: Hutchinson, 1984.

MacKenzie, Kenneth M. *The Robe and the Sword: The Methodist Church and the Rise of American Imperialism.* Washington, D.C.: Public Affairs Press, 1961.

Matthews, Donald G. *Slavery and Methodism: A Chapter in American Morality, 1780–1845.* Princeton: Princeton University Press, 1965.

Richey, Russell E., and Kenneth E. Rowe, eds. *Rethinking Methodist History.* Nashville, Tenn.: Kingswood Books, 1985.

Walker, Clarence E. *A Rock in a Weary Land: The African Methodist Episcopal Church during the Civil War and Reconstruction.* Baton Rouge: Louisiana State University Press, 1982.

Wearmouth, R. F. *Social and Political Influence of Methodism in the Twentieth Century.* London: Epworth Press, 1957.

Mexico

A federal republic in North America, Mexico gained independence from Spain in 1821. Most of Mexico's 95 million people consider themselves Roman Catholics, and some 40 percent attend church services regularly. There is also a growing Protestant minority. Protestantism—especially Pentecostal sects, which emphasize individual experiences of spiritual gifts, expressive worship, and evangelism—has increased in Mexico to between 15 and 19 percent of the population. Some Protestants have held important political posts. In the late 1990s, however, Protestants were increasingly divided among themselves over religious and political issues.

Historical Background

No other Latin American country has had more contention between church and state than Mexico. Mexico's tradition of official anticlericalism, or political antagonism toward the clergy, lasted until 1991 and was rooted in the country's past. The colonial *encomienda* system granted Spanish nobles, soldiers, and the Roman Catholic Church large tracts of land. Although the church was one of the few institutions concerned with the welfare of the indigenous people and the impoverished *mestizos* of mixed race, thus contributing to the lower classes' conservatism and piety, it nonetheless grew wealthy through gifts and bequests. By 1859 the church owned one-third of all property and land, and for many Mexicans, it became associated with tradition and the landowning class. A rigid class system, which placed Spanish-born persons in the highest colonial civil and church offices, also bred resentment among people of mixed race, Native Americans, and those of European descent who were born in New Spain.

Mexico's struggle for independence and its early years as a nation were marked by conflict between Centralists—a conservative group of church leaders, rich landowners, and army officers determined to maintain a highly centralized, colonial form of government—and Federalists—a liberal, anticlerical faction that supported a federation of sovereign states and sought control over the church as a political opponent.

In 1859 President Benito Juárez—a man of humble origins and Zapotec descent—decreed the nationalization of church property and attempted to suppress religious orders. He was impeded in these reform efforts by occupying French forces and political turmoil. With the dictatorship (1876–1880, 1884–1911) of Porfirio Díaz, the church began to recover much of its lost fortune and established new schools.

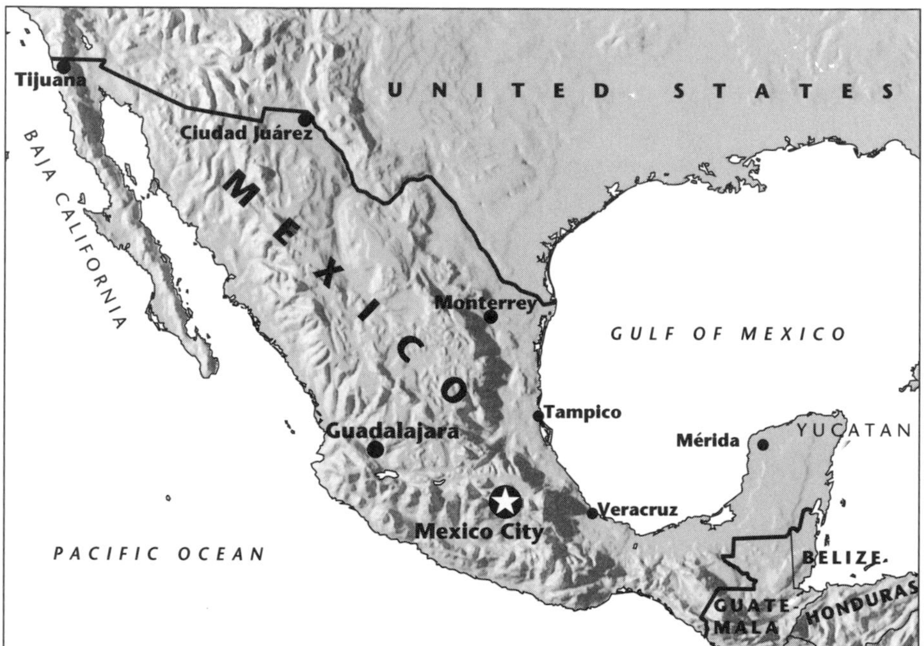

The clergy's return to open political activity, beginning in the 1890s, drew fierce attacks from revolutionaries, especially after the 1911 overthrow of Díaz that brought a period of civil war. Venustiano Carranza, Francisco Villa, and others committed outrages against the clergy and church property. Revolutionary leaders drafted the 1917 constitution, which forbade Catholic schools and the public expression of religion, stripped priests of the right to vote, and deprived churches of the right to own property. But these anticlerical provisions went unenforced until President Plutarco Calles (1924–1928) announced his intention to carry them out. Church leaders openly resisted compliance.

Church-state relations further declined in the 1920s, when the militant Catholic *Cristeros* presented the first largely lay, ideologically committed opposition to the secularization of the revolution. The government deported many priests and executed several for political activities.

Church and government begin moving toward conciliation during 1926–1946. President Lázaro Cárdenas (1934–1940) opened the way in 1936, allowing the church more freedom in practice than the constitution did by law. Bishops negotiated informally with state officials to gain control at least of religious activities, but the state was not ready to grant full juridical standing to the church as an institution capable of influencing national policy or political rights, in the form of votes, to the clergy.

Since 1929 the Institutional Revolutionary Party (PRI) has dominated Mexico's political system. The PRI has maintained a hierarchical organization that controlled politics through cronyism and electoral fraud. PRI presidents continued to offer limited freedom to the church and permitted reestablishment of theological schools.

Social and Political Change

Following the reforms of the Second Vatican Council (1962–1965)—with their emphasis on a new ecumenical openness toward other Christian churches, the collective responsibility of bishops in the church's mission, more acute concern for political and social issues, reform of priestly education, and partial acceptance of diversity in theology and local practices—priests and Catholic laity became more formally active in Mexican public affairs. After Pope John Paul II's first visit to Mexico in 1979, individual bishops and groups of bishops were more openly critical of the government. Bishops of all persuasions spoke out on sensitive social and political issues, especially electoral fraud.

Despite reservations among many Catholics and anticlerical Mexicans, President Carlos Salinas de Gortari (1988–1994) began changing church-state relations. Salinas and the Vatican established formal diplomatic relations. Within Mexico, legal reforms affecting the churches were debated and eventually voted through. The legislature amended the constitution (Articles 3, 5, 24, 27, and 130), giving freedom to the faithful to organize, allowing some outdoor religious ceremonies, permitting the church to own property, and granting the clergy the right to vote.

The heritage of past church-state relations has marked lay Catholics. Mexican Catholics were indoctrinated in nineteenth-century Mexican liberalism in almost universal public schooling but they have a strong attachment to Catholic-Latin values at home. In the early 1990s most Mexicans believed that the church should refrain from political activism but placed more confidence in it than in any other social institution.

PRI Presidents Salinas and Ernesto Zedillo (who took office in 1994) encouraged other parties to participate more in governing Mexico. Catholics at all levels have been active in promoting free and fair national and local elections. Grassroots Catholic groups have joined with other organizations to form social assistance movements, especially after the 1984 Mexico City earthquake that killed more than 7,000 people. The focus of protests has been the PRI, which is marked at times by inability to respond to crises and by repressive control. Since 1984 a strong human rights movement addressing a wide array of issues, especially clean elections and police brutality, has emerged. These groups seek to strengthen civil organizations as the basis for more participation by the people in democracy.

In January 1994 an uprising in Chiapas by an indigenous group calling itself the Zapatista National Liberation Army focused world attention on the Zapatistas' demands for government reform. Mexican Catholics and Protestants alike have shifted their focus from church-state issues to religious faith and political issues as a new era unfolds in the country.

See also *Anticlericalism; Vatican Council, Second.*

Edward L. Cleary

BIBLIOGRAPHY

Camp, Roderic A. *Crossing Swords: Politics and Religion in Mexico.* New York: Oxford University Press, 1996.

Cleary, Edward L. "Human Rights Organizations in Mexico: Growth in Turbulence." *Journal of Church and State* 37 (autumn 1995): 793–812.

Hanratty, Dennis M. "Church-State Relations in Mexico in the 1980s." *Thought* 63 (September 1988): 207–223.

Mecham, J. Lloyd. *Church and State in Latin America: History of Politico-Ecclesiastical Relations.* Rev. ed. Chapel Hill: University of North Carolina Press, 1966.

Migration

See *Nativism*

Millennialism

The religious belief that a divinely ordained utopia will arise on earth at the end of time, perhaps following a vast global catastrophe, is called millennialism (or millenarianism). This belief has taken many forms throughout history, often with profound political ramifications. These, too, have varied widely, depending on the group involved and the social context.

Sources of Millennial Belief

Millennialism figures most prominently in the three major monotheistic religions, Judaism, Christianity, and Islam, often in the form of a belief that at some future time the Messiah (identified in Christianity and Islam as Jesus) will establish an earthly reign of peace and justice. At the end of this era, human history will end and eternity will begin. In the Jewish prophetic scriptures, the messianic hope typically focuses on the salvation of the Children of Israel and the destruction of their enemies. In a series of Jewish apocalyptic works beginning about 200 B.C., however, the coming Messiah vanquishes the forces of evil everywhere and establishes dominion over the whole earth.

The first Christians linked such messianic expectations to the imminent return of Jesus Christ. Following a brief but terrible interlude dominated by a demonic figure, the Antichrist, they believed, Jesus would return with the martyred saints to rule the earth from Jerusalem. In the New Testament Book of Revelation, a Christian apocalyptic work dating from about 100 A.D., this reign lasts for one thousand years (hence, the millennium, from the Latin *mille,* "thousand," and *annus,* "year"). At the end of this interval, Satan is briefly loosed, but after a final battle he is forever consigned to "the lake of fire and brimstone." History ends, a "new heaven and a new earth" arise, and Christ and the saints reign forever. In the Islamic variant of millennialism, a messianic leader, the Mahdi, will arise in the last days. He will defeat an Antichrist-like figure, al-Dajjal, and establish Islam worldwide, after which Jesus will return to launch his reign.

Although without the specific thousand-year component, the belief in a glorious future age appears in other religions as well. In Hindu thought, blessedness is achieved as the individual gains self-knowledge through many lifetimes, eventually transcending earthly passions to attain oneness with *Brahman,* the universal reality. In modern times, Indian spiritual leaders such as Raja Rammohun Roy (1772 –1833), Vivekananda (1863–1902), and Mohandas Gandhi (1869–1948) added a social dimension to Hindu mysticism, supplementing renunciation of earthly desire with efforts for a purified society and a peaceful, harmonious world. In Buddhism, which arose in India in the sixth century B.C., the principle of reincarnation gave rise in popular piety to belief in the eventual return of the Buddha himself to inaugurate an era of justice and happiness.

In different places and times, specific movements within these major religions have highlighted the millennial theme. Buddhist millennialism, for example, flourished in thirteenth-century Japan, as spiritual leaders sought to make Buddhism more accessible to ordinary folk by encouraging worship of the Buddha's image as a path to Nirvana, or enlightenment. Like the ancient Hebrew prophets, these reformers portrayed society as corrupt and ripe for destruction. The most prominent of these reformers, Nichiren (1222–1282), prophesied earthquakes, epidemics, and an enemy invasion as punishment for the people's wickedness. Nichiren's apocalyptic message lived on. One militant group of his followers, called Nichiren Shoshu, remained active into the twentieth century, vigorously seeking converts and elevating Nichiren to messianic status as the Great Holy One, a Buddha for the last days.

Postmillennialism and Social Reform

Because millennialism anticipates a transformed social order within human history, it has exerted a major and sometimes dramatic effect on politics, society, and culture. In some contexts, millennial belief has inspired reformist efforts to better the human condition. In Protestant Christianity, this reformist impulse historically has characterized postmillennialists, who believe that Christ's earthly reign will succeed a long upward march of human progress and moral advance. In early nineteenth century America, postmillennial fervor inspired religious revivalism and an array of social reforms, from communal utopias to antislavery movements. Millennial hope suffuses Julia Ward Howe's Civil War anthem, "The Battle Hymn of the Republic" (1863), with its soaring opening line: "Mine eyes have seen the glory of the coming of the Lord."

In the late nineteenth and early twentieth centuries, postmillennial visions inspired the Social Gospel, whose advocates exhorted those who longed for Christ's kingdom to work for improved conditions in the nation's factories and slums. Theologian Walter Rauschenbusch, in such works as *Christianity and the Social Crisis* (1907) and *A Theology for the Social Gospel* (1917), explicitly linked millennialism and social reform.

Postmillennial beliefs also reenforced Americans' sense of mission. The Puritans, who founded a colony in New England in the seventeenth century, clothed their enterprise in millennial imagery. Nineteenth-century politicians and religious leaders alike pictured westward migration and imperial expansion as a further unfolding of God's divine plan. In 1917–1918, President Woodrow Wilson, the son of a Presbyterian minister, invoked a secularized millennialism to justify America's entry into the First World War, portraying the war as a spiritual crusade to "make the world safe for democracy" and lift humanity to a higher plane.

Revolutionary and Anticolonial Movements

Although millennialism has inspired optimistic reform efforts that viewed the existing political system as an instrument for fulfilling God's purposes, it has also fueled more radical movements that repudiated the established order as irredeemably evil. Seventeenth-century English revolutionaries quoted biblical prophecies as they battled what they saw as a satanic civil and religious establishment. In antebellum America, thousands embraced the message of William Miller, who preached Christ's return on October 22, 1844, to remove his saints from earthly wickedness. When the appointed day passed, some disappointed Millerites reformulated their end-time scenario and founded the Seventh-day Adventist Church, which by the late 1990s boasted nine million members worldwide.

In a very different setting, Christian millennialism helped fuel the Taiping Rebellion, which convulsed China in the mid-nineteenth century. The uprising, in the aftermath of China's defeat by the British in the Opium Wars, was led by Hong Xiuquan, a rural youth who repeatedly had failed the rigorous exams for admission to the imperial civil service. Encountering a Christian tract that described the destruction of human society in a violent end-time struggle and the establishment of Christ's kingdom, Hong not only embraced the millennialist message but concluded that he himself was "God's Chinese son." Soon he had organized his Taiping ("Great Peace") movement to overthrow the demonic imperial system and create an earthly paradise of harmony, justice, and sexual purity. Peasants rallied to the cause, and in the 1850s Hong's army overran much of China and established the movement's headquarters in Nanjing. In 1864 the imperial army, aided by Western forces, captured Nanjing, killed Hong, and crushed his movement. Fifteen years of fighting left an estimated twenty million Chinese dead.

Millennialism burst forth in Sudan in 1881, when Muhammad Ahmad proclaimed himself the long-awaited Mahdi. Preaching holy war against unbelievers, he launched a struggle to throw out Sudan's Anglo-Egyptian occupiers. In 1885, after a ten-month siege, the Mahdi's forces stormed the garrison at Khartoum and killed the English commander, Charles George Gordon. The Mahdi himself died in 1885, but his followers fought on until Lord Kitchener defeated them in 1898, solidifying British control of Sudan.

Millennial aspirations would later help inspire Islamic fundamentalism, which challenged the political order in many countries in the late twentieth century. Drawing on the anti-Western, anti-imperialist thought of such figures as Jamal al-Din al-Afghani (1838–1897), Islamic Shi'ite leaders such as Ayatollah Ruholla Musavi Khomeini of Iran (1900–1989) repudiated the secular West as the "Great Satan" and called for an undefiled society ruled by strict Islamic principles.

The Rastafarian movement in Jamaica further illustrates the interaction of millennialism and anticolonialism. The movement began in 1930, inspired by the crowning of Haile Selassie as emperor of Ethiopia. Drawing on Jewish and Christian apocalyptic literature, early Rastafarian leaders viewed Selassie as the returned Christ. They identified Jamaica's British colonial rulers with the Babylon whose destruction is foretold in the Book of Revelation and regarded the United States as the evil northern power whose fate is described in the Book of Ezekiel. In the coming age, the Rastafarians taught, black people everywhere would rise to power under Selassie. Appealing to the poor and outcast, Rastafarian millennialism sharpened anticolonial sentiment in Jamaica and elsewhere in the Caribbean. The movement remains a cultural influence.

Another perspective on the political ramifications of millennialism is offered by Japan's Soka Gakkai movement, a Buddhist sect founded in the 1930s by two Tokyo schoolteachers. Affiliated with the Nichiren Shoshu branch of Buddhism, Soka Gakkai recruited aggressively, denounced all other faiths, and offered a millennial agenda: converting Asia to true Buddhism by 2020, when a utopian age would begin. With an estimated ten to fifteen million members, Soka Gakkai by the 1970s was Japan's fastest growing religion. Like many such movements, it especially attracted the poor, the ill-educated, and the marginal.

In the 1960s, as part of its campaign to "purify the world," Soka Gakkai formed the Komeito ("Clean Government") Party to compete in Japanese politics. While denouncing the established parties as corrupt, Komeito leaders soon formed alliances with those same parties as they maneuvered for political power. A millennial movement rooted in radical hostility to the established order had become a part of that order.

Premillennialism and Rejection of the Social Order

In the United States the antigovernment, anti-establishment position has most often been embraced by premillennialists. Assembling an array of Bible passages like a picture puzzle, premillennialists hold that before Christ's earthly reign, wickedness, warfare, and natural disasters will intensify. As conditions worsen, some believe, Christians will be taken from the earth in a supernatural event known as the Rapture. After a seven-year Tribulation, culminating in the Antichrist's global dictatorship, a final cosmic conflict will be fought at Armageddon (an ancient battle site near Haifa in Israel). The Antichrist will be vanquished and the Millennium will begin.

The most widespread variant of this prophetic system, known as premillennial dispensationalism, was formulated in the 1830s by a British churchman, John Nelson Darby, a founder of the Plymouth Brethren, who in his preaching and writings popularized the doctrine of the pre-Tribulation Rapture. Darby embedded his end-time scenario within a larger interpretive scheme in which all history, from the Creation to the Last Judgment, is divided into seven periods, or dispensations, each with a distinct plan of salvation for Jews and gentiles. The present dispensation, the Church Age, Darby taught, while of indeterminate length, will end soon in the Rapture.

Premillennial dispensationalism was promulgated in the United States and Canada by Darby's frequent evangelistic tours (1859–1874) and by influential proponents, including Cyrus Scofield, an American who wrote the *Scofield Refer-*

ence Bible (1909). Premillennial dispensationalism has been spread more recently by television evangelists and paperback popularizers. Hal Lindsey's *The Late Great Planet Earth* (1970), a premillennialist book written for a mass readership, was the nonfiction best-seller of the 1970s. By the end of the century, premillennial dispensationalism was embraced by millions of people in North America, Latin America, Africa, and other regions where evangelical Protestant missionaries carried the doctrine.

The Jehovah's Witnesses movement, founded in the 1870s (incorporated in 1884) by Charles Taze Russell, espoused a variant of premillennialism with certain unique features, such as the doctrine that those who have not heard of Jesus will have a second chance for salvation during the Millennium. Firm in their faith, Jehovah's Witnesses worship in Kingdom Halls, promulgate their beliefs through publications such as *The Watchtower,* and tirelessly proselytize door to door. By the mid-1990s the sect claimed 4.5 million members worldwide. Viewing earthly governments as demonic, Jehovah's Witnesses have endured persecution in many countries, including Nazi Germany. In the United States, they have faced legal challenges for their opposition to blood transfusions, military service, and the Pledge of Allegiance.

Proclaiming the wickedness of all human institutions, premillennialists find abundant evidence for their position. For them, the United States, having long since fallen from divine favor, is sinking ever deeper in sin and apostasy. During the cold war that followed World War II, premillennialist popularizers found the Soviet Union's destruction prophesied in the Book of Ezekiel and a thermonuclear holocaust foretold in II Peter 3:10: "[T]he heavens shall pass away with a great noise and the elements shall melt with fervent heat, the earth also and the works that are therein shall be burned up."

For premillennialists the Jews' return to Palestine, the establishment of Israel in 1948, and Israel's recapture of the Old City of Jerusalem in 1967 represented prophetic signs of the first importance. Interpreting literally God's promise to Abraham, recorded in Genesis, of all the land from the Euphrates to the "river of Egypt," they foresaw Israel's vast future expansion. Marshaling other prophetic texts, they anticipated the rebuilding of the Jewish Temple in Jerusalem on its original site—now occupied by the Dome of the Rock, a sacred Islamic shrine. But premillennialists also found a darker side in the prophesied destiny of the Jews. The long history of anti-Semitic persecution, including the Nazi Holocaust, many argued, was God's "chastisement" for the Jews' failure to accept Jesus as the Messiah. And they cited various biblical passages to argue that during the Tribulation, the Antichrist will outdo Hitler in killing millions of Jews.

Political Implications

In short, popularized premillennialism with its focus on current events has had obvious political implications, fostering passivity toward issues that others considered the most urgent of the day. If nuclear war, the physical annihilation of the Soviet Union, and the mass slaughter of the Jews are all part of God's prophetic plan—essential stages leading to the Millennium—why resist any of these developments?

In the 1990s, as the nuclear threat receded and the Soviet Union collapsed, premillennial popularizers turned to different end-time themes. They noted environmental hazards such as global warming as the fulfillment of biblical prophecies of natural catastrophes in the last days. They cited a variety of social developments—radical feminism, New Age mysticism, AIDS, abortion, drugs, and illegitimacy—as evidence of the approaching end. Even more urgently, they pointed to multinational corporations, international trade agreements, global political institutions, worldwide satellite communications, and a computer-based economy as a prelude to the Antichrist's universal rule.

This latter strand in the premillennialist scenario, too, had political implications, fostering a conspiratorial, almost paranoid view of current events. Powerful and sinister forces, the popularizers suggested, were creating conditions that would soon give rise to the demonic world order foretold in the Bible. In such a climate, all major institutions, from the federal government and the public school system to big corporations and media conglomerates, became deeply suspect. Only the divinely ordained destruction of the present world order in a spasm of violence, this belief system implied, would clear the way for the Millennium.

The televangelist Pat Robertson, founder of the influential and politically conservative Christian Coalition, contributed to this conspiratorial mindset. "A giant plan is unfolding," Robertson warned in *The New World Order* (1991); "everything is perfectly on cue." Among the conspirators Robertson identified the Masons, the eighteenth-century "Bavarian Illuminati," the first U.S. Congress, the Rothschilds, the Trilateral Commission, the Council on Foreign Relations, the Beatles, and credit cards. As the conspiracy deepened, he proclaimed, the Antichrist's "counterfeit world order" would emerge. But beyond all the unsettling developments lay the ancient millennial hope: the Antichrist's dictatorship will fail, Christ's kingdom will come.

Radical Separatist Movements

In its more extreme manifestations, millennialism has led some groups to withdraw from the world entirely to defend themselves against the gathering forces of evil. The results have sometimes been catastrophic.

In 1534 the followers of a Dutch mystic named Jan Mathys took over the Westphalian city of Münster, cut it off from the outside world, and proclaimed Christ's New Jerusalem in which all property would be held in common. Mathys was succeeded by Jan Bockelson (known as John of Leiden), a twenty-five-year-old Dutch tailor who proclaimed himself the Messiah. Besieged and starving, the Münsterites surrendered in 1535 to the expelled civil and religious authorities and were slaughtered en masse. The bodies of Bockelson and two followers were suspended in cages from a church tower. The cages remain to this day.

The Church of Jesus Christ of Latter-day Saints (Mormons), founded by Joseph Smith in upstate New York in 1830, had a strong millennial strain that looked to the establishment of an American Zion. Persecuted in New York, Ohio, and Illinois for their practice of polygamy, their economic exclusiveness, and their defiance of state power, the Mormons migrated to Utah after the murder of Smith. Here, in 1847, they founded Salt Lake City, the prophesied Zion. In 1857 they came under siege by the U.S. Army, when President James Buchanan declared them in rebellion. Only in 1896, after the Mormon leadership abandoned polygamy and made other concessions, did Utah gain statehood.

In 1965 the Reverend Jim Jones, the popular minister of a racially integrated church in Indianapolis, Indiana, moved to California, where he established the People's Temple in San Francisco. Jones's movement was millennialist in the sense that he isolated his followers from the world and promised them a new social order based on racial equality. He insisted that converts give him all their assets, call him "Dad," and obey him implicitly. Dissidents endured public beatings. In 1976, increasingly dictatorial and drug dependent, and facing legal problems, Jones with a thousand followers moved to a remote settlement in Guyana. In November 1978, responding to reports from worried family members of Jones's followers, California representative Leo J. Ryan went to investigate "Jonestown." When Ryan and four members of his party were murdered by Jones's lieutenants, Jones ordered his followers to commit suicide by drinking cyanide-laced punch. When police arrived, they found 912 bodies; among them was Jones himself, shot in the head.

Fifteen years later, in Waco, Texas, young David Koresh held sway over the Branch Davidians, a millennial sect that had arisen in the 1930s as an offshoot of the Seventh-day Adventist Church. Koresh had gained control of the sect in 1983 and turned it in an ominous direction. Warning that the forces of evil Babylon would soon attack, he gathered his followers into a compound that he turned into an armed fortress. Claiming divinity and quoting Bible prophecy, he imposed absolute authority and insisted on his right of sexual access to any women of the sect, including young girls.

In February 1993, when federal agents tried to arrest Koresh on firearms charges, gunfire erupted. Four federal agents and six Davidians died. A fifty-one-day FBI siege followed, amid massive media attention. In rambling letters and taped sermons, Koresh blended millennial visions and apocalyptic warnings. On April 19, as armored vehicles moved in, several fires broke out simultaneously inside the main building. When the inferno had cooled, some eighty Davidians lay dead.

In Japan, meanwhile, Shoko Asahara was recruiting members to his apocalyptic sect, Aum Shinri-kyo (Supreme Truth). Asahara attracted highly educated, but spiritually adrift, young technocrats and scientists. Blending Tibetan Buddhism, Hinduism, Yoga, and Christian beliefs, Asahara added his own prophecies of disaster ahead, including nuclear war and a natural catastrophe that would inundate Japan. After these horrors, Asahara assured his followers, Aum Shinri-kyo would bring forth a righteous new age. Converts must hasten this outcome, he insisted, to rescue people from their suffering and lead the world to enlightenment. On March 20, 1995, members of the sect released sarin, a deadly nerve gas, on Tokyo's crowded subway system. Ten commuters died, and more than five thousand suffered injury.

Clearly, millennialism looms large in the history of many religions. Just as clearly, the alluring spiritual vision of a brighter future free of the sorrows and conflicts of the present has had profound political consequences. In different times and places, millennial belief has inspired reform efforts, fueled revolutionary and anticolonial movements, and encouraged passive withdrawal from the public arena. Tragically, especially when manipulated by unscrupulous or megalo-

Shoko Asahara, leader of the Japanese millennialist cult Aum Shinri-kyo (Supreme Truth), was indicted for ordering a 1995 nerve gas attack on the Tokyo subway system.

maniac leaders, the shimmering prospect of a glorious tomorrow has all too often produced only suffering and death today.

See also *Cults; Mahdi; Social Gospel; Survivalism; Utopianism.*

Paul Boyer

BIBLIOGRAPHY

Adas, Michael. *Prophets of Rebellion: Millenarian Protest Movements against the European Colonial Order.* Chapel Hill: University of North Carolina Press, 1979.

Boyer, Paul. *When Times Shall Be No More: Prophecy Belief in Modern American Culture.* Cambridge: Harvard University Press, 1992.

Capp, B. S. *The Fifth Monarchy Men: A Study in Seventeenth-Century English Millenarianism.* London: Faber, 1972.

Hadden, Jeffrey K., and Anson Shupe, eds. *Prophetic Religion and Politics.* New York: Paragon House, 1986.

Olson, Theodore. *Millennialism, Utopianism, and Progress.* Toronto: University of Toronto Press, 1982.

Sandeen, Ernest R. *The Roots of Fundamentalism: British and American Millenarianism, 1800–1930.* Chicago: University of Chicago Press, 1970.

Spence, Jonathan D. *God's Chinese Son: The Taiping Heavenly Kingdom of Hong Xiuquan.* New York: Norton, 1996.

Underwood, Grant R. *The Millenarian World of Early Mormonism.* Urbana: University of Illinois Press, 1993.

Weber, Timothy P. *Living in the Shadow of the Second Coming: American Premillennialism, 1875–1982.* Chicago: University of Chicago Press, 1987.

Wright, Stuart A., ed. *Armageddon in Waco: Critical Perspectives on the Branch Davidian Conflict.* Chicago: University of Chicago Press, 1995.

Miracles

Miracles are extraordinary events that are regarded as manifestations of supernatural power or divine will. In the Judeo-Christian tradition miracles have frequently served political purposes, in some cases legitimizing regimes but in others providing support for dissidents who sought divine sanction. Miracles have also played a political role in other religious traditions and have helped to inspire resistance to European imperialism in both Africa and Asia.

The biblical account in Exodus of God's intervention to free the Jews enslaved in Egypt illustrates this double-edged connection between miracles and politics. The plagues sent to punish the Egyptians and the parting of the Red Sea legitimized the leadership of Moses and Aaron and reassured the Jews in their resistance. In medieval France and England the belief that consecrated kings had the miraculous ability to heal scrofula by means of their "royal touch" following their consecration helped to legitimize royal authority; the practice was last employed by Charles X of France in 1825.

The Political Connection

For Catholics, miraculous apparitions of Jesus, the saints (particularly Mary), and other divine beings have been an important vehicle for communicating advice and admonitions about those who held and aspired to political power. Apparitions have frequently been linked to shrines, cultic centers where pilgrims seek healings and communities ask relief from drought and plague. Over the past two centuries shrines as sites of miraculous power have also functioned as political centers, places around which believers mobilized in the face of foreign threats and domestic anticlericalism.

Miracles played an important role in the wars of religion that troubled Europe in the sixteenth and seventeenth centuries. Protestants and Catholics traded claims about miraculous support for their causes, as manifested through healings and apparitions. Dissenters who objected to the establishment of a particular orthodoxy were comforted and inspired by miracles, which became an important source of political opposition in early modern Europe. George Fox (1624–1691), the founder of the Society of Friends (Quakers), for example, was reputed to have miraculous healing powers that helped his followers persevere in the face of repression by the Anglican Church. In France the Jansenists, who advocated a rigorous moral theology and opposed papal authority, felt assured of divine favor in part because of miracles attributed to a holy thorn reputedly from Jesus' crown of thorns. Jansenist dissenters consistently appealed to a general church council rather than pope or king as the ultimate religious authority, an argument that contributed to the critique of absolutism and the defense of representative institutions that fueled the French Revolution of 1789.

Following the French Revolution, religion in Europe played a crucial role in determining the loyalties of an expanding electorate and defining nationalist sentiments that emerged as a major principle of political organization. Miracles and miraculous shrines helped to generate solidarity among Roman Catholics and support for their political positions. During the nineteenth century a series of apparitions of the Virgin Mary occurred in France, the most famous of which took place in the town of Lourdes in 1858. These formed the basis of shrines that drew a national audience of Catholics who generally supported the royalist position favored by the Catholic hierarchy and were sympathetic to the defense of the pope and the Papal States, which had been absorbed by the newly unified Italian state during the 1860s. Although the apparitions and healing miracles at Lourdes bore no explicit political message, they nonetheless helped to link Catholic devotion to Mary with royalism, papal power, and French nationalism.

Modern Examples

Apparitions of Mary, which became implicated in political programs, became increasingly common in the late nineteenth century, with incidents occurring in Germany, Italy, Belgium, Portugal, and Spain. The most prominent of these occurred at Fatima, Portugal, in 1917, inspiring a shrine that became associated first with opposition to the anticlerical policies of the Portuguese Republic and in the 1930s with Catholic anticommunism. During the cold war of the late 1940s and 1950s, Our Lady of Fatima was a major devotion whose promises to convert Russia helped mobilize Catholics against communism throughout the world.

Older miracle-working shrines and shrine images were also politicized. Two examples are Our Lady of Guadalupe in Mexico and Our Lady of Czestochowa in Poland, which became symbols of national identity and banners for movements of national independence from, respectively, Spain and Russia. In 1920 the newly created Poland was at war with Russia over disputed borders. Many Polish Catholics believed that their victory against the Russians on the Feast of the Assumption was a miracle that should be attributed to the intervention of Our Lady of Czestochowa. The shrine at Czestochowa continued to serve as a focal point for Polish nationalism during the 1980s and thereby contributed to the movement for independence led by the Solidarity trade union. The political importance of miracle-working shrines can also be gauged by the attacks they have provoked, as was the case in France during the wave of dechristianization in 1792–1793 that followed the French Revolution, and in the Soviet Union, whose government destroyed miracle-working icons as part of its antireligious campaign in the 1920s.

The apparitions in the village of Medjugorje in Bosnia–Herzegovina (then part of Yugoslavia) in 1981 illustrate the continuing and complex relationship between miracles and politics. Mary's appearances to a group of children lent support to the Franciscan friars, who staffed the local parish, against the bishop of Mostar, who was seeking to replace them with diocesan clergy. Mary's call for peace and reconciliation allowed the cult that emerged in the 1980s to serve for a time as a vehicle for reconciling groups of Serbs and Croats engaged in violent feuding. With the dissolution of Yugoslavia, however, the nationalist dimension of the cult became more prominent, and some Croats now see the apparitions as sanctioning the inclusion of Medjugorje as part of Roman Catholic Croatia rather than of Eastern Orthodox Bosnia–Herzegovina.

Over the past two centuries European expansion throughout the world has provoked politico-religious opposition that frequently was accompanied by a belief in the miraculous powers of anticolonialist leaders and movements. Muhammad Ahmad, who claimed to be the Mahdi (the guided one) who would restore the unity and purity of Islam, led a Sudanese uprising (1881–1885) against Egyptian and British rule. His power was based in part on his supporters' belief in his miraculous visions and in supernatural help in battle. The Boxer Rebellion in China (1899–1900), directed against foreign influence, was based on a sectarian society that believed its charms and rituals could evoke supernatural intervention against European soldiers. Local holy men such as the Buddhist Saya San, who led a Burmese revolt against the English in 1930–1932, were able to build on their reputation as healers and assume the role of prophet, calling on indigenous people to throw off European colonial rule.

The relationship between miraculous healings and individual political authority is not one that has been restricted to former European colonies, however, for miracles have frequently been discussed on the American evangelist Pat

Robertson's television show in the 1980s and 1990s and have thereby been integrated into his claims to be a political leader of America's fundamentalist Christians. For emerging states and political dissidents, miracles have been a potent argument for mobilizing support, as they can be used to demonstrate divine approbation, the righteousness of the cause, and its inevitable success.

See also *Cults; Sacred places.*

Thomas Kselman

BIBLIOGRAPHY

Adas, Michael. *Prophets of Rebellion: Millenarian Protest Movements against the European Colonial Order.* Cambridge: Cambridge University Press, 1987.

Bax, Mart. *Medjugorje: Religion, Politics, and Violence in Rural Bosnia.* Amsterdam: VU University Press, 1995.

Blackbourn, David. *Marpingen: Apparitions of the Virgin Mary in a Nineteenth-Century German Village.* New York: Vintage Books, 1995.

Christian, William A., Jr. *Visionaries: The Spanish Republic and the Reign of Christ.* Berkeley: University of California Press, 1996.

Kselman, Thomas. *Miracles and Prophecies in Nineteenth-Century France.* New Brunswick, N.J.: Rutgers University Press, 1983.

Perry, Nicholas, and Loreto Echeverria. *Under the Heel of Mary.* London and New York: Routledge, 1988.

Soergel, Philip. *Wondrous in his Saints: Counter-Reformation Propaganda in Bavaria.* Berkeley: University of California Press, 1993.

Missionaries

Missionaries are representatives of a religion who take on the task of converting others to their religious practices and vision of truth. The missionary activities of Buddhism, Islam, and Christianity provide a special perspective on religion and politics. Each of these religions claims universal validity, and in the determination to absorb nonbelievers each has been drawn into the processes by which cultural, political, and economic influence move around the world. A simple definition of mission stresses individual persuasion leading to conversion, but such person-to-person exchanges are only part of a larger picture. Whatever their individual motivation, when missionaries take their religious message across cultural boundaries, they typically do so as agents of sophisticated and politically significant organizations devoted to bringing fundamental change to the collective lives of others.

These organizations have rarely confined their attention to a single dimension of people's lives and have rarely worked in a field free of political complications. Not only have missions competed against each other, they have often been able to enter into other cultures only because opportunities were opened and resistance weakened by expanding international commerce, colonization, or military conquest. Whatever their religious philosophies, they have been involved in those broader processes. Today as in the past, they focus most of their energy on areas destabilized by internal social turmoil and disruptive external influences. This is not because the objectives of missions are directly derived from those of the secular parties with whom they must interact; indeed, their interests may be at odds with those of their nonmissionary compatriots abroad. But despite the episodic differences between religious and secular organizations, in the long run their agendas overlap and each from time to time provides something of value to the other.

Recognizing this uneasy religious-secular interdependence is a starting point for understanding the politics of the missionary phenomenon. Seen from the receiving end, both those who oppose missionaries and those who welcome them can see that they come not just as religious messengers but as part of a diverse cast of related characters from the outside world. That perception affects the reception given to missionaries. In the history of European colonialism, for example, relatively privileged indigenous families, looking to a future of external domination, have seen the wisdom of sending their children to mission schools to learn the language, cultural habits, and technical skills of these powerful outsiders. In time the mission's beliefs may also be internalized, but religious "seeking" or successful "conversion" is rarely the point with which the relationship begins.

Attracting adherents in this rather oblique way may secure a foothold for a mission, but converts in sufficient numbers to form a religious community are likely to come from subjugated, alienated, or deprived groups who have little to expect from the old ways and less reason to cling to them in unsettled times. In addition to the children of elites, nineteenth-century Christian missionaries in Africa often made a special place for slaves, ex-slaves, orphans, outcasts, and the physically stigmatized. For such marginalized people, the attraction of a new religion may be that it offers simple sustenance in a stable community and the opportunity to make a living, free of past disfavor, in a new division of labor. In time, the dignity and communion surrounding their new identity may replace the disrepute and isolation that defined their old lives, and their religious commitment to the emerging community may grow as a consequence.

Missionary appeals to women have displayed some of the same dynamics. In Christian outposts around the world female missionaries have assumed the task of "liberating" indigenous women from customs that Christians see as degrading and inducting them into the Western ideal of domesticity. Paradoxically, the missionary women who took on this work were imparting an essentially patriarchal message about gender relations (often in effect replacing an indigenous patriarchy with a Western one), but in doing so were themselves pursuing active roles outside the home that, in many ways, were at odds with the rhetoric and practices of their own cultures.

When appeals to marginal groups are effective, converts, both men and women, will absorb a new self-definition that is incompatible with their positions in the indigenous social order. If converts are clustered in enclaves, they may prosper because of their association with the missionaries and with the influential outsiders with whom the missionaries are linked. In time, their shared experiences may lead them to behave as a political community, motivated by their new conception of self, conditioned by their new material advantages, strengthened by their new sense of community, and guided by a new cluster of expectations about their relations with other groups in society. If their numbers are large, their defection from the old order will weaken it, and those who remain attached to the old system may well resist such changes. The visibility of the converts may mark them for political resentment and persecution.

In short, the propagation of religion across cultural boundaries is caught up in much larger cultural, economic, and political processes. Looking at Buddhism, Islam, and Christianity historically calls attention to patterns in missionary activity that are common across a wide range of circumstances. Buddhism and Islam will be addressed first, and briefly, because Christianity supports by far the largest number of international missionaries today.

Buddhism

The teachings of Gautama Buddha, the Enlightened One, became an organized body of thought in the sixth century B.C. In the third century B.C., King Asoka renounced war and embraced the nonviolent principles of Buddhism as the foundation of his rule in what is now northern India. Seeking to extend his rule and the ethical system that was its foundation, he called for the propagation of Buddhism throughout India and into Sri Lanka and the Mediterranean region. Where the diffusion of an established religion abroad is the official policy of the state, the missionaries are in effect political agents because they are involved in an intrinsically political process. As Buddhism evolved and divided internally, and as further contacts between cultures developed, it spread throughout Asia. It flourished and persisted in China, and in many areas—Japan is one example—it became the official state religion, at least for a time. But it was to remain so only in Tibet, Sri Lanka, Burma, Thailand, Laos, and Cambodia.

In the twentieth century, though Buddhism has not been an aggressive missionary religion, there has been significant Buddhist missionizing. Within individual countries where it has long been established, it has continued to expand in ways that have political implications. In India, for example, a Buddhist revival that began in the 1950s has appealed primarily to the Harijans (outcasts), in a strategy reminiscent of those used both by the earliest Buddhists and by Christian missionaries in India at a much later time. In Japan, a lay movement called Soka Gakkai (Value Creation Society) has been active in directly political ways. Associated with Nichiren Buddhism, Soka Gakkai was formed in the 1930s. Since the 1950s it has used the conversion techniques of a missionary religion, based on the conviction that Buddhism must be socially engaged and outward looking, bringing about tangible changes in people's lives. The society has participated in the political arena, even to the extent of forming its own reformist political party. In recent years, it has looked abroad, and affiliated organizations now exist around the world. Perhaps the most significant new conversions to Buddhism have taken place in Europe and North America, where representatives of Theravada Buddhism from Asia have been missionaries.

Islam

In Islamic belief and practice, a sharp distinction between political and religious activity does not exist. The prophet Muhammad taught that all aspects of life are unified under one collection of egalitarian religious values. Religious uniformity, together with strong family ties, would supplant tribal loyalties as the basis of social and political cohesion. Wealthy merchants and tribal leaders disagreed with this aspect of Muhammad's religious worldview and forced him to leave Mecca in 622. He settled in Medina, where his revelations continued, his movement grew, and in fairly short order, he took his place as Prophet and chief lawgiver, judge, and head of state. After several years of war and negotiation, Muhammad and his followers took control of Mecca in 630.

For Muslims, Muhammad was the final prophet in the line that began with Adam and included Abraham, Moses, and Jesus. In the periods following all previous prophets, people had strayed from God's ordained path. God called Muslims to the urgent and final missionary task of "reforming the earth," which they were to do by bringing the Prophet's message and the social institutions consistent with his teachings to all the earth's inhabitants. Because of their place in the Abrahamic prophetic tradition, Jews and Christians in areas under early Islamic control could continue their religious practices, but the adherents of other religions were often absorbed into the Islamic community, whether by their own choice, through persuasion, or in some cases by force.

After Muhammad's death in 632, disputes over the leadership became the basis for lasting divisions in Islam. But despite their internal differences, the Muslims expanded their control and promulgated their religion throughout the Middle East. Before a hundred years had passed, their armies, together with Muslim traders, educators, and preachers, had carried Islam into Iraq and Persia, into Egypt, then west across North Africa to Morocco, and from there (in 711) over the Mediterranean into Spain. Islamic influence reached India and China in roughly the same period. At its peak, the Islamic empire reached from Morocco and Spain to Indonesia. The Ottoman Empire, which ruled most of the Middle East from the fourteenth century until after World War I, also brought Islam to southeastern Europe. The Muslim community remains sizable there, a fact that continues to affect the politics of that region, as the ethnic and political strife in Bosnia and Herzegovina amply demonstrates.

When Christian missionaries began to go abroad in large numbers during the periods of European colonial expansion, they often found Islam firmly established. Muslim missionary activity had preceded their own by hundreds of years. The strategies of Islamic expansion over the centuries can be grouped under three principal categories: Conformity by conquest, conversion through individual persuasion, and the missionary efforts of organized religious movements. These distinctions are useful for purposes of discussion, but in reality the three processes intertwined in complex ways.

Conquest and conformity. Historically, the expansion of Islam as a religion has often accompanied military conquest by Islamic nations. Whether the words *conversion* or *missionary* apply to the adoption of a new religion in these circumstances depends on whether those terms refer only to psychological persuasion or encompass all methods, including force in some cases, of extending the reach of universal religious claims. The picture is especially complicated where victorious Islamic forces brought liberation from another, even more resented source of external control. In such circumstances, many among the local population might welcome the new rulers with their new religion, as was the case, for example, when the Muslim Arabs displaced the Christian Byzantine rulers of Egypt in 655.

A similar kind of calculus is implied when, given the opportunity, those who were religiously marginal or despised in their old religion converted freely to Islam (or in some places to Christianity) because it gave them a new identity free of the old stigma and persecution. Although such transformations often occurred in the context of conquest or other foreign intrusion, it is inappropriate to refer to them as "forced conversion" or "conversion by the sword." Such complex mixtures of compulsion, strategic personal choice, and genuine voluntary conversion are by no means unique to Islam; strategies of missionary outreach and patterns of religious expansion are always affected by the "geopolitics" of the time and by the material, social, and psychological circumstances of potential converts.

Individual persuasion. Active individual proselytizing has been a second strategy of Muslim expansion, one that is of immense cumulative historical importance. Islamic hegemony prevailed in large parts of the world for more than a millennium, and this provided numberless opportunities for those with strong religious convictions to pursue individual missionary work. Compared with conquest and compulsion, this version of mission is closer to the common meaning of missionary activity. It is also closer to the Islamic ideal that sees a Muslim as one who freely embraces the teachings of the Prophet. All of those among the faithful share the calling to combat the evils they encounter in the world. One such evil is nonbelief, which Muslims must not passively tolerate but rather are obliged to address with their own powers of persuasion. This missionary calling, sometimes called "conversion by the tongue," was carried forward very effectively by merchants and traders, religious educators, clerics, and travelers of all sorts—all energetically sharing their faith with any receptive audience and working to establish Islamic worship and governance in the cities that emerged along major trade routes. For Islam, the cumulative gains of such missionary activities, with their lasting religious aftereffects, are beyond calculation.

Organized religious movements. Alongside individual efforts to spread the faith, popular religious movements representing spiritual, revivalist, and messianic interpretations of Islam have been the third major source of expansion, from the eighth century to the present. What is different about these movements is the level of organization they bring to the missionary calling. Sufi brotherhoods, to take the most prominent example, are movements inspired by charismatic religious leaders who offer a pious, often mystical version of Islamic spirituality. They are by no means a relic of the past; they exist in many forms around the world today. Historically, the emotional energy of Sufism and its stress on individual mystical experience have given it widespread popular appeal and help to account for its effectiveness as a missionary strategy. These same features, however, have sometimes contrasted sharply with orthodox belief and practice. For this reason, the earliest brotherhoods were often regarded with suspicion by the orthodox *ulama* (Islamic scholars) and sometimes were suppressed. The movements that have survived and been most successful, both religiously and politically, have been the ones that stayed close enough to orthodoxy to be accepted or even encouraged by mainstream Islam. Over the centuries the leadership and proselytizing resources of these organizations have contributed greatly to Islamic missionary success.

One of many such enterprises that have had profound political ramifications is the highly organized popular movement called Sanusiyyah. Inspired by Muhammad bin Ali al-Sanusi (1787–1859), this movement proliferated through the eastern Sahara region of Africa and its missionaries ventured successfully into areas of central and west Africa in the mid-1800s. The religious followers of the "Grand Sanusi" have been deeply involved in the politics of modern Libya. They led the struggle against French and Italian colonialism, and al-Sanusi's grandson, Idris, became King of Libya when it gained its independence in 1951. Idris was overthrown in 1969 by Muammar al-Qaddafi, whose regime is rooted in its own politically revolutionary vision of Islam.

Other religious movements in Islam are similar to the Sufi brotherhoods in their missionary zeal and popular appeal, but for them the emphasis on individual spirituality is less central or in some cases rejected. Rather than concentrating on spiritual communion with God, for example, some revivalist groups press for a return to the earliest forms of Islamic belief and practice. The best known movements of this type have emerged in periods of Islamic decline and crisis. A striking example among many is the militant Wahhabi movement, named for Muhammad ibn Abd al-Wahhab (1703–1792), who insisted that departures from strict Islamic doctrine had been the cause of moral decline and therefore were responsible for the Muslim world's vulnerability to foreign domination. Abd al-Wahhab led a fundamentalist revival that gave rise to vigorous proselytizing and equally vigorous military activity in the politically turbulent eighteenth and nineteenth centuries in Arabia. The Wahhabi movement spread throughout that region by either persuading or compelling large numbers of people to submit to its rule and embrace its ascetic (some say "puritanical") version of Islam. The movement's fortunes were closely tied to those of the Saud family, whose dynasty founded and has dominated the politics, religion, and social institutions of Saudi Arabia for much of the twentieth century. Pilgrims to Mecca during the Wahhabi reformation took its vision of Islam with them when they returned home. Its influence proliferated and had ripple effects throughout the Islamic world, far beyond the context in which it originated.

Two other examples of politically important religious movements in Islam are the nineteenth-century messianic movement called al-Mahdiyyah and the Muslim Brethren, an organization that has existed in Egypt since the 1920s. Al-Mahdiyyah emerged in Sudan in the late nineteenth century as the instrument of Muhammad Ahmad. He claimed to be the Mahdi, or messiah, who communicated directly with God and who would stamp out infidelity and drive out the infidels. He succeeded briefly, establishing an Islamic state patterned on the earliest model of Islamic rule in the time of the Prophet. His regime lasted from 1885 to 1899, when the British swept it aside. Egypt's politically powerful Muslim Brethren, founded by Hasan al-Banna as an Islamic revival movement in 1928, is a more recent variation on this religious and political theme. Although Banna was assassinated in 1949 for his political activities, his organization survived him and has been intricately involved in the politics of contemporary Egypt.

The broad religious and political appeal of such movements, and ultimately the power they wield, can be traced in large part to their missionary skill. Above all, their impact reflects their success in combining religious purpose with political clarity in a climate of social crisis. Unlike other missionary efforts that focus on nonbelievers, each of the four movements described here has urged Muslims, not infidels, to embrace their renewed vision of Islam. Each has argued in its own way that the departure from the founding principles of Islam is to blame for the religion's decline and for the resulting intrusion of external non-Islamic influences. Fertile ground was provided for such appeals by the instability caused by the long decline of the Islamic empires and by the later turmoil that accompanied the relentless expansion of Western influence in the Muslim world.

A contemporary religious development of a different sort, one outside the Islamic mainstream but with clear missionary dimensions, is the movement called Ahmadiyya, named for Ghulam Ahmad, an Indian born in Qadian in 1835. From its center in Rabwah, Pakistan, Ahmadiyya consciously uses the methods of the Christian missions that flourished in the nineteenth and early twentieth centuries. Contrary to the predominant Muslim belief that Muhammad was the last of the prophets, Ghulam Ahmad declared himself a messenger in the same line of succession that ran from Adam to Muhammad. For this reason, many Muslims consider Ahmadiyya to be non-Islamic, and persecutions have resulted. The followers of Ghulam Ahmad embrace the outlines of Islamic law but refrain from direct participation in governing; however, this has not insulated them from the political complications that began with the colonial era. In India, where they began, for example, they were supporters of British rule, and in Africa they achieved their greatest gains in this century in the former British colonies on the west coast, including Ghana, Nigeria, and Sierra Leone. In those areas they are not the largest Islamic group, but they have appealed effectively to marginal categories such as former Christians, recent migrants to cities, new professionals, and women.

The Expansion of Christianity

There is a special missionary urgency in the belief that everyone, everywhere must be exposed to the "Good News" of the Second Coming of Christ so that they will know the path that leads to personal salvation. Christianity has never had a time when impassioned heralds of some segment of the Christian community were not spreading their version of this story. Through the centuries many methods of evangelization have been used, and a wide variety of political compromises and alliances with secular interests have been found tolerable, as long as they have allowed the central mission, spreading the Gospel, to proceed.

In the earliest days of Christianity the political expansion of Rome unintentionally provided a crucial resource for the efforts of the first missionaries: they were able to travel great distances by taking advantage of the networks of administrative control and land and sea transportation established by the Romans. The clearest mark of the missionaries' success in exploiting this resource is that from its beginning, as a troublesome, persecuted sect, Christianity became the established religion of the Roman Empire in 393. Even as the empire declined, the Church grew until it was consolidated throughout Europe, where it shared in the exercise of worldly political power for more than a thousand years.

The missionary zeal of this now established church and the continual intermingling of religious and secular impulses were never more visible than during the Crusades. From the eleventh through the thirteenth centuries Catholic Christendom tried repeatedly to establish religious, military, and commercial control over the region of Christianity's origin, and especially over Jerusalem. That goal remained elusive, but the political ramifications of the Crusades have continued down the centuries and are visible today in the uneasy coexistence of Christians, Jews, and Muslims in that city.

When waves of expansion were launched by the Christian rulers of Spain and Portugal in the explorations of the fifteenth century, the church gave its permission and blessing. In the ensuing conquests, Catholic missionaries witnessed and sometimes aided colonial incursions into the Caribbean and into Central and South America. At times, however, they vigorously opposed some of the practices associated with those incursions. A full understanding of the politics and economics of this era therefore requires an awareness of the missionary projects that were interwoven with them.

In North America an equally close correlation of religious and nonreligious activities was apparent in the chain of late eighteenth and early nineteenth century Franciscan missions established by Junípero Serra in California. "Conversion" of the indigenous people was accompanied by virtually complete control of their material and cultural lives. Across the continent in the east, a faction of the Puritans of colonial Massachusetts extended missions to the native people of that region. Like Serra's, these missions were expressions of theocratic authority aimed not just at conversion but also at pacification, territorial acquisition, and worldly dominion. For all their differences, where the original inhabitants of California and New England were concerned, the

Catholic and Puritan missionaries fused politics with religion in similar ways.

These diverse missions were complex in their guiding philosophies and in their practical implementation. At least equally complex has been the modern Protestant missionary movement, which with all its many forms became the largest social movement of the nineteenth century. The fervor of this movement was a product of the waves of "awakening" and mass revival that swept across Britain and North America from the mid-1700s onward. Timely opportunity to put this religious energy to work came with the expansion of international commerce and the competition for political hegemony that began opening Asia and Africa to Western influence. In time, scores of European and North American organizations, representing all the major Protestant churches, many nondenominational and interdenominational coalitions, and a number of newly formed Catholic missions, had joined the movement. Missionaries sometimes followed their secular colleagues abroad, but at other times they boldly took the lead as adventurers for Christ, in the confident expectation that where they established a presence the protection of the flag would eventually follow.

In this movement, missionary societies had ample reason to present themselves as detached from politics. On one level it was a question of purity: worldly agendas could not be seen as contaminating the purely religious rationale that missions offered for their undertakings. Moreover, missions relied on financial and moral support from diverse sources within the larger community, ranging from influential national churches to local voluntary (usually women's) associations. Being visibly engaged in partisan politics or obviously identified with narrow secular interests could undermine that broad-based support. Finally, nonconformist (non-Anglican) missions in Britain occupied an uneasy position in the shadow of the established church, while mission societies created in North America were conditioned by the constitutional separation of church and state. Beyond a diffuse patriotic identification with their homeland, therefore, missionary rhetoric usually stressed political detachment, and missions admonished their recruits to avoid political entanglements in their work as much as possible.

But more often than not, such rhetoric did not describe reality. However strategically wise it was for these organizations to profess political detachment at home and abroad, detachment is not an accurate description of their day-to-day activities. The expansion of Western influence abroad that provided most of their opportunities was defended as a "civilizing" enterprise, and a close correlation (though not an equation) was drawn between civilization and Christianity. Missions naturally embraced this popular conception and sent their members out to illuminate the "heathen darkness" with the blended light of Christianity and Western culture. To the greater good of all, the salvation of the primitive and idolatrous would go forward together with material progress and political domination.

It pays to be cautious in characterizing this period, however. Because of the connections just mentioned, missionaries are sometimes cast as mere apologists for Western imperialism, or it is assumed that they uncritically supported the activities of their secular counterparts abroad. Reality is more complicated. To be sure, there were complex affinities and opportunistic alliances between the missionary movement and international politics and economics, but the only generalization supported by the evidence is that missions pragmatically supported those things that advanced their evangelical progress and opposed whatever blocked it. Missions can be found on both sides of many controversial issues, and that is why their relationship with other Western interests abroad must be described as one of uneasy interdependence.

For their own reasons, traders, settlers, and colonial administrators were eager to be seen as Christian in their pursuits, and they often made use of missionaries because of their organizational skills, schools, language facility, and ability to broker contacts with indigenous cultures. But just as often these secular agents were reluctant to welcome missionaries into their zones of control because they saw them as meddlesome and unrealistic, always capable of taking a "principled" stand against what was "practically" necessary. For their part, missionaries were eager patriots, who often sought the protection of colonial authorities in their conflicts with local people and with the missionaries and administrators of other colonial powers. They contributed in many ways to the whole pattern of colonial domination, but at the same time they frequently were harsh opponents of many of the activities of their secular compatriots.

To take just one striking example, it was the slave trade that initially opened much of west Africa to European influence and the depredations of the trade attracted missionaries to that region. Similarly, the first British missionaries to the West Indies ministered to the slaves in that plantation economy. Despite their best efforts, the missionaries were drawn into the politics of servitude and liberation in fairly short order. In the earliest days, in the interest of political neutrality, some of them insisted that the question of the continuation of slavery was best left to secular authorities to resolve. Most missionaries taught slaves to accept their lot and simultaneously reassured slave owners that Christian slaves would be compliant slaves. Increasingly, however, as they encountered the implacable resistance of many plantation owners, missionaries spoke of the moral contradictions of slavery, and their thinking evolved quickly toward the belief that this institution was simply an abomination in Christian terms. When they gave widespread voice to this conviction at home, their (sometimes reluctant) sponsoring organizations were impelled to move closer to the abolitionist campaign that eventually ended slavery in the British Empire. This was the case, for example, when the missionary William Knibb, an agent of the Baptist Missionary Society, returned from Jamaica to England to express his moral opposition to slavery and his support for immediate abolition. The widespread favorable attention Knibb drew in his public appearances caught the society's leadership by surprise and led the organization to support the abolition campaign officially.

Missions and Colonialism

Oscillation between strategic acquiescence and strategic political engagement was also apparent in missionary activities in Asia. From 1600 until the 1830s the British East India Company enjoyed a near monopoly on trade between Britain and Asia. For much of that time the company functioned as de facto government in the areas under its sway and in this capacity strictly limited the activities of missionaries. The company's concern was that by seeking native converts missions would exacerbate the tension that already existed among Hindus, Muslims, and others. Missionaries from several countries found ways to evade the company's ban, but their work in India was precarious at best.

That was the environment that faced William Carey, the first person posted abroad to represent the newly formed Baptist Missionary Society, when he left England for India in 1792. Carey is one of the best known figures in the Protestant missionary movement, and his career is emblematic of the political and economic compromises missionaries made in order to get their work done. He supported himself at first by taking a partnership in an indigo plantation, where he confined his religious work to the bonded plantation workers under his control. Later, he moved to the Danish settlement at Serampore, near Calcutta. While Carey lived under the protection of the Danish crown, his missionary activities were less subject to the control of the East India Company. But at the same time he supported himself, his family, and the ministry of his Baptist colleagues by working as a language professor in a college operated by the East India Company. He also put the Baptist mission's presses to work printing government documents for the company. In other words, Carey, the missionary, was also a civil servant, supported by the generous wages, contract payments, and (in time) the pension he earned from the same political authority that officially banned, occasionally blocked, and often condemned his missionary activity.

Robert Morrison, the first Protestant missionary to China, had a similar arrangement with the East India Company at about the same time. Morrison, who was in the service of the London Missionary Society, worked for the company as translator and diplomatic consultant in Macao and Canton, all the while striving to translate the New Testament into Chinese and to lay the groundwork for an eventual missionary outpost on the mainland. (Both of these projects were illegal under Chinese law.) Some of his translations were carried to India, to be printed there at company expense on Carey's presses. In Canton and Macao, Morrison also worked with William Jardine and James Matheson, whose shipping firm brought to China a commanding share of the opium that had become the East India Company's chief source of export revenue and was the key to a favorable balance of payments between Britain and China. From the profits of this trade, Jardine funded a number of missionary projects, among them the Morrison Educational Society (committed to the continuation of Robert Morrison's work after his death), at the same time that his partner Matheson was condemning missionaries (whom he contemptuously called "the saints") in the press and before Parliament for their foolish disapproval of the opium business.

Because of these complicated and contradictory entanglements, Carey in India and Morrison in China can (depending on how the story is told) be used to illustrate the kinds of worldly compromises missionaries made to keep their work alive, or to demonstrate how resourceful they were in continuing their work in the face of opposition from powerful secular interests. In their personal lives, these pragmatic maneuvers troubled the missionaries, as did the insecurity that came from having no official permission for their work. Their parent organizations at home urged them to preserve their autonomy, and in the meantime the leadership pressed Parliament for legislation freeing mission access to the Indian subcontinent and other areas under the East India Company's administration.

In this struggle, the leaders of the large missionary organizations maintained close contact with political leaders, including prime ministers, and influential members of both houses of Parliament. The evangelical societies also developed impressive skill in manipulating public opinion, by using tracts, simultaneous nationwide sermons, and petitions (one reported to contain a million signatures) to get their message before the public and strengthen their hand in their dealings with political authority. Their campaign to break the East India Company's control over their activities stretched over many years, but in 1813 it was successful. The prohibition on missionary activity in India was rescinded. Whatever may be said about missionary organizations during this period, neither strict aloofness from politics and economics abroad nor political reticence at home are terms that describe them accurately.

A second political watershed for the missionary movement came at midcentury when two wars—later called the Opium Wars—forced the Chinese to tolerate the importation of opium from British India and to open the doors wider to Western commercial and diplomatic interests. Some missionaries in China supported those wars and others opposed them. In the end, however, the same treaties that opened the door to Western commerce also forced the Chinese to cede territory (Hong Kong) to the British and give Western missionaries freer movement on the Chinese mainland. British, European, and North American missionaries quickly established a network of outposts, and their presence there, resented by nationalists and Chinese authorities but protected by the West, was a continuing factor in Chinese politics from then until the Communists expelled them in the late 1940s.

The same missionaries who followed the warships, drug merchants, and diplomats into China also launched an unrelenting campaign against the opium trade. As with slavery, they had arrived at the conviction that this trade was irredeemably evil once they understood how it undermined their evangelical efforts. They carried on their crusade against it in China, in churches throughout Great Britain, in Parliament, and in religious and political circles in the United States. They argued that the opium traffic made a mockery of Western pretensions about the civilizing influence of Christian commerce. As had been the case earlier in India and the West Indies, the missionaries in China were able to benefit from the access provided by the expansion of Western influence while simultaneously undermining one of the economic pillars of that expansion.

At roughly the same time that China was being forced open for missionary work, Britain assumed direct imperial control of India, and soon thereafter the "scramble for Africa" of the 1880s reduced that continent to a patchwork of European colonial prizes. Every stage in the Western expansion across three continents opened opportunities for British and European missions. The foreign policy of the United States kept it on the periphery of the competition for colonies, but this did not deter American missions from posting agents to many places in Africa, India, and the Far East.

Closer to home, American missionaries were increasingly active among the indigenous peoples as the United States frontier moved westward. These missionaries were involved in the politics of that era just as their British and European counterparts had been caught up in the colonial adventures that were taking place in other parts of the world. Indeed, one of the clearest cases of official mission-government collaboration took place when Protestant missionaries, beginning with the Quakers (who were otherwise known for their strict commitment to church-state separation), agreed to administer some of the reservations that were central to President Ulysses S. Grant's strategy to pacify the Native Americans in the West. The Quakers were chosen because of their reputation for incorruptibility and their previous work among Native Americans; nevertheless, in this short-lived experiment they served as government agents exercising religious and secular control over a conquered people.

By the time World War I had begun in 1914, Christian missionaries from North America, Britain, and Europe numbered in the thousands, and there was hardly any place in the world that remained beyond their reach. Seen in broad historical perspective, these organizations have been and continue to be an important part of the process by which Western political, economic, and cultural influence has grown around the world. There is also a more intimate dimension of the missionary movement that must be briefly considered because it, too, reveals the intersection of religion, economics, and politics.

Beyond Conversion

At the level of daily missionary life, the evangelical enterprise is often described as a voluntary activity, undertaken by individuals with a personal calling to carry the message abroad. The emphasis in most accounts has been on person-to-person persuasion leading to conversion, where new belief encounters old belief and the former prevails over the latter. What is less often emphasized is that the same scriptural mandate that motivated Christian missionaries to spread their faith also imbued them with a martial spirit as it called upon them to eradicate non-Christian beliefs and practices, which were regarded as ignorant at best, idolatrous and sinful at worst. The result is that for converts, identification as Christians has often meant alienation—even expulsion—from the traditional community.

Regardless of how unidimensionally they describe their purpose, until comparatively recently most missionaries have worked to bring about fundamental changes in all aspects of social reality for their converts. They have often begun with linguistic research, Bible translations, literacy campaigns, and formal education and then deepened their impact by imparting to the emerging Christian community new definitions of the nature and responsibility of the individual; new gender relations; new mandates for family life, kinship, and nomenclature; new rules for relations among the generations; new modes of dress; new conceptions of the physical, biological, and temporal dimensions of life; new expectations for work; new rules for accumulating wealth and property; and sweeping new judgments about what is religiously acceptable in the way of economy, polity, and social discipline.

In other words, the realization of Christian goals in non-Christian cultures goes far beyond simple conversion. It requires a restructuring of daily lives at the local and personal levels. Every element of that restructuring has a political aspect. Local people who embraced such programs of change in the past and their descendants today have formed the core of increasingly independent Christian communities around the world. In the postcolonial period those communities, including the many leaders among them who were educated in mission schools, have often (and paradoxically) taken the lead in throwing off Western cultural and political domination. Others, in contrast, resisted the intrusion of missionaries from the outset and defined their arrival as the beginning of Western subjugation. For both converts (who see liberation in Christianity) and resisters (who have seen cultural destruction in the missionary message), life has been irreversibly changed.

Since the end of World War II, in 1945, many Western missionary organizations have placed less emphasis on the exclusivity of their Christian beliefs and have become less eager to proclaim that either the West or Christianity has the secret to "civilization." In the process they have become increasingly willing to engage in ecumenical dialogue with other faiths and more oriented toward social service programs than toward conversion. Fundamentalists, Pentecostals, and Latter Day Saints are conspicuous exceptions to this pattern, each pursuing in its separate way a politically and religiously conservative and closely scripted conception of Christian salvation. The impressive number of missionaries these groups are able to send out and their visible successes, particularly among the displaced and poor in Latin America but also in Africa, Asia, and the former Soviet Union (which has taken drastic steps to curtail their activities), suggest that they will be the leading subject of future essays on missionaries and politics.

See also *Christianity in Asia; Colonialism; Conversion; Crusades; Islam; Jihad; Nongovernmental organizations.*

Jon Miller

BIBLIOGRAPHY

Comaroff, Jean, and John Comaroff. *Of Revelation and Revolution: Christianity, Colonialism, and Consciousness in South Africa.* Vol. 1. Chicago: University of Chicago Press, 1991.

Fisher, Humphrey J. *Ahmadiyya: A Study in Contemporary Islam on the West African Coast.* Oxford: Oxford University Press, 1963.

Huber, Mary, and Nancy Lutkehaus, eds. *Gendered Missions: Women and Men in Missionary Discourse and Practice.* Ann Arbor: University of Michigan Press, forthcoming.

Jackson, Robert H., and Edward Castillo. *Indians, Franciscans, and Spanish Colonization: The Impact of the Mission System on California Indians.* Albuquerque: University of New Mexico Press, 1995.

Miller, Jon. *The Social Control of Religious Zeal: A Study in Organizational Contradictions.* New Brunswick, N.J.: Rutgers University Press, 1994.

Moorhouse, Geoffrey. *The Missionaries.* Philadelphia: Lippincott, 1973.

Neill, Stephen. *A History of Christian Missions.* Revised for the 2d ed. by Owen Chadwick. New York: Penguin, 1986.

Rahman, Fazlur. *Islam and Modernity: Transformation of an Intellectual Tradition.* Chicago: University of Chicago Press, 1982.

Reiter, Frederick J. *They Built Utopia: The Jesuit Missions in Paraguay, 1610–1768.* Potomac, Md.: Scripta Humanistica, 1995.

Stanley, Brian. *The Bible and the Flag: Protestant Missions and British Imperialism in the Nineteenth and Twentieth Centuries.* Leicester: Apollos, 1990.

Modernism, anti-

See *Traditionalism*

Moral Majority

See *Conservatism*

Morality

Morality is generally considered to involve issues of personal deportment or behavior, such as sexual conduct, substance abuse, and certain questions of free expression. The regulation of such behaviors is often a high priority for politically active religious conservatives, and religious beliefs and values appear to have their strongest effects on attitudes toward moral issues.

Morality represents the behavioral manifestation of religious belief. As such, questions of morality involve the behavioral consequences of holding particular beliefs or adhering to a particular religious tradition or denomination.

Religion is not the only possible source of moral attitudes. Many analysts and political activists have sought to use sociobiology or science or the like as justification for moral judgments. However, religious justifications for moral positions are the most common in the United States, and religious attitudes and affiliations are important sources of state policy on issues of personal morality. Thus, in American politics, questions of religion and morality are most often intimately connected.

Morality as a Rhetorical Resource

The concept of morality is a very important rhetorical resource for those who seek to apply religious principles to political affairs. Although Americans are more religious than the citizens of other industrialized nations, religious influence on political decision making is limited by two important cultural characteristics. First, the political culture of the United States is characterized by a pervasive individualism. That is, Americans take seriously the notion that there exists a "private sphere," within which individual choices tend to be of paramount importance. The effects of widespread religious belief on political decision making (especially with respect to issues of personal deportment) are often inhibited by a reluctance to interfere with the private affairs of other people. Second, the very pervasiveness of religious belief in the United States has led to a bewildering array of denominational choices. This diversity, in turn, has led to a sense of religious particularism among many believers, that is, to a belief that one's own religious principles should be promoted regardless of the sometimes contrary beliefs of others. The tendency of people to look on their own faith as superior and to emphasize differences among religious traditions has often rendered political cooperation among those of different faiths and denominations difficult.

By focusing attention on the consequences of acts in which the "victims" are unable to defend themselves, religious activists have often been able to use the concept of morality to overcome the arguments of individualism and religious particularism. This can be seen most clearly with respect to the issue of abortion, in which religiously motivated activists have argued that the personal autonomy of the woman must give way to the "rights" of the unborn. Indeed, abortion is a fascinating issue when considered from the standpoint of the individualistic tradition in the United States, since the identity of "persons" bearing "rights" is precisely at issue. If the humanity of the fetus is granted, abortion is no longer considered a private, self-regarding act but is, rather, one that has consequences for other "persons" and that can therefore be regulated by government.

Other moral issues also involve that part of religious values concerned with consequences, although the consequences of certain "private" acts may be more elusive. A common rhetorical strategy among religious activists is to focus attention on the consequences of certain "immoral" acts for children. Children are often regarded as incapable of making morally informed choices (and, therefore, are not entitled to the personal autonomy granted to adults). Moreover, children are often described as lacking control over their environments and thus are involuntarily subject to the consequences of the moral choices made by the adults who define the children's surroundings.

For example, two moral issues have received attention in recent years. One of these involves the control of "indecent" images and messages transmitted by computer across the "information superhighway." Congress has attempted to regulate such communications, despite the fact that the content of such messages would normally be protected by the First

Amendment to the Constitution. Proponents of such regulation have focused their arguments almost exclusively on the ease with which very young children can gain access to the Internet. They have suggested that government must monitor and control electronic communications to shield innocent children from "adult" communications. A similar desire to protect children has provided the rhetorical basis for the "V-chip." This device would allow parents to block the transmission of certain television shows into their homes on the basis of descriptions of the programs' content.

A second recent issue involving the protection of children involves the access of married couples to the option of divorce. Since the end of World War II marriage has come to be regarded in the United States as a voluntary institution, which unhappy spouses should be allowed to leave. A trend has developed since the 1960s toward "no fault" divorce, in which uncontested divorces can be granted relatively quickly and easily. During the 1990s a countermovement to no-fault divorce has been generated, in which many people (mainly religious conservatives) have sought to render divorce more difficult. The pervasive individualism of American political culture has caused many Americans to regard marriage as a private contract between two autonomous individuals and to resist any alternative characterization of matrimony. Thus opponents of easy divorce have typically invoked the (negative) consequences of marital termination for children as the principal justification for their position. A consideration of the results of a supposedly "private" action (divorce) for innocent third parties provides the ground on which religious conservatives can rationalize support of government regulation of personal, intimate relations.

This point can be generalized. Many evangelical Protestants who are active in politics have come to avoid explicitly religious arguments in favor of "family values" or a "pro-family" agenda. By raising the issue of the effects of personal moral behavior on children, such activists are able to counter assertions that they are attempting to "legislate morality" or to interfere with personal choices.

Morality, as a rhetorical resource, can also limit the effects of religious particularism. In many instances, potentially formidable religious coalitions have been fragmented by theological or doctrinal differences. For example, it has frequently been suggested that the support received by the presidential candidate Pat Robertson in the 1990s was limited by the unpopularity of Robertson's pentecostal beliefs among other evangelicals. Similarly, the effectiveness of a potentially large "pro-life" coalition is likely limited by mutual antipathy between evangelical Protestants and Roman Catholics. By focusing on the behavioral consequences of religious belief, religious activists are occasionally capable of sidestepping doctrinal differences that may divide supporters.

From a religious standpoint, such a strategy involves making a distinction between the duties owed to God by humanity and the obligations humans have to one another. In the mid-nineteenth century, the French historian and political theorist Alexis de Tocqueville perceived the political consequences of this distinction and observed that, despite numerous differences between "sects" in the United States, all were subsumed under the "great unity of Christianity." Moreover, he noted that Christian morality is the same everywhere. Thus, while the duties owed to God were a potential source of political division, that part of religion concerned with consequences was, according to Tocqueville, a source of cohesion and consensus. The conservative activist Jerry Falwell appears to have had a similar intuition when he argued that his group, the Moral Majority, was not a religious organization but a political one in which people of all faiths (or, indeed, no faith) were quite welcome.

It has been argued that the Prohibition movement of the 1920s resulted from the efforts of a coalition of evangelical and mainstream Protestants. The key to the success of the Prohibition movement was the ability of religious leaders to deflect attention from religious justifications for abstinence and to focus on the common goal of eliminating alcoholic beverages from public consumption. Mainstream Protestants, with their emphasis on the Social Gospel (that is, the use of Christian principles to attack social problems), were able to use alcoholism as a manifestation of the sickness of contemporary urban life, while more doctrinally conservative evangelicals could invoke biblical injunctions against intoxication.

More recently, abortion activists have turned to more secular, consequentialist language as well. Antiabortion rhetoric has become much less religious since the *Roe v. Wade* decision of 1973 in which abortion was made legal. Pro-life activists have increasingly used scientific arguments (concerning the characteristics of the developing fetus, for example) at the expense of theological considerations in their attempts to recriminalize abortion in the United States. This refocusing of the abortion debate has enabled antiabortion activists to deemphasize differences between the "natural law" theology of Roman Catholics (which also prohibits contraception) and the Bible-based heuristics of evangelical Protestants.

Morality as a Link between Religion and Politics

Questions of public policy on morality pose some difficult problems. Democracy is often regarded as a persuasive system, in which government coercion is limited by the respect accorded individual citizens. To this extent, those who would make or influence public policy must provide commonly agreed-upon reasons for their stand. Although some analysts have suggested that religion can provide such reasons, other observers have realized that theology or (to a lesser extent) morality is an unlikely source of agreement in a religiously pluralistic society.

Given that a commonly shared basis for moral judgments is elusive in the contemporary United States, the role of religion and morality in American politics has become problematic. The question is, In the absence of general agreement on principles of religion or morality (in a society in which, for example, the morality of abortion and homosexuality is contested), is there any manner in which personal behavior can legitimately be regulated? Indeed, the very appropriateness of religious language in public debate has become contested.

It has been argued that religious sensibilities should give way to generally shared (or publicly accessible) points of view when the latter are available. However, in many cases, such publicly shared views simply do not exist. In such situations, some believe there is no reason to exclude religious discourse from the debate. It has also been argued, in contrast, that basing public policy moral judgments on religious values entails an unconstitutional "establishment" of particular religions. Finally, some observers have invoked the language of free exercise of religion to support government policies regulating personal behavior. By permitting unregulated contraception, pornography, and the like, government arguably has made religious adherence (particularly the religious socialization of the young) more difficult. The concept of morality provides an impetus for this sort of debate, by focusing attention on the public consequences of private behavior.

Thus, while religious belief and adherence are widespread in the United States, the political expression of religious beliefs faces formidable obstacles in American politics. The translation of religious values into public policy is limited, among other considerations, by a societal consensus on the value of individualism and by the effects of religious particularism. "Morality" provides a link between religion and politics by directing the political agenda to the consequences of personal behavioral transgressions. The concept of morality warrants the regulation of private behavior by public authorities and may offer common ground on which adherents of different religious traditions can cooperate. Although the notion of a publicly justified morality does not solve the problem of religious involvement in political life, it may provide a means of overcoming the practical problems associated with political religion in a pluralistic society.

See also *Abortion; Conservatism; Homosexuality; Individualism; Pluralism; Sexuality; Social Gospel; Temperance movements.*

Ted G. Jelen

BIBLIOGRAPHY

Carter, Stephen L. *The Culture of Disbelief: How American Law and Politics Trivialize Religious Devotion.* New York: Basic Books, 1993.

Falwell, Jerry. "An Agenda for the 1980s." In *Piety and Politics: Evangelicals and Fundamentalists Confront the World,* edited by Richard J. Neuhaus and Michael Cromartie. Washington, D.C.: Ethics and Public Policy Center, 1987.

Green, John C. "Pat Robertson and the Latest Crusade: Religious Resources and the 1988 Presidential Campaign." *Social Science Quarterly* 74 (1995): 157–168.

Greenawalt, Kent. *Religious Convictions and Political Choice.* New York: Oxford University Press, 1988.

Grindstaff, Laura. "Abortion and the Popular Press: Mapping Media Discourse from *Roe* to *Webster.*" In *Abortion Politics in the United States and Canada: Studies in Public Opinion,* edited by Ted G. Jelen and Marthe A. Chandler. Westport, Conn.: Praeger, 1994.

Neuhaus, Richard John. *The Naked Public Square.* Grand Rapids, Mich.: Eerdmans, 1984.

Reichley, A. James. *Religion in American Public Life.* Washington, D.C.: Brookings Institution, 1985.

Thiemann, Ronald. *Religion in Public Life: A Dilemma for Democracy.* Washington, D.C.: Georgetown University Press, 1996.

Tocqueville, Alexis de. *Democracy in America.* Edited by Phillips Bradley. 2 vols. New York: Vintage Books, 1945.

Wilcox, Clyde. *God's Warriors: The Christian Right in the Twentieth Century.* Baltimore: Johns Hopkins University Press, 1992.

Mormons

See *Latter-day Saints, Church of Jesus Christ of*

Morocco

Located in northwest Africa, Morocco is a constitutional monarchy that has both an Islamic and a Mediterranean identity. The ruling Alawi dynasty, like some of Morocco's earlier ones, bases its legitimacy on descent from the prophet Muhammad and periodic contractual renewal of a covenant *(bay'a)* between the monarch and his subjects, as represented by community leaders and Islamic scholars. The covenant reaffirms that the monarch is governing in accord with Islam and the popular will.

The king (called "sultan" until 1957) is "commander of the faithful," a concept with profound Islamic roots and enshrined since 1962 in successive Moroccan constitutions. In popular terms, peasants and tribespeople still refer to Morocco's king as caliph, or "God's deputy on earth," assured of God's special blessings and protection, a notion powerfully reinforced by Moroccan popular understandings of Islam.

French colonial rule in Morocco (1912–1956), supplemented by Spanish rule in the north and the Saharan south, preserved the monarchy and its claims to religious legitimacy intact. Spain withdrew from the Sahara only after Hasan II, who succeeded his father in 1961, led a peaceful march of hundreds of thousands of civilians in 1975, a charismatic event that reaffirmed his religious and political leadership.

Morocco's political parties, which acquired legal status after independence, were obliged to work within the framework of monarchic rule, in large part because the monarchy's strong religious credentials survived the colonial era intact. As Hasan II said before parliament in 1984—Morocco has had local and parliamentary elections at irregular intervals since the early 1960s—his "school" of politics directly follows from that of Muhammad. Political parties are banned from using Islamic symbols, or speaking in the name of Islam, as the monarchy reserves to itself appeals to religious legitimacy.

The religious aura of the monarchy remains strong, although rising educational levels contribute to causing many youth, at least in private, to challenge the monarchy's religious claims. Morocco's rapidly rising population growth, population shifts from rural areas to towns, diminishing prospects of economic emigration, and stagnant economy and dramatically rising levels of unemployment, especially among Morocco's educated youth, have created a politically volatile situation in which Islamic radicalism has appealed increasingly to some Moroccans. Twenty percent of Morocco's university students are estimated to be sympathetic to Islamic radicalism. The specter of neighboring Algeria, rent by violence since its military intervened to prevent an Islamist victory in late 1991, however, has limited the popular

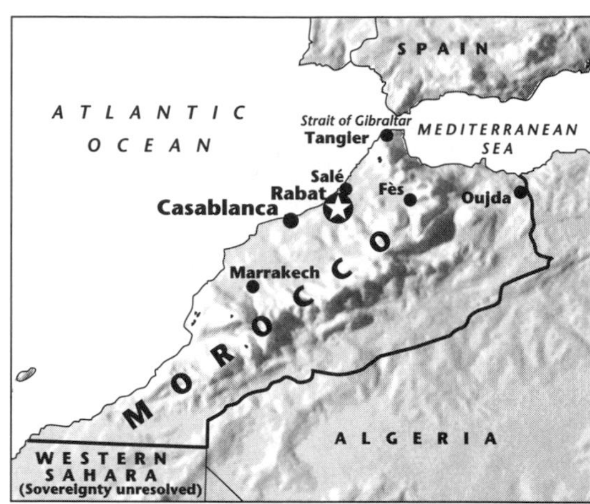

appeal of radical alternatives to the current rule in Morocco.

In his speeches and public acts, the monarch does not hesitate to explain how the state, in becoming more open and accountable, also fulfills an Islamic mandate, sometimes by co-opting the language of Islamic radicals. The monarchy's claims to religious legitimacy remain strong, although not unchallenged, and its policies are sufficiently adaptable to changing political and economic circumstances to continue to offer more hope for the immediate future to most Moroccans than do alternative ideas of political rule.

See also *Algeria; Covenant; Islam.*

Dale F. Eickelman

BIBLIOGRAPHY

Bennani-Chraïbi, Mounia. *Soumis et rebelles: Les jeunes au Maroc.* Paris: CNRS Editions, 1994.

Eickelman, Dale F. *Knowledge and Power in Morocco.* Princeton: Princeton University Press, 1985.

Geertz, Clifford. *Islam Observed.* New Haven: Yale University Press, 1968.

Hammoudi, Abdellah. *Master and Disciple: The Cultural Foundations of Moroccan Authoritarianism.* Chicago: University of Chicago Press, 1997.

Munson, Henry, Jr. *Religion and Power in Morocco.* New Haven: Yale University Press, 1993.

Muhammad

The prophet of Islam. Islamic sources tell us that Muhammad (c. 570–632) was born into the Arab tribe of

Muhammad's ascension from Jerusalem into heaven is depicted in this painting from a Persian manuscript, "The Ascension of the Prophet."

Quraysh, which was settled in Mecca in the southern Hijaz, around 570. As a young man he became the commercial agent of a rich Meccan woman, who later married him. He began to receive monotheist revelations (later collected as the Qur'an) at the age of forty. When he started to preach the message in Mecca, strong tensions developed between his followers and the traditional Meccan polytheists. He was thus constrained to seek political protection outside Mecca, and in due course he was invited to Yathrib, the later Medina, an oasis of the northern Hijaz that was in a state of internal turmoil.

His move to Medina (the *hijra*) took place in 622. During his ten years there he continued to receive revelations and established a rudimentary state that extended its military and political power, together with the new religion, over a significant part of Arabia. After his death in 632 his followers created an empire ruling large territories outside Arabia, resulting in the further spread of Islam and the emergence of Islamic civilization.

Muhammad's career must be understood against the background of Arabian society. Arabia was an arid land (some 97 percent desert). As a result, state structures had only a limited existence on the fringes of the peninsula and were entirely lacking in the interior, including the Hijaz. Here each oasis was politically independent of the others, and even individual oases did not have rulers. Groups of nomadic pastoralists were likewise politically independent and internally fragmented. In the absence of states the structures of Arabian society were tribal—that is to say, based on extended kinship. Political and military activity in this society involved a large part of the male population, with raiding and feuding as central features of the tribal way of life. It was virtually impossible for any tribal leader to create a strong state out of such material: there was little to levy taxes on, and the population was too mobile and warlike to be easily coerced into paying them. So far as we know, no major state had ever arisen in Arabia before the time of Muhammad.

Two things may have been crucial to Muhammad's unprecedented success. The first was conceptual: his religious message enabled him to synthesize a type of authority that had not previously existed in Arabia. He thus brought into existence a religious community that, although it remained embedded in tribal loyalties and traditions, to a significant extent transcended them. This made it possible for his followers to think in terms of a new level of sustained collective action. The second had to do with material rewards: collective action delivered goods on a larger scale than the traditional tribal structures, both through raiding (booty, especially livestock and women) and conquest (tribute and other fruits of power). These features of Muhammad's state continued after his death on a larger scale: the unification of the peninsula led to the conquest of much richer lands outside it.

This religious mode of state formation had a long future ahead of it in the tribal lands of the more arid parts of the Islamic world, specifically in Arabia and northern Africa (but not, in general, in the Turkic tribal world of the Eurasian steppes). Outside such an environment, in the agriculturally richer and more urbanized regions of the Islamic world, Islam tended to be yoked to the more patrimonial forms of state power that were already characteristic of these areas in pre-Islamic times. In modern times, as these patrimonial states have been transformed or swept away and their nationalist successors have stumbled, the values associated with Muhammad's venture in state formation have achieved strong resonance under the very different conditions of modern mass politics. This resonance has given rise to a religious populism that is a strong, and sometimes revolutionary, force in many parts of the Islamic world today. The link is no doubt the high level of political and military participation characteristic of both contexts.

See also *Islam; Mecca.*

Michael Cook

BIBLIOGRAPHY

Cook, Michael. *Muhammad* (Past Masters Series). Oxford: Oxford University Press, 1983.

Crone, Patricia. *Meccan Trade and the Rise of Islam.* Princeton: Princeton University Press, 1987.

Watt, W. M. *Muhammad: Prophet and Statesman.* London: Oxford University Press, 1961.

Muhammad Abduh

Egyptian reformer and pioneer of Islamic modernism and nationalism. Of peasant stock from Lower Egypt, Abduh (1849–1905) studied at the village Qur'an school, the Ahmadi mosque in Tanta, and the great mosque-university of al-Azhar in Cairo. Sufism (Islamic mysticism) and his apprenticeship with the Iranian pan-Islamist Jamal al-Din al-Afghani (1839–1897) strongly influenced his outlook. When Afghani was expelled from Egypt in 1879, his disciple Abduh was dismissed from teaching duties at al-Azhar and returned to his village.

Abduh came back to Cairo in 1880 as editor of the government's *Official Journal.* Because he supported a revolt against Egypt's domination by Europeans and the Turkish-speaking elite in the army and palace, the British (after occupying Egypt in 1882) exiled Abduh to Beirut in what is now Lebanon.

In 1884 Abduh joined Afghani in Paris to publish a short-lived journal, *The Indissoluble Bond,* which preached Muslim unity against Western imperialism. In 1888 he returned to Egypt and became a judge on the National Courts; eleven years later he became grand mufti, Egypt's highest official interpreter of the *shari'a* (Islamic law). From his seat on al-Azhar's administrative council, he tried unsuccessfully to reform the institution. Conservatives blocked his efforts, and shortly before his death in 1905 he resigned in frustration.

Abduh and Afghani believed that Muslims everywhere must cooperate to reverse internal decline and counter European imperialism. They called for a return to the spirit of early Islam and a reinterpretation of the Qur'an and the *sunna* (precedent) of the prophet Muhammad in light of modern times. They believed that limited borrowing from Western ideas was permissible and that properly used reason could not conflict with religious revelation.

Although the shock of defeat and exile, and Afghani's spell, had briefly drawn him back into political activism in Paris, Abduh came to believe that political protest was futile without reform from within. This belief led him to limited cooperation in social reform with Lord Cromer, the British consul general and real ruler of Egypt from 1883 to 1907. It also alienated him from the local ruler, Khedive Abbas Hilmi II, and Mustafa Kamil's circle of nationalists, all of whom pushed for immediate independence from the British.

After Abduh's death his closest disciple, the Syrian reformer Muhammad Rashid Rida (1865–1935), continued to carry his message throughout the Islamic world. Rida's magazine, *al-Manar,* spoke for the Salafiyya movement, which sought inspiration in the example of virtuous early Muslims (the *salaf,* or ancestors). Rida grew more anti-Western and intransigent after World War I, deeply influencing Hasan al-Banna and the Muslim Brethren. Islamist radicals today prefer Afghani, the relentless activist, to Abduh, the patient reformer.

Abduh's legacy also lived on among his secular nationalist and liberal followers. These men—mostly lawyers and teachers rather than *ulama,* or scholars of Islam—set the tone of Egypt's dominant liberal nationalism until a military coup in 1952 overthrew the government. Thereafter liberal Egyptian nationalism was on the defensive, first against Gamal Abdel Nasser's Arab nationalism and socialism and then against the Islamist resurgence that began in the late 1960s.

See also *al-Afghani, Jamal al-Din; Banna, Hasan al-; Egypt; Islam; Muslim encounters with the West.*

Donald Malcolm Reid

BIBLIOGRAPHY

Adams, Charles C. *Islam and Modernism in Egypt.* 1933. Reprint, New York: Russell and Russell, 1968.

Ahmed, Jamal Mohammed. *The Intellectual Origins of Egyptian Nationalism.* Oxford and New York: Oxford University Press, 1960.

Enayat, Hamid. *Modern Islamic Political Thought.* Austin: University of Texas Press, 1982.

Hourani, Albert. *Arabic Thought in the Liberal Age, 1798–1939.* London: Oxford University Press, 1970.

Kerr, Malcolm H. *Islamic Reform: The Political and Legal Theories of Muhammad Abduh and Rashid Rida.* Berkeley: University of California Press, 1966.

Muslim Brethren

See *Banna, Hasan al-*

Muslim encounters with the West

Islam's experience with the world of Europe and the Americas is best reviewed and interpreted from within Islam's own sense of how politics and religion fit together. The Mediterranean Sea was the main theater and lasting symbol for the course of Islamic endeavors. In the *hijra,* or emigration of 622 from Mecca to Medina, Muhammad made himself a ruler to further his vocation as religious prophet. Ever since, in a union of creed and community, Islam has been the most essentially politicized of religions.

When the new faith expanded its power, it rapidly established itself across the African shore of the Mediterranean. Most of Spain, which was conquered by Muslims in 711, was ruled for more than a century from the caliphate (successors of Muhammad) in Damascus, in what is now Syria. Muslim domination of Spain long delayed the ambition of European Christendom to repossess Muslim-held territory in the Holy Land. The Crusades, beginning in the late eleventh century, were impelled by politico-religious motives that ultimately yielded the Latin Kingdom of Jerusalem. Mediterranean islands—Rhodes, Cyprus, and Sicily—figured notably over the centuries in the East-West conflict, with resounding clashes like the naval battle of Lepanto (1571) off the coast of Greece between a Venetian coalition and the Ottoman Turks or the prolonged revenges throughout the Mediterranean of Barbary corsairs from Algiers.

Sharp entanglements, both religious and political, dominated much of the nineteenth and twentieth centuries, but a strangely mutual superior-inferior complex in the psyches of both the Muslim and the Western worlds has marked their entire exchange. As the final religion ("religion with God is Islam," Surah 3.19), Islam perceived other faiths as, at best, inferior to its own, at worst, misguided and idolatrous. Corroborated by the idea of infallible Scripture and a divinely sanctioned social, moral, and political order, Islam legitimated a deep superiority complex, which it saw vindicated in its rapid and irreversible expansion west and east of its native Arabia. That belief and the claim of dominance brought a sense of physical and spiritual inferiority to Eastern Christendom. The Islamic sense of greatness was further stimulated by the majesty of the Ottomans in the sixteenth century, symbolized by Sulayman the Magnificent (1520–1566) and by the Safavid dynasty in Persia.

The West, for a variety of reasons, denigrated Islam, partly in reaction to Muslim success and partly because the initial thrust of Islam in its first centuries acquired the sophistication of its theology, its architecture, and its arts in appreciable measure from the lands and cultures it overran. Insofar as it was pupil, however, Islam appreciably bettered its tuition. It put Western thought into its debt by preserving classical knowledge in the Middle Ages, with polymaths like Ibn Sina, known in the West as Avicenna (980–1037), and its influence on the Western Renaissance at its height in the fifteenth century. Accordingly, when Western science and technology came riding into Islamic realms in the nineteenth century, Muslims felt decadent where they had once been dominant, inferior to pupils of their own past. The far-reaching Western penetration into the Muslim realm in the modern world, although bringing material changes not to be refused, spelled deep resentments for its implied disparagement of Muslim peoples and a perceived threat to their pride and tradition. This love-hate relationship forms a continuing feature of the whole encounter between the Muslim East and the Christian West. That culture and technology were accompanied by political power and empire only made the experience, as Muslims knew it from within, all the more vexing and ambiguous.

Faith and Governance

It makes sense to begin with the political in this encounter between the Muslim world and the West. It is where every Islamic instinct begins and where history is best first analyzed. Napoleon's invasion of Egypt in 1798 is symbolic.

Seeking to recover the Holy Land from the Muslims, European Christians waged a series of wars known as the Crusades between the eleventh and fourteenth centuries. This painting, "La Prise de Jerusalem," records the Christian conquest of the Holy City in 1099.

The invasion was fueled by Anglo-French imperial rivalry expressed in British India, where for decades the British had been established in the form of the East India Company, later to be taken over by the British Crown. Napoleon's tactical sponsorship of Islam was short lived, as was his tenure on Egyptian soil. The subsequent regime in Cairo of an Albanian adventurer, Muhammad Ali, marked the first significant breach of Ottoman suzerainty. The nineteenth century saw steady European penetration into Ottoman power.

Trade and finance helped pave these inroads into the Muslim world. The Ottomans conceded consular and community rights to European merchants—rights known as "capitulations"—an ironic word, in the event. Although the meaning referred to documented concessions, the effect was to weaken Muslim authority and to erode the image of a prestigious caliphate. A restiveness was fostered within the Arab provinces of the Ottoman lands. Istanbul lost the heady magnificence of its great Sulayman. With the disintegration of the Ottoman Empire, and European interest in its territory, "the sick man of Europe" became "the Eastern question" of Western diplomacy: European powers began to scheme to take advantage of fading Ottoman power.

Whether the British in India, the Dutch in the East Indies, the French (from 1830) in Algeria, the British in Egypt (from 1887 in the wake of financial collapse), European imperial inroads into *Dar al-Islam,* "the realm of Islam," called into radical question a fundamental principle of Muslim identity—namely, the inherent role of political power in religious faith. From the time of Muhammad and his caliphal successors in the *Dawlah,* or state-regime, Islam assumed the right to govern. It had a readiness to tolerate *dhimmis,* or non-Muslim religious elements, if they submitted politically.

Muslims, however, ought always to be ruled by Muslims, seeing that, ever since the Prophet's own emigration from Mecca, power was the due accompaniment of *Din,* or religion.

Disruption of this order of things by Western imperialism was not only emotionally unsettling, it was religiously flagrant. Forfeiture of the principle that Muslims govern Muslims might be broadly likened to Jews being deprived of the temple and holy land that define their full identity. Muslim subjection to non-Muslim political authority, even if they still enjoyed religious rites and liberties, was inimical to their true being.

Nor was the situation eased when, after the First World War, the caliphate itself was abolished by a nascent Turkish nationalism. For the Western factor was still at work in the fragmentation of the Muslim community into Western-style nation-states, seen by purists as sundering the true *Ummah,* or "single Nation of Islam." These developments posed the basic question about Dar al-Islam. They had worried Indian Muslims in the aftermath of the 1857 Indian mutiny in which Muslims had participated. After bloody pacification, it had to be asked whether this entrenched British Raj constituted Dar al-Islam, authentic Islamic being. Mosques were open and Islamic rites fulfilled, but a non-Muslim queen, Victoria, reigned as empress.

Thinkers like the Indian Muslim reformer Sayyid Ahmad Khan (1818–1897), an Anglophile, aimed to persuade a disheartened community to cease lamenting and embrace Western mores and appreciate their imperial mentors. Islam, too, was progressive and could be just religious. Half a century later, however, when the British Raj was in exodus from the subcontinent, Indian Muslim opinion in the areas where Muslims predominated favored the costly creation of Pakistan—Islamic statehood when and where it could be had—rather than continuing to live in a pluralist India in equality with non-Muslims. That development in the late 1940s marks the clearest of pointers to the mind and genius of Islam in response to the West and its legacy.

Although Western withdrawal from Muslim realms is tactically complete, it has many lingering forms in the global power equation. If, by and large, Muslims are now ruling Muslims, the dilemma of the due form of Islamic politics is far from resolved. There are, moreover, large Muslim minorities—in India, Europe, farther Asia, and Africa—in permanent lack of an Islamic statehood. There are others, notably in Africa (for example, Nigeria, Uganda, Sudan), where nationhoods are shared by other religions. In either case the Islamic debate about faith and governance is Westernized in the sense that secular criteria of law, human rights, extent of suffrage, and the forms of power clash with the classic concepts of traditional Islam.

The age-long, though much tried, caliphate has not been revived. After its demise with the final collapse of the Ottoman Empire after World War I, as early as 1925 there was a lively disavowal by Egyptian writer and scholar Ali Abd al-Raziq of the caliphate's necessity to a right Islam on the grounds that its appropriateness in the aftermath of Muhammad's death and in the early centuries had been long superseded by developments in the self-perception of Islam and of law in and between nations. Islam could be happily rid of it and still fulfill itself in fully religious terms through a partial secularization of the state. The debate continues.

Experience through half a century of Pakistani constitution making and abrogating demonstrates how unresolved the issues remain for Muslim legists and leaders, civil and military—how disconcerting too for their populations. The encounter with the West that has spawned many of the issues, and certainly fevered the climate, has had a dubious relation to their solution. If Islam sees itself as having a divinely given blueprint for its society in the *shari'a* (sacred law), how is that consistent with democracy? The Sunni Muslim concept of consensus of the community might be, but is that consensus subject to supervision only by rigorist expertise as to Islamic quality—an expertise the masses do not possess?

There are those who would like to argue that Islam should readily accommodate a secular polity, like that of Turkey under Kemal Atatürk, on the grounds that the primary message and mission of the Prophet were essentially religious. To others, this would spell a complete betrayal. Exegesis of the Qur'an may yield categorical answers for some Muslims, but others find ground for secular readings. Encounter with the West brought Muslims a prolonged and strenuous crisis over the nature of Muslim experience and yearning for fulfillment in a polity at once authentic and modern.

Mind and Spirit

Questions of caliphate and state, of power and law, of religion and polity reach into mind and spirit. Napoleon's incursion into Egypt was militarily brief, but the scholars, Egyptologists, and pundits he brought with him had a more subtle effect. Muhammad Ali was enamored of military imports and made famous use of them, but they could not be isolated from a ferment of ideas and the desires they provoked. Later, the Suez Canal and developing Western-style economic efficiencies quickened the attitudes and the pace of thought. Later still, exploitation of oil in the Persian Gulf region and its trappings disturbed static assumptions and required anxious reflection on new perspectives of how theocracy might combine with human competence and Islamic authority with the spread of change.

Islam, with its deeply rooted theism, was not likely to succumb to that recession in the sense of God that occurred in the West in response to a perceived human self-sufficiency. But how was rationality, so seemingly convincing in science and its fruits, to be reconciled with the Qur'an as revelation, with dogma as God given? Where suspicion spread that even revelation, as given in the Qur'an, might for good or ill be susceptible to scholarly inquiry, the burden of religious loyalty became the more acute. The few who acknowledged the issue were burdened with anxiety about its implications for the authority of Scripture.

Education, especially higher education, was the most important proving ground, for the school had long been the pride of Muslim culture, and calligraphy of the Qur'an, its most cherished art. Preserving the firm structures of belief and piety had to reckon with new and exacting tests of such continuity. Some naively thought that the new sciences could be avidly absorbed for their techniques without the mind-set that produced them—a mind-set that would not spare sacrosanct religious claims but would put them to the same empirical scrutiny that the pious fear.

Indian Muslim and North African intellectuals showed themselves ready to acknowledge and undertake the tasks of criticism and scholarship concerning dogma and tradition, but they were often either too cautious or too erudite to carry others with them. Taha Husain (1889–1973), a blind Cairo scholar and a pioneer reaching far into Western academia (he attained his doctorate in France at the Sorbonne), published *The Future of Education in Egypt* in 1938, insisting that the spiritual and intellectual destiny of Egypt was toward Europe. Egyptians were heirs of the Mediterranean and Alexandria, its great cultural center, and intellectually were Westerners.

Such confident Europeanism, however, was resisted by those Muslims for whom Egyptian thinker Sayyid Qutb (1906–1966) was representative. Revered leader of the Muslim Brotherhood, Qutb rejected an early Western-style literary interest for a defense of traditional faith. He wrote an influential commentary on the Qur'an and paralleled in Egyptian Islam the role of Sayyid Abu al-Ala Mawdudi, who founded the Islamic Party *(Jama'at-i Islami)* in India in 1941. Never losing sight of the role of political action and the risks of being subversive, such conservators of a rigorous Islam have tended to place their hope in a discipline of devout practice and social action. By and large, academic scholarship across Islam stays cautious and tentative in its approach in terms of Western norms of investigative theology and textual study of religious sources—or those who have adopted such critical procedures have found themselves exiles in the West. But there is no doubt that a growing number of Muslims are recognizing the need for critical inquiry.

There is, however, a large problem around what might be called the politics of scholarship. Proud cultures resent what they see as Eurocentrism or Westernism somehow claiming a universal writ. At times, from inside Western academia come voices protesting distorted portrayals of the East and of Islam, such as Palestinian scholar Edward Said's *Orientalism* (1979). It is true that the West has romanticized its vision, seen what it wanted to see. It is also true that some oriental scholarship has been funded by vested interests and been corrupted accordingly. Yet it remains possible that, in all this indicting, there is an occidentalism in reverse.

One Muslim response to perceptions of arrogance or falsity in Western treatment of Islam is to cultivate a total intellectual self-sufficiency within Islam. It is expounded, for example, in Isma'il al-Faruqi's *Cultural Atlas of Islam* (1986) and his proposal for an Islamicization of all knowledge. Western sciences, especially psychology and sociology, tend to relativize all truth and so undermine Muslim loyalty to Islamic finality. It is therefore argued that all these disciplines must be brought inside Islamic norms, thus resuming the former, splendid Islamic hegemony of arts and sciences and also immunizing Muslim youth against the corrosive influence of secularized scientism and sciences. The ambition is understandable in the psyche but hardly feasible in the context of growing secularization.

Muslim Society and the West

When Napoleon brought guns and savants, power and politics, into Egypt, the world was not what it would become. The Suez Canal, not to say Zionism and Ayatollah Ruholla Khomeini, oil and nuclear fission, independence and diasporas, were far below the horizon. The Napoleon who troubled the Muslim and Coptic scene had no intimations of the Ottoman demise, no European vistas of the Versailles treaty that ended World War I nor of Adolf Hitler and his legacy. Interreligion was there in 1798, but since then it has greatly enlarged and quickened. Minority communities of Muslims extend across Europe; Western tourism reaches into the remotest confines of Islam; and technicians disconcert traditional Muslims wishing to defend their faith against secular challenges. Races, nationalities, and cultures have mingled together in a ferment that takes Muslims beyond their own self-sufficiency.

Growth of population, the duty of a present generation to the next and of that prospectively to the next again, the burden of technology on the environment, majority-minority relationships in lands where different groups mix, the chronic imbalance in the exploitation and distribution of the wealth of nations—all these create the necessary intermingling of cultures yet challenge their sense of exclusiveness and assurance and vex their souls.

In this context the Islamic revolution of 1979 in Iran was of the utmost significance. It stemmed from a sense of being swamped by Western norms, Western goods, and Western mores, with the ruling shah their evil accomplice. Antagonism proved capable of rallying decisively behind a determined Ayatollah Khomeini who was able, even from exile in France, to muster a popular uprising. So doing, his clerical protest movement could carry all before it in a dramatic dethroning of state power ironically equipped with all the instruments of Western expertise and sustained by the endless generosity of oil wealth.

Iran provides a classic example of the strength of reaction produced by the encounter with the West. Such a reaction had been anticipated in a powerful pamphlet circulated during the shah's final years, entitled *Gharhzadegi,* which might be translated as "plagued by Westitis"—Westitis being a deplorably endemic and destructive disease. The author, Jalal Al-e-Ahmad, unloaded pent-up resentment of invasive, deleterious Western culture with its Pepsicolonization, its films and brazen styles, corrupting the precious heritage of Persian pride and poetry. He excoriated the vulgarity of the commodity culture that the West was promoting in Iran, a culture that ignored the beauties of a landscape and a poesy and an architecture it would not, or could not, comprehend.

The indictment no doubt ignored generations of scholars and other Westerners in authentic love with Persia, but even so it struck a resounding chord in political Iran. More intellectually perceptive and—at long range—representative were the writings of Iranian thinker Ali Shari'ati (1933–1977). He sensed what he called "alienation from ourselves" in listless piety and drew perceptively on the writings of Franz Fanon, penman of the Algerian revolution. From the Qur'an's words about Allah as "the God of the people" (Surah 114.3), he read Muhammad's leadership after the *hijra* as essentially a Marxist-style mission to the masses. Shari'ati, however, perceived the dangers of clerical exploitation of mass emotion, decrying the vested professional interest that motivated the clerics. His laicization of the Islamic mind—if it may be so described—and his quest for an integrated intellectualism underlined a widespread debate throughout Arab and Indian Islam about whether the public mind of Muslims needed, or did not need, the sanction of free inquiry unburdened by concern with the minutiae of exegesis and jurisprudence.

The opening of the gate of *ijtihad,* of free inquiry, was crucial to an Islam setting itself abreast of the ever multiplying ethical and social perplexities ensuing from nuclear power, genetic engineering, the birth control pill, drug culture, and the rest. It was through the likes of Shari'ati that something of the feel of liberation theology in its Latin American context could make some way into Muslim thought. In the 1930s Muhammad Iqbal (1876–1938), the patron saint of Pakistan, had stirred a new assurance, a European-style vitalism in Muslim thinking, drawing alike on the Qur'an and on Western mentors, philosophical and sociological. It was problematic to reconcile French social theorist Emile Durkheim's thesis about religion as a societal device—a theory that called in radical question divine sanction of a revealed order in a holy *shari'a*—with the basics of Islam, which Iqbal tried to do. But the sense of the positive societal tasks of religion had to militate against the kind of static conservatism that had hardly noted there were any.

What comes into existence after doubt, anxiety, and agitation has value: belief after unbelief. The prophets came essentially to produce controversy, to plant, as Shari'ati said, contradiction and conflict in a stagnant people—a sentiment that could be both suspect and reprehensible only if the words were Western meant for the East. Coming from Islamic minds, it may be some measure of what the encounter with the West has produced. Such an encounter must be reciprocal and open ended.

See also *Ahmad Khan, Sir Sayyid; Durkheim, Emile; Egypt; Fundamentalism; Iqbal, Muhammad; Iran; Islam; Khomeini, Ruholla; Mawdudi, Sayyid Abu al-Ala; Muhammad; Qutb, Sayyid; Turkey.*

Kenneth Cragg

BIBLIOGRAPHY

Ahmad, Aziz. *Islamic Modernism in India and Pakistan, 1857–1964.* Oxford: Oxford University Press, 1967.

Akhtar, Shabbir. *A Faith for All Seasons.* London: Bellew, 1990.

Cragg, Kenneth. *Counsels in Contemporary Islam.* Edinburgh: Edinburgh University Press, 1965.

———. *Returning to Mount Hira': Islam in Contemporary Terms.* London: Bellew, 1994.

Esposito, John, ed. *The Oxford Encyclopedia of the Modern Islamic World.* 4 vols. New York: Oxford University Press, 1995.

al-Faruqi, Isma'il, with Lois Faruqi. *The Cultural Atlas of the Islamic World.* New York: Macmillan, 1979.

Hourani, Albert. *Arabic Thought in the Liberal Age, 1798–1939.* Oxford: Oxford University Press, 1961.

An-Na'im, Abdullahi Ahmad. *Towards an Islamic Reformation, Civil Liberties, Human Rights, and International law.* Syracuse, N.Y.: Syracuse University Press, 1990.

Sardar, Ziauddin. *Islamic Futures: The Shape of Ideas to Come.* London and New York: Mansell, 1985.

Smith, Wilfred Cantwell. *Islam in Modern History* Princeton: Princeton University Press, 1957.

N

Nasser, Gamal Abdel

Egyptian political leader and first president of the Egyptian Republic. Nasser (1918–1970) helped to organize a clandestine army officers' organization and coup that toppled the Egyptian monarchy in July 1952. He became prime minister in 1954 and then president (1956–1970).

Nasser strongly believed that Egypt should gain independence from the dominance of foreign powers, and he enacted social and economic reforms. Among the most important were land reforms aimed at limiting the size of holdings owned by wealthy landlords. He also nationalized Egypt's large industries and banks. To gain control over the strategic Suez Canal, owned mainly by British and French interests, he nationalized the canal in July 1956. This act put him in direct confrontation with Britain and France. These two powers, together with Israel, attacked the canal and occupied it in 1956, but they were forced to retreat under pressure from the United States and the Soviet Union. For Nasser and the Arabs, the resolution of the Suez Canal crisis was a major victory, and Nasser became an instant hero in the Arab world.

Nasser challenged the West by purchasing arms from the Soviet Union and other socialist countries. In addition, he received loans from the Soviets to help finance the Aswan High Dam, aimed at increasing irrigated land in Egypt. In 1955 he continued his anti-Western policies by attending the Bandung conference, a meeting of leaders of developing countries in Asia and Europe. At the conference the countries agreed on a position of positive neutrality as a challenge not only to the West but also to the Soviet Union.

Nasser's ideas of Arab nationalism were influential in creating a union between Syria and Egypt, the United Arab Republic, which lasted from 1958 to 1961. They also inspired several successful military coups that toppled monarchies in other Arab countries, among them Iraq (1958), Yemen (1962), and Libya (1969).

Opposition to his ideas and policies within and without Egypt came mainly from pan-Islamic movements that opposed his secular pan-Arabism, the old landed and wealthy classes, and Marxists and communists, who opposed him despite his cordial official ties with socialist countries. His greatest defeat, however, came in June 1967, when Israel staged successful attacks against Egypt, Syria, and the West Bank of the Jordan River, taking valuable Arab land. Before Nasser could regain Israeli-held Egyptian territory, he died unexpectedly from a heart attack in September 1970.

Nasser's legacy still lives in the Arab world. Several political parties and groups claim Nasserism—defined as Arab unity and independence—as the source of their ideology and inspiration.

See also *Egypt; Nationalism.*

Louay Y. Bahry

BIBLIOGRAPHY

Dekmejian, Hrair R. *Egypt under Nasir: A Study in Political Dynamics.* Albany: State University of New York Press, 1971.

Nutting, Anthony. *Nasser.* London: Constable, 1972.

O'Brien, Patrick. *The Revolution in Egypt's Economic System: From Pri-*

Gamal Abdel Nasser is greeted in August 1956 by a cheering crowd upon his return to Cairo from Alexandria, where he announced that he had nationalized the Suez Canal.

vate Enterprise to Socialism, 1952–1965. London: Oxford University Press, 1966.

Stephens, Robert. *Nasser: A Political Biography.* New York: Simon and Shuster, 1971.

Nationalism

Although the term "nationalism" is sometimes loosely used to describe an attitude of fanatical loyalty to a nation, it also indicates any social philosophy, ideology, or set of shared values that undergirds the concept of nationhood. It refers especially to ideas legitimating the secular nation-state that emerged in eighteenth-century Europe and America and that by the mid-twentieth century had become accepted in most of the modern world. Advocates of secular nationalism have an ambivalent attitude toward religion: they have rejected it, tacitly employed it, and, in the last decades of the twentieth century, in some cases stridently embraced it in new movements aimed at creating a religious nation-state.

Ambivalence toward Religion

When modern secular nationalism emerged in the eighteenth century as a product of the European Enlightenment's political values, it did so with a distinctly antireligious, or at least anticlerical, posture. The ideas of seventeenth-century English philosopher John Locke about the origins of a civil community and the social contract theories of eighteenth-century French thinker Jean-Jacques Rousseau required very little commitment to traditional religious beliefs. Although they allowed for a divine order that made the rights of humans possible, their ideas had the effect of taking religion—at least church religion—out of public life. At the time, religious enemies of the Enlightenment protested religion's public demise, but their views were submerged in a wave of approval for a new view of social order in which secular nationalism was thought to be virtually a natural law, universally applicable and morally right.

Yet as religion was becoming less political, the secular political world was adopting a religiousness of its own. The French Revolution, which began in 1789, was the model for much of the nationalist fervor that developed in the nineteenth century. It infused a religious zeal into revolutionary democracy, taking on the trappings of church religion in the priestly power meted out to its demagogic leaders and in the slavish devotion to what the revolutionaries called the temple of reason.

According to nineteenth-century French statesman and

political theorist Alexis de Tocqueville, the French Revolution was much like a religious revolution. The American Revolution also had a religious side: many of its leaders had been influenced by eighteenth-century Deism, a religion of science and natural law. As in France, American nationalism developed its own religious characteristics, blending the ideals of secular nationalism and the symbols of Christianity into what has been called a civil religion.

The latter part of the nineteenth century fulfilled de Tocqueville's prophecy that secular nationalism would overrun the world. It was spread throughout the globe with an almost missionary zeal and was shipped to the newly colonized areas of Asia, Africa, and Latin America as part of the ideological freight of colonialism.

Secular nationalism reached its zenith in the mid-twentieth century after the end of World War II as colonial empires crumbled and new nations proliferated in Africa, Asia, and the Middle East. Formerly colonial governments turned their political and economic infrastructures from territories into nation-states, and the ideology of secular nationalism infused efforts to create public loyalty and a sense of legitimacy for public institutions in what came to be known as nation building.

Leaders like India's Jawaharlal Nehru (1889–1964) and Egypt's Gamal Abdel Nasser (1918–1970) symbolized the modern and Westernized nationalist who had little tolerance for what was perceived to be the irrationality of religion's customs and the divisiveness of its loyalties.

Yet though the masses in newly independent countries such as India and Egypt expressed a great deal of nationalist pride, their acceptance of a secular basis for national identity was not extensive. As it had in the West in previous centuries, in the late twentieth century secular nationalism in the formerly colonized countries came to represent one side of a great encounter between two vastly different ways of perceiving the sociopolitical order and the relationship of the individual to the state—one informed by the notion of a secular compact, the other by the authority and community conveyed through traditional religion. Given the fundamental character of the division, and the intensity of the loyalties to each side, it is no wonder that in the last decades of the twentieth century the encounter was so violent.

Criticisms of Secular Nationalism

The religious rejection of secular nationalism emerged as a major motif in the latter decades of the twentieth century, especially among areas of the Middle East and Asia that had been colonized or that had come under the West's economic and cultural influence. In these parts of the world, secular nationalism has been criticized for being by its nature Western, a charge leveled by the Ayatollah Ruholla Khomeini (1900–1989) against the policies of the shah during Iran's successful religious nationalist revolution in 1979. Though Iran had never been colonized, the Ayatollah claimed that American and European economic control and cultural influence amounted to colonialization all the same. In Algeria the Islamic Salvation Front took a similar position during the 1991 elections, claiming that the secular nationalism promulgated by Algeria's military leaders was an extension of French colonial rule. Religious nationalism is also seen as the unfinished business of anticolonialism in Egypt, India, Sri Lanka, and elsewhere in Africa, Asia, and the Middle East.

Religious nationalists in other parts of the world—including industrialized countries—have criticized secular nationalism for other reasons, including their conviction that it is the enemy of religion. The claim that secular nationalism is hostile to any political identity or ideology related to religion was a major theme of Jewish movements for religious nationalism in Israel and many of the religious nationalist movements that erupted in Tajikistan, Uzbekistan, Ukraine, Azerbaijan, and Chechnya in the 1990s. In many of the nations formerly associated with the Soviet Union, religious activists saw the ideology of communism as a foil for an irredentist Russian nationalism, which barred religion not only for Marxist ideological reasons but also to keep national identities associated with religion from rising in the Soviet-dominated states. Following the Soviet Union's demise in 1991, many in these nations saw their religion as a locus of renewed national identity and loyalty.

Radical religious activists in the United States and Japan have criticized secular nationalism for promoting a unified world order. According to these critics the global ideology of secular nationalism sets the stage for the establishment of a new world power, one that promotes a single central political authority and a unified world society and culture. In the 1990s the Christian Identity and Christian Reconstruction movements in the United States fostered fears over the global aspirations of secular political leaders, anxieties that were shared by Japan's Aum Shinrikyo, a breakaway Buddhist group involved in a nerve gas attack on Tokyo's subways in 1995. In the views of these groups it was religion that protected national interests against the internationalism that they thought was secular nationalism's ultimate goal.

Ethnic and Ideological Religious Nationalism

Religious nationalism has been associated both with loyalties to particular ethnic religious communities and with commitments to certain political-religious ideologies. In some movements the ethnic aspects have been primary, in some the ideological issues have been paramount, and in others both aspects have been equally important. The struggle of the Irish—both Protestant and Roman Catholic—to claim political authority over their land is an example of ethnic nationalism. The former Yugoslavia has witnessed three groups of ethnic religious nationalists pitted against one another: Orthodox Serbs, Catholic Croats, and Muslim Bosnians.

The most confrontational movements of religious nationalism in the late twentieth century, however, have been ideological. Messianic Zionist organizations for Jewish nationalism in Israel and radical forms of Muslim nationalism have aimed at establishing a political order based on religious law, as have the Christian Identity and Christian Reconstruction groups associated with militia organizations in the United States. Movements that have been both ethnic and ideological in character have had double sets of enemies: their ethnic rivals and the secular leaders of their own people. The Hamas movement in Palestine, for example, simultaneously waged a war of independence against Israel while sparring with the secular Palestinian Authority led by Yasir Arafat.

Religious Nationalist Movements

By the end of the twentieth century virtually every religious tradition in the world had provided justification for some form of religious nationalism. The theoretical constructs of modern Islamic movements were linked to the writings of Pakistan's Mawlana Abu al-Ala Mawdudi (1903–1979), who founded the Jamaʿat-i Islami (Islamic Association) in 1941 in British India before Pakistan was created, and Egypt's Hasan al-Banna (1906–1949), who established the Muslim Brotherhood in 1928. These thinkers identified Western imperialism as an enemy of Islamic society and called for political organization to overthrow Western influences, if necessary by force, in order to establish a political order based on Islamic law.

In Egypt successors of al-Banna included Muslim Brotherhood leaders Sayyid Qutb and Abd Al-Salam Faraj, both of whom were executed by the Egyptian government—Qutb in 1966, and Faraj in 1982 after he was accused of taking part in the assassination of President Anwar Sadat. Faraj had argued that Muslims had a neglected duty to undertake a *jihad* (sacred struggle) against the secular forces that threatened Islam, and he was associated with an extreme faction of the Muslim Brotherhood, the Jamaat al-Jihad. Another radical group at the fringe of Egypt's Muslim Brotherhood was the Gamaa al-Islamiya (Islamic Group) led by Sheik Omar Abdul Rahman. The movement was implicated in the 1993 bombing of New York City's World Trade Center and a string of bombings in Egypt, including an assault on a group of tourists at the Temple of Hatshepsut in Luxor in 1997. The aim of these movements was to remove American and other international support for Egypt's secular nationalism.

In nearby Gaza and the West Bank of Palestine, these Egyptian groups and the thinking of Mawdudi, al-Banna, Qutb, and Faraj influenced a growing Muslim movement of Palestinian nationalism that eventually rivaled the secular Palestine Liberation Organization headed by Arafat. The Muslim movement was founded by Sheik Ahmed Yassin and other religious activists in 1987 and named Hamas, a word that means "zeal" and serves as an acronym for the phrase Harakat al-Muqawama al-Islamiyya, "Islamic Resistance Movement." Hamas supported the intifada, the grass-roots Palestinian resistance movement, and rebelled against Arafat and the Palestine Liberation Organization after the Palestinian leader signed a peace agreement with Israel's Yitzhak Rabin in 1993.

In other Arab regions the power of new Islamic political movements has also been felt. In Syria Islamic activists have attempted to unseat the secular Baʿth Party of Hafiz al-Asad, and in Saudi Arabia, Kuwait, and the other Gulf emirates, where an official Islamic culture prevails and Islamic law is honored, rebel Islamic nationalists are also feared. In elections held in Jordan after the Persian Gulf War in 1991, members of the Muslim Brotherhood became the largest single bloc in the Jordanian parliament.

In Iran the ideology of Islamic nationalism that emerged during and after the 1979 revolution was propounded by the Ayatollah Khomeini and Ali Shariʿati. Shariʿati employed socialist notions of revolution in formulating a Shiʿi Islamic political philosophy not unlike the liberation theology of Latin American Christianity. These ideas and Iran's example of a successful Islamic revolution encouraged leaders of Shiʿi Islamic movements elsewhere, including the Hezbollah and

Amal organizations based in Lebanon that targeted both American and Israeli military units in the 1980s.

In Afghanistan Muslim groups seized the leadership of the liberation struggle against the Soviet-backed government, and an Islamic state was established in 1992. In 1995 an even more radical group, the Taliban, succeeded in establishing military control over most of the country, including the capital, Kabul. Led by members of the Pathan ethnic community who were former students of Islamic schools, these religious revolutionaries established an autocratic state with strict adherence to traditional Islamic codes of behavior.

In Pakistan conservative Muslims who helped to oust Benazir Bhutto from office in 1990 and again in 1997 supported legislation that made the tenets of the Qur'an the supreme law of the land. India was torn by a violent encounter in the mid-1990s between the Indian army and rebels in Kashmir supporting the establishment of an autonomous Muslim state. In Indonesia Islamic activists led a separatist movement in the Aceh region, where they instituted strict Islamic moral codes and engaged in a violent struggle with the army. Other Islamic leaders in Indonesia supported the successful revolt against Suharto in 1998 and endorsed Muhammadiya, a Muslim nationalist party.

In Algeria protests mounted by the Islamic Salvation Front led to enormous electoral successes in December 1991. The movement, in soundly defeating the party that had ruled Algeria since its independence from the French in 1956, promised to give the former colony what its leader called an Islamic state. Scarcely a month later, however, the army annulled the elections and established a secular military junta, outlawing the Islamic Front. The violent resistance to the junta's actions that followed included a series of bombings in Paris subways in the mid-1990s in protest against what was perceived to be France's support for the secular military leaders. In neighboring Tunisia the outlawed Islamic Renaissance Party organized an opposition to the secular Tunisian government.

In Sudan Lieutenant General Omar Hassan Ahmed Bashir established one of the world's most influential Islamic regimes in 1989, masterminded by Muslim leader and theoretician Hassan Abdullah Turabi. Sudan is alleged to have been a training ground for Islamic activists worldwide, and the articulate, urbane Turabi has been an international spokesman for Islamic nationalism.

In Turkey the Islamic-oriented Welfare Party briefly came to power in 1996; its leader, Nejmettim Erbakan, was forced to resign in 1997, and the party was banned in 1998. In northern Nigeria Islam has fused with ethnic tribal politics; and in the Philippines, Islam has been tied to a separatist movement in the southern islands. Islam has also been linked to the rise of ethnic Muslim politics in Croatia and Bosnia-Herzegovina in Yugoslavia; Serbia's Kosovo province adjoining Albania; Xinjiang, Ningxia, Gansu, and Yunnan provinces in China; and Uzbekistan, Azerbaijan, Turkmenistan, Kazakstan, Kyrgyzstan, Tajikistan, and the Islamic regions of central and southern Russia in the Commonwealth of Independent States.

Islam is not the only religious tradition to include movements for religious nationalism and political change. Jewish nationalism, for example, has been tied to the creation of an independent state of Israel in 1948. Rabbi Avraham Yitzhak ha-Kohen Kook (1864–1935), the chief rabbi of pre-Israeli Palestine, and his son and successor, Z.Y. Kook (1891–1982), maintained that the secular state of Israel was religiously useful and that its purification could help precipitate the return of the Messiah. After the 1967 war in which Israel gained land from adjacent Arab states, some Jewish nationalists thought that the time had come for the biblical nation of Israel to be re-created. Rabbi Moshe Levinger and others established the Gush Emunim, an organization that encouraged Jews to establish settlements on the West Bank of the Jordan River to recover what was regarded as biblical lands from Palestinians.

An even more extreme form of Jewish nationalism was articulated by Rabbi Meir Kahane, who immigrated to Israel from the United States in 1971 and founded the Kach (Thus!) Party dedicated to the creation of an Israeli nation based on Torah (biblical law) rather than secular principles. Kahane advocated a catastrophic form of Messianic Zionism that urged confrontation with Arabs, secular Jews, and others perceived to be enemies of a Jewish religious state. Although Kahane was assassinated in New York City in 1990 by Muslims associated with the Gamaa al-Islamiya, his movement continued to advocate violent encounters. One of his followers, Dr. Baruch Goldstein, killed Muslim worshippers at the Shrine of the Cave of the Patriarchs in Hebron in 1994. Yigal Amir, propelled by ideas similar to Kahane's, assassinated Prime Minister Yitzhak Rabin in 1995.

Christianity has been associated with political power since Roman emperor Constantine embraced it in the fourth century and has had a history of clerical influence on political authority. Recent Christian nationalists have traced their ideas to the sixteenth-century Protestant reformer John Calvin, who advocated a Christian religious basis for political order and established Geneva, Switzerland, as a Christian city-state.

In the 1980s religious activists in the United States adopted Calvin's thinking in a movement of Christian Reconstruction that called for America's economic system and legal order to be based on Christian principles. A similar strand of revolutionary religious activism, the Christian Identity movement, has been associated with militia movements and has provided the ideological basis for such religious communes as the Freeman Compound in Montana and Elohim City in Oklahoma. In the 1990s followers of both Christian Reconstruction and Christian Identity were involved in the bombing of abortion clinics and in violent encounters with the U.S. government, which they regarded as their ideological enemy.

India's nationalist movement has had a religious side since the late nineteenth century, when political activists such as Bankim Chandra Chatterjee (1838–1894) and Aurobindo Ghose (1872–1950) added a specifically Hindu spiritual dimension to India's emerging movement for independence. In 1925 the Rashtriya Swayamsevak Sangh (National Volunteer Organization), basing its ideas on the writings of Vinayak Damodar Savarkar (1883–1966), advocated the political preservation of what Savarkar called *hindutva,* a national identity based on Hindu culture. During the 1980s members of the organization formed a new political party, the Bharatiya Janata Party (Indian People's Party) based on Savarkar's ideas. The party won state elections and in 1998 was able to establish a coalition national government led by Atal Bihari Vajpayee, one of its more moderate leaders.

Sikhs in India's Punjab state expressed a much more strident form of religious nationalism in the 1980s. The movement, led by Sant Jarnail Singh Bhindranwale, who was killed in the Indian army's assault on the Sikh's Golden Temple in 1984, aimed at creating Khalistan—a new nation to be established in the Punjab and based on Sikh religious principles.

The Theravada Buddhist tradition has had a long history of political interaction and religious warfare. In Thailand kings are expected to have had training as monks, and members of monastic orders influenced twentieth-century political reforms. In Sri Lanka Buddhist dynasties have ruled that island kingdom since the time of Mahinda in the third century B.C. Buddhist monks were at the forefront of Sri Lanka's independence movement in 1948, and in 1953 an influential pamphlet, *The Revolt in the Temple,* began a religious critique of secular nationalism and the claim that secular leaders had betrayed Buddhism. The demand for a Buddhist state came to a head in the 1980s, when thousands of monks joined the revolutionary Janatha Vimukthi Peramuna (the People's Liberation Front). In Myanmar (Burma) Buddhist monks supported the unsuccessful democracy movement in 1988.

In China Mahayana Buddhist and traditional Chinese ideas fused with Protestant Christian millenarianism in the ideology of the Taiping Rebellion (1848–1865), aimed at establishing a peaceful dynasty. In Japan Buddhism and Shinto concepts were employed in support of Japanese nationalism during World War II and in neonationalist ideologies in the 1980s and 1990s. The Aum Shinrikyo movement derived its ideas from a variety of Buddhist, Hindu, and Christian sources and aimed at the religious purification of the Japanese nation. In Tibet the push for national liberation from Chinese control—and the restoration of the Dalai Lama—is both a religious and political cause. In Mongolia the revival of Tibetan Buddhism as the national culture after the end of communist rule led in 1992 to establishment of a Mongolian Buddhist Party.

In some cases religious ideas have been fused with secular ones in nationalistic civil religions. Among the most strident examples in the late twentieth century were the *juche* philosophy propagated by North Korea's Kim Il Sung and his son and successor, Kim Jung Il—which blended Confucian, Korean shaman, and Marxist ideas—and the ideology of Iraq's President Saddam Husayn, which mixed Sunni and Shiʿi Islamic and ancient Iraqi images with the dictatorial socialism of the Baʿth Party.

Critics of Religious Nationalism

Some of the most severe critics of the new movements for religious nationalism have come from within religious quarters. Among them have been religious utopians who prefer their own isolated political societies, religious liberals satisfied with the existing secular nation-state, and religious conservatives who tend to ignore politics altogether. Some Muslims have accused their religious activists of making Islam into a political ideology, thereby reducing it to the terms of modern politics. In Iran a leading Muslim theologian, Abdolkarim Soroush, claimed in the mid-1990s that the political involvement of Islam in his country corrupted the purity of religion. In Egypt and elsewhere in the Middle East, Muslim clerics have accused religious activists of being nationalistic and not appreciative of the transnational character of Islam. Other religious nationalist movements, such as the Indian People's Party, have moderated their ideological positions after attaining political power, a trend that will likely continue when movements of religious nationalism attempt to accommodate their visionary agenda with the existing secular nation-state.

See also *Afghanistan; Algeria; Banna, Hasan al-; Buddhism, Theravada; Buddhism, Tibetan; Calvinism; China; Civil religion; Colonialism; Dalai Lama; Egypt; Enlightenment; Gush Emunim; Hinduism; India; Indonesia; Iran; Iraq; Ireland; Islam; Japan; Khomeini, Ruholla Musavi; Liberation theology; Mawdudi, Sayyid Abu al-Ala; Nasser, Gamal Abdel; Pakistan; Qutb, Sayyid; Revolutions; Russia; Sadat, Anwar; Shinto; Sudan; Syria; Tocqueville, Alexis de; Turkey; Yugoslavia; Zionism.*

Mark Juergensmeyer

BIBLIOGRAPHY

Anderson, Benedict. *Imagined Communities: Reflections on the Origin and Spread of Nationalism.* London: Verso, 1983.

Casanova, José. *Public Religions in the Modern World.* Chicago: University of Chicago Press, 1994.

Hobsbawm, E. J. *Nations and Nationalism since 1780: Programme, Myth, Reality.* Cambridge: Cambridge University Press, 1990.

Juergensmeyer, Mark. *The New Cold War? Religious Nationalism Confronts the Secular State.* Berkeley and Los Angeles: University of California Press, 1993.

Kotkin, Joel. *Tribes: How Race, Religion, and Identity Determine Success in the New Global Economy.* New York: Random House, 1992.

Rudolph, Susanne Hoeber, and James Piscatori, eds. *Transnational Religion and Fading States.* Boulder: Westview Press, 1997.

Smith, Anthony D. *The Ethnic Origins of Nations.* Oxford: Blackwell, 1986.

van der Veer, Peter. *Religious Nationalism: Hindus and Muslims in India.* Berkeley and Los Angeles: University of California Press, 1994.

Westerlund, David, ed. *Questioning the Secular State: The Worldwide Resurgence of Religion in Politics.* London: Hurst, 1996.

Nation of Islam

The Nation of Islam is a sectarian, militant religious and cultural movement that has preached black nationalism and separatism in the United States. It was established in 1930, in Detroit, by a peddler who became known as Wali Fard Muhammad. Fard (c.1877–?1934) claimed that he brought the true religion of the black men of Asia and Africa that would liberate black people from white oppression by giving them true self-knowledge. He told his followers that they were not Americans, owed no allegiance to the American flag, and should refuse to vote or serve in the American military. Instead, they were citizens of the Lost-Found Nation of Islam, which had the goal of establishing a separate nation for black people somewhere in the United States or in Africa.

Fard's trusted lieutenant was Robert Poole (1897–1975), who joined the Nation in 1931 and was given the Muslim name Elijah Muhammad. When Fard mysteriously disappeared in 1934, there was a leadership struggle. Elijah Muhammad moved his family and close followers to the Southside of Chicago, where Temple of Islam No. 2 was established as the headquarters of the movement. He reshaped the Nation of Islam by establishing the doctrine that Master Fard was Allah, that God was a black man, and that he, the Honorable Elijah Muhammad, knew Allah personally and was the anointed messenger of Allah. Both beliefs are considered heretical by the orthodox majority of Muslims (Sunni Muslims), who believe that Muhammad, the founder of Islam, was the last prophet and who consider God beyond human comprehension.

Under Elijah Muhammad's guidance, the Nation focused on the development of economic independence and emphasized the importance of recovering an acceptable black self-identity. "Do for self" became the rallying cry of the movement, which encouraged economic self-reliance for black people. Hard work, frugality and the avoidance of debt, self-improvement, and a conservative lifestyle enabled Elijah Muhammad and his followers to establish more than one hundred temples nationwide; innumerable grocery stores, restaurants, bakeries, and other small businesses; and the Nation's own farms.

Stressing the slogan "know yourself," Elijah Muhammad diagnosed the vulnerabilities of the black psyche as stemming from a confusion of identity and self-hatred caused by white racism; the cure that he prescribed was forming a separate black nation. Elijah Muhammad taught that the white man was a devil by nature, unable to respect anyone who was not white, and that he was the historic and persistent source of harm and injury to black people.

Malcolm Little (1925–1965), who was to become the most prominent spokesman for the Nation of Islam, converted to the Nation in prison, in 1947, and became known as Malcolm X. Dropping one's surname and taking on an X, standard practice in the movement, was considered an out-

Malcolm X

ward symbol of inward change: it meant ex-Christian, ex-Negro, ex-slave. The charismatic Malcolm X expanded the membership by establishing temples across the country and founding the newspaper, *Muhammad Speaks.* As the minister of Temple No. Seven in Harlem, he became the national representative of the Nation, second in rank to the messenger himself.

Malcolm's keen intellect, incisive wit, and ardent radicalism made him a formidable critic of American society and of the civil rights movement, challenging Martin Luther King's principal notions of integration and nonviolence. His biting critique of the "so-called Negro" and his emphasis on the recovery of black self-identity and economic independence for the black community provided the intellectual foundations for the black power and black consciousness movements of the late 1960s and 1970s in American society. In contrast to King's nonviolence, Malcolm urged his followers to defend themselves "by any means possible." He also articulated the bitterness and rage felt by the dispossessed black masses—the grass roots. He eventually broke with the Nation of Islam and was assassinated in 1965.

After Elijah Muhammad died in 1975, his son Wallace D. Muhammad was chosen to succeed him as the chief minister of the Nation of Islam. Changing his name and title to Imam Warith Deen Muhammed, he rejected his father's radical teachings, removed all racial restrictions on membership, and led the Nation into the fold of orthodox Islam. He called his new movement the American Muslim Mission.

In 1977, dissatisfied with these changes, Louis Farrakhan, leader of the New York temple and one of Elijah Muhammad's ministers, worked to rebuild the old Nation of Islam. He held the 1995 Million Man March in Washington, D.C., the largest black gathering in history, which embraced the Nation's traditional goals of community building. Farrakhan has allowed his followers to participate in electoral politics and has expanded the international contacts of the Nation of Islam.

See also *Civil rights movement; Islam; King, Martin Luther, Jr.*

Lawrence H. Mamiya

BIBLIOGRAPHY

Essien-Udom, E. U. *Black Nationalism: The Search for Identity in America.* Chicago: University of Chicago Press, 1962.

Gardell, Mattias. *In the Name of Elijah Muhammad: Minister Louis Farrakhan and the Nation of Islam.* Durham, N.C.: Duke University Press, 1997.

Lincoln, C. Eric. *The Black Muslims in America.* 3d ed. Grand Rapids, Mich.: Eerdmans, 1994.

Malcolm X, and Alex Haley. *The Autobiography of Malcolm X.* New York: Grove Press, 1965.

Mamiya, Lawrence H. "From Black Muslim to Bilalian: The Evolution of a Movement." In *Islam in North America: A Sourcebook,* edited by Michael A. Koszegi and J. Gordon Melton. New York: Garland, 1992.

Native Americans

The descendants of those who inhabited the Americas before European colonization, Native Americans are diverse peoples with strikingly varied political and religious systems. As with other societies around the world, Native American or Indian politics and religion have been intimately intertwined. Religion traditionally helps shape and sanction political arrangements and decisions, and political circumstances affect the forms and content of religious life.

Historically, Indian political systems have ranged from small, face-to-face bands composed of a few extended families to large, complex chiefdoms or states incorporating tens of thousands in far-flung economic, religious, and political networks. Political and religious order among Native Americans has usually been attuned to particular natural, supernatural, and social landscapes, and differing environmental and geopolitical conditions can help to explain the diverse political and religious arrangements among Indian peoples, although they alone did not determine them.

Diversity of Cultures

Among the most extensive and complicated political and religious systems in North American history was the Mississippian (so-named by archeologists), which organized inhabitants of almost the entire Mississippi River watershed through a collection of major and minor chiefdoms into a single religious, political, and economic complex. At its center was the city of Cahokia (near present-day St. Louis, Missouri), which at the height of its power in about the year 1000 contained a population of some 30,000, covered an area of five square miles, and encompassed some 100 ceremonial mounds, the largest of which rose 100 feet over a central plaza. Although some descendants of Mississippians encountered Spanish explorers in the southeastern woodlands in the sixteenth century, neither first-hand European accounts nor archaeological remains allow scholars to explain definitively pre-Columbian Mississippian life or its abrupt decline in the thirteenth century. Most agree, however, that common ritual practices—evidenced by the symbols and motifs incised, engraved, or embossed on materials recovered throughout the region—and commerce, as well as a political and religious hierarchy, bound members of the complex together.

In other places, as among the Iroquoians of the U.S. Great Lakes region, multitribe federations emerged, which integrated culturally similar but politically distinct peoples into larger entities through real or imagined kinship. Often such new political structures were chartered by religious and political myths, which explain a people's origins and prescribe forms of organization and behavior. Although lineages, clans, and villages remained essentially autonomous within the Iroquois League, this confederation encouraged peace among its members and helped create a common moral universe. Religious societies and ritual practices common throughout the confederation helped to cement common identity. Iroquois League chiefs, not typically religious figures, commanded respect and enjoyed power through their wisdom and generosity, not through coercion. Iroquoians reckoned kinship descent through female lines and organized households around the residences of female elders. Among them, women wielded considerable religious and political authority, including designation of league chiefs and important spokesmen. Women's religious and political power has varied greatly among Native Americans.

In other areas, a looser band organization predominated and could embrace from handfuls to thousands of people in political groupings that were related though autonomous. Northern Arctic and Subarctic hunting people, for example, tended to be individualistic and egalitarian, and the composition of their small bands was flexible, in large part to serve subsistence and survival in their extreme environments. Linguistically similar people shared use of land and resources and often intermarried. Religious practice typically centered on individuals and their personal relationships with the supernatural. Persons with special powers to engage the spirit world, or shamans, aided others; such power—through sorcery or witchcraft—could also be used to cause harm.

On the North American plains, band and village organization could be elaborated into tribes, with populations in the thousands. The Teton Sioux, or Lakotas, for example, who ventured onto the plains in the early eighteenth century, were subdivided into seven component tribes by the mid-nineteenth century. Though linked by common language, culture, interests, and intermarriage, these tribes operated independently and in shifting alliances with other Lakotas. At least once a year, tribes assembled to hunt buffalo. They were further integrated by common religious rituals, beliefs, and practices. Shamans joined civil chiefs, speakers, and war leaders in council to discuss problems and also shape opinions. Civil and wartime leaders could also be religious figures. As religious leaders, shamans interpreted dreams, cured afflictions, promoted successful hunting, and generally helped individual Lakotas and their communities remain in harmony with their natural and supernatural worlds. Such examples only begin to suggest the diversity in politics and religion among native people of the Americas.

The Colonial Era

Native American political and religious life and institutions have changed dramatically since the arrival of Europeans after 1492. In the colonial era European soldiers, traders, settlers, missionaries, and officials penetrated Native American worlds. Through both cooperation and conflict, native people and colonists forged a New World. Physical encroachment; new ideas, customs, and practices; European material culture (including metal implements, cloth, firearms, and alcohol); and especially deadly diseases to which Native Americans had little resistance all worked to transform Indian life and challenged Native American political and religious systems.

Demographers estimate that native populations were reduced by 90 percent within the first century of their contact with Europeans. Some native peoples—like the Massachusetts of coastal North America and the Tainos of the Caribbean region—disappeared as social and political entities. Not only did epidemics of diseases like smallpox, measles, and influenza drastically reduce Indians' numbers, but they also weakened native people when they required the greatest physical and cultural strength to negotiate the challenges of European colonization. In some cases, Native Americans questioned their religious beliefs, practices, and leaders in the face of their helplessness against such widespread epidemics. Other Indians attributed this devastation to their own religious transgressions or interpreted such affliction as European sorcery or witchcraft. Over generations, depopulation, destruction and dispossession of land, and growing economic dependence on whites eventually reduced Native American power and required Indians to adjust, often fundamentally, to their new circumstances.

For Indian peoples, religious crisis was a fundamental part of the larger predicament that colonialism presented, especially as missionaries worked to convert them to Christianity. Native responses were often as religious as they were political, social, or economic. Different groups reacted in different ways, depending on when and how often they encountered Europeans or Euro-Americans; how close white settlements were; the national, ethnic, and religious backgrounds of colonists; what these newcomers wanted; and especially the cultural and material resources different native societies had.

The Micmacs of the Canadian Maritime provinces, for example, were beset by early epidemics but managed to avoid political dissolution. Despite their reduced circumstances and dependence on Europeans, they were able to conserve their ethnic identity through creative adaptation of Christianity. Micmacs forged a new, hybrid Christianity, one that clearly reflected Micmac traditions but that nonetheless classified them as Catholics. Mayas of the Guatemalan Highlands and Nahuas of Central Mexico did much the same, merging their ancient practices and gods with Catholic rituals and saints. In these cases, however, conversion represented something other than mere capitulation and assimilation; it was a political as well as religious choice that promoted ethnic survival. St. Anne's Day (July 26), for example, has become a national holiday for contemporary Micmacs (honoring St. Anne the teacher as well as Anne of Austria, the seventeenth-century patron of the missionaries who first converted the Micmacs), and Catholicism has become Micmac traditional religion, even though such a tradition dates only to the seventeenth century.

The Zunis, a Pueblo people of the U.S. Southwest, offer perhaps the best example of a Native American group able to avoid Christian acculturation and maintain ancient religious beliefs and practices. Zuni relations with Europeans began early with the violent intrusion of the Spaniard Francisco Vásquez de Coronado in 1540. Sporadic contact continued, including unsuccessful Spanish attempts to set up Catholic missions and Zuni rejection of colonialism and Catholicism in the Pueblo revolt of 1680, but there were no Spanish-speaking communities in Zuni territory until the 1860s. Although they established new forms of secular government to deal with the outside world, Zunis continued to be ruled by religious leaders and to maintain their autonomy and self-sufficiency. In the late nineteenth century, increased infiltration by traders, Protestant missionaries, western travelers in search of gold or grazing land, and anthropologists changed Zuni life considerably. Zuni traditions came under increasing scrutiny by whites, and ancient religious practices were condemned as barbarous. By 1900, following intervention of agents from the U.S. Bureau of Indian Affairs to suppress Zuni witchcraft trials, the political power of the Zunis' senior Bow Priests—the guardians of the statues of the Zuni war gods who symbolize the strength, aggression, and heroism that guide and protect the Zunis—was undermined. In the twentieth century a secular tribal council grew in size and political importance. Nonetheless, relatively few Zunis became Christian converts, and the traditional ceremonial system and world view continue to predominate among the Zunis.

Revitalization

The greater the degree of independence and autonomy Native Americans continued to possess, the less likely they were to convert to Christianity or submit to efforts by white missionaries and reformers to transform their systems of government, land ownership, work, gender relations, sexual practices, housing, dress, and manners. The Senecas, one of the Six Nations of the Iroquois, for example, neither adopted Christianity nor held fast to a relatively unchanged, traditional religion. Isolated in the territory that later became western New York State, and commanding power as members of the Iroquois League, Senecas effectively resisted missionaries through the period of the American Revolution in the latter eighteenth century. Even when Iroquois power and unity were later undermined, Senecas maintained considerable control over religious life, in part because Quaker missionaries among them allowed liberty of conscience and promoted the secular aspects of assimilation. Nonetheless, the Senecas' post-Revolution crisis was religious as well as political, social, and economic. A new religion emerged, based on the teachings of Handsome Lake, a prophet who blended traditional Iroquoian and Christian ideas and prescriptions, which followers accepted and modified as a way to survive in the early nineteenth century. The Old Way of Handsome Lake thus helped to revitalize the Senecas and other Iroquois people and to conserve religious and political autonomy.

Other revitalization movements—like the Ghost Dance, which was intended to call back the dead and renew the world, and peyote religions, which honored the hallucinogenic peyote as a sacramental food, of the late nineteenth and twentieth centuries—also promoted invention or adaptation of traditions, rather than appropriation of Christianity, as the best means to cultivate power, revive native communities, maintain separate ethnic identities, and resist assimilation. Although revitalization among Native Americans—or white fear of that phenomenon—sometimes led to conflict and violence, such movements were largely peaceful, introspective, and accommodating rather than aggressive. For Native Americans, revitalization movements were religious in their appeal to the supernatural and their emphasis on transformation; these movements were also fundamentally political in their efforts to regain power over their lives.

It would be difficult to overstate the devastation Native Americans suffered as a result of white expansion, destruction and expropriation of land and resources, and promotion of Christianity and cultural transformation. Few whites questioned the notion that Native Americans would and should disappear, either through extinction or assimilation, and few saw any value in protecting Native American culture. Instead, native religions were suppressed; political organizations were manipulated, corrupted, or ignored; and native bands, tribes, or nations were assaulted in the interest of "pulverizing" (in the words of one well-intentioned white reformer) these collective Indian bodies and transforming Indians into discrete American individuals. After the Dawes General Allotment Act of 1887 broke up communally owned reservation lands and allotted them to individual Indian families, Native Americans lost two-thirds of their remaining holdings, more than ninety million acres. And government agents, reformers, and missionaries continued their assault on tribalism and culture. Nonetheless, by the 1920s a new recognition began to emerge among some government officials and reformers that Indians would not disappear and that cultural persistence was legitimate. In 1924 Native Americans became U.S. citizens, regardless of their tribal affiliation or degree of assimilation. But more important, Native Americans themselves continued to adjust and conserve native identities, beliefs, and cultural practices and began to develop new means to assert themselves in white political arenas.

In 1930, under the direction of John Collier, the activist commissioner of Indian Affairs, the U.S. federal government took steps to stop the practice of allotting Native American lands in severalty (that is, by individual right rather than as shared property), to end persecution of Indian religion and cultural expression, and to promote Indian self-determination. The Indian Reorganization Act of 1934 (also known as the Wheeler-Howard Act) was designed to halt the erosion of Indians' land base, to encourage economic development, to ensure religious freedom, and to provide for Indian self-government. Some Native American communities rejected the legislation, however, because they believed its provisions ran counter to their traditions or best interests.

World War II, which the United States entered in 1941, proved to be a watershed for Native Americans as it was for the rest of the country. Many Indians served in the armed forces and worked in war-related industries, activities that drew them from their separate communities and exposed them to non-Indian life but also subjected them to new forms of discrimination. After the war an older form of assimilationism reasserted itself in a new guise through Congress's attempt to terminate Indians' special status as recog-

Devil's Tower National Monument, in Wyoming, has religious significance for some Native American tribes on the Northern Plains. The monument, a favorite of mountain climbers, has been at the center of the battle for Native American civil rights. The U.S. National Park Service instituted a voluntary ban on climbing in June, when many tribes celebrating the summer solstice converge on the monument to conduct religious services.

nized tribes with rights and privileges guaranteed under the Constitution and specific treaties. Urbanization programs also sought to resettle Native Americans as individuals and families in urban areas where economic opportunities were available. Thousands found themselves in Chicago, Minneapolis, Denver, and Los Angeles, living in substandard apartments, working menial jobs, and trying to adjust to urban noise, congestion, and crime. Relocation gained the reputation among Indians as a missing-persons factory, but it also created a new kind of urban Indian. Many returned to their rural homelands. Such integrationist policies reflected U.S. governmental efforts to encourage dissolution of Native American tribes and reservations.

Activism

Indian activism—especially through new organizations that transcended tribal bounds and were allied with non-Indians committed to cultural pluralism and Indian rights—challenged these assimilationist acts and asserted Native American self-determination. Native American political awareness and pride exhibited itself in Chicago, in 1961, in the American Indian Charter Convention. The convention, which was restricted to Indians with whites attending as silent observers, represented a broad array of native peoples from North America. It issued a Declaration of Indian Purpose that articulated a far-reaching Native American political agenda. A new militancy emerged among Native Americans in the United States, with calls by some for Red Power and with acts of civil disobedience, including fish-ins in the Northwest and the occupation of Alcatraz in San Francisco Bay, the former site of a federal prison, in 1969. Although organizations like the militant American Indian Movement—born of the grim urban Indian experience in Minneapolis—garnered headlines, they did not represent the politics of all North American Indians or provide the only means for Native American political assertion. By the 1980s American Indians in the United States worked nationally through more conventional organizations, like the Native American Rights Fund, as well as on reservations to maintain civil rights and to protect or regain land and resources. Religious issues and leaders have been at the heart of these efforts.

Among the most important gains of the Native American civil rights movement was the American Indian Religious Freedom Act of 1978. This act was designed to confirm American Indians' constitutional rights under the First Amendment guaranteeing them free exercise of religion as U.S. citizens. It has often failed, however, because Native American religions do not conform easily to expectations about religion based on Christian experience and are not widely understood. Because Indian religious practice is often spatial, situated in particular places—spiritually significant mountains or woods, for example—free exercise depends on uncompromised access to specific sites, yet many such places are no longer controlled by native people. The U.S. Supreme Court has often ruled that government intervention to protect such undisturbed access was government advocacy of religion and thus was unconstitutional.

Native American struggles to protect their religions, cultures, and lands now join native peoples of North America with those in Central and South America in networks of indigenous peoples. For five hundred years Latin America's native peoples have survived through both resistance and accommodation. From the sixteenth-century anti-Spanish "Dance Sickness" movement in Peru, which envisioned a utopian return of local Andean control, to the mid-nineteenth-century Caste War in Yucatan, which mixed quasi-Catholic teachings with Mayan separatism, to contemporary indigenous activism in the Chiapas region of Mexico, in the greater Amazon basin, or in northern Argentina, native people have sought to maintain their identities, homelands, and ways of life. The 1992 Noble Peace Prize awarded to indigenous Guatemalan activist Rigoberta Menchú focused international attention on the cause of Native American survival.

Nonetheless, the fate of these efforts by Native Americans to overcome poverty and oppression and to preserve their ways of life remains unclear. But through the past five centuries, Native American religion and politics have proved themselves nothing if not creative, resilient, and enduring.

See also *Constitution, U.S.; Conversion; Missionaries; Sacred places.*

Matthew Dennis

BIBLIOGRAPHY

Cornell, Stephen. *Return of the Native: American Indian Political Resurgence.* New York: Oxford University Press, 1988.

Dennis, Matthew. *Cultivating a Landscape of Peace: Iroquois-European Encounters in Seventeenth-Century America.* Ithaca, N.Y.: Cornell University Press, 1993.

Harrod, Howard L. *Becoming and Remaining a People: Native American Religions on the Northern Plains.* Tucson: University of Arizona Press, 1995.

Josephy, Alvin M., Jr., ed. *America in 1492: The World of the Indian Peoples before the Arrival of Columbus.* New York: Knopf, 1992.

Lockhart, James. *The Nahuas after the Conquest: A Social and Cultural History of the Indians of Central Mexico, Sixteenth through Eighteenth Centuries.* Stanford: Stanford University Press, 1992.

Martin, Joel W. *Sacred Revolt: The Muskogees' Struggle for a New World.* Boston: Beacon Press, 1991.

Stewart, Omer C., and David F. Aberle. *Peyotism in the West.* Salt Lake City: University of Utah Press, 1984.

Sturtevant, William C., ed. *Handbook of North American Indians.* 20 vols. Washington, D.C.: Smithsonian Institution, 1978– .

Nativism

Nativism, the dark underside of nationalism, usually refers to the impulse to exclude immigrant populations from a polity on the grounds that they threaten to undermine civic solidarity. In its broadest sense, the term refers to the hostility of majority populations in the United States and western Europe toward minority groups. The term also has been used to describe movements among indigenous populations to ward off the encroachment of a technologically advanced power—as in the efforts spearheaded by the American Indian leader Tecumseh in the early nineteenth century to form a pan-tribal alliance opposed to the westward expansion of white settlers, or the repudiation of citizenship rights for residents of Chinese, European, and Indian descent by the recently restored indigenous governments of Fiji and New Caledonia. While one might distinguish between ethnocentric prejudice in the first example and anti-imperialist sentiment in the second, both reflect the same fear that alien values will strip traditional structures of meaning and the same desire to preserve those structures at any cost. This discussion focuses on the first phenomenon, nativism as organized xenophobia expressed by members of a politically dominant group.

Historians have described nativism as the expression of many different kinds of conflict generated or exacerbated by the movement of populations. Economic competition, class struggle, intercultural misunderstanding, linguistic confusion, legal formulations, and other social shifts all have been credited with fomenting nativist sentiment. Although it is generally underemphasized in the literature, religion also may play a crucial role in the dynamics of intergroup hostility. Religion has been instrumental both in defining an immigrant group as alien and in providing a rationale—or even a mandate—for discrimination.

Religion and Xenophobia

In the United States and elsewhere, religious convictions have provided much of the foundation for nativist sentiment. Opposition to Irish immigration in the pre–Civil War period (1815–1860), for example, was expressed in diatribes against the evils of Roman Catholicism, and semipornographic texts such as the perennially popular *The Awful Disclosures of the Hotel Dieu Nunnery by "Maria Monk"* (1836) portrayed nuns as unwilling slaves to clerical lusts.

In 1915 a former circuit-riding minister who took religious commitments very seriously revived the Ku Klux Klan as a nativist fraternity. As the self-appointed defenders of white Protestant womanhood, Klansmen believed they had to don the armor of righteousness; church attendance was compulsory. In the 1920s automobile magnate Henry Ford assailed Jewish immigrants by reprinting the spurious *Protocols of the Elders of Zion* and other works of conspiratorial anti-Semitism. More recently, Arab Americans have been methodically harassed on the untenable grounds that Islam is a fanatical faith. The outlook of many nativists is captured in the pointed slogan of one white supremacist organization: "God is a racist."

Some observers may dismiss these examples as simply recurrent manifestations of deeply rooted patterns of religious prejudice. After all, modern anti-Catholic writings have drawn on rhetoric coined during the Reformation (the sixteenth-century movement against the Catholic Church that led to the establishment of Protestantism), and unflattering characterizations of Muslims and Jews have an even more venerable lineage in the Christian West. Nevertheless, religious identity is so central to nativist ideology that it merits further explication.

Nativists do not object to all forms of immigration equally. Religious identity is vital to the process by which nativists characterize one group and not another as alien. In the late nineteenth century, for example, American xenophobes rose in protest to immigration by Jews and Catholics from southern and eastern Europe but did not object to arrivals from such predominantly Protestant countries as England, Germany, or Holland. Today, Europeans identify emigrants from Islamic countries as problematic while accepting those from Christian countries. Because religion is understood to be an essential component of personal identity, nativists may present members of different faiths as irreconcilably deviant. In 1835 an anti-Catholic publication described a convent as "wholly *foreign;* having been founded, in 1820, by two *foreigners,* who imported four Ursuline *foreigners* into this country [with] *foreign money."* The echoing use of *foreign* suggested that not only were Catholics fundamentally alien, unassimilable, and insular but also that they represented a palpable political threat.

The danger presented by religious outsiders was understood to be not only civic but spiritual. Since the colonial era, Protestant nativists generally have embraced an eschatological interpretation of American history that has admitted no distinction between the theological and the political. In this scheme, America was identified as the New Israel, the site where the Kingdom of God was to be modeled on earth in preparation for the Second Coming of Christ, when humanity would be redeemed. Impediments to the realization of this design were identified as emissaries of Satan. The presence of non-Protestant populations in the United States, then, took on cosmic significance in the battle of the forces of Darkness against the forces of Light.

In the early nineteenth century this dualistic perspective was intensified by the spread of Christian perfectionism, the belief articulated by John Wesley, the founder of Methodism, that individuals who adopted a lifestyle of personal holiness could be purified from sin, sanctified, and restored to God. Perfectionism provided evangelical Protestants with a political mandate—if the individual could be perfected, then so could the entire society. By portraying evil as an externalized force, radical perfectionism also lay the groundwork for a politics of demonization. Although Christian perfectionism gave rise to numerous progressive reform initiatives in the early nineteenth century (among them, the movements to abolish slavery and to grant women equal rights), this theology also engendered many nativist movements, including that peculiar amalgam of nondenominational Protestantism, Anglo-Saxon mythography, racism, and anti-Semitism known as "Christian Identity."

Nativism in U.S. History

The earliest recruitment pamphlets for emigration to America—Richard Hakluyt's *Discourse of Western Planting* (1584), for example—explained the role British settlements in America would play as necessary bulwarks against the growth of Catholic power. And in the seventeenth century when Puritans conceived their model state, the "City upon a Hill," they imagined it to be free of the "Romish corruptions" that marked religious practice in the Old World. In the colonies Catholics were not imprisoned for their beliefs as they had been in England, but throughout the colonial era they were prohibited from celebrating Mass, denied voting rights, barred from public office, and widely slandered. In the seventeenth century "papists" were so vilified that even clergyman Roger Williams (1603–1683), the champion of religious freedom, was moved to intolerance; his writings are suffused with the same vivid anti-Catholic rhetoric that echoed throughout the colonial period.

After the War of Independence (1775–1783), American political leaders drafted a Constitution and a Bill of Rights, finally ratified in 1791, that guaranteed religious liberty but could not mandate religious toleration. Although Anglo-Americans soon ceased to burn effigies of the pontiff at Pope Day festivals, many retained the old Protestant dread of the "Romish Church." Agnostics cited the English philosopher John Locke (1632–1704), one of the founders of modern liberal theory, who asserted that Catholics' fealty to the pope made them untrustworthy participants in a democratic polity. In 1798, to ward off the threat of insurgency from French Catholics and Bavarian Illuminati, Congress passed the Alien and Sedition Acts, which required immigrants to wait fourteen years before naturalization and authorized the deportation of resident aliens deemed "dangerous to the peace and safety of the United States." Although the acts were undermined once the Federalist Party lost its footing in 1800, they were periodically resurrected, particularly during wartime.

With the influx of Irish immigrants after 1830, American nativism entered a new phase. Ireland contributed over 41 percent of the more than four million immigrants who entered the United States between 1831 and 1855; demagogues compared it to an invasion. Tracts by Protestant clergymen and polemicists such as William C. Brownlee, Lyman Beecher, and Samuel F. B. Morse charged the pope with attempting to conquer the United States. Exposés of convent life purportedly by ex-nuns became bestsellers. In 1834 a convent in Charlestown, Massachusetts, was burned, violence erupted across the country, and job applicants were told that "No Irish need apply." The Native American Democratic Association, organized in 1835 to address the immigrant problem, met with little success. But later ventures were more successful. The American Party ("Know-Nothings"), founded in 1844 as a fraternal order and dedicated to excluding Catholics and foreigners from political office, had become a major political force by 1855, when more than one hundred of its members were elected to Congress. A poor showing in the presidential race of 1856 and the advent of the Civil War in 1861 put an end to the party but not to political expressions of xenophobia.

In the 1870s disaffected laborers in California protested the arrival of Chinese immigrants, who were willing to work in mining and construction projects at reduced wages. As anti-Asian violence spread throughout the West, Congress passed a statute in 1882 banning immigration from China; the law was renewed in 1892 and 1902. Negotiating with Japan to exclude further immigration from that country, President Theodore Roosevelt effectively put an end to the "Yellow Peril" in 1907.

While menacing Orientals continued to dominate the pages of popular adventure fiction, political nativists shifted their attention in the last decades of the nineteenth century to the legions of "new immigrants" from southern and eastern Europe who were arriving in record numbers. Between 1880 and 1924, the year the National Origins Act imposed country-specific ceilings on immigration, 27 million people emigrated to the United States. Even sympathetic observers characterized these new arrivals in unflattering terms. In her poem "The New Colossus" (1883), which adorns the Statue of Liberty in New York Harbor, Emma Lazarus welcomed "the wretched refuse of [the Old World's] teeming shore." Many of Lazarus's contemporaries were less enthusiastic about the arrival of these tired, poor "huddled masses yearning to breathe free." Prominent journalists, educators, clergy, and statesmen, including Presidents Theodore Roosevelt and Woodrow Wilson, propounded a pernicious theory that predicted the pollution of the Anglo-Saxon race and the dissolution of national unity by these aliens who were, in the words of nativist author Lothrop Stoddard, "American citizens but not American."

This anti-alien rhetoric had widespread repercussions, affecting policies at all levels of society, from hiring practices to wildlife management. The most visible fruits of resurgent nativism, however, were the new "patriotic" leagues that sought to purge America of Catholic, Semitic, and radical elements. The American Protective Association, founded in 1887, was the first such organization to gain national recognition since the demise of the Know-Nothing Party thirty years earlier. Stridently anti-Catholic, the American Protective Association attracted 2.5 million members before its dissolution in 1896. Over the next fifty years, scores of similar groups rose and fell—the United American Mechanics, the Daughters of Liberty, the United Order of Pilgrim Fathers, and many others. The largest and most notorious of these nativist fraternities was the Ku Klux Klan, which in its second incarnation (1915–1928) harassed Jews and Catholics as well as blacks. The collapse of the Ku Klux Klan enabled other nativist leaders to rise to prominence. In the 1930s demagogues such as Gerald L. K. Smith, William Dudley Pelley, and Gerald Winrod labored to advance the cause of fascism. Their contemporary, Father Charles E. Coughlin, pastor of the Shrine of the Little Flower in Royal Oak, Michigan, became famous for his weekly broadcasts extolling the Nazis and attacking Jews and communists. The anti-Semitic cast to much of the agitation against radicalism before World War II, including the Red Scare of 1919–1920, stemmed from the widespread belief that Bolshevism was a Jewish conspiracy for world domination.

Many historians suggest the importance of World War II (1939–1945) as a turning point in American pluralism; government propaganda, military experience, and popular books and movies all emphasized that ethnic identity was not incompatible with patriotism. Even Japanese Americans, interned during the war, were swiftly reincorporated into the national polity. But nativistic sentiments persisted in the postwar era. In a best-selling book first published in 1955, Paul Blanshard asserted that "Catholic Power" posed an imminent danger to "American Freedom." And in 1960 opponents of Catholic presidential candidate John F. Kennedy rehearsed many of the same arguments that had been directed against Catholic candidate Alfred E. Smith in the presidential campaign of 1928.

Anti-Semitism also continued to find popular expression: a 1946 opinion poll found 55 percent of Americans attesting that Jews had too much power in the United States; forty years later a Harris poll revealed that 27 percent of Americans believed farmers were exploited by "international Jewish bankers." And there were new demons: during the cold war Americans of Eastern European descent were suspected of being worshippers at the "godless altars" of communism. Since the 1978–1979 Iranian revolution, Arabs have been the targets of widespread animosity, expressed less in government policy than in popular media portrayals of Muslims as evil zealots. And Hispanic Americans have borne the onus of exaggerated concerns about the economic threats of illegal immigration.

Although violent opposition to supposedly un-American populations is restricted today to small groups at the margins of society, such as Aryan and militia organizations, contemporary nativists continue to launch widespread political movements that seek to limit participation in democratic processes—the drive to define English as the official language of the United States, for example.

The Global Context

Although nativism is usually referred to as a North American phenomenon, religiously informed xenophobia has found organized expression in every country that sponsors a nationalist movement. Outside the United States, however, identifying the subject of nativism becomes more complicated. One may easily use the term to label the anti-immigration movements of western Europe. But elsewhere the line between nativism and ethnocentrism may be extremely thin. Present-day Serbian aggression in Bosnia, for example, is predicated on a nationalist myth that labels Muslims as intruders, despite the fact that the legacy of each group in the Balkans is equally venerable. Pogroms against Jews and gypsies in eastern Europe, the extermination of Armenians by the Turks, the expulsion of Palestinians by Israeli extremists, anti-Bengali agitation in the Indian state of Assam—these are a few of the many examples that might be included in an expansive catalogue of nativism.

Defined more narrowly as a reaction against recent or continuing immigration, nativism is most clearly evidenced in western Europe, where the influx of people who once were defined as colonial subjects has evoked strong opposition. French Muslims were systematically harassed during Algeria's war for independence (1954–1962), with these *ratonnades* (rat hunts) culminating in the Paris riots of 1961. As immigration rates continued to rise in the 1970s and 1980s, anti-alien agitation escalated dramatically. In a 1989 poll between 11 and 14 percent of the population of the European Community affirmed xenophobic attitudes. The restrictionist platforms of right-wing political parties—including the

Austrian Freedom Party *(Freiheitliche Partei Österreichs,)* Flemish Bloc *(Vlaams Blok)* in Belgium, National Front in England, *Front National* in France, Republicans *(Die Republikaner)* in Germany, National Alliance *(Alleanza Nazionale)* in Italy, Center Democrats *(Centrumdemocraten)* in the Netherlands, and New Democracy *(Ny Demokrati)* in Sweden—have garnered increasing levels of success. Populist demagogues in Europe have been joined by neo-Nazi groups and loosely organized gangs of disaffected youths ("skinheads") who see themselves as heirs to a prewar fascist legacy. The racial and religious foundations of European nativism are underscored by the fact that attacks have not been on resident aliens from the United States, Australia, or New Zealand but on laborers and refugees from Turkey, the Maghrib (Morocco, Algeria, and Tunisia), and other parts of Asia and Africa.

Outside North America and Europe, the country whose nativist traditions have been most thoroughly analyzed is Japan. During the earliest years of the Tokugawa period (1603–1867), intellectuals cultivated the notion of a unique and sacred Japanese identity. Based on the exegesis of classical texts, the movement for national learning *(kokugaku)* soon acquired religious and political overtones. The influential scholar Hirata Atsutane developed a Shintoist theology that promised eternal rewards to those who served the divine will; his students located divinity in the figure of the emperor and spearheaded the imperial restoration movement that saw an end to the Tokugawa shogunate. Other intellectuals identified a religious mandate for isolationism. Touting the xenophobic slogan "Revere the emperor, expel the barbarians," the scholar Aizawa Seishisai argued that the preservation of Japanese sovereignty was predicated on the repulsion of foreign influences, including Christianity and Islam. As these views were extended during the Meiji period (1868–1912), ideologues developed the concept of a national polity or essence *(kokutai),* which was embodied in the figure of the emperor. This provided the basis for the transcendent ultranationalism of the decades immediately preceding World War II. Nativist rhetoric has been muted in the postwar period, but notions of Japanese cultural superiority still find expression and have led to the maltreatment of resident minorities from Korea and the abuse of laborers from Bangladesh, Pakistan, and the Philippines.

Religion and Tolerance

Although religion often has fostered xenophobic sentiments, it also has served as a foundation for efforts to promote tolerance and diversity. If the deity of the nativists is the God of judgment, then that of the antinativists is the God of love. In his *Bloudy Tenent of Persecution* (1644), Roger Williams presented powerful arguments for the preservation of religious freedom and the separation of church and state that have been echoed by religious liberals ever since. In 1893 the World's Parliament of Religions presented a well-publicized model of universal harmony. And in the twentieth century a series of worldwide ecumenical conferences, as well as the Second Vatican Council (1962–1965), sought to eradicate old animosities through constructive dialogue.

In the United States a number of interreligious organizations were established to combat the new nativism—among them, the Anti-Defamation League of B'nai B'rith (established in 1913) and the National Conference for Community and Justice (originally the National Conference of Christians and Jews, founded in 1927). A series of monographs published in the 1950s, most notably Will Herberg's influential *Protestant–Catholic–Jew* (1955), promoted the idea that Americans of all stripes are characterized by a broad spiritual consensus in their devotion to a common way of life. The "melting pot" model propounded by these scholars did not prove attractive to people who wished to maintain a sense of ethnic distinctiveness. In recent years religious liberals have moved away from this assimilationist ideal in favor of one that not only acknowledges pluralism but celebrates it.

See also *Anti-Semitism; Ethnicity; Fascism; Genocide and "ethnic cleansing"; Nationalism; Pluralism; Traditionalism.*

Bradford Verter

BIBLIOGRAPHY

Barkun, Michael. *Religion and the Racist Right: The Origins of the Christian Identity Movement.* 2d ed. Chapel Hill: University of North Carolina Press, 1995.

Bennett, David H. *The Party of Fear: From Nativist Movements to the New Right in American History.* New York: Vintage Press, 1990.

Bjørgo, Tore, ed. "Terror from the Extreme Right." Special issue of *Terrorism and Political Violence* 7 (spring 1995): 1–300.

Franchot, Jenny. *Roads to Rome: The Antebellum Protestant Encounter with Catholicism.* Berkeley: University of California Press, 1994.

Harootunian, H. D. *Things Seen and Unseen: Discourse and Ideology in Tokugawa Nativism.* Chicago: University of Chicago Press, 1988.

Higham, John. *Strangers in the Land: Patterns of American Nativism, 1860–1925.* 2d ed. New York: Atheneum, 1963.

Horowitz, Donald L. *Ethnic Groups in Conflict.* Berkeley: University of California Press, 1985.

Perea, Juan F., ed. *Immigrants Out! The New Nativism and the Anti-Immigrant Impulse in the United States.* New York: New York University Press, 1997.

Ribuffo, Leo. *The Old Christian Right. The Protestant Far Right from Depression to Cold War.* Philadelphia: Temple University Press, 1983.
Takaki, Ronald. *Iron Cages: Race and Culture in Nineteenth-century America.* New York: Oxford University Press, 1990.

Natural Law

Natural law is a moral theory about the principles that underlie the duties and rights of free human persons; it also serves as moral grounding for human behavior. The concept is based on two key ideas: first, that the origins of human morality lie in a description of what human persons are by nature, and, second, that this moral law is discoverable by the light of human reason alone. Natural law is not an external law or a system of laws so much as an internal law. Indeed, it can be more accurately described as "the logic of law."

The theme of natural law as an almost instinctive moral law governing all human activity was formulated by the Greek philosopher Aristotle three centuries before the Christian era and developed in philosophical terms in early Christian centuries by the Stoics, members of a Greek school of philosophy founded by Zeno of Citium about 308 B.C. In the second century A.D., the Greek theologian St. Justin the Martyr took up the Stoic idea and developed it in connection with theological concepts, as St. Thomas Aquinas, the Italian theologian and philosopher, was to do in the thirteenth century in a detailed moral theory.

In the period immediately following the sixteenth-century Reformation, jurists Hugo Grotius of Holland and Samuel von Pufendorf of Germany, as well as English philosopher John Locke, stoutly defended a liberal interpretation of natural law in a formulation of the theory whose force was independent of notions of sin. Even Christian authors who claimed that natural law theory must presuppose the existence of God lay stress on the metaphysical aspect of natural law, as well as on the fact that the principles are self-evident and not dependent on divine Revelation.

Already in the thirteenth century, Aquinas had moved this rather general, abstract moral theory closer to the realities of day-to-day moral decision making by formulating intermediate moral foundations. He broke down the general idea of human nature into three basic and specific moral dynamisms. The first: resist destruction and continue in existence. From this it is possible to deduce the moral duty of respect for human life, caring for human health, and creating the conditions for the flourishing of human welfare and well-being. In connection with this dynamism and the principles deduced from it, one can analyze detailed matters of medicine, ecology, and bioethics. The moral grounding of smoking, drugs, driving under the influence of alcohol, human cloning, and "green" questions concerning the environment, for example, are implications of this dimension of natural law.

The second dynamism is one shared with all members of the animal kingdom: ensure the survival of the species. It serves as the foundation of moral principles used by some religious bodies to direct all sexual behavior. Sexual actions judged to block natural and essential human outcomes are to be classified as unethical. Understandings of this kind led in the twentieth century to controversies on matters such as contraception, abortion, and homosexuality.

In human persons there is a third and distinctive dynamism connected with rationality and human speech: seek the truth and foster life in community. Detailed applications of principles in this area would extend not simply to speaking the truth in day-to-day matters but to truthful dealings in insurance, financial markets, public policy, and political affairs. Matters of fraud, the need for transparency in organizations, and freedom of information are all included in this dynamism.

The theory of natural law, therefore, can be taken beyond the first principle of practical reasoning that "good is to be done and bad to be avoided" and extended to provide for positive fuller human fulfillment. It operates at three levels: first, to govern individual conduct; second, to govern communal life in terms of solidarity; and, third, to govern the institutional frameworks that create the conditions for human flourishing. Natural law theory, then, embraces personal and structural morality.

Two objections often are advanced against natural law theory. The first is that the theory is procedurally unsound in deriving "ought" from "is." The second is that the theory is ahistorical in the sense that it rests on a traditional concept of an unchanging and universal human nature; it should give way to some form of "situation ethic" that takes account of human existence as it actually is in all its experience and historical diversity. This, it is claimed, would overcome the unvarying and absolutist tendencies that have accompanied natural law as a moral theory.

Several present-day scholars—among them Germain

Grisez, John Finnis, and Bruce Renton—argue cogently that many criticisms of natural law theory result from an ignorance of the classical texts and from important twentieth-century developments in the study of natural law. At the simplest level, the replacement of the term *human nature* by the more psychologically grounded *human person* as the basic criterion for a reasoned morality has allowed the development of richer, more nuanced applications of moral principles to conditions of modernity. So also the classification of eight or nine "modes of responsibility" or "requirements of practical reasonableness," as suggested by Grisez and Finnis, has helped to reconstruct the ancient theory of natural law in ways appropriate to the solution of contemporary ethical and moral problems.

Francis P. McHugh

BIBLIOGRAPHY

Crowe, M. B. *The Changing Profile of Natural Law.* The Hague: Martinus Nijhoff, 1977.

Finnis, John. *Natural Law and Natural Rights.* Oxford: Clarendon Press, 1980.

Grisez, Germain. *The Way of the Lord Jesus.* Chicago: Franciscan Herald Press, 1983.

O'Connell, T. E. *Principles for Catholic Morality.* San Francisco: Harper and Row, 1990.

Renton, Bruce. "Finnis on Natural Law." *Kingston Law Review* 2 (April 1981): 30–68.

Netherlands

See *Low Countries*

New religious movements

See *Cults*

Nhat Hanh, Thich

Zen Buddhist monk, writer, poet, and champion of nonviolent Buddhist activism. Born in central Vietnam, Thich

Thich Nhat Hanh

Nhat Hanh (1926–) joined the Buddhist monkhood in 1942 at age sixteen. On becoming a full monk at age twenty, he assumed the religious title of *thich.*

In 1950 Nhat Hanh became associated with the An Quang pagoda in Saigon, the center of an activist Buddhist movement. The movement was viewed with suspicion by Ngo Dinh Diem, a Roman Catholic who became president of the Republic of Vietnam (South Vietnam) in 1954, when international agreements led to the establishment of two independent Vietnamese states. The popular support for the Buddhist movement, however, contributed significantly to bringing down the Diem government in 1963.

At the time of Diem's assassination in 1963, Nhat Hanh was in the United States where, since 1961, he had been studying and teaching. In 1963 he returned to Vietnam and soon became a leader in a Buddhist-led movement that sought to promote through nonviolent protests a "third way" in what had become a war between the anticommunist government of South Vietnam and the communist government of North Vietnam. But Nhat Hanh's "engaged Buddhism" and advocacy of reconciliation were condemned by both sides, and his writings were censored in both countries. Undeterred, the Buddhist monk extended his activism beyond the political arena. In 1964 he founded the School of Youth for Social Services, which sent people into the countryside to set up health clinics and schools and, later, to rebuild bombed villages.

By the mid-1960s Nhat Hanh had become well known both outside and inside Vietnam as a peace activist whose moral stance was based on Buddhism. In a meeting with Pope Paul VI in 1966 he urged Catholics and Buddhists to work together to seek peace and reconciliation in Vietnam. In 1967 American civil rights leader and friend Martin Luther King Jr. nominated Nhat Hanh for the Nobel Peace Prize. And when negotiations aimed at ending the Vietnam conflict began in Paris in 1969, Nhat Hanh organized and led a Buddhist delegation to the talks.

Both sides in Vietnam, however, continued to view the activist monk as a threat. In 1973 while outside the country, Nhat Hanh was denied permission by the government of South Vietnam to return home. Thus he was outside Vietnam in 1975 when the Republic of Vietnam was conquered by communist forces (and the present-day communist government of a united Vietnam continues to ban him from the country).

Nhat Hanh took refuge in France, but he remained engaged. In 1976–1977 he led efforts to rescue the men, women, and children fleeing southern Vietnam—the "boat people"—who, in overcrowded vessels, were in danger of drowning or at risk of attack by pirates.

In 1982 Nhat Hanh founded a Buddhist meditative community in southern France called Plum Village. This community attracts activists from around the world who are seeking a place for spiritual renewal. Nhat Hanh draws on Zen Buddhism in accentuating the importance of "mindfulness," which entails making oneself fully aware of one's body and surroundings. Through mindfulness, he teaches, one is able to engage the world without succumbing to worldly desires. Although a Buddhist, Nhat Hanh also draws on the moral and spiritual teachings of other religions.

In addition to his work at Plum Village, Nhat Hanh travels outside France to encourage others to embrace "engaged Buddhism." During his visits to the United States at least every other year, he leads retreats and gives lectures on the principles of mindful living. Indeed, Nhat Hanh is widely considered to be a holy person who serves as an exemplar for those who link the cultivation of spirituality with moral engagement in the world to effect social and political change.

See also *Vietnam*.

Charles F. Keyes

BIBLIOGRAPHY

Cao, Ngoc Phuong. *Learning True Love: How I Learned and Practiced Social Change in Vietnam*. Berkeley, Calif.: Parallax Press, 1993.

Nhat Hanh, Thich. *Love in Action: Writings on Nonviolent Social Change*. Berkeley, Calif.: Parallax Press, 1993.

———. *Vietnam: Lotus in a Sea of Fire*. New York: Hill and Wang, 1967.

Niebuhr, Reinhold

American clergyman and theologian known for the doctrine of Christian realism. In the middle third of the twentieth century, Niebuhr (1892–1971) was the most influential public theologian in the United States. A spellbinding speaker, an original religious thinker, and an indefatigable political journalist and organizer, he modeled in his life what he maintained in his thought: unless one was called to a path of saintly asceticism, religious belief led necessarily to political commitment. At its best religion stood in a paradoxical relation to politics: it gave politics an indispensable transformative power while also subjecting politics to constant "prophetic" criticism. The self-sacrificial love *(agape)* preached by Jesus was the standard by which worldly justice was to be measured. Having come of age in the political conflicts of the 1920s and 1930s, when many intellectuals joined socialist and communist parties, Niebuhr concluded that, although the quest for justice always needed a religious spark, it also required religious restraint lest it careen into one or another form of fanaticism.

Born in Missouri, Niebuhr was raised in the German Evangelical Synod of America, a heavily midwestern immigrant denomination of which his father was a liberal-leaning minister. Even before studying at Yale Divinity School, Niebuhr had embraced the liberal gospel according to which the law of love was in principle applicable to all of human affairs, social as well as individual. Liberals believed that love, if preached steadfastly, would spread like a contagion and ultimately vanquish selfishness throughout society. They trumpeted cooperation not only as end but as means. Yet Niebuhr's experience as a preacher in Detroit, Michigan, between 1915 and 1928—in which he did battle with such formidable opponents as the Ku Klux Klan, Henry Ford, and pacifists and isolationists sickened by World War I—persuaded him that the liberal understanding of love was flawed.

In his classic volume *Moral Man and Immoral Society*

Reinhold Niebuhr

(1932), Niebuhr contended that once individuals entered the social arena they were in the realm of power, not of love, and the means they chose in the pursuit of justice should be judged not only by the standard of love but by their potency in resisting evil. Liberals, Niebuhr thought, were poorly equipped to stand up for either justice or for love because they could not grasp the place of power in human affairs. They mistakenly thought that love was the power to trump all others, and that in the long run love was the state of fellowship in which calculations of justice would certainly be superfluous. In this utopian dream they resembled the Marxists with whom they often allied themselves during the ideological wars of the 1930s and 1940s. Where the liberals shared the Marxists' hope for a final historical stage of peaceful harmony, Niebuhr shared their realism about power. Indeed, much of his authority as public theologian at midcentury derived from his aura of being as realistic as the communists about power without embracing their alleged fanaticism.

Niebuhr's mature work *The Nature and Destiny of Man* (1941, 1943) insisted that, although liberal professions of love were indeed worthless without concrete political fights for justice, so quests for justice were futile without concrete acts of self-sacrificial love. Love was a lived experience in religious and secular communities, and lasting justice depended on the uncompromising militance of those who loved God and neighbor alike. Niebuhr's lifelong thinking about love and justice exercised a profound effect on later thinkers and activists, among them Martin Luther King Jr.

See also *King, Martin Luther, Jr.; Public theology; Social Gospel.*

Richard Wightman Fox

BIBLIOGRAPHY

Fox, Richard Wightman. *Reinhold Niebuhr: A Biography.* Ithaca, N.Y.: Cornell University Press, 1996 [1985].

Kegley, Charles W., ed. *Reinhold Niebuhr: His Religious, Social, and Political Thought.* Rev. ed. New York: Pilgrim Press, 1984.

Lasch, Christopher. *The True and Only Heaven: Progress and Its Critics.* New York: Norton, 1991.

Lovin, Robin W. *Reinhold Niebuhr and Christian Realism.* Cambridge: Cambridge University Press, 1995.

Meyer, Donald. *The Protestant Search for Political Realism, 1919–1941.* Hanover: University Press of New England, 1988 [1960].

Nietzsche, Friedrich Wilhelm

Nineteenth-century German philosopher. Nietzsche (1844–1900) is one of the most controversial and influential figures in modern philosophy. Yet he never held an academic appointment in philosophy, and poor health ended his initially brilliant but brief academic career, as a professor of classical philology at Basel, Switzerland, in his mid-thirties. He spent the next ten years in boarding houses in Switzerland and Italy, before suffering a physical and mental collapse in 1889, from which he never recovered.

Nietzsche was born in the village of Röcken in Saxony. The son of a Lutheran pastor (who died when he was four), he came of age during the unification and rise of Germany under Otto von Bismarck. He repudiated both origins, becoming a vehement critic of the Christianity and the Germany of his time. A champion of the artistic, literary, and intellectual achievements of Western culture at its best, he was passionately critical of much in that culture, which he took to be decadent, mediocre, and detrimental to the enhancement of human life. Calling for a "revaluation of all values" and a naturalistic reinterpretation of ourselves and our lives that would be "beyond good and evil," he sought to inaugurate a philosophy that would be capable of showing the way beyond the nihilism he foretold as the inevitable and potentially disastrous outcome of what he called "the death of God." By this he meant both the cultural demise and the in-

Friedrich Wilhelm Nietzsche

tellectual bankruptcy of belief in anything like the Christian god.

Nietzsche is commonly taken to have been unqualifiedly hostile to both morality and religion. In fact, his hostility focused on their most familiar and common forms. In styling himself an "immoralist," he took as his target the kind of morality that would legislate categorically for all, heedless of human differences, and that employed concepts of good and evil fleshed out in ways detrimental to human flourishing. Similarly, his attack on Christianity, in *The Antichrist* (1895) and elsewhere and on the Judaism that set the stage for it, was directed primarily at certain prevalent forms of both religions, less for the absurdity of their theologies than for their detrimental effect on the vitality and quality of human life.

Nietzsche deemed all forms of otherworldly religion (and metaphysics) to be untenable and ill motivated, reflecting dissatisfactions, resentments, and wishful thinking compounded by intellectual shortcomings. He took a more positive view of religions (and moralities) conceived and developed as value systems that contribute to human efforts to come to terms with life. In *Thus Spoke Zarathustra* (1883–1892), he invoked the possibility of a kind of ecstatically naturalistic religious attitude celebrating the creative-destructive phenomenon of life and its enhancement. It was symbolized by the idea of the *Übermensch* ("overman"), representing the endowment of life with meaning through its creative enhancement.

Nietzsche's hostility to democracy and socialism alike, together with his fondness for the language of warfare and domination, his celebration of "higher" exceptions to the human rule, and his contempt for the human "herd" all are commonly taken to show that his politics were either reactionary or an anticipation of fascism. But his hostility to democracy and socialism arose from what he regarded as their leveling and pandering tendencies, and his elitism reflected his conviction that all human excellence is at once rare and the key to rendering human life worthy of affirmation.

Nietzsche well understood the cultural (and therefore social and institutional) character of all forms of human excellence, as well as the threats posed to them by other dynamics of social and psychological life. He envisioned a "great politics" revolving around the fundamental question of how societies might best be arranged (or rearranged) to promote the enrichment of human life in this larger context. It is one of the sad ironies of his intellectual legacy that the political caricature associating him with his fascist admirers has long obscured his antipathy to everything they represented.

Richard Schacht

BIBLIOGRAPHY

Bergmann, Peter. *Nietzsche: "The Last Antipolitical German."* Bloomington: Indiana University Press, 1987.

Hayman, Ronald. *Nietzsche: A Critical Life.* Oxford: Oxford University Press, 1980.

Kaufmann, Walter. *Nietzsche: Philosopher, Psychologist, Antichrist.* 4th ed. Princeton: Princeton University Press, 1974.

Schacht, Richard. *Nietzsche.* London: Routledge, 1983.

Warren, Mark. *Nietzsche and Political Thought.* Cambridge: MIT Press, 1988.

Nigeria

The multireligious Federal Republic of Nigeria, located on the coast of western Africa, is the most populous of African states, with about 110 million people. The capital of the federation of thirty-six states is Abuja, in central Nigeria. Approximately 50 percent of the people are Muslim (primarily Sunni), 40 percent are Christian, and 10 percent are explicitly "traditional." There are more than two hundred ethnic groups; the major ones are the Hausa and Fulani in the north, the Yoruba in the southwest, and the Igbo in the east. Nigeria became a British colony in the late nineteenth century and gained its independence in 1960.

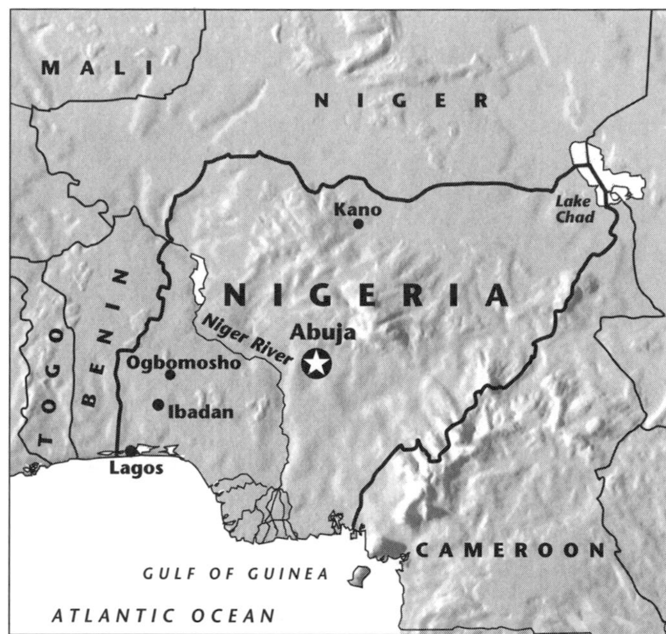

The Muslims

The three predominant Muslim areas in Nigeria are the "emirate states" (that is, states with a symbolic Islamic ruler, or emir) in the northwest; the historic Borno state in the northeast, which includes one of the oldest Islamic communities in sub-Saharan Africa, dating from the eleventh century; and certain parts of Yorubaland in the southwest, especially the areas that became Oyo, Ogun, and Lagos states. Lagos and Ibadan, the two largest cities, are major urban bases for Yoruba Muslim populations. All three of these areas are multilingual, although English is the official language of Nigeria. The Hausa language tends to predominate as the lingua franca (the language used in trade and commerce). Other languages include Fulfulde, Yoruba, Nupe, and several minority languages.

Brotherhoods of Sufis (Islamic mystics) evolved throughout the nineteenth and twentieth centuries. In the nineteenth century the Qadiriyya and the Tijaniyya became the two major Sufi brotherhoods in northern Nigeria. During the twentieth century the Tijaniyya spread extensively in Kano, the commercial and industrial capital of the north, and then throughout Nigeria (including Ibadan) and, indeed, throughout western Africa.

Shortly after Nigerian independence in 1960, Shaykh Abubakar Gumi, an outstanding Arabist and legal scholar, was appointed Grand Kadi in northern Nigeria and hence was responsible for the *shari'a* (Islamic law) legal system. A legalist who was against "innovation," that is, development after the time of the Qur'an, Gumi became the teacher of many university-educated young people and many of the civil servants and professionals in northern Nigeria. Among the urban youth of the new towns in the north, especially cities such as Jos and Kaduna without a brotherhood tradition, social organizations and teaching networks developed under the umbrella name of Izala. While some of the Izala groups were directly influenced by Gumi, others set off in their own directions. This led to some confrontations between the Izala and the youth wings of the brotherhoods, especially in Kano, since the Izala condemned the brotherhoods as "innovations." Gumi's translation of the Qur'an into the Hausa language was the basis of a fundamental reassessment or "reformation" within the Muslim community, which now had direct access to holy writ in a vernacular language.

The intellectual reformers—often members of departments of Islamic studies, Arabic studies, or legal studies in the universities—represent both those who refer back directly to the time of the prophet Muhammad (570?–632) and those who refer back to a later period as a source of ideas and values. For the most part, such intellectuals join in debate within an academic setting, but their influence in the media and in political life is considerable.

The antiestablishment syncretists (those who prefer a combination of beliefs) emerged in the late 1970s when the oil boom in Nigeria brought with it the powerful forces of rapid change, urbanization, and modernization. Their "syncretism" was a blend of traditional Hausa folk beliefs and highly selective bits and pieces of the Qur'an. They tended to represent the "dispossessed" newcomers in the urban centers, who saw the Muslim establishment getting richer and more Westernized to the detriment of the poor and non-Western. The most significant of such fringe cults to emerge was led by an itinerant preacher, Muhammad Marwa, also known as Maitatsine, in Kano in the late 1970s. A violent confrontation between his followers, the Yan Tatsine, and the authorities in Kano City occurred in December 1980, with thousands of resulting deaths. Even with the death of Maitatsine in these Kano riots, his followers violently challenged authorities in some parts of the north throughout the 1980s.

The antiestablishment Ikhwan, or "Muslim Brothers," emerged in the late 1980s and early 1990s. This younger generation of semieducated and better-educated youth, finding that they had no employment prospects in the economic austerity of the time, began to challenge the corruption and wealth of the Muslim establishment on Islamic grounds. The leader of the group was Ibrahim El-Zak Zaky, who had graduated in economics from Ahmadu Bello University in Zaria. Because he had received training in Iran and there appeared to be Iranian funding involved, his movement was termed "Shiʿite" by the larger Nigerian community, an attempt to marginalize his influence. Throughout the 1990s there were clashes between the Ikhwan and the authorities, culminating in the arrest of Ibrahim on September 13, 1996, in Zaria. Subsequently, his followers protested in Zaria and Kaduna, and about forty were killed in direct clashes with the police. In February 1997, at the end of the sacred month of Ramadan (the ninth month in the Islamic year), several of the followers tried to take over the central mosque in Kano and were killed in the resultant clash with police. The exact nature of this "Shiʿite" movement remains obscure, but the antiestablishment challenge is clear.

The early Muslim ecumenical movement of the 1960s in Nigeria was extended to a national arena, mainly through the vehicle of the Nigerian Supreme Council for Islamic Affairs (NSCIA), established in 1974. The head of the NSCIA was the sultan of Sokoto; the vice president was the *shehu* (a religious and political leader) of Borno; and the secretary-general was a leading Yoruba Muslim lawyer. The vice presidents are drawn from all thirty-six states and include distinguished emirs and other Muslim notables. The NSCIA has regular meetings bringing Muslim leaders from all states of the federation to deliberate on matters of common interest. At the international level, the council maintains close links with counterparts in other countries and cosponsors the Islamic Council in London. The NSCIA cosponsored the Islam in Africa conference in 1989, which resolved to establish Islam in Africa organizations with headquarters in Abuja, the federal capital.

In 1987 the federal government established a National Council for Religious Affairs (NCRA). In modified form this council ultimately came to have twelve Christian and twelve Muslim leaders, who were supposed to discuss matters of mutual concern and report directly to the Ministry of Interior. In practice the NSCIA represented the Muslims, and the Christian Association of Nigeria (CAN) represented the Christians. After a period of deadlock in the council, the Christian leaders stopped attending, and the NCRA became moribund.

A second Muslim umbrella organization, similar to the NSCIA, is the Federation of Muslim Women's Associations in Nigeria (FOMWAN). In the mid-1980s Muslim women began to feel more clearly the effect of the spread of education. As a result of such education many women developed a more Western attitude. Some Muslim women participated in organizations such as Women in Nigeria. Others began to reclaim their own sense of Muslim identity, and the Muslim Sisters Organization was established in Kano. Later, FOMWAN was established to give coherence to Muslim women's organizations throughout Nigeria. FOMWAN focused on the need to counteract the role of "custom" in Nigerian Muslim societies. By the early 1990s FOMWAN included about four hundred member organizations throughout Nigeria, but a majority of these members were in the Yoruba-speaking areas. Each state selects representatives to a national committee, which publishes a magazine and holds annual conferences on topics of special concern to Muslim women. The main language of communication is English, and FOMWAN acts as a liaison with other national and international Muslim women's organizations.

The Christians

The Christian Association of Nigeria, organized in the early 1980s, is an uneasy alliance between the mainstream groups (Protestant and Roman Catholic) that have always led CAN and the localized "African" syncretists, evangelicals, and inspirational, or pentecostal, churches. These groups may be divided into two larger clusters: hierarchically organized establishment churches and localized nonestablishment churches.

In the nineteenth century, as a result of the British presence in the port city of Lagos and surrounding Yoruba areas, early forms of mainstream Protestant denominations, especially Anglican and Methodist (plus Scottish Presbyterian), were incorporated into the educated elite culture of southern Nigeria. In the 1980s and 1990s the original "low church" character of Protestantism in Nigeria began to shift to more of a "high church" set of structures and rituals. Hence, Methodists became more like Anglicans in their organization and Anglicans became more like Roman Catholics, perhaps reflecting the general sense of hierarchy in Nigerian social and political (and military) life. The original dominant British influence in Nigeria was partly offset by Roman Catholic priests from Ireland who engaged in missionary work in Nigeria, often through education and health services. The occasional tension between Irish priests and British administrators may mirror the tensions that developed between Igbo and Yoruba communities in the 1950s and 1960s. During this time party coalitions were formed that linked northern Muslims and eastern Roman Catholic Igbos against the predominantly Protestant Yoruba in the west. During the civil war (1967–1970) a realignment took place, in which northern and western Nigerians confronted the secessionist state of Biafra, with its predominant Igbo population and strong ties to the Roman Catholic Church within and outside of Africa. The first sixteen years of CAN leadership came from the Roman Catholic Church, and only in the late 1990s did it shift to the Methodists.

The "African" churches developed from the mainstream Protestant denominations. Some, such as the Aladura, focused on faith healing through prayer. Others were based on a particular vision of the founder. These churches became popular in the Yoruba-speaking areas and are seen by some as blends of Christian beliefs and the rich panorama of Yoruba deities.

There has been a high degree of North American evangelical missionary activity in the middle belt, mainly in the states of Plateau (and later, Nassarawa) and Benue, but including Taraba (formerly southern Gongola) and Kogi (formerly western Kwara). Schools and clinics attracted those residual ethnic populations who had resisted Muslim advances. The Sudan Interior Mission (SIM), based in Toronto, Canada, had extensive facilities in Jos, high on the plateau, where it was cooler than in the rain forest to the south or the savanna zone to the north. Bible literature was translated into local languages, and many local churches began to develop indigenous leadership.

When the government took over all "private" (that is, parochial) schools in 1975 and many expatriate missionaries began to retire, the first generation of indigenous evangelical leaders began to assume control and tried to work out new relationships with the religiously mixed urban authorities. SIM and other groups, such as the Sudan United Mission, reorganized into the Evangelical Church of West Africa (ECWA). Subsequently, the term "ECWA" has been used to describe a wide variety of autonomous evangelical Protestant churches. Because of the opportunities for Western education, many of the middle-belt Christians had a disproportionate representation in institutions of higher education and in the military. Some evangelicals have found themselves in direct confrontation with their evangelical counterparts from the Muslim Izala movements.

The inspirational, or pentecostal, churches most frequently had broken away from the mainstream Protestant churches and drew constituencies from common people, especially in the south. Although there has generally been an attitude of live-and-let-live, tensions have occasionally arisen in the mainstream community over some of the more extreme forms of group therapy or traditional culture represented by the inspirational churches.

With the downturn of the economy in the 1980s and 1990s, pentecostal churches in the south proliferated. Essentially, these nonpolitical churches represent highly personalized forms of prayer worship that are intended to "overcome" personal hardship and facilitate the acquisition of jobs and health care.

Religion and Constitutional Law

The Nigerian state has a mixed constitutional mandate. The 1989 constitution (not expected to change when the 1995 constitution is resolved), on the one hand, guarantees a great deal of religious freedom to Nigerians, including giving citizens the right to "freedom of thought, conscience, and religion" and forbidding both the federal government and the states to adopt any religion as a state religion. On the other hand, it gives state *shariʿa* courts of appeal jurisdiction over civil proceedings in which Islamic law is involved and all the parties are Muslims. In addition, it requires the president of the country to ensure that justices of the Supreme Court and the federal court of appeal include those learned in Islamic law as well as those learned in customary law.

Because of the long experience in Nigeria with colonial rule and military rule, the role of the judiciary in the interpretation of fundamental rights has been uncertain at best. Many of the issues of conflicts of rights or limits of rights have been determined by edict or decree. The limits of unorthodox opinion, especially in religious matters, is a delicate but essential judgment that is made by political leaders, religious leaders, and constitutional lawyers. The general practice in Nigeria is not to use legal services in pursuit of fundamental or religious rights. Rather, grievances are addressed through the political process, even when that process is military rather than civilian. The lack of federal case law is partly the result of the fragility of constitutional order and the high stakes placed on political solutions.

Religion and Electoral Politics

During the first republic (1960–1966) the dominant Northern Peoples' Congress made every effort to find allies among the Christian middle belt factions and ended up with a coalition that included northern Muslims and middle belt and eastern Christians. This coalition faced an alliance of Muslims and Christian Yorubas. The same alliance pattern prevailed in the second republic (1967–1983).

During the election in 1993, which was intended to be a transition to a third republic, the Yoruba-based dominant alliance excluded many of the emirate states and the Christian east. Ironically, the winners in the June 1993 election were a Yoruba Muslim (Moshood Abiola) for president and a Borno Muslim for vice president. Those defeated were a Muslim from Kano and a Christian from the east.

Clearly, electoral politics do not divide along Christian-Muslim lines in Nigeria. To the contrary, every effort has been made, through different combinations of elements, to link coalitions that include both Christians and Muslims. The stated intent of the 1995 constitution was to create a rotational system for the highest federal offices, so that no one zone or region would predominate and cross-zonal and cross-religious coalitions would be mandatory.

Religious and ethnic political parties have been banned in Nigeria since the first republic. Since the civil war of the late 1960s, it has been required that each of the states, and hence religious segments, be represented at the federal executive level. Because the critical swing area—Yorubaland in the southwest—is almost equally divided between Christians and Muslims and because politics tends to revolve around city and state loyalties, the tendency to politicize religion has decreased. Yet whenever there is a political "crisis"—including a military coup—the question of religious balance is a matter of immediate calculation.

Religion and Military Politics

On July 29, 1975, General Murtala Ramat Muhammad emerged as the first Muslim military head of state in Nigeria. He replaced General Yakubu Gowon, a Christian from the middle belt, who in turn had replaced Major General Johnson Aguiyi-Ironsi, an Igbo Christian. On February 13, 1976, Muhammad was assassinated in a failed coup attempt apparently led by Christian middle belt officers. Muhammad was replaced by his next in command, General Olusegun Obasanjo, a Christian Yoruba from Ogun, who, for the next three and a half years (prior to the return to civilian rule in 1979) worked to continue the policies of his predecessor, including the creation of a new federal capital at Abuja. The next-in-command to Obasanjo was Shehu Musa Yar'Adua, a dynamic Muslim personality from Katsina emirate.

The general pattern of top military leadership has usually been a Muslim-Christian or a Christian-Muslim team. Military politics has not been much different from electoral politics on the matter of religious balance, despite some of the prevailing perceptions that Hausa Muslims have dominated top military leadership. The larger issue is whether military leaders, of whatever religious persuasion, are willing to return to the barracks and transfer power to elected civilians. The annulment of the June 1993 election was clearly not an example of religious obstacles, since both Abiola and his opponent were Muslims, but of more complex factors.

The Key to Future Stability

The Muslim establishment in the emirate states, Borno, and Yorubaland, has normally felt comfortable working with its mainstream Christian counterpart. Still, at the grassroots level the highly localized Muslim and Christian groups, often competing for land or jobs or educational opportunity, have found cause to challenge the establishment or to withdraw from worldly affairs into a religious mode. The boom-and-bust cycles of an oil economy have created a rich drama of religious expression based on the hopes and fears of ordinary people. Whether popular discontent will take the form of religious organization remains to be seen. Within the emirate states, a cleavage seems to be forming that may result in confrontation between Muslims, which in turn may affect relations between Muslims and Christians. At the same time, the hard-driving evangelism of some Christian groups, who have made it their mission to convert Muslims, also may prompt a religious confrontation.

The key to stability in Nigeria is the continued pattern of religious balance, within both the military and the political class. Nigeria remains a multireligious (rather than a secular) society, and as such its practical policies and its constitutional guidelines may hold lessons for other religiously plural societies in Africa. The larger issues of democratic rule and human rights will have to take account of the fragile balance of geocultural and religious zones in Nigeria.

See also *Africa, Christian; African traditional religions; Christianity; Evangelicalism; Islam.*

John N. Paden

BIBLIOGRAPHY

Gumi, Sheik Abubakar. *Where I Stand.* Ibadan: Spectrum Books, 1992.

Hackett, Rosalind. "New Religious Movements." In *Religion and Society in Nigeria,* edited by Jacob Opulent and Toying Fall. Ibadan: Spectrum Books, 1991.

Kastfelt, Niels. *Religion and Politics in Nigeria: A Study in Middle Belt Christianity.* London: British Academic Press, 1994.

Kukah, Matthew Hassan. *Religion, Politics, and Power in Northern Nigeria.* Ibadan: Spectrum Books, 1993.

Laitin, David. *Hegemony and Culture: Politics and Religious Change among the Yoruba.* Chicago: University of Chicago Press, 1986.

Ogbu, Kalu. *The Embattled Gods: Christianization of Igboland, 1841–1991.* Lagos Jacob: Minaj Publishers, 1996.

Olupona, Jacob, ed. *Religion and Peace in Multi-Faith Nigeria.* Ife: Obafemi Awolowo University, 1992.

Paden, John. *Ahmadu Bello, Sardauna of Sokoto: Values and Leadership in Nigeria.* London: Hodder and Stoughton, 1986.

———. *Religion and Political Culture in Kano.* Berkeley: University of California Press, 1973.

Sulaiman, Ibrahim. *The Islamic State and the Challenge of History: Ideals, Politics, and Operations of the Sokoto Caliphate.* London: Mansell, 1987.

Nongovernmental organizations

Nongovernmental relief and development organizations sponsored by religious denominations support socioeconomic programs worldwide, especially in the developing nations of the world. The oldest international nongovernmental organizations (NGOs) in Western societies were created by church denominations more than four hundred years ago. Beginning in the sixteenth century, religious orders and congregations from Spain and Portugal sent missionaries and resources to the Americas, East Africa, Southern Asia, and the Far East. In the late eighteenth and early nineteenth centuries new Christian missionary societies were created throughout sub-Saharan Africa and Southeast Asia. American and Canadian Christian missionaries joined them in the same regions by the late nineteenth and early twentieth centuries.

In addition to proselytizing, these organizations carried out a variety of welfare activities. Missionaries often pioneered in modern education, medicine, and surgery in China, Africa, and much of India. The Europeans also received substantial subsidies from their home governments for their religious and social activities because they were considered promoters of Western culture and allies of colonial administrations.

Today many of these same missionary organizations continue to support religious and social activities in Asia, Africa, and Latin America. Of the largest two hundred Western international nongovernmental organizations engaged in relief or development work on these continents, twenty-one are missionary societies founded between 1798 and 1912.

Twentieth-Century Expansion

The number of religiously affiliated and secular NGOs grew in the first half of this century in the wake of devastating wars. World War I, World War II, and the Korean War all stimulated national Red Cross societies in Europe and the United States to expand activities. To aid victims, orphans, and refugees, Christian groups founded new international relief agencies such as American Friends Service Committee (1917), the Mennonite Central Committee (1920), Christian Children's Fund (1938), Catholic Relief Services (1943), Lutheran World Relief (1945), Church World Service (1946), and Adventist Development and Relief Agency (1956).

In the early twentieth century, the U.S. Jewish community also created its own nongovernmental organizations to assist increasing numbers of Jewish migrants to Palestine. The American Jewish Joint Distribution Committee (1914) and the American Federation for Rehabilitation through Training (1922) aided Jewish settlers in self-help projects and, later, gave assistance during the Arab-Israeli war in 1948, when Israel fought for its independence.

Most of these new religiously sponsored relief organizations received U.S. government financial or material assistance because they worked in countries that were allies of the United States. In recent decades they have all expanded their scope to include development activities, and some remain among the largest international NGOs functioning today.

From the 1950s through the 1970s there were several reasons for expanded NGO activities. The cold war competition between East and West for the allegiances of newly independent nations in Africa and Asia, growing demands for economic and social development by leaders in the developing world (often voiced in the United Nations), and the need to find cost-effective conduits of aid to developing countries all created new work for NGOs.

As Europe, the Middle East, and Korea recovered from the aftermath of war in the 1950s, many of the religious relief agencies began to focus on the developing world. In the face of the chronic poverty these agencies found, they expanded their activities to include technical assistance, such as building schools, health clinics, water systems, and prefabricated housing and providing small farmers and business people with training and credit. Many older missionary societies operating in the same countries also expanded their activities to include a development focus rather than a strictly religious-and relief-focus. Some of the European mission societies (long identified with colonial policies) wanted to prove their usefulness (and credibility) to leaders of newly independent nations by contributing to social and economic development.

In the late 1950s and throughout the 1960s churches in Canada and Western Europe created new organizations designed to deliver development rather than relief aid to nations south of the equator. Among the larger religious NGOs founded during these years were the Canadian Catholic Organization for Development and Peace (1967); the (Catholic) Campaign against Hunger and Disease in the World, or MISEREOR (1958), in Germany; the (Protestant) Interchurch Coordination Committee for Development Projects (1964) and the (Catholic) Central Agency for Joint Financing in Development (1969), in the Netherlands; the Catholic Committee against Hunger and for Development (1961), in France; and the Catholic Fund for Overseas Development (1962), in Great Britain. All remain active in overseas development work today.

Of the approximately 3,500 Western NGOs engaged in overseas relief and development in 1990, approximately 326 (almost 10 percent) have a religious affiliation. They account, however, for far more than 10 percent of the overall resource transfers of NGOs to Asia, Africa, and Latin America. In 1981, for example, 65 religiously affiliated NGOs alone (all with annual budgets of more than $1 million) accounted for nearly one-third of all NGO overseas assistance ($1.4 billion of $4.5 billion) that year.

Governments and NGOs in the 1960s and 1970s

By the early 1960s the growing presence of African and Asian nations in the United Nations led to demands in that forum for increased development aid from communist as well as from capitalist countries. Western nations wanted not only to provide aid but also to expand Western influence in these areas to keep them from turning to the Soviet bloc. Western governments also realized that private aid networks operated by religious and secular NGOs could deliver small-scale development assistance more effectively to the citizens in these new nations than government-to-government programs because their overhead costs were low and they worked directly with indigenous private groups at local levels. From the late 1960s on, several governments in Western Europe, as well as in Canada and the United States, began to channel increasing amounts of their own development aid through nongovernmental organizations, including those with a religious affiliation, to target some of their assistance to the grassroots level and to do so in the cheapest way possible.

Some of these governments, such as the United States, were also amassing large amounts of surplus food bought from farmers to keep domestic agricultural prices high. To avoid depressing domestic markets, they looked for opportunities to dispose of this food abroad.

Western governments again turned to NGOs as useful allies for overseas objectives. They gave NGOs increasing amounts of public moneys and food to assist the poor abroad. As a result, by the 1980s significant percentages of the operating budgets of these nongovernmental organizations (including those that were church-related) came from public sources. In the early 1980s, 46 percent of the income ($1.3 billion) of the largest two hundred Western nongovernmental organizations involved in relief or development work came from their home governments.

Although contributions to religious organizations constitute a considerable portion of charitable donations in the United States, most of this money is earmarked for domestic, not international, programs. U.S. private donations to international charities in 1994, for example, amounted to only

$2.2 billion, or 1.7 percent of the total amount of U.S. philanthropy that year. Moreover, the tax laws in Canada and Western Europe have not been as conducive to charitable giving as in the United States, and philanthropy has never been as extensive in these other Western nations.

Consequently, as church-sponsored NGOs expanded their overseas work in the 1960s and 1970s and took on new development tasks, they turned to their home governments for assistance. By the early 1980s some were receiving the preponderant share of their resources from home governments. Others continued to raise most of their support from private citizens, but a significant amount of their resources originated from their governments.

Current Government-NGO Relationships

In the 1980s and early 1990s governments relied on NGOs to build stronger domestic bases for overseas aid in their own countries. With the end of the cold war, cyclical economic recessions, and growing demands for lower taxes, foreign aid programs became harder to justify. Many NGOs in Europe, Canada, and the United States now dedicate substantial amounts of their income (some up to 10 percent) to education programs at home to make donors and the general public more aware of the continuing needs of the poor in developing countries. In the United States NGOs have been vocal supporters of foreign aid, testifying frequently at congressional hearings for continued economic assistance to developing nations. In turn, governments have provided some of the resources to expand NGO development education programs at home, including those run by organizations with a religious affiliation.

In Canada and Europe many NGOs are also working to change home government policies they consider harmful to developing nations—sales of weapons to less developed nations, official aid to repressive regimes, tariff restrictions on imports from developing countries, and immigration quotas. Although NGO advocacy efforts have not yet had a significant effect on governmental policies on these issues, NGOs have kept alternative viewpoints before the public eye and engaged in continuing debate with policymakers.

Governments, in turn, have tried to influence NGO decision making. During the cold war, for example, NGOs in the United States could not use U.S. government subsidies in any country "red marked" because of its communist ideology. In the early 1990s government policymakers were increasingly interested in using NGOs to help open up new markets for U.S. goods abroad by helping them to carry out more commercially oriented programs.

The U.S. Congress since 1986 has insisted that NGOs receiving governmental subsidies must generate at least 20 percent of their income from private sources. European and Canadian governments have provided NGOs with expanded subsidies to be used in regions that are their foreign policy priorities (former colonies, for example) or for specific issues of government concern (AIDS, women in development, support for democracy, refugee assistance). Many Western governments on both sides of the Atlantic have insisted on systematic evaluation of NGO projects abroad to justify continued support for these activities.

Some of the governmental pressures on NGOs clearly will enhance their efficiency, independence, and creativity. The benefits are more professional evaluation of overseas activities, greater reliance on private rather than governmental resources, willingness to enter into new areas of social need, and more focus on making recipients self-reliant. Some strings attached to governmental subsidies, however, might limit the flexibility or damage the integrity of NGOs. Among the potential drawbacks are demands that they avoid working in some countries or concentrate on countries of political or economic interest to home governments and pressures to work in certain types of programs that they may not have capacities for (AIDS treatment, commercially oriented projects) or with which some may have a moral problem (birth control and abortion services).

Trends in Development Work Abroad

Over the past several decades nongovernmental organizations in Europe, Canada, and the United States have transferred increasing amounts of resources overseas, and there has been a growth of indigenous private organizations receiving and administering this aid in Latin America, Africa, and Asia. Because Christian missionary societies have long worked among the poor in these countries, many of these new NGOs in the developing world were created by churches. In recent years some have spun off and become nondenominational but remain on good terms with churches and continue to receive support from international religious NGOs. Increasing numbers of secular NGOs were created in developing countries in the 1970s and 1980s to assist the grassroots poor, and many of these also receive foreign church assistance for their development work through religious NGOs.

Mainline Protestant and Catholic NGOs from North Atlantic countries now channel some of their assistance to secular indigenous NGOs if the work fits their development priorities. Evangelical NGOs still prefer to work with church-related groups abroad because they consider their social efforts closely related to and supportive of their goals of making and keeping converts.

Some estimates in the early 1990s numbered national and regional indigenous NGOs from 30,000 to 35,000 in Latin America, Asia, and Africa, with hundreds of thousands of smaller ones operating at the grassroots. These NGOs have focused most of their efforts on enhancing the skills and resources of the poor with projects in basic health, credit and management training for small producers and merchants, small-scale agriculture and water development linked with environmental preservation, and production and consumer cooperatives (increasingly among women).

Very few of these indigenous NGOs engage in direct political action, but they do increase the self-confidence and social awareness of low-income groups participating in their projects. This effect sometimes spills over into growing demands by recipients for better social services from their governmental agencies.

In some repressive regimes, such as Latin American military governments in the 1970s and 1980s, NGOs supported politically sensitive projects in legal aid and social assistance to dissidents and their families. Often, these projects were given protection under the auspices of churches and received support from international religiously affiliated NGOs. At times, this support led to church-state tensions and harassment by secret police agents angry over humanitarian aid to government opponents.

In some Middle Eastern, African, and Asian countries Muslim NGOs have emerged as important conduits for assistance from those in wealthy Arab nations desirous of helping poor Muslims in these regions. At times, these NGOs have clashed with their respective governments over human rights violations and official policies that chronically have neglected the poor or disregarded traditional Muslim teachings about the role of women in society and the availability of liquor and gambling.

The vast majority of religiously affiliated NGOs—both those that send funds to developing nations and those that receive them—try to avoid political entanglements and concentrate on relief and development projects. Sometimes, however, the environment in which they operate gives their work unavoidable political implications.

See also *Community organizing; Economic development; Humanitarianism; Jesuits; Lobbying, Religious; Maryknoll; Missionaries; Philanthropy; World Council of Churches.*

Brian H. Smith

BIBLIOGRAPHY

Carroll, Thomas F. *Intermediary NGOs: The Supporting Link in Grassroots Development.* West Hartford, Conn.: Kumarian Press, 1992.

Clark, John. *Democratizing Development: The Role of Voluntary Organizations.* West Hartford, Conn.: Kumarian Press, 1991.

Fisher, Julie. *The Road from Rio: Sustainable Development and the Nongovernmental Movement in the Third World.* Westport, Conn.: Praeger, 1993.

Lissner, Jorgen. *The Politics of Altruism: A Study of the Political Behaviour of Voluntary Development Agencies.* Geneva: Lutheran World Federation, 1977.

Schmidt, Elizabeth, et al. *Religious Private Voluntary Organizations and the Question of Government Funding.* Maryknoll, N.Y.: Orbis Books, 1981.

Smilie, Ian. *The Alms Bazaar: Altruism under Fire—Nonprofit Organizations and International Development.* Ottawa: International Development Research Center, 1995.

———, and Henny Helmlich, eds. *Non-Governmental Organizations and Governments: Stakeholders for Development.* Paris: Organization for Economic Cooperation and Development, 1993.

Smith, Brian H. *More Than Altruism: The Politics of Private Foreign Aid.* Princeton: Princeton University Press, 1990.

———. "Nongovernmental Organizations in International Development: Trends and Future Research Priorities." *VOLUNTAS* 4 (December 1993): 326–344.

Northern Ireland

See *Ireland*

Orthodoxy, Greek

Greek Orthodoxy—the official religion of Greece, Cyprus, and of the Greek Diaspora (the approximately 4.5 million people of Greek ethnic origin, language, and religion spread throughout the world)—is part of the historically continuous Church of Eastern Christianity out of which the Russian Orthodox Church and the Orthodox churches of the Balkans were established from the tenth century onward. Greek Orthodoxy has unbroken continuity with primitive Christianity.

The first Christian communities around the eastern Mediterranean were established by the Apostles. St. Paul's Hellenic education, and the fact that the books of the official canon of the New Testament were initially written in Greek, gave a Greek cultural character to the Eastern church from the beginning. The Greek Fathers in the fourth and fifth centuries consolidated Greek Orthodoxy by synthesizing Platonic and Neoplatonic philosophy with biblical teaching and liturgical practice to form the basic doctrines of the Holy Trinity—God as Father, Son, and Holy Spirit—and of the divinity and humanity of Christ and general Orthodox theology.

The composite terms *orthodox* and *orthodoxia* appear in the fourth century and carry a double meaning—the right belief and the right worship. The reasons for their appearance were theological just as they were political. The theological controversies over the heresies of Arius (fourth century) and Nestorius (fifth) had direct political significance because they threatened the unity of the empire.

The Roman emperor Constantine, having converted to Christianity, transferred the capital from Rome to Byzantium (330). For Constantine's successors Orthodoxy became the cement that held together what gradually became the Byzantine Empire. Through the Ecumenical Councils, they established a particular relationship of religion and politics and of church and state in the Orthodox world, which, in principle, has prevailed to the present day.

Following Christ's command, Orthodox theology claims that the "things of Caesar" should not be confused with the "things of God." The religio-spiritual realm should be kept out of the administration of power and the administration of the things of the world. The church has always claimed its autonomy and its independence from the state because their functions are separate and are delineated by two different sets of canons—the law of the state and the sacred canons of the church. But because the church "is in the world" and consequently part of society, it cannot be kept out of its conflicts and struggles. This creates a deep-seated ambivalence and tension between religion and politics, and consequently between church and state.

In Byzantium, according to many scholars, that ambivalence led to *Caesaropapism,* subjugation, that is, of the church to the state. But others believe religion and politics were both diffused and inseparably connected. Many emperors lost not just their thrones but also their heads for their stance on Orthodoxy. The power of the patriarch, the clergy, the monks, and of religion at large was a constant factor in Byzantine politics. This became clear, above all, during the iconoclastic struggles under Emperors Leo III (726–787) and Leo V (813–843) that shook Byzantine society to its foundations. The Orthodox faithful viewed icons, or religious images, as representations of the divine and instruments of veneration. The iconoclasts, who wanted to purge the use of icons, drew on Old Testament prohibitions against the worship of images. But according to defenders of icons, Christ's human birth had made possible his representations and rejecting them was, in essence, rejecting Christ's divinity. The iconoclasts were ultimately defeated, and icons remain important in Eastern Orthodox theology and worship.

The Church and National Identity

By the eleventh century Orthodoxy was transmitted to the Russians and the Slavs and the Bulgarians in the Balkans by Greek missionaries who translated the Bible and the liturgy into Slavonic. Mainly for political reasons, these ethnic groups gradually formed independent ethnic Orthodox churches more or less under the general jurisdiction of the ecumenical patriarchate.

But the fall of Constantinople (1453) to the Turks initiated a new era in religion and politics in the Greek Orthodox world. The conqueror Mehmet II granted the ecumenical patriarch certain privileges, not just for the Greeks but for all the Orthodox groups *(millet)* in the Balkans, which included a certain degree of autonomy to practice their religion. In return the patriarch had to guarantee the collection of taxes and obedience of Christians to the sultan. This enhanced the political role of the patriarchate of Constantinople, which undertook most civil functions over Orthodox subjects. The power of the patriarch and the bishops, however, although significant, was never absolute because they were subject to the sultan and his political whims. So, despite a certain degree of corruption, which the church suffered as a result, its ethnic aspect was consolidated and enhanced during Ottoman rule because the hopes of the enslaved Greeks were entrusted to that institution.

Orthodoxy, to a large extent, formed the cultural background for the revolution and the acquisition of national independence of the Orthodox people in the Balkans in the nineteenth century. Especially for the Greeks, involvement of the church in the struggle for independence (1821) was direct, and many clergy, including Gregory V, patriarch of Constantinople, paid with their lives. National independence, however, brought about subjugation of the church to the new-born Greek state, as well as a strong nationalist influence on Greek Orthodoxy. The ecumenical patriarchate resisted this influence by not recognizing the 1833 declaration of independence of the Greek church. But in 1850 the patriarchate had to give in to a fait accompli and recognized the Orthodox Church of Greece as autocephalous, or independent and headed by its own archbishop.

The religio-political situation in the new-born Greek state (1830) was altogether anomalous. After the assassination of Ioánnis Kapodistrias, the first president of Greece, Britain, Russia, and France invited Prince Otto of Wittelsbach, the seventeen-year-old son of King Ludvig of Bavaria, to become monarch of Greece. Not only was the young king a Catholic, invited to rule over an Orthodox church and an Orthodox nation, but the three-man regency council that was in fact to rule was also Bavarian and Protestant. The church was to be administered by a Holy Synod under the authority of the king, who was also supreme bishop, in conformity with the Bavarian prototype.

The church thus became subordinate to the state despite strong resistance at the grass roots and by the monasteries, most of which were closed down and their properties passed to the Crown. The church became virtually part of the state, and religion in general became entangled with party politics, which hindered modernization and democratization of the country. During the second half of the nineteenth century Greek Orthodoxy was infused with Greek nationalism and the nostalgic vision that Greece would again be great and would encompass its pre–Ottoman occupation boundaries. That vision ended in what is known as the Asia Minor catastrophe (1922), when Turkish troops routed the Greek army at Smyrna and more than a million refugees fled Turkey for Greece.

The church itself has rarely been left free to administer its own affairs according to its sacred canons. Throughout the twentieth century, not a single archbishop has been elected without the intervention of the state, and most of them have been dethroned during political upheavals. During the military dictatorship (1967–1974) the image of the church was severely tarnished because of the way it was used to legitimize and support the regime. The church, on the other hand, has enjoyed the financial support of the state because all parish clergy and the bishops are paid and pensioned out of state funds. Also, as the official church, it has enjoyed a certain cultural hegemony over Greek society.

Since 1975 the whole situation has changed significantly. The government of the Panhellenic Socialist Movement in 1981 proclaimed in its manifesto "the administrative separation of church and state." But such separation proved impossible without a radical revision of the constitution. The government, however, introduced civil marriage (nonexistent before 1982) as optional and made a rather unsuccessful attempt to expropriate the major part of church property for the state in 1987. In the 1990s religion and the church seem to be used less and less for political purposes, and tensions between church and state have significantly eased, but there is no talk of formal separation. With Greece now a member of the European Union and looking toward modernization, chances are that church and state relations and the relation of Greek Orthodoxy to Greek society are entering a new era.

Ethnic or Universal Religion?

Despite various attempts in the past to reform church and state relations in Greece, in substance things have remained unchanged. The constitution, which opens with an invocation of the Holy Trinity, safeguards Orthodoxy as the official religion of the country (article 3) but also guarantees religious freedom as an absolute right (article 13) for all known religions. More than 95 percent of the population acknowledge themselves as Orthodox Christians, and, over the centuries, the ethnic identity of the Greeks has become interwoven with their religion. Indeed, many of them have no difficulty in identifying and fusing Hellenism with Orthodoxy. Religion also permeates civil rituals, and there is hardly an official public occasion from which the church is absent, from swearing in a new government to blessing large or small technological projects. Furthermore, at all major national and local religious festivals, state functionaries are officially present.

The geographical and cultural boundaries of Greek Orthodoxy, however, are not limited to the Church of Greece, which is in full communion with and is only one among the family of the other self-governed Orthodox churches. Greek Orthodox Churches outside Greece are under the jurisdiction of the Ecumenical Patriarchate, and the autocephalous Church of Cyprus is Greek Orthodox.

The Orthodox Church of Cyprus has influenced the island's recent political history considerably. In 1950, while Cyprus was still under British rule, Mihail Mouskos, the bishop of Citium of Cyprus, was elected archbishop as Makarios III. He also became de facto leader of the Greek Cypriot community and organized a plebiscite among the Greek community, who voted 96 percent in favor of *enosis* (Greek, "union")—the political amalgamation of Cyprus and the kingdom of Greece. The British denied the petition.

An independent Cyprus was established in 1959, and Makarios was elected its first president. He continued as president and archbishop during the turbulent 1960s and 1970s, when Greek and Turkish Cypriots clashed over what the Turks viewed as Greek efforts to disenfranchise them, and the governments of both Greece and Turkey intervened in Cypriot affairs. Makarios was ousted as president during a 1974 Turkish invasion, and the island was eventually divided into separate Greek and Turkish Cypriot states. Although no longer directly involved in Cypriot government, the Orthodox Church still wields considerable political power.

Historically, Greek Orthodoxy has coexisted with various religions and cultures, and its theology is essentially ecumenical, universalist, and democratic because its prototype is the *person* as represented by Christ.

See also *Balkan states; Religious organization; State churches.*

Nikos Kokosalakis

BIBLIOGRAPHY

Frazee, Charles. *The Orthodox Church and Independent Greece.* Cambridge: Cambridge University Press, 1969.

Kokosalakis, Nikos. "Greek Orthodoxy and Socioeconomic Change." In *Religion and the Transformation of Capitalism,* edited by Richard Roberts. London: Routledge, 1995.

Nicol, Donald. *Church and Society in the Last Centuries of Byzantium.* Cambridge: Cambridge University Press, 1979.

Runciman, Stephen. *The Great Church in Captivity: A Study of the Patriarchate of Constantinople from the Eve of the Turkish Conquest to the Greek War of Independence.* Cambridge: Cambridge University Press, 1968.

Ware, Timothy. *The Orthodox Church.* London: Penguin, 1964.

Orthodoxy, Russian

Russian Orthodoxy has been the main religion of the Russian people since 988, when the pagan Prince Vladimir, eventually canonized as Saint Vladimir, embraced Christianity and led his people, the Rus, to the Dnieper River in what came to be called the Baptism of Russia. Vladimir married Anne, sister of the Byzantine emperor Basil II, inviting missionaries to Kiev from the church in Byzantium. In 1488, under Metropolitan Iona (the primate of the province of Moscow), the Russian Church became autocephalous (independent) of the patriarch of Constantinople, the head of the Eastern Orthodox Church.

After the fall of Constantinople (the Second Rome) to

the Ottoman Turks in 1453, Moscow saw itself as the Third Rome and the heir to pure Orthodoxy. In 1589 Tsar Boris Godunov (1551–1605) founded the Russian Orthodox patriarchy in Moscow. The church in Russia was closely connected with the state power and for most of its history was completely subordinate to it. Because of Orthodox belief in humility and obedience, the absence of ideas about natural human rights, and the tradition of veneration of the monarch, the Russian Orthodox Church has actively contributed to the formation of an authoritarian centralized state.

There have been dissenters from the official doctrine, and, rare as they were, they are now of great significance to church reformers. In a strongly antiheretical age that also encouraged the church to accumulate great wealth, the leader of the Non-Possessors, Saint Nil Sorsky (c. 1433–1508), believed the whole church was called to poverty and that heretics should be treated with patience and understanding. Moscow Metropolitan Philip Kolychev protested against the tyranny of Ivan the Terrible in the sixteenth century.

In 1658–1667, in Patriarch Nikon's time, the Russian church split. Nikon introduced reforms of ritual that were practiced among the Orthodox outside Russia but that the Russian Church Council of 1551 had declared heretical. Many worshippers broke with the state church, refusing to recognize the reforms of the rite, unification, and bureaucracy of the church life. They found themselves persecuted, pursued, and excluded from the mainstream of Russian life. Since that time, these traditionalist dissenters known as the Old Believers have been radically opposed to the mainstream Orthodox Church and secular authority. In the early twentieth century they amounted to more than 10 percent of the Russian population.

Patriarch Nikon was deposed by Tsar Alexei Mikhailovich for striving to ensure church independence and to expand its rights. The schism and deposition of Nikon weakened the church, allowing Peter I to abolish the patriarchate in 1721. Church administration was vested in the entirely secular bureaucratic organization known as the Holy Synod. Russian liberal and left-wing movements regarded the church as an instrument of ideological control, and anticlerical trends grew during the nineteenth century. Until 1905 the Orthodox Church was structured as an establishment of the authoritarian administration and absolutely submitted to it.

Revolution and the Church

In the early twentieth century the Russian church saw a short period of revival. There appeared a generation of well-known religious philosophers (Vladimir Soloviev, Nicholas Berdyaev, Pavel Florensky, Sergei Bulgakov), and liberal ideas spread among the clergy. After the edict of religious tolerance of 1905 and, especially, after the March Revolution of 1917 that led to the abdication of the tsar and, ultimately, to the end of the tsarist regime, social movements were rapidly developing in the church. In the summer and autumn of 1917, there was a quiet church revolution that established a democratic administrative system like that of most U.S. Protestant denominations. The Council of 1917–1918 sanctioned the democratic reforms, restored the patriarchate, and elected Tikhon (Belavin) patriarch. But the church democratization was too late. Coming to power in October 1917, the Bolsheviks openly aimed at annihilating all religion, Orthodoxy first of all, because they regarded it as an autocratic institution.

Mass repression of clergy and believers began in the first days of the revolution. After Patriarch Tikhon's death in 1925, government authorities allowed the church, which was in a state of anarchy, to reorganize. The campaign against the church was carried on not only by means of repression but also by infiltrating it with agents and supporting all kinds of dissenters, renovationists—radical reformers advocating a union with communism—chief among them. Supported by the Bolsheviks, the renovationists became strong opponents of the traditionalist followers of Tikhon. In the early 1920s the submission of legal church organizations to the political authorities made the champions of church independence break with these organizations and go underground (the Catacomb Church).

In the early twentieth century the Russian Orthodox Church was also shaken by nationalist movements. After the fall of the tsarist regime, there was a push to establish the Autocephalous Orthodox Church in Ukraine, which was founded in 1921 and abolished by Stalin in 1930. The church survived among Ukrainian immigrants, and in the West, Russian Orthodox Church leaders who had fled after the revolution organized the Russian Orthodox Church Abroad.

After Estonia and Latvia declared independence, their Orthodox churches broke with the Moscow patriarchy and became subordinate to the patriarch in Constantinople. When Stalin occupied the Baltic countries in 1940, their

Orthodox communities were again subordinated to the Moscow patriarchy.

In Belorussia there existed an influential movement for an independent Belorussian church, a demand that was partially met with the foundation of the Autocephalous Orthodox Church in Poland. The church united the worshippers of Western Belorussia, which belonged to Poland after the revolution.

The Church and State Propaganda

During World War II Stalin reconsidered his church policy. In September 1943 Stalin ordered a council of bishops to meet, a patriarch was elected, proper church administration was restored, and some churches and monasteries reopened. The church became once again an obedient servant of the regime and symbol of Russian nationalism and authoritarianism.

In an attempt to revive communist antireligion ideals, in 1958–1962 Soviet President Nikita Khrushchev subjected the church to more repressions; closed many parishes, seminaries, and monasteries; and further restricted the clergy's rights.

Since the 1960s the state has made use of the church on the international scene—the Moscow patriarchy became a member of the World Council of Churches and other international organizations and became one of the instruments of Soviet foreign policy.

In the 1960s to 1980s dissident initiatives arose within the church. Led by priests Gleb Yakunin and Pavel Adelgeim, they opposed church discrimination and church submission to the authorities and were persecuted by the church itself.

After the Fall

As the Soviet Union weakened and eventually collapsed during 1988–1991, the church was liberated from state restriction and began intensive building of churches and opening of monasteries and theological schools.

In 1990 Alexi II was elected patriarch. Shortly after his election he allied himself to Boris Yeltsin's regime and began supporting nationalistic and authoritarian movements.

Now free to govern itself, the administration of the Russian Orthodox Church lacks experience in mounting social programs. It directs most of its efforts to consolidation with government, restitution of church property, financial and commercial activity, which cause regular scandals. For example, controversy surrounded Metropolitan Cirill, head of the church's department of interior affairs, which was revealed to have had secret (and possibly illegal) exemptions from customs and taxes on trade in alcohol and tobacco. In Ekaterinburg funds were twice stolen from a trust to build a memorial cathedral of Tsar Nicholas II and his family. The media have also accused church leadership of having ties to organized crime.

Nationalist in outlook and fearing competition with Protestants and Catholics, since 1992 the Russian Orthodox Church has been fighting for legislative and other forms of discrimination against Christian minorities. The authoritarian system within the church, a holdover from Stalin's time, has begun to arouse protest and threaten schism.

Since the collapse of the Soviet Union 1991, thousands of parishes have found themselves in the territory of the new independent countries. In some of them (Estonia, Ukraine) independent Orthodox churches have formed with government support; in others, the authorities contribute to the greater autonomy of the Russian patriarch.

See also *Anticlericalism; Orthodoxy, Greek; Russia; State churches.*

Sergey Borisovich Filatov

BIBLIOGRAPHY

Anderson, John. *Religion, State, and Politics in the Soviet Union and Successor States.* Cambridge: Cambridge University Press, 1994.

Buss, Gerald. *The Bear's Hug: Christian Belief and Soviet State, 1917–1986.* Grand Rapids, Mich.: Eerdmans, 1987.

Ellis, Jane. *The Russian Orthodox Church: A Contemporary History.* Bloomington: Indiana University Press, 1986.

———. *The Russian Orthodox Church: Triumphalism and Defensiveness.* London: Macmillan, 1996.

Hill, Kent R. *The Soviet Union on the Brink: An Inside Look at Christianity and Glasnost.* Portland, Ore.: Multnomah Press, 1991.

Pospelovsky, Demitry. *The Russian Church under the Soviet Regime: 1917–1982.* 2 vols. Crestwood, N.Y.: St. Vladimir's Seminary Press, 1984.

Ramet, Pedro, ed. *Eastern Christianity and Politics in the Twentieth Century.* Durham, N.C.: Duke University Press, 1988.

P

Pacifism

Pacifism, in the absolute sense in which the word is here used, is a political stance that is unusually indebted to religion. Its insistence that war is never justified—not even in self-defense—originated in attempts by Christian sects to promote what they believed to be the authentic scriptural position. Pacifism developed into a movement, albeit a very small one, in certain Protestant countries—those, of which Britain and the United States are the leading examples, characterized also by liberal political cultures and a relatively high measure of security from invasion. Elsewhere pacifism has mostly been confined to individuals or sects whose beliefs have become a matter of public knowledge only when brought into the open by their refusal to serve in the military. And although in recent years its legitimacy has increased in many countries, this growing acceptance can partly be attributed to the fact that its support has everywhere been too limited to threaten the defense effort.

The unconditional rejection of war is also unusual among political viewpoints in the high degree of etymological and semantic confusion that has surrounded it. It has even lacked an agreed word to describe it. Before *pacifism* was coined in 1901 by French peace activist Emile Arnaud, who thought the peace movement should have its own "ism," the most commonly used label in English-speaking countries was *nonresistance,* but this was far from ideal because it also had other meanings, including in England the almost antithetical one of unconditional obedience to a legitimate ruler. The coining of *pacifism* did not wholly solve the problem. Especially at first, this new word was ambiguous: it could apply not only to nonresistance but also to a separate and more moderate antiwar viewpoint that condemned militarism and asserted that war could ultimately be abolished yet did not unconditionally reject military force. In 1957 this moderate viewpoint was labeled *pacificism* by the celebrated British historian A. J. P. Taylor. From a strictly etymological point of view, Taylor's choice of label was unfortunate because pacificism had been an early variant of pacifism on which English-language purists had unsuccessfully tried to insist. But it conveyed the essence of the viewpoint that he was describing, namely that it is pacific rather than unconditionally opposed to fighting. For that reason, and in the absence of an obvious alternative, Taylor's term *pacificism* (italicized in the interests of clarity) will be adopted here.

In continental Europe, where absolute pacifism has been very rare, the primary meaning of pacifism has always been *pacificism,* and an adjective such as "absolute" or "integral" has been added on the rare occasions when it has been necessary to refer to the unconditional rejection of war. For English speakers, however, among whom a rejection of even defensive war has been somewhat more common, pacifism came by the mid-1930s to have a predominantly unconditionalist meaning.

Variations on Pacifism

The complexity of pacifism as an ideology is rarely acknowledged. Pacifism exists in a number of variants. It can be inspired by different beliefs—though originally inferred from Christianity, it has subsequently been derived from socialist, utilitarian, and humanitarian principles as well. And different pacifists object to different things. The most stringent object not merely to war but also either to force of any kind (in which case they object also to a domestic police force) or, more moderately, to any form of killing (in which case they object also to the death penalty). But the most permissive object to military force only when used between states and allow it when used within a state (for example, in a revolution or a civil war) on the grounds that this does not count as war.

Pacifism must be distinguished from nonviolence, conscientious objection, or a demand for special exemption from military service. Nonviolence is older than pacifism, and has no necessary connection with it. *Ahimsa* (noninjury) was first preached by Buddhists twenty-five hundred years ago but was a doctrine of personal salvation for a spiritual elite and did not entail repudiating warfare. Indeed, Buddhism failed to generate either pacifism or a tradition of nonviolent domestic politics. In the twentieth century nonviolence has been widely adopted as a political tactic by campaigners on a wide range of issues—for example, by opponents of racial discrimination—who, for the most part, have not been pacifists.

Conscientious objection to military service is a repudiation of the authority of the state that can be inspired by beliefs other than pacifism. Some Christian sects have objected not to military service as such but to its incidental requirements such as an "idolatrous" oath of loyalty or taking orders from "unbelievers." More recently some conscientious objectors have been voluntarists whose objection is to compulsion, not fighting. And even when the objection has been to the war in question, it has sometimes been inspired by *pacificism* rather than pacifism, as when socialists refused to fight for their capitalist governments while avowing a willingness to participate in a people's war.

Special exemption from military service has sometimes been claimed by those who approve of conscription when applied to others. For example, priests have generally been successful in asserting a vocational claim to exemption from serving even in just wars, though attempts by creative artists to do the same have met with little sympathy. Exemptionism of this kind is profoundly different from pacifism, which hopes that everyone will refuse to bear arms.

Origins

The historical origins of pacifism are disputed. According to pacifists, they are to be found in the practice of the early Christian church, which undoubtedly disapproved of its members serving in the Roman army and dropped this disapproval only after the emperor Constantine accepted Christianity in 313. According to nonpacifist Christians, however, the early church's initial disapproval of military service was a rejection not of war but of an idolatrous military oath, and they also point to the fact that by 170 a few Christians were nonetheless serving as Roman solders. Pacifists have probably been correct about the stand of the early church but have been wrong to imply that Christianity could have developed into a major and enduring world religion had it not abandoned pacifism and developed the doctrine of the just war.

Historians are generally agreed, however, that after Constantine's conversion, pacifism disappeared for more than eight centuries and that during the next four centuries it surfaced only intermittently, when expounded by some of the radical Christian sects—the first being the Waldenses in France in the 1170s—that appeared in Europe at times of acute social tension. The history of pacifism as a continuous tradition begins only in the early sixteenth century, as part of the general questioning of church practices in much of western Europe at that time. In espousing a nonresistant version of Anabaptism in Zurich during the 1520s, the Swiss Brethren launched what was to prove the first enduring pacifist sect, the Mennonites. Pacifism was also preached by a tiny but growing number of Christian radicals, mystics, and pietists—although Dutch scholar Desiderius Erasmus (1466?–1536), whose powerful antiwar writings have a strikingly modern tone, stopped just short of this position. It was sufficiently established as a heterodox viewpoint by 1563 for the Church of England to require its clergy to agree: "It is lawful for Christian men, at the commandment of the magistrate, to wear weapons and serve in the wars."

The sect that in the long run did most to spread pacifist ideas was the Society of Friends, better known by its nickname the Quakers. It emerged in the early 1650s in an England that was undergoing its greatest ever upheaval—a civil war in which the king and bishops had been overthrown had encouraged various radical-puritan movements to try to establish the rule of the saints on earth. In 1660, however, this politico-religious experiment collapsed, and the crown and church were restored, presenting all radical puritans with a stark choice between armed revolt and acquiescence. Opting for acquiescence, in January 1661 the Quakers issued a Declaration against Wars and Fightings, which committed them to nonresistance.

This declaration proved of great importance in the history of pacifism because the Quakers not only survived as a sect and achieved a measure of influence on both sides of the Atlantic but also consistently refused to serve in the militia, hire substitutes, pay fines instead (thus suffering seizure of their property), or supply goods or services to the armed forces (even when it was highly profitable to do so). The peace testimony of the Quakers was clearly pacifist rather than exemptionist, especially when contrasted with that of the Mennonites, who were willing to pay militia fines and provide horses and fodder for the army.

Pacifism and Politics

It was at the end of the eighteenth century that pacifism made the breakthrough from being a peculiarity of historic peace sects to being a viewpoint open to all Christians and from being a doctrine motivated by the avoidance of personal sin to one concerned with finding a new way of conducting international relations. This was an era of profound change. Under the stimulus of the American, French, and Industrial Revolutions, modern political processes were developing, and under the influence of evangelicalism—a religious impulse that, by appealing to members of many churches, also helped to forge ecumenical cooperation between Quakers and mainstream Christians—philanthropic associations were being established.

It was thus because of its timing as well as its length that Britain's war of 1793–1815 with France produced the world's first peace campaign worthy of the name. Although this campaign was predominantly *pacificist,* pacifism played its part too. From 1796 onward the first pacifist tracts not to emanate from a historic peace sect began to appear, and when in the war's immediate aftermath (and that of the Anglo-American conflict of 1812–1814) the first peace associations were created on both sides of the Atlantic in 1815–1816, pacifists played a leading role.

As pacifism thus organized itself, it had to work out its attitude toward political activity. At one extreme, pacifism could be apolitical, presenting itself as a faith capable of developing only through the slow process of individual conversion rather than as a policy capable of immediate application to politics. This pessimistic orientation has had the most appeal when both the domestic and international environments are particularly inimical to peace activism. At the other extreme pacifism could be seen as a practical national policy on the grounds that a disarmed country either would be left alone or could protect itself by nonviolent resistance. This optimistic orientation has been most popular either in moments of unusual hope or when *pacificist* policies have run into difficulties. Pacifism could also steer a middle course and take the view that its followers can participate in political campaigning but only in support of *pacificist* policies rather than pacifist ones. This collaborative orientation has been adopted when *pacificist* ideas have been in the ascendant.

During their early years the first pacifist associations generally opted for the pessimistic orientation. They did not aspire to alter government policy but witnessed to Christian truth by issuing pacifist literature. Admittedly, an evangelical faith led some of their members to imply that a truly Christian and therefore nonresisting nation could expect to be preserved, but this would come through divine intervention rather than enlightened political behavior. From the 1840s *pacificist* ideas, such as referring international disputes to arbitration and promoting interdependence among countries by means of free trade, found such favor with an emergent liberal movement that British and American pacifists switched increasingly to the collaborative orientation. This affiliation enabled them to feel that they were making a practical contribution to war prevention by promoting *pacificism,* though it did so at the price of playing down pacifism's distinctive views. In addition, the lapsing of the militia system meant that, except during the American Civil War, there was no compulsory military service in the English-speaking world to focus attention on the absolutist position.

Growth of Pacifism

Thus, although *pacificism* continued to make progress, pacifism stagnated intellectually on both sides of the Atlantic during the second half of the nineteenth century and the beginning of the twentieth, which helps to explain why the word *pacifism* originally had the imprecise meaning it did even in Britain and the United States. In this period the absolutist cause derived its biggest stimulus from an unlikely source—Russia, a repressive, expansionist, and conscriptionist state, where in the late 1870s the aristocrat and novelist Leo Tolstoy espoused an extreme anarcho-pacifism that rejected even noninjurious force. Though drawn to this position by his reading of the New Testament, Tolstoy grounded his pacifism in a universal humanism rather than a distinctively Christian ethic. As a result his "law of love" attracted some support from socialists who rejected Christianity.

These socialist Tolstoyans, few in number but found in several countries, thus became the first pacifists to derive their stand from an explicitly non-Christian (and moreover nonreligious) inspiration.

As could have been anticipated from the protest by vocal minorities in Australia and New Zealand when these recently autonomous British dominions, worried about their security, introduced military training from 1911, pacifism was reinvigorated in the English-speaking world by the introduction of conscription in Britain and the United States during the First World War. Both countries made legal provision for conscientious objection, as did a very few others. This was a major step in the recognition of pacifism as a legitimate viewpoint within a liberal state. In Britain, which was by far the most generous, this recognition was in principle extended not only to Christians outside the historic peace sects but even to those whose objection was not religious; and dispensation was in practice allowed not only from military service but also from alternative service. But even in Britain the tribunals that applied the law discriminated against nonreligious objectors and those seeking an unconditional exemption. The sufferings of that significant minority of conscientious objectors who went to prison rather than accept their tribunals' rulings—a group among whom socialist pacifists were prominently represented—raised the profile of pacifism and began the process whereby that word acquired an absolutist connotation in English-speaking countries. Thus during the First World War pacifism benefited from the prejudices of society as well as from the comparative liberality of the state on both sides of the Atlantic.

Pacifism reached its peak of influence during the mid- to late 1930s when the *pacificist* policies of general disarmament and collective security through the League of Nations, which achieved much support in the disillusioned aftermath of the First World War, were discredited by the intransigence of Japan, Italy, and Germany. It was then that the English word *pacifist* came to be reserved for those who refused to defend themselves even against a regime as evil as Nazi Germany. This was the position of Britain's Peace Pledge Union, which—founded in May 1936 and reaching a membership of 136,000 at its peak in April 1940—became the largest pacifist association in history. Although founded by an Anglican clergyman, Dick Sheppard, its pacifism was more humanitarian or even utilitarian than Christian, reflecting the influence of such intellectuals as Aldous Huxley (1894–1963) and Bertrand Russell (1872–1970). In other words, its essential message was that nothing could be worse than the suffering and damage to be expected from a modern war in which aerial bombardment would be the principal mode of fighting. At first the Peace Pledge Union experimented with the optimistic orientation, in the hope that the nonviolent techniques that the Indian nationalist Mohandas K. Gandhi (1869–1948) had recently been pioneering might prove at least as effective against Hitler and his air force as against the British colonial regime. As this came to seem improbable, however, many leading pacifists retreated to the pessimistic orientation, accepting that theirs was a faith rather than a policy.

World War II and After

The Second World War proved both a breakthrough and a setback for pacifism. Provision for conscientious objection was further improved, though it still did not extend beyond the Protestant-liberal regimes of the English-speaking world, the Netherlands, and Scandinavia, and social prejudice against conscientious objectors was less than in the First World War. Yet this was in large part because, its limitations as a policy having been clarified by Hitler, pacifism had shown itself to be a demanding viewpoint that only a small minority could be expected to endorse. Even in Britain, where pacifism was strongest, only 1.2 percent of conscripted males professed a conscientious objection, and comparatively few of them felt justified in behaving intransigently toward a state and society that treated them well.

Since 1945 the story of pacifism has continued to be one of increasing legitimacy but negligible political influence. As liberal values have spread, an increasing number of countries—for example, Roman Catholic states such as France (1963) and Italy (1971)—have made provision for conscientious objection. But many of those refusing military service, such as the Greens in West Germany or white radicals in South Africa under apartheid, have been protesting more against their own domestic regimes than against war as such, and Gandhian techniques have been applied most readily to domestic contexts, such as the civil rights struggle in the United States or land reform in India, rather than international ones. Admittedly, pacifists took up a wide range of cold war issues, though they tended to support *pacificist* campaigns—those against weapons of mass destruction (especially nuclear weapons), particular wars (notably the Vietnam War), and the arms trade—rather than to promote their own, unvarying, absolutist agenda. Indeed, they sometimes seemed embarrassed by the absolutist stance—most notably, many self-styled pacifists in the United States responded to the Vietnam War by declaring support for wars of national liberation.

The end of the cold war has not so far helped the pacifist cause. The collapse of the Soviet bloc revealed that many of its former subjects valued national self-determination more highly than peace, and a significant element of progressive opinion in the West favored military intervention to protect the Muslim population from the Serbians after Bosnia-Herzegovina's declaration of independence. Thus, although pacifism is increasingly accepted as the stance that humanity must aspire ultimately to adopt, the fulfillment of this aspiration is generally understood even within the peace movement to be still a very long way off.

See also *Anabaptists; Civil disobedience; Civil rights movement; Friends, Society of; Gandhi, Mohandas Karamchand; Violence; War.*

Martin Ceadel

BIBLIOGRAPHY

Brock, Peter. *Pacifism in Europe to 1914.* Princeton: Princeton University Press, 1972.

———. *Pacifism in the United States: From the Colonial Era to the First World War.* Princeton: Princeton University Press, 1968.

Carter, April. *Peace Movements: International Protest and World Politics since 1945.* London: Longman, 1992.

Ceadel, Martin. *The Origins of War Prevention: The British Peace Movement and International Relations, 1730–1854.* Oxford: Clarendon Press, 1996.

———. *Pacifism in Britain, 1914–1945: The Defining of a Faith.* Oxford: Clarendon Press, 1980.

Paganism

A countercultural revival of pre-Christian Western traditions, contemporary Paganism (also referred to as Neopaganism, Witchcraft, Wicca, or the Old Religion) is a religious movement that shows a strong concern for environmentalism and feminism and has spread primarily in English-speaking nations (Britain, Australia, and the United States). The term *pagan* (literally, "country dweller") was long used derogatorily to refer to all non-Christian religions. Although major world religions such as Islam or Buddhism are now exempted from that label, it continues to be applied to small-scale, nature-based religions. Today's Paganism must be distinguished from the New Age movement (much of which derives from Eastern religions) and Satanism (the worship of the devil).

Origins and Beliefs

Resistant to the notion of a unified creed, most Neopagans believe in a polytheistic pantheon in which the high deity is usually female (the Great Goddess) and may or may not have a male consort. Their worship emphasizes ritual (focused on the cycle of nature) and the use of magic (the harnessing of supernatural forces for desired ends). The community is decentralized, and there is no attempt to convert others. Estimates of the size of the movement vary widely, ranging from ten thousand to several hundred thousand adherents in the United States alone.

Although many Pagans see themselves as carrying on ancient, pre-Christian traditions, there is little reliable evidence that European paganism continued as a religion after its suppression by the Inquisition in the fifteenth century. The contemporary Pagan movement was born in late-nineteenth-century Great Britain when Gerald Gardner, an English folklorist, blended elements from Western magic and European folk tradition to create what we now know as Wicca (the Old English word for witches) or Neopaganism. Claiming to have been initiated into a secret coven that represented one of the last remnants of the Old Religion, Gardner initiated into his own tradition hundreds of people, including Raymond Buckland, who brought it to the United States. Americans combined Gardnerian witchcraft with ideas from science fiction, feminism, and various ethnic sources other than Western Europe (such as Greek and Egyptian mythologies). Neopaganism thus now includes a wide variety of groups ranging from Aryan supremacist followers of Norse gods to radical lesbians devoted to the Earth mother.

Most Pagans are not politically active, with those who are usually liberal in orientation. Although politically conservative Pagans exist, they represent a small minority within the larger Pagan movement and have not been active in politics. The primary areas of political activism are feminism and environmentalism.

Environmental and Feminist Concerns

Because the Goddess is identified with nature, the environment is a key political concern for Pagans. Many see the destruction of nature as a direct result of the Judeo-Christian belief in a God who is transcendent and above nature and who has given man dominion over the earth and its creatures. By contrast, the Goddess is seen as present in nature, so reverence for her by definition requires respect for the environment. Thus many Pagans are politically active on environmental issues, such as opposing nuclear power and toxic waste dumps and promoting animal rights.

Another concern is women's rights. Although many Christian and Jewish feminists believe that their respective traditions can be reformed, more radical feminists reject them as inherently patriarchal and have seized on Paganism as an alternative. Imagining God as female is seen as empowering women. The myth of an ancient matriarchy that was later suppressed by the Judeo-Christian tradition provides an explanation of why women are oppressed and proves that patriarchy is not inevitable. The anti-authoritarian structure of Pagan ritual (circular worship space, rotating leadership, creative liturgy) affirms the feminist belief in equality of all people, and the permissive ethics ("do as thou wilt but harm none") is consistent with feminist calls for a woman's control over her own body and the support of lesbianism as an alternative lifestyle. Thus many Pagans are politically active on feminist issues, among them fighting rape and pornography and promoting reproductive choice and gay rights.

For many Pagans, concern for the environment and women's rights are interrelated. They believe that the attitude of domination and exploitation that has led to oppression of women has also led to destruction of the environment and assert that respect for women will naturally follow from renewed reverence for the earth. These Pagans have become part of the Ecofeminist movement that combines activism for women's rights and environmentalism and overlaps with liberal Christianity.

Politics and Identity

Pagans engage in grassroots political activism (writing letters to Congress, participating in protest marches, putting together newsletters), but they also believe that spiritual practices (celebrating menstruation in rituals, visualizing pollution reduction, casting a spell to catch a rapist) can have a political impact. This belief has led some critics to accuse Pagans of escapism, a charge that is largely unfair as many Pagans engage in both kinds of activism. Prominent among them are Starhawk, the most widely known Pagan priestess and writer in America, who has long been active in the antinuclear movement, and Z. Budapest, founder of one of the first feminist covens, who has organized protests against rape and for abortion rights.

Starhawk

Their rejection of Christianity and support for abortion and gay rights has pitted many Pagans directly against the Christian right, which they see as their most dangerous enemy. The Christian right in turn has lost no time in (wrongly) identifying Pagans with Satanism and labeling them a threat to America's children. Yet, unlike the Christian right, the Pagan movement has not been able to make a direct political impact or become a visible political constituency that members of Congress respond to. There are several reasons for this.

One is widespread misunderstanding about what Paganism is. Thanks to media coverage that does not distinguish Paganism from the larger New Age movement and pronouncements by Christian right leaders who identify Paganism with Satanism, Pagans continue to fight a negative public image that few politicians want to be associated with. Another reason is the decentralization of the movement. No one leader represents Pagans the way that, say, televangelist Pat Robertson speaks for conservative Christians. Pagans pride themselves on not adhering to a unified creed or political dogma, but this also prevents them from acting in a unified manner. Finally, some Pagans reject the American political system itself as an outgrowth of the patriarchal, imperialistic outlook of Judeo-Christian culture, seeing any participation (including voting) in that system as implicit support for it. Although the Pagan movement has only indirectly had any political effect, it has provided spiritual sustenance and moral support to many environmental and feminist activists who are making a difference.

See also *Environmentalism; Feminism; Inquisition; Witchcraft.*

Christel J. Manning

BIBLIOGRAPHY

Adler, Margot. *Drawing Down the Moon: Witches, Druids, Goddess Worshippers, and Other Pagans in America Today.* Rev. ed. Boston: Beacon Press, 1996.

Eller, Cynthia. *Living in the Lap of the Goddess: The Feminist Spirituality Movement in America.* New York: Crossroad, 1993.

Luhrman, T. M. *Persuasions of the Witch's Craft: Ritual Magic in Contemporary England.* Cambridge: Harvard University Press, 1989.

Manning, Christel. "Embracing Jesus and the Goddess: Towards a Reconceptualization of Conversion to Syncretistic Religion." In *Magical Religion and Modern Witchcraft,* edited by James Lewis. Albany: State University of New York Press, 1996.

Merchant, Carolyn. *The Death of Nature: Woman, Ecology, and the Scientific Revolution.* San Francisco: Harper and Row, 1980.

Neitz, Mary Jo. "In Goddess We Trust." In *In Gods We Trust: New Patterns of Religious Pluralism in America,* edited by Tom Robbins and Dick Anthony. New Brunswick, N.J.: Transaction, 1993.

Spretnak, Charlene, ed. *The Politics of Women's Spirituality: Essays on the Rise of Spiritual Power within the Feminist Movement.* New York: Doubleday, 1982.

Starhawk. *Dreaming the Dark: Magic, Sex, and Politics.* Boston: Beacon Press, 1982.

Pakistan

Pakistan was created in 1947 as a homeland for Muslims of South Asia. With an estimated population of 150 million, it is the world's second largest Muslim country after Indonesia. Today it is an avowedly Islamic republic, wherein Islamic standards dominate national political discourse and influence discussions about democratization, economic reform, and state-society relations.

Pakistan was the culmination of the Muslim demand for separatism at the twilight of British rule in India. Many Muslims, including thinkers like Abul-Kalam Azad (d. 1958) and religious institutions such as the Jamʿiat-i Ulama-i Hind (Society of Indian Ulama), remained involved in the independence movement under the leadership of the Indian Congress Party. Others followed intellectuals such as Muhammad Iqbal (d. 1938) and politicians such as Muhammad Ali Jinnah (d. 1948) in the Muslim League; they questioned the belief that the struggle against the British ought to be the paramount concern of Muslims. These Muslims were apprehensive about living as a minority in a predominantly Hindu state and sought to safeguard and further Muslim communal interests before an uncertain future.

For the leaders of the Pakistan movement, however, Muslim nationalism was not so much a religious notion as a communal one. Himself secular, Jinnah wanted to identify Muslims as a people belonging to a distinct cultural group and sharing a common identity separate from that of the majority population. The promise of Pakistan for Jinnah lay not in its religious potential, but in the fact that it would serve as a political arena in which a Muslim's aspirations would not be limited by his identity. But Jinnah was not able to keep Pakistan a secular ideal. The separatist struggle, especially during its last phase, was compelled to appeal to Islamic symbols to mobilize public support, opening the door to thinking of Pakistan as an Islamic ideal.

Soon after Pakistan was created, the place of Islam in the national political discourse was put to debate. The secular political elite at first resisted giving Islam a role in national politics. But a state built in the name of Islam and as a Muslim homeland and confronted with insurmountable ethnic, linguistic, and class conflicts, economic collapse, a serious refugee problem, and war with India quickly succumbed to the temptation of mobilizing Islamic symbols in the service of state formation. This practice was only reinforced over the years as the state failed to address fundamental socioeconomic issues, carry out meaningful land reform, and contend with ethnic and provincial demands and consolidate power in the center.

Islam and the Secular State

The turn to Islam opened the door for Islamic parties to enter the fray. They have disagreed over how to create an Islamic state, but their collective as well as their independent activities strengthened the impetus for Islamization. The secular state resisted this trend only briefly. By 1949 the elite had accepted a political role for Islamic forces, compromising their original conception of Pakistan as a thoroughly secular state. In that year the government adopted the Objectives

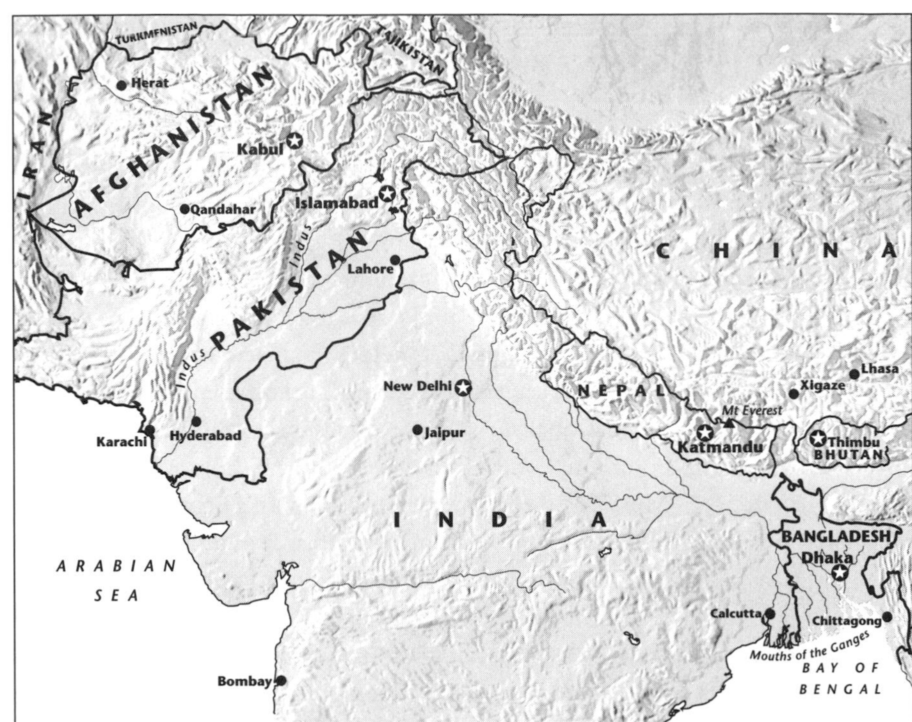

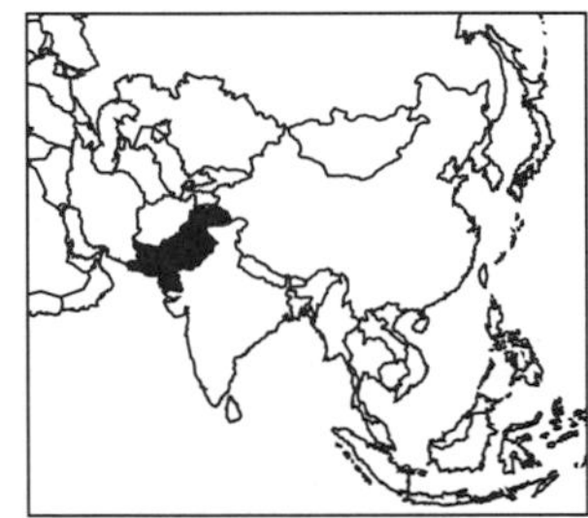

Resolution, which Islamic forces demanded as a statement of intent for the future constitution. The resolution formally introduced Islamic concerns into constitutional debates. Subsequent state policy, culminating in the constitution of 1956, only reinforced this trend. As a result, by the end of Pakistan's first decade Islamic forces were fully included in its politics and had moved to appropriate the national political discourse from the state.

Although the state accepted a place for Islamic forces in national politics it was not willing to abandon secularism or to permit Islamization of society and politics outside its direct control. The government therefore resorted to regulating the flow of Islam in politics, hoping gradually to negotiate arrangements with Islamic parties to that effect. But frictions and confrontations, the most notable and significant of which was the anti-Ahmadiyya riots of 1953–1954, pitted the state against Islamic forces.

In 1953 Islamic forces demanded that the Ahmadiyya sect, which Muslims consider outside the pale of Islam, be declared a non-Muslim minority and Pakistan's Ahmadi foreign minister, Sir Chaudhri Zafaru'llah Khan, be dismissed from his post. They argued that if Pakistan was an Islamic polity, then the Ahmadiyya could not enjoy full rights in it. The dispute put the Islamicness of the state into question and enabled Islamic forces to force the government to more clearly commit itself to Islamization. The government reacted by imposing martial law and arresting and trying anti-Ahmadi religious activists on charges of sedition.

The strong government reaction did not, however, end the problem inherent in a secular government seeking to use Islam selectively to shore up its authority. After the constitution of 1956 formally committed Pakistan to some form of Islamicness, declaring the state an Islamic republic, Islamic forces once again demanded adoption of Islamic laws and precepts.

Resisting Islam

The government of General Muhammad Ayub Khan (1958–1969), which assumed power after a military coup, sought to resolve the Islamist problem once and for all. Soon after he assumed office, Ayub Khan attacked Islamic parties and institutions. His government sought to redefine the ideology of the state and to anchor it in his vision of development in lieu of Islam. His government nationalized religious endowments and assumed guardianship of religious shrines, restricted religious education, introduced a new secular family law, and in the constitution of 1962 removed "Islamic" from the official name of the state. Ayub Khan was not able to completely subdue Islamic forces or to undo the preceding decade's gradual politicization of Islam and Islamization of politics. And it was evident that as a Muslim homeland, Pakistan would always have to be defined, in some degree, in Islamic terms.

Unable to extricate Islam from politics, Ayub Khan accepted its involvement but then sought to define Islam along modernist lines. He encouraged thinkers such as Fazlur Rahman (d. 1986) and Khalifah Abdul Hakim (d. 1966) and such forums as the Islamic Research Institute and Institute of Islamic Culture to formulate a modernist interpretation of Islam to undergird state ideology and provide a different relationship between Islam and Pakistan. State patronage of Islamic modernism increased tensions with Islamic forces, who refused to be marginalized and relinquish the right to interpret Islam to the state. These forces organized resistance to Ayub Khan's policies and ultimately contributed to his fall in 1969.

The Ayub Khan regime collapsed before a rising tide of prodemocracy and leftist activism across Pakistan and ethnic nationalism in East Pakistan. The growing influence of the left and the appeal of ethnic identities in lieu of loyalty to the Islamic state put to question the role of Islam in Pakistan. The civil war of 1971, which brought the separation of East Pakistan into the independent state of Bangladesh, however, led many Pakistanis to turn to Islam for solace. They faulted the military, its misguided policies, and its secularism for the loss of East Pakistan.

Throughout the 1970s Islamic activism would gain ground, dominating student politics, labor unions, and professional associations. It would evolve into the main voice of dissent, eventually drowning leftist ideology and putting on the defensive the populist government of Prime Minister Zulfiqar Ali Bhutto (1971–1977). The prime minister, who had risen to power on the crest of a widely popular left-of-center movement, eventually adopted the demands of the Islamic opposition. It was Bhutto who finally declared the Ahmadiyya a non-Muslim minority in 1974 and in 1977 banned the serving of alcohol, closed casinos and nightclubs, and prohibited gambling and all other social activities proscribed by Islamic law. He had hoped that by surrendering to the demands of the Islamic groups he could mollify them. But Islamic parties were in no mood to be placated. They were now determined to use Islam to take over power. They continued the anti-Bhutto campaign, which ended only when the military, under the command of General Mohammad Zia ul-Haq, staged a coup in July 1977.

Harnessing the Power of Islam

During the Zia period (1977–1988) the state adopted a radically different approach to the role of Islam in public life. Zia was himself a devout Muslim, but more important, he understood that the state would gain more by harnessing the energies of the Islamic forces than by resisting them. He was, however, careful to protect the position of the state and to keep Islamic forces under state control. Zia opened state institutions and policy making to Islamic movements. The bureaucracy and the military became more openly Islamic, the state provided patronage to an array of Islamic activities, and Islam colored its policy making. In the process, Zia co-opted Islamic forces and protected the supreme position of the state. To do so the state itself became the initiator of Islamization, which was introduced through a series of legal and policy initiatives in 1979–1984.

The Islamization package included the introduction of Islamic penal, commercial, and inheritance laws and religious taxes and public observance of Islamic strictures, especially in women's dress. Zia's initiatives had a greater influence as Pakistan became an integral part of the Islamically charged anti-Soviet war in Afghanistan in the 1980s.

Co-opting Islamic forces, however, was not always easy, nor did it completely resolve the dilemma of controlling Islamization and its advocates. Zia proved willing to accept a greater sociopolitical role for Islamic forces and to give them considerable power and autonomy of action but only in matters that were limited to religious questions. Hence, symbolic measures such as selective application of Islamic penal laws, ceremonial applications of Islam's anti-usury laws, addition of the adjective "Islamic" to the titles of a whole host of programs and institutions, patronage of religious seminaries, festivals, and institutions, paying greater lip-service to Islam, restriction of social activities of women and minorities, and application of Islamic law in issues pertaining to personal conduct abounded.

The state, however, guarded its political and economic turf jealously. For instance, although Zia instituted a Federal Shari'at Court to review the compatibility of all laws with Islamic dictums, he was careful to exclude economic questions that would affect state policy from the court's activities. The state kept Islamization at bay and ran its affairs with the aid of the same constellation of social classes and interest groups, and in the same manner, that it had since 1947. Moreover, the state's tight control limited the power and autonomy that the Islamic parties enjoyed. Zia successfully prevented Islamic parties from exercising power independently of his regime, and especially in lieu of his authority. He resisted holding elections during the months immediately following the coup, when the Islamic parties might have fared well and found an independent base of support.

Meanwhile, through his patronage of Islamization Zia gained legitimacy and institutionalized his regime. He used the state's open advocacy of Islamization to control and even silence the Islamic parties, to postpone elections repeatedly, and to resist real economic and political changes or the meaningful restructuring of state policies. The fact that the state was so openly Islamic placed the Islamic parties in a very difficult position. In fact, Zia's pro-Islamization strategy divided Islamic activists over the extent to which they ought to support this champion of Islam even as he kept them under tight control and manipulated the role of Islam in politics. As a result, Zia deftly kept the Islamic parties in line without transferring real power to them.

During the Zia period Pakistan became more Islamic, levels of public observance increased, and Islam influenced all aspects of public policy and political interactions. Islamization did not, however, alter the country's sociopolitical structure and economic regime. After Zia was killed in a plane crash in 1988 and Pakistan moved swiftly toward democracy, economic grievances, ethnic tensions, and rivalries among the elite determined the political dynamics. Islam continued to influence politics but decreasingly and no longer directly. For a time Islamic parties wielded some power in the democratic arena but were eventually overshadowed by the rise to prominence of the Muslim League, which since 1993 has successfully created a broad right-of-center coalition that includes the Islamic vote but is not an exclusively Islamic party, further constricting the avowedly Islamic parties. In fact, many activists have turned to militancy, looking to the radical Taliban movement in Afghanistan as the model to follow.

After five decades of statehood, there is little doubt that Islam is important to Pakistan's identity and influences the country's politics. How exactly popular piety and religious activism shape the relationship between Islam and the state has become more complex with time, so that in this Muslim homeland, Islam is ubiquitous in public life, but Islamic parties are weak. Commitment to Islam is strong but is little reflected in the real political, economic, and social struggles in the country. The state has struggled with Islam; first resisting its influence, then suppressing it, but eventually learning to coexist with it, and even to control it.

See also *Afghanistan; India; Iqbal, Muhammad; Islam, Southeast Asia; Jinnah, Muhammad.*

Seyyed Vali Reza Nasr

BIBLIOGRAPHY

Abbott, Freeland. *Islam and Pakistan.* Ithaca, N.Y.: Cornell University Press, 1968.

Ahmad, Mumtaz. "Islam and the State: The Case of Pakistan." In *The Religious Challenge to the State,* edited by Mathew Moen and Lowell Gustafson. Philadelphia, Pa.: Temple University Press, 1992.

Binder, Leonard. *Religion and Politics in Pakistan.* Berkeley and Los Angeles: University of California Press, 1961.

Iqbal, Afzal. *Islamisation of Pakistan.* Lahore: Vanguard Books, 1986.

Kennedy, Charles H. "Islamization and Legal Reform in Pakistan, 1979–89." *Pacific Affairs* 63 1990: 62–77.

Nasr, Seyyed Vali Reza. *The Vanguard of the Islamic Revolution: The Jama'at-i Islami of Pakistan.* Berkeley and Los Angeles: University of California Press, 1994.

———. "Islamic Opposition in the Political Process: Lessons From Pakistan." In *Political Islam: Revolution, Radicalism, or Reform?* edited by John L. Esposito. Boulder, Colo.: Lynne Rienner, 1997.

Weiss, Anita, ed. *Islamic Reassertion in Pakistan.* Syracuse, N.Y.: Syracuse University Press, 1986.

Papacy

The papacy is the ecclesiastical office held by the pope, the bishop of Rome, who enjoys a primacy of honor and jurisdiction over every Roman Catholic bishop in communion with him. Together, these bishops teach, serve, and lead the world's one billion Catholics. The pope resides in the Vatican, a city-state in Rome, where he occupies the Holy See, the central administrative and governing body of the universal church.

Pope John Paul II (served 1978–) was the 261st successor of St. Peter, the first bishop of Rome, and he inherited the full powers and responsibilities promised by Jesus in Matthew 16:18–19, the biblical passage known as the Petrine Commission: "And so I say to you, you are Peter, and upon this rock I will build my church, and the gates of the netherworld shall not prevail against it. I give you the keys to the kingdom. Whatever you bind on earth shall be bound in heaven; and whatever you loose on earth shall be loosed in heaven." Although Catholics differ among themselves on the fine points of this doctrine of papal primacy, they stand apart from other Christians by their acceptance of its general teaching.

Pope Pius IX

The Battle against Liberalism and Modernism

The papacy entered the modern era possessed of a decidedly antimodern attitude. The longest-reigning pope in history, Pope Pius IX (served 1846–1878), bitterly presided over the loss of the Papal States (the central region of what is now Italy) to the forces of Italian national unification. With this defeat came an end to any effective papal claim to temporal sovereignty or direct political power, and the papacy entered a period of retrenchment known as "fortress Catholicism."

Earlier, in 1832 and 1834, Pius IX's predecessor, Pope Gregory XVI (served 1831–1846), had condemned modern liberalism and its principles of church–state separation, religious liberty, and freedom of the press. The target of his condemnation was a liberal French priest, Félicité Robert de Lamennais (1782–1854), and his progressive newspaper, *L'Avenir.* In 1864 Pius IX followed suit by issuing the *Syllabus of Errors,* a broad-based rejection of modern science and naturalism, "progress" pursued apart from the moral guidance of the church, and all forms and expressions of political and theological liberalism. With the aim of bolstering the church's defenses against such "acids of modernity," Pius IX convened the First Vatican Council at Rome five years later. In 1870 the council fathers solemnly defined the doctrine of papal infallibility, thereby empowering the pope to act alone as necessary (that is, without convening or directly consulting the bishops) to define Catholic doctrine and defend the apostolic faith. The foundations of the Catholic fortress were now securely in place.

Perhaps it was Pius IX's zealous opposition to modern ideas and political institutions that enabled his successor, Pope Leo XIII (served 1878–1903), to attempt a partial rapprochement with modernity. For Catholics concerned with reversing the church's image as the final refuge of monarchists and theocrats, the twentieth century effectively began in 1891 with the appearance of the encyclical letter *Rerum Novarum* ("The Condition of Labor"), the initial articulation of modern Catholic social doctrine. Applying the philosophy of natural law to the political economy, Leo XIII denounced socialism for violating man's natural (and sacred) right to own private property—an error the pope attributed to socialism's atheistic ideology. He also turned a critical eye toward laissez-faire capitalism and the inhumane excesses of the unfettered market. To fight worker exploitation and ensure the payment of a "just wage" by employers, Pope Leo urged Catholics to organize Christian workingmen's associations (modeled, by his description, more along the lines of medieval guilds than modern labor unions).

While sharing his immediate predecessor's attitude toward the loss of the Papal States and the church's political clout in Europe, Leo XIII was a political realist. Accordingly, he crafted a more flexible approach to international politics, one based more on diplomacy than denunciation. Thus, although he forbade Catholics to participate in elections in the new Italian state and warned against certain spiritual and ecclesial tendencies collected under the rubric of "Americanism," the pope boldly encouraged French Catholics to support the Third Republic, successfully blocked or modified anticlerical legislation in Germany, Spain, Mexico, and Chile, and praised the United States for allowing the Catholic Church to flourish there.

In its relative openness to the modern nation-state and to democracy (as a temporary, if not ideal, arrangement), Leo's pontificate established a precedent that later popes would develop. Pope Leo XIII's immediate successor, however, chose the name "Pius," signaling a preference for the antidemocratic, antiliberal animus of Pius IX. The political orientation of Pope Pius X (served 1903–1914) was reflected in his attitudes toward two French sociopolitical movements.

While he tolerated the right-wing, monarchist *Action Française,* Pius X condemned the politically liberal and religiously ecumenical movement *Le Sillon.* His conservative-reactionary secretary of state, the Spanish cardinal Rafael Merry del Val, immediately set to work to fashion a less accommodating relationship to secular governments. Merry del Val preferred to confront secularizing or secularized states rather than bargain with them, a policy that placed the church in Portugal and France in a weakened, albeit less dependent, position vis-à-vis the state. Similarly, the Vatican chose vigorous and uncompromising advocacy of the rights of Catholic minorities in Ireland and Poland over compromise and concordats with their political masters, England and Russia.

At times the hard line seemed to backfire. For example, Pope Pius X alienated the American public in 1910 when he refused to receive Theodore Roosevelt because the ex-president was scheduled to speak at the Methodist church in Rome. The pope also risked alienating the Catholic working classes when he opposed trade unions that were not exclusively Catholic.

Pius X also perceived a dark force building within the church itself, a "synthesis of heresies," composed of previously condemned theological and philosophical errors revived under the auspices of the new Darwinian thought, subjectivist and agnostic philosophies, and the so-called higher criticism of the Bible (a method of examining the historical and literary character of the Bible as if it were just another book). In the thinking of Pius X's curial theologians, the small and scattered company of scholarly, progressive priests in France, England, and Italy who were corresponding with one another and contributing articles to one another's journals constituted a dire threat to the supernatural worldview undergirding Catholicism. (The priests did perhaps constitute a potential threat to one prominent school of theology known as neoscholasticism and its control over the expressions of that supernatural worldview, which was enough to mark them for censure.) In 1907 Pius X issued a sweeping condemnation of their "movement" and the "heretical synthesis" of ideas and methods it promoted, which he designated as "Modernism."

The subsequent systematic campaign to extirpate all traces of Modernism within the church, bolstered by a mandatory clerical oath against the heresy and a network of informants to report on deviations from doctrinal orthodoxy, had a profound, and partly ironic, impact on twentieth-century Catholicism. On the one hand, it undermined what had been the primary strength of Catholic intellectual life—theological and philosophical thought—by discouraging Catholic scholars from pursuing new, nonscholastic lines of inquiry in their teaching and research. On the other hand, the crackdown meant that the best and brightest of the clergy would turn their attentions to the elaboration and application of the nascent social doctrines of the church that were papal in origin and thus beyond reproach. In this way, Pius X inadvertently promoted the legacy of Leo XIII.

The World Wars, the Rise of Communism, and "Catholic Action"

Pius X's successor, Pope Benedict XV (served 1914–1922), tried to move the church beyond the factionalism of the modernist controversy, but his pontificate was inevitably defined by the First World War (1914–1918). Initially Benedict XV maintained a neutral posture, and in 1917 he proposed a seven-point peace plan calling for the renunciation of war indemnities and the return of all occupied territories. Both the Allies and the Central Powers, however, ignored his plan. Later, believing that Benedict XV had harbored hopes of a German victory that might have returned Rome to the Holy See, the Allies and Italy agreed to exclude him from negotiations to end the war.

After the war Benedict XV supported the establishment in 1920 of the League of Nations (predecessor of the United Nations) and worked to restore the Vatican's diplomatic relations with the erstwhile combatants. His canonization of French heroine Joan of Arc (1412–1431) in 1920 was an attempt to repair the breach with France. Similarly, the pope permitted Italian Catholics to participate once again in the political process, and he sent an emissary to Benito Mussolini, Italy's fascist prime minister from 1922 to 1943, for the purpose of regularizing the status of the Holy See within the Italian state.

Benedict XV did not live to see the result of the latter initiative; his successor, Pope Pius XI (served 1922–1939), signed the Lateran Treaty of 1929, which established the Vatican city-state as a separate and independent political entity. Under its terms, the Catholic Church officially recognized the Italian state, and Italy compensated the Vatican financially for the loss of the Papal States, repealed its anticlerical laws, recognized Catholicism as the official religion of the country, and mandated religious instruction in secondary schools.

Pope Pius XI also is remembered for, among other things, his virulent anticommunism and his support of Catholic Action, a series of European and American social movements of workers, students, and married couples, designed to involve lay Catholics in the work of spreading the Gospel and modeling Christian behavior to a secularized world. The pope believed that atheistic communism was the supreme social evil threatening church and world, and he went so far as to bolster its natural enemy, fascism, by signing agreements or concordats with Mussolini and German Nazi dictator Adolf Hitler and by supporting Spanish dictator Francisco Franco during Spain's civil war (1936–1939).

Pius XI soon came to regret his initial openness to Italian fascism and Nazism. The break with Mussolini came in 1931 after the dictator dissolved Catholic youth organizations in Italy; in response, Pius XI issued an encyclical critical of the Italian version of fascism. In 1933 the pope began to protest formally the Nazi government's oppression of the church. In 1937 he promulgated the encyclical *Mit Brennender Sorge* ("With Searing Anxiety"), a powerful denunciation of Nazism as fundamentally racist and anti-Christian which he ordered to be read from every German pulpit. Infuriated, the Nazis intensified their persecution of the church and its priests.

Pius XI chose the fortieth anniversary of *Rerum Novarum* to advance Catholic social doctrine to the next level of elaboration. His 1931 social encyclical, *Quadragesimo Anno* ("Fortieth Anniversary"), addressed the sources and effects of the worldwide economic depression, repeating and developing Leo XIII's criticism of both the radical individualism associated with capitalism and the extreme collectivism of the socialist left. At the same time, he argued that the right to own private property does not give people license to ignore the requirements of social justice and the common good.

Quadragesimo anno also introduced the principle of subsidiarity, which quickly became a cornerstone of the evolving Catholic social tradition. It holds that nothing is to be done by a higher agency that can be accomplished at a lower, or more local, level. A curb on the encroachments of the modern nation-state, subsidiarity also reflected the Catholic affirmation of the family as the primary educator of children.

Pope Pius XII (served 1939–1958) shared his predecessor's horror of the evils of communism and promoted devotion to the Blessed Mother (Virgin Mary) as a means of battling the menace. In 1950 he exercised papal infallibility to proclaim the dogma of the Assumption (of Mary ascending bodily into heaven).

When war threatened Europe in 1939, Pius XII called for diplomatic initiatives to resolve differences peacefully. When World War II (1939–1945) finally erupted, he adopted an impartial stance, reluctant to speak out forcefully and publicly in behalf of the Jews and other persecuted minorities—a failure that history has judged severely as a case of moral cowardice or implicit anti-Semitism. His defenders claimed that Pius XII condemned genocide only in general terms because he feared that stronger and more explicit denunciations would lead to even greater reprisals, and they pointed to his personal support of efforts to rescue Jews from the Holocaust. (After the German army occupied Rome in September 1943, for example, Pius XII offered Vatican City as a haven for many refugees, including Jews.)

Overshadowed by the controversy over Pius XII's reaction to Nazism was his dynamic leadership of the church as it entered a period of renewal. Unfortunately, his leadership found full official expression only after his death, in the Second Vatican Council (1962–1965). Indeed, the encyclicals of Pius XII were truly pioneering. *Mystici Corporis* ("On the Mystical Body," 1943) borrowed a scriptural metaphor to describe the church as the mystical body of Christ, a reality encompassing laity as well as clergy, and spiritual as well as institutional markers of membership. *Divino Afflante Spiritu* ("Inspired by the Divine Spirit," 1943) made the "turn to Scripture" explicit by permitting Catholic biblical scholars to employ the (previously condemned) tools of critical science and critical history to interpret the Bible in its original historical and theological contexts. This opening to the "new" biblical criticism eventually revolutionized the way Catholics thought about other Christians, the church, and revelation itself. *Mediator Dei* ("Mediator of God," 1947) described the laity—previously subordinate and passive observers of the Catholic Mass—as central participants in the worship of the church.

These openings to a new way of being Catholic remained inchoate and ambiguous during Pius XII's pontificate; indeed, he issued an encyclical in 1950, *Humani Generis* ("Of the Human Race"), that condemned much of the theological ferment presaging and accompanying his progressive encyclicals of the forties. It was left to the relatively obscure patriarch of Venice, Angelo Roncalli, who took the name John XXIII on his election in 1958, to usher the Catholic Church fully and finally into the modern world.

Developing Catholic Social Doctrine

Elected by the College of Cardinals as a compromise candidate, "good Pope John," as Pope John XXIII (served 1958–1963) was affectionately called, surprised the world by convening the Second Vatican Council in 1962. In doing so, he proclaimed that the church needed "updating" (*aggiornamento*) in order to more effectively celebrate what was good and refine what was promising in the modern world. He saw the church as a beacon of hope, a community of disciples of Christ, and a company of spiritual pilgrims open to dialogue and collaboration with other Christians, non-Christians, and nonbelievers.

Pope John XXIII's social encyclicals reflected this hopeful appraisal of the church and its responsibilities to the modern world. *Mater et Magistra* ("Mother and Teacher," 1961), released on the seventieth anniversary of *Rerum Novarum,* set Catholic social teaching on property, the rights of workers, and the obligations of government within the new global context of socialization. The pope defined socialization as the science and technology-driven "multiplication of social relationships, that is, a daily, more complex interdependence of citizens . . . introducing into their lives and activities many and varied forms of association." Such a world required greater levels of international and governmental collaboration and leadership, Pope John XXIII observed, in order to serve the common good. *Pacem in Terris* ("Peace on Earth," 1963) linked world peace to the universal recognition and protection of human rights and responsibilities. Urging the community of nations to strengthen its collaborative governing institutions such as the United Nations, the pope called for global nuclear disarmament, decolonization of the developing world, and an even-handed approach to economic development.

Pope John XXIII's pontificate thus set the church on a path-breaking and exhilarating journey that led to the affirmation of innate human dignity, rather than theological orthodoxy and Catholic Church membership, as the authentic source of civil rights and political self-determination. Proclaimed in Vatican II's *Dignitatis Humanae* ("Declaration on Religious Freedom"), the relocation of fundamental human rights in the person rather than in the church or the state further aligned the modern church with democratic polities and against all forms of totalitarianism.

Pope Paul VI (served 1963–1978) upheld and advanced Pope John XXIII's legacy, focusing especially on the growing and scandalous disparity between the developed and underdeveloped nations. "The world is sick," Pope Paul VI wrote in *Populorum Progressio* ("On the Development of Peoples," 1967). "Its illness consists less in the unproductive monopolization of resources by a small number of men than in the lack of brotherhood among individuals and peoples." Calling on the wealthy to embrace the spirit of brotherhood, Pope Paul VI linked economic justice to political stability, proclaiming that "the new name for peace is development."

Embodying a new awareness and appreciation of Catholicism as a truly global and multicultural church, Paul VI traveled more widely than any previous pope. In terms of long-range impact on the international church, Pope Paul's greatest contribution might have been his transformation of the College of Cardinals (the Catholics designated to elect the pope) into a truly multinational, multicultural body by his elevation of bishops from all corners of the globe to the rank of cardinal. By 1976 the college had 148 members, of whom Italians constituted a small minority.

Paul VI was succeeded in 1978 by Pope John Paul I, who died after thirty-three days in office. His successor, Pope John Paul II, was the first Slavic pope in history and the first non-Italian pope since Hadrian VI (served 1522–1523). He also has been the most well-known and well-traveled pope in history, one of the most prolific popes in exercising his teaching office, and perhaps one of the most influential in world-historical terms.

Many political analysts have credited John Paul II, in his lifelong opposition to Marxism and Soviet state socialism and in his outspoken support, as pope, of the Solidarity movement in the 1980s in his native Poland, with providing the political inspiration and the moral courage necessary for the masses to topple communism in Eastern Europe in 1990–1991, a historic event that contributed mightily to the 1991 collapse of the Soviet Union. Pope John Paul II's fervid opposition to Marxist influence also extended to the church itself; in the 1980s the Congregation for the Doctrine of the Faith, led by Cardinal Joseph Ratzinger, issued statements highly critical of Latin American priests who were practicing Marxist-influenced liberation theology. A tireless advocate for social and economic justice and a defender and promoter of human rights, the pope ordered Catholic priests to follow his example, so to speak, by offering powerful social and cultural criticism and moral witness rather than by holding political office or participating in narrowly partisan politics.

The social magisterium of John Paul II developed Vatican II's teaching on religious freedom and other human rights by advocating pluralism—the principled embrace of religious plurality—as the sine qua non of civil society. A vibrant civil society with strong voluntary associations and religious institutions, John Paul taught, strengthens the political will of citizens to resist the encroachment of the modern secular state into realms beyond its competence and authority.

Pope John Paul II's progressive and often courageous social teaching was couched in, and accompanied by, bracing reaffirmations of traditional Catholic morality. His early social encyclicals such as *Redemptor Hominis* ("Redempter of Humanity," 1979) and *Laborem Exercens* ("On Human Work," 1981) grounded denunciations of human rights abuses, consumerism, and environmental exploitation and advocacy of workers' rights and responsibilities in an incarnational theology that emphasized the inviolable dignity and worth of every human person. Other major social encyclicals followed: *Sollicitudo Rei Socialis* ("Solicitude for Social Concerns," 1987) updated the themes of *Populorum Progressio,* including the need for development; *Centesimus Annus* ("The Hundredth Year") marked the centennial of *Rerum Novarum* by reaffirming the church's "preferential option for the poor" and by praising democratic political systems for ensuring the participation of all citizens in government. In the 1990s Pope John Paul II issued *Veritatis Splendor* ("On the Splendor of Truth," 1993), a profound and stern condemnation of moral relativism and the ethical position known as proportionalism, followed by the encyclical *Evangelium Vitae* ("The Gospel of Life," 1995), which condemned birth control, abortion, and euthanasia as expressive of a secular and materialistic "culture of death" infecting Western society.

See also *Catholicism, Roman; Fascism; Holocaust; Liberation theology; Vatican; Vatican Council, Second.*

R. Scott Appleby

BIBLIOGRAPHY

Gremillion, Joseph, ed. *The Gospel of Peace and Justice: Catholic Social Teaching since Pope John.* Maryknoll, N.Y.: Orbis Books, 1976.
McBrien, Richard P. *Lives of the Popes: The Pontiffs from St. Peter to John Paul II.* San Francisco: HarperCollins, 1997.
O'Brien, David J., and Thomas A. Shannon. *Catholic Social Thought: The Documentary Heritage.* Maryknoll, N.Y.: Orbis Books, 1992.
Reese, Thomas J. *Inside the Vatican: The Politics and Organization of the Catholic Church.* Cambridge: Harvard University Press, 1996.
Weigel, George. *Soul of the World: Notes on the Future of Public Catholicism.* Washington, D.C., and Grand Rapids, Mich.: William B. Eerdmans and the Ethics and Public Policy Center, 1996.

Pax Christi

See *Catholicism, Roman*

Pentecostalism

Pentecostalism is a Protestant movement that originated at the turn of the twentieth century in the United States but since has spread to other countries, particularly in Latin America. The movement takes it name from the Christian feast of Pentecost, which celebrates the descent of the Holy Spirit upon the disciples of Jesus.

The United States has many pentecostal denominations and a vast number of independent pentecostal congregations. The two largest pentecostal denominations are the Assemblies of God and the Church of God in Christ. Historically, most North American pentecostalists have assumed that the church has no direct place in politics. Rather, congregations train people, instilling moral principles and a sense of identity and meaning. Those trained individuals then blend into the larger culture as "salt" and "leaven." Some may choose careers in government and politics, while many more simply opt to live out their conceptions of citizenship, stewardship, and care for one's neighbor.

American pentecostalism emerged gradually after 1900 out of radical evangelical contexts. Many of its early adherents already had forsaken historic Protestant denominations for the warmth and fervor of independent and Holiness congregations. When they embraced pentecostalism's distinctive view that the baptism with the Holy Spirit always would be evidenced by speaking in tongues, they found themselves on the margins of radical evangelicalism. They created new networks bound by periodicals and camp meetings that nurtured their renewed sense of urgency about their overwhelming conviction that the world was about to end in cataclysmic divine judgment (also known as end times) and world evangelization. Self-consciously other worldly in piety, they also manifested entrepreneurial and pragmatic instincts that helped to assure their rapid expansion.

Early pentecostalists found themselves uncomfortable in the Protestant establishment for many reasons. For one thing, their belief that the world would end in cataclysmic divine judgment distanced many from the Social Gospel and its political implications (the Social Gospel was an attempt by theologically liberal American Protestants to bring the power of faith to bear on social problems). For another, they considered mainline congregations spiritually "dead" and culturally ingrown.

A few spoke out on public issues and some devoted their lives and resources to assisting the needy, but the movement adopted no corporate stance on the urgent political issues of the day, with the exception of the pacifist stance adopted by movement leaders during World War I (1914–1918). What views early pentecostalists had were shaped by their conviction that pentecostalism was a revival that signaled the imminent end of the world. They eagerly looked for signs that biblical prophecies related to the end times were being fulfilled. They saw God and Satan locked in combat everywhere in life's small annoyances, illness, the loss of a job, or the problems of nations. Indeed, life for them was lived out in the context of the ultimate conflict between God and Satan. Political involvements had little appeal: evangelism in the face of imminent divine judgment seemed all that mattered.

Origins of American Pentecostalism

Speaking in tongues occurred in many settings in nineteenth-century America, from Mormons and Adventists to spiritualists, immigrant pietists, and Holiness people. Charles Fox Parham, a one-time Methodist who in 1900 supervised a healing home, city mission, and Bible school in Topeka, Kansas, is generally credited with first linking speaking in tongues to the baptism with the Holy Spirit. Over time, this view came to be called "uniform initial physical evidence." It resolved the troubling question of how one could be certain one had received the baptism with the Holy Spirit (a subject of intense concern among radical evangelicals in the 1890s). It also gave identity to a fledgling movement otherwise indistinguishable from an array of contemporary groups that also shared an emphasis on the end times, healing, evangelism, and holiness.

In January 1901 Parham began promulgating his view of tongues speech and its link to baptism with the Holy Spirit. For the next four years, he traveled through Kansas, Missouri, Oklahoma, and Texas, where he gained a following for the "apostolic faith." New Testament religion had been restored in the end times, he maintained; the "full gospel" included healing, holiness, and the baptism with the Holy Spirit, evidenced by speaking in tongues.

While Parham had an interest in persuading unchurched Americans to respond to his gospel, he and his followers also directed their energies toward church members. He found strong support in the Houston area, where, among others, he influenced William Seymour, a black preacher. Seymour brought Parham's message to Los Angeles in 1906, and a revival resulted, centered in an abandoned Methodist church building on Azusa Street (in what is now the city's Little Tokyo). Within a few months revival news from Los Angeles circulated around the world, first among the radical evangelical groups whose periodicals carried reports. The reports generated controversy and sparked curiosity, drawing people to the meetings. The convinced regarded what was happening as a sign of the imminence of Christ's return. It was the fulfillment of prophecy and an "enduement with power for service" for the rapid evangelization of the world.

The revival progressed without reference to the political issues of the day. Its message was premillennialist, and the expectation that Christ might burst through the clouds at any moment nurtured a preoccupation with individual readiness for the hereafter rather than concern for current issues. If early pentecostalists manifested political activism at all, it was directed primarily toward foreign policy—especially Israel. Charles Parham, a Zionist, spoke eloquently in behalf of Theodor Herzl (1860–1904), the Hungarian Zionist leader who in the 1890s advocated the establishment of a Jewish state in Palestine. Before his teaching spawned the pentecostal movement, Parham also had publicly advocated women's suffrage and the Kansas temperance movement. But during the busy years that followed the first outburst of tongues at his Topeka Bible school, Parham apparently neglected his earlier political pursuits. Yet when dissension within early pentecostal ranks effectively marginalized him after 1908, he used his periodical, *The Apostolic Faith,* to comment in a rambling fashion on selected issues of the day. By then, however, others were setting the direction of the pentecostal movement.

One of those whose curiosity about revival led him to Azusa Street was Charles Harrison Mason, a black Holiness preacher from Arkansas and Tennessee. Mason was one of several evangelists who worked with Charles Price Jones, a Baptist Holiness preacher from Mississippi whose followers often shared the name the Church of God in Christ. Another name popular among them—and the one Mason used for his own congregation in Memphis until at least 1920—was Church of the Living God.

Eventually, Mason embraced the pentecostal message. His colleague Charles Price Jones did not and renamed his following the Church of Christ (Holiness) USA. The Church of God in Christ became a pentecostal denomination. Incorporated first in the state of Mississippi, it was predominantly black.

The Assemblies of God was formed in Hot Springs, Arkansas, in 1914. It united various regional networks of pentecostal pastors, evangelists, and missionaries, predominantly white, into a national group. Unlike the Church of God in Christ, the Assemblies of God was not expressly a Holiness pentecostal denomination.

In founding the Assemblies of God, in 1914, its leaders, including J. Roswell Flower (left), and E. N. Bell, formed a national organization from regional Reformed congregations and networks of individual pentecostal ministers.

Pentecostalism and Politics

World War I forced these fledgling pentecostal denominations to face political issues, but debates about pacifism and military service for the most part did not translate into advocacy of any political party agenda. Pentecostalists disagreed sharply about whether Christians should fight. Strong pacifist voices were countered by others who manifested deep antipathies toward Germany and Germans. Some worried about the hatred and bigotry fostered by the war. Frank Bartleman, an itinerant pentecostal evangelist and prolific writer, maintained that the war climate made it impossible to preach a gospel of love—after all, love for a German was sedition. An ardent pacifist, Bartleman concluded that war precluded the preaching and practice of true Christianity and mandated civil disobedience; therefore, it was wrong. Charles Mason's friendship with some pentecostalists of German birth as well as his own pacifism were noted by the federal government, and he was arrested in Lexington, Massachusetts, on charges of sedition. But a white supporter posted bond, and Mason ultimately was cleared. The Assemblies of God published articles with a clear pacifist message in its official periodical, but soon responded to constituents who strongly supported the war by also airing their views. The paper came to favor conscientious objection but revealed a wide range of views among clergy. No other event resulted in a similar engagement in public issues.

World War I also intrigued pentecostalists with its prophetic implications. The end of time seemed to them ominously near. In the decades after the war, a continuing fascination for end-times prophecies prompted what little political awareness pentecostal denominations manifested.

Fascist Italian prime minister Benito Mussolini, Nazi German dictator Adolf Hitler, President Franklin D. Roosevelt's New Deal in the United States, and the creation of the state of Israel all took their places in the prophetic calendar. The 1960 U.S. presidential election and the candidacy of Roman Catholic John F. Kennedy elicited warnings from individual leaders (most notably Assemblies of God general superintendent Thomas F. Zimmerman) against electing a Catholic president—a warning couched more in religious terms than in political terms.

The reluctance of early pentecostal denominations to engage the political sphere was rooted, as noted, in the conviction that the church's mission was primarily to prepare for the end of time and to evangelize. The church trained good citizens by inculcating Christian values and encouraging voter participation guided by individual conscience. Evangelist Aimee Semple McPherson of Los Angeles, founder of the International Church of the Foursquare Gospel, was a case in point. She occasionally spoke out on local issues that had moral overtones. A pioneer gospel broadcaster, McPherson commanded a huge following in the Los Angeles area in the 1920s. She orchestrated patriotic displays second to none in her day, and her people rushed to scenes of disaster to offer relief. In the 1930s her commissary fed and clothed hundreds of thousands of people impoverished by the depression. In the 1940s she promoted war bonds. She encouraged patriotism, civic involvement, community service, and humanitarian aid, but she stopped short of political endorsements.

Individual pentecostalists, then, occasionally expressed an interest in politics and political action. And they have done so with more frequency since World War II (1939–1945), serving in local, state, and national government in both elective and appointive roles. James G. Watt, secretary of the interior from 1981 to 1983 under President Ronald Reagan and an Assemblies of God layman, was the first pentecostal cabinet appointee. Pat Robertson, a Southern Baptist and unsuccessful contender for the 1988 Republican presidential nomination, embraced the charismatic movement and thus entered an extensive network of people who cultivate pentecostal forms of spirituality without joining a pentecostal denomination. He found a following among so-called classical pentecostalists as well. Missourian John Ashcroft, also an Assemblies of God layman, served two terms as governor of Missouri (1985–1993) before moving to Washington, D.C., in 1994 to take a seat in the U.S. Senate. In 1998 a handful of other pentecostalists served in the House of Representatives.

While the Assemblies of God as a denomination largely ignored the civil rights movement in the 1960s, the Church of God in Christ emerged as a significant presence in local and national civil rights activism. In 1964 a strike by Memphis garbage workers gained the support and cooperation of the Church of God in Christ, which offered its large denominational headquarters church in Memphis as a meeting place for the strikers.

The civil rights movement represented something of a turning point for black pentecostalists who, some argue, had tended to emphasize the economy of salvation rather than the secular political economy. Since the 1960s, with varying urgency, Church of God in Christ pastors and congregants across the country have been providing community leadership, addressing the problems of juvenile delinquency, and delivering social services. They band together with other community churches more readily than before, although their historic tendency toward pietistic individualism still sometimes sets them apart. This community involvement, however, is not entirely new to black pentecostalism. In the 1930s, for example, a female black pastor, Lucy Smith, provided social services in Chicago's impoverished Bronzeville neighborhood through her pentecostal Church of All Nations.

Today, the Church of God in Christ is the largest black pentecostal denomination in the United States, but black pentecostalism itself is much larger. Indeed, it is one of the most powerful expressions of black faith in the world, with more adherents and more influence than the historic black denominations. Independent pentecostal preachers, as well as pastors whose activities rather than denominational affiliation define them, manifest political agendas far more ambitious than those their predecessors in the pentecostal movement would likely have embraced. Al Sharpton, a pentecostal minister from Brooklyn, has no pulpit but preaches a radical street politics that molds a following. Eugene Rivers of Boston is perhaps the most prominent of a group of urban pastors whose efforts to reclaim neighborhoods and people for civil society have won the applause of law enforcement and made them contenders for tax dollars. In an era of welfare reform, some urban black pentecostalists stand at the cutting edge of alternative programs.

Adherents of the Assemblies of God, by contrast, often demonstrate an inclination toward the Christian right. They tend to be social conservatives, supporters of Israel, advocates of prayer in public schools, and opponents of abortion and homosexual rights. Anglo pentecostal views on such issues have been influenced by television evangelists, most notably in the 1980s by preacher Jimmy Swaggart and Jim and Tammy Bakker and their PTL (Praise the Lord) Club, and in the 1990s by preacher Oral Roberts, Phil and Jan Crouch of TBN (Trinity Broadcasting Network), and Pat Robertson. The Assemblies of God has promoted Senator Ashcroft, a favorite of the Christian right who supports legislation on issues of morality and tax support for private and parochial schools. The social conservatism and vision for America outlined by, among others, James Dobson of Focus on the Family and Pat Robertson also have substantial followings of North American pentecostalists.

Black and Latino pentecostalists always have been active in the cities, home of many of their adherents. As minorities, they have been forced to confront city hall and government policies in ways that Anglo congregations have not. In the 1980s Anglo pentecostalists began to build an urban presence—thus they too sometimes find themselves part of efforts to renew communities. Meanwhile, some pentecostalists outside the United States were taking up corporate political activism in ways that North American pentecostalists generally had not.

Pentecostalism in Latin America

In parts of Latin America, pentecostal leaders have intentionally chosen to enter the political arena. When Brazil held elections for a constitutional assembly in 1986, eighteen pentecostalists were among the thirty-three Protestants elected. The International Church of the Foursquare Gospel, independent of its U.S. parent body since 1980, ran its own candidates, chosen by the pastors, in the election. Other pentecostal churches also led efforts to elect a pentecostalist from each state. Those who won church endorsement tended to be men who had distinguished themselves in the work of the church or well-to-do businessmen who wielded financial influence in the churches. They were not ordinary members who announced their own candidacies and built grassroots support through trade unions or other local agencies. As Brazil made the transition from military to democratic government in the late 1980s, pentecostal denominational leaders decided to get involved by identifying candidates from their membership and then mobilizing the membership to vote. Although pentecostal leaders in Brazil often support conservative political agendas, at the local level adherents of pentecostal churches sometimes participate in labor unions and political party structures that pentecostalists once shunned. Some large denominations still officially frown on political involvement, but most are now finding their way into the system. As they climb the social ladder, pentecostalists in state and national parliaments are forced to deal with issues, such as debt crises, that once seemed utterly remote to the primary pentecostal task of evangelization.

Perhaps nowhere have pentecostalists attained higher office than in Guatemala. There, pentecostalists, like other Protestants, traditionally have been conservative, endorsing little or no social involvement. But in Guatemala, Efraín Ríos Montt became the first pentecostalist to serve as head of state (1978–1983). Although Montt was not a member of a missionary-established denomination, leaders of the North American Assemblies of God proudly posed with him, as he was widely regarded as a symbol of the growing acceptance of pentecostalists in Latin America.

Meanwhile, in Chile Gen. Augusto Pinochet, who led a four-man ruling junta, attended the dedication of a huge pentecostal church, thereby recognizing both the size of this pentecostal congregation and promises of political support from pentecostal pastors. Chilean pentecostal leaders have tended to be conservative, rejecting violence and class warfare and advocating private property. Nevertheless, a minority among pentecostalists in Chile affiliated with the World Council of Churches and in 1988 in Nicaragua signed a document entitled "Kairos Central America: A Challenge to the Churches of the World" that called for (in terms unusual for pentecostalists) economic justice.

In violent places in Latin America, pentecostalists—like other Protestants who have refused violence and taken no side—sometimes have been martyred. In Colombia the quest for peace led the pastor of one of Bogota's largest evangelical churches, the International Charismatic Mission, to seek office in the Colombia House of Representatives. Elected in 1998, Cesar Castellanos expressed his sense of mission in terms also relevant in other parts of South America: he is determined to work on the social and political fronts as well as on the spiritual to bring peace and justice to his world.

Pentecostalism is growing most rapidly outside the United States, and where it is growing, indigenous movements thrive side by side with missionary churches and often outpace them. The approaches of U.S. pentecostalists to politics and government are not necessarily replicated abroad. In the United States pentecostal reluctance to participate in politics beyond individual activism shows signs of erosion. Early pentecostalists did not expect to be around for long. Now after nearly a century of existence, and disappointed by what it perceives as the erosion of America's moral core, the pentecostal movement is slowly expanding the fronts on which it pursues its visions of power and righteousness.

See also *Brazil; Communication; Conservatism; Evangelicalism; Herzl, Theodor; Latin America; Millennialism; Social Gospel; Zionism.*

Edith L. Blumhofer

BIBLIOGRAPHY

Alvarez, Carmelo. *People of Hope: The Protestant Movement in Central America.* New York: Friendship Press, 1990.

Blumhofer, Edith. *Restoring the Faith.* Champaign, Ill.: University of Illinois Press, 1993.

Frazier, E. F. *The Negro Church in America,* and C. Eric Lincoln, *The Black Church since Frazier.* New York: Schocken Books, 1974.

Hollenweger, Walter. *The Pentecostals.* Minneapolis: Augsburg, 1972.

Lincoln, C. Eric, and Lawrence Mamiya. *The Black Church in the African American Experience.* Durham, N.C.: Duke University Press, 1990.

Martin, David T. *Tongues of Fire: The Explosion of Protestantism in Latin America.* Oxford: Basil Blackwell, 1990.

Stoll, David. *Rethinking Protestantism in Latin America.* Philadelphia: Temple University Press, 1993.

Wilmore, Gayraud W. *Black Religion and Black Radicalism.* Maryknoll, N.Y.: Orbis Books, 1983.

Philanthropy

Philanthropy is the social relation of care in which individuals (and groups) respond to the moral invitation to expand the horizons of their self-interest to include meeting the needs of others.

Philanthropy as a Social Relation of Care

Many definitions of philanthropy have been offered. Some stress its voluntary nature and welfare goals. Others focus on what is legally demarcated as charity. And still others emphasize the institutional sector in which the giving occurs. None of these definitions does justice to the fundamental essence of philanthropy as a social relation revolving around the moral virtue of *caritas* (love for others in their true needs) and extending beyond the legal and sectoral meanings of the term *philanthropy* itself.

As just defined, philanthropy conjoins a resolute sentiment of sympathetic identification with the fate of others, a thoughtful discernment of what needs to be done, and a strategic course of action aimed at meeting the needs of others. This definition does not differentiate philanthropic relations from commercial and political relations—all are voluntary in nature, dedicated to the "public good," and occur in civil society or the nonprofit sector. Rather, the distinctive attribute of philanthropy is the kind of signal or moral claim that mobilizes and governs the matching of resources to needs.

Most efforts to conceptualize philanthropy emphasize the presence of a special dedication to the public good or philanthropy's voluntary nature. Neither of these aspects, however, gets to the essence of what distinguishes philanthropy from politics and commerce in a positive, rather than derivative, way. First, attending to the public good is not a claim that can be made exclusively in behalf of philanthropy. Commerce and politics also enjoy many moral and philosophical—not to mention ideological—arguments extolling their contribution to the public good. Philanthropy is not distinctive in having an intention to meet people's needs, but in the kind of signals it pays attention to in deciding what needs of which people are important to allay.

Second, to delimit philanthropy by its "voluntary" character is equally unpersuasive, if by voluntary one means free from obligation. Hallowed religious and ethical traditions speak unapologetically about the *obligation* of attending to the needs of others. It is simply not the case that philanthropy is sheltered from external pressures. For example, many wealthy donors recount the array of pressures or imperatives—business, tax, community, personal, political, and moral—that do in fact compel their philanthropic activity. Again, philanthropic relations are not distinctive because of the absence of obligation but because of the moral nature of the obligation and the signals of entreaty by which the obligation is brought within the conscience of the donor.

Indeed, philanthropy is a particular kind of interactive production process. It is a social relation governed by a moral obligation that matches a supply of private resources to a demand of unfulfilled needs and desires that are communicated by entreaty. The defining characteristic of philanthropy is in the *type of social signals* it responds to rather than in some formal, institutional characteristic such as its tax status, its normative attribute such as its being voluntary, or its particular goal such as service of the public good.

Commercial activity is mobilized by the medium of financial capital in the form of revenue and income. Political activity is mobilized by the medium of political capital in the form of votes and campaign contributions. Philanthropic activity is mobilized by the medium of moral or cultural capital in the form of symbolic expressions of need. In *commercial* relations, needs elicit a response largely to the extent that they become expressed in dollars—that is, translated into what economists call "effective demand." Similarly, in *political* relations needs elicit a response largely to the extent that they can become expressed as campaign contributions or as votes—what in fact is another form of effective demand. Just what makes commercial and political demand "effective" in eliciting a response? It is that these forms of demand are presented through a medium that suppliers (those offering economic or political goods and services) must receive to remain viable. Neither businesses nor politicians can long afford to ignore such concrete indications of their clients' will. For example, automobile companies and U.S. senators eventually must bow to the desires of their constituencies or risk losing the revenue that keeps them in existence. Thus attention to needs is generated not directly by the inherent importance of the needs themselves but indirectly by the functional importance of the medium (income, votes, contributions, and so forth) through which the needs are expressed.

In philanthropic relations the medium for communicating needs is neither votes nor dollars but the symbolic medium of words and images. In contrast to commercial and political relations, philanthropy thus utilizes "affective" rather than "effective" demand. The demand of needs is expressed through the medium of entreaty whereby the needs themselves, rather than the medium through which they are presented, become the immediate object of attention. In French novelist Victor Hugo's 1862 play *Les Misérables* the main character, Jean Valjean, consoles the dying prostitute he has befriended, Fantine, by agreeing to bring Fantine's daughter, Cosette, under his care. This is a philanthropic relation with both Fantine and Cosette not simply because Valjean is attempting to do good, nor simply because it is voluntary—in fact, in many ways he is bound by his conscience. Nor is it because his help is tax-deductible or housed within the boundaries of a nonprofit sector. It is philanthropy because it matches the resources of the giver to the needs of the recipient through a social relation that is directly mobilized and governed by force of a morally armed entreaty. As such, philanthropic relations occur within economic and political organizations just as commercial and political relations occur within nonprofit organizations and civil society.

The Primacy of Charity in Philanthropy

Philanthropy, then, is not simply the giving of money or time but a reciprocal social relation in which the needs of recipients—and the recipients themselves—present a moral claim to which donors may choose to respond. As such, the quality, indeed the existence, of the philanthropic relation is contingent on the moral sentiments of the donor in the sense of being willing to take up the ancient virtue—as opposed to the nineteenth-century practice—of charity. It is important, however, to understand charity in view of its cognate *care* (*caritas*), understood to be the aspect of love that seeks to involve others in good.

The Jesuit philosopher Jules Toner has defined *care* as the attention dedicated to loving others in their true needs. Care is the practical or "implemental" side of *radical love.* For Toner radical love is the irreducible affection by which a lover "affirms the beloved for the beloved's self" and "affectively identifies with the loved one's personal being, by which in some sense the lover is the beloved affectively." Care, then, says Toner, is affirmative affection toward someone in need. The need or what is needed is not the object of radical care; rather, the object is persons in their need.

Toner's notion that in care "the lover affectively identifies with the loved one's personal being" brings the issue of love as identification to center stage. This is not unlike Scottish economist Adam Smith's emphasis in the eighteenth century on "sympathy" or "fellow-feeling" as the elementary sentiment regulating social intercourse. Many centuries earlier, Italian theologian and philosopher Thomas Aquinas (1225–1274) had maintained that "love has the property of uniting lover and beloved." Such identification is the basis for that paradoxical unity between duty and pleasure (satisfaction) which today's most committed donors cite as the linchpin of their giving and volunteering.

The discourse and practice of identification are clouded by the modern notion of self-identity that focuses on the individual as the hub of moral consciousness and moral decision. Sociologist Robert Bellah and his associates have spoken of the utilitarian, biblical, civic, and expressive varieties of individualism. In each variety a different set of ambiguities arises surrounding the perennial problem of bridging the gulf between personal fulfillment and public involvement.

Admittedly, it is hard to concoct a formula to supplant this dualism, but Bellah and his colleagues reported that many Americans have displayed individualism that reflects their active identification with various communities and traditions. Additional language for obviating the false dualism of self and other lies in the discourse of *caritas* properly understood—that is, *caritas* as "the implemental aspect of love." But such an approach has its own problems, mainly revolving around the fact that the discourse of love is not as prominent in the American cultural heritage as notions of citizenship and civic responsibility.

If the modern sense of self-identity stresses *self* as an individual personality and as a rights-bearing citizen, the reconceptualization revolving around the virtue of charity stresses *identity* as the formative motivation for determining the content of moral sentiment and moral biography. This emphasis on self-identity as identification (or self-identity with) is precisely the heart of the Thomistic concept of charity. Although Aquinas did not speak of identity in the modern sense, his concept of love does presume an understanding of identification that sees love transform the lover into the beloved.

The Unity of Love of Self and Love of Neighbor

Ironically, today the notion of the unity of love of neighbor and love of self may be more readily embraced in action than in thought. With self-development becoming a purposive, reflective activity for many people, one hears a lot about "creative selfishness" along with the more credible phrase of French historian Alexis de Tocqueville (1805–1859) "self-interest properly understood." For some, such notions are bothersome because they provide too wide a berth for justifying private interest under the guise of the common good.

Although the temptation to be self-serving is ever present, philanthropy is at its best when derived from heartfelt engagement. It is ironic that the ideal of selflessness is offered as the epitome of morality precisely in those arenas of temporal and material commitment where the *quality* rather than the *absence* of self matters most. This means that efforts now directed toward extricating donors from their supposedly flawed self-attachments would be better invested in strengthening the sensitivity, intensity, extent, and insight of their identifications.

Defining philanthropy as a social relation of *caritas* revolving around self-identity with others in their needs suggests how important it is for individuals to expand the horizons within which they experience an obligation of identification, a vocation of communion, with other human beings as radical ends. The failure of William Shakespeare's King Lear to do so is his tragic flaw. In search of expiation, Lear beckons the pompous to expose themselves to identification with the forsaken:

"Expose thyself to feel what wretches feel, / That thou mayst shake the superflux to them, / And show the heavens more just."

With this in mind, one can see the significance of defining philanthropy as the social relation in which one feels obligated to extend one's self-interest to include meeting the needs of others. Philanthropy as one of many important defining acts of self is the relationship in which people directly attend and respond to noncoercive affective (rather than effective) expressions of need. For such charity to be caring rather than controlling or self-aggrandizing, some personal knowledge of the object of love is necessary. This is why Aquinas perceived love to be an act in which one person "affectively" associates with another, hoping that they will be united in a state of mutual happiness. Because such communion may be achieved with temporal, financial, and psychological resources, charity is never the special preserve or obligation of any one income group. All are implicated in the vocation and moral identity of *caritas*.

See also *Humanitarianism; Voluntarism*.

Paul G. Schervish

BIBLIOGRAPHY

Bellah, Robert N., Richard Madsen, William M. Sullivan, Ann Swidler, and Steven M. Tipton. *Habits of the Heart: Individualism and Commitment in American Life.* New York: Harper and Row, 1985.

Gilleman, S. J. Gerard. *The Primacy of Charity in Moral Theology.* Westminster, Md.: Newman Press, 1959.

Martin, Mike W. *Virtuous Giving: Philanthropy, Voluntary Service, and Caring.* Bloomington: Indiana University Press, 1994.

Ostrander, Susan A., and Paul G. Schervish. "Giving and Getting: Philanthropy as a Social Relation." In *Critical Issues in American Philanthropy: Strengthening Theory and Practice,* edited by Jon Van Til. San Francisco: Jossey-Bass, 1990.

Schervish, Paul G. "Major Donors, Major Motives: The People and Purposes Behind Major Gifts." In *Developing Major Gifts,* edited by Dwight F. Burlingame and James M. Hodge III. San Francisco: Jossey-Bass, 1997.

Schervish, Paul G., with Obie Benz, Peggy Dulany, Thomas B. Murphy, and Stanley Salett. *Taking Giving Seriously.* Indianapolis: Indiana University, Center on Philanthropy, 1993.

Smith, Adam. *The Theory of Moral Sentiments,* edited by D. D. Rapheal and A. L. Macfie. Oxford: Clarendon Press, 1976.

Toner, Jules. *The Experience of Love.* Washington, D.C.: Corpus Book, 1968.

Van Til, Jon. "Defining Philanthropy." In *Critical Issues in American Philanthropy: Strengthening Theory and Practice,* edited by Jon Van Til. San Francisco: Jossey-Bass, 1990.

Philippines

An archipelago consisting of more than seven thousand islands, the Philippines is located in Southeast Asia, on the eastern side of the South China Sea. Approximately 85 percent of the population are Roman Catholic, 5 percent are indigenous Christians, 5 percent are Muslim, 3 percent are Protestant, and the rest are divided between Buddhists and Animists. Of these religious groups, Catholics and Muslims have played the most predominant role in politics since Philippine independence in 1946.

Catholicism was introduced to the Philippines in the 1500s by the Spaniards, who ruled the country as a colony until 1898, when they were defeated in the Spanish-American War. Indigenous Christian churches emerged during the Spanish colonial period in response to Filipino demands to serve as clergy. They eventually split with Rome, and many were involved in millennialist movements. Today, the strongest indigenous organizations include the Philippine Independent Church (known as the Aglipayans) and the Iglesia ni Kristo.

The introduction of Islam predated the Spaniards by almost one hundred years. Muslim Filipinos, known as Moros, are concentrated in the southern part of the country, particularly on the islands of Mindanao and Sulu. Since the 1500s Muslims had felt their cultural values, economic interests, and political power threatened by central authorities. Animosity increased as American colonial rulers began resettling northern Christians to Mindanao. By the 1950s Muslims became a minority in the region, when President Ramón Magsaysay (1907–1957) defeated the Christian Huks, a Communist-led group of former guerrillas against the Japanese who had organized a rebel government on the northern island of Luzon, and relocated Huk soldiers and their families to farms in Mindanao.

Declining Muslim control of the south coincided with increasing support to the region from Muslim countries

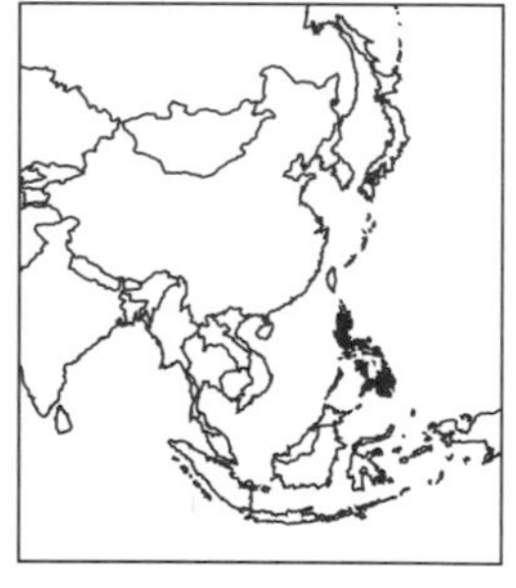

such as Indonesia, Malaysia, Pakistan, Egypt, and Saudi Arabia. These countries sent missionaries to Mindanao, helped organize local Muslim groups, and included Filipinos in international Muslim organizations. This aid strengthened Filipino Muslim consciousness and led Muslims to work for regional autonomy.

Protestant missionaries came to the Philippines during the American colonial period, which lasted from 1898 to 1946 (excluding the Japanese Occupation, from 1942 to 1945). Today, there are more than two hundred Protestant sects represented in the country. As in Central and South America, Protestantism is now gaining followers in the Philippines, and in 1992 the country elected a Protestant president, Fidel Ramos.

Authoritarian Rule and Religious Activism

In 1972 President Ferdinand E. Marcos (1917–1989) declared martial law and installed an authoritarian regime. The Muslim community saw martial law as a direct threat, and their response was immediate and intense opposition. As the armed forces began village-by-village searches throughout Mindanao for weapons, the Moro National Liberation Front, formed in 1971 to establish an independent Islamic state in the south, immediately responded with armed insurrection. The front received support from several foreign countries, particularly Malaysia and Libya, and thus was able to conduct a protracted separatist war. Although Marcos and the Moros signed several cease-fire agreements, none of them succeeded because Marcos refused to grant independence to the south and the front splintered into several armed guerrilla groups.

Roman Catholic opposition to Marcos's regime emerged gradually. The church consisted of three groups, each with its own religious mission and reaction to martial law. The church hierarchy characterized the conservative group, which was composed of a majority of the Catholic Bishops Conference of the Philippines, as well as several religious superiors. Although the Philippine church accepted the Second Vatican Council (1962–1965) reforms, it did not aggressively carry them out. Rather, the church hierarchy valued its ecclesiastical role, administering sacraments and educating people, over working for socioeconomic initiatives or political reforms. Because the Roman Catholic Church had traditionally held a prominent position in society, the hierarchy at first did not fear Marcos's regime. Instead, it saw the choice in 1972 as between the communists and Marcos, and sided with Marcos.

A majority of the Association of Major Religious Superiors of the Philippines and several bishops belonged to the moderate group within the church. This group embraced the Vatican II reforms and liberation theology, calling for the church to address the economic and political roots of poverty in the Philippines. Deteriorating economic conditions and rising human rights abuses under martial law led the moderates to break with the hierarchy's position of critical collaboration and to speak out against the regime. They organized base communities to promote political awareness among parishioners, created the Justice and Peace Commission to engage in social action, and formed the Task Force Detainees to monitor and report human rights violations. (The National Council of Churches in the Philippines, which represented nine Protestant sects, supported these efforts.)

The revolutionary group within the church included some bishops and religious superiors but was mostly drawn from church workers involved in grassroots organizations. A minority within the church, this group had become frustrated and radicalized by its work in local development programs. The revolutionary members organized a parallel grassroots church that decentralized church structures and traditions and instead focused on the people of God. Applying historical structuralism to analyze societal problems, some members came to accept the use of violence as a last resort in the struggle for reform. These church workers adopted as their role model Camilo Torres, a Colombian priest and sociologist who came to believe that social justice would be achieved only through armed struggle, and joined the New People's Army (the military wing of the Communist Party of the Philippines) and the Moro National Liberation Front in the mountains as priest-guerrillas.

Church fragmentation increased through the 1970s. In retaliation against church members' active opposition to his regime, Marcos attacked the church. Church-owned newspapers and radio stations were closed; church workers were arrested, tortured, and killed; and foreign missionaries were deported. Rather than intimidating the moderate and revolutionary groups, the regime's actions strengthened their resolve. Eventually, the church hierarchy realized that the only way to unify the church was to adopt the moderates' position and oppose authoritarianism openly. In 1979 Jaime Cardinal Sin, archbishop of Manila, called for Marcos to step down.

The 1983 assassination of opposition leader Senator Benigno Aquino spurred the church to the forefront of the opposition. When Marcos called for presidential elections to be held in 1986, Cardinal Sin convinced the democratic opposition to support one ticket with Corazon Aquino, the senator's widow, as the presidential candidate. The church mobilized voters for Aquino and helped the National Movement for Free Elections create an independent ballot count. When Marcos claimed victory, the free election movement announced that Aquino had won, and the church supported her. Defense Minister Juan Ponce Enrile, Acting Chief of Staff Fidel Ramos, and the Reform the Armed Forces of the Philippines Movement rebels threw their support behind Aquino, and Cardinal Sin used Radio Veritas to call for People Power. More than eight hundred thousand people protected the rebels from loyalist troops and demanded that Marcos resign. This tense four-day period ended with Marcos fleeing the country and Aquino being sworn in as president.

Democratic Restoration

With democracy restored in 1986, both the Roman Catholic Church and the Moro National Liberation Front began to shift from confrontation with the government to reconciliation. After Corazon Aquino was sworn in as president, the Catholic Church remained active in politics. Individual church members served as advisers to Aquino, as members of the commission that drafted the 1987 constitution, as cabinet ministers, and as members of the committee that negotiated cease-fire agreements with the New People's Army. When Marcos loyalists and Reform the Armed Forces of the Philippines Movement rebels initiated more than seven coup attempts, the church supported her regime to bolster its stability. But the church hierarchy also saw the return of democracy as an opportunity for it to retreat to its ecclesiastical role and to rein in activist members, leaving political participation to the laity.

Many moderate and revolutionary church members disagreed with the church hierarchy's decision to withdraw from politics and return to its ecclesiastical mission. They argued that church efforts, such as organizing base communities and building a parallel grassroots church, are still needed because the structural causes of poverty and powerlessness have not been removed. They feared that the church hierarchy's suspicion that social action work aided communism would increase tension within the church and cause it to fragment again.

Moro leader Nur Misuari left exile in Libya to return to the Philippines when Aquino became president. The Moro National Liberation Front engaged in a series of cease-fire negotiations with the administration, and in 1996 an accord was finally reached with President Fidel Ramos. The front agreed to give up its goal of secession in exchange for creation of a permanent autonomous government. Although the Philippine government was successful in negotiating with the front, it has not succeeded in signing similar agreements with various Muslim splinter groups. The Moro Islamic Liberation Front has refused to enter into peace talks because it is still committed to creating an independent Islamic state. To date, it has not compromised and accepted the idea of an autonomous government. The Abu Sayyaf group has also refused to negotiate with the government and has engaged in political violence, including assassinations, bombings, and kidnappings targeted against Christian churches in Mindanao.

Given the experiences of religious groups under authoritarian rule, it is unlikely that they will completely withdraw from politics in the future. Rather, Catholics and Muslims will remain involved, the Catholic Church lobbying for the socioeconomic and political reforms espoused by Vatican II, and the Moro National Liberation Front seeking greater political freedom.

See also *Base communities; Catholicism, Roman; Christianity in Asia; Islam, Southeast Asia; Liberation theology; Protestantism; Vatican; Vatican Council, Second.*

Gretchen Casper

BIBLIOGRAPHY

Casper, Gretchen. *Fragile Democracies: The Legacies of Authoritarian Rule.* Pittsburgh: University of Pittsburgh Press, 1995.

McCoy, Alfred W. *Priests on Trial.* New York: Penguin Books, 1984.

Noble, Lela Garner. "The Moro National Liberation Front in the Philippines." *Pacific Affairs* 49 (fall 1976): 405–424.

Rafael, Vicente L. *Contracting Colonialism: Translation and Christian Conversion in Tagalog Society under Early Spanish Rule.* Ithaca, N.Y.: Cornell University Press, 1988.

Youngblood, Robert L. *Marcos against the Church.* Ithaca, N.Y.: Cornell University Press, 1990.

Pilgrimage

See *Sacred places*

Pillarization

See *Low Countries*

Pluralism

Religious pluralism is a condition of religious diversity within a political community and is both a political problem and a political principle. Human history always has been marked by religious diversity. Prior to the modern age, however, the differences among religions coincided largely with the differences among more or less separate cultural traditions and political communities. In the medieval West, European civilization displayed an overwhelming religious uniformity sustained by the authority of the Christian church.

Religious plurality within a single political community emerged through the fragmentation of Christianity in the Reformation of the sixteenth century and through other social and cultural transformations that increasingly eroded the acceptance of religious authority. The new political problem became starkly apparent when ruinous religious wars, especially between Protestants and Catholics, devastated seventeenth-century Europe.

To some observers, war seemed inevitable because religious beliefs are comprehensive convictions—that is, convictions about the ultimate context of human life and about the fundamental grounds on which all moral issues should be decided. Based on such fundamental differences, a conflict between religions seemed beyond political resolution because the conflict was about the grounds for adjudicating all conflicts. A plurality of religions internal to the same civil order appeared to be, in principle, a prescription for civil instability. This logic counseled religious uniformity within a given political community. Thus the continuing emergence of nations in seventeenth- and eighteenth-century Europe was marked by the political establishment of one or another form of Christianity. "Establishment" means that, in a given nation, some religion was declared to be the official religion or church. It was united with and supported by the state, and all people within the nation were expected to acknowledge that this church provided the religious grounds for political life. Still, the religious plurality within most European nations could not be reversed. Official toleration of "nonestablished" or "dissenting" religious communities was increasingly advocated and, though sometimes fitfully, increasingly practiced—even up to the present day.

Some political thinkers argue that this solution is conceptually unstable. Establishing one religion and, at the same time, tolerating others seems to imply that the political community both is and is not united by religious uniformity. In other words, members of "dissenting" religious communities have to affirm two different religions, and, given the comprehensive character of religious commitments, that seems impossible. It is true that some European nations in which there is both an official religion and toleration of others have proved nonetheless to be stable or enduring. But one is led to suspect that this practical success occurs only because the differing religions are in fact substantially in agreement with respect to political purposes or because the established religion has more or less withdrawn from official political power.

In any event, religious pluralism as a political problem became acute in the American colonies at the time of their union in the late eighteenth century. Although most of the separate colonies themselves practiced some form of religious establishment, settlement in the colonies as a whole had, for many reasons, drawn on the diversity of European religious communities. Moreover, Rhode Island and Pennsylvania had forsworn religious establishment altogether. As a result, no church was in a position to make a bid for supremacy in the new nation. If the European experience counseled that no civil order could have integrity without an established religion, the facts in the colonies dictated that they could not be united with one. In the U.S. Constitution, specifically in the religion clauses of the First Amendment (ratified in 1791), religious pluralism became a political principle, often called the principle of religious freedom: "Congress shall make no law respecting an establishment of religion, or prohibiting the free exercise thereof."

The Dominant Interpretations

It is widely thought that the principle of religious freedom—or, as some people say, the separation of church and state—is an unsurpassed expression of distinctively modern politics and that the First Amendment contains its classic statement. There also is wide disagreement about what this principle means. To be sure, most people affirm that freedom of conscience is among the most important of the liberties government ought not to invade. Moreover, there is a general consensus that this freedom helps to prevent the concentration of power that is the greatest threat to democracy. In themselves, however, these considerations are not sufficient to identify what the principle of religious freedom means. They define that principle in terms of its prohibition on the government—that is, what politics cannot do. Although this prohibition is clearly a part of the principle, a democratic constitution also is meant to unite the political community, and the problem of religious pluralism is this: How can a diversity of comprehensive convictions be politically united? Somehow, the principle of religious freedom also must make sense as a principle of union; this too must be a part of its meaning—and this is where interpretations differ.

In the twentieth century, contention about this meaning has increased because of the expanding role of government in our common life and the growing plurality of religious convictions or comprehensive convictions. The issue is important not only for political unity but also for religious reasons. Because religious freedom is a part of the Constitution, all citizens of the political community are expected to affirm the principle. Every religious adherent, therefore, has reason to ask whether citizenship is consistent with her or his religious beliefs, and the answer cannot be affirmative unless the kind of political unity religious freedom prescribes does not violate her or his comprehensive conviction.

There are two dominant interpretations of this modern political principle, each of which is at odds with the other. The first holds that separating religions from the state simply means that the basic political norms or values uniting the community are divorced from any and all religious beliefs. Many thinkers who advance this interpretation hold that it defines modern political liberalism. By their account, the liberal tradition began with the recognition that religious wars were inevitable unless the norms of politics could be independent of religious differences. Political liberals typically assert that this divorce is possible because the ultimate questions answered in differing ways by differing religious faiths transcend rational understanding and discourse, while political norms express a common morality that can be agreed on by all reasonable citizens. Thus liberal politics is neutral to all religions because it does not offer answers to ultimate questions, and it unites all religious believers because they can distinguish between matters of faith and those of reason.

For many religious adherents, however, this "separationist" reading is unacceptable because it is secularistic. The idea that political norms or values can be divorced from ultimate questions implies that the true answers to these questions have no importance for political life. But this implication seems to violate every religious conviction, whatever its content, because a comprehensive conviction is about the fundamental grounds on which all moral issues should be decided. Sometimes this objection is expressed by saying that the separationist view of religious freedom implies the "privatization" of religion. Since privatizing religion is inconsistent with the comprehensive character of religious beliefs, modern politics seen through this liberal understanding does not legitimate religious plurality but in truth denies that any religion can be true.

Many who are persuaded by this objection assert a "religionist" interpretation of modern politics: religious freedom does not deny that religion is important to civic virtue and to the well-being of the civil order; the principle merely prevents the state from discriminating among religions. This reading is the second of the two dominant interpretations. It agrees with the first that answers to ultimate questions transcend rational understanding and discourse and that political union is based on a common morality accessible to reason. But this second view insists that a commitment to rational norms in politics, in contrast to the mere pursuit of one's own self-interest, is itself a moral or political virtue that citizens do not develop unless they also are religious believers. Only the belief that human life relates to the ultimate or transcendent reality provides the motivation to accept political principles accessible to reason. Thus religious freedom does not prevent the government from affirming and supporting the practice of religions generally—and thereby opposing secularism—as long as the state does not prefer one religion to another.

But the religionist interpretation also is subject to objections. For one thing, it implies that citizens who do not affirm any religious faith cannot be fully committed to rational norms in politics. In addition, critics point out that there is no such thing as religion in general. Belief that human life relates to an ultimate or transcendent reality has no politically relevant content until the nature of ultimate reality is articulated in some particular faith, and whether the belief then supports civic virtue depends entirely on the content of one's faith. The gods that religions affirm may be racist or aristocratic instead of democratic or emancipating. Thus government support for religion has no purpose unless it is support for some particular religious content—but that would be the establishment of a religion. There also is a third criticism of the religionist reading: religious adherents themselves should object to it because it makes the differences among religions indifferent to politics, and this seems again to violate every comprehensive conviction because each purports to identify the fundamental grounds for all moral decisions.

Alternative Interpretations

Because neither of the dominant interpretations seems convincing, some thinkers have concluded that the only general meaning of the religion clauses is that they have no general meaning. They do not express a political principle but merely a pragmatic solution to an inescapable problem with which the architects of the nation were faced. Thus the question of political unity cannot be given a general answer. Any particular issue about the relation between government and diverse religions can be resolved only in the context of legal precedents set by previous particular resolutions and with due attention to the peculiarities of the current dispute. But this recourse seems unwittingly to assert its own principle—namely, that the relation between politics and religion is always a wholly contextual matter. Moreover, this meaning of religious freedom would seem to contradict the affirmation that every religion makes, regardless of its content—namely, that all human life should be informed by a comprehensive truth. On that affirmation, no constitutional provision can be merely pragmatic.

A more promising understanding of the principle of religious freedom opens with the suggestion that none of the three previous interpretations expresses the intent of the First Amendment's principal architects. Although the principle of religious pluralism or religious freedom was variously understood by differing individuals and groups in the new Republic, its most convincing rationale was provided by the Founders such as Thomas Jefferson, James Madison, and Benjamin Franklin. They were children of what is commonly called the Enlightenment, an eighteenth-century intellectual movement that affirmed only experience and reason as the final basis for truth and therefore rejected any final appeal to authority. The Founders believed, in contrast to the common assumption of the three interpretations just reviewed, that the religious question is itself subject to rational discourse. Thus religious freedom articulates the fundamental commitment of modern politics to government by discussion and debate. Perhaps Thomas Jefferson best expressed the point: "Truth is great and will prevail if left to herself; . . . she . . . has nothing to fear from the conflict [among religions] unless by human interposition disarmed of her natural weapon, free argument and debate."

On this reading, the principle of religious freedom unites a plurality of religious or comprehensive convictions by constituting a full and free public discourse among them. Political union requires only that all religious adherents, whatever the content of their convictions, be committed to public discourse or the way of persuasion whenever they seek to advocate the political importance of their religious beliefs. Moreover, this interpretation is consistent with any religion that citizens might affirm because the commitment to discourse is present whenever one claims that one's conviction is true. Religious freedom prohibits the state from taking part in this debate by teaching or seeking to prevent the teaching of any particular comprehensive conviction, including secularistic ones, because this political principle asserts only that the way of reason is the process by which "we the people" govern ourselves.

See also *Constitution, U.S.; Enlightenment; Freedom of religion; Liberalism; Separation of church and state.*

Franklin I. Gamwell

BIBLIOGRAPHY

Gamwell, Franklin I. *The Meaning of Religious Freedom: Modern Politics and the Democratic Resolution.* Albany: State University of New York Press, 1995.

Greenawalt, Kent. *Private Consciences and Public Reasons.* New York: Oxford University Press, 1995.

Mead, Sidney E. *The Lively Experiment: The Shaping of Christianity in America.* New York: Harper and Row, 1963.

Murray, John Courtney. *We Hold These Truths: Catholic Reflections on the American Proposition.* Kansas City, Mo.: Sheed and Ward, 1960.

Rawls, John. *Political Liberalism.* New York: Columbia University Press, 1993.

Smith, Steven D. *Foreordained Failure: The Quest for a Constitutional Principle of Religious Freedom.* New York: Oxford University Press, 1995.

Poland

Situated in east central Europe on the Baltic Sea, Poland was drawn into the Soviet orbit after World War II (1939–1945) and remained a communist republic until 1989 when political reformers with the help of the Roman Catholic Church succeeded in wresting the country from communist domination. Although religious activity is not officially encouraged in Poland, 90 percent of the Polish people are said to maintain religious beliefs. Of these, 93 percent are Catholic, 5 percent are Eastern Orthodox, and 1 percent adhere to various Protestant denominations. Most of Poland's Jews were killed in the Holocaust in which over six million European Jews were systematically destroyed by Nazi Germany both before and during World War II. State-church relationships in Poland are regulated by law, including those adopted by Parliament on May 17, 1989, giving the Catholic Church legal status, the right to buy and sell property, and the right to operate businesses, and authorizing the government to return church property it had seized in the 1950s.

After World War II the victorious Allies agreed to place Poland within the Soviet orbit of Eastern European states. The Polish United Workers' (Communist) Party proceeded to establish a rigid police state. In 1956 Wladyslaw Gomulka assumed power as Communist Party chief and with him

came hopes for greater freedom from the strictures of communist life. Gomulka, however, quashed such hopes with his attacks on the church and the intelligentsia. He was succeeded in 1970 by Edward Gierek, who during his ten-year tenure managed to help modernize Poland's economy but turned a blind eye to the accompanying corruption and graft. In the summer of 1980 Gierek was overthrown, largely as a result of the strikes called by the labor union Solidarity in the Gdansk shipyards. Gen. Wojciech Jaruzelski, who took over leadership of the party and the government, responded to Solidarity's calls for democratic reforms with the imposition of martial law. Solidarity was forced to go underground, only to resurface in 1985 when Mikhail Gorbachev's assumption of Soviet leadership presented an opportunity to resume calls for democratic reform. Fueled by the leadership of Solidarity member Lech Walesa and the active support of Polish pope John Paul II, reformers were able to force the communists to the negotiating table in 1989.

Under the 1989 roundtable agreements between the state authorities and Solidarity and other groups, open elections were held on June 4, 1989, for the first time in forty years. At stake were 161 open seats in the 460-member Sejm, or lower house of parliament, and 100 seats in the newly created Senate. Candidates sponsored by Solidarity won 160 Sejm seats and 92 Senate seats. On July 19, 1989, the reconstructed National Assembly elected General Jaruzelski, general secretary of the United Workers' Party and head of state since 1981, as Poland's president. Tadeusz Mazowiecki, a Solidarity official, was elected as Poland's first postwar noncommunist prime minister and took office on July 29, 1989. In elections held in December 1990, Solidarity leader Lech Walesa replaced General Jaruzelski as president.

The Catholic Nation versus the Communist State

In the postwar period all attempts by the communist regime to sever the links between the Catholic Church and Polish nation ended in failure. The church's prestige was at an all-time high, and its identification with the nation was reinforced by the fact that almost the entire population of Poland was, at least formally and for the first time in modern Polish history, homogeneously Catholic as a result of the eradication of Polish Jewry before and during the war and the massive Polish–Ukrainian resettlements and the redrawing of Poland's borders after the war. By contrast, the prestige of the Polish communists had never been high. The practical liquidation of the entire Polish Communist Party by Soviet Communist Party leader Joseph Stalin did not help matters, and its replacement, the Polish United Workers' Party, was, like the regime, regarded as being of foreign conception.

The ultimate goal of the communist state was clear: the complete elimination of the church and religion from Polish life. But it also was understood that, like the final phase of communism, this goal was far away, possibly requiring many detours. All strategies of forced secularization used relatively successfully first in the Soviet Union and then throughout Eastern Europe were variously tried in Poland but with little success.

The strategy of neutralization and control of religion through the official incorporation of the church into the state also failed. Unlike the Orthodox Church, the Catholic Church proved relatively immune to socialist subordination of the church to the state. Neither the creation of "patriotic priests" nor that of "progressive Catholics," neither the support given to the schismatic Polish National Catholic Church nor the attempt to deal directly with the Vatican and thus bypass the unyielding Polish hierarchy, was able to divide the church or undermine its prestige.

The strategy of coercion also did not succeed. The selective repression of representative bishops, priests, and nuns only served to turn them into martyrs or national heroes, as attested by the triumphal popular acclamation produced by the release of Cardinal Stefan Wyszynski, influential leader of the Polish Catholic Church imprisoned by the communist regime from 1953 to 1956.

Socialist resocialization failed as well. The attempt to establish a new civil religion and to create a new "socialist man"—a far from successful endeavor elsewhere in Eastern Europe—was a total failure in Poland. In spite of state control of all official means of communication, education, and socialization, the church and the Polish family were able to counteract socialization and defend the right of all Poles to a religious education. Indeed, all attempts to rewrite Polish history and to depict the church as the enemy of the nation backfired; rather, the church became the cherished trustee of the nation's history, culture, and traditions, and of the collective memories of the Polish people.

The marginalization of religion to a private religious sphere also ultimately failed because neither Catholic principle nor Polish tradition could be easily reconciled with a conception of religiosity borrowed from Protestantism and restricted to the private and unmediated relationship between the individual conscience and God. Neither could Soviet socialism recognize in earnest the right of an autonomous sphere to exist where "antisocialist" (antisystem norms and values) could develop.

Although Marxist sociologists of religion collected every promising sign that the laws of secularization were operating in Poland in the communist era, most indicators pointed to a reverse process of desecularization: there was an absolute and relative increase in the number of bishops, priests, nuns, seminarians, and so forth, when compared with precommunist Poland, and an increase in the number of Catholic parishes, churches, and publications. Indicators measuring the religious beliefs of the population, which had always remained inordinately high, even showed some tendency to rise, most significantly among the young. The figures on religious practice were even more overwhelming since even those who did not consider themselves "believers" participated in religious ceremonies as a symbolic opposition to the regime.

Clearly the church had won the war of secularization. Every time there was a direct confrontation between the Catholic Church and communist regime over the control of religious education and of ecclesiastical appointments, the curriculum in the seminaries, the millennium celebration, even constitutional revisions, the regime had to withdraw and the power and prestige of the church were enhanced in the process.

Cardinal Wyszynski was most directly responsible for the church's victory. As primate of Poland, he served as spokesman not only for the church but also for the Polish nation. In a sermon at the Warsaw Cathedral on February 7, 1974, elaborating on his conception of the relations among church, nation, and state in Poland, Cardinal Wyszynski attributed the victory of the church to the primacy of the relationship between church and nation over that between church and state.

The Catholic Church and the Rise of Solidarity

The striking image in the late 1980s of the Gdansk shipyard workers on their knees partaking of Holy Communion manifested the extent to which traditional popular Polish religiosity, with its typical undifferentiated fusion of sacred and profane time and space, had survived the thrusts of modern Polish history. Catholic intellectuals associated with the

Catholic Intellectual Clubs (KIKs) also played an important role in this survival, first in the founding of Solidarity and later as official and unofficial advisers to the democratic reform movement. Finally, there was the impact that the election and the 1979 visit of Pope John Paul II had on public opinion and on the Polish collective consciousness.

While few would question the positive role of Polish Catholicism in the emergence of Solidarity, the role of the church and Polish Catholicism was much more ambiguous later in the martial law period (1981–1983), the reemergence of Solidarity in 1985, and the transition to democracy. The ease with which the church, after the establishment of martial law, reverted to its traditional role as mediator between the communist state and Polish society should have served as at least a warning of the threats the institutional power of the Polish church would pose to a fully autonomous civil society.

Not surprisingly, the Polish Catholic Church rejects the liberal principle of privatization as a self-interested secularist prescription for the marginalization of religion into public irrelevance. But because the church plans to maintain a public presence in Poland, the question is at which level of the polity will the church choose to make its public presence felt? Will it want to intervene and play a public role at the state level? Will it mobilize its resources for the battle in political society? Or will it limit itself willingly to playing a role in the public sphere of an open and differentiated civil society? Judging from the ambiguous and relatively restrained interventions of the church in Polish politics since 1989, those questions remain open.

The present primate, Cardinal Jozef Glemp, has repeatedly expressed his preference for a confessional Catholic state. In 1988 in an internal document of the Polish episcopate, Cardinal Glemp defended the traditional Catholic position against the principle of religious freedom and separation of church and state, arguing, like the traditionalists at the Second Vatican Council (also known as Vatican II, 1962–1965), that the church cannot tolerate falsehood or recognize that error has the same rights as truth. But in the face of some public resistance, and apparently the disapproval of the Vatican, the church did not press the issue. For the time being, at least, it appears that the Polish Catholic Church has resigned itself to accepting the constitutional separation of church and state. Whatever its preferences, the Polish hierarchy could hardly publicly defend a position that goes against the new doctrine of religious freedom proclaimed at Vatican II, against the repeatedly expressed views of the Polish pope, and against general historical trends in Europe and throughout the Catholic world.

Before becoming Pope John Paul II, Cardinal Karol Wojtyla had played a prominent role in the Polish church and in Vatican II, where he joined the American bishops in defending the principle of religious freedom. Cardinal Wojtyla was the main force behind the movement for post–Vatican II reform in Poland, and, as an intellectual, he found it easier than Cardinal Wyszynski to develop close ties with the reform-minded Catholic intellectuals who often internalized Vatican II's message sooner and deeper than much of the Polish hierarchy.

But the formal acceptance of constitutional separation of church and state does not necessarily mean that the Polish church is ready to refrain from intervening in state affairs privately through corporatist avenues. In the fall of 1990, under obvious pressure from the church, the Ministry of Education of Prime Minister Tadeusz Mazowiecki's Solidarity government put religious education back into the public school curriculum. The church's heavy pressure was equally evident in the 1991 passage by the Solidarity-controlled Senate of a bill criminalizing once-legal abortion. The bill was passed practically without debate—only one female senator dared to raise some questions; all senators virtually echoed the official Catholic position. The majority of Poles, however, opposed the criminalization of abortion, leading President Aleksander Kwasniewski, under pressure of public opinion, to sign on November 20, 1996, a bill liberalizing abortion. These two examples raise a fundamental question: to what extent is the church ready to refrain from using its extraordinary corporate power to bypass the normal democratic process by establishing itself as an extraconstitutional and extraparliamentary tutelary power over certain reserved domains of policy making, such as religion, education, and family morality?

Religious Pluralism in a Democratic Society

The church has the right and the duty to speak up publicly on any issue it considers of public relevance, from the evil of abortion to the personal and societal need for religious and moral education to the need to establish norms of solidarity to limit and counter market laws and state administrative measures that are impervious to human needs and to the damage they produce in the social fabric. As the pope did in his June 1991 visit to Poland, the church also is entitled to urge Poles to avoid and resist what is seen as the Western European path of secularization, materialist and hedonist consumerism, utilitarian individualism, and liberalism. But will the church strive for Catholic hegemony in the public sphere to stifle and silence dissonant voices or will it respect the right of these voices to be heard publicly? Much depends on the courage of Polish intellectuals, particularly Catholic intellectuals, to express their differences of opinion publicly, especially when their opinions differ from those expressed by the church hierarchy.

But even in Poland, where the hierarchical, centralized, and clericalist nature of the Catholic Church, along with traditional elements of Catholic culture, would seem to press in the direction of Catholic hegemony, one finds strong countervailing forces. Once the need for a unified societal resistance against the communist state disappeared, Polish society exhibited an increasing pluralism of interests, norms, and values, belying any notion of a homogeneous Catholic national community. Any attempt to impose Catholic solutions on societal problems not only may open up religious–secular cleavages, but, given the increasingly pluralistic nature of Polish Catholicism, also could lead to internal conflicts and divisions within the Catholic community and the church.

If the church maintains its uncompromising attitude and insists on enforcing Catholic morality publicly, there is still a danger that the institutionalization of some form of Polish national Catholicism could serve as an obstacle to the consolidation of an open, pluralist Polish civil society. Given the disposition proposed by the Polish pope, the Polish Catholic Church could learn to accept modern secularization—that is, the relatively autonomous differentiation of the secular spheres—without necessarily resigning itself to the decline or the privatization of Catholicism in Polish civil society.

See also *Catholicism, Roman; Communism; Europe, Eastern; Orthodoxy, Russian; Papacy; Separation of church and state; Vatican; Vatican Council, Second.*

Leonard T. Volenski

BIBLIOGRAPHY

Gagnere, Nathalie. "The Return of God and the Challenge of Democracy: The Catholic Church in Central Eastern Europe (Czech Republic, Hungary, Poland, and Slovakia)." *Journal of Church and State* 35 (August 1993): 859–884.

Giles, Thomas, and Bill Yoder. "Is Catholic Influence on the Wane in Poland?" *Christianity Today,* May 16, 1994, 49.

Monticone, Ronald C. *The Catholic Church in Communist Poland 1945–1985: Forty Years of Church–State Relations.* New York: Columbia University Press, 1986.

Neuhaus, Richard J. "Poland: Reflections on a New World." *First Things* 40 (February 1994): 19–22.

Pater, Dobroslew K. "Grandiose Visions: Changes in the Catholic Church in Poland after 1989." *Religion in Eastern Europe* 15 (August 1995): 1–16.

Pawlikowski, John T. "The Holocaust: Its Implications for Contemporary Church–State Relations in Poland." *Religion in Eastern Europe* 13 (April 1993): 1–13.

Swatos, William H., ed. *Politics and Religion in Central and Eastern Europe: Traditions and Transitions.* Westport, Conn.: Praeger, 1994.

Waters, Philip, ed. "Overcoming the Old, Creating the New: The Role of Churches in the New Europe." *Religion, State, and Society* 25 (1997): 11–101.

Population control

See *Sexuality*

Pornography

See *Censorship*

Prejudice

Prejudice can be cited when people prejudge a group and its members, are intolerant or unfair to them, or look upon them with an unfavorable or unjustifiably negative attitude. "Blatant" prejudice occurs when people openly report being prejudiced; "modern" or "subtle" or "automatic processing" prejudice takes place when prejudicial acts are not acknowledged. Everyone spontaneously knows what is meant by the term, but its definition becomes more problematic the more it is investigated.

Defining Prejudice

All agree that a stereotypical prejudgment of a person based solely on group membership without recognition of the individual's characteristics and without seeking out more information is prejudice. Acting prejudicially contrasts with judging individuals on their own characteristics regardless of group membership. However, further elaboration of the definition with other terms often produces difficulties.

The phrase "unjustifiably negative attitude" raises the

questions of who feels the attitudes are unjustified and why. Adding to the definition such words as *unfair* just adds the same problem again: what group or subcultural standard is being used to define *fairness?* Even greater problems are found with prejudice defined as "unfavorable attitude." This addition to the definition implies that either there are no differences between groups (since someone might see that difference as favoring one or the other group) or that we should pretend there are no differences between groups. Is a negative attitude toward the group called "war criminals" prejudice? Or is it an appropriate response to their crimes? The narrower definition of prejudice as a stereotyped response to one person based solely on that person's group membership appears more defensible than a broad definition of "negative attitude."

The traditional method of measuring prejudice is by using questions about negative and positive attitudes toward a group or by using a measure of social distance. The latter includes questions about whether a group's members should be allowed in the country, allowed to become citizens, allowed to be a member of the family by marriage, and so on. The social distance measure allows an interesting check on the definition of prejudice: rating one's own group along with others.

Prejudice Sources

It is generally found that those who have negative attitudes toward one social group, even their own group, also have negative attitudes toward other groups. This finding suggests that some people are misanthropic, wishing to keep everyone at a distance. Thus one source of high scores on scales measuring prejudice are those people who are negative toward all human groups (but may not be particularly biased toward the group being measured over and above that general attitude).

In addition to misanthropy, another personality variable has been consistently related to prejudice: authoritarianism. In the measurement of prejudice it is currently defined as the favoring of submission to authority, aggression, and conventionalism and is properly labeled "right-wing authoritarianism."

Before the civil rights movement, research on prejudice focused on blatant types of prejudice. Now, however, it is no longer socially correct to admit prejudice by supporting segregation and other such policies. Thus, attempts have been made to measure "modern" prejudice, that which is subtle or automatic. "Subtle" prejudice is prejudice that is in a socially acceptable form, and "automatic" prejudice is prejudicial action done without awareness. The latter occurs when a person makes a decision based only on group membership without realizing that he or she is doing so. It is hypothesized that automatic prejudice is a function of past learning within a prejudiced subculture.

The problem of defining prejudice continues in some of these modern scales. For example, some social scientists score people as having subtle prejudice if they believe another group has a religion different from their own or speaks another language. When dealing with immigrants, as these researchers were, it appears that anyone knowing that the other group did have another religion and spoke a second language would be labeled prejudiced whereas those ignorant of the information would be rated nonprejudiced. Thus the scale could only be used with groups that were known to have the same language and religion as the respondents.

In addition to the stereotypic judgments arising from the personality characteristics of misanthropy and authoritarianism, prejudicial judgments and negative attitudes arise from ethnocentrism based on in-group membership. Each group values itself and its members more highly than other groups even if there is no basis for doing so. Other groups are derogated. This ethnocentric bias is found in every group. For example, even when the "groups" are just arbitrary labels attached randomly by researchers, such as "group bb" and "group nn," ethnocentric bias occurs. The only time it is not found is when there are no identifiable groups. The more easily the group membership is observed, the more likely it is that ethnocentric bias will occur. Hence, theoretically, everyone who has a strong group identification will show ethnocentric bias. If that is so, such people will have higher prejudice scores when rating others not identified with their group; and those who are unconnected to any group will be the least prejudiced.

Both religion and politics are related to prejudice, although the understanding of the relationship between these two areas is unclear. Some researchers have found religious membership to be associated with prejudice. In particular, fundamentalism—whether Christian, Hindu, Jewish, or Muslim—is related to greater prejudice. Because fundamentalists have a very strong group identity, they are the most likely to show ethnocentric bias.

The prime evidence contrary to the above interpretation

of ethnocentric bias for religions is the finding that active Christians are less prejudiced than inactive Christians. Since activity is one measure of group identification, the prediction would be that active Christians would show more ethnocentric bias than inactive Christians. It is possible that this reversal of prediction is a function of those aspects of Christian theology that stress acceptance of others.

Under the group membership theory, the more that members identify with a political group, the more likely they will show ethnocentric bias. Hence it has been predicted that those deeply involved in politics who strongly identify with a political party will show the same ethnocentric bias. Any developments that make the group identity more prominent will accentuate the ethnocentric bias. Under this interpretation, right-wing authoritarianism correlates with prejudice because it is one kind of political group identification. It would be expected that a measure of left-wing group identification would also be related to ethnocentric bias toward outsiders. Contemporary research on prejudice is more likely to find prejudice among political conservatives because they are less likely to see minorities as part of their group. (It would seem that those identifying with left-wing politics are more likely to be prejudiced toward those seen as part of the right wing, and so not a part of their own group, but this research has yet to be done.)

The interaction of politics and religion is most notable in the "religious right." Members of this group are concerned with "traditional" values and strongly identify with the coalition. Therefore we would expect them to show bias toward others. This would register as prejudice toward any group associated with left-wing politics.

See also *Anti-Semitism; Civil rights movement; Ethnicity; Genocide and "ethnic cleansing."*

Richard L. Gorsuch

BIBLIOGRAPHY

Altemeyer, Bob. *Enemies of Freedom: Understanding Right-Wing Authoritarianism.* San Francisco: Jossey-Bass, 1988.

Hunsberger, Bruce. "Religious Fundamentalism, Right-Wing Authoritarianism, and Hostility toward Homosexuals in Non-Christian Religious Groups." *International Journal for the Psychology of Religion* 6 (1996): 39–49.

Myers, David. *Social Psychology.* New York: McGraw-Hill, 1993.

Zanna, Mark P., and James M. Olson, eds. *The Psychology of Prejudice.* Hillsdale, N.J.: Lawrence Erlbaum Associates, 1994.

Presbyterians

Presbyterians are part of a larger family of churches within the Reformed tradition. In this context, *Reformed* denotes those Christian churches that trace their origins to sixteenth-century Protestant leaders such as the Swiss reformer Ulrich Zwingli (1484–1531) and his disciple Heinrich Bullinger (1504–1575); the French theologian John Calvin (1509–1564), who moved to Geneva, Switzerland, and developed Calvinist doctrine; and John Knox (1513–1572), leader of the Scottish Reformation and influential in founding the Presbyterian Church of Scotland. The term distinguishes the Reformed churches from the other major streams—Lutheran and Anabaptist—of the Protestant Reformation in the 1500s. In continental Europe, Reformed churches generally made that word itself part of their formal designation, but the frequent practice in the English-speaking world was to assume the name Presbyterian.

The differences in nomenclature notwithstanding, Presbyterians have shared a common ethos with other members of the Reformed community. Although the Reformed tradition has produced neither a single statement of belief nor become a monolithic identity, certain themes recur: a profound sense of the majesty of God as revealed in Jesus Christ, an iconoclasm toward any lesser allegiance threatening to usurp the place of God, a conviction that the Bible provides a comprehensive guide for the ordering of all of life, and a strenuous moral activism among believers seeking to subject themselves, the church, and the world to God's discipline. These theological emphases have had significant implications for the manner in which Presbyterians have governed their ecclesiastical life as well as the ways they have dealt with political questions.

Church Government

Presbyterian, derived from the Greek *presbyteros* (elder) in the New Testament, refers to a form of church government. The individual Presbyterian congregation is governed by a board of lay elders, usually called the session, and moderated by the minister. Congregations are grouped in a district, or presbytery. All ministers within the boundary of the presbytery are members of that body along with those elders who have been designated as representatives to the presbytery by their sessions. Each congregation elects its own pastor, but the presbytery must approve the decision and ordain and install the minister. Presbyteries in turn are supervised by synods whose membership is composed of representatives—elders and ministers—sent by the presbyteries. At the highest level, delegated clergy and elders gather in the General Assembly, usually meeting once a year, to direct the work of the entire church. Presbyterianism, in short, is a system of government by hierarchically structured church courts.

Presbyterians have not always agreed among themselves about all features of the system of government. The eldership, for example, is, in one sense, a lay office, for its members do not receive the formal theological education given to the clergy. They do not preach, administer the sacraments, or receive the stipends paid to professional clergy. Some Presbyterian theorists have, in fact, contended that elders are lay helpers in the administration of religious affairs. Others have stressed that both the clergy and the elders are equal as presbyters—the clergy as teaching elders ordained to the ministry of the word and sacrament and the others as ruling elders set apart for the ministry of governance. At different times in Presbyterian history, disputes have arisen about the terms of service for elders. Once chosen, does the ruling elder serve for life or for a stated period? In recent years, most Presbyterians have held that the ruling eldership is an ordained office and that ordination is for life, though the length of active service depends upon election (or reelection) by a congregation to specified terms.

Presbyterians have also differed about the degree to which their polity is given by divine rule *(iure divino)*. Some have insisted that the Bible prescribes the specifics of polity and that the church therefore has little freedom in devising new practices or organizations. Others have maintained that presbyterian polity, while deriving its ultimate legitimacy from the principles of biblical Scripture, allows considerable leeway for the church to formulate policies and structures expedient in particular circumstances—provided that these measures are consistent with the standards set forth in Scripture.

Yet despite disagreements, several basic assumptions lie at the heart of the Presbyterian system. First, the polity presumes that congregations are not separate, autonomous entities. They are part of one church, the body of Christ. This organic connection is appropriately expressed through an ascending system of church courts. Second, Presbyterians emphatically believe that church power should be exercised collectively and that all ministers are equal. Although in some places, such as Hungary, Reformed churches have accepted the office of bishop, they have rejected the notion that the clergy are divided into ranks and that those of higher rank have the power to make decisions unilaterally. Third, Presbyterian polity emphasizes the importance of the laity. Ecclesiastical governance does not rest solely in the hands of the clergy; it belongs to representatives of the whole people of God. Suffusing all of these principles is the central axiom of Presbyterian polity: God in Christ, speaking through the witness of Scripture by the illumination of the Holy Spirit, is the ultimate authority in the church.

John Knox

The Scottish Reformation

When the Reformed churches emerged in the sixteenth century, the vast majority of Christians assumed that church and state were part of a comprehensive Christian civilization, the *corpus christianum*. The state was obliged to uphold true religion, and the church was to work closely with the civil authority.

The Reformed churches added their own peculiar twists to this assumption. More than Lutherans, for example, the Reformed sought to define a sphere of ecclesiastical independence apart from the civil power. This idea gave the Reformed tradition, at least initially, a greater ability to establish and maintain itself in places where it did not enjoy the favor of the state. Moreover, Reformed theory and practice lent themselves to a peculiarly dynamic relationship with the political order. Convinced that God wished all of life to be subjected to his law and committed in their own internal life to a polity emphasizing a representative and collective (rather than autocratic) exercise of power, the Reformed were poised to intervene in politics in a revolutionary fashion.

In Scotland in 1559–1560, John Knox was one of those working to depose the Roman Catholic regime and install a government that moved the Scottish church in a Reformed direction. Subsequently, the Stuart monarchs' notions of the divine right of kings (the idea that monarchs rule by the will of God, not by the will of the people, and therefore cannot be replaced) and their suspicion of Presbyterianism threatened the Scottish Reformation. In response, some Scottish leaders issued a National Covenant, in 1638. Affirming Reformed faith and Presbyterian polity, the covenant pledged the entire Scottish nation, much after the analogy of God's biblical covenant with Israel, to walk in God's ways. In 1643 this document served as a model for the Solemn League and Covenant whereby the Scots and the English parliamentary forces struggling against Charles I promised mutual support. The Solemn League in effect fused the political liberties of the Scottish and English Parliaments with the religious struggle for the preservation of Presbyterianism in Scotland and the reform of the Church of England in accord with the Scottish pattern. The calling in 1645 of the Westminster Assembly to prepare a statement of faith and a directory of worship for the English church was a tangible outcome of that agreement.

Once they gained ascendancy in the English Civil War, however, the English parliamentary forces under Oliver Cromwell gradually receded from the terms of the Solemn League. During Cromwell's rule (1653–1658), the diversities within the Puritan coalition, as well as Cromwell's own Congregationalist sympathies, prevented the imposition in England of the kind of uniform Presbyterian pattern that the Scots had envisioned. In Scotland the National Covenant and the Solemn League and Covenant remained powerful ideals, particularly during a period of persecution (1661–1686) of Presbyterianism by the restored Stuart monarchy. A group of strict Covenanters refused to acknowledge the legitimacy of the monarchy for failing to endorse the Solemn League.

American Presbyterians

For the future political attitudes of their church in America, it is significant that Presbyterian immigrants—most of them Scotch-Irish or Ulster Scots from what is today Northern Ireland—first settled in great numbers in the middle colonies, particularly in New York, Pennsylvania, and Maryland. The middle colonies, with the possible exception of Rhode Island, were the most religiously diverse in British North America. In this environment, Presbyterians had to abandon old assumptions about the state's obligations to support the church. When the main body of American Presbyterians adopted the Westminster Confession of Faith as their own statement of faith in 1729, they did so with a significant demurral: they no longer accepted the assumption that the civil magistrate should favor one Christian group over another. Only those American Presbyterians, a relatively small number, who stood in the strict Covenanter tradition resisted this redefinition of the relationship of church and civil order.

Yet even as they moved toward acceptance of the separation of church and state, Presbyterians remained politically engaged. During the controversy (1767–1770) over the possible introduction of an Anglican bishop to America, many Presbyterians protested against this policy, regarding it as a step toward political tyranny. When the Second Continental Congress declared independence from Great Britain in 1776, most Presbyterians supported the cause as a righteous one. Some even saw the American venture as a sign of potential millennial glory, when Christ would reign for a thousand years. In sermons on behalf of the Revolution, Presbyterian clergy synthesized two major strands of revolutionary thought. First was the liberal notions of the state symbolized by the thought of John Locke, an English political theorist of the previous century. According to Locke, a social contract exists between individuals and states; if the contract is broken a government can be dissolved by the people. The other revolutionary strand was the classical republican tradition of ancient Rome that the civic humanists of the Renaissance had revivified and that writers in the English radical Whig tradition had adopted.

Presbyterian support for the American Revolution was, however, not uniformly enthusiastic. In the back country of North and South Carolina during the late 1760s and early 1770s, so-called Regulation movements, with Presbyterians often prominent members, had expressed grievances against the tidewater aristocracies that controlled the government of the two colonies. With those same aristocrats leading the Revolution a few years later, some Presbyterians in the Carolinas were at best lukewarm revolutionaries and at worst were politically indifferent or British-leaning in sympathy.

In the years following independence, Presbyterians were engaged politically along several fronts. They played an important role in the making of new constitutions in several colonies—for example, in New Jersey, Pennsylvania, and North Carolina. Also, in the person of James Madison—many of whose political ideas were shaped by John Witherspoon, his Presbyterian professor and president of the College of New Jersey (Princeton)—the denomination exercised at least indirect influence on the shape of the federal constitution. Presbyterians' involvement in constitution making was in some respects the logical extension of their own long-standing effort to define and circumscribe the use of power in the church, an effort that had grown more intense in the years 1741–1758, when the Presbyterian Church, divided over the issues raised by the revivalist movement known as the Great Awakening, had been forced to think precisely how the privileges of majorities and the rights of minorities could be balanced and reconciled.

During the early nineteenth century, Presbyterians sought to mold American society through a series of new institutions. Along with the Congregationalists, their cousins in the Reformed faith, they played a prominent role in the creation of numerous voluntary societies. Among them were the American Tract Society, the American Bible Society, the American Education Society, and the American Home Missionary Society. Although these groups (sometimes known collectively as the evangelical united front or benevolent empire) were not overtly partisan, they were political in a broad sense. Each sought to shape the cultural ethos in accord with Protestant values by promoting its own peculiar cause. Eventually, involvement in the benevolent empire became one of the many sources of a bitter schism as Presbyterians split into separate Old School and New School denominations in 1837.

Presbyterians sometimes tried to do more than influence mores and occasionally advocated specific public policies or candidates. For example, the General Assembly in 1815 asked the U.S. Congress to close the mails on Sunday, and Presbyterians remained for decades among the most ardent defenders of restrictive "blue laws." In 1827 a prominent Philadelphia Presbyterian, Ezra Stiles Ely, recommended that his denomination and other Protestant bodies should constitute a Christian political party—one pledged to vote only for candidates exhibiting Christian values. Ely found such a candidate in his friend Andrew Jackson, who became president in 1829, but many other Presbyterians disagreed. During the 1830s the Jacksonian Democrats were pitted against the Whigs, and Presbyterians could be found on both sides of the divide. The New School appears to have been strongly Whig, while the Old School had considerable sentiment for both parties within its ranks.

Agitation over slavery and the eventual dismemberment of the Union in 1861 forced Presbyterians to grapple with their public role. Although the General Assembly in 1818 had called the slave system incompatible with the Gospel, it subsequently tried to avoid the question, especially after 1833, with the emergence of radical forms of antislavery thought generally known as abolitionism. Both New School and Old School Presbyterianism contained abolitionist elements, but these were more numerous in the New School denomination, which was slightly more inclined to speak against slavery than was the Old School. When secession split the nation in 1861, the Old School, which had a sizable Southern component, divided along sectional lines.

The new Southern church emphasized as one of its doctrines the notion of the spirituality of the church, a concept forged in the controversies over slavery and given classic expression by James Henley Thornwell (1812–1862), one of the foremost theologians of Southern Presbyterianism. The doctrine averred that the church, as a purely spiritual society, had no mandate for pronouncing upon political or social questions unless Scripture provided a specific warrant. Yet, as individuals, prominent Southern Presbyterian clergy such as Thornwell and Benjamin M. Palmer played a major role in advocating secession. During the war the Northern portion of the Old School ever more vocally allied itself with the Union and eventually with emancipation. The shared bond of vigorous patriotism contributed significantly to the reunion of the Old School (at least its Northern portion) and the New School in 1869–1870.

In the late nineteenth and early twentieth centuries, Presbyterians gradually absorbed the spirit of the Social Gospel, a movement that sought to apply Christian principles to modern industrial society and to soften the asperities of laissez-faire capitalism. In 1903 the Northern Presbyterians appointed Charles Stelzle to head the first denominational agency designed to implement the Social Gospel, though ten years later a conservative backlash cost him his job. Following a long tradition of support for temperance, Presbyterians also backed Prohibition during its thirteen years of legal ascendancy starting in 1920. Presbyterians ardently endorsed America's participation in World War I and gave equally strong, though less chauvinistic, support in World War II. Given their notion of the spirituality of the church, Southern Presbyterians usually were slower and more circumspect in efforts to address political questions than were their Northern counterparts.

The Contemporary Church

Following World War II, Presbyterians adopted a style of more direct advocacy in the political realm. Even Southern Presbyterians, having abandoned Thornwell's interpretation of the spirituality of the church (in "A Brief Statement of Belief," 1962), exhibited the trend. Except for a few select issues or except at moments of special urgency, the older style of Presbyterian political engagement had entailed efforts to inculcate public moral values while avoiding entanglement in specific issues of policy or program. The new style called for direct engagement. In 1963 Eugene Carson Blake, the stated clerk, or chief executive officer, of the Northern Presbyterian Church, provided a powerful symbol of this new style. After joining black and white leaders attempting to integrate an amusement park in Baltimore, Maryland, he was arrested. Newspapers around the nation carried photos of him entering a police van. Blake's action, one of many instances of Presbyterian involvement in public protest during the turbulent 1960s, was mirrored in the style of direct advocacy adopted in the social pronouncements of both the Northern and Southern churches—and, after 1983, by a single Presbyterian denomination at last reunited across sectional lines.

Since the 1960s various meetings of the General Assembly have expressed grave reservations about the Vietnam War, opposed particular weapons systems, approved economic boycotts, supported women's right to terminate pregnancy, endorsed the proposed equal rights amendment, and argued that the private sexual behavior of consenting adults should not be regulated by the state. Although these pronouncements have generally tended toward liberal politics, many opinion surveys have suggested that Presbyterians in the pews are politically more conservative than their leaders. Since the 1960s organizations such as the Presbyterian Lay Committee have sought to move the church in a more conservative direction.

See also *Calvinism; Covenant; Enlightenment; Reformation; Religious organization; Separation of church and state; Social Gospel.*

James H. Moorhead

BIBLIOGRAPHY

Balmer, Randall, and John R. Fitzmier. *The Presbyterians.* Westport, Conn.: Praeger, 1994.

Carwardine, Richard J. *Evangelicals and Politics in Antebellum America.* New Haven: Yale University Press, 1993.

Hessel, Dieter T. *The Social Teaching of the Presbyterian Church.* New York: Program Agency, Presbyterian Church, 1984.

Hunt, George L., ed. *Calvinism and the Political Order: Essays Prepared for the Woodrow Wilson Lectureship of the National Presbyterian Center, Washington, D.C.* Philadelphia: Westminster Press, 1965.

Leith, John H. *An Introduction to the Reformed Tradition: A Way of Being the Christian Community.* Rev. ed. Atlanta: John Knox Press, 1981.

McNeill, John T. *The History and Character of Calvinism.* New York: Oxford University Press, 1954.

Noll, Mark A. *Religion and American Politics: From the Colonial Period to the 1980s.* New York: Oxford University Press, 1990.

"Presbyterians and the American Revolution: An Interpretive Account," edited by James H. Smylie. Entire issue of *Journal of Presbyterian History* 54 (spring 1976).

Presidents, American

The American president, the person who holds the top elective office in the United States, is both head of government and chief of state. Because the United States maintains a high degree of separation between church and government, the presidency does not play a formal religious role in the American political system. Nonetheless, because the president serves as the focal point of the political system and the office is the symbolic embodiment of the United States, the president has often taken on religious significance in the minds of many Americans.

Religious Affiliation of Presidents

For most of American history, serious aspirants for the presidency have been members of the largest and most socially prestigious Protestant denominations. Belonging to one of these denominations was not a legal requirement for holding office, something expressly forbidden by the prohibition on "religious tests" for public office in Article VI of the Constitution. Nonetheless, from 1788 through 1924, the men who served in the White House were mostly Episcopalians, Unitarians, Presbyterians, Methodists, and members of smaller denominations from what would later be described as the "mainline" wing of Protestantism. Even those presidents who were not formally affiliated with a church, such as Thomas Jefferson and Abraham Lincoln, were men of intense personal faith who were deeply imbued with Protestant religious principles.

Just how powerfully the Protestant norm operated was demonstrated in 1928, when the Democrats conferred their presidential nomination on a Roman Catholic, Gov. Alfred E. Smith of New York. In one of the most bitter presidential campaigns in American history, many Protestant clergy and some Republican campaign officials charged that Smith would threaten American freedom by imposing Catholic rule on the United States. Attacked as the embodiment of the corrupt big-city, Irish political machines, alcohol, and a despotic church ruled by the pope, Smith went down to one of the greatest defeats in American political history. Because of defections by many Protestant voters, Smith lost six Southern states that had voted reliably Democratic since the Reconstruction period that followed the Civil War (1861–1865) and also lost support in other Protestant areas. Smith's support among his fellow Roman Catholics enabled him to carry the formerly Republican states of Massachusetts and Rhode Island, but these additional votes did not offset the losses caused by Protestant opponents of a Catholic president.

More than thirty years later, when Catholicism had grown to become the single largest religious denomination in the United States, the political taboo against Roman Catholics was finally broken. In the 1960 election Sen. John F. Kennedy of Massachusetts managed to overcome some of the same pressures faced by Smith and won the presidency on a narrow popular vote. Unlike Smith, who spoke in a strong New York accent and symbolized an alien cultural presence to many Americans, Kennedy was a wealthy and well-educated member of the American elite. His social credentials and pledge to keep his religious faith out of his political judgment enabled him to avoid the full extent of the controversy that engulfed Smith in 1928.

Even so, Kennedy's candidacy was haunted by the Catholic issue. His drive for the nomination was aided by a decisive victory in the West Virginia Democratic primary, reassuring many Democratic leaders that Kennedy could do well in states without many Catholic voters. The Democratic campaign also found it necessary to send the candidate to a meeting of Protestant ministers in Houston, Texas, where he pledged his respect for the separation of church and state and promised to govern in a religiously neutral manner. Although Kennedy also lost votes from Protestants in the South, the losses in 1960 were smaller than those Smith had experienced in 1928 and were more than offset by huge increases in Roman Catholic and Jewish support for the Democratic ticket elsewhere. There was nothing particularly Catholic about the way Kennedy governed, further diminishing fears that he would somehow attempt to favor or impose Catholic doctrine on the United States.

Since Kennedy's election, major candidates for national office have better reflected American religious diversity, and the religious loyalty of candidates has seemingly played a lesser role in voter deliberations. Roman Catholics have won vice presidential nominations from both major parties and have also been strong contenders for the presidential nomination. The prospect of a Catholic in the White House no longer commands much interest or concern from the public. The largest non-Catholic denomination and the mainstay of the evangelical wing of American Protestantism, the Southern Baptist Convention, has produced three Democratic presidents in the last half of the twentieth century, Harry Truman (1945–1953), Jimmy Carter (1977–1981), and Bill Clinton (1993–). Smaller denominations, such as the Greek Orthodox Church, have also achieved representation through the nominations of Spiro Agnew (Republican vice presidential candidate in 1968 and 1972) and Michael Dukakis, the 1988 Democratic presidential nominee. Americans tell pollsters that they would not be reluctant to vote for a Jewish presidential candidate and that they would withhold votes in large numbers only from an avowed atheist. If Americans no longer require their president to be a Protestant or even a Christian, they still draw the line at the absence of any religion.

Religious Symbolism and the Presidency

Does the religion of the president matter in how the nation is governed? Few scholars have been able to trace the distinctive behavior or philosophies of presidents to their religious backgrounds. For example, on the contentious issue of abortion, the most "pro-life" presidents of recent years—George Bush (1989–1993) and Ronald Reagan (1981–

1989)—came from religious denominations that were generally "pro-choice" on the abortion question. On the other side of the issue, both Jimmy Carter and Bill Clinton supported liberal access to abortion despite the strong anti-abortion sentiment that prevails in their Southern Baptist denomination. This example suggests that presidents reflect their party or ideology more than their personal religious denomination.

Whatever their religious differences on specific issues, presidents clearly recognize the value of maintaining good relationships with religious communities. Presidents have welcomed national and international religious leaders to the White House, with one prominent evangelist, the Reverend Billy Graham, serving as unofficial chaplain to several presidents. The White House prayer breakfast, an interdenominational gathering for officials, staff, and press, has become a common event. Most presidential administrations have appointed a government official to serve as formal liaison between the White House and major organized religious groups. Presidents have also used the platform of various religious organizations to announce major public initiatives and to spread their campaign messages.

The presidency may still have religious significance even if the inhabitant of the office does not act in a particularly religious manner. Presidents have been inclined to invoke one of two different kinds of "civil religion," a term used to describe the tendency of Americans to invest their nation with religious significance. In what has been called the "high priest" role, some presidents have emphasized the moral virtue of the United States as a nation blessed by God. In foreign policy, this tendency has encouraged Americans to perceive the United States as acting from altruistic motives rather than from narrow self-interest. Other presidents have been more comfortable in the role of "prophet," calling on the nation to follow a righteous path. The role of prophecy generally carries a more critical tone than that of high priest. George Bush illustrated the priestly strain when he suggested that American military effort during the Persian Gulf war against Iraq in 1991 was blessed by God. Abraham Lincoln is often cited as the best example of the prophetic strand of civil religion. In his second inaugural address (1865), Lincoln told his audience that the bloody Civil War was God's punishment on the South for the sin of slavery and on the North for the sin of moral complicity.

See also *Catholicism, Roman; Civil religion; Evangelicalism; Fundamentalism; Graham, Billy; Jefferson, Thomas; Pluralism; Protestantism; Separation of church and state; United States of America.*

Kenneth D. Wald

BIBLIOGRAPHY

Alley, Robert. *So Help Me God: Religion and the Presidency: Wilson to Nixon.* Richmond, Va.: John Knox Press, 1972.

Fairbanks, James David. "The Priestly Functions of the Presidency." *Presidential Studies Quarterly* 11 (1981): 214–232.

Hutcheson, Richard G., Jr. *God in the White House: How Religion Has Changed the Modern Presidency.* New York: Macmillan, 1988.

Lichtman, Allan J. *Prejudice and the Old Politics: The Presidential Election of 1928.* Chapel Hill: University of North Carolina Press, 1979.

Prohibition

See *Temperance*

Protestantism

Protestantism as a religious movement originated in the reforms of Christianity in sixteenth-century Europe. Five centuries later, the movement has spread around the globe and is known for its considerable diversity of religious doctrine, ethics, and ecclesiastical structures. Its most visible form is the hundreds of separate church bodies that have arisen, but it may also be thought of more broadly as an "ethic," "spirit," or "culture." By its very nature, Protestantism cannot be identified with any of the particular forms it has produced or by reference to any single historical or cultural period. Born out of a spirit of protest, and thus set in contrast to medieval Roman Catholicism, the movement has continued to evolve and is best understood through its many transformations and adaptations over the course of history.

Early History

Histories of the Protestant Reformation identify three major strands of religious figures and ideas: the Lutheran, the Calvinist, and the radical free-church movements. In Germany in the sixteenth century, Reformation leader Martin Luther (1483–1546) challenged practices and interpretations within medieval Catholicism by defending two principles that would become widely accepted as key Protestant doctrines: one, salvation by grace through faith alone; and two, Scripture as the sole basis of religious authority and interpretation. Luther recognized only two sacraments, baptism and the Eucharist. Luther remained very much a traditionalist, retaining strong sacramental views of both practices despite his emphasis on the preaching of the Word. He argued for cooperation between church and state but looked on the two as separate spheres.

French theologian John Calvin (1509–1564), in Geneva, was the second great leader of the Protestant movement. Father of the Reformed tradition, Calvin published in 1536 his major work, *Institutes of the Christian Religion,* a systematic treatise stressing the sovereignty of God in creation and salvation. He taught that the standard for the Christian is the law of God as found in Scripture, thereby breaking, as did Luther, with the Roman Catholic reliance on tradition. His was a rather austere church, designed to encourage contemplation of the Word as revealed through Scripture by deemphasizing the aesthetic and liturgical aspects of worship. Calvin held to a doctrine of predestination, or divine choice of election for some and damnation for others, that is, a view of the atonement limited to the elect. Both the church and the civil government were regarded as divinely established for the maintenance of society, and Calvin himself worked to mold the city of Geneva into a model of a theocratic society.

Among the radical reformers were Jacob Hutter (d. 1536) in Moravia, Thomas Muntzer (c. 1489–1525) in Germany, and Menno Simons (1496?–1561) in Holland. What united them was largely their opposition to any form of state church and their rejection of infant baptism. The Anabaptists, as the members of this movement came to be known, were influential in establishing "free churches," that is, local associations of regenerated Christians that were united as the body of Christ through adult baptism. They refused to bear arms or take any form of oath. Some groups like the Hutterite Brethren lived communally. Apocalyptic and even social revolutionary thinking and militancy were not uncommon in this, the left wing of the Protestant movement, which found its greatest followings in Germany, Switzerland, and the Netherlands.

Protestantism—or more correctly, the various Protestant movements—quickly gained followings across northwestern Europe. The term *Protestant* first appeared in 1529 in a formal protest against the Roman Catholic majority in the German Reichstag (legislature), who were seeking to abolish the Lutheran territorial churches. By 1552 Lutheranism had

King Henry VIII

gained legal recognition in Germany (alongside Roman Catholicism) and had spread to Scandinavian countries, where it became politically established. By the end of the sixteenth century, Denmark, Iceland, Norway, and Sweden were all Protestant countries, by political imposition if not by popular approval. Calvinism grew in Switzerland and spread to France, to the Netherlands, and especially to Scotland. "Presbyterianism," as the Reformed faith in Scotland came to be called (owing to its New Testament–based structure of government by presbyters), spread rapidly. In 1690, after decades of strife, the Westminster Confession of Faith was ratified by the Scottish Parliament as the creed of the realm. This Confession remains a major statement of faith in the Calvinist tradition down to the present, with emphasis on original sin, the "covenant of works," and the "covenant of grace" through Christ.

In England, Parliament created the Church of England by decree in 1534 when the pope denied King Henry VIII his request for a divorce. Anglicanism, as the faith came to be known, retained much of Roman Catholic tradition and ecclesiastical structure but rejected the papacy and the sacraments other than baptism and the Eucharist. During the reign of Queen Elizabeth I, the Thirty-nine Articles became the statement of faith for the church, and the first version of The Book of Common Prayer was adopted. The late sixteenth and seventeenth centuries brought considerable religious and political strife when the Puritans, influenced by Reformed and Presbyterian thinking, sought to "purify" the church of its Roman Catholic vestiges. The Puritans themselves, although quite diverse in religious outlook and understanding, were drawn together in their defiance of tyranny and the abuse of power, whether in church or state. Radical Separatists among the Puritans sought complete separation from the Church of England, while non-Separatists worked to reform the church from within. Left-wing Separatists were dissenters who drew from both the Reformed tradition and the radical reformers. These left-wing Separatists—most notably, Baptists, Congregationalists, and Quakers—organized voluntary associations of individual believers who were committed to a church covenant and to simple practices of worship in "meetinghouses." During this time dissenting groups contended with one another and with religious establishments over issues of church order and the relations of church and society, generating blueprints for both the church and society that would greatly shape the Protestant future, particularly in America.

Diversity

Protestantism today is known for its continuing, ever-evolving diversity. Its proliferation on a worldwide basis is due partly to an evangelical spirit and partly to tendencies toward institutional schism. The vast majority of the more than 20,000 separate Christian denominations worldwide are Protestant. Still, defining what is Protestant or non-Protestant is not easy. Some Anglicans, for example, prefer to be linked to the historic Catholic tradition. Likewise, the nineteenth-century restorationist movement, which sought a return to the early New Testament church and is known in the United States as the Disciples of Christ, resists easy identification with Protestantism as a historic, evolving movement.

The United States has been a particularly fertile ground for Protestantism. Nearly 1,500 organized Protestant religious groups have been counted. Of these, almost 550 might be thought of as "classic Protestant," in the sense that their roots can be traced to the Protestant reformers. More than 200 others claim varied relationships to that line of descent; among these are Christian Scientists, Jehovah's Witnesses, Mormons, and Seventh-day Adventists. In addition, there are vast numbers of small splinter groups, independent fellowships and communities that are rather invisible. Particularly in the United States, Protestant beliefs and principles have meshed well with secular notions of democracy and individualism, making it virtually impossible to establish clear-cut boundaries between many religious constituencies. Doctrinal disputes are indeed a factor in creating Protestant diversity, but often underlying these are social and economic differences. Nationality, social class, ethnicity, and race are major sources of religious division on every continent today, just as H. Richard Niebuhr, the twentieth-century American Protestant theologian, argued were the social factors shaping Protestant life in the United States in the nineteenth and early twentieth centuries. Gender and lifestyle are more recent influences.

Diversity in the political organization of the different Protestant denominations dates from the early days when Protestants found biblical support for quite differing conceptions of church structure. Authority for Anglicans as well as Lutherans in Scandinavian countries resides with bishops, buttressed by a doctrine of apostolic succession, or the notion that authority is passed down through ordination. In the Reformed tradition, there are synodical and presbyterial forms of church government for Lutherans and Presbyterians, respectively, consisting of clergy and laity within a particular region. In the radical Reformation tradition—for example, Congregationalists and Baptists—the local congregation claims autonomy. In the modern context, conflicting pressures blur differences in organization: none of the traditions, not even those claiming local autonomy, has escaped bureaucratization, or tendencies toward centralization of power and authority; at the same time, greater individualism in matters of faith and practice on the part of the laity has eroded traditional religious authority of all kinds.

There is ideological diversity as well, reflecting a mix of theological and political elements. In the early decades of the twentieth century, the confrontation of modern science and biblical scholarship with traditional Protestantism led to the modernist-fundamentalist controversy, thus widening the split between theological liberals and theological conservatives. Today, Protestant bodies can be arrayed on a liberal-conservative spectrum with regard to a wide range of doctrinal views and personal and social ethics. Much attention has been given to the polarization between the more established, liberal Protestants, such as Episcopalians and members of the United Church of Christ, and the more rapidly growing conservative Protestants, a split that has intensified since World War II. The public posture of conservative Protestantism in this more recent period shifted in the direction of increased mobilization around moral and religious issues, most notably with regard to abortion, homosexuality, women's ordination, prayer in public schools, and euthanasia. Alliances in the United States such as the Moral Majority in the 1980s and the Christian Coalition in the 1990s have given expression to a resurgent religious force in politics; their efforts at mobilizing voters and shaping public opinion through televangelism, newsletters, and direct mailing have sparked new debate over religion's public role in a pluralist society. Moreover, polarization within religious bodies appears to have increased as a result of the growth of special interest groups, both liberal and conservative, all making direct appeals to individuals on behalf of their causes.

Common Themes

Despite this diversity of social context, organization, and ideology, common themes for Protestants do exist. The most basic of these is what is often called the "Protestant Principle." This amounts to a spirit of creative protest and self-correction derived from belief in the sovereignty of God and in the sole authority of the Word of God. Protest and correction target many objects: false gods, icons, cultural captivity, greedy institutions. In this way Protestantism cultivates a critical capacity for viewing any and all human claims—including its own claims. While Protestantism, no less than any other religious tradition, is prone to make such claims, still it contains within itself the possibility of theological critique, and thus of continuing reformation and renewal. No single ecclesiastical organization, creedal formulation, or cultural formation can be held up as constituting normative Protestantism, since as a movement it attests to a faith that expresses itself ever in new ways as circumstances change.

A second common theme among Protestants is the emphasis on religious individualism. Closely bound up with the modernization of the West, Protestantism has encouraged a more autonomous role for the individual believer. If faith alone is sufficient for salvation, it follows that individuals have opportunities for making their own religious choices. The doctrine of the priesthood of all believers further affirms a direct connection between individual believers and God and thus elevates the believer's accountability in matters of faith and morality. This belief in a direct connection serves as a basis for a concept of religious vocation, which is understood to mean that one can express faith in all types of work, with none deemed more important than any other. In the United States, especially, religion is viewed largely as a matter of conscience and personal responsibility, which gives believers considerable latitude in faith and practice.

A third, closely related theme is that of the church as a gathered body of believers. Historically, the church was understood in Protestant theology as the community sharing faith in God through Christ and observing the sacraments of baptism and the Eucharist, as opposed to the Roman Catholic and even Anglican traditions, where church was defined more in relation to the authority of bishops and apostolic succession. In democratic, pluralist settings, the church may more clearly be seen as a voluntary association, a gathering of those who profess the faith and are of like mind in religious outlook. In the categories of the German philosopher Ernst Troeltsch, churches in such settings where there is no territorial or state church take on "sect-type" characteristics, a sect being a voluntary gathering of committed believers as opposed to the established churches. The Lutheran establishments in Scandinavian countries would seem to constitute major exceptions; in actual practice, however, the relatively small number of devoted church followers in these countries approximate the norm of a voluntary fellowship.

Still another theme, most pronounced in New England Puritanism, is the notion of a covenant between God and man and among church people. Likened to the covenant between God and Israel in the Old Testament, this new covenant committed Puritans to faithfulness to God and, in turn, they would be God's people. The covenant was a means of stressing human responsibility while also giving expression to the Puritan concern for ordering all of life under God. Drawing on biblical imagery, they saw themselves on an "errand into the wilderness" to fashion a new beginning—a recurring theme in American religious culture, occasionally taking on millennial and apocalyptic qualities. Although the binding quality of the covenant in a religiously pluralist society has diminished over time, it retains some meaning in the form of the nation's unofficial civil religion, with its themes of chosenness and national obligation. Protestant churches have had to adjust both to pluralism and to a loss of cultural hegemony. Increasingly they see themselves in a struggle with other faiths and secular ideologies in shaping public life.

Shifting Centers

As these themes suggest, American churches have very much helped to shape Protestantism in the contemporary period. Individual choice, direct relationship with God, voluntary association, and tolerance of others are its distinguishing features. These religious themes take on even greater importance in view of the American churches' crucial role in the worldwide missionary movement. Throughout the nineteenth and early twentieth centuries, American-style Protestantism was exported to many places around the globe. It is a normative religious style shaped not only by New England Puritanism but also by such later developments as the great revivals stemming from the German Pietist and Methodist movements, the dynamics of a pluralist religious environment, and the constitutional separation of church and state—all of which contributed to the formation of a voluntary, denominationally based religious order.

Contemporary Protestantism is characterized by two types of shifts: geographic and ideological. The geographic center for Protestantism, once located in northwestern Europe prior to its shift to North America, is now shifting to Latin America, sub-Saharan Africa, and the Pacific Rim. Here, amidst largely nonwhite indigenous populations, evangelical Protestant zeal and growth currently is at its greatest. The ideological shifts are more subtle: an American imprint remains on forms of Christianity in these new settings, even though the normative style for large sectors of Protestantism is changing as it adapts to new cultural contexts. Pentecostalism, the fastest-growing Protestant movement worldwide, for example, appeals especially to those who want a more experiential and expressive form of religion. At present the churches in these newer settings make use of modern communication technology and are in a phase of addressing the felt concerns of the masses; as their numbers increase in coming decades, we can expect more clearly defined ideological Protestant styles and reconfigurations of religion, culture, and politics globally.

See also *Anabaptists; Anglicanism; Baptists; Calvinism; Catholicism, Roman; Christian Science; Conservatism; Covenant; Friends, Society of; Individualism; Jehovah's Witnesses; Latter-day Saints, Church of Jesus Christ of; Lobbying, religious; Lutheranism; Methodism; Millennialism; Missionaries; Pentecostalism; Pluralism; Presbyterians; Reformation; Revivalism; Separation of church and state; Seventh-day Adventists; State churches; Voluntarism.*

Wade Clark Roof

BIBLIOGRAPHY

Dillenberger, John, and Claude Welch. *Protestant Christianity Interpreted through Its Development.* New York: Scribner's, 1954.
Marty, Martin E. *Protestantism.* New York: Holt, Rinehart, and Winston, 1972.
Miller, Perry. *Errand into the Wilderness.* Cambridge: Harvard University Press, 1956.
Niebuhr, H. Richard. *The Social Sources of Denominationalism.* New York: Holt, 1929.
Pauck, Wilhelm. *The Heritage of the Reformation.* Rev. ed. New York: Oxford University Press, 1968.
Roof, Wade Clark, and William McKinney. *American Mainline Religion: Its Changing Shape and Future.* New Brunswick: Rutgers University Press, 1987.
Walker, Williston. *A History of the Christian Church.* New York: Scribner's, 1959.
Wuthnow, Robert. *The Restructuring of American Religion.* Princeton: Princeton University Press, 1988.

Public theology

Public theology turns religious visions of a nation and its people toward moral judgment of the ways they live together and govern themselves. Whether construed narrowly to refer to denominational statements on public policy or broadly to take in the social teaching of the Christian churches and their counterparts among world religions, the idea of public theology offers an instructive counterpoint to conceiving religion and politics in terms of a unitary civil religion or public philosophy. In doing so, it develops insights long shared by the social study of religion and the cultural history of theology into how religion enters into the cultural constitution of all social institutions, particularly the polity, even as social differences imprint the structures of religious community and belief. History and theology grow out of each other, which diversifies publics in both politics and religion yet makes for coherence of conversation among them.

Public theology is "an effort to interpret the life of a people in the light of a transcendent reference," writes the historian Martin Marty in *The Public Church* (1981). It focuses less on any saving faith than the ordering faith that helps constitute civic, political, and social life from a theological point of view. Public theology engages a diverse people in the larger context of American public culture as distinct from the public church understood as a specifically Christian polity, people, and witness. In Marty's usage, drawn from American statesman Benjamin Franklin instead of French philosopher Jean-Jacques Rousseau on civil religion, the public church is a partial Christian embodiment within a public religion that overarches rather than displaces traditional faiths and their continuing contributions to public virtue and the commonweal.

American Christianity counterposes diverse forms of public theology—beginning with the Constantinian ethos of theocratic rule in the Catholic colonies and the Calvinist covenant of Puritan New England; the antitheocratic, religiously tolerant theology of the dissenting Roger Williams, who founded the Rhode Island colony in 1636; the evangelical ordering of civil affairs to promote the work of redemption of early eighteenth century revivalist Jonathan Edwards; and the immanence of the holy republic arising from redemption and Christian nurture, as envisioned by nineteenth century theologian Horace Bushnell, the father of American religious liberalism, and revised by the Social Gospel, which appealed to Christian principles to inspire social reform. Varieties of public theology have multiplied in twentieth-century America with the cultural disestablishment of Anglo-Protestantism amid broader recognition of Roman Catholic and Jewish social teaching, exemplified by the National Conference of Catholic Bishops' pastoral letters on peace (1983) and the economy (1986) and the development of Jewish social ethics. The distinctive social witness of the African American churches has emerged nationally. Religious pluralism has grown to include communities of Muslims, Buddhists, Hindus and other faiths. Religious intellectuals have nurtured liberationist, feminist, black womanist, ecological, and related theologies among religious leaders and encouraged them to tackle the task of constructing a public theology.

From the beginning, public theologies have coexisted with various forms of public philosophy in America, predicated on traditions of civic republicanism, the democratic social contract, natural law, and constitutionalism. These philosophies extend from the Enlightenment faith in "the laws of Nature" professed in the Declaration of Independence by American president Thomas Jefferson through ideals advanced by political critic Walter Lippmann and Catholic theologian John Courtney Murray of a lawful moral consensus capable of sustaining civil debate over public goods to current debates over the public sphere, multiculturalism, and the politics of recognition.

Public Theology and Civil Religion

Varieties of public theology complement the sociological construct of a generalized civil religion, seen as an institutionalized ideology for a whole national society. Marty attempts to discern two kinds of civil religion, featuring the priestly blessing or prophetic challenge of alternative visions of America as "one nation under God" or the moral embodiment of "liberty and justice for all." The diversity of public theology figures in his rehearsal in *The One and the Many* of a rich repertory of diverse national narratives and rites, conversationally commingled across group boundaries, to restory and restore the bodies politic of the American Republic into an association of associations through cohesive sentiments and symbols. These sentiments stem less from veneration of the Constitution than from family reunions, civic volunteering, and Labor Day weekend baseball games. Their mutual affection owes more to Jonathan Edwards and the common sense corollaries of Adam Smith than to the solidarity sentiments of Rousseau or French sociologist Emile Durkheim.

Conversely, sociologist Robert Bellah elaborates the idea of civil religion in terms that clarify the meaning of public theology. Lacking both an established church and a classic civil religion on the model of Plato's Laws or Rousseau's social contract, the American republic has institutionalized the free exercise of religion in ways that mediate tensions in its ambiguous political identity. It is a democratic republic that depends on the participation of public-spirited citizens for its shared self-government and a liberal constitutional state that pledges to secure the individual rights of self-interested citizens who pursue wealth and wisdom through free markets for economic and intellectual exchange.

Religion mediates this tension, first, by fixing an ultimate moral sovereignty above the sovereignty of the state and the people. Thus the Declaration of Independence (paragraph 1) begins by referring to "the laws of Nature and of Nature's God" that stand above the laws of humankind and judge them. Solemn reference to a distinctly if not entirely biblical God who stands above the nation and ordains moral standards to judge its conduct becomes a permanent feature of American public life. But civil-religious ideals are thinly if securely institutionalized within American government, without explicit legal sanction or support in the Constitution or the liberal side of the American cultural heritage it expresses. The religious needs of a genuine republic can hardly be met by such a formal and marginal civil religion. In addition, the religious community entirely outside any formal political structures provides the ultimate order of the national community, in which the civic virtues and values of a republic make moral sense, in terms of public theology as distinct from civil religion, beginning with the civil millennialism of the revolutionary period.

From the beginnings of the American nation, the diversity and range of its public theology are significant morally as well as analytically because it grounds most of what is good and most of what is bad in American history, according to Bellah. Every movement to make America realize more fully its professed values has arisen from some public theology—from abolitionism through the Social Gospel to the civil rights movement and labor movements. But every expansionist war and every form of oppression of minorities and immigrants has also grown out of a public theology.

Religion in the American republic also brings together civil religion and public theology. Although the liberal state is constitutionally incapable of inculcating civic virtue in its independent citizens, federalism permitted the nation to foster schools of republican virtue in the institutions of state and local government, in the public schools, and most of all, in religious congregations and denominational bodies. In addition to teaching republican values, religious communities nurtured the mores of their self-governing members by offering them practical lessons in public participation. Because it contributed so centrally to the creation of American citizens and the moral order of the life they shared, nineteenth century French political thinker Alexis de Tocqueville concluded that religion should be considered "the first of their political institutions."

Current research confirms that religious communities continue to provide a cradle for democratic citizenship and civic aptitude, one of particular importance for Americans who are otherwise institutionally disadvantaged or excluded from voice and equality in public affairs. Those most active in religious institutions, notably churchgoing African Americans and lower-middle-class white evangelicals, offer the only striking exceptions to the rule of classbound declines in political participation and civic voluntarism in American society since the 1970s, with greater fall-offs found the further down the social ladder one goes. With the sole exception of trade unions, now shrunk to less than one-half their share of the U.S. labor force forty years ago, religious institutions provide the single most democratic counterweight to the cumulative process that favors those with more education, income, occupational clout, and connections when they take part in public life.

Recent studies of public theology within specific religious institutions—for example, the National Baptist Convention and its Women's Convention—shift focus from the religious dimension of the public realm in society as a whole to the public dimension of religious denominations and congregations. Studies of the African American church in particular as a church with the soul of a nation—in contrast to civil-religious visions of the nation with the soul of a church—tend to close the distance between civil religion and church religion and expand the institutional range of public theology. They also point up the value of theoretical efforts to diversify the public sphere, understood as a society-wide realm of rational critical communication surrounding the state in which citizens settle social questions on the merits of reason-giving argument. These efforts yield a picture of multiple publics and counter-publics of special significance for those barred by racial caste, class, or gender from full standing in the public at large—or the church at large—and betrayed by ostensibly universal representations of the meaning of such membership.

Other studies stress the integrity of the African American Christian tradition, rooted in the biblical vision of the parenthood of God and the kinship of all peoples, as a culturally encompassing framework for the social teaching of the black churches and a globally inclusive matrix for conjuring culture. They underscore the prophetic authority of figures such as abolitionist Frederick Douglass and civil rights leader Martin Luther King Jr., no less than President Abraham Lincoln and theologian Reinhold Niebuhr, to recast public theology from sources across the whole of American life and culture, sacred and secular, to call upon its people to practice what they preach.

Public theology, in sum, has always unfolded as an argument and a conversation within communities of faith, as well as among them and in their relations to public dialogue in the polity. In societies around the world today debates continue among counterposed public theologies within every major religious tradition about the relationship of religious rule or establishment to religious freedom and the rights and duties of citizens. Such debates focus, for example, on what truly constitutes a Jew in Israel, a Christian church in Russia, or a lawful government in Algeria or Iran. In the United States, compare the Social Gospel and the Gospel of Wealth, for example, or the movements to abolish slavery and alcohol or outlaw abortion and nuclear arms. Specific social issues and religious traditions describe dimensions of diversity and change in the history of public theology in America, marking shifts in its relationship to political ideology on one side and church religion on the other. So, too, do the institutional forms and settings of public theology, particularly those situated in between communities of faith and the national community.

Public Theology and Political Ideology

In 1960 there were barely thirty nondenominational religious organizations devoted to governmental and public affairs on the U.S. national scene. A generation later there are more like three hundred, including the Christian Coalition, for example, and The Interfaith Alliance. The tenfold growth of these politically oriented parachurch groups, as they have come to be called, has far outpaced the growth of denominational churches themselves. But their yield is dwarfed in turn by the concurrent mushrooming of some two thousand nonreligious national political associations, from Common Cause to the American Enterprise Institute. They stand formally free of political parties yet often couple public-interest advocacy, policy research, and civic education with political lobbying, sometimes backed by direct electoral mobilization and organizing.

The recent rise of such freestanding political associations, religious and nonreligious alike, comprises one element in a system of increased interpenetration between an expanded state and other sectors of society, changing how other institutions work and how they think and communicate. Not only commerce, defense contracting, and agribusiness but also churches, schools, and families grow more legalized and politicized. The polity itself grows more crowded and densely organized. It builds up a more nationally integrated yet more contested and multivocal argument about how people ought to live together.

A decade's sociological evidence indicates that the members of politically oriented parachurch groups tend to divide into two contrasting social clusters. Typically, older, less educated cultural conservatives fill the ranks of groups that fight abortion and pornography and champion creationism, school prayer, and family values. Younger, more educated cultural liberals usually belong to groups dedicated to nuclear disarmament, racial and gender quality, environmental protection, and economic justice. Armed with such evidence, some observers warn against the social-class divisions and culture wars they see parachurch groups declaring. Little evidence has emerged of more polarized or ideologized social opinions among Americans generally, or among religious liberals and conservatives in particular, with the exception of attitudes on abortion and differences between Republican and Democratic Party identifiers.

Within religious institutions, however, major denominations and some congregations show caucus-church signs of growing more politicized if not polarized along the lines of identity politics. In media wars waged by direct-mail campaigns, fax blitzes, and televised sound bites, religious lobbies turn public theology in the direction of political ideology insofar as they bypass the unified demands of congregational religious practice and teaching in strategic efforts to manage public opinion, mobilize partisan constituencies, and play group-interest politics with public officials.

To balance the view that Americans now face a dangerous split of civil religion into separate and competing moral galaxies or an uncivil war of orthodox and progressive believers with world views that are worlds apart, it is also worth weighing the notion that America is in the midst of a fertile if painful broadening of public theology's contested ambit among a larger, more educated, and urbanized middle class. Into this nonetheless coherent argument over how we ought to order our lives together have come culturally conservative Protestants, Catholics, Jews, and others in sufficient numbers and with sufficient eloquence as well as clout to make their voices heard.

If Americans are willing to keep listening to one another and trying to persuade one another by example and critical, conciliar dialogue alike, then this broadening of public theology promises to deepen and enrich the moral argument of public life as a whole. In a sense it has already done so, particularly for those problems such as abortion, gender and the family, peace and the poor, which have no neat solutions within the one-dimensional moral universe of individual interests, rights, and entitlements crowned by the national interest. For the counterposed ideologies of free market capitalism and welfare state liberalism at the core of American party politics today are equally mortgaged to individualist axioms that leave citizens blinded to their interdependence and unmoved by their need to share responsibility for the commonweal, which public theologies persist in proclaiming.

Public theologies proclaim these themes within an ongoing cultural conversation that embraces multiple moral traditions and languages inseparable from the social practices and institutional settings that embody them. So Americans often disagree, and understand one another when they do. Even as philosophical liberals and their communitarian critics debate the role of religion in forging or fragmenting political consensus, the moral argument of public life continues comprehensively. The United States is held together by the coherence of disagreement among its citizens, not by some comprehensive cultural agreement conceived as a value-consensus or a value-neutral set of procedural rules and individual rights, because all of its people share a common culture woven of traditions that themselves embody continuities of conflict over how they ought to live. And all Americans lead lives that span the different social institutions and practices to which moral traditions and public theologies ring more or less arguably true, including a polity that is at once a religious republic and a liberal constitutional democracy.

See also *Citizenship; Civil religion; Civil rights movement; Civil society; Communitarianism; Durkheim, Emile; Enlightenment; Holidays; King, Martin Luther, Jr.; Liberalism; Lobbying, Religious; Niebuhr, Reinhold; Pluralism; Social Gospel; Tocqueville, Alexis de; Voluntarism.*

Steven M. Tipton

BIBLIOGRAPHY

Bellah, Robert N. "Religion and the Legitimation of the American Republic." In *Varieties of Civil Religion,* edited by Robert N. Bellah and Phillip E. Hammond. San Francisco: Harper and Row, 1980.

Bellah, Robert N., Richard Madsen, William M. Sullivan, Ann Swidler, and Steven M. Tipton. *Habits of the Heart.* 2d ed. Berkeley and Los Angeles: University of California Press, 1996.

———. *The Good Society.* New York: Vintage Books, 1992.

Casanova, José. *Public Religions in the Modern World.* Chicago: University of Chicago Press, 1994.

Higginbotham, Evelyn Brooks. *Righteous Discontent.* Cambridge: Harvard University Press, 1993.

Hunter, James Davison. *Culture Wars.* New York: Basic Books, 1991.

Marty, Martin E. *The Public Church.* New York: Crossroad, 1981.

Thiemann, Ronald F. *Religion in Public Life.* Washington, D.C.: Georgetown University Press, 1996.

Verba, Sidney, Kay Lehman Schlozmann, and Henry Brady. *Voice and Equality.* Cambridge: Harvard University Press, 1995.

Wuthnow, Robert. *The Restructuring of American Religion.* Princeton: Princeton University Press, 1988.

Puritans

See *English revolution*

Q

Qaddafi, Muammar al-

Libyan political leader. Qaddafi (1942–) is a devout Muslim who has served both formally and informally as head of the North African state of Libya since 1969, when he led a bloodless coup against the Libyan monarchy. Qaddafi's parents were members of a nomadic Bedouin tribe, the Gadadfa, from which he derived his last name.

In 1951, when Qaddafi was only nine, Libya, which had been administered by French and English military governors, became independent and was proclaimed the Kingdom of Libya. Idris al-Sanusi, head of the Sanusi, a Sufi (mystic) Islamic order, became the country's first king. The order and its teachings had permeated all aspects of life and behavior of the people of Libya for more than a century.

Throughout his childhood Qaddafi was saturated with Islamic teachings and filled with hatred for colonial powers. As a high school student, he was a strong advocate of Gamal Abdel Nasser, a proponent of pan-Arabism and anticolonialism who served as president of Egypt from 1956 to 1970. Meanwhile, King Idris al-Sanusi was being denounced by the Libyans because of his close relationship with the British authority in Libya and vilified as a deviant from real Islam.

In 1964, while studying at the Libyan Military Academy, Qaddafi formed the Free Unionist Officers, modeled after Nasser's Free Officers organization and based on strict observation of the Qur'an, the holy book of Islam. After graduating from the military academy in 1965, Qaddafi organized his fellow military officers to topple the unpopular Sanusi family. In 1969 King Idris al-Sanusi was overthrown by the

Muammar al-Qaddafi

Qaddafi-led military junta; Libya was proclaimed an Islamic socialist republic. Denouncing the Sanusi and all other orders, Qaddafi announced he would adhere to no specific order but to the Qur'an and the instructions of the prophet Muhammad, the founder of Islam. His philosophy of domestic and foreign policy is enshrined in *The Green Book,* a slim volume based on Islamic belief and the instructions of the Qur'an and intended to serve as a guideline for the people of Libya.

Upon assuming leadership of Libya, Qaddafi took steps to cement his popularity by undertaking equitable distribution of the country's rich oil revenues while proclaiming the country's independence and nonalignment. Among other things, he also nationalized the country's banks and oil resources and abolished all private-sector economic activities. The dictator sought as well to establish himself as the center of a united Arab world. In doing so, he was particularly forceful in his hostility to Israel and Western countries such as Great Britain, France, and the United States.

In the 1970s Qaddafi's popularity waned abroad and at home as he began to support terrorist activities, provide military training and arms to rebel groups, and harshly impose the socialist principles of his *Green Book.* Although he resigned from his formal government positions, his personal power continued to grow behind a public facade of revolutionary government. In 1981, in retaliation for Libya's support of terrorist activities, the United States shot down two Libyan fighter planes and initiated further air attacks in 1986 against Libyan targets linked to terrorist activities. In April 1992 the United Nations banned arms sales and flights to Libya after Qaddafi refused to allow extradition of two Libyan officials suspected of terrorist involvement in the December 1988 crash of a Pan Am flight in Lockerbie, Scotland.

Despite coup attempts in 1970, 1975, and 1984, and the erosion of his popularity nationally because of the continuing foreign embargoes and sanctions, Qaddafi remains Libya's political leader. Indeed, he has no serious rivals, thanks largely to the continued support of the Libyan military.

See also *Islam; Libya; Nasser, Gamal Abdel.*

Mamoon A. Zaki

BIBLIOGRAPHY

Gadaffi, Mu'ammar. *The Green Book.* London: Martin Brian and O'Keefe, 1967 and 1981.

Tremlett, George. *Gadaffi: The Desert Mystic.* New York: Carroll and Graf, 1993.

Quakers

See *Friends, Society of (Quakers)*

Qur'an

See *Islam*

Qutb, Sayyid

Egyptian educator, Islamic activist, and leading ideologist of the Muslim Brethren. Born in a village in Upper Egypt, Qutb (1906–1966) was a life-long opponent of the British, who kept Egypt in semicolonial subordination into the 1950s. Qutb grew up reading the nationalist newspaper *al-Liwa,* to which his father subscribed. Moving to Cairo, after attending a government primary school, he eventually attended Dar al-Ulum, a college that prepared future Arabic teachers with a mix of religious and modern courses. Graduating in 1933, he began an eighteen-year career as a teacher and official in Egypt's Ministry of Education.

In the 1930s Qutb wrote for the literary and political press. In 1937 he left the nationalist Wafd Party, which had been prominent in winning greater independence from Britain, and joined the splinter Sa'dist Party. Both were secular nationalist parties, and their split owed more to leadership rivalries than to ideological differences. In the 1940s, however, Qutb left the Sa'dists and began denouncing the sociopolitical order in Islamist terms. This stance drew him closer to Hassan al-Banna, founder of the Muslim Brethren, a group that sought to restore Islamic principles and create an Islamic state.

During an interval in the United States (1948–1950), Qutb earned a master's degree, but he also came to despise Western civilization. In letters to the press back home, he denounced American licentiousness, racism, hostility toward Islam, and prejudices favoring Zionism and the new state of Israel.

When Qutb returned to Egypt in 1951, he resigned from the Ministry of Education and became a leader in the Muslim Brethren. The Brethren initially welcomed the military coup of 1952, led by the Free Officers who deposed the king and set up a republic. Col. Gamal Abdel Nasser, one of the leaders of the coup, became prime minister in 1954. Nasser was essentially secularist and refused to share power with the religiously oriented Brethren. Qutb was jailed early in 1954. He emerged for a few months to edit a Brethren paper in which he denounced Nasser for making concessions to the British in the treaty that finally won the evacuation of British troops from the Suez Canal Zone. Qutb was rearrested that fall after an attempt by the Brethren on Nasser's life.

Torture in Nasser's jails radicalized Qutb and others in the Muslim Brethren. He spelled out his radicalized Islamism in *Milestones,* which he wrote in the prison hospital and published in 1964. He attacked the political order as corrupt and illegitimate, in a state of non-Islamic ignorance, *jahiliyya,* a term applied primarily to sinful, pagan Arabian society before the dawn of Islam. He saw Islam as a timeless essence, not as a historically conditioned phenomenon needing reinterpretation for each time and place. *Milestones* discussed the obligation of individual believers to wage *jihad* (holy struggle) against governments that were only nominally Muslim, stopping just short of explicitly calling for Nasser's overthrow. Qutb unconvincingly maintained that his teachings on democracy and social justice derived entirely from Muslim sources and owed nothing to Western thought. He also wrote a commentary on the Qur'an and other works while in jail.

Granted amnesty in 1964, Qutb was rearrested in 1965 in connection with another conspiracy. In 1966 he and two other brothers were hanged. The Brethren maintain that these plots were trumped up for political reasons. Banna's successor as head of the Muslim Brethren repudiated *Milestones* as heretical, but its ideas still inspire radical Islamists in Egypt and throughout the Islamic world. The pamphleteer who wrote the tract justifying the assassination of President Anwar al-Sadat in 1981 drew on Qutb's ideas. Qutb remains one of the most influential radical Islamist thinkers of the century.

See also *Banna, Hasan al-; Egypt; Fundamentalism; Islam; Jihad; Muslim encounters with the West; Nasser, Gamal Abdel.*

Donald Malcolm Reid

BIBLIOGRAPHY

Abu-Rabi', Ibrahim M. *Intellectual Origins of Islamic Resurgence in the Modern Arab World.* Albany: State University of New York Press, 1996.

Akhavi, Shahrough. "Sayyid Qutb: The 'Poverty of Philosophy' and the Vindication of Islamic Tradition." In *Cultural Transitions in the Middle East,* edited by Şerif Mardin. Leiden: Brill, 1994.

Kepel, Gilles. *Muslim Extremism in Egypt: The Prophet and the Pharaoh.* Berkeley: University of California Press, 1958.

Moussalli, Ahmad S. *Radical Islamic Fundamentalism: The Ideological and Political Discourse of Sayyid Qutb.* Beirut: American University of Beirut, 1992.

Shepard, William E. *Sayyid Qutb and Islamic Activism: A Translation and Critical Analysis of Social Justice in Islam.* New York: Brill, 1996.

R

Reformation

The Reformation, a sixteenth-century religious movement in Europe, broke the monolithic authority of the Roman Catholic Church and opened the way to Protestantism. It profoundly changed the nature not only of Western Christianity but also of social, political, and economic relations in Western civilization. The conventional date for the beginning of the Reformation is October 31, 1517. On this day a German priest, monk, and scholar named Martin Luther posted his Ninety-five Theses on the door of the castle church at Wittenberg. Posting a document in this manner was the typical way of signaling a scholarly debate. In the Ninety-five Theses, Luther applied his understanding of "salvation by faith alone." He attacked the authority of the institutional church to mediate salvation, specifically by selling indulgences, which were pardons granted by the pope to ensure or assist in salvation. Luther saw this practice as a flagrant example of the corruption of ecclesiastical power.

To say even this, however, is already to oversimplify. The ideas that led to the Reformation had been fermenting for almost a century before Luther's deed. Furthermore, subsequent commentators, such as Max Weber (1864–1920), a German sociologist, have viewed Luther as traditionalistic, suggesting that his theses in themselves would not have produced the significant sociopolitical changes that today are associated with the Reformation. Weber would point to the theological heirs of John Calvin, a younger contemporary of Luther's, as more important "carriers" of the Reformation spirit. The German theological historian Ernst Troeltsch, on the other hand, does not see the Reformation fully realized until the work of the eighteenth-century founder of the Methodist movement, John Wesley. It is perhaps best to consider the Reformation as a collection of sociocultural processes focused on religious themes that intersected in time and place to produce an outcome not necessarily intended or anticipated by any specific thinker or group of the period.

This last point raises what may be the most important key to understanding debates among scholars of the Reformation: there may be, and generally are, significant differences between the *intentions* of reformers, on the one hand, and the actual *outcomes,* on the other. These two historical viewpoints are further complicated in current discussions by psychohistorical approaches that seek to uncover the "real" or "hidden" motivations in reformers' lives (for example, Was Luther trying to resolve a conflict between himself and his father?) and by anachronistic readings that fail to distinguish between contemporary and historical uses of terms (Protestant, for example). Careful scholars make clear the historical specifics of their arguments, and students should take care to note them.

Reformation Theology

The Reformation produced the term "Protestant" and the distinction between Protestants and (Roman) Catholics that most Westerners now take for granted. Christian theology might be said to rotate on two axes: one has to do with the afterlife, the other with the proper ordering of the present life. The two are related. The dominant theme of the Reformation is the conviction that a person's eternal salvation

Martin Luther by Lucas Cranach

is in God's hands alone; no human effort can effect or affect eternal reward or punishment. As a result, a priesthood enshrined in a church hierarchy and acting as mediator is useless, even a fraud. The individual stands before God with only Jesus as his or her mediator. At the same time, however, the conduct of one's present life is not irrelevant, for the present life can serve as a sign of one's eternal standing. People can receive assurance of their "election" (God's choosing of them) for salvation by the success they achieve as they seek to fulfill God's call to them.

Government, according to this view, is primarily instituted by God to put down wickedness and establish righteousness. The Bible contains within it a complete plan for the ordering of society, and the duty of rulers is to implement that structure. Proper government is carried out by Christian men in light of God's law. The elect will enjoy being under godly authority, while the reprobate will abhor it and need punishment. Proper government arises through a covenant among the godly to rule and be ruled according to biblical mandates. In this respect, the invention of the printing press in the mid-sixteenth century cannot be overemphasized as an essential material condition to the success of the Reformation. The printing of the Bible created an accessible textbook, potentially available to all (even though most of the people were illiterate).

The implementation of Protestant theories of government varied widely, but some notion of consent is inherent in all of them. Protestant theories reject the idea of any infallible earthly ruler, although some notions of the divine right of kings—the idea that kings ruled as direct agents of God—veered in this direction. Calvin, for example, rejected as blasphemous the claim, in the Act of Supremacy of 1534, that Henry VIII was "Supreme Head" of the Church of England.

There is also an element of freedom in Reformation thought. Precisely because God's sovereignty is the ultimate arbiter of salvation, a foreground is opened for innovation. This notion may seem contradictory. It is certainly ironic. Yet in Weber's seminal work, it became a fulcrum for the shifting of leverage away from medieval to modern worldviews. Weber argued that Protestant theology opened the way for a new "ethic" that rewarded successful political and economic innovation. Precisely because the issue of salvation was settled "once for all" by the sacrificial crucifixion of Jesus, individuals could turn their energies to other pursuits. Success in these pursuits, as measured (within limits) by economic returns, could be taken as signs of God's favor. Thus the activities of this world appeared to gain divine approval in Reformation theology.

This combination of government and freedom had consequences for the expression of Christian faith in both worship and church organization. For at least a thousand years the primary form of church government had been monarchical episcopacy—that is, rule by a hierarchy of bishops. Reformers introduced presbyterian and congregational forms of polity, in which governing authority was vested either in elders (presbyters) or in individual congregations. The role of the clergy and the nature of worship changed greatly under these forms. Although the Anglican and some Lutheran national churches retained an episcopal church governance and continued a liturgy similar to the Roman Mass, these other forms emphasized preaching as the predominate task of the clergy. Liturgical vestments and the instrumental and choral musical traditions of Christian worship were set aside. Congregationalism, though a radical innovation even among the reformers, set the groundwork for the increased tolerance, toleration, and pluralism that came to flower in America.

Protestantism and Economics

Weber's essays, published as *The Protestant Ethic and the Spirit of Capitalism,* originally written in 1904–1905, but revised by Weber shortly before his death, have probably been the most significant contribution to the Reformation debate in the twentieth century. They have produced volumes of claims and counterclaims almost from the day they were published. Weber answered some of these himself; the appearance of these works in translation has been so piecemeal, however, that misunderstanding has been amplified with the passage of time.

At the heart of Weber's position lie the notions of *irony* and *elective affinity.* First, according to Weber, an ironic coincidence of historical circumstances led some aspects of Reformation outcomes to enlarge even as others receded. Those that enlarged pulled loose from their theological moorings and free-floated through sociocultural systems, taking on a "reality" and value of their own. This is what Weber meant by the "spirit" of capitalism; that is, certain aspects of normative Protestant action (the Protestant "ethic") became transvalued into beliefs in their own right. Second, a historically specific convergence of ideal and material interests led groups of people of similar economic position to be attracted to some ideas rather than others and to try to implement these values in ways that were consistent with their position. Third—and this is a crucial point in Weber's argument—religious convictions led to actions that served to advance their proponents economically as these ideal and material interests converged. An example is the Quaker "fixed price" policy, which is the now taken-for-granted view that everyone should pay the same price for an item, rather than haggling or experiencing discrimination.

Many writers have attempted to challenge Weber's thesis; most of these challenges are based on misreadings, in whole or in part, of Weber's argument. Protestantism in Weber's use has a clear, historically specific, limited definition (Puritans, Baptists, Methodists and other pietists, Mennonites, and Quakers) and, as Randall Collins has phrased it, constitutes a "last intensification" in a long causal chain of interactions of ideal and material conditions that can be traced back at least to the high Middle Ages of the twelfth and thirteenth centuries. An analogy that might convey the structure of Weber's thought is to say that the appearance of the modern rational-capitalist system was like the outburst of a firecracker for which Protestantism served as the fuse. When it was lit amazing things happened. To the extent that we can say the lit fuse "caused" the fireworks display to happen, we can say that the Protestant ethic "caused" modern rational capitalism to appear where and as it did.

A variant on Weber's thesis is Guy E. Swanson's *Religion and Regime* (1967). Swanson argues that state structures led to the adoption or rejection of Protestantism and that these same structures had a relation to economic activity. For Swanson, state structure is more important to understanding subsequent Reformation outcomes than is Protestantism itself. William Garrett, in "Reinterpreting the Reformation" (1990), however, has shown that there is no real conflict between Swanson's thesis and Weber's thesis; the concept of elective affinity can encompass and accommodate Swanson's thesis because state structures developed concurrently with religious ideas and economic patterns.

It is instructive to compare England and Spain in this respect: in the early 1500s Henry VII sought an alliance with Spain through the marriage of Catherine of Aragon to his son, later to become Henry VIII. By the end of that century the British had defeated the Spanish Armada and began to sail to the ends of the earth as a Protestant superpower. The British still were at enmity with Catholic France (which was part of the inspiration for the earlier Anglo-Hispanic alliance), but England had experienced fundamental shifts in values away from the worldview that permeated Catholic Spain. Consistent with Weber's view of Lutheran traditionalism, a similar argument can be advanced to show the differences between England under the Hanoverian monarchs of the eighteenth century and their German cousins at home.

The Nation-State and Democracy

There seems to be general agreement that the Reformation and the rise of the nation-state were powerfully intercorrelated. To understand how this could come to be so, we must look at the Reformation in its own historical sequence rather than from the conditions of our day. Specifically, this means the end of the medieval period—the era of the plagues that destroyed huge numbers of the population and the presence of what Weber terms "salvation anxiety," an intense concern about avoiding damnation upon one's death. Today, for example, we have many religious options from which we may pick and choose—or walk away. Why was it necessarily the case that the emergence of differences in

Christian thought about the afterlife ("how to get to heaven") should cause such enormous sociopolitical upheaval?

The answer is that for at least five hundred years the Western Church (what is now called Roman Catholicism, but that term itself is a product of the Reformation) had been consolidating itself as a politico-ecclesiastical empire. In the early centuries of the Church, tribal or national groups generally had converted to Christianity through the formal submission of their leader to the pope (the bishop of Rome) in spiritual matters; the pope, in turn, recognized the leader's right to administer the temporal affairs of his realm, subject always to papal approval. Church and people became identified, and as political administration became more complex, this arrangement became known as the union of church and state. A person was "born into" the church because a person was born to some parents of some nation of some people. The idea of "choosing" a religion was no more a part of sixteenth-century experience than flying to the moon.

Thus, when Reformers began to put forth specific "protests" against the Church of Rome, and the Church rejected these, one of two things had to happen: either the protesters (hence the term "Protestants") had to be silenced by the ruler on order of the hierarchy, or the ruler—along with his or her people—would be excluded from participation in the Church's sacraments, the means of salvation to Catholic believers. For centuries, the Church had turned "heretics" over to the state for persecution, and state authorities tended to be compliant. Matters had reached such an extreme by the sixteenth century, however, that gradually one ruler after another came to say "no" to the Church. Different factors motivated different rulers, but a trend began to manifest itself in clear succession.

Consider England, for example: Henry VIII wanted a divorce from Catherine of Aragon because he believed she was incapable of producing a male heir. The pope would not authorize the divorce. Henry with the consent of Parliament created the Church of England, separate from Roman jurisdiction. The basis for this action was quite simple: English Christianity had been placed under papal authority by the decision of the monarch Oswy in 664 after the Synod of Whitby; what one monarch could give, Henry reasoned, another could take back. In other parts of Europe, things were not in every case this simple, and the Thirty Years' War (1618–1648) was fought over conflicting claims across much of what was the Holy Roman Empire (at various times from the German states to Spain). Local lords would decide either for the faith that was produced by the Council of Trent (which met intermittently, 1545–1563) of the Catholic Counter Reformation or for one of the principal Protestant confessions.

Nevertheless, the general pattern became clear: a ruler would decide which competing set of doctrines to follow, and that would become the religion of his or her people. (This formula, *cuius regio, eius religio,* adopted in 1555 at the Peace of Augsburg, roughly means "in a ruler's country, the ruler's religion.") Hence the nation-state was born. Wandering tribes had settled into specific geographical areas, and technology had advanced to the point where borders could be drawn on maps and described in words. Over time, the nation-state came to supersede the ruler. For example, in England's "Glorious Revolution" of 1688–1689, when James II refused to abandon Roman Catholicism, he was forced from the throne and was replaced by his Protestant son-in-law, William of Orange. Other European monarchs on occasion formally abdicated to accept another faith. In Protestant Europe, particularly, the formation of nation-states was aided by the translation of the Bible from Latin into English, German, Swedish, Icelandic, and so on. In this way, the material invention of the printing press entered into elective affinity with culture (language), religion (biblical literacy as a precondition for faith), and politics (the differentiation of nation-states on the basis of differences in language).

Finally, James Duke and Barry Johnson have demonstrated a connection in contemporary nation-states between Protestantism and democracy. Using the massive dataset of the *World Christian Encyclopedia,* Duke and Johnson show that the presence of Protestant Christianity in a nation-state stands in an unambiguous causal relation to the presence and quality of a democratic regime. This is clearly a Reformation outcome, since none of the major Reformers supported anything like democracy as we know it, and the few writers who did do so were persecuted both by other Protestants and by Roman Catholic authorities. Nevertheless, as the English Revolution of the 1640s shows, the seeds of democracy were already planted in Protestant soil, and, once allowed exposure, they yielded their logical fruit.

See also *Anabaptists; Anglicanism; Calvinism; Christianity; English Revolution; Lutheranism; Presbyterians; Protestantism; Puritans; Religious organization; State churches; Weber, Max.*

William H. Swatos Jr.

BIBLIOGRAPHY

Collins, Randall. *Max Weber.* Beverly Hills, Calif.: Sage, 1986.

Duke, James T., and Barry L. Johnson. "Protestantism and the Spirit of Democracy." In *Religious Politics in Global and Comparative Perspective,* edited by William H. Swatos Jr. New York: Greenwood, 1989.

Garrett, William R. "Reinterpreting the Reformation." In *Time, Place, and Circumstance,* edited by William H. Swatos Jr. New York: Greenwood, 1990.

Kent, Stephen A. "The Quaker Ethic and the Fixed Price Policy." In *Time, Place, and Circumstance,* edited by William H. Swatos Jr. New York: Greenwood, 1990.

McGrath, Alister E. *The Intellectual Origins of the European Reformation.* Oxford and New York: Blackwell, 1993.

Swanson, Guy E. *Religion and Regime.* Ann Arbor: University of Michigan Press, 1967.

Swatos, William H., Jr. "Charismatic Calvinism." In *Charisma, History, and Social Structure,* edited by Ronald M. Glassman and William H. Swatos Jr. New York: Greenwood, 1986.

Troeltsch, Ernst. *Protestantism and Progress: The Significance of Protestantism for the Rise of the Modern World.* Translated by W. Montgomery. Philadelphia: Fortress Press, 1986.

Weber, Max. "Anticritical Last Word on *The Spirit of Capitalism.*" *American Journal of Sociology* 83 (1978): 1105–1131.

———. *The Protestant Ethic and the Spirit of Capitalism.* New York: Scribner's, 1930.

Refugees

See *Sanctuary*

Religious organization

Religious organization concerns the formal governance and control of religious institutions and faith communities. It relates to the legal, normative, and doctrinal framework designed to regulate internal religious activities. The modes of regulation are quite varied: organization is complex and formal in some traditions but simple and informal in others. Some Christian churches and denominations, such as the Roman Catholic Church or the Lutheran Church, are legalistic and hierarchical, whereas formal organization is at a minimum within other groups, such as the Quakers or the Amish. There are also formal organizations in Islam and Judaism, but the degree of formal organization is lower in Buddhism, Hinduism, Shinto, and Sikhism.

Nevertheless, continuity in belief and practice is problematic in all religions unless the authority of certain precepts, roles, and institutions is acknowledged. The ways in which authority is institutionalized has political implications for each religion and for each religion's relations with the rest of society.

Types of Christian Organization

Three German-born scholars—Max Weber (1864–1920), Ernst Troeltsch (1865–1923), and Joachim Wach (1898–1955)—pioneered sociological analyses of religious organizations. According to their analyses the core ideas and values of the Christian tradition had tended to crystallize into three organizational types: church, sect, and mysticism. Each type was a translation of theology, ethics, and religious experience into a distinctive social form with its own implications for admitting initiates into the group, training religious specialists, regulating the moral life of the community, and guiding relations with nonmembers.

The church-type organization was an inclusive, formal, and sometimes compulsory body, controlled by hierarchical authority, which tended to reach out to all and favor supportive relations with legitimate secular powers in states where it was situated. The administration of sacraments by professional priests was also characteristic of the church-type. By contrast, the sect-type organization was an exclusive, less formal body of enthusiasts who had to earn their membership and who spurned professional ministers and sacraments. Sects tended to show indifference to secular politics and were often marginalized as a result. Mysticism paid little heed to formality, allowing individuals the freedom to seek their own paths to salvation with the minimum of control.

In a departure from this framework, an American clergyman, H. Richard Niebuhr, in 1929 emphasized the political significance of American religious denominations by claiming that they mirrored "the caste system of human society" in their conformity with the social class contours of modern industrial society. But the growing concern with denomination as a distinctively American type of Christian collectivity after World War II reflected the belief that the relative openness and mobility of middle-class American society required the type of Christian organization that was pragmatic, adaptable, and tolerant. The competition between conservative and liberal denominations for members was also said to reflect the existence of a religious "market" and to show people's willingness to change their denomination in accordance with their changing circumstances, self-identity, and political outlook.

Sociological Thought since the 1950s

Four major developments in sociological thinking about types of organization in Christianity have occurred since the 1950s. Each illustrates the close link with politics.

The first was Bryan Wilson's classification of sects into seven subtypes based on different views of the world, ranging from manipulationism to revolutionism. For example, Christian Scientists hold relatively conservative opinions and are at ease with much of modern life, whereas Jehovah's Witnesses hold radically "other worldly" views and are widely persecuted in many countries because of their strict moral code and their opposition to governments as the work of Satan. Each subtype of sect represents a micropolity whose political relations with the rest of society are shaped by its theology and form of authority.

The second development was a series of attempts to show that Troeltsch's mysticism was the forerunner of the cult, a loosely structured assemblage of independent-minded seekers after unconventional religious truths who tended to be uninterested in politics. Ironically, the popular usage of "cult" has come to designate a controversial religious group widely accused of manipulating and exploiting its members for the benefit of unscrupulous leaders. Questions about the political and legal consequences of trying to control controversial cults that are viewed as a threat to society are currently of concern to legislators in France, Germany, Japan and the United Kingdom as well as in the United States.

The third revision of ideas about types of religious organization is the radical claim that the most significant effect of religion on politics at the end of the twentieth century cuts across churches, sects, cults, and denominations. According to Robert Wuthnow, special-purpose religious groups draw their support from conventional types of religious organizations, but they operate in relatively independent lobbies, campaigns, agencies, and movements to manifest a bewildering variety of broadly political purposes alongside the central activities of worship, instruction, and pastoral support. Examples in the United States in the nineteenth and early twentieth centuries included missionary movements, abolitionism, and temperance.

The number and diversity of present-day special-purpose groups are overwhelming. In the United States alone, examples include such disparate groups as the Fellowship of Christian Athletes, the Christian Legal Society, and nine different associations for chaplains. They are politically significant not only because many of them campaign for secular political goals but also because their activities are in large part responses to the expansion of the state's involvement in areas such as education, social welfare, and civil rights. Indeed, the crucial role played in the American civil rights movement by the Southern Christian Leadership Conference (founded by Martin Luther King Jr.), the American Baptist Black Caucus, and the National Black Catholic Clergy Caucus, among others, is evidence of the political responsiveness and influence of special-purpose groups.

Interdenominational and nondenominational special-purpose groups may therefore be in the process of replacing conventional types of religious organization as the main vehicles for bringing Christianity to bear on American public life. The risk, however, is that they may reinforce the political fracturing of American society along the conservative-liberal divide. The proliferation of campaigns to mobilize conservative Christians from a wide range of denominations to oppose abortion and homosexuality, for example, or to restore prayer in schools has had a major impact on American politics since the late 1970s. The Moral Majority, founded in 1978 by Jerry Falwell, and the Christian Coalition, founded by Pat Robertson in 1989, are only the most famous examples of the "religionization" of politics. These groups capitalize on the advantages of "televangelism," computerized mailing lists, and the growing popularity of Christian schools to get their message out.

The fourth development is a revision of scholars' assumptions about churches' presumed alignment with the interests of nation-states. For example, Jose Casanova has depicted concordats and other constitutional agreements between the Roman Catholic Church and the governments in Italy, Spain, and Brazil as incompatible with modern principles of citizenship and damaging to the capacity of established churches to exercise independent religious influence over political life. From this point of view, one might conclude that the established churches of England, Scotland, and some Nordic countries might exert greater influence as religious organizations if they became independent of the state and could resist or counteract the forces of rationalization, secularization, and privatization at the state level in order to pursue universal values on a global level. Casanova claims that evidence of this transition from a state-oriented to a global society–oriented church can be found in Polish and American Catholicism, although, as the history of strained relations between the Catholic Church and African Americans in large cities has shown, ethnic and "racial" prejudices have also shaped the church's political stance in the recent past.

These four developments in thinking about Christian organizations emphasize not only the variety and variability of their organizational structures but also the close connection between these structures and their political stances. Put simply, organizations controlled by hierarchies based on sacramental theology and professional clergy tend to exercise authority from the top down, whereas organizations based on the notion of the priesthood of all believers, who are responsible for their own personal relationship with God, tend to be more responsive to grassroots opinion.

Religious politics are shaped by these very different organizational frameworks only in part, however. Resistance to hierarchical authority has been a feature of, for example, feminists, religious progressives, civil rights and human rights activists, and some members of religious orders in various churches. Similarly, lay opposition from conservatives to clergy-backed liberalism has been a feature of some other denominations. Thus it is unwise to equate each type of religious organization closely with a particular political orientation, though the type of organization undoubtedly influences the kind of disputes that develop within them and the way in which the disputes are conducted.

Beyond Christianity

Buddhism, Hinduism, Islam, Judaism, Shinto, and Sikhism have produced relatively few central and authoritative bodies such as churches, sects, or denominations, but the absence of these structures does not mean that these faith traditions and philosophies are devoid of formal organizations. It means that their religious activities are centered in families, kinship networks, ethnic and tribal cultures, local communities, and local centers of worship and teaching. Some of these domestic, local, and regional activities are articulated through mosque, synagogue, or temple committees; shrine associations; monastic orders; brotherhoods; legal systems; and centers of learning at regional, national, and international levels. In relatively few cases, however, do any of these bodies function as independent organizations with the authority to exercise centralized control over doctrine and practices, the training of religious professionals, the administration of property, the disciplining of individual "members," and relations with political officials. Outside Christianity it is unusual for people to practice religion as a matter of exclusive commitment to, or identity with, a single organization giving religious authorities the power to sanction people's beliefs and actions.

Although the major religions other than Christianity are not dominated by highly centralized and authoritative organizations of religious professionals, they nevertheless have extensive networks of coordinating bodies, representative councils, missionary agencies, lay societies, publishing enterprises, and interfaith associations. Matters of doctrine, philosophy, religious practice, and law are the preserve of, for example, universities and other institutions of religious training, religious or monastic orders, brotherhoods, councils of religious experts, and judicial bodies. Few of them command the loyalty and obedience of all members of their respective faith communities, so disputes between them are not uncommon, but there may also be informal agreements about the relative authority of particular institutions, official positions, or individuals. Thus leading monks and priests, lamas, *ulama* and *imams,* rabbis, *pandits,* and *granthis* can influence political policies and conduct by contacting governments directly in some cases, by mobilizing public opinion in others, or merely by exercising charisma in still others.

Indeed, the distinction between politics and religion means little in some faith traditions. A close association of religion, law, and politics has been especially evident in Islamic countries, with Iran being the extreme case of a total conflation of the three. Following the Islamic revolution of 1979, political power and legal authority in Iran were largely in the hands of Muslim clerics who installed a virtual theocracy. The collapse of communist regimes in Central and Eastern Europe after 1989 also created conditions in which Catholic and Eastern Orthodox Churches were able to recreate organizations with strong links to political forces and state agencies.

Faith traditions and their organizational structures are rarely static for long. There is a constant tension between the forces of institutionalization and revitalization, centralization and decentralization, or power seeking and maintenance of purity. The legitimacy of religious authority is therefore called in question each time new movements challenge old orthodoxies. Above all, the extent of alignment between religious and political forces is constantly shifting in response to changes in the internal condition of religious communities and in their relations with the world.

See also *Christianity; Cults; Denominationalism; State churches; Weber, Max.*

James A. Beckford

BIBLIOGRAPHY

Beckford, James A. "Religious Organization: A Trend Report and Bibliography." *Current Sociology* 21 (1973): 1–170.

Casanova, Jose. *Public Religions in the Modern World.* Chicago: University of Chicago Press, 1994.

Kurtz, Lester R. *Gods in the Global Village: The World's Religions in Sociological Perspective.* Thousand Oaks, Calif.: Pine Forge Press, 1995.

Niebuhr, H. Richard. *The Social Sources of Denominationalism.* New York: Holt, Rinehart, and Winston, 1929.

Wilson, Bryan R. *Religious Sects: A Sociological Study.* London: Weidenfeld and Nicolson; New York: McGraw Hill, 1970.

Wuthnow, Robert. *The Restructuring of American Religion: Society and Faith since World War II.* Princeton: Princeton University Press, 1988.

Revivalism

The relationship between revivalism and politics has been as complicated as revivalism and politics are themselves. Moreover, the relationship never has been fixed, and revivalism has been associated with many kinds of politics—liberal, conservative, and midstream—despite its stereotypical association in twentieth-century America with conservatism. This fluidity holds true for the nineteenth and twentieth centuries, and major changes in this complexity do not seem to be making their appearance for the twenty-first century.

So many different movements and episodes have been labeled "revivals" that the phenomenon always has been difficult to define. Generally, both participants and scholars have meant broad-scale movements to increase religious reform and commitment, usually led by powerful, sometimes charismatic religious figures. These revival leaders typically urge followers to reshape individual behavior and refashion "traditional" societies to honor God and uphold divine moral commands as ways of vanquishing contemporary irreligiosity, immorality, and blasphemy. As a result, modern revival movements often foster powerfully symbiotic relationships between individual salvation and national character that frequently plunge revivalists into politics.

Considerable variation has long typified revivals. For example, American revivals in the past century often have emphasized large-scale public gatherings with vivid preaching, emotionalism, and frequent public testimonies by the converted, including confessions of sins. Yet some of these elements also might be missing. From the 1940s into the 1970s the Reverend Oral Roberts encouraged open displays of personal emotion to demonstrate God's ability to act in modern, secular times, but revivals in the same decades by the Reverend Billy Graham typically discouraged emotional displays by the converted, and Graham's sermons were substantially more sedate than Roberts's, although still powerful.

Revivalism's relationship to politics also has been highly varied. This complexity was signaled in the first modern revivals. These revivals originated in Prussia in the so-called Pietist movement within German Lutheranism in the late 1690s and stressed personal introspection and moral living, not politics. They spread throughout German-speaking Europe and stimulated the growth of the Moravian movement, led by Count Nikolaus Zinzendorf (1700–1760), whose early followers came from Moravia and stressed personal piety and evangelism, and the Mennonite movement, a pacifist offshoot of sixteenth-century radical Anabaptists originally led by Menno Simons (1496?–1561). Finally, the revivals reached England, Scotland, and the British colonies in the United States.

Some governments, such as that of Prussia, actively supported the revivals. In Austria, Catholic authorities persecuted Protestant revivalists, both for their revivalism and their Protestantism. In Britain, revivalism prospered among longtime religious dissenters, such as Welsh Baptists, but also within the Church of England in the "Methodist" societies of John and Charles Wesley. The great revival meetings in Cambuslang, Scotland, drew thirty thousand participants in July 1742 with little apparent connection to the persistent political tension and upheavals that brought Scotland to civil war in 1745–1746 after the arrival from France of Charles Stuart (1720–1788), the pretender to the British throne.

Indeed, the Protestant revivals in the mid-eighteenth-century American colonies, later termed the "Great Awakening" by the nineteenth-century historian Joseph Tracy, illustrate their complex character and their fitful relationship to politics. The revivals were disparate. They occurred in New England and the middle colonies in the 1740s but were not common in the southern colonies until the 1760s. They were eclectic. They put forth conflicting theologies, ranging from Calvinism with its belief in predestination, to Arminianism, which emphasized the individual's ability to affect salvation, to a near-mysticism that trumpeted direct communication with God. And they bore confusing relationships to politics. The revivalist preacher James Davenport encouraged laymen to preach in the place of ordained clergymen and burned books and luxury goods in New London, Connecticut, to demonstrate his followers' new life. But Davenport was declared insane and soon lost his following. The Presbyterian Gilbert Tennent (1703–1764) attacked "unedifying" ministers and urged parishioners to listen to sanctified itinerants, but he was no egalitarian. He criticized lay preachers for their ignorance and supported a new Presbyterian synod to increase oversight of ministers. Ironically, although no revivalists preached against government or promoted social or political reform, historians have argued that revivalists' attacks on opponents formed an important model for criticism of the British government and policy on the eve of the American Revolution.

The beginning of the nineteenth century witnessed dramatic changes in the relationship between revivalism and politics and established models important to that relationship for the next two centuries. In the United States antebellum revivalism included a wide variety of social and political reforms. The ubiquitous Protestant revivalism of the 1820s through the 1850s led to major critiques of American society and a panoply of crusades to reshape it. Activists who promoted women's rights, temperance, and abolitionism, such as Phoebe Palmer, Henry Ward Beecher, and Charles Finney, often either directed or worked closely with Christian revivalism. Abolitionism's most ardent supporters often interpreted their activity in Christian millennial terms, believing that they were ushering in not only the end of slavery but the second coming of Christ.

Political crusades in other societies, some supportive of the government and some opposed, intertwined with revivalism in ways that demonstrate its peculiarities and even contradictions. In France a vigorous defense of Catholicism, whose adherents had been persecuted during the French Revolution, and a widening promotion of Mariology, the devotional adoration of the Virgin Mary, became associated with the return of the monarchy and the rise of French nationalism, including the expansion of the French overseas empire. Although the English historian E. P. Thompson has blamed the success of Methodist revivalism for England's failure to develop a politically conscious class solidarity among the working poor between 1780 and 1820, in the early twentieth century the Labour Party took root in the still-revivalistic dissenting denominations, especially Methodism. It was widely joked that Labour Party gatherings were just Methodist annual meetings without Methodist bishops. Events in Britain's empire also contradict Thompson's thesis about the inverse relationship between revivalism and political agitation. In India Arya Samaj, or Society of Aryas, founded in 1875 by Swami Dayananda Sarasvati (1824–1883), regarded many "modern" Hindu practices as corrupt and unfaithful and sought to revive adherence to the earliest Hindu scriptures. The Arya Samaj movement won support from educated and upper-class Hindus and served as an important vehicle for Hindu nationalism under British colonial rule.

Although twentieth-century revivalism has been stereotypically associated with political conservatism, this has not always been true. The Progressive Movement in the United States, with its many proposals for social welfare, had vital origins in liberal Protestant revivalism and the Social Gospel in the late nineteenth and early twentieth centuries, which stressed the social teachings of the New Testament, especially the Sermon on the Mount, as the basis for improving working and living conditions for laboring men and women. The civil rights crusade of the 1960s in turn bore strong witness to these Social Gospel and liberal revivalistic heritages, and its crowning public achievement—the rally at the Lincoln Memorial in Washington, D.C., in August 1963, capped by Martin Luther King's "I Have A Dream" oration—almost perfectly replicated a Protestant revival meeting. Still, much twentieth-century revivalism in both the United States and the Middle East has put forward conservative political agendas intended to restore "traditional" religious values to society. Fundamentalist revivalists in the United States, epitomized by Billy Sunday in the 1910s and Jerry Falwell in the 1970s, bitterly denounced modernism and secularism, the liberal state, and the decline of "Christian morality" in law and society. Shiʿite Islamic fundamentalism and revivalism in the Middle East in the 1970s and 1980s likewise denounced secularization. Based on traditional readings of the Qurʾan, Islamic revivalists like the Ayatollah Khomeini (1900–1989) in Iran and Shaykh Muhammad Mutawalli al-Shaʿrawi in Egypt demanded a return to traditional Islamic religious law, *shariʿa,* to guide secular and religious life.

Revivalism's complex relationship to modern politics is suggested both in its history and in contemporary developments. Despite occasional antiauthoritarian rhetoric among a wide variety of revivalists, most embrace the state rather than reject it. The object is to discipline the state, not dismantle it. King and Falwell each sought to bend government to serve the religious, moral, and ethical ends they believed the Bible sanctioned, but each had markedly different interpretations of what those ends might be. In 1979 Iran's Shi'ite fundamentalists overthrew the modern secular state created under Reza Shah Pahlavi (1877–1944) and restructured it to serve a conservative, theocratic government. Based in part on the Iranian success, the Sunni Islamic assassins who murdered Egypt's president Anwar Sadat (1918–1981) in 1981 believed that Sadat's murder would usher in a rebellion by faithful Muslim followers who would regain a state corrupted by secular technocratic elites.

Twentieth-century revivalism has widely embraced modern technology in both proselytizing and politics. Revivalists who condemn modern culture have long typically employed modern technologies in pursuing revivals and political change. Eighteenth-century revivalists perfected elaborate letter-writing techniques to create a "concert of prayer" on both sides of the Atlantic Ocean that would promote spiritual reform. They and their nineteenth-century successors adroitly employed printed tracts easily distributed to thousands of readers to spread their message quickly and cheaply. Twentieth-century revivalists welcomed both radio and television. Chicago's Moody Bible Institute and Los Angeles's Pentecostal evangelist Aimee Semple McPherson quickly purchased radio licenses in the 1920s—for WMBI in Chicago and KFSG in Los Angeles. And in the early 1950s the major U.S. revivalists, including Billy Graham and Oral Roberts, rapidly developed production teams to master television. Iran's Islamic revolution of 1979 prospered through clandestine radio broadcasts and taped speeches of the Ayatollah Khomeini smuggled into prerevolutionary Iran in small cassettes.

Revivalism and politics share remarkably similar strategic needs for doctrinal and ideological simplification. The revivalist's techniques of heightening religious commitment in brief religious services strongly parallel the politician's methods of shaping public sentiment among distracted citizens. They compress intricate theologies or complex ideologies into easily recognizable slogans that listeners will remember and act upon. George Whitefield (1714–1770), often described as the originator of modern English and American revivalism, asked the question "What must I do to be saved?" thousands of times on his seven tours of the British mainland colonies between 1740 and his death in 1770. His pithy, simple inquiry anticipated the catch words and slogans that have typified modern revivalism and politics since 1800, most of which boldly catalog dramatic problems and simple solutions while masking dilemmas and entanglements that raise doubt, hesitation, and critical inquiry.

Revivalism also has frequently targeted the activist, middle-class clientele that drives modern politics. Most revivalism refutes the erroneous stereotype that emerged in the United States during the Scopes trial in Dayton, Tennessee, in 1925. Critics like the journalist H. L. Mencken suggested that revivalists and their followers were ill-educated, poor, and remarkably unsophisticated. This has grossly distorted revivalism's typical clientele and seriously underestimated revivalism's potential for stimulating cultural and political change. Indeed, in the United States, Europe, and the Middle East, the middle and upper classes often have criticized the union of revivalism and politics, especially when it has promoted conservative social engineering. Yet participants in nineteenth-century U.S. revivals typically were literate middle- and lower-middle-class adults, while participants in twentieth-century revival crusades typically have attended college and carry substantial expectations for upward mobility. If Islamic revivalism with its attendant fundamentalism alienated many members of the middle and upper classes in Iran and Egypt, it also has drawn surprisingly strong support from the middle and lower-middle classes, who see in Islamic revivalism's religious certainty, "traditional" values, and resurgent nationalism an affirmation of spiritual purpose amidst the moral emptiness of modern secularism.

Ultimately, revivalism's chief political appeal rests in its capacity to confer transcendent values upon secular politics. Since most religions claim to speak for God or represent what the theologian Paul Tillich (1886–1965) calls the "ground of being" that informs every individual's moral and ethical life, religious revivalism holds attractive political assets for those who cultivate it. Numerous politicians and activists have adopted the claim of Christian, Muslim, and Hindu revivalists that the divine is present in their work and favorable to their causes. Antebellum Christian abolitionists in the United States tied their crusades to end slavery directly to the Bible and millennialistic expectations of Christ's return to earth. Late-twentieth-century evangelical conservatives have boldly stated their intent to restore the United States as a "Christian society" and have embraced the arguments of the evangelist Jerry Falwell and the activist Ralph Reed that political involvement is not only a requirement but is historically sanctioned in American history and the Bible. Hindu and Islamic revivalists have seen divine retribution in the calamities befalling both Great Britain and the United States in the nineteenth and twentieth centuries.

However, this appeal to divine sanction also carries crucial limitations on revivalism's usefulness in politics. In democracies revivalism's frequent inclination to advance absolutist religious claims and to suggest divine support for only one kind of union between politics and religion may conflict with both the political process and the need for parties to accommodate rather than sharpen differences among their constituencies. Islamic revivalists in Egypt and Turkey in the 1980s and 1990s found it difficult to move from minority to majority positions when they implicitly and explicitly condemned the life lived by the very voters they courted. Christian conservatives in the United States won many unexpected election victories between 1970 and 1990 but experienced substantial frustration when they failed to win legislative majorities in state and national politics. For example, Christian conservatives won control of state Republican Party machinery in Minnesota in the 1980s and 1990s but lost crucial elections when voters perceived them as intolerant extremists. Similarly, Christian conservative efforts to use the national Republican Party to restore the United States as a "Christian society" alienated Jewish and Catholic Republican voters in the U.S. presidential election in 1992; they saw the strategy as a return to long-discarded Protestant attempts to dominate American politics and society. In this regard, revivalism's image of intolerance and its not infrequent antagonism toward competing religious and political views can undermine its political attractions and advantages.

See also *Abolitionism; Civil rights movement; Communication; Conservatism; Evangelicalism; Fundamentalism; Graham, Billy; Hinduism; Islam; Khomeini, Ruholla Musavi; King, Martin Luther, Jr.; Millennialism; Pentecostalism; Social Gospel; Temperance movement.*

Jon Butler

BIBLIOGRAPHY

Bonomi, Patricia U. *Under the Cope of Heaven: Religion, Society, and Politics in Colonial America.* New York: Oxford University Press, 1986.

Bruce, Steve. *The Rise and Fall of the New Christian Right: Conservative Protestant Politics in America, 1978–1988.* Oxford: Clarendon Press, 1988.

Butler, Jon. "Enthusiasm Described and Decried: The Great Awakening as Interpretative Fiction." *Journal of American History* 69 (1982): 305–325.

Hunter, Shireen T., ed. *The Politics of Islamic Revivalism: Diversity and Unity.* Bloomington: Indiana University Press, 1988.

Marty, Martin E., and R. Scott Appleby, eds. *Fundamentalisms Observed.* Chicago: University of Chicago Press, 1991.

Noll, Mark A., ed. *Religion and American Politics from the Colonial Period to the 1980s.* New York: Oxford University Press, 1990.

Sen, Amiya P. *Hindu Revivalism in Bengal, 1872–1905: Some Essays in Interpretation.* New York: Oxford University Press, 1993.

Smith, Timothy L. *Revivalism and Social Reform: American Protestantism on the Eve of the Civil War.* Baltimore, Md.: Johns Hopkins University Press, 1980.

Revolutions

Revolution is a fundamental change in political organization and its social basis. Karl Marx's famous verdict on religion as the opiate of the masses should be assessed with the perspective that the system he was constructing was, in fact, a gigantic secular religion. Revolution was one of the central myths of this new secular religion, the historic event that served as its model being the great French Revolution of 1789. While dismissing the old religion to propagate his new one, Marx adopted the modern myth of revolution as the moment of redemption in history. Revolution became in Marxism what the millennial myth and the messianic idea had been in the Judeo-Christian and Islamic religions. A more dispassionate view of both religion and revolution than Marx's, however, reveals a more varied and complicated relationship between the two. In such a view, both the revolutionary potential of religion and the religious dimension of modern revolution will be conspicuous.

Major changes in social life brought about by a new religion have been described as revolutionary even when they did not entail a political revolution. In the *Decline and Fall of the Roman Empire,* for instance, English historian Edward Gibbon (1737–1794) referred to the spread of the cult of saints during the conversion of the Roman Empire to Christianity in the fourth century, as a revolution that made the Christian martyrs into celestial protectors of the empire. German sociologist and economist Max Weber (1864–1920) is the foremost figure in social theory to see the world religions of salvation as a major force for social change in human history. In his best-known thesis he argued that the Protestant ethic gave birth to the spirit of capitalism and was thus a major cause of the development of capitalism in the West.

Weber himself paid relatively little attention to the influence of religion on politics and the relation between religion and political revolutions, even though he considered the idea of a God-willed social and political revolution the distinct contribution of ancient Judaism to world history. Some contemporary social scientists, however, have used his theoretical perspective to throw light on the relation between religion and political change in general and revolution in particular.

It has been argued, for instance, that religious ethics had a major influence on the authority structure of Iran after the establishment of Shiʿi Islam by a millenarian movement in 1501 and on the political modernization of Japan as a result of the Meiji restoration of the emperor in 1867. More specifically, scholar Michael Walzer has argued that, although the ascetic ethic of Calvinism may have been a precondition for the emergence of capitalist entrepreneurs in the long run, it first produced, in the Puritan preachers, a class of political entrepreneurs who shaped the new politics of revolution by shifting the focus of political thought from the hereditary prince to the saint as the instrument of God, driven by a sense of vocation. The Puritan saints, as we shall see, played a major role in the English civil war (1640–1660), a role that justifies calling that great rebellion the revolution of the saints, or as its nineteenth-century historian S. R. Gardiner (1829–1902) called it, the Puritan Revolution.

Messiahs and the Millennium

Weber's remark on the emergence of the idea of a God-willed revolution in ancient Judaism points to instances of revolution in antiquity. The Maccabean revolt in the mid-second century B.C. was undoubtedly religiously motivated and had important consequences in world history despite its immediate failure. It resulted in the emergence of the apocalyptic view of politics and millennialism that were incorporated into the Judeo-Christian and Islamic religious traditions through the Book of Daniel. The accommodation of apocalyptic millennialism, which came to include the idea of the Messiah as savior, henceforth endowed the Abrahamic family of religions with the conception of a final, complete, God-willed social and political transformation.

A revolutionary potential was thus built into these religions, even though it was as a rule contained by projecting the end of time to the remote future. The revolutionary potential of the Abrahamic religions is reinforced by the ethical character of their solutions to the problem of theodicy, or justice of God. In this respect the medieval Christian interpretation of theodicy as the suffering and redemption of humanity through the Son of God differs sharply from the purely ethical theodicy of the Old Testament and the Qurʾan, and, alongside the Augustinian idea of the church as the city of God, accounts for the severe containment of the millennialism of pristine Christianity. According to sociologist Peter Berger, the medieval Christian theodicy of suffering caused an otherworldly transposition of the millennial idea of total transformation, and its eventual collapse during the Enlightenment in the eighteenth century ushered in the era of modern revolutions.

The rise of Islam (622–632) was a religious revolution that saw itself as the realization of messianism. It entailed a political revolution in Arabia and immediate expansion into the Roman and Persian empires. Islam's social integration, which resulted in the integration of the converted non-Arab population of the vast conquered lands from North Africa to Central Asia and Northern India, came in the mid-eighth century and has rightly been called the Abbasid revolution. The Abbasid revolution covers a protracted power struggle from 744 to 763 that ended with the definitive victory of the partisans of the Abbasid house. By the time of the Abbasid revolution, a number of messianic titles had gained currency. Of these, the one that was to outlast all others and become the general term for the divinely inspired (literally, "the rightly guided") restorer of religion in a new era was the mahdi. The Abbasid movement had typically considered itself a mission *(daʿwa)* and vied with other revolutionary and millennial movements for the correct interpretation of Islam. The Abbasids and the charismatic leaders of contending revolutionary movements competed in claiming to be the mahdi and assumed lesser messianic titles.

An important trend in modern scholarship considers the so-called Investiture Contest, which began with the papacy of Gregory VII (1073–1085), the Papal Revolution. It grew out of the Cluniac reform movement, which aimed to detach Christianity from worldly entanglements, and involved considerable mobilization of urban support under the slogan of "the freedom of the church" from temporal power. The idea of the Papal Revolution can be justified in terms of the major change in the authority structure as a result of the consequent independence of the church and the tremendous growth of its power, as well as in view of the effective integration of Western Christendom through the Roman Catholic Church in an era of feudal political fragmentation. It was a revolution initiated by the pope and leaders of the Catholic hierarchy to protect and promote the interests of the religious institution.

In contrast to the Papal Revolution, none of the medieval European movements that arose in the pursuit of the millennium—the thousand-year reign of Christ—succeeded in bringing about any revolutionary political change. A series of millennial movements that proclaimed the dawn of a new era under charismatic leaders who claimed mahdihood also failed in the fourteenth and fifteenth centuries in the Ottoman Empire, Iran, and Central Asia. In 1501, however, one mahdist movement succeeded in conquering Iran and established the Safavid empire (1501–1722). It can be argued that the ensuing conversion of Iran to Shi'i Islam and the important long-term changes this conversion entailed justify calling the rise of the Safavids in Iran a revolution.

Another world religion with an important millennial bent that provided a major stimulus to various revolutionary movements in premodern Asia is Buddhism. In China, from the second century of the common era onward, Buddhism converged with independently emergent Daoist ideas of the Way of Great Peace and the Way of the Celestial Masters. Expectations of imminent cataclysmic destruction were soon added in the blending of Daoism and Chinese Buddhism. The Buddhist idea of the Chakkavatti, the world conqueror who would usher in the age of the Future Buddha and universal redeemer, Maitreya, was used time and again by charismatic leaders who claimed to be Bodhisattvas (reincarnations of the Buddha) in a chain of heterodox rebellions from the latter part of the second to the end of the nineteenth century.

The revolt of the Yellow Turbans, who are said to have numbered 360,000, broke out in 184. The rebels wore yellow headgear, and their movement was called the Way of Great Peace. Their notion of the Buddhist redeemer and the Daoist Perfect Ruler, who would become manifest to reestablish Heaven and Earth in good order, seemed to merge with Buddhism thereafter. The Buddhist Maitreya sects were involved in numerous rebellions down to the sixth century. From the tenth to the nineteenth century, their position as the nucleus of heterodox rebellions was taken by the followers of the White Lotus teachings. Through these centuries the White Lotus sects provided the organizational network for several millennial uprisings; elements of the White Lotus millennial ideology were still to be found in the Boxer rebellion in 1900.

Two decades after the Safavid revolution in Iran, religion emerged as a major factor in several revolutionary upheavals in Europe during the Reformation. In the Peasant Wars in Germany the rebellious peasants of Swabia called for Christian freedom in their Twelve Articles (February 1525) and appealed to Martin Luther (1483–1546), only to be disowned by the reformer of Wittenberg. Further east, Thomas Muntzer (ca. 1489–1525), an apocalyptic preacher who had founded the League of the Elect and prophesied the ending of the fifth empire or monarchy of the world as the new Daniel in 1524, took over the leadership of the rebellion in Thuringia in May 1525 in which five thousand peasants perished.

A decade later Anabaptist millenarians expelled the godless from the city of Muenster and declared it the New Jerusalem. Within a few months a certain John of Leiden (ca. 1509–1536) established himself and twelve elders as the government of the city. Shortly thereafter, in September 1534, he was anointed as the King of New Zion. The uprising was suppressed in June 1535 and all the male insurgents slaughtered. These spectacular episodes apart, the German Reformation did not produce a political revolution because the reformers were successful in winning over a number of German rulers and achieved their religious aims within the status quo.

Reformation and Rebellion

It was otherwise with Calvinism, whose political influence became immediately evident in the French wars of religion (1562–1598) and the revolution in the Netherlands (1566–1589) that resulted in the creation of the Dutch Republic. While John Knox (1514–1572) and other English Calvinists in exile, who formed a congregation in Calvin's Geneva during the reign of the Catholic Queen Mary (1553–1558), were developing a distinctly radical and prophetic view of politics as saintly warfare in their letters of admonition sent to England, Calvinist missionaries and preachers were being dispatched from Geneva to France, Germany, Switzerland, and the Netherlands. Some ninety Calvinist missionaries were sent to France between 1555 and 1561, and more than one hundred in 1562, the year of the outbreak of the first French war of religion.

The ecclesiastical organization of Calvin's Geneva was dominated by a consistory, a collegial body comprising both pastors and lay elders, and stressed communal discipline and lay participation. At the psychological level, the Calvinist ethic of strict self-discipline tended to produce a type of personality Weber described as ascetic and bent on the mastery of the world. Organizationally, the Calvinists' replication of consistories, their emphasis on congregational autonomy, and their proclivity for colloquies and synods were distinctly proto-republican. Indeed, the Huguenots (French Calvinists) immediately formed a sort of autonomous republic within the French polity, a republican state within the state, thus creating a situation of dual power that Russian Marxist revolutionary Leon Trotsky (1879–1940) considered characteristic of revolutions. The era is also marked by Calvinist militancy: a wave of iconoclasm—breaking of statues and images of saints—in southern and western France in 1559 and the iconoclast fury in the Netherlands in 1566, which was followed by a lesser wave.

The Massacre of St. Bartholomew in France in August 1572 resulted in a sharp radicalization of Huguenot political thought, which now justified tyrannicide and the right of the lesser magistrate to rebel against ungodly rulers. Meanwhile, the organization and intense activism and pamphleteering of the Huguenots provoked the formation of a series of Catholic Leagues and Catholic countermobilization. It is interesting to note that the politics of the Catholic League, in which the clergy played a major part, became increasingly radicalized and populist as King Henry III (1551–1589) sought a rapprochement with the Huguenots, whose leader, the future Henry IV (1553–1610), became his legitimate successor according to the Salic Law in 1584. The theorists of the Catholic League discussed regicide and opted for elective kingship. In the Day of the Barricades the league militants forced Henry III to flee Paris (May 1558) and gained power in the capital and a number of other cities. In December 1588 the Catholic League set up a revolutionary tribunal known as the Sixteen and elected a new king.

Outside France the radical, post-1572 Huguenot ideas traveled fast among Calvinist communities, including some sixty thousand exiles in the Netherlands, and affected the rebellion in the Netherlands. Though but about one tenth of the population of the Netherlands, the Calvinists acted as a disciplined revolutionary force devoted to building the New Israel and were responsible for the escalation and radicalization of the revolt. The new, radical phase began with uprisings in Ghent and Bruges in 1577, where the Calvinist-dominated republics were later suppressed by the Spanish king Philip II (1527–1598), and culminated in the Union of Utrecht (1578) and the Act of Abjuration (1581), which permanently established the Dutch Republic in the united northern provinces of the Netherlands. The Calvinists dominated the political reconstruction that followed independence and shaped Dutch institutions.

The English Revolution

If the Dutch revolt of the sixteenth century, in which the Calvinists unquestionably played a major role, has a good title to being considered the first modern revolution, the English revolution, whose title to such consideration is more widely acknowledged, was dominated by the Puritans from the beginning to the end. It was punctuated by sermons and frequent prayer meetings in Parliament and the army, monthly fasts and days of public humiliation, and parliamentary purges of the ungodly. When the New Model Army was created in 1645, Puritan chaplains were appointed to instill the soldiers with religious zeal, which manifested its results in the decisive victory of the Royalist forces in June of that year.

Puritanism was, in fact, the single most important factor contributing to the English revolution of both ideology and organization. Puritan insistence on popular literacy as a prerequisite for reading the Bible in the vernacular, which English political theorist Thomas Hobbes (1588–1679) considered the main cause of the revolution, and on popular preaching were a major stimulus to political mobilization, mass petitioning, and publication of books and pamphlets. John Pym (1584–1643), Oliver Cromwell (1599–1658), and other leaders of the English revolution belonged to the generation of Puritan gentry who had studied Calvinist works under the direction of Puritan dons at the universities. Cromwell had been reborn in Cambridge. Like these leaders, the Puritans on the benches of the House of Commons were molded by the Calvinist conception of public service as a calling and saw themselves as godly magistrates and the Elect of God.

For decades before the English revolution, the Puritan movement had served as a mechanism for the social integration of the dislocated laborers or "masterless men" who drifted into the cities. The organizational framework for revolutionary political action grew out of an embryo of Puritan organizations: the Presbyterian classes laymen already attended in the 1570s, new associations based on Solemn Oath and Covenant, and especially the congregations around the Puritan lecturers in urban churches in the 1620s and 1630s. As these lectureships took root in English towns, laymen became the patrons and paymasters of the Puritan lecturers, and the congregations that clustered around them began to look like ideological party organizations. Furthermore, the Puritan clergy mobilized the populace with their celebrated sermons, which propagated the Puritan ideology of the revolution that glorified the English as the chosen people and the House of Commons as God's chosen instrument for rebuilding Zion.

The Puritans, however, were divided over the question of religious establishment. The majority were Presbyterians, who favored a national church. During their dominance, the Parliament, in fact, voted for the establishment of a Presbyterian national church (1646). This was opposed by the Independents, including Cromwell, on the grounds of the freedom of conscience, by those Puritan ministers who favored congregational autonomy and by other sectarians whose number increased during the revolution. Notable among the new sectarian groups were the radical Levellers, who preached egalitarian communism, gained considerable influence in the New Model Army, and became temporary allies of Cromwell and the Independents in opposing establishment of a national church.

In 1649 Cromwell purged Parliament of the Presbyterians, executed the king, Charles I (1600–1649), abolished the House of Lords, established the Commonwealth and Free State, and crushed several Leveller mutinies in the army. In December 1653 Puritan army officers who saw Cromwell as God's instrument to execute judgment on his enemies installed him as the head of the state, declaring him its Lord Protector.

Millennialism is also present in the English revolution in two forms: in the mild form of the general expectation of building a new world by the thorough reformation both of church and commonwealth and in the spectacular form it took among the Fifth Monarchy Men, the sect that took the execution of Charles I in 1649 as the signal of the end of the fourth empire of world domination, predicted in the Book of Daniel, and the rise of Cromwell as the beginning of the Fifth Monarchy, the thousand-year reign of Christ and the saints. Their millennial hope, which survived the revolution itself by a year, was extinguished with the bloody suppression of their uprising in 1661.

American Independence

A century later and across the Atlantic, the providential millennialism of the Great Awakening (1735–1765) was fostering the psychological disposition shortly to be harnessed to the cause of the American Revolution. Unlike the Puritans in England, the leaders of the American Revolution were shaped by the political ideas of the Enlightenment and derived their republicanism from the humanistic reconstruction of the ancient Greco-Roman heritage. These leaders shaped the ideology of the American Revolution and the institutions of the new republic accordingly. The primary goals of the revolution were therefore set not by religion but by the rationalist ideas of the Enlightenment and its political science. It was, however, in the psychological motivation of the bulk of the patriots to revolutionary action that religion was of fundamental importance.

The Puritan heritage had been transferred to New England in the seventeenth century, and the Puritan colonies considered themselves the chosen race with a covenant with God. The Great Awakening had added to this a sense of millennial mission to which elaborate rituals of public repentance gave the quality of tense anxiety rather than triumphalism. Appeals to religious motives in support of the revolutionary cause are evident from the outset. In June 1775, in a measure reminiscent of the Puritan revolution in England, the Continental Congress recommended "a day of publick humiliation, fasting and prayer" on July 20. From that point onward, the revolutionary energy of the ordinary citizens and the ranks of militia were tapped by the rhetoric of national guilt and punishment and the ritual of occasional fasts and public penitence. It is doubtful whether the philosophy of natural law and rationalist ideas of inalienable rights and social compact would by themselves have motivated the average patriot to sustain the prolonged revolutionary struggle. Religious discourse had far greater emotive power than the language of political rationalism, and the incidence of sermons was far greater than that of secular political debates. Once the radical Whig political ideas and the rhetoric of natural rights became incorporated into the religious discourse of the Puritans, dissenters and alienated Anglicans alike, as they readily were, they acquired a psychological power that far outweighed their rational appeal.

The thinkers of the Great Awakening, especially American theologian Jonathan Edwards (1703–1758), had reinterpreted Christian millennial beliefs to demonstrate the American destiny to be God's New Israel with a divine mission for the salvation of mankind. The Great Awakening had also been remarkably cross-denominational in its appeal and had affected all the Protestant population of the thirteen colonies. The idea of the Christian union it had promoted inspired the revolutionary motto *e pluribus unum* (from the many, one). The surviving New Lights of the Great Awakening—like American clergyman John Witherspoon (1723–1794), who was the president of the New Light college that would become Princeton University and served in the Continental Congress—carried its millennial providentialism into the American Revolution. Clergymen of all denominations supported the revolution from the pulpit and harnessed the millennialism ingrained in the American culture by the Great Awakening to the cause of the revolutionary war of independence. Furthermore, many of them served in the revolutionary army as chaplains and officers.

The Rise of Civil Religion

It has been argued persuasively that the American Revolution itself had a religious dimension, in that it transformed the providential millennialism of the Great Awakening into a civil millennialism and, further, that the act of foundation of the republic by the Founders created religious symbolism for a national religion—in short, that the American Revolution created a civil religion. The autonomous religious dimension of the French Revolution is even more unmistakable, and it was during that revolution that a conscious attempt was made to institutionalize what eighteenth-century French philosopher Jean-Jacques Rousseau (1712–1778) had called civil religion in his *Social Contract*. The autonomous religious dimension was forcefully brought out by nineteenth-century French statesman and thinker Alexis de Tocqueville (1805–1859) in *The Old Regime and the Revolution*.

Of the passionate idealism of the French Revolution, according to Tocqueville, was born a new religion. With the perspective of the communist and fascist revolutions of the twentieth century, this new religion can be typified as political religion. Unlike earlier political upheavals, according to Tocqueville the French Revolution aimed at the political, secular salvation of humanity. If anything, it can be asserted that Tocqueville underestimated the importance of the numerous revolutionary festivals as its distinctive form of communal ritual. These revolutionary festivals were a powerful force in the growth of French nationalism, and their symbolism became permanently embodied in the communal ceremonies of the French civil religion. Furthermore, the French revolutionaries marked the beginning of a new era with a new calendar and, under Maximilien Marie Isidore Robespierre (1758–1794), even attempted to institute a cult of Reason with a Supreme Being as its deity. Above all, however, the new political religion of the French Revolution that passed unto the international political culture was the ideology of Jacobinism, so named after the radical egalitarian Jacobin revolutionary clubs in which it took shape. Through Jacobinism, revolution itself became a new political myth in modern culture, a myth or value-idea with an autonomous power akin to the millennial myth of the old religion.

Tocqueville also noted that the political religion of the French Revolution was not incompatible with traditional religion. The essence of the revolution was the love of liberty and the passion for equality. In the past these objectives had been striven for through religious revolutions rather than political struggles. The revolution was anticlerical because the church was closely identified with the state and hated as a part of the old regime. But as Tocqueville points out, its purpose was not essentially anticlerical.

It can be said in support of this interpretation that the lower clergy, which constituted two-thirds of the representatives of their estate at the Estates General in 1789, supported the revolution at the early stage and consistently sided with the commoners of the Third Estate. Clergymen such as the Abbé Sieyès (1748–1836) gained prominence among the moderates, but lower clerics could also be found among the radical groups. Jacques Roux (d. 1794), a leader of the extremist Enragés, was a priest and saw the revolution as the manifestation of the spirit of Christianity. And traditional religion persisted among the insurgent masses during the French Revolution, its vitality manifesting itself in such spontaneous phenomena as the cult of the patriotic saints and the cult of the martyrs of liberty. It is interesting to note that the effort to dechristianize the cult of the martyrs came from the militants in positions of political authority and ran counter to the religious propensity of the masses. Yet it is clear that Tocqueville exaggerated the compatibility of the civic religion of the revolution and traditional Christianity.

The clash of the two became inevitable with the Civil Constitution of the Clergy (July 1790), which made the clergy salaried officials of the state, to be elected by the citizens, and required an oath of loyalty from them. The clergy protested vigorously, and many refused to take the oath. The pope condemned the measure as heretical. The refractory priests were involved in subsequent religious disturbances and were persecuted and imprisoned. In March 1793 a mass rebellion against the revolution broke out in the Vendée region of western France under the leadership of refractory priests.

At least in one significant respect, the political religion the French Revolution generated went beyond the civil religion of the American Revolution. The idea of revolution itself was an integral part of it. The apocalyptic perspective in general and political messianism in particular, as they had developed in the Judeo-Christian and Islamic traditions, were fundamentally religious and therefore not autonomous as political phenomena. They remained so for two millennia until the French Revolution secularized messianism into the modern myth of revolution. Only then did the idea of revolution become an autonomous political phenomenon, conceived as a redemptive people-guided social and political revolution. The myth of revolution generated the modern revolutionary tradition, which did not lose its vigor until the collapse of communism in 1989. Communism and fascism, both of which have been aptly described as (secular) political religions, substituted the modern myth of revolution for traditional messianism as their motive force. The Bolshevik revolution of October 1917 in Russia thus put communism in place of the messianic idea of Moscow as the Third Rome that was still potent in the religious and nationalist thought of other revolutionary groups that had participated in the revolutions of 1905 and February 1917. The Nazis proudly compared their revolution to the inferior revolutions of the French and the Russians, and their secular millennialism is evident in their idea of the Third Reich as what they termed the Thousand Year Reich of national freedom and social justice.

England remained politically stable during the age of democratic revolutions ushered in by those of America and France. The fact that England in this very period experienced the Methodist Revival stimulated an interesting thesis on the relation between religion and political revolution. The thesis was first put forward by the French historian Elie Halévy (1870–1937) in 1906 and has been reiterated by a number of contemporary historians with varying modifications. As Halévy noted, the Methodist Revival was a mass movement that swept through the new industrial towns of England for three quarters of a century. Although a branch of the movement, known as the Primitive Methodists, was politically radical and participated in the early nineteenth century protests, Methodism as a whole was politically conservative. The spread of Methodism as an evangelical and highly emotional religious movement in England in the period of rapid urbanization when, in other Western countries, the masses were swept into revolutionary politics suggested that religious revival may be a substitute for political revolution. Halévy's broad idea has been more finely tuned by subsequent historians to generate several hypotheses: that Methodism was the earlier prepolitical phase of a political movement—namely socialism; that it was England's version of the democratic revolution; or that the Methodist Revival was a substitute for political revolution and gained momentum on political reversals of the revolutionary movement in England. None of these narrower hypotheses, however, finds as much support as the original idea that revolutionary politics and religious revivalism can be substitutes as the mechanism for mass mobilization and for the social integration of a recently urbanized population.

Western Influence and Cultural Identity

The spread of Western culture and political domination to the rest of the world during the age of imperialism produced various millennial revolts and anticolonial revolutionary movements that were mainly defined by religious nationalism. The millennial response both to Western political domination and to the influence of Western ideas is quite typical. The millennial reaction to colonial intrusion can take the form of the yearning for the apocalyptic destruction of the hated colonial order and the appearance of a charismatic savior. In the second quarter of the nineteenth century in Shiʿi (Zaydi) Yemen and in Buddhist Burma we witness the appearance, respectively, of a mahdi as the Lord of the Sword and a Buddha-Ruler as the Lord of the Weapon. In Burma this instance was the first in a century-long series of peasant revolts motivated by messianic folk Buddhism and led by charismatic leaders who claimed to be the Lord of the Weapon (Setkya Min). The last such claimant was hanged in November 1931, but the cult of Setkya Min survived him.

The mid-nineteenth century is remarkable for giving us a spectrum both of modern revolutions and millennial uprisings, the former in Europe, the latter in Asia. The revolutions of 1848 in Europe, in which religion played no significant role, were enactments of the myth of revolution central to modern political messianism generated by the French Revolution. At that very time older forms of messianism were the motive force in two millennial uprisings in Asia: the Babi movement in Iran and the Taiping movement in China. The

Babi movement was launched in Shi'i Iran on the thousandth anniversary of the birth of the hidden *imam* identified with the mahdi by a young merchant who first claimed to be the gate (Bab) to the mahdi, then the mahdi himself, bringing a new revelation.

The Babi armed rebellions began in 1848, and the last one was suppressed in 1850. It failed as a political revolution. The Taiping uprising, which began in 1851, by contrast, created a revolutionary state that lasted for a decade (from the capture of Nanjing in 1853 until a few months before its collapse in 1864) in a prosperous area in southern China with a population of some thirty million. The Babi movement was primarily a millennial movement in the mahdist tradition and only secondarily a response to Christian influence through Western missionaries. The Taiping was a Chinese Christian movement whose leader was inspired by missionary tracts and was briefly instructed by an American Baptist missionary in Canton.

The founder of the Taiping movement, Hong Xiuquan, a village teacher who had failed the examination for entering the imperial bureaucracy, was convinced that he was the younger son of God the Father whom he had visited, together with his Heavenly Elder Brother, Jesus, in a heavenly ascent. He organized a Society of God Worshippers around the Thistle Mountain in Guangxi in the late 1840s. In 1848, when Europe was in the grips of modern revolution, Jesus came back to earth many times and spoke to the Society of God Worshippers through Xiao Chaogui, a peasant who became his mouthpiece. In the same year Yang Xiuqing, a charcoal burner who had just joined the movement, began to speak with the voice of God the Father. The armed uprising began on the first days of 1851, and within a few months, Hong Xiuquan, using the terms for the Kingdom of Heaven in the Chinese translation of the New Testament, declared the existence of the Heavenly Kingdom of the Great Peace *(Tai-ping tien-kuo)*. Jesus gave his blessing to the enterprise and twenty-three of its named leaders through his mouthpiece, thereby inaugurating the distinct divinely inspired political ritual of the Taiping, which combined policy directives with rewards for the virtuous and punishment for backsliders.

During the fall of 1851 the Taiping established their new state in the walled city of Yongan and marked the beginning of their era with a new calendar. Hong became the Heavenly King and the Lord of Ten Thousand Years; Yang, the East King; and Xiao, the West King, followed by two kings for the two remaining cardinal points and a Wing King, being, respectively Lord of Nine to Five Thousand Years, in descending order. The Taiping forces that had grown to some forty thousand suffered colossal casualties in June 1852, including many of the veterans. The losses in number were, however, more than made up by massive recruitment from the secret societies or brotherhoods that had mushroomed in the aftermath of the Opium Wars (1839–1842). The Taiping forces captured the rich provincial capital of Wuchang in January 1853 and moved six hundred miles further along the Yangzi River to capture Nanjing in March. Their exodus, begun two years earlier from the Thistle Mountain, now ended in the promised earthly paradise, and Nanjing was declared the New Jerusalem.

With the broadening of recruitment in 1852, a strong nationalistic element entered Taiping propaganda. The demons whom the Heavenly King was to eradicate were identified with the Manchu rulers. The emperor was the Manchu demon of barbarian origin, the Tartar dog and the "mortal enemy of us Chinese." Nevertheless, the religious motive remained primary in the Taiping revolution. Like the Puritans, the Taiping militants were instilled with anxiety about sinfulness and practiced rituals of atonement and supplication by praying on their knees. The intense activism of the Taiping is reflected in the fact that the militants received military and religious instruction together and at the same time. The disciplinarian asceticism of the Taiping movement was, however, markedly collective. Strict collective discipline was maintained by ritual shaming, dismissal from military posts for failure to answer ritual religious questions, severe exemplary punishment of deviants, and execution of retrograde demons.

The Taiping authority structure was shaped accordingly. Officials of all ranks held both military-political and religious authority. When the victorious new regime reorganized Nanjing as a puritanical city of virtue, the quarters of men and women were separated; adulterers, homosexuals, and opium smokers were executed; and the whole army prayed regularly before meals.

The Taiping movement recruited from humble social classes, in particular enlisting women widely and opening unprecedented social and political careers to them. Religious movements often open an avenue for social participation by marginal social groups, notably women, and recruit from them disproportionately. The Taiping movement likewise tapped women's energy for revolutionary militancy. Women participated vigorously in the Taiping army and administration. This participation went hand in hand with the segregation of the sexes, and with austere sexual asceticism from which the kings, however, were exempted.

Although Jesus motivated Taiping militants to revolutionary political action from the beginning of the movement to the death of his earthly mouthpiece, Xiao Chaogui, in 1853, the revolutionary power struggle thereafter was marked by constant intervention of God the Father, whose earthly mouthpiece, Yang Xiuqing, made his bid for primacy in the Heavenly City, Nanjing. Far from countermanding the typical dynamics of this power struggle in which the revolution, like Saturn in Greek myth, devours his own children, God the Father let the history of revolution in the Heavenly Kingdom of Great Peace take its natural course. At the end of 1853, well within a year of the conquest of Nanjing, Yang Xiuqing began to criticize the Heavenly King with the voice of God the Father and to overturn his decisions. In 1854 Yang, the East King, forced the Heavenly King to declare him the Paraclete and the Wind of the Holy Spirit. He overstepped the mark in 1856, however, by demanding the same millennial rank as the Heavenly King with the title of the Lord of Ten Thousand Years. This was too much for the Heavenly King and two rivals whom Yang Xiuqing had recently demoted from the kingly rank. A revolutionary coup was successfully executed in September 1856. The East King and his entire family were killed, and thousands of his supporters in Nanjing massacred.

The Taiping Heavenly Kingdom survived the bloody revolutionary purge of 1856 for eight years, but it became increasingly corrupted by the hereditary principle that had been recognized from the beginning and now worked to the benefit of the incompetent and rapacious family of the Heavenly King. The Heavenly King became increasingly withdrawn and devoted himself to revising the Bible and refashioning himself for posterity as the priest-king Melchizedek, and presenting the Heavenly Kingdom of the Great Peace (renamed God's Heavenly Kingdom in 1861) as the fulfilled New Jerusalem of the Book of Revelation.

Latin American Liberation

The presumption that only Protestantism could be revolutionary and Catholic Christianity was inherently conservative and incapable of oppositional activism has been decisively dispelled by the developments in contemporary Latin America. But it resulted in the systematic neglect of popular Christian insurrections in the last two centuries. A few important cases can be mentioned. In Mexico there was a massive peasant rebellion of 1810, led by two parish priests, Father Hidalgo and Father Morelos. In the 1830s in Spain, there is the case of the Carlist movement in which the clergy led the prosperous yeomanry in Basque and Aragon in defense of their local autonomy against the encroachments of the central government and created a de facto monkish democracy. In the twentieth century the Cristero movement during the Mexican revolution was organized by priests and lay Catholics in reaction to the anticlerical policies of the central government; it gathered a massive following under the motto "Long Live Christ the King" in 1927 and 1928. The Cristero movement is comparable to the clerically led uprising of the Vendée in 1793 in revolutionary France as instances of mass religious countermobilization against anticlerical policies of revolutionary regimes.

Nevertheless, the potential of Catholicism for radical political activism and popular mobilization was greatly enhanced after Vatican II in the 1960s. The saying of the Mass in the vernacular, a shift of emphasis away from the hierarchical conception of the church and toward the idea of the church as the pilgrim people of God, the emphasis on the work of the church in the world, on collegiality, and on the enhanced authority of the councils of bishops, and finally, the new emphasis on the dignity of the laity and the priesthood of all believers—all of these factors contributed to the increased political activism of the Catholic Church and its potential for involvement in revolutionary politics.

If the Second Vatican Council brought the Catholic Church into the modern world, the second Conference of Latin American Bishops convened in Medellín, Colombia, in August 1968, brought the Latin American churches into the modern revolutionary tradition at a time when revolution was in the air everywhere. Some 130 bishops attended the conference, which focused on the work of the church in this world and combined biblical and sociological themes to propose that political action was necessary to change the social structure that caused poverty. The word "liberation" was frequently used during the conference, and reference was made to base communities organized by lay Catholics in poor urban and rural districts.

Medellín was followed by another Conference of Latin American Bishops in Puebla, Mexico, in 1979, which discussed pastoral themes and the need for evangelization while affirming the preferential option for the poor. The theology of liberation was born between the two conferences. It supplemented the traditional Christian theodicy of suffering with a new one that had clear revolutionary potential by interpreting Christian faith in terms of the suffering, struggle, and hope of the poor. The distinctive theodicy of liberation theology identifies suffering with the struggle of the poor and substitutes liberation from this suffering in the world for other-worldly redemption (at any rate, as the objective of action here and now). It can therefore absorb the modern myth of revolution as a redemptive act in history and has considerable revolutionary potential.

The full acceptance of the idea of revolution as a historical act of social and political liberation accounts for the fact that the Catholic Church played an important role in the Nicaraguan revolution, and many radical priests and lay activists in the Christian (base) communities expressly supported it out of religious motives. In the 1970s the church in Nicaragua was infused with the spirit of Vatican II and Medellín by a new generation of clergy and young lay activists, some of whom led religious activities in rural areas not served regularly by a priest, and important contacts were made with the Sandinista Front of National Liberation. In 1977 the priest and poet Ernesto Cardenal publicly joined the Sandinistas, and shortly thereafter a Christian group significantly calling itself the Twelve, which included two other priests, Fernando Cardenal and Miguel D'Escoto, declared their opposition to the Somoza regime. Fernando Cardenal, a Jesuit, was the organizer of a Christian Revolutionary Movement that, according to him, supplied the Sandinista front with as many as four hundred young people. In January 1978 the Nicaraguan bishops denounced the Somoza regime in a pastoral letter, thereby encouraging many church people and the activists in the Christian base communities to give open support to the Sandinistas, who succeeded in overthrowing Somoza in July 1979. The three radical priests served in the Sandinista revolutionary government, respectively, as ministers of culture, education, and foreign affairs, as did a fourth radical priest who held the Ministry of Social Welfare. Other priests have served in the Council of State, and several lay Catholics have held important positions.

The Nicaraguan revolution is also instructive of other ways religion and revolution relate. The pope's visit to Nicaragua in 1983 highlighted the tension between the Catholic Church and the Sandinista Marxist regime. In 1984 Fernando Cardenal was forced to leave the Jesuit order to become minister of education, and in 1985 Ernesto Cardenal and Miguel D'Escoto were suspended from the priesthood, and the clerical minister of social welfare asked to be released from his vows.

The Nicaraguan church had meanwhile distanced itself from the regime with the waning of revolutionary enthusiasm and began to speak out against it. Cardinal Miguel Obando y Bravo, the archbishop of Managua, indeed became the chief opponent of the Sandinista regime. The independence of the church from the state enabled it to change its position from conditional support to outspoken opposition that contributed to the downfall of the Sandinista revolutionary regime.

Evangelical Protestantism grew phenomenally during the Sandinista revolution. Conversion to evangelical Protestantism gained rapid momentum during the revolutionary period, and the Protestant population of Nicaragua grew from around 5 percent to probably more than 20 percent. Evangelical Protestantism has grown rapidly throughout the region. Like evangelical Methodism in England, evangelical Protestantism in Latin America is an intensely emotional religion of justification by faith in Jesus. Furthermore, the parallel with the growth of Methodism in England during the age of democratic revolutions is as clear as it is theoretically suggestive and supports Halévy's thesis of the substitutability of political revolution and religious revival as alternative mechanisms for the social integration of recently urbanized masses. In Nicaragua Protestant revivalism progressed along with the Sandinista revolution; elsewhere in Latin America, Protestant revivalism has possibly foreclosed the possibility of mass mobilization to revolutionary movements and helped prevent political revolution.

Revolution in Iran

Like the Vendée uprising and the Cristero movements in France and Mexico, the Islamic revolution of 1979 in Iran was a clerically led revolutionary mass mobilization against the decades-long secularization that was a part of the modernization of the Iranian state by the Pahlavi shahs. For three centuries after Shi'i Islam was established in Iran, a Shi'i hierocracy had grown in Iran and secured its independence from the monarchy. A dual structure of authority, consisting of a state and a hierocracy, prevailed in the nineteenth century. The modernization of the state in the twentieth century entailed secularizing the judiciary and the educational systems and transferring many of the functions of the hierocracy to the state. It did not, however, impair the independence of the hierocracy and the religious authority of the high-ranking Shiʿi clerics, the ayatollahs.

Clerical opposition to state building and secularization was ineffective in the 1920s and 1930s. In the 1970s, however, under the charismatic leadership of Ayatollah Ruholla Khomeini (1900–1989), clerics launched a massive campaign of revolutionary mobilization that succeeded in overthrowing the shah and reversing his secularization policies with a vengeance. For this campaign Khomeini used the younger clerics and seminarians whose professional status had declined and who had dim prospects for social mobility under the shah. Under Khomeini's leadership, these dispossessed clerics became a revolutionary counter-elite that eventually seized power and took over the state.

Rapid social change during the two decades preceding the revolution had created favorable conditions for Khomeini's project of replacing monarchy with an Islamic government. Urbanization and the expansion of higher education, in particular, contributed to the rise of an Islamic revival movement and its swift revolutionary politicization. Thousands of religious associations spontaneously came into being in the fast-expanding cities, Islamic associations appeared in the universities, and the growth of religious publications outpaced that of other categories. The popular religious associations, which were to provide a platform for the militant preachers and later for playing of cassettes of the exiled Khomeini's sermons, acted as the mechanism of social integration for a significant proportion of migrants into the cities. The Islamic associations in the universities similarly integrated many first-generation students who had come to big-city universities from small towns or a traditional lower-middle-class background. These young men crucially contributed to the revolutionary politicization of the Islamic revival of the 1970s and shaped the ideology of the Islamic revolution.

Max Weber once remarked that if any hierocracy wishes to retain its power after the advent of modern mass politics, it must establish a party organization. Khomeini chided his clerical colleagues and followers for leaving political mobilization to leftist atheistic parties and factions. Rapid urbanization and the shah's failure to integrate the uprooted and especially the socially mobile, newly educated elements into his political system offered Khomeini and the Islamic militant clerics an unparalleled opportunity for creating an Islamic revolutionary mass movement, to which they proved equal. Using the organizational network of mosques, lay religious associations, and Islamic university students, the militant clerics periodically organized massive anti-shah demonstrations and closings of the bazaar. The secular opposition and the nonclericalist Islamic radicals and modernists acknowledged Khomeini's leadership and became partners in a revolutionary coalition firmly dominated by him.

After the overthrow of the shah in February 1979, the secular and Islamic nonclericalist partners in the revolutionary coalition were eliminated in the revolutionary power struggle of the next two and a half years. Clerical control over the Iranian state was tightened, and Khomeini's clericalist theory of government as the basis of the mandate of the supreme religious jurist to rule was carried out in institutional form. The Islamic revolution thus created the first theocratic republic in world history. The constitution of the Islamic Republic of Iran gives the supreme religious jurist, called its leader *(rahbar),* the position created for Khomeini, extensive religious and secular powers, including the appointment of the commanders of the armed forces and of the head of the judiciary, the confirmation of the elected president, and the naming of the six clerical jurists of the Council of Guardians, which automatically reviews all parliamentary enactments and must approve all candidates for the parliament and the presidency.

Many of the globally televised millions of people who crowded into Tehran to welcome Khomeini in January 1979 did so with some apocalyptic expectation stimulated by his assumption of the title of *imam,* hitherto reserved for the hidden *imam* who was expected to reappear as the mahdi at the end of time to save the world. Khomeini did not claim to be the mahdi, but the temptation to see him as the forerunner of the latter was irresistible, just as had been the case with Ismaʿil, the leader of the Safavid revolution four and three-quarter centuries earlier. This messianic disposition was captured in one of the most frequent slogans of the Islamic revolution: "O God, preserve Khomeini until the revolution of the mahdi." Over and above this largely implicit substratum of traditional messianic beliefs, the myth of revolution as the quintessential form of modern political messianism was also fully and explicitly operative. The Islamic ideologue, Ali Shariʿati, who died in 1977 shortly before the revolution, interpreted the idea of the return of the mahdi as an allegory of revolution. Many revolutionaries, and certainly the revolutionary clerical leadership, did not accept this assimilation and subordination of the old Shi'i political messianism to the modern political myth of revolution. Nevertheless, the latter, too, accepted the idea of a people-willed revolution as an autonomous principle and certainly used it as a pillar of their legitimacy.

See also *Anabaptists; Anticlericalism; Base communities; Calvinism; Catholicism, Roman; Central America; China; Civil religion; Communism; English Revolution; Enlightenment; Evangelicalism; Fascism; France; Hobbes, Thomas; Iran; Islam; Khomeini, Ruholla Musavi; Latin America; Liberation theology; Lutheranism; Mahdi; Marxism; Methodism; Mexico; Millennialism; Papacy; Reformation; Revivalism; Weber, Max.*

Said Amir Arjomand

BIBLIOGRAPHY

Arjomand, S. A. *The Turban for the Crown. The Islamic Revolution in Iran.* New York: Oxford University Press, 1988.

Berdiaev, N. A. *The Russian Revolution.* Ann Arbor: University of Michigan Press, 1961.

Berryman, Phillip. *Liberation Theology. The Essential Facts about the Revolutionary Movement in Latin America and Beyond.* Philadelphia: Temple University Press, 1987.

Dodson, M. "Nicaragua: The Struggle for the Church." In *Religion and Political Conflict in Latin America,* edited by Daniel H. Levine. Chapel Hill: University of North Carolina Press, 1986.

Gorski, P. S. "The Protestant Ethic Revisited: Disciplinary Revolution and State Formation in Holland and Prussia." *American Journal of Sociology* 99 (1993): 265–316.

Halévy, Elie. *The Birth of Methodism in England,* translated with an introduction by B. Semmel. Chicago: University of Chicago Press, 1971.

Lewy, G. *Religion and Revolution.* New York: Oxford University Press, 1974.

Miller, P. "From the Covenant to the Revival." In *The Shaping of American Religion,* edited by J. W. Smith and A. L. Jamison. Princeton: Princeton University Press, 1961.

Sarkisyanz, M. *Buddhist Backgrounds of the Burmese Revolution.* The Hague: M. Nijoff, 1965.

Spence, J. D. *God's Chinese Son. The Taiping Heavenly Kingdom of Hong Xiuquan.* New York: W. W. Norton, 1996.

Thrupp, S. L., ed. *Millennial Dreams in Action: Studies in Revolutionary Religious Movements.* New York: Schocken, 1970.

Walzer, Michael. *The Revolution of the Saints.* Cambridge: Harvard University Press, 1965.

Romero, Oscar A.

Roman Catholic archbishop of San Salvador, modern martyr, and a symbol of the Catholic Church's option for the poor. On March 24, 1980, Romero (1917–1980) was shot and killed while saying Mass. In his relatively short tenure as archbishop he had defended the poor at a time when El Salvador was plagued by poverty, paramilitary violence, and guerrilla insurrection; disorder and repression were increasing; and civil war seemed inevitable.

Archbishop Oscar A. Romero

Romero became archbishop in February 1977 at a moment of sharply escalating crisis: in front of the cathedral an opposition vigil protesting fraud in the election of Gen. Carlos Humberto Romero to the presidency was broken up as government troops beat people, killing several dozen of them. Within days Rutilio Grande, a respected pastor, was murdered for his work with the poor; shortly afterward another priest was murdered; and the army carried out a sweep and occupied the town of Aguilares, using the church as a barracks and holding captive the Jesuit priests. During this time leftist guerrillas were also kidnapping business people for ransom. Before he became archbishop Romero had been regarded as an honest, serious, if conservative priest and then bishop; indeed, his theological and pastoral conservatism facilitated his appointment by the Vatican. This climate of violence, and especially the murder of Grande, led him to take the side of the poor.

Romero's first actions foreshadowed what was to be his style: he denounced acts of violence, defended the legitimacy of people's struggle for their rights, and placed the church and its resources at the disposal of the poor. During his time in office Romero received a constant stream of poor people, who often told of violence used against them. In 1978 the archdiocese began to monitor human rights violations systematically. At his Sunday Masses Romero would reflect on general trends in the country—always from a Gospel viewpoint, he insisted. This increasingly took the form of describing incidents of political violence that the media, controlled by the military and the oligarchy, would not publish. Romero came to be called the "voice of the voiceless." In four pastoral letters he took up the issues arising out of the role of the church in a situation of escalating conflict—for example, the stance of the church toward militant mass organizations.

Tensions increased in October 1979 after a group of military officers took power and claimed to be installing a reformist or even revolutionary government, but in fact violence by government forces and right-wing death squads increased. Romero insisted that the new government should be given a chance but continued to denounce human rights violations. By early 1980 approximately a thousand people a month were being killed, almost all civilians murdered by official forces and right-wing death squads. Romero ended his Sunday sermon on March 23, urging, even commanding, soldiers not to obey orders to kill peasants. He was murdered the next day by a death squad sharpshooter, probably ordered by ex-major Roberto D'Aubuisson, leader of an ultrarightist group. Romero's outdoor funeral was interrupted by bombs and shooting, and seventy-five thousand people had to flee in terror (approximately twenty-six were left dead).

Formal procedures for Catholic canonization are underway, but for many Salvadorans and Latin Americans, Romero is already a saint and martyr.

See also *Central America; Latin America; Liberation theology.*

Phillip Berryman

BIBLIOGRAPHY

Brockman, James R. *Romero: A Life.* Maryknoll, N.Y.: Orbis Books, 1989.

———, ed. *The Violence of Love: The Pastoral Wisdom of Archbishop Oscar Romero.* San Francisco: Harper San Francisco, 1988.

Sobrino, Jon. *Archbishop Romero: Memories and Reflections.* Maryknoll, N.Y.: Orbis Books, 1990.

Rushdie, Salman

See *Censorship*

Russia

An independent republic in eastern Europe and Asia established on December 25, 1991, Russia was formerly the Russian Soviet Federated Socialist Republic of the Union of Soviet Socialist Republics (USSR). It is now officially the Russian Federation. Church and state have long been closely associated in Russia.

The support of the Russian Orthodox Church for the prevailing political system of the day originated in Byzantine times, when the Eastern Christian Church was subordinate to the emperor. The otherworldliness of the Orthodox Church is often more apparent than real. The timelessness of the liturgy, virtually unchanged in a thousand years, often conceals not merely political passivity but even active support for nondemocratic or occasionally totalitarian regimes.

The Church under the Tsars

The ancient territory of Kievan Rus (located within present-day Ukraine) inherited this absolutism directly from Byzantium when it adopted Christianity in the tenth century, though it exercised this power in a moderate way. The shift of power north to Muscovy saw the emergence of a true theocracy in which the tsar and the patriarch were equally important in maintaining the political system. Moscow came to see itself as the Third Rome (Constantinople, before its conquest by the Turks, had been the second).

To bring the church under state control, Peter the Great's Spiritual Regulation of 1721 abolished the office of patriarch and replaced it with a state functionary, the over-procurator of the Holy Synod (Peter had taken a Germanic Protestant

model for his reduction of the temporal power of the church).

Tsarist power, indeed, was never open to reform; this intransigence was to lead eventually to its toppling in March 1917 and the supplanting of the provisional government by the Bolsheviks six months later. It would not be true to say that there was no criticism of the political system within the Orthodox Church during the nineteenth century, but this came almost exclusively from lay intellectuals (novelists Fyodor Dostoevsky and Leo Tolstoy, for example) who had no relation to the power structure of the Russian Orthodox Church itself. Toward the turn of the century, however, a movement for reform grew within the church. Clergy were active in the first revolution of 1905, which led to some liberalization, and by 1917 there was a specific agenda within the church for reducing the absolute control of church affairs by the state and—in its turn—of the church's unconditional support for state policy.

It is a little-known fact about the Revolution of 1917 that the Russian Orthodox Church was actively attempting to bring about internal reform at the very time the old order was being overthrown. A Sobor (the church's governing body, which had long since fallen into desuetude) was summoned, and its first act was to elect a patriarch (Tikhon) for the first time in almost two hundred years. Revolution leader Vladimir Ilyich Ulyanov Lenin (1870–1924) and the Bolsheviks immediately (January 1918) sought to break the power of the church, beginning by nationalizing its property and seizing its schools. The rest of the reforming agenda had to be shelved, and the Sobor would not meet again until 1944, but neither then nor subsequently has there been any free discussion of the whole agenda of reform within the Orthodox Church.

Soviet Rule

Patriarch Tikhon's position was precarious from the first. He opposed the Bolsheviks' confiscation of church valuables and condemned Soviet power for its lawlessness. After his arrest and probable torture in prison, he declared that he was no longer an enemy of the Soviet government. When

Tikhon died in 1925 Stalin did not allow the appointment of a successor. Under even more duress, Metropolitan Sergi, designated as deputy in charge of the patriarchate, signed a declaration in 1927, the words of which were to remain standard policy for the church until the very end of Soviet power in 1991 and would link it to the Soviet regime.

It is true that the Moscow Patriarchate, as the governing body of the church is now called, did not call for a restoration of the Soviet Union at the moment of its collapse, though strong elements within it supported the coup against Soviet leader Mikhail Gorbachev. The sixty-four years between Sergi's declaration and the end of the Soviet Union illustrate how far the Orthodox Church could go in endorsing a godless regime. There was no time in war or peace when the official voice of the church did anything other than echo state policy—even claiming on many occasions that what was in fact an aggressively atheist regime provided sufficient space for the religious needs of the people.

In 1929 the Stalinist power removed the last vestiges of religious liberty with the promulgation of the Law on Religious Associations. Although the Soviet constitution continued to proclaim separation of church and state, this new law decreed that the only legal religious activity would be worship within the four walls of a registered church. Religious education in all its forms would be barred. The state had total control over registration of every worshipping community—only a local *dvadtsatka* (group of twenty believers), the membership of which had to be explicitly approved by the local soviet, could apply for registration.

The German invasion of 1941 followed this virtual annihilation of the church. Metropolitan Sergi managed to appeal to Orthodox believers to oppose the Fascists, which led in 1943 to Joseph Stalin's acknowledgment of the role the church had played in the war effort. He permitted it to reestablish a central body (the Moscow Patriarchate) and to elect Sergi as patriarch after convening a Sobor.

In the postwar Soviet Union the Russian Orthodox Church, now gaining strength, played an overtly political role, not only in subjugating the Greek-Catholic (Uniate) Church in Ukraine (1946) but also in helping to shore up Soviet power in those newly conquered countries where Orthodoxy was strong (Bulgaria, Romania, and, to a less successful extent, Yugoslavia).

Spokesmen for the Moscow Patriarchate now overtly backed every military initiative of the Soviet regime: suppression of the Hungarian uprising (1956), the erection of the Berlin Wall (1961), the invasion of Czechoslovakia (1968) and of Afghanistan (1979).

Less obvious, but perhaps more insidious, was the attempt to dominate the agenda of international church relations. In 1961 the Russian Orthodox Church successfully applied for membership in the World Council of Churches. The temporary opening of Soviet archives has revealed how concerted were the efforts of the KGB (Committee of State Security) to dictate the political agenda of countless religious meetings, not only in the World Council forum but also elsewhere. The full history of this attempt is yet to be written: the World Council of Churches continues to deny that it was taken in by such tactics, but there is a body of evidence to the contrary. There were attempts to influence the Vatican as well.

The New Russia

The end of the Soviet period saw the church leadership claim that it had opposed Soviet policies all along. As early as 1988, during the millennium celebrations of the Christianization of Russia, Metropolitan Yuvenali stated at one of the great public gatherings of the time that there were both priests and laity among the many thousands who had been subjected to mass repression.

Before long, however, the Moscow Patriarchate would embrace a very different regime, a post-Soviet one. In a state suddenly seeking an ideology and a raison d'être, the Orthodox Church saw an opportunity unique in history. Here there was tremendous potential for good. The Russian people did indeed need firm footing on which they could stand after the collapse of the official ideology. To some extent Russian Orthodoxy filled this void, and there is much good to be found in the reestablishment of parish life throughout the country.

With the demise of the Soviet Union, traditional non-Orthodox religions have also asserted themselves (especially Baptists and Catholics), and there have been innumerable incursions of foreign religious movements, both Christian and non-Christian. The Orthodox Church has opposed these, not primarily by strengthening its own teaching and evangelism but by prevailing upon the Duma (parliament) in 1997 to introduce discriminatory legislation, reinstating something of the primacy Orthodoxy enjoyed before 1917.

According to the new law, Judaism, Buddhism, and Islam now count as traditional religions as well, giving them a status above that of Protestants and Roman Catholics but still below that of the Russian Orthodoxy, which is cited as the greatest influence on the development of Russian culture. Curiously, some of the most traditional of all religions do not receive comparable recognition. The Old Believers represent the Russian Orthodox Church as it was before the reforms of the seventeenth century, and the True Orthodox Church claims continuity with the pure Orthodox tradition before church leaders' compromises with the communists.

The Moscow Patriarchate also continues to justify even the most controversial policies of Boris Yeltsin's regime. There was, for example, no single word of condemnation of the genocide in Chechnya. On the contrary, the church hierarchy continued to enjoin young men not to shirk their patriotic duty of serving in the army, even if that meant shooting their fellow citizens.

Although over the centuries the Russian Orthodox Church has explicitly endorsed state policy, in all its vicissitudes, there has also been opposition to this stance from within the church itself. Dissenters among the intelligentsia in the nineteenth century were excommunicated; in the Soviet period they formed a large group in such early prison camps as Solovki; in the postwar period they were persecuted as political dissidents. In 1997 Orthodox priests lost their parishes or teaching posts in seminaries for opposing the new laws on religion. There are countries, such as the United States and Australia, with a considerable number of adherents to the Orthodox Church, where a completely different attitude to politics has emerged, and it is possible that one day this will influence Russia itself.

See also *Communism; Europe, Eastern; Marxism; Orthodoxy, Russian.*

Michael Bourdeaux

BIBLIOGRAPHY

Bourdeaux, Michael. *Patriarch and Prophets: Persecution of the Russian Orthodox Church Today.* London: Macmillan, 1969.

———. "The Russian Church, Religious Liberty, and the World Council of Churches." In *Religion in Communist Lands.* Journal of Keston College 13 (spring 1985): 4–27.

Davis, Derek H. "Editorial: Russia's New Law on Religion: Progress or Regress?" *Journal of Church and State* 39 (autumn 1997): 645–655.

Fletcher, William C. *A Study in Survival: The Church in Russia 1927–1943.* London: SPCK, 1965.

Spinka, Matthew. *The Church in Soviet Russia.* Westport, Conn.: Greenwood Press, 1980.

S

Sabbatarianism

See *Seventh-day Adventism*

Sacred places

Holy places—sites that are regarded as sacred, taboo, or worthy of special veneration—are characteristic of all religions. Closely associated with them are the notions of boundary (the demarcation of the taboo locale from the surrounding profane areas); cult acts or rituals particular to that place; the identification of who may cross the boundaries to perform the rituals forbidden to others (in short, a priesthood); the enshrinement or adornment of the place to identify or honor it; and, finally, the practice of pilgrimage, a visit to a place to acknowledge and in some manner share in its sanctity.

What Makes a Place Holy?

Historians of religion are uncertain about the origins of holy places, as they are about the origin and nature of holiness itself. The witnesses to the sanctity of places, as opposed to those who merely describe or analyze the phenomenon, are unanimous in believing that certain places possess an intrinsic holiness, typically by reason of a divine presence in that place, a manifestation or act of God. Such places often have another attribute. A divine apparition (theophany) prompted the biblical Jacob to call a place in Palestine Beth-el, "the house of God" (Genesis 28:17), and then, immediately, "the gateway to heaven," where the messengers of God moved between God's dwelling and ours. This was one of the sites where the heavenly and the earthly domains intersect along a cosmic axis. Such too were Jerusalem and Mecca, Delphi in Greece, and the Hindu temples where the devotee alone may leave the external secular world and enter the cosmic center within.

Animists have always regarded some form of the divinity as resident in nature, and natural features like springs, rivers, trees, and mountains have received a marked reverence in almost every culture, from the Buddhists' veneration of the bodhi tree to the Greeks' regard for Mount Olympus and the Hindus' for the Ganges River of India. Eventually, some such objects become personified as everything from major deities to the minor sprites and nymphs who dwell in woodland and water. Quite different from the immanent but universal sanctity of elements of nature is the intrinsic but quite specific holiness of the Land of Israel in Jewish eyes. It is God's own: "The Land is Mine; for you are strangers and sojourners with Me." (Leviticus 25:23) And so it enjoys an innate holiness that is, in its developed understanding, a far more existential concept than the more familiar instances of attributed holiness due to the presence of the sacred in a place and a far more historical one than the sanctity of nature.

Judaism knew the holiness of presence as well. There are explicit boundary markings and purifications in preparation for Yahweh's appearance on Sinai (Exodus 19). God's continuing presence among the nomadic Israelites crossing the Sinai wilderness was visible by day and night and was housed in a ceremonial tent (Exodus 25:8; 40:38). And finally there is God's presence in the Holy of Holies of the Jerusalem temple, which put that city too at the vertical intersection of heaven and earth and the intense center of horizontal rings of diminishing holiness drawn by the rabbis on the sacred geography of the Land of Israel *(Eretz Israel).* Surrounding the sacred center were the graduated outer precincts of the temple into which those of progressively austere degrees of purity were admitted: priests, Israelite males, Israelite women, and finally Gentiles in the remotest court of all. Jerusalem itself became a bounded taboo: a corpse had to be removed from within its limits before sunset, and certain holy festivals like Passover could be observed only within those same municipal limits.

Jerusalem and Pilgrimage

Christians never regarded Jerusalem in quite the same way. Its sanctity to them was of a historical, memorializing type—the final great events of Jesus' life had taken place in specific locales there—but neither it nor the land enjoyed the singular and abiding presence of God that it did for Jews. The sacred Jerusalem of Israelite history was explicitly abandoned by Paul on behalf of all Christians in a famous passage in Galatians (4:21–28). Thereafter Christian eyes were raised away from the ruins of the historical city (destroyed by the Romans in A.D. 70) to a heavenly Jerusalem. The earthly Jerusalem was holy by remembrance, however, a specifically Christian remembrance. In the fourth century the now-Christian emperor Constantine promoted a well-financed and well-publicized project to identify the Jesus sites in Jerusalem and the rest of Palestine and to enshrine them with appropriate structures. Thus Constantine by identifying and enshrining the Palestinian sites associated with Jesus began converting Palestine into a Christian holy land, not in the intrinsic Jewish sense but as a network of discrete holy places, each connected with Jesus or one of the figures of early Christianity and linked together by a practice associated with sacred places everywhere, pilgrimage. Not terribly different is the Buddhist identification of major events in the life of Buddha—his birth, enlightenment, first sermon, and death—with specific locations and their subsequent development as both shrines and pilgrimage sites.

Jewish law required residence in holy Eretz Israel for the perfect fulfillment of the Torah and presence in Jerusalem for the full celebration of the highest of holy days, Passover, Shabuoth, and Succoth—the first obligation was made progressively more difficult by the Jewish dispersion and the second nullified by the destruction of the temple when the city was destroyed—but Christians' pilgrimage to their holy places was voluntary, though made progressively more attractive by the spiritual rewards attached to pilgrimage by the church. After Constantine, the number of sites included in the pilgrims' itinerary grew ever greater (and more specific), but the center remained the empty tomb of Jesus in Jerusalem.

Tombs and Shrines

In almost all religious communities, even those like the early Greeks and the rabbinic Jews in which there is no strongly developed sense of the afterlife, the living have found it difficult to believe that the powerful or saintly in life should lose all of their *mana,* or inherent power, at death, and tomb sites are among the most widely dispersed form of sacred places. Jews and Muslims, for example, regard a corpse as a powerful source of ritual impurity, and the orthodox of both groups have struggled for centuries to discourage tomb cults. They have sprung up nonetheless, and one of the most spectacular shrines in the Abode of Islam is the prophet Muhammad's tomb in Medina, even now being enlarged and enhanced by the descendants of the puritanical Wahhabis who destroyed all the other Muslim tombs in Mecca and Medina.

Christianity's view of tomb-shrines was different from these at the outset: the tomb of Jesus was the site of the founding and sustaining miracle of Christianity, Jesus' resurrection from the dead. This triumph over death (and the impurity of the flesh) soon spread to the other heroes of the early Jesus movement, the "witnesses" *(martyres)* who affirmed the faith by their willingness to die for it. Their burial places in suburban Roman cemeteries became early Christian cult sites, but with the transformation of Christianity from persecuted sect to imperial church, the remains of the sainted martyrs were translated from those remote cemeteries to the centers of the empire's cities and graced with splendid domed *martyria* erected above and around their now publicly venerated relics. In much the same way, the remains of the cremated Buddha were distributed to the princes of all the nations and were enshrined in elaborate pagoda-shrines *(stupas),* where they are venerated to this day.

Thus the Christian church building, once a room or a shrine or an oratory in a private house, was supplanted by

Muslim pilgrims gather in the large inner courtyard of the Great Mosque in Mecca, Saudi Arabia, the holiest city of Islam.

monumental new edifices built through imperial or aristocratic patronage. Some of the new churches commemorated previously holy sanctified places and so were essentially shrines, but many of the churches were merely new Christian temple buildings in which the Christian eucharistic liturgy could be solemnly celebrated. That developing liturgy—half synagogue service, half transformed temple sacrifice—clearly shows forth its Jewish origins, and the Christian church and altar complex displayed many of the characteristics of the Jerusalem temple, with a male priesthood, a separated sanctuary, a gender-segregated community, and rules governing ritual purity and contamination.

Mecca and the Hajj

Islam's premier holy place, the cubical Kaʿba and its surrounding *temenos* (taboo zone) set down in the midst of Mecca, long antedated Muhammad's seventh-century promulgation of the Qurʾan. Its origins are lost to us—a sacred spring, the Zamzam, located nearby perhaps—and lost too are whatever myths the local Arabs recounted to explain its presence in their midst. There are reports of animal sacrifice outside what was ancient Mecca's only stone construction, but most traces of the Meccan cult were swept away by Islam or integrated into a new founding myth that traced the Kaʿba and its surviving rituals back to Abraham and his son Ishmael's residence in Mecca (Qurʾan 2:125–127). The Meccan Kaʿba was not Mecca's only pre-Islamic sacred place; there were additional shrine sites within the town's *temenos* and others scattered in the environs. We know of them chiefly because Muhammad sanctioned their continued (though somewhat modified) use for Muslims in the complex of site- and time-tied ritual practices known as the pilgrimage, or *(hajj),* par excellence (Qurʾan 2:196 ff.) and that climaxed not at the Kaʿba in Mecca but in the standing on the hill known as Arafat eleven miles outside Mecca.

The narrow Meccan *temenos*—there is a more extended zone of taboo surrounding the town—known as the taboo shrine *(al-masjid al-haram),* or simply as the Haram, had all the familiar characteristics of a holy place: it offered the privilege of immune sanctuary, and it was banned to the ritually impure. The actual Kaʿba, on the other hand, despite its resemblance in shape and function to the Jerusalem Holy of

Holies—it was, even before Islam, regarded as the *Bayt Allah,* the House of God (Qur'an 106:3)—was not governed by the same severe access taboos as the Jerusalem house of Yahweh, where only the high priest was permitted entry and that but once a year.

Jewish holy place and sanctuary notions seem to some modern scholars to have been pervasive at pre-Islamic Mecca, but be that as it may, many purely pagan practices regarding sacred places survived the coming of Islam. The veneration of the dead, which is, as has been remarked, as offensive to Muslim purity sensibilities as it was to Jewish, was common in pagan Arabia and continues to this day in most Muslim venues, from the simple and solitary domed tombs *(qubbas)* of holy men that still dot the landscape in the Middle East and North Africa, through the numerous convents *(zawiyas)* built around the tombs of the saintly founders of Sufi religious orders, to the spectacular Iraqi tomb-shines of the Shi'ite eminences Ali at Najaf and his son Husayn—Shi'ite Islam's protomartyr—at Karbala.

The Politics of Holy Places

The identification and containment of sanctity within a defined place creates a locus of authority and, in consequence, a field of political force. Power is immanent in the place by reason of its holiness, but it also resides in the control of access and the regulation of the rituals that take place there. Possession brings power. As a legacy of the long Islamic rule over Jerusalem, a Muslim family is still in at least nominal possession of the keys to the Church of the Holy Sepulcher in Jerusalem, and though Israel ceded ownership of the Temple Mount to the Muslims when they occupied the Old City in 1967, it is their security concerns and political goals that regulate much of the access and traffic there. Some elites control by reason of their own intimate connection with ritual, as the Jewish priesthoods did in the Jerusalem temple. The temple's attraction was spread across a wide network (called the Diaspora) by reason of the scripturally based obligation of every Jew to sacrifice there, and, after 621, only there. Both Jewish law and Jewish ritual demanded a broad band of human activity in connection with the Jerusalem temple and its priesthoods, and wealth, power and prestige followed. According to one plausible interpretation of the evidence of the Gospel, Jesus went to his death for challenging that power and prestige.

The semisecular Israelite kings had always to reckon with their priestly rivals on the Temple Mount in Jerusalem, never very successfully, and even the powerful Herod and his Roman procuratorial successors preferred to rule Palestine from maritime Caesarea rather than in the upland shadow of Jerusalem's holy place. But Herod, like others before him, had tried to put his signature on the Jerusalem holy place by constructing a new architectural frame around the site to enhance the importance and so the allure of the holy place. Popular piety often enshrines, but monumental architectural enshrinement on the order of Solomon's temple, of Constantine's basilicas over the sites of Jesus' birth in Bethlehem and death in Jerusalem, or the Saudis' spectacular enlargement of the Haram at Mecca and Muhammad's tomb-shrine at Medina are major political projects financed out of royal exchequers; they speak as loudly to the religious certification of the rulers who built them as to the site they were intended to glorify. Hence upstart regimes—like that of Herod in Judaea in the turn of the Christian era; of Asoka, a new Buddhist convert in India in the third century B.C.; or of the Mamluks in Egypt in the thirteenth and fourteenth centuries—poured both money and energy into the holy places for which they were responsible in the hope that such well-publicized gestures of piety would redound to the glory of the ruler.

Islam knows no resident priesthood. Its religious elite, the muftis and mullahs of the learned *ulama,* were, like the rabbis of Judaism after the destruction of the temple, linked to the interpretative control of a book rather than of a place or a ritual. Thus control of the Muslim holy places in Mecca and Medina became a centuries-old contest between the only obliquely religious authority of the secular caliph-sultans and the obliquely political authority of the local rulers of Mecca termed *sharifs,* nobles of the blood descended from Muhammad. From the tenth century to the first quarter of the twentieth, sharifs have lorded it at Mecca and Medina under the envious and watchful eye of a caliph in Baghdad or Cairo or Istanbul. The sharif had possession and pedigree; the caliph, money and arms. The two lived in dangerous equilibrium until the opening of the twentieth century, when British wartime diplomacy succeeded in detaching the sharif Husayn (d. 1931) from his Ottoman caliph sovereign. Today there is neither sharif nor caliph to contest Islam's sacred places; rather, republics and monarchies, Muslim powers and a Jewish state, struggle for possession and control of Mecca and Medina and the sacred places of Jerusalem.

See also *Jerusalem; Mecca.*

F. E. Peters

BIBLIOGRAPHY

Carmichael, David, et al., eds. *Sacred Sites, Sacred Places.* London: Routledge, 1994.

Eade, John, and Michael Sallnow, eds. *Contesting the Sacred: The Anthropology of Christian Pilgrimage.* Routledge: London and New York, 1991.

Peters, F. E. *The Hajj: The Muslim Pilgrimage to Mecca and the Holy Places.* Princeton: Princeton University Press, 1994.

———. *Jerusalem and Mecca: The Typology of the Holy City in the Near East.* New York: New York University Press, 1987.

———. *Jerusalem: The Holy City in the Eyes of Chroniclers, Visitors, Pilgrims, and Prophets from the Days of Abraham to the Beginning of Modern Times.* Princeton: Princeton University Press, 1985.

Smith, Jonathan Z. *To Take Place: Toward Theory in Ritual.* Chicago and London: University of Chicago Press, 1987.

Wilken, Robert L. *The Land Called Holy: Palestine in Christian History and Thought.* New Haven: Yale University Press, 1992.

Sadat, Anwar

Egyptian soldier and politician, who succeeded Gamal Abdel Nasser as president of Egypt in 1970 and became the first Arab leader to make peace with Israel. Sadat (1918–1981) was born in the village of Mit Abul Kum, forty miles north of Cairo, and was in the first class to graduate from the Cairo Military Academy (1936–1938). While posted to a remote district in Upper Egypt, Sadat met Nasser and with ten other junior officers formed the Free Officers, a group that in 1952 overthrew the Egyptian monarchy and worked toward the expulsion of the British from Egypt and the Middle East. Sadat quickly rose through the ranks of the new revolutionary government until he became Nasser's sole vice president in 1969. After Nasser's death in 1970, he was elected president.

Sadat reversed Nasser's domestic and foreign policies, which had brought Egypt to the edge of bankruptcy and lost the Sinai peninsula to Israel in a six-day war in 1967. He expelled Soviet military advisers in 1972, to minimize Egypt's dependence on the Soviet Union, and launched the 1973 Arab-Israeli War to recapture the Sinai. Although Egypt's military campaign ended in defeat, its initial victories restored Egyptian pride, convinced Israeli military leaders that Egypt was a threat, and won the respect of the United States, achievements crucial to the success of Sadat's subsequent diplomatic initiative. Sadat cooperated with U.S. secretary of state Henry Kissinger in negotiating the reopening of the Suez Canal, which had been closed in 1967, and the Sinai Disengagement Agreements of 1974 and 1975,

Anwar Sadat

which brought a partial Israeli withdrawal from the Sinai. But it was his dramatic visit to Jerusalem in November 1977 that opened the way for the signing of the Egypt-Israel peace treaty of March 1979 and the complete return of the Sinai to Egypt in 1982. Both Sadat and Israeli prime minister Menachem Begin won the 1978 Nobel Peace Prize for their efforts.

In the Arab world Sadat was vilified for making a separate peace with Israel, and many states cut their relations with Egypt entirely. At home, economic dislocation, brought on by half-hearted free-market reforms, combined with Sadat's tolerance toward political parties, contributed to the rapid growth of opposition groups. The most important were the fundamentalist Muslim Brethren and the Islamic associations (Jamaʿat al Islamiyah). Sadat at first believed he could use the Islamic fundamentalists to counter the growing influence of the left. Leaders of the Muslim Brethren were freed from jail in 1974, and Islamic organizations spread rapidly on campuses where they won more than one-third of all student union elections.

In 1977 violent riots broke out in Cairo and Alexandria to protest cuts in food subsidies. The president arrested many fundamentalist leaders, a policy that was expanded in 1981, when more than 1,500 Egyptian political leaders were arrested. The peace with Israel caused Egypt's radical Islamic groups to declare open war on Sadat. On October 6, 1981, Sadat was assassinated by an Islamic extremist who announced that he had "killed Pharaoh." Sadat was not deeply mourned in the Middle East, but his policies became the centerpiece of his successor Husni Mubarak's regime.

See also *Egypt; Nasser, Gamal Abdel.*

Joshua M. Landis

BIBLIOGRAPHY

Haikal, Muhammed Hasanain. *Autumn of Fury: The Assassination of Sadat.* New York: Random House, 1983.

Hirst, David, and Irene Beeson. *Sadat.* London: Faber and Faber, 1981.

Israeli, Raphael. *Man of Defiance: A Political Biography of Anwar Sadat.* Totowa, N.J.: Barnes and Noble Books, 1985.

Kepel, Gilles. *Muslim Extremism in Egypt: The Prophet and the Pharaoh.* Translated by Jan Rothschild. Berkeley: University of California Press, 1986.

Sadat, Anwar. *In Search of Identity: An Autobiography.* New York: Harper and Row, 1978.

Saints

Saints are men and women recognized by their communities as exemplars of religious excellence and as mediators of knowledge and power from the invisible to the visible world. In all pre-industrial and in many industrial societies the visible world is seen as just part of the picture. There is more to the world than meets the eye. Somewhere, behind that common sphere where the rules of common sense and practical reason apply, there exists another, invisible sphere. The inhabitants of the invisible sphere are a heterogeneous group: gods, angels, demons, fairies, and souls of the dead. They possess enormous powers, much greater than those held by dwellers of the visible world. They know what people desperately try to conceal and what they desperately try to find out: private sins, public lies, the future. The invisible sphere's inhabitants can break the rules of nature and of logic: they work miracles, do the impossible, offer hope where none was expected, and bring calamity where none was feared.

The visible and the invisible worlds are not neatly separated. There are hidden and public routes that connect the two. Every once in a while, it is reported, gods, demons, ghosts and other supernatural beings emerge from behind the screen that conceals them and communicate with ordinary mortals. Most people, however, are able only to deduce the presence of supernatural forces from their effects; they remain unseen to the ordinary eye. If they wish to communicate with the unseen world, they need help. Saints traditionally provide such help.

The Politics of Saintliness

All religious systems are obsessed with the unseen world. They consider it more important than the seen; they shape it in their form and image and try to shape human society as a footnote to it. In their theologies and mythologies the religious experts describe the history, the topography, and the demography of the unseen world (heaven, hell, purgatory, limbo). They propose a set of procedures for communicating with it and offer a group of communications experts—the mediators.

Who are the mediators? Priests, rabbis, imams, shamans—all profess to help the laity make its wishes and needs known to God and his entourage and to protect them from divine chastisement and diabolical mischief. They do this through dogma and theology, religious law and education, scholarly exegesis and public ritual, through prayers and sacred rites. Religious establishments intercede. They stand between the simple believer and the unseen world—as much obstruction as protection.

One can distinguish between two kinds of charisma, cold and warm. Cold charisma consists of the mediatory powers that reside in religious officials by nature of their office. Priests and rabbis are endowed with divine inspiration as they interpret Holy Scriptures or pronounce religious rulings, for example. Catholic priests can work miracles (turning the host into the flesh and blood of Jesus Christ); the pope is infallible when he makes certain dogmatic pronouncements. Warm charisma consists of all the supernatural powers that individuals claim to have through a special, nonformal relation with the divine.

Institutional charisma is always cautious and impersonal. It makes vague promises to people in need of concrete and quick solutions for their burning problems. Where the priest may demand a long process of becoming worthy of divine grace and then make it conditional on God's inscrutable will, the saint would simply lay hands on you and cure you. Warm charisma is a demonstration of immanence—an invisible power is present and active. The ability of people outside the priestly ranks to channel powers directly and immediately has deep religious and political consequences.

Warm charisma appears in answer to a social and psychological demand: people, dissatisfied, or not fully satisfied, with the mediation religious authorities offer are looking for substitutes or additives. It is also the result of a different demand—that of the suppliers. People who want to become active participants in the religious game use it as a trump card. Because the charismatic claims to have a unique personal relationship with supernatural beings, he or she is not bound by the rules that bind others. The priest's authority comes from his institutional status (he is an ordained priest, an orthodox theologian, an authorized religious judge), the charismatic's from his or her alleged ability to move between the worlds. He or she goes into a trance in the presence of others, foretells the future, heals, exorcises demons, stops or starts rains, speaks in tongues. These manifestations of power mark the performer as a go-between who can deliver what the representatives of cold charisma often only promise: visible goods from the invisible world.

All power is political; spiritual power is no exception. Those who claim to have special powers, to have the right, given them from on high, not to play by the rules are making a claim to a greater slice of political power and authority than they supposedly had the right to have. God cannot be confined to the religious sphere. He has things to say about other spheres too. And so do his messengers and protégés. Those who speak in the name of the divinity do not need to be well trained or properly ordained; those who work miracles need no certificates. In the name of He who has sent them (whose presence they manifest through their powers), they claim the right to meddle in other people's business.

The Dominican tertiary St. Catherine of Siena (1347?–1380), for example, though of humble origins and of no official standing in the church (she was never more than a simple member of her order), became a figure of international importance. Through her visions and prophecies she claimed to be God's mouthpiece. As such she preached a crusade, convinced the pope to return from Avignon to Rome, and intervened in the disputes between Florence and the papacy. Without the reputation of sainthood and divine grace, no woman of her class and position could ever have dreamed of achieving such influence.

Charisma is by its nature a usurpation. It allows its holder powers that were not legitimately his or hers. Because it is a shortcut to power, it has a tendency to emerge in the margins. The powerless have much more to gain from not playing by the rules than do those who have made the rules to their advantage. This does not mean that the powers-that-be are totally lacking in charisma. There are people from within the elite who become career-charismatics, but, having less to gain by it, they are fewer than are those outside the circles of power. On closer inspection, furthermore, they are often found to be people who, though part of the elite, face serious obstacles in their ways to power, obstacles that charisma helps them overcome.

Managing Miracles

What is to be done with uncertified charismatics, delivering uncalled-for messages and performing unauthorized miracles? Different religions give different answers to this question. It is possible, as post-exilic Judaism has succeeded in doing to a large extent, to delegitimize all forms of non-institutional charisma. "After the destruction of the [second] temple, prophecy ceased in Israel," declares a famous rabbinical maxim. This, however, has a price. The unruly charismatic powers of mediation that crop up spontaneously in the religious field are trouble, it is true, but they can also rejuvenate a religion and add to it a much needed enthusiasm. The miracles and the fresh messages from out there, if they are performed and delivered in the right spirit, prove to the faithful that God has not forsaken his flock, that he is observant and active—just as his priests have always been saying.

A notable example of the extraordinary services a charismatic can render institutional religion is the case of St. Bernadette Soubirous (1844–1879). Not only did the apparitions that appeared to this simple French peasant girl aid in promoting the dogma of the immaculate conception—in one of her apparitions the Virgin Mary referred to herself by that name—but she also helped make Lourdes a major pilgrimage site and the focus of Catholic revival in the late nineteenth century. In much the same way a modest folk healer without much education, Rabbi Israel Baal Shem Tov (c. 1698–1760), the initiator of the Hasidic movement, started one of the most profound religious revivals in Judaism.

In most religions, then, charismatics need to be controlled and their charisma bridled, but once properly church broken, they can become an aid rather than a threat to the authorities. The notion of sainthood is a crucial mechanism for controlling wild charisma. A saint, so all religious authorities insist, is a person who is not simply a transmitter of supernatural powers. He or she is not just a miracle-worker but a model of moral excellence and of religious devotion. What exactly is moral excellence? The answer varies with time and with space.

One element, however, seems crucial in all religious systems. The saint must set himself or herself apart by religious excess—almost always by one form or another of asceticism. The saint denies himself or herself pleasures and comforts that ordinary human beings crave, even those that are considered legitimate; he or she strives after a religious perfection that goes way beyond normal religious piety. This is often accompanied by strong affirmations of worthlessness and modesty: the saint must seem not to seek power and status; he or she is powerful and famous in spite of him- or herself.

A typical example is St. Francis of Assisi (1182?–1226). The saint exercised all forms of religious asceticism—from long fasts to the denial of basic comforts like sleep and proper clothing. His heroic self-abnegation gained him the reputation of a saint second only to Christ, but Francis himself always insisted he was nothing but a sinner and a fake.

Sainthood and Supernatural Power

Now, supernatural power does not naturally go hand in hand with moral and religious excellence. The field of charisma is much broader than the straight and narrow field of moral excellence. The Latin *sacer* and *sanctus,* just like the Greek *agios* and the Hebrew and Arabic roots *q-d-s,* all mean "holy" in the sense of set apart, belonging to the gods. They could originally denote both good and evil persons and places. It is only gradually that they came to mean "saintly." The same linking of power and values can be observed in the change that occurred in the meaning of the Latin word *virtus.* Originally it has simply meant "power"; with time it has come to mean our much less neutral "virtue."

The virtuous saint is a compromise. Instead of rejecting all charisma as potentially dangerous to established religion, religious establishments are willing to accept charismatics—cautiously—as long as they are willing to play by the rules. When religious establishments put saints on symbolic pedestals, it is as exemplars. They are said to possess piety and devotion, orthodoxy, and especially religious conformism. Whether this attribution is true or false is beside the point. It is their pass into the religious pantheon.

In the thirteenth century the Jewish theologian and philosopher Moses Maimonides formulated the hierarchy's idea of the relationship between institutional authority and charismatic power. A prophet, he argued, is not to be judged a true prophet solely because of his performance. The ability to foretell the future accurately was given to false prophets, just as true prophets may err because of a divine change of plans. What establishes a prophet's authenticity is his orthodoxy. A prophet speaking against the precepts of the Torah is, by definition, a false prophet. In the end, then, charisma is judged by religious experts who use rational criteria of orthodoxy and morality. Christian and Muslim authorities would have agreed. True saints would never say or do anything that would jeopardize established religion.

From the point of view of the authorities, all new saints start as dangerous pretenders. The saint begins his or her career by making social noises (displaying exceptional piety) and exhibiting his or her spiritual muscles (working miracles). If these manifestations are acceptable to a large enough circle of followers, the aspirant saint must pass the examination of the local representative of the religious authorities. Is that person, referred to as a saint by his or her admirers, orthodox? Does he or she obey the moral norms relevant to his or her status? Are his or her followers behaving in an acceptable way? A negative answer to any of these questions could mark the aspiring charismatic with one of the dangerous labels available to the authorities: heretic, lunatic, false prophet, witch, idiot, demoniac. In some historic periods such social tags would be no more than a slap on the wrist and a loss of religious face; in others they could mean the difference between life and death.

Institutional resistance, however, is not necessarily the end of religious innovation. What begins as a religious aberration might be the initiation of a new orthodoxy. Jesus was considered a blasphemer (and possibly a magician) by Jewish authorities, and his followers, heretics. Joseph Smith (1805–1844), the founder of the Church of Jesus Christ of Latter-day Saints—the Mormons—was considered an impostor, a forger, and possibly insane. In both cases, the movements survived institutional opposition and public ridicule to become respected and powerful new orthodoxies.

The Problem of Living Saints

Of all religious establishments, the Roman Catholic Church has brought the method of examining saintly aspirants closest to bureaucratic perfection. The process of canonization has its roots in the late twelfth century under Pope Innocent III (served 1198–1216), but it reached maturation in the seventeenth, during the pontificate of Urban VIII (served 1623–1644). It has the form of a legal investigation, followed by a trial of the candidate. It deals only with persons who enjoy a reputation of sanctity among, at least, some faithful Catholics. A prophet may not be honored in his own country, but a prophet who is honored in no country at all is no prophet at all.

The community must approach the Holy See for a ruling on whether a specific person is truly worthy of veneration. The papal investigators first establish that the said individual had really enjoyed the reputation of being a saint and then examine his or her life and works to determine whether this reputation was well founded. If the candidate was orthodox, lived a virtuous life (or died a virtuous death), and performed a certain number of certified miracles, he or she was added to the catalogue of saints and his or her cult was made universal. If the candidate's supporters failed to prove their case, the pope could either allow a local cult or disallow any sort of veneration.

Impressive though canonization might seem, as an expression of the papal will to control saintly activity, it was never—indeed could never be—more than a symbolic gesture. Not only is the number of aspiring local saints too great for any establishment to control effectively, it is probably also counterproductive, politically, to be too specific about too many saints. Tastes change. People who were once useful may later prove an embarrassment. It is safer to maintain a level of ambiguity. Other religions did not bother to waste energy on similar procedures.

Canonization is concerned solely with dead saints. The papacy cautiously avoided giving its seal of approval to living persons. Living persons, no matter how great a reputation they have enjoyed, remained, at least somewhat, suspicious. One can never be sure what they would do next. It is best not to give them more power than they already have.

Dead saints, in contrast, could be more effectively controlled—their bodies safely guarded by the authorities and their images reshaped by clerical hagiographers. No matter how radical they might have been in their lifetime, they tend to be politically and religiously conservative post-mortem. A classic example is St. Thomas á Becket (1118–1170). A serious political nuisance as the living archbishop of Canterbury, he became, thanks to the clever manipulation of the English crown, a monarchist and a patriot—the protector and supporter of those he died opposing.

Living saints, once they have passed the initial tests—in terms of moral standards and charisma—become increasingly difficult to manipulate. If as beginning saints they are quite willing to be guided, as well-established saints with large followings and a heavy dossier of miracles, they are much less keen on taking orders from anyone. They now have strong views on what is morally acceptable and what is orthodox. These views do not always correspond with those of the authorities.

Living saints, then, are a mixed blessing. They can be rallied in support of the hierarchy's causes; they provide moral support and photo opportunities. As long as they play the game, they are treated with reverence; praise and privileges are heaped upon them. Their idiosyncrasies are tolerated and their political faux pas borne patiently. They can be extremely useful. But saints may also take problematic advantage of the traditional privilege of making their voices heard on whatever they see fit, without respect of persons. Saints with impeccable moral credentials and impressive spiritual powers may adopt a strongly critical attitude toward the establishment, declare it corrupt and immoral, and call for painfully popular reforms.

Because saints derive their power and authority from problematic sources (formally God, informally their admirers), they are unstable and unpredictable political dancers. They are hard to impeach or fire. If they choose to dance along, they can be very graceful partners in the collective waltz. But then they may, without warning, change partners and step on all political toes.

See also *Heresy; Miracles; Papacy; Witchcraft.*

Aviad M. Kleinberg

BIBLIOGRAPHY

Ben Ami, Issachar. *The Veneration of Saints among the Jews in Morocco.* Detroit, Mich.: Wayne State University Press, 1998.

Christian, William A., Jr. *Visionaries: The Spanish Republic and the Reign of Christ.* Berkeley and Los Angeles: University of California Press, 1996.

Gellner, Ernest. *Saints of the Atlas.* London: Weidenfeld and Nicolson, 1969.

Kieckhefer, Richard, and G. D. Bond, eds. *Sainthood: Its Manifestations in World Religions.* Berkeley and Los Angeles: University of California Press, 1988.

Kleinberg, Aviad M. *Prophets in Their Own Country: Living Saints and the Making of Sainthood in the Later Middle Ages.* Chicago: University of Chicago Press, 1992.

Tambiah, Stanley, J. *The Buddhist Saints of the Forest and the Cult of Amulets: A Study in Charisma, Hagiography, Sectarianism, and Millennial Buddhism.* Cambridge and New York: Cambridge University Press, 1984.

Sanctuary

The concept of sanctuary originated thirty-five hundred years ago when Yahveh (God) commanded the prophet Moses, who led the Israelites out of Egypt, to set aside cities and places of refuge (sanctuary) in Canaan, the "Promised Land," where the persecuted could seek asylum from "blood-avengers." Indeed, Judeo-Christian faith was born in the travail of escape. Yahveh liberated the Israelites, or Hebrews, from the bondage of the Egyptian pharaoh's dictatorship. God's identity thus was rooted in action—leading refugees from slavery to freedom.

Inspiration for the Sanctuary Movement

Sanctuary draws inspiration from the centrality of the exodus and rearticulates the covenantal relationship between God and the faithful and between the faithful and their neighbors. Both the Old and New Testaments call for strangers or sojourners to be taken in because the Hebrews "were once sojourners in the land of Egypt." Jesus immortalized a foreigner, the Samaritan, to illustrate the lesson of neighborly love.

The notion of sanctuary draws not only on scriptural tradition but also on the civic tradition that was recognized in Roman law, medieval canon law, and English common law. In the seventeenth century the entire North American continent was viewed as a sanctuary from political and religious persecution. Two of the most heroic expressions of sanctuary date from the 1850s in the United States and World War II (1939–1945) in Europe. In the United States Congress passed the Fugitive Slave Act in 1850 which made it illegal to harbor or assist a slave. In response, Northern churches, in defiance of federal law, became stations on the underground railroad, an escape route for slaves from the South to free states or Canada. In the 1940s monasteries in Europe hid Jews fleeing the Holocaust, the Nazi-led destruction of Jews before and during World War II. In southern France the Protestant minister André Trocme inspired the entire village of Le Chambon to become a sanctuary for over three thousand Jews. Later, during the Vietnam War (1965–1975), Boston and California churches harbored war resisters by invoking the tradition of sanctuary. More recently, in the 1980s and 1990s, the U.S. sanctuary movement inspired European churches in Switzerland, Germany, and Scandinavia to offer sanctuary to Turkish, Nigerian, and some Eastern European refugees.

The U.S. Sanctuary Movement

The U.S. sanctuary movement of the 1980s and 1990s was born from an encounter of North Americans and Central Americans—not around a conference table but on the road, in the desert, along the barbed wire of border crossings. Central Americans fleeing their homelands because of terror and torture were being deported back to that violence. In Guatemala, of fifty-five thousand documented killings throughout the thirty-six-year war, the bishops' diocesan human rights document *Guatemala: Never Again* (1998) held the Guatemalan army responsible for 85 percent of the violence. In the twelve-year war in El Salvador, eighty thousand people were killed, the majority peasants and workers. One million fled into exile and another million were made homeless. In 1981–1982, as the sanctuary movement was beginning, the United States was the only country in the world sending Salvadorans directly back to their homeland, deporting an average of one thousand per month.

On March 24, 1982, the second anniversary of the death of the martyred Salvadoran archbishop Oscar Romero, assassinated for defending the poor majority, the Southside Presbyterian Church in Tucson, Arizona, and five East Bay, California, churches declared themselves public sanctuaries for Guatemalan and Salvadoran refugees. The sanctuary signs told the U.S. Immigration and Naturalization Service (INS) to stay out or risk breaking the ancient law of sanctuary.

In spite of the sacred and civil claims of sanctuary, the U.S. government considered the "harboring or transporting of illegal aliens" a felony punishable by five years' imprisonment and a $2,000 fine. Sanctuary organizers, however, argued that the U.S. government was violating its own law, the U.S. Refugee Act of 1980, which stipulated that any person having a grave fear of persecution must not be returned to his or her homeland. Sanctuary advocates also argued that the government's treatment of refugees violated international accords and protocols. For example, the United Nations High Commission on Refugees charged (as recorded in the *Congressional Record*) that the United States had failed to uphold its international obligation to refugees and that the State Department and INS were not in compliance with the 1949 Geneva Convention protocols (ratified by the Senate in 1955) which prevent all signatory nations from returning refugees to war-torn nations. Every Protestant adjudicatory body supported public sanctuary as did the Rabbinical Union.

By 1984, as the death toll mounted in El Salvador, the INS was turning down Salvadoran political asylum applications at the rate of 98 percent. The INS stipulated that peasant applicants were not refugees fleeing death threats or torture but seekers of a better economic life. Marc Van Der Hout, director of the Central American Refugee Program of the Most Holy Redeemer Church in San Francisco, countered that Salvadorans had the best case for political asylum he had ever seen. Antonio Rodriguez, director of the Los Angeles Center for Law and Justice, claimed that if the U.S. Refugee Act were upheld, it would mean indicting the State Department's policy of support for the Salvadoran military.

In fact, in 1980 Archbishop Romero had written a letter to U.S. president Jimmy Carter imploring the United States to cease sending not only military aid to El Salvador but also all economic and humanitarian aid because it was used for the "repression of the Salvadoran people." Nevertheless, the United States continued to funnel $1.5 million in aid each day for ten years (a total of $4.8 billion).

Efforts to stop U.S. funding for a war producing refugees sparked an ideological struggle within the sanctuary movement. Tucson leaders Jim Corbett and John Fife considered such an objective too political. The Chicago Religious Task Force on Central America, an organizing center for refugee placement in churches and synagogues in the north, invoked Romero's insistence that in the face of massive repression the people have an obligation to organize themselves to stop the violence. According to Romero, the church, faced with the "most basic option of faith," had to choose between life and death—that is, serving the life of Salvadorans or acting as "accomplices in their death." For one segment of the sanctuary movement, which later became the National Sanctuary Alliance, the most efficacious way to choose life was to stop the source of death which they saw as U.S. support for military campaigns against Salvadoran and Guatemalan populations. For another segment, the role of the faith community was to offer assistance to war victims but not to organize to confront U.S. government intervention.

These splits became moot in 1986 after the government began to arrest sanctuary workers. The nine-month trial and investigation, based on the testimony of government informants and sanctuary infiltrators, cost $1 million and ended in the successful prosecution of eleven people—nuns, lay and ordained ministers, deacons, and priests. But the government's crackdown did not seem to deter the movement. An open "railroad" caravan from Chicago to the Weston Benedictine monastery in Vermont brought a Mayan family of seven into sanctuary days after the government's triumph. The trial did, however, leave the divided movement without a common strategy for future action.

From 1986 onward, sanctuary continued as a more or less pluralistic, humanitarian effort while the war in El Salvador continued. It was not until the Salvadoran military assassinated six Jesuit priests and their housekeeper and her daughter during a guerrilla offensive in 1989 that military officers were held legally accountable for murder—a Truth Commission report linked the Jesuits' murders to the Salvadoran High Command. The assassinations and the international denunciations that followed were critical factors in the 1992 peace accords in El Salvador.

The sanctuary movement of the 1980s located both the spirit and practice of the ancient tradition of defending the defenseless by invoking the moral right of faith communities to harbor fugitives. In the mid-1980s Central American refugees held at El Centro, a California detention center, best articulated that moral claim. Upon hearing that a group of sanctuary workers were driving out to the desert to view the camp conditions at El Centro, the refugees tore up bed sheets and made a sign whose letters were painted with a mixture of punch they saved as well as their own blood. As the small group of religious women approached El Centro, they saw the bed sheet thrown over the barbed wire fence. Pointed north: it bore the words *En el nombre de Dios, ayudanos* ("In the name of God, help us"). That claim impelled eighty thousand North American ordinary church and synagogue members to risk felonies, and was the type of claim that gave rise to the historical tradition of sanctuary which insists that strangers be defended from persecution as commanded by God.

See also *Abolitionism; Central America; Civil disobedience; Holocaust; Humanitarianism; Latin America; Romero, Oscar A.*

Renny Golden

BIBLIOGRAPHY

Bau, Ignatius. *This Ground Is Holy: Church Sanctuary and Central American Refugees.* New York: Paulist Press, 1987.

Bibler Coutin, Susan. *The Culture of Protest: Religious Activism and the U.S. Sanctuary Movement.* Boulder, Colo.: Westview Press, 1993.

Golden, Renny, and Michael McConnell. *Sanctuary: The New Underground Railroad.* Maryknoll, N.Y.: Orbis, 1986.

Hallie, Phillip. *Lest Innocent Blood Be Shed: The Story of the Village of*

Chambon and How Goodness Happened There. New York: Harper and Row, 1979.
Hollyday, Joyce, and Don Mosley. *With Our Own Eyes.* Scottdale, Pa.: Herald Press, 1996.
Lorentzen, Robin. *Women in the Sanctuary Movement.* Philadelphia: Temple University Press, 1991.

Saudi Arabia

Containing Mecca, the center of the Islamic religion, oil-rich modern Saudi Arabia occupies most of the Arabian peninsula, which is located between the Indian Ocean, Red Sea, and Persian Gulf. Islam and politics in Saudi Arabia are closely intertwined and mutually interdependent. Most Saudis are Sunni Muslims, the majority Islamic sect.

The holy cities of Mecca (Makkah) and Medina in western Arabia were the birthplace of Islam in the seventh century. Muhammad, the founder of Islam, was born in Mecca and moved to Medina in 622. Although both cities continued to be pilgrimage sites, they soon lost much of their prominence as the capital of the Muslim empire shifted elsewhere. Ruling Mecca conferred some prestige on later external rulers such as the Ottoman dynasty, who protected and encouraged the pilgrimage to it, but most of Arabia was too arid to support agriculture and too poor to tempt foreign empires. The isolation of central-eastern Arabia was broken in 1745, when Muhammad ibn Abd al-Wahhab, a Muslim religious reformer, formed an alliance with a local prince, Muhammad ibn Sa'ud. This religious-political alliance has endured through many generations and has served as the basis for the creation of three Saudi kingdoms in Arabia.

The doctrines and ideas of Muhammad ibn Abd al-Wahhab were called Wahhabism by his enemies; his followers rejected this term, believing themselves to be the only pure Muslims. The Wahhabis emphasized such core beliefs as the unity of God. They opposed intercession by invoking the prophet Muhammad, objected to the veneration of graves, violently fought followers of the minority Shi'ite sect of Islam and the mystical Sufi tradition, condemned a merely surface adherence to the faith, and sought to eradicate all innovations that they believed had marred the original practices of Islam.

Acting on the basis of this puritanical but appealing approach to Islam, Muhammad ibn Sa'ud and his successors in the Saudi royal family rapidly conquered much of central Arabia, thereby establishing the first Saudi kingdom. This expansion was stopped when the Saudis seized Mecca and Medina, thereby impelling the Ottoman Empire and Egypt to invade Arabia, capture the Saudi capital in 1818, and execute the ruling Saudi prince.

Seemingly, the Saudi-Wahhabi political-religious experiment was at an end, but the faith lived on in the desert and towns of eastern Arabia, and a second Saudi kingdom with its capital at Riyadh replaced Egyptian domination in 1824, gradually conquering most of the territory held earlier. The Saudis gained experience in exercising power, concentrating their rudimentary institutions of government on administering justice, collecting taxes, and fostering Islam. A disputed succession in the royal family in the 1870s, however, led to civil war, foreign intervention, and, by 1891, the overthrow and flight into exile of the Saudi ruler.

The Third Saudi State

A young Saudi prince, Abd al-Aziz (born about 1880), regained control of Riyadh in 1902 and began the third Saudi kingdom. Abd al-Aziz, who was known in the West as ibn Sa'ud, demonstrated good judgment, leadership skills, and extraordinary courage as well as a deep personal and political commitment to Islam. Once again the Saudis reconstituted their empire in central and eastern Arabia. In addition to employing town militias, Abd al-Aziz helped to raise an enthusiastic army from among the former nomads who had been settled and trained as warriors for the faith.

Abd al-Aziz expanded first into coastal eastern Arabia, a region subsequently famous for its oil deposits but then thought to be poor. In 1924–1925 the Saudis added to their realms the crucial cities of Mecca and Medina, thereby expelling the Hashimite royal family. The new united state, officially designated as the Kingdom of Saudi Arabia in 1932, suppressed internal opposition and established peace with its neighbors, thus abandoning further armed expansion of Wahhabi Islam.

After the end of World War II, in 1945, revenues from oil steadily grew, eventually reaching staggering amounts whose allocation and disposal challenged the ingenuity and skills of the royal family. The new prosperity transformed the austere life of the Saudi subjects, enabling dramatic increases in the standard of living, the building of infrastructure, the movement of people to the big cities from the countryside, and the expansion of public education. All these changes brought

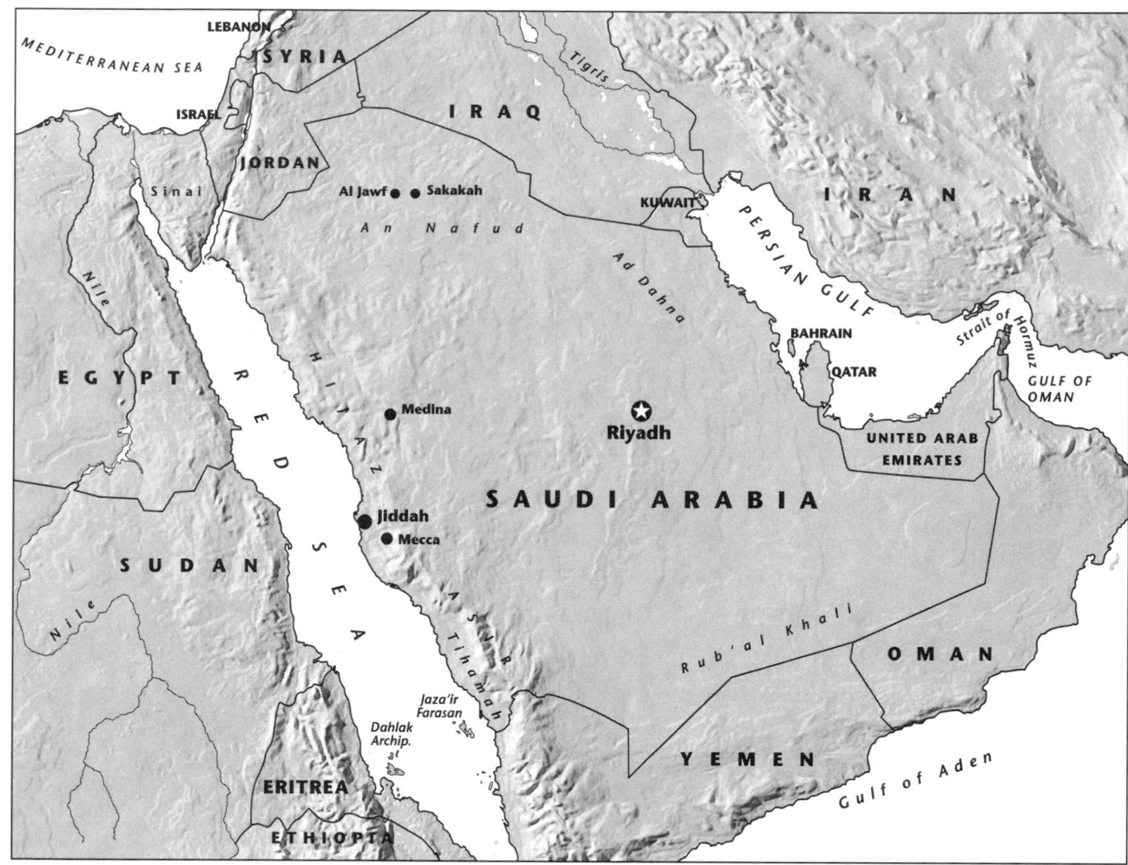

into question the internal relationship between government, religion, and society.

After the death of Abd al-Aziz in 1953, four of his sons ruled in turn, retaining most political power in their hands. The Saudi official view was that the kingdom needed no written constitution, legislature, and political parties since the Qur'an, the sacred book of Islam, served as the basis of the state and the political system. Religious education dominated the formation of values in the schools and universities, and the *ulama* (scholarly men of religion) provided legitimacy to the ruling elite. In return, the kings and the expanding bureaucracy maintained the supremacy of conservative religious values in law, social customs, gender roles, the media, and in culture generally.

Saudi foreign policy was also based in part on religious considerations: the government opposed both Jewish Israel and the atheist Soviet Union. In the 1990s, with the collapse of the Soviet Union and the movement toward peace between the Palestinians and Israelis, Saudi Arabia could turn its attention elsewhere. Since the onset of oil prosperity, the kingdom has donated large sums of money to support the spread of Islam and to back various Muslim nations and groups. Saudi Arabia has also served as the chief patron of the Muslim duty to make a pilgrimage to Mecca, expanding arrangements to house and transport the millions of pilgrims who come from all over the world. Saudi contributions played a major role in the World Muslim League, a religious-propagation agency founded in 1962 with its headquarters in Mecca, while Saudi Arabia was also highly influential in the Organization of the Islamic Conference, a multinational grouping of Muslim countries that periodically organizes summit conferences of government leaders.

Challenges to the Political-Religious Alliance

On the first day of the Muslim year 1400 (November 20, 1979), a group of fundamentalist Islamic militants seized control of the Ka'ba, Islam's most sacred place, in the Grand Mosque in Mecca. They called for the overthrow of the Saudi dynasty and a return to strict Islamic practices. Although this uprising ultimately was suppressed, the regime recognized that its legitimacy was threatened and continued vigorously a policy of co-opting religious conservatives. Most of the Islamic Middle East, other than the Islamic Republic of Iran, had gradually become more secular in the post–World War II period, but Saudi Arabia remained strongly committed to fostering a large role in public life for religion. Many Muslims in Saudi Arabia nevertheless criticized the regime for the corruption prevalent among government officials and members of the large royal family as well as a perceived exemption for princes from the equal application of the sacred law.

Three crises have posed a dramatic challenge to Saudi Arabia in recent years. A sharp fall in revenue from oil exports in the mid-1980s continued for most of the next decade to curb government revenues. War between Iraq and Iran (1980–1988) threatened Saudi Arabia both with military confrontation and with the threat of Shi'ite Islamic revivalism from revolutionary Iran. Most dangerous of all was Iraqi leader Saddam Husayn's invasion and annexation of nearby Kuwait in 1990. Hundreds of thousands of foreign troops, including many non-Muslims from such countries as Britain and the United States, defended Saudi Arabia against possible Iraqi attack. Then, with the approval of the United Nations, Saudi Arabia and its allies launched a war in early 1991 that successfully forced Iraq to withdraw from Kuwait.

Domestic critics and some foreign Muslim governments criticized on religious grounds Saudi dependence on the non-Muslim United States for protecting its security against Iran and Iraq. In 1992–1993 King Fahd instituted a broad range of political reforms, including the appointing of a consultative council (Majlis al-Shura), an institution long desired both by secularizing liberalizers and conservative Islamic revivalists. The reforms did not stop the growth of underground religiously oriented opposition groups, particularly among young people in the cities, university students, preachers, elements of the *ulama,* some professionals, and a few of the Shi'ites living in the wealthy Eastern Province. Although the fragmented opposition was generally peaceful, two bombings directed against American military forces stationed in Saudi Arabia in November 1995 and June 1996 may have been the result of Saudi underground religious factions.

Despite serious challenges, Saudi Arabia has continued the alliance of religion and the state begun in 1745 and articulated during the three Saudi kingdoms. Using enormous new wealth arising from oil, the Saudi dynasty and the *ulama* have maintained a mutually interdependent relationship while substantially expanding their influence in the world.

See also *Islam; Jordan; Mecca; Sacred places.*

William Ochsenwald

BIBLIOGRAPHY

Dekmejian, R. Hrair. "The Rise of Political Islamism in Saudi Arabia." *Middle East Journal* 48 (autumn 1994): 627–643.

Long, David. *The Kingdom of Saudi Arabia.* Gainesville: University Press of Florida, 1997.

Ochsenwald, William. "Saudi Arabia." In *The Politics of Islamic Revivalism: Diversity and Unity,* edited by Shireen T. Hunter. Bloomington: Indiana University Press, 1988.

Salibi, Kemal. *A History of Arabia.* Delmar, N.Y.: Caravan Books, 1980.

Al-Yassini, Ayman. *Religion and State in the Kingdom of Saudi Arabia.* Boulder, Colo.: Westview Press, 1985.

Scandinavia

The term *Scandinavia* refers to the Scandinavian-speaking countries, Denmark, Iceland, Norway, and Sweden; however, Finland is generally included in their political collaboration, and the five are called the Nordic countries. During the nineteenth and early twentieth centuries, the region went through a period of upheaval. New nations were formed (Finland, Iceland, Norway), and a great part of the population moved from the rural areas to the expanding industrial towns.

Two important movements were born at this time: the revival movement and the labor movement. The revivals were based mainly in the rural areas, whereas the labor movement was based in the large industrial towns. These movements collided with the political, economic, and church leadership. The manifestos of the Social Democratic (labor) Party declared that "religion is a private matter" and proposed to separate the church from the state. The labor movement tended to see the church as a tool of bourgeois power.

During the Finnish Civil War (1918), the clergy were generally associated with the White faction in its struggle with the Red (socialist) faction. Similar, though less dramatic, confrontations occurred in other Scandinavian countries. The split between Social Democrats and Communists implied a difference in religious views: the Communists followed an atheistic, anticlerical line, whereas the Social Democrats stood for a moderate reform policy.

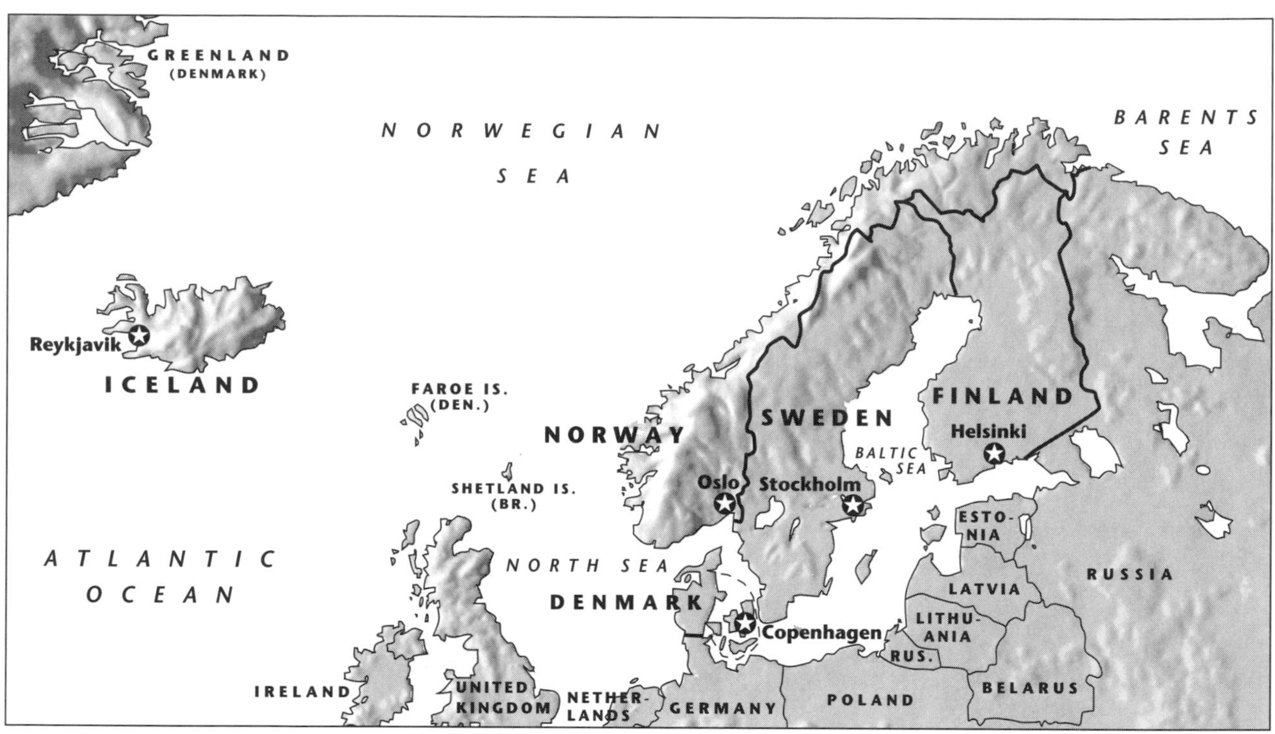

During Finland's Winter War (1939) against the Soviet Union and the Nazi occupation of Norway and Denmark (1940–1945), the state church of each of these countries became generally accepted as a religious symbol for the whole nation. With increased political influence, the Social Democratic Parties modified their church policy. The church has gradually come to be regarded as a valuable part of the public services in all these welfare states. The ideological view is that legitimate welfare needs, which it is the duty of the state to support, include religious needs. The reconciliation of the labor movement and the church in Finland is evidenced by meetings between the archbishop of Finland, John Wikström, and leaders of the Social Democratic Party in the 1980s. In addition, several leading figures within the Scandinavian labor parties have declared Christian views.

The bourgeois parties are traditionally pro-church. The ideology of the Conservatives (or Moderates) stresses the role of the church as carrier of national traditions and values and therefore strongly supports the church establishment. The reforms that excluded the church from control of the school system were therefore criticized by the Conservatives. Conservative voters, however, do not differ much today from Social Democratic voters in their attitude toward the state church. Some of the bourgeois parties have a strong revivalist or free-church influence among their membership. This can be traced in a strong support for the church among Liberal and Center voters in Scandinavian countries. The critique of the church is most noticeable among the left-wing parties and the right-wing populist parties.

Religion and church affairs as political issues are not only infrequently discussed in Scandinavian politics; they can even be said to be political anathema. Sweden is partially an exception to the rule. The political parties there have participated in parish council elections since the 1970s, and state church reform has been much debated. Religion is regarded as a personal matter. Laws stressing religious freedom have been introduced in all the Scandinavian countries since the Second World War.

The liberalizing laws on abortion, pornography, and so forth have been criticized with regard to Christian ethics. This debate cuts across the former ideological cleavages between labor and bourgeois parties because both sides supported the laws. The formation of Christian parties in several of the Scandinavian countries may be interpreted as a reaction against this liberalization. Norway was the first country to form a Christian party, and in this country the party has had the most support and influence. It was formed in 1933 and was initially supported by people affiliated with revivalism in western Norway. Its breakthrough on the national political scene occurred at the election following liberation from the Nazis in 1945, in homage to courageous clergymen who stood up during the occupation. Since then the party, characterized by a combination of a progressive social policy, a conservative economic policy, and moral strictness, has risen to become the third largest in Norway. In the other Scandinavian countries Christian parties were established in the 1960s and 1970s, mainly in protest against what was seen as legitimation of moral decay. The electoral support of these parties is small, and their influence on the political scene is hardly traceable.

See also *Revivalism; Separation of church and state; State churches.*

Ole Riis

BIBLIOGRAPHY

Madeley, John. "Scandinavian Christian Democracy: Throwback or Portent?" *European Journal of Political Research* 5 (1977).

Montgomery, Ingun, and S. U. Larsen, eds. *Kirken, Krisen og Krigen.* Oslo, Norway: Universitetsforlagt, 1982.

Pettersson, Thorleif, and Ole Riis, eds. *Scandinavian Values.* Uppsala, Sweden: AUU, 1994.

Science and technology

Science is the study of the natural world through observations, measurements, and experiments that can be duplicated to demonstrate or modify general law, although some contemporary explanations of scientific cosmology as yet lack plausible proofs. Technology is the practical application of knowledge to augment human power over the environment. Inevitably, religious faiths intersect in different ways with both.

In the United States no major religious sect is either wholly anti-science or anti-technology, although some groups such as the Old Order Amish have rejected modern technology in favor of a simple life—that is to say, an earlier form of technology. Some fundamentalist Christians have vocally rejected aspects of modern science and technology, although they may at the same time enthusiastically embrace others (like advanced mass communications techniques). Even the largely pro-science and pro-technology mainline Christian faiths have opposed certain applications of science and technology at various times in their histories. The inevitable consequence is recurrent political controversy. Such continued uneasiness is curious because modern science arose only in Western Europe at a time when intellectual life still fell under the sway of Christian dogma.

In the twentieth century most of the major religions of the world have accepted modern science. Modernizers of Islam and Buddhism, for instance, have enthusiastically argued that their faiths are particularly hospitable to science. But many societies have resisted certain implications of technology, particularly those affecting reproduction and marriage. It is not Protestant fundamentalists alone who pick and choose which elements of modern science and technology to support.

In all societies religion engages both science and technology as different forms of a distinctly human understanding and intervention in nature and culture. Advances in theoretical science can challenge deeply held theological assumptions about the origins of the universe or conflict with the purposes of human existence described in religious texts. Technology, on the other hand, may confront religion because it empowers human beings to alter the natural world and what is assumed to be human nature in ways that clash with traditional beliefs.

In the United States as elsewhere, the dialogue between science and religion tends to divide along conservative and liberal lines. For instance, conservative businessman and philanthropist John Templeton has concluded that science and religion, properly understood, can bolster the values and principles of a competitive, capitalist society. He has promoted this notion through the Templeton Foundation, which sponsors conferences, publications, and courses, and through the Templeton Prize for Progress in Religion, awarded annually to the most important contribution to modern religion. For him, this complements the annual Nobel Prizes granted to scientists. On the other hand, Ian Barbour, a physicist and religious writer, has been deeply critical of modern, consumption-oriented, competitive society. In addition to a very large number of books on the subject, a number of U.S. organizations are devoted specifically to studying the relationship between science and religion. These include the American Scientific Affiliation, the Creation Research Society, the Genesis Institute, the Institute on Religion in an Age of Science, the Religious Research Association, and the Society for the Scientific Study of Religion. These too tend to divide over conservative or liberal interpretations of the relation of science to religion.

Outside the United States, there has also been considerable interest in reconciling science and religion, leading to a large literature, published primarily in Western Europe. Periodic European conferences on science and religion, like one held in the Netherlands in 1988 and the International Conference on Science and Religion, held in New Delhi, India, in the same year, suggest the worldwide dimensions of this interest. Publications and conferences on creation science (which contests Darwinian theories of natural selection) are largely confined to the United States, although there are creation science organizations elsewhere such as Skapelsetro (the Biblical Creation Society of Sweden) and the Creation Science Foundation of Australia.

On specific issues, the same kinds of divisions between liberal and conservative appear, attracting the attention of institutional religions and individual faiths, and often developing into controversies that have been played out in the political realm. This is especially true in the twentieth century because the modern state increasingly encourages and fosters science and technology. Although older controversies around the nature of the universe and the placement of earth, sun, stars, and galaxies are no longer matters of life and death, as they once had been in societies where church and state were intertwined, important disputes about religion and science still enter contemporary political life. Since World War II (1939–1945), science and technology have incited even more religious commentary partly because religious positions on issues such as creationism, abortion, and birth control have hardened (particularly among Protestant fundamentalists) and partly as governments have become more interested in exploring, expanding, and regulating the application of scientific and technological advances.

The State, Science, and Religion

In most societies the modern state encourages and regulates science and technology, although funding research with implications for religious groups can lead to controversy. Governments also sponsor science exhibits and museums. They regulate the sale and availability of drugs and medicines and medical procedures, some of which demand ethical guidelines for their use. In warfare, government designs and builds weapons of mass destruction, such as the atomic bomb or other lethal and controversial weapons. At all levels of society, government fosters and regulates education, deciding what sort of science shall be taught. In the United States the power of local and state school boards means that any education plan, however general, must at least consider subjects such as creation science or other religion-based substitute scientific theories.

Creationism and Evolution

The argument over Darwinism in educational institutions is most prominently an American dispute. Elsewhere, theologians, church hierarchies, and ordinary citizens have had to confront rapid innovations in science and technology. In some modernizing societies in the Islamic world (such as Iran), religious dogma maintains strict vigilance over the social life and the content of education—including science. But such encounters have been most widely noted in the United States because it is the most scientifically advanced nation in the world. The 1925 trial of John T. Scopes in Dayton, Tennessee, for example, had enormous and abiding impact. Scopes, a high school biology teacher, was accused of violating the Butler Act, a Tennessee law that forbade teaching evolutionary theory in public schools because it contradicted the biblical account of creation.

For several years before this trial, William Jennings Bryan (1860–1925), former secretary of state and candidate for president of the United States, and other fundamentalists had lobbied state legislatures in the southern United States to ban the teaching of evolution based on the theories of English naturalist and author Charles Darwin (1809–1882). Darwin's theory proposed that species originate from earlier forms through natural selection of those best adapted for success in their environment. The trial became a national media event, and the press heaped ridicule on Bryan for his inconsistent defense of biblical literalism and naive notions of science. The defense, conducted by criminal lawyer Clarence Darrow (1857–1938), argued that the Butler Act was unconstitutional. Scopes was convicted on a misdemeanor, although the case never reached the Supreme Court, as opponents of the law had hoped it would.

This public relations defeat for fundamentalism did not, however, end the political disputes surrounding the teaching of evolution. Several states continued to ban the teaching of Darwinism. Citizens did not relinquish the notion that they, and not just scientists, could decide what was or was not legitimate science. This populist impulse continued to affect public school curriculums throughout the country for many years.

As late as the 1980s two states—Arkansas and Louisiana—passed laws mandating the teaching of creation science wherever evolutionary science was to be taught in the public schools. Although the Supreme Court later struck down these laws, local school boards continue, on occasion, to debate whether to grant equal time to creation science in biology classes.

Weapons, Science, and Religion

Although church and state are constitutionally separated in the United States, the dialogue between religion, science, and technology has often entered the political arena as religious and scientific groups lobby government to alter policy. Because religion in the United States encompasses so many different faiths and denominations, however, this pressure is sometimes less effective than it might be coming from a single major group. Nonetheless, there have been many successful citizen protests that affected U.S. science and technology policy. Churches and religious groups have had a profound effect on issues of nuclear warfare, for example. Although religious groups alone did not prevent further use of atomic weapons after the end of World War II, many have been vigilant and politically active in their protests over weapons development and testing.

From the very beginning, public debate over atomic weaponry has involved a variety of religious groups, many of whom lobbied for peace and disarmament. This is particularly true in the United Kingdom, certain European nations such as Sweden and Germany, and the United States. Catholic leadership and many Protestant groups found dropping atomic bombs on Japan to be morally indefensible. Yet some of the defenders of their use, such as President Harry S. Truman, invoked biblical language to support their deployment.

There is also no doubt that religious groups in the United States helped to shape the political climate during the 1970s and 1980s in favor of detente with the Soviet Union and various limited gestures of disarmament through the Strategic Arms Limitations Treaties of 1972 and 1979.

Genetics and Biomedical Ethics

In 1997 the cloning of Dolly the sheep at the Roslin Institute in Edinburgh, Scotland, also raised considerable controversy. The creation of a genetically identical individual from the borrowed cells of an adult animal immediately suggested the potential for applying this technology to humans, creating human beings in the likeness of a living individual. This possibility had once been the subject of science fiction; now it had become practical. Religious commentators immediately raised objections to cloning because it appeared to push dangerously close to tampering with creation and the existence of stable species and because it raised a host of ethical issues about the potential manipulation of individuals and society. In 1997 U.S. president Bill Clinton asked the National Bioethics Advisory Commission to study the implications of cloning. The commission, set up in 1996, includes members from business, medical ethics, law, public health, and religious studies.

The issue of ethics in medicine is as old as the Hippocratic Oath, developed in ancient Greece to guide the activities of physicians. But World War II raised these issues again because of the activities of German doctors and scientists who conducted medical experiments on concentration camp inmates and prisoners of war. The 1946 international Nuremberg Code (based on the 1945–1946 trials of German doctors) defined the rights of medical patients. A number of countries, including the United States, used these guidelines to limit medical experiments on human subjects. Since then, the same sorts of rules have been extended to such techniques as gene therapy. Most universities and research hospitals that conduct experiments have set up biomedical ethics centers often staffed by people trained in philosophy and religion as well as medicine.

Abortion and Birth Control

Perhaps the most volatile political discussion of issues in science, technology, and religion revolved around the abortion issue. Before the 1973 *Roe v. Wade* Supreme Court decision established a woman's constitutional right to an abortion in the United States, such procedures were illegal in most jurisdictions. Only a few years before, even access to birth control devices was either illegal or heavily regulated. In its 1973 ruling the Supreme Court made both a moral (and religious) statement and a scientific assertion. Rejecting Catholic teaching that a human being appeared with conception, the Court defined human existence as beginning far later during pregnancy, basing its decision on scientific evidence. After this ruling, the Catholic Church hierarchy, many individual Catholics, and many Protestant groups began to support a human life amendment to the Constitution to outlaw abortion. This issue has been raised in almost every presidential and congressional election since the 1970s.

This issue of science, technology, and morality preoccupies much of the rest of the world too. Laws and attitudes toward abortion range widely from outright prohibition to the use of abortion for population control. With a few exemptions, most African, Middle Eastern, and South American countries severely restrict or ban abortion. In Europe, law and practice vary from very restrictive laws in Ireland to much more lenient practices in France. In some nations, such as China and Singapore, abortion is accepted as a way of limiting population growth.

In the United States debate over abortion intensified with the development in France of the drug RU486, which could induce abortion in the very early stages of pregnancy. Although this drug has been thoroughly tested and is widely prescribed in Europe, it did not immediately become available in the United States, largely because of intense opposition from religious groups.

Such cases exemplify the problems of rapidly developing science and technology in societies in which religion maintains an important cultural and political influence. In the past, and, most likely in the future, this will continue to evoke dispute, debate, and, ultimately, some form of social compromise.

See also *Abortion; Communication; Environmentalism; Fundamentalism; Holocaust; Medicine.*

James B. Gilbert

BIBLIOGRAPHY

Barbour, Ian. *Issues in Science and Religion.* London: SCM Press, 1966.
Brooke, John Hedley. *Science and Religion: Some Historical Perspectives.* Cambridge: Cambridge University Press, 1991.
Gilbert, James. *Redeeming Culture: American Religion in an Age of Science.* Chicago: University of Chicago Press, 1997.
Larson, Edward L. *Trial and Error: The American Controversy over Creation and Evolution.* New York: Oxford University Press, 1989.
Numbers, Ronald L. *God and Nature: Historical Essays on the Encounter between Christianity and Science.* Berkeley: University of California Press, 1986.
White, Andrew Dickson. *A History of the Warfare of Science with Theology in Christendom.* New York: Appleton, 1876.

Secular humanism

Secular humanism is a philosophy or outlook that advocates human values rather than religious ones. By 1980 secular humanism had emerged in the United States as an important concept adopted by the new right in its critique of modern society and was popularly embraced by conservatives from a variety of religious backgrounds. By secular humanism, conservatives mean the belief they feel that some people hold that ultimate questions of human existence and morality are to be decided by human beings themselves without reference to God. *Secular* means of the temporal world rather than of a timeless spiritual domain, and *humanism* means a system of thought concerned with human, as opposed to divine, interests. In the secular humanist view, conservatives assert, the moral order of human life is expected to change over time to accommodate new needs and interests, or better knowledge.

What distresses conservatives most is that this view denies the existence of timeless and unchanging absolutes, moral standards they see as divinely ordained, evident in Holy Scripture or in natural law, and constituting the only true guide for human life. Beliefs are all the more telling and powerful, conservatives point out, when they are tacit and taken for granted. Furthermore, conservatives assert that secular humanists, in making human beings rather than God the measure of morality and meaning, ignore the evil tendencies in humankind, which require that humanity be held to standards not of its own making.

The popularity of the idea of secular humanism among new right activists may have been strengthened when the Supreme Court referred to it as a *religion* as early as 1961 (*Torcaso v. Watkins,* 367 U.S. 488). Conservatives often cite that statement to support their argument that removing traditional religious beliefs from public life rests on the assumption that human beings themselves should determine the ultimate grounds of reality and morality and, hence, that it amounts to establishing a religion, contravening the First Amendment of the U.S. Constitution. Considering secular humanism the dominant religion in contemporary America, commentators of the new right see it most heavily entrenched in the small but influential educated middle class—especially in higher education, the media, and government officialdom—and feel that it works against their own freedom of religion and expression. For this reason, they have militated against secular humanism and for a return to religious beliefs and morality as the basis for governance.

See also *Conservatism; Constitution, U.S.; Secularization*.

James M. Ault Jr.

Secularization

The term *secularization* refers to a decline or marginalization of religion in public life. The concept of secularization, obviously important in considerations of politics and religion, has often been criticized by scholars as imprecise or unwarranted. But in fact, common usage is fairly consistent when discussion is clearly limited to the secularization of a society, an institution, an activity, or a mentality. Political institutions, ideas, and activities have had a powerful effect on religion in each of these areas. Sometimes, as in England, political development has been the cause of the various processes of secularization. Other times, as during the French and Russian Revolutions, the guiding political ideas were already secular as a result of prior social and intellectual changes.

The secularization of a society (society considered as a structure, not as a population) is best thought of as structural differentiation. In the West the separation of religious and political institutions dates back at least to late antiquity. The fact that the religion (Christianity) that succeeded in establishing itself was not native to its political host (Rome) kept alive the sense that these two powers might find themselves in competition.

Western Europe

Throughout the medieval period a Christian Church that was gaining in strength tended to relativize the emerging states. Popes and emperors, bishops and kings, tended the boundaries between sacred and secular realms, refining their arguments regarding the respective rights of the two spheres. Rivalry over the appointment or investiture of church officials provided the most usual arena for contests between political and religious powers. Neither power was all-sufficient, however, and there were continuing efforts to find terms of accommodation.

Among the changes associated with the Renaissance and Reformation was a shift in favor of the emerging state's power over both the church and persisting popular religious cultures. During that time, the consolidating nation-states sometimes adopted divine right theories of monarchy, which were less successful in creating a sacred aura around the monarch than in establishing an independent secular sovereignty. Attempts to advertise the monarch's powers of healing suggested a transfer of religious authority to the state, but the divine right monarchy principally served to break the competing power of the papacy. The idea of Reason of State was developed in opposition to earlier religious inhibitions on political action. A growing nationalism began to serve as a source of legitimation within such states, competing with religious loyalties. This nationalism might even be considered to be religious in a loose, functional definition of the term.

Confusion over attempts to define religion have complicated the study of secularization. It may be observed that most definitions (especially those from phenomenological and ethnographic schools) slip in the element of power at some point, making religion that which gives access to supernatural power, or to the presence of such powers. This is not always the power of some over others, as would be the case in defining politics. But it easily becomes that, as religion is institutionalized. It is for this reason, of course, that relations between state and church have been such a central theme in history, at least until states achieved their present dominance.

Legal Secularization

While divine right monarchies were creating a sovereignty that was effectively secular, Protestant regimes had an even easier time promoting a more secular politics. Protestant theology directly promoted a redefinition of the religious, concentrating on a spiritual core and excluding much that had previously been included within a religious culture. In England, for example, the first use of the term *secularize* was in reference to the seizure of monastic personnel, lands, and wealth in the 1530s. This was only part of a rapid secularization of much else in government and law. In this, Henry VIII had the essential aid of a national parliament. Critical to the legitimacy of his parliaments was the traditional presence of bishops and abbots, who now were trapped in the position of political hostages and outvoted.

Using legislative precedents from an aborted fourteenth-century attack on church power and wealth, Henry's state curtailed every aspect of clerical authority and substituted its own. In a period of only four years (1532–1536) the king became the court of appeal in all cases involving the church, required that all laws used in the church's courts receive his approval, abolished the study of church (canon) law, eliminated the need for anyone's approval of his appointments in the church, pocketed the taxes formerly sent to Rome, surveyed the whole wealth of the church and began to nationalize it (which involved ending the monastic and mendicant forms of religious life), issued a statement defining heresy and religious truth, took responsibility for calling and presiding over the church's governing assembly (convocation), executed a cardinal, and authorized an official translation of the sacred writings into the language of the laity. Thus, the state established a secular authority over the religious institutions of the realm, with all the appearance of ordinary political process. This was done without giving the monarch any religious duties, which would have suggested a transfer of sacred authority.

Thus we see a secularization of *activities,* in that activities once performed by religious institutions were *transferred* to existing political institutions. Administration of social welfare programs was an immediate example. The transfer of perjury jurisdiction to state courts was another, despite the sacred oaths involved. Although all these things might still have been thought of as religious activities, the laicization of their administration led to the notable secularization of thinking about politics, law, and society that we associate with sixteenth- and seventeenth-century England.

England also offers examples of the secularization of *institutions* as a result of state action. That is, institutions that had once been considered religious were *transformed* to bear a more secular character. For instance, the English stage was secularized when the state ended dramatic performances of a religious nature and allowed secular plays to replace them. Artistic expression of all sorts took on a more secular tone as clerical patronage gave way to aristocratic and royal patronage. Political oaths were multiplied, which seemed to have mainly temporal rather than divine sanctions. Ecclesiastical buildings were profaned to secular uses, including St. Stephen's Chapel, Westminster, which became the first permanent home of the House of Commons.

The very process of making these vast changes established the supremacy of statute and of Parliament in English political thought and legal practice. And this, in turn, fostered more secular political theories. As so often in history, the state's contest with religious institutions had sharpened its sense of its own needs and powers.

Henry's Protestant successors radically reformed the religious life of the country, eradicating what they considered to be magical and superstitious practices. Historians who assume that religion means Christianity fail to recognize the secularizing effect of this campaign, since it was done under Protestant auspices. But the state eliminated sacred shrines and holy days, which were part of the traditional magical economy, and thereby began the secularization of notions of space and of time. This made England particularly receptive to the abstractions of the new science. Thus the state's action led even to the secularization of *mentalities,* diverting attention from ultimate to proximate considerations. As another example, the state's elimination of clerical immunities and distinctiveness led to secularized ideas of personhood, and thereby encouraged English leadership in social theory.

Secularization is not necessarily irreversible, and many Protestant regimes were faced with religious millenarian reactions to these secularizing trends. It did not prove possible to institutionalize a transcendent millenarian authority in the England of Oliver Cromwell or in the New England colonies. Massachusetts Bay was notably secular, in marriage law for example, and Rhode Island was the first political entity in Western history that had no religious establishment and full religious liberty (as differentiated from toleration for nonconformists).

Toleration Policies

Protestant encouragement of institutional secularization sometimes extended to the doctrine that jurisdiction over what are counted sins belongs to the secular power rather than to the church, which has a more exclusively spiritual function. This doctrine is known as Erastianism after the sixteenth-century Swiss theologian Thomas Erastus (1524–1583), and was more fully developed in the next century by the Dutch philosopher Hugo Grotius (1583–1645). A major element in political liberalism, Erastianism may be considered to be a development of certain religious ideas as much as a rejection of others.

The enactment of religious toleration laws in England in 1689 signified that religion was seen as a mere political issue—to be decided by institutions of another character—rather than a political power in its own right. No longer could popes bring nations to heel by pronouncing a curse of anathema. There would be no question of a dominant religious authority, under which the powers of a parliament would be decided by a panel of bishops, or the proper dynasty determined by a conclave of prophets.

Such policies of toleration became widespread after Europe's exhausting religious wars (1560–1650) following the Reformation. Adopted far in advance of the development of feelings of tolerance, they demonstrate how political developments often fostered the secularization of thought. The success of such measures encouraged the view that social and political unity could be based on something besides religious agreement, such as property or other utilitarian concerns. This experience naturally led to much theoretical reflection on politics.

In line with these theories, the federal authority established over the newly independent American states was designed to be religiously neutral, given the various ecclesiastical arrangements adopted by those states. That religious neutrality was later imposed upon the states by incorporating state law within these constitutional arrangements, including the First Amendment regarding religious freedom. But in the case of *Reynolds v. United States* (1879) the Supreme Court began to define what "religion" was and was not, since, as it observed, the U.S. Constitution had not done so.

The power to define what is and is not religion per se is the ultimate power over religion and therefore the final stage of institutional secularization. Since the 1940s in the United States this has been the focus of much consideration, and the admitted confusion of the courts has caused much scholarly comment. Part of the confusion has been over whether religion is bounded by belief or includes behavior, and how far "religion" can be broadened by functional definition.

Revolutionary Secularization

France represents a different model of secularization. The governments of the French Revolution (1789–1799) found themselves in a growing rivalry with religious institutions, which was not altogether foreseen. The revolutionaries were without the *religious* justifications for secularization that Protestantism had provided in England. Indeed, the slogan adopted by the revolutionaries—liberty, equality, and fraternity—can be seen as a generalization of the religious ideals of spiritual responsibility, respect for the individual, and charity. But the revolutionary state developed precisely in order to promote a national regeneration in the face of the Catholic Church's opposition. Accordingly, the church was seized and run as a department of state. A popular cult of reason and a state-supported Rousseauist cult of the Supreme Being were meant to offer the legitimation that religion had long provided to the state. But it was a more secular nationalism that would effectively fill that need, with revolutionary oaths and a terroristic mania for national solidarity. The ambiguous legacy of this revolution and the subsequent restoration of Louis XVIII to the throne kept tensions between politics and religion high in France and in "enlightened" circles in Europe throughout the nineteenth century.

By the time of the Bolshevik Revolution in Russia in 1917 the situation regarding secularization had been clarified. Liberalizing regimes had gradually shorn religion of many of its social, political, and legal functions without threatening the churches' cultic activities. But for a regime that was unequivocally atheistic, the meaning of secularization was quite straightforward: stripping religious institutions of their property, razing their buildings, harassing their clergy, and indoctrinating the young in the official ideology.

Methodological Considerations

Such a conscious secularism has not proved to be the standard pattern of subsequent times. The sociologist David Martin has shown how many patterns are needed to describe just the Western experience of secularization. It is notable that the most important variables within Martin's patterns are political. Such work is a necessary caution to those who use an economic determinist model of secularization. The United States itself is often taken as an example of the "paradoxical" situation in which institutional secularization of a society can coexist with high levels of religious profession in a population.

At present, the limits of secular authority are often defined by various formulations of a right of religious liberty. Given the sovereignty of modern states, this would be better described as religious toleration, since it is always subject to legislative revision. But it is symbolic, at least, of the sense that there are "human" rights that stand forever beyond the state's reach, whatever the transcendent sanctions for such rights may be.

The conceptualization and measurement of "religion" remain problematic for those trying to study the processes of secularization. The religions with which the West is most familiar seem to involve mostly beliefs and occasional rituals, which are commonly measured by opinion polling and membership or attendance statistics. Matters are very different in some other societies and in earlier periods of Western history. In such societies and periods the recourse to agricultural magic and to vows, the observance of sacred times and places, and the respect for certain persons and taboos might have struck contemporaries as more obvious marks of religiosity. Even at the present time, other criteria might well be considered in the measurement of religion, like the sale of religious publications or donations to religious charities. And even the usual marks of religious adherence, like church attendance or denominational membership, should be used carefully, since they mean very different things within different traditions.

Finally, the concept of secularization can be applied consistently only in accordance with a generic definition of religion, which will involve more than the officially recognized or normative religion. Otherwise, what looks to one scholar to be the decline of religious culture will strike another as a progressive spiritualization. Most studies of secularization are, actually, of de-Christianization.

See also *Anticlericalism*.

C. John Sommerville

BIBLIOGRAPHY

Berman, Harold J. *Law and Revolution: The Formation of the Western Legal Tradition*. Cambridge: Harvard University Press, 1983.

Kantorowicz, Ernst H. *The King's Two Bodies: A Study in Medieval Political Theology*. Princeton: Princeton University Press, 1957.

Martin, David. *A General Theory of Secularization*. Oxford: Basil Blackwell, 1978.

Sommerville, C. John. *The Secularization of Early Modern England: From Religious Culture to Religious Faith*. New York: Oxford University Press, 1992.

Tackett, Timothy. *Becoming a Revolutionary: The Deputies of the French National Assembly and the Emergence of a Revolutionary Culture (1789–1790)*. Princeton: Princeton University Press, 1996.

Senegal

A secular republic in western Africa, Senegal has a governmental structure and system of laws adapted from the French and modified to suit national needs. Only the civil code relating to family matters contains an option allowing self-professed Muslims to follow a version of Islamic law in marriage, divorce, family authority, child custody, and inheritance. Senegal is nonetheless a Muslim country. (Ninety-five percent of the population is Muslim.) The major leaders in government, including the president and prime minister, are Muslim. Muslim national holidays are celebrated, and most children are educated in Qur'anic schools, beginning before they attend Western-style schools. Islam is a powerful political force in Senegal even today, but fundamentalist militants do not dominate and are still subordinate to the conservative but basically laissez-faire rural Muslim leaders.

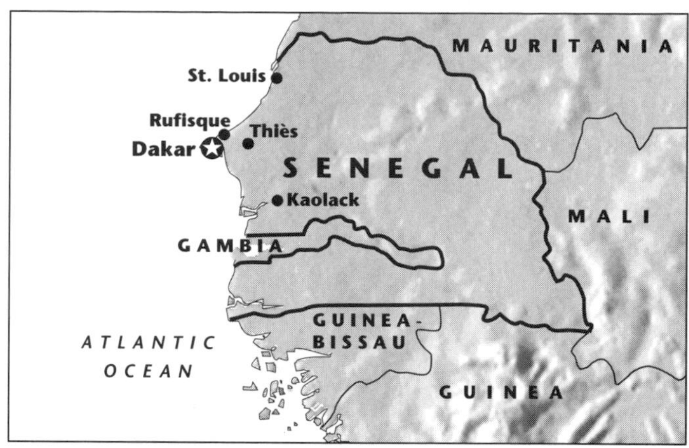

The government of Senegal has paid increased attention to asserting connections to the rest of the Muslim world, especially since the first president of Senegal, Léopold Sédar Senghor, departed and was replaced by Abdou Diouf, in 1981. The government, however, seeks its aid primarily from the West and uses Muslim leaders in the countryside to get support from the population while maintaining its own control over government institutions. Religion is intimately involved in politics in Senegal, but the two have not merged.

The relationship between religion and politics is still an uneasy partnership, much as it was before independence from France in 1960. The French used Muslim leaders *(marabouts)* to get support for their programs and obedience to their edicts. These leaders in turn received government assistance and even used French support to eliminate rivals within their brotherhoods. President Diouf has attempted to include better-trained technocrats in his government, to streamline government, and to eliminate some of the patronage inherent in the old system. But he still does not have the national support needed to bypass the *marabouts* completely, and, in the various crises that plague the economically fragile nation, he still turns to the religious leaders. Thus, in the hotly contested 1993 presidential election, Diouf again won by a comfortable margin, based on his ability to mobilize support from the rural Muslim leaders. Islamic leaders, then, have a major voice in Senegal and, although they do not make policy, they certainly influence the shaping of the society and polity.

Origin of the Political Power of the Marabouts

The political importance of Islamic leaders in Senegal—and the limits to their power—dates back to the colonial period. In the late seventeenth and early eighteenth centuries the territory of present-day Senegal included several precolonial kingdoms, each ruled primarily by leaders of one of the distinct ethnic groups located in the region. But over time a mixture of peoples developed as other ethnic groups migrated inward and conquered or merely settled in the polity that already existed. In this period, Islamic traders and missionaries were already present, although the majority of the various ethnic groups had not yet converted. Thus *marabouts* are noted among the Wolof people even in the fifteenth century, although they were not completely converted until the end of the nineteenth century.

The three largest ethnic groups are the Wolof (36 percent), the Tukulor and Fulani (26 percent), and the Serer (17 percent). The Serer were already settled in central Senegal by the eleventh century, and the Wolof began to appear in their kingdoms by the end of that century. By the end of the fifteenth century the Wolof had established a large kingdom pushing the Serer-controlled area to the south. By the end of the sixteenth century there were four Wolof and two Serer kingdoms in the central zones of what is now Senegal. The Tukulor, also of a related language group, were Fulani people whose name originates from their settling in the Tekrour, the Senegal River valley to the northeast, where they had founded the kingdom of Tekrour by the eleventh century.

Before the French arrived, the influence of Islam in politics appears to have been strongest in the Tukulor kingdom because the Tukulor people were introduced much earlier to the religion than were the Serer or Wolof. The first dynasty had Muslim rulers among its members, and Islam was introduced to the majority of the Tukulor in the eleventh century. In contrast, the Wolof were not Islamicized until the end of the nineteenth century, and the Serer began to convert in large numbers only in the twentieth century. Thus, among the two centrally located ethnic groups, Islam remained largely intermingled with preexisting values and customs. Pre-Islamic customs played an important role in the lives of the Tukulor as well, but Islamic traditions were more central to both state and society.

The situation in Senegal was complicated by the fact that Islam was not the only major influence from the outside that would distort and even destroy the social, political, and economic structures of society. The French brought perhaps even more change. French conquest of Senegal was a violent undertaking, despite periods of calm and superficial negotiations backed by the constant threat of reprisal should the French not achieve whatever goal they had then set. The French invasion distorted, even destroyed, the political systems that had already existed there. Traditional rulers lost their authority, and it is in this atmosphere that the *marabouts,* and especially the few leaders of the largest brotherhoods, became rural political powers. The *marabouts* drew followers from all castes and classes as people sought to find a new, positive definition of themselves and their society. As the old leaders became powerless, they turned to the *marabouts.* The nobles and warriors intermarried with maraboutic families until these were practically indistinguishable from the upper castes of earlier times. Now the leaders of the clan alliances, through which politics continued to run, were *marabouts.* The French had created the vacuum into which the Muslim leaders would step.

Aware that they had actually helped to spread Islam, the colonial authorities did not intend to support or increase the power of Muslim leaders. In practice, though, the French needed effective channels to the rural people. Because their numbers were few and their language and customs so different, the French could not communicate directly with the mass of the Senegalese. To maintain control and to get their own needs met—such as collecting taxes—or to embark on any new plan—such as spreading cultivation of peanuts throughout the country—strong rural leaders were useful. The French interfered in brotherhood politics when they felt it necessary, but generally they left the *marabouts* to do as they pleased as long as they did not challenge French authority. The French used the *marabouts* and were used by them; the reciprocal relationship worked well for both. Indeed, the French presided benignly over the continued conversion of the country. In 1912, 66 percent of the population was Muslim, but by 1960, the year of independence, this figure had grown to 90 percent.

Muslim Political Power in the 1990s

In the late 1990s a handful of Muslim fundamentalists in Senegal called loudly for conversion of the government to a Muslim regime, but few heeded their cry. What was established in Senegal was a state based on collaboration between Muslim leaders and secular rulers, with the rulers having the upper hand in terms of military power and technology. This collaboration remains in effect, and reliance on the West (meaning the United States and Europe rather than just France) is still far more important than the public efforts of the Senegalese government to be seen as a Muslim state—for example by joining the Organization of the Islamic Conference.

Senegal has many ethnic and cultural groups and different religious groups as well, many of whom are Muslim. There are many secular Muslims of the middle and working classes (who would certainly deny the term "secular") who behave as their Christian counterparts do in France or the United States. These Senegalese follow general rituals, such as attending mosque and fasting during the month of Ramadan but otherwise living according to the dictates of their work and the expectations of a Western state and Western-dominated business and trade networks. These men (and women) are not very interested in establishing the pure Muslim state. They piously condemn the corruption of the West, but their lives follow a moral path not too dissimilar from those of their foreign counterparts.

There are conservative Muslims as well who may be members (or often leaders) of brotherhoods or who may be called orthodox, for want of a better term, meaning not belonging to a brotherhood and usually part of the educated elite. These people are more concerned with the moral decline of their society, more likely to be seriously disturbed about Western corruption of the moral values of the land, and more likely to be assiduous in the observation of the rituals of their religion. When threatened by any attack to their religion, their response is to defend it against further encroachment by secular society. They call for a Muslim state, meaning the adoption of the *shariʿa,* or Islamic law, but they have been, and will be, satisfied with a coexistence of their organization with a secular state unless it begins to infringe on what they view as their rights. There is also a range of fundamentalist groups who call for a radical revision of society and the creation of a Muslim state following *shariʿa* law. Some of these groups are more radical than others, but at present they remain a small, elite element with little influence in society.

In the late 1990s the government of Abdou Diouf and his functionaries was dependent on support from Western nations and institutions and bent on pushing Senegal to emphasize the private sector and to liberalize laws and social attitudes. They were opposed to the notion of establishing an autocratic Muslim state governed by the *shariʿa.* But there was considerable dissatisfaction in Senegal because of economic instability. Structural adjustment reforms increased the price of goods and services privately available, as well as the number of unemployed, and decreased available government services.

The crowning blow came in January 1994 with the devaluation of the local currency. Despite government subventions and controls on prices, people in Senegal found themselves paying more for domestically produced food, for utilities, and for necessary imports like gasoline. In this environment, support for the radical fundamentalist leaders who opposed the government began to grow. Ironically, many of these Muslim leaders were relatives of the rural *marabouts* who have colluded with the Western-style government throughout the years. One of the better known is Moustapha Sy, whose followers, called Moustarchadines, are primarily young men, some even of secondary-school age. This group was the core of riots in March 1994 that followed devaluation.

President Diouf, however, was still able to create workable coalitions, drawing together, when needed, a larger and more powerful support group with which to defeat his opponents. He could also co-opt, where necessary, his rivals (as he did when he drew Abdoulaye Wade, head of the major opposition party, the Senegalese Democratic Party, into his government as minister of state in March 1995).

Although democracy has a tenuous hold in Senegal, it seems to be deepening its roots. Opposition is open and vocal, with only occasional surges of repression. The power of the rural *marabouts* is waning but still strong. Muslim fundamentalists clamor at the borders of the political arena, occasionally threatening political stability and always representing a menace that could intensify if the economic situation worsens or if some Islamic issue unites the presently diverse conservative Muslim groups scattered throughout the society. For now, however, the fundamentalist threat to democratic development does not appear very large.

Lucy Creevey

BIBLIOGRAPHY

Behrman, Lucy C. *Muslim Brotherhoods and Politics in Senegal.* Cambridge.: Harvard University Press.

Coulon, Christian. *Le Marabout et le prince: Islam et pouvoir au Sénégal.* Paris: A. Pedone, 1981.

Creevey, Lucy. "Islam, Women, and the Role of the State in Senegal." *Journal of Religion in Africa* 26 (1996): 268–307.

———. "Muslim Brotherhoods and Politics in Senegal in 1985." *Journal of Modern African Studies* 23 (1985): 715–721.

O'Brien, D. B. Cruise. *The Mourides of Senegal: The Political and Economic Organization of an Islamic Brotherhood.* Oxford: Clarendon Press, 1971.

———. *Saints and Politicians: Essays in the Organization of a Senegalese Peasant Society.* Cambridge: Cambridge University Press, 1975.

O'Brien, D. B. Cruise, and Christian Coulon, eds. *Charisma and Brotherhood in African Islam.* Oxford: Clarendon Press, 1988.

Villalón, Leonardo. *Islamic Society and State Power in Senegal: Disciples and Citizens in Fatick.* Cambridge: Cambridge University Press, 1995.

Separation of church and state: a potent, dynamic idea in political theory

Separation of church and state refers to a division or disconnection in one form or another between religious organizations and secular government. Although the principle often is considered a powerful American contribution to political theory and a core value in American politics, such a claim both overstates reality and presupposes a clearer understanding of the principle than actually exists. Ironically, separation of church and state is a widely accepted concept in the United States precisely because it has several specific, sometimes contradictory, meanings—a situation that has spawned no small number of legal controversies.

A society that professes, usually through constitutional provisions, to support separation of church and state is fundamentally different from a society that professes to support a unitary form of government. Unitary forms may be either theocratic, in which the state is subordinate to the church, or Erastian, in which religion is subject to the state. Examples of theocratic societal systems are the Islamic nations of Iran, Afghanistan, and Saudi Arabia, which insist that there can be no separation between the religious and secular spheres; both spheres are under God and must be ruled by God's law. Most non-Islamic societies, by contrast, are committed to some form of separation, although communist China has an Erastian system.

Five Types of Separation

Five types of separation of church and state are distinguishable. *Structural separation* is the most ancient and fundamental. As theory, it may be traced to Jesus' statement in Matthew 22: 21: "Render therefore unto Caesar the things which are Caesar's; and unto God the things that are God's." As a part of Western political culture, structural separation may be traced to the two swords (spiritual power and temporal power) theory of Pope Gelasius I (served 492–496). Much of the history of Western Europe revolved around the relationship between the papacy (spiritual power) and various secular governments (temporal power). While there were many battles for dominance and many cooperative efforts, particularly against nonbelievers, the structures of religious and governmental organizations developed separately, including recruitment and training of professional administrators, systems of law, and ownership of property. Still, structural separation is a rather minimalist type of separation with a fair amount of overlap—for example, secular rulers attempt to influence selection of religious leaders and enforce religious laws, and clerics attempt to influence the selection of secular rulers. It may be compatible with an established church such as in England where the monarch is the titular head of the Church of England.

Absolute separation is sometimes referred to as strict or "no aid" separation. Adherents argue that refusal to aid religion is the underlying value of the First Amendment to the U.S. Constitution, which specifies that Congress "shall make no law respecting an establishment of religion, or prohibiting the free exercise thereof." Perhaps the best expression of the absolute separation doctrine is that of Supreme Court Justice Hugo L. Black in *Everson v. Board of Education* (1947): "Neither a state nor the Federal Government can set up a church. Neither can pass laws which aid one religion, aid all religions, or prefer one religion over another. . . . No tax in any amount, large or small, can be levied to support any religious activities or institutions, whatever they may be called, or whatever format they may adopt to teach or practice religion. Neither a state nor the Federal Government can, openly or secretly, participate in the affairs of any religious organizations or groups and vice versa." Over a century earlier, in his letter to the Danbury Baptist Association dated New Year's Day 1802, President Thomas Jefferson had asserted that the clause against establishment of religion by law was intended to erect "a wall of separation between Church and State." Absolute separation often is referred to as an ideal by its adherents, but it has never been strictly practiced or enforced in the United States. Its most forceful expression and enforcement have been in Supreme Court decisions about financial aid to primary and secondary schools with religious affiliations.

Advocates of *transvaluing separation,* whose underlying value is the removal of all religious influence from the public education and political culture of a nation, see religion as a strictly personal, private affair that has no place in the public affairs of a society. This type of separation was expressed in the constitution of the former Soviet Union, which had an explicit bias toward atheism. While it is not widely popular in the United States, transvaluing separation does have some adherents. They may be simply agnostic toward religion, but they do have a commitment to secularism in the public square.

Perhaps the clearest expression of transvaluing separation is a statement made fifty years ago by the American Humanist Association which argued that attempts by the church to either promote or discourage passage of legislation favorable or unfavorable to church interests was precisely the kind of religious–political activity that the Founders "tried desperately to prevent on American soil by adopting the First Amendment and the corresponding state laws." Most scholars reject this interpretation of the Founders' intent, and indeed in *Harris v. McRae* (1980) the Supreme Court dismissed the argument that religious influence on the passage of laws renders them unconstitutional. Nonetheless, this argument remains a viable meaning of separation, particularly for those opposed to attempts by religious interest groups to influence public policy.

Supportive separation, better known as the accommodation theory, holds that government and religion may support each other so long as government does not favor or support one religion over all others. Perhaps the best expression of the supportive separation position remains the statement of Supreme Court Justice William O. Douglas in *Zorach v. Clausen* (1952): "We are a religious people whose institutions presuppose a Supreme Being. We guarantee the freedom to worship as one chooses. . . . When the Government encourages religious instruction and cooperates with religious authorities by adjusting the schedule of public events to sectarian needs, it follows the best of our traditions. For it then respects the religious nature of our people and accommodates the public service to their spiritual needs."

Obviously, supportive separation is entirely incompatible with absolute or transvaluing separation. As a result, it has had many opponents over the years and, except in a few cases, has never garnered a majority of the Supreme Court. Even Justice Douglas changed his mind later in his career. Nonetheless, it remains the constitutional value of a large number of citizens.

Equal separation is sometimes called the neutrality or, more recently, the nondiscrimination theory. It rejects all political or economic privilege, coercion, or disability based on religious affiliation, belief, or practice, or lack thereof, but guarantees to religiously motivated or affiliated individuals and organizations the same rights and privileges extended to other similarly situated individuals and organizations. In other words, it provides protection to religion without providing privilege. It treats the right to religious belief and practice as a human right to be protected along with other human rights in an even-handed manner. It protects the right of religiously motivated groups and individuals to participate in the political process and the economic system in the same manner and to the same extent that it protects the rights of other similar groups and individuals to participate. The roots of equal separation are found in a 1785 article "Memorial and Remonstrance," written by then-Virginia legislator James Madison.

Separation and U.S. Political Theory

Each of these theories is defended as the "authentic" understanding of separation of church and state and a statement of the "true" meaning of the First Amendment religion clauses, yet they are not all compatible. Moreover, the dilemma cannot be resolved by searching for the intention of the Founders. In early America there were two main threads of thought about separation. The first was that of the English-born religious leader Roger Williams (1603–1683) who promoted the idea of a wall of separation between the garden of religion and the wilderness of the secular world. Separation was a means of keeping the corrupting influence of government out of religious affairs and allowing the churches to pursue their spiritual mission.

The second thread is properly traced to President Jefferson, who, in his famous 1802 letter to the Danbury Baptists, referred to the "wall of separation between Church and State." In President Jefferson's words, "Believing with you that religion is a matter which lies solely between Man & his God, that he owes account to none other for his faith or his worship, that the legitimate powers of government reach actions only, & not opinions, I contemplate with sovereign reverence that act of the whole American people which declared that their legislature should make no law respecting an establishment of religion, or prohibiting the free exercise thereof, thus building a wall of separation between Church and State." Recent scholarship concludes that Jefferson had two main concerns: to keep the divisive and oppressive tendencies of religion out of the federal government and to keep the federal government clear of all religious action or expression. For this reason he refused even to call for a day of thanksgiving or for national days of fasting, a practice common at the time.

These two threads weave through the history of separation in American political thought, although the Jeffersonian thread is far better known. They hold together the basic value of separation, yet pull in opposite directions, ensuring ongoing tension between the adherents of each tradition. The Williams thread aims to protect religion from all government; the Jefferson thread works to protect the federal government from religion.

These tensions have reappeared in numerous Supreme Court decisions. In *Everson v. Board of Education,* which provided the classic text for an absolute separation theory, Justice Black's majority opinion upheld New Jersey's payment of bus transportation for parochial schoolchildren. But in something of a defense of the equal separation theory, Black also pointed out that New Jersey could not exclude "members of any other faith, because of their faith, or lack of it, from receiving the benefits of public welfare legislation."

In 1983 in *Marsh v. Chambers,* the Court held that a state legislature could indeed pay a chaplain for opening legislative sessions with a prayer and counseling legislators without violating the Constitution—a clear example of supportive separation.

Lemon v. Kurtzman (1971) provided the Court with a rule or test for determining whether laws violate the First Amendment's establishment clause. Now known as the Lemon test, it holds that a statute must meet three criteria to be constitutionally permissible: "First, the statute must have a secular legislative purpose; second, its principal or primary effect must be one that neither advances nor inhibits religion; finally, the statute must not foster an excessive government entanglement with religion."

For a quarter of a century the Lemon test was used to reach anomalous results. For example, it upheld state financial aid to religious colleges and universities and denied such aid to religious grade and high schools. The latter was justified on absolute separation/no-aid grounds. In 1997, however, the Court in *Agostini v. Felton* reversed itself, holding that state funding of special education classes held in religious schools but not teaching religion is constitutionally acceptable. The Court utilized the Lemon test but justified its change on the grounds of neutrality.

Separation of church and state, even with its multiple meanings, remains a potent and dynamic idea in political theory. In the United States the Supreme Court has decided cases inconsistently, using different theories of separation. Yet there are signs of doctrinal development. In recent years several scholars and justices have begun to develop a consensus that focuses more on government neutrality and equality of treatment than on separation. One formulation is that set forth by law professor Douglas Laycock which he calls substantive neutrality: "the religion clauses require government to minimize the extent to which it either encourages or discourages religious belief or disbelief, practice or non-practice, observance or nonobservance." Under this formulation religious organizations may participate in and receive government funding for social services on an equal basis with similar agencies (equal separation). They can be free of regulations that would limit religious expression or symbols while providing those services (supportive separation), but would be ineligible for celebration or honoring of religion by government (absolute separation). Whether such a formulation will end the tensions between varieties of separation of church and state or simply add a level of complexity has yet to be seen.

See also *Civil religion; Holidays; Jefferson, Thomas; Separation of church and state: a principle advancing the struggle for human rights; State churches; Theocracy.*

Paul J. Weber

BIBLIOGRAPHY

Dreisbach, Daniel L. "Sowing Useful Truths and Principles: The Danbury Baptists, Thomas Jefferson, and the *Wall of Separation.*" *Journal of Church and State* 39 (summer 1997): 455.

Esbeck, Carl H. "A Constitutional Case for Governmental Cooperation with Faith-based Social Service Providers." *Emory Law Journal* 46 (winter 1997): 1.

Feldman, Stephen M. *Please Don't Wish Me A Merry Christmas: A Critical History of the Separation of Church and State.* New York: New York University Press, 1997.

Gaustad, Edwin S. *Liberty of Conscience: Roger Williams in America.* Grand Rapids, Mich.: Eerdmans, 1991.

Laycock, Douglas. "The Underlying Unity of Separation and Neutrality." *Emory Law Journal* 46 (winter 1997): 43.

Luper, Ira C. "The Lingering Death of Separationism." *George Washington Law Review* 62 (1994): 230.

Monsma, Stephen V. *When Sacred and Secular Mix.* Lanham, Md.: Rowman and Littlefield, 1996.

Weber, Paul J. *Equal Separation: Understanding the First Amendment Religion Clauses.* Westport, Conn.: Greenwood Press, 1990.

Separation of church and state: a principle advancing the struggle for human rights

The principle of separation of church and state—religion and politics—on which the United States as a nation was founded, has advanced the struggle for human rights by allowing the separate development of these two spheres with mutually reinforcing effects. President Thomas Jefferson (served 1801–1809) summed it up in his aphorism "Divided we stand, united we fall," by which he meant dividing the sphere of state authority from that of religion, thereby erecting a wall of separation between church and state. Jefferson believed that uniting church and state would bring ruin to both institutions, but dividing them into mutually antagonistic spheres would be equally damaging. The well-being of human beings demands that they flourish spiritually and politically.

The original sixteenth- and seventeenth-century Puritan proponents of separation recognized the importance of religion in the political democratic state by conceding an autonomous but mutually hospitable domain to each of the two spheres. Religion became even more central when, under the pressure of growing pluralism and of political demand, it was cleansed of its territorial "Christendom" complex and allowed to merge into a culture of choice and moral agency. The territorial "domain" that cradled medieval Christianity eventually was discarded as the framework for organized religion.

This principle of nonterritoriality was carried to the New World and enshrined in the Declaration of Independence (1776). But the assertion in the Declaration that all citizens are endowed by their Creator with certain inalienable rights, among which are life, liberty, and the pursuit of happiness, concludes where it did not begin. Life is the Creator's gift, unearned and undeserved, and liberty is of a piece with that—the unconditioned, unqualified abatement of divine omnipotence to make room for human choice and freedom. But the pursuit of happiness, a phrase dear to Jefferson, comes as an anticlimax to the Declaration's exalted opening, and in fact falls pretty close to what French writer and politician Alexis de Tocqueville (1805–1859) suggested about the useful trumping the moral. Tocqueville was right that happiness is a by-product rather than an object in its own right. Thus the Declaration's own theocentric logic looks to justice rather than to happiness as having equal value with life and liberty.

Separation Necessary but Inadequate

The subject of separation can be taken in its own right as representing a genuine religious insight that allows for real political innovation. Its use in the First Amendment to the U.S. Constitution (1791) as the removal from the state of the power to enjoin religion is accompanied by the complementary rule of religion protected from state control. By law, then, the liberal democratic state may not prescribe religion, but it may not proscribe it either.

The state is implicated, however, in the effects and consequences of religious practice. For example, murder is a crime not because it threatens the public order (Mafia-style executions can enforce a certain order and deterrence) but because life is sacred. "Thou shalt not kill" as a religious commandment is founded on the divine right of personhood, the same warrant that fostered notions of human rights and minority rights. Thus separation is *necessary* in distinguishing and safeguarding the political rule in public life from the religious end in the moral life. Separation is *inadequate,* however, in grasping the convergence of interests and values at the level of practice. In a liberal democratic state such as the United States, religion has the space to flourish, and as such has had effects, both good and bad, on national life and politics.

A liberal democratic society thus presumes the free exercise of religion as an inalienable right. As the seventeenth-century divines put it, religion forced on individuals becomes an impeachment of God's honor, for a person so compelled ceases to be a fit subject for religious regeneration. Thus in the antebellum South a Baptist leader petitioned the Georgia legislature to condemn slavery as a violation of God's law. "Soul-liberty," he said, is rightfully inherited by all God's moral creatures. Civil authority has no power over the religion of the slave nor over that of the citizen. (The irony here is that it was by federal legislative authority that slavery was ended in the United States.)

In the new ethical scheme so envisaged, freedom is an act of faith based on spiritual commitment rather than merely a state concession. Freedom in this notion is self-evident in the sense of being uncontestable as a source-value and thus shares with the gift of life the quality of divine warrant. Freedom is not ultimately a subject of state sanction but its controlling axiom because freedom is grounded in the fundamental truth of our moral origin though its expression and effects are practical and social.

Church and state are thus united in the common recognition of separation as a necessary safety net between them. Political pragmatism and religious commitment are joined in the allegiance of free citizens, though in terms of the moral scheme social facts and religious truths are distinct and separate. The political contract and the religious covenant, each proper in its own sphere, nevertheless share a common conception of human well-being grounded in moral agency, whether that be in the ballot box, in law, or in worship of God, with religion offering a transcendent scope vis-à-vis the more limited natural sphere.

The operative axiom of liberal jurisprudence that persons who are impaired to the degree that they cannot tell the difference between right and wrong are deemed incompetent to stand trial is of a piece with the religious doctrine of the knowledge of good and evil. The crucial difference, however, between the political and the moral is that the political is provisional and penultimate while the moral relates to our normative and ultimate destiny. It is the case, therefore, that on only pragmatic grounds we are not all equal in the competition for political goods, some people being better endowed than others in that sphere, though from the religious point of view we are ultimately all equal as prescribed in the law of God. Equal citizenship, backed by law, is the application in the public realm of that theocentric idea.

Natural Law Theory

The natural law theory of politics demands not so much that we be able to prove the objective truth of its central metaphysical assumptions as we be able to recognize that striving for perfection invests our actions with a credible but penultimate character, with plenty of room in that striving for differences, contests, and self-restraint. It may be the case today that jurisprudence no longer seeks to deduce fundamental principles from metaphysics, as did the old jurisprudence, but rather seeks to base law and policy on social facts and social operation. Yet modern jurisprudence has not entirely abandoned the notion of separation even when it advocates a social activist view of the state. In this sociological view the state is not preoccupied with the individual rights and the moral independence of the believer from state control, things that Puritan doctrine promoted. For, according to the Puritans, the state was not an arbitrary power free of all moral constraints. For example, the English-born founder of Rhode Island, Roger Williams (1603–1683), insisted that God's commandments were written on the two tablets of conscience and civil obedience and that while both were intended for our well-being, they were not identical and therefore were not to be confused. On the divine tablet was inscribed our eternal security and on the worldly tablet our political welfare. Accordingly, the separate branches of church and state have a single religious root and, by extension, a common moral source.

Even though the new jurisprudence sought to overthrow this Puritan scheme of the appeal to rights, it did not jettison the principle of separation, a principle important to limiting state power. In other words, the new jurisprudence would take from the visible hand of institutional curbs on state power what it declined from the invisible hand of what Supreme Court justice Oliver Wendell Holmes Jr. (1841–1935) called "a brooding omnipresence in the sky." Thus the religious habit would have conditioned the state to accede to norms of self-restraint until the time came for these norms to be based on public reason. All that may be involved here is religion as an unacknowledged source of political minimalism and as a bulwark against state tyranny.

In any case, while sociological theories of the state, such as those of Supreme Court justices Louis Brandeis (1856–1941) and Oliver Wendell Holmes and educator Roscoe Pound (1870–1964), would wish to free the state of a higher law of nature on the grounds that that law restricts the power of government, those theories would resort to other checks and balances, such as separation of powers or the balancing effects of competitive social and political interests, to limit state power. Pound and Holmes, for example, reduced Puritan effusions on rights and freedom to nothing more than a pious attempt by prudes to stop pigs from putting their feet in the trough. Yet with those natural law safeguards removed, the state would be left unchecked in its despotic power. Holmes thus proposed sterilizing those considered socially unfit and economically burdensome—in other words, those considered politically intolerable, all this on the pretext that freedom was not absolute but relative. It is hard to see how the democratic state can avoid being imperiled by this teaching.

Natural theology establishes a similar safeguard for religion, so that objective merit may accrue to human effort on the grounds of common humanity rather than by virtue of adherence to any particular creed. Natural theology overlaps with natural law theory in this important sense—both are designed to avoid the extremism of the right and left at the same time. And it moderates the extreme Puritan notion of an unbridgeable gulf between God and humanity, so that any business with God, and with one another, is conducted on contested, sectarian ground. The "other" is the enemy, and God will help one hunt and contain the enemy. It is a notion that makes one ask of any institution whether it is of God, in which case one falls down and worships it, or whether it is of "man," in which case one attacks and destroys it. Natural theology softens this dialectical extremism by harmonizing the natural sphere with the religious, at least in terms of the public interest.

Yet the theological moderation of natural theology is accompanied by the radical religious posture that the whole created order stands within the comprehensive doctrine of the providence and sovereignty of God. For example, in his reflections on Christianity in the empire, St. Augustine (354–430), a founder of the early Christian church, answered those who claimed that the teachings of Christ, being so idealistic and impractical, were inimical to civil law and custom. Turning the other cheek, going the extra mile, not repaying evil for evil, or not taking up arms, the critics charged, may be perfectly sound moral teachings, but they undercut the public interest. Augustine responded that the commonwealth was the repository of the interests of the people, interests that were common to all, including the state. In fact, he insisted, the state itself was a community of people united by a bond of agreement. The conduct of public affairs required more than the rule of efficiency; it required sanctions to restrain evil, norms to produce works of mercy, precepts to guide and direct, warrants to instill and commend virtue, and sacraments to change and transform life. Let those who say that Christ's teaching is in opposition to the commonwealth, declared Augustine, make up an army of the kind of soldiers Christ's teaching commands—that is, ordinary citizens, including masters and servants, rulers, judges, taxpayers, and tax collectors—and then let them say that "this doctrine is in opposition to the commonwealth!" Rather, this teaching, if obeyed, "would be the salvation of the commonwealth." Even in this Augustinian view, then, separating the natural sphere from revelation does not deny their connection at the level of what is prudent and expedient, or at that of the public good and in matters of personal ethics.

War

In few other areas are politics and religion more controversially linked than in the idea and practice of war. This is so in part because war deals with both political method and moral end, thereby pushing at the wall of separation between church and state, and in part because war as such looks beyond individual freedom and rights to national commitment and personal sacrifice, which is the highest moral act. Implicated in war, then, is the ultimate conception of human life, with limited military objectives—for example, begging the source question about the limitless value of human life. In this sense, the political state can scarcely be indifferent to moral ends when its method in war involves so final and comprehensive a moral act as the taking of human life.

Oliver Wendell Holmes expressed the view that war is the state's weapon to discipline and rehabilitate a heedless and irresponsible modern youth, a view that ends up moralizing the state instrument and giving it comprehensive monopoly of the public interest. It gives the state exclusive warrant to command citizens' obligation on the questionable basis that the state knows what is good for them better than they themselves. In Holmes's opinion, the state, like the universe, is a blind machine indifferent to the fate of men and women. Idealism and sentiment are politically meaningless, which indicates that in war the state may do whatever is necessary to save and protect itself. However, apart from dismissing pacifists and other conscientious objectors, Holmes had no answer for why the unpopularity of war, which should be suppressed as an impertinence, should force a democratic state to retreat from war, the great discipliner, or even to avoid war, suggesting there are moral constraints on state power that political prudence would come to heed. Holmes embraced the austere Darwinist principle that the struggle for life requires the instruments imperative to success. That comes pretty close to the doctrine expressed by seventeenth-century English philosopher Thomas Hobbes that compacts without the sword are but mere words. All of that transforms the state into a combative superstructure and society into a battlefield. It is a setback for freedom, justice, and pluralism.

Common Security

State encroachment on the moral sphere thus has in certain circumstances provoked religious activism with the aim of capturing the state instrument to serve the truth claims of religion. Consequently, a combative secular state evokes its religious doublet. Implied in the theocratic contest for state takeover is not a weakening of the state but its growing supremacy, with religion seeking to sequester it for its own end. Theocracy is still statism exalted. Instead of fostering the sharing of a common security interest, a theocratic reaction to state fundamentalism reproduces on the right a perfect replica of its secular foe on the left. It comes to the same thing whether the state instrument serves religious truth claims, or religious truth claims serve the state. In these circumstances, the religious reaction produces results that are no better or worse than those of state encroachment on the moral sphere. Moralization of political ends comes to the same thing as the politicization of moral truth. In either case, the principle of separation is destroyed. The sword of the magistrate that is supposed to rule only in the outward sphere would acquire a twin blade to rule in the inward sphere as well. State jurisdiction would now extend over the temporal as well as the spiritual domain, with human rights a casualty.

The cautionary lesson here is that a left-wing secular fundamentalism begets its nemesis in a right-wing religious fundamentalism, a situation that results in separation being only a fiction in either case. The alternative to such extremism and its unpalatable consequences is recognizing that politics and religion do overlap, that truth claims and political values do converge, and that such convergence need not result in the denial of the rule of functional separation. Thus qualified separation is necessary to maintain the separate spheres of the outward and inward jurisdiction, so that political method may advance the moral end, and vice versa, without the moral and political becoming wholly identical. Accordingly, rules of procedure need not become matters of substance, for laws may be effective without their being necessarily just, and technically sound laws may abort the ends of honor and fair play. As was first expressed in the promulgation of Pope Gelasius I (served 492–496), the divine and the temporal are two interdependent ends, with church and state "each equal to the other when acting in its own sphere, and each equally dependent on the other when acting in the sphere of the other."

The way forward, then, between politics and religion lies in preserving their common security zone. It involves a fine balancing act in which the state is not so out of step with the church—neither so far ahead in terms of a messianic state, nor so far behind in terms of prescriptive atheism, that it provokes the risk of strategic intransigence in every political action, leaving the state with coercion and repression as its signature tools. By the same token, the state should not become so identical with religion that political acts assume the status of moral dogma. Moderate versions of separation, then, tailored to suit different situations, would be required to prevent all conflict and disagreement from becoming a fight to the finish, with politics and religion each other's hostage. Some such mildly prescriptive rule will need to accompany all meaningful struggle for human rights.

The Global Scene

In a good deal of global political and religious turmoil and unrest, the secular role of religion has remained a burning issue for religions of the left and right equally. The future of religions in a world energized by new-found freedoms and marked by growing pluralism is fundamentally bound up with the issue of freedom and choice, and that in turn is connected with separation, however it is defined. Therefore, any effective understanding or any long-lasting solution to the struggle for human rights requires attention to the relation of politics and religion, in particular to preventing areas of overlap between the two centers of life from becoming grounds for mutual hostility or collusion. The issue is not whether proselytization and tolerance, for example, are compatible or in conflict, but whether tolerance is meaningful at all in the absence of religion, suggesting that tolerance is a function itself of religious freedom. One could express the issue thus: religion is important and comprehensive enough for it not to overlap with politics, but it is too important and comprehensive for politics to co-opt it. As Tocqueville hinted, government by habit prefers the useful to the moral and will, if tempted, require the moral to be useful. The otherwise religiously based argument that freedom to believe in God belongs with the truth claim of God's design for human well-being turns out to have public rationale for the liberal democratic enterprise—that is, a free environment marked by political and moral choice.

In any event, the liberal democratic enterprise as such is constrained to promote a certain secular worldview, say, a Jeffersonian liberalism, as its own precondition and to demand universal acceptance. Yet to speak of universal acceptance, to speak of a general, impartial allegiance in a diverse, pluralist society, is to make an objective natural law claim about the political community as the moral community, even if the political is not synonymous with the moral. Such a view is expressed, for example, in the Miltonian doctrine of men and women having been "created in the image and resemblance of God." As Jefferson himself testified: "I have no fear but that the result of our experiment will be that men may be trusted to govern themselves without a master. Could the contrary of this be proved, I should conclude either there is no God or that he is a malevolent being." The religious premise invoked in that statement, and defended by the American philosopher John Dewey (1859–1952), is necessary to the liberal democratic enterprise, even if that be from a position of separation.

The political expression of this separation is thus also important for religion, largely because religion is its source. The state is not its own orthodoxy, and the church exists as public safeguard of that truth. Religion thus offers a longer-range view of our interest than the goals of political organization. The liberal democratic enterprise and the religious vocation under this conception run on parallel but unequal courses, leading to church and state being independent of each other in their own spheres, but interdependent when each acts in the sphere of the other.

In America and elsewhere the independence of church and state has conceived a society of diverse interests and pursuits and is at the same time well designed to elevate human rights to the center of politics where the state is constrained by the higher law—the law that says that state authority is subordinate to the general ethical norms of human rights, freedom, and justice. As such, separation could scarcely be confined to American shores, and so in time the idea, or some forms of it, was carried into other societies and cultures where it produced new currents of thought and the framework for political and religious action and reaction. Church–state separation has been an indispensable safeguard for personal freedom as well as one of the most crucial factors behind the rise (and crisis) of national secular states in non-Western societies.

See also *Civil religion; Freedom of religion; Hobbes, Thomas; Jefferson, Thomas; Natural law; Separation of church and state: a potent, dynamic idea in political theory; Theocracy; War.*

Lamin Sanneh

Seventh-day Adventism

Seventh-day Adventism is a Christian denomination with a conservative, even literalistic, approach to the Scripture. Its adherents observe Saturday, the "seventh day," as the Sabbath. Adventist evangelists focus on the apocalyptic visions of the biblical books of Daniel and Revelation, interpreting them to show that the second advent of Christ is near (and so the name "Adventism"). Such preaching tends to draw relatively poor converts. Because of their emphasis on education and their system of educational institutions, however, Adventists in the United States typically have experienced considerable upward mobility, especially in the second generation.

Formally organized in 1863, Seventh-day Adventism has become a global movement that in the twentieth century has grown rapidly, especially in the developing world: in 1997 it was active in 207 countries and claimed an adult membership of more than nine million people. Its centralized structure, global presence, and extensive educational, health care, and publishing institutions have led it into a complex web of relationships with governments. Adventists in the United States have been an influential force in advancing religious liberty and in protecting the separation of church and state.

Origins and Development

The Seventh-day Adventists arose from a revivalist movement inspired by the preaching of William Miller (1782–1849), a Baptist lay preacher in New York State. Miller prophesied that Jesus' Second Coming, in 1843, would be followed by the millennium, his thousand-year reign. The Millerite movement attracted a wide following in the northeastern United States. When the prophecy failed to come true, the Adventists broke into several smaller groups, most of which did not survive. Seventh-day Adventists became the most prominent of the ones that did survive.

Early Adventism's apocalyptic beliefs led to ridicule and tensions with government authorities. Its followers, who identified the United States with the second beast of Revelation 13, believed the beast would join together with the "apostate churches" to persecute Adventists. Arrests of Adventist farmers between 1850 and 1895, peaking at more than one hundred arrests during the final decade of that period, were seen as evidence that the expected persecution was already waxing. The farmers, who worked on Sunday after resting on Saturday, were arrested for breaking state "blue laws." During the American Civil War (1861–1865), Adventists, who regarded the taking of human life as the transgression of the commandment "Thou shalt not kill," declared themselves conscientious objectors and refused to fight; they were treated with scorn and their loyalty was questioned.

After the Civil War, Adventists sent out missionaries, and the movement grew internationally as well as within the United States. They built schools, hospitals, and publishing houses. As the movement put down roots and spread, the urgency of its apocalyptic vision became less intense. Ellen White (1827–1915), the influential Adventist prophet, counseled rapprochement with civil authorities to facilitate missionary work around the world. She encouraged Adventists to help prolong America's future so that the Adventist message might flourish.

In 1888 the National Reform Association launched a campaign to extend the Sunday blue laws in effect in some states to the national level. Although Adventists saw the passage of a national "Sunday law" as the culmination of the prophecy of persecutions that would precede the millennium, they felt obliged by Ellen White's counsel to respond boldly to this threat. They established a magazine devoted to religious liberty in 1883; they participated in the lobby that helped defeat legislative bills requiring the observance of Sunday as the day of rest in 1888 and 1889; and they founded the National Religious Liberty Association in 1889. By 1892 their involvement included petitions to both houses of Congress and, eventually, the presentation of legal briefs for their causes in court.

Moves toward Accommodation

In the twentieth century Adventists continued seeking ways to make accommodations with the secular world and maintain their own beliefs. They became identified as strong proponents of the separation of church and state. They built coalitions with other religious groups to lobby for legislation they supported or argue against legislation they considered threatening.

When the United States entered World War I in 1917, Adventists modified their position on military service. By allowing conscripted members to serve as noncombatants (soldiers without arms), usually in medical units, they could uphold their faith while expressing their patriotism. Service in medical units also helped to resolve the other major problem posed by conscription, the threat to observance of the Sabbath. Adventists regarded medical work on the Sabbath as legitimate since it was "doing good." They still faced problems concerning Sabbath observance during basic training, however, and many were imprisoned for disobeying officers.

During the years between World Wars I and II, Adventists sought accreditation for their educational institutions. With the new focus on accreditation, colleges sent their faculty members to secular universities for doctoral studies. The quality of education improved, and secular content in curriculums was expanded. These changes prepared the way for increased upward mobility of graduates.

With the outbreak of World War II in Europe, in 1939, Adventists reached out to cement relationships with the American military and, through them, with political authorities. To make their members attractive to medical units, they again established a program to give medical training to potential draftees. Their American Medical Cadet Corps was directed and supervised by regular army officers, through cooperation with the armed forces. Adventists had become "conscientious cooperators."

During the Korean War in the 1950s, Adventist military chaplains, who were paid by the armed forces and had regular military careers, were appointed for the first time. In 1954 the U.S. Army established a special camp where all noncombatants could receive basic training. More than half the men trained there were Adventists. That same year the U.S. surgeon general contacted Adventist headquarters, seeking approval for the army to ask Adventist draftees to volunteer in biological warfare research. With the encouragement of church leaders, 2,200 Adventists participated in the program between 1955 and 1973.

The Adventist relationship with the state in America had clearly become more comfortable. In 1943 the U.S. Supreme Court, in *Barnette v. West Virginia State Board of Education,* reversed an earlier decision that allowed school boards to expel Jehovah's Witnesses who refused to salute the flag, thus strengthening religious liberty, and President Franklin D.

Roosevelt included religious freedom as one of his four basic freedoms. The editor of the church's paper commented that the millennium lay further in the future. After the war there was considerable debate within American Adventism over the extent to which it should accept the government aid that had become available to private institutions, such as schools and hospitals. The decision to accept aid for its institutions, with some restrictions, compromised the Adventists' previously unyielding stand on the separation of church and state.

In the early 1980s, church leaders discovered that vast sums in government aid were available for relief and development work. They transformed the church's disaster relief agency into the Adventist Development and Relief Agency (ADRA), which they viewed as an "entering wedge" that could penetrate regions where conventional missionaries were often unwelcome. In many ways, however, the source of the funds and the restrictions placed on their use gave the appearance of making this agency an arm of American foreign policy. For example, during the 1980s, when the U.S. government opposed the Nicaraguan government, ADRA distributed aid generously in Honduras but provided nothing to the people of Nicaragua.

Adventists and the U.S. Courts

Until the coming of the five-day work week in the 1930s, almost all Adventists who needed employment (unless they worked for the church or for other members) faced problems in gaining and keeping jobs. Thereafter, any who were required to work shifts continued to face problems. In spite of the arrests of Adventists during the nineteenth century for working on Sunday, and the extent to which they continued to be at a disadvantage in the twentieth-century job market, Adventists developed no concerted legal response. They had few attorneys among their members and lacked grounds for defense. Even though the adoption of a five-day week opened many jobs to them, they were still excluded from shifts that required work on Friday night or Saturday. As Adventist members became urbanized in the interwar years, and as many employers sought to increase efficiency by working factories multiple shifts, pressures mounted for the church's General Conference to work for change.

Responding to these pressures, the General Conference took the first step toward building a legal department in 1936. Moreover, the development of the legal doctrine of incorporation about the time of World War II obliged the states to honor the constitutional guarantee of religious freedom. The doctrine of incorporation refers to the process in which the Supreme Court identified certain rights—those in the Bill of Rights—as inherently "incorporated" in the Fourteenth Amendment concept of due process. Incorporation meant, in effect, that such rights were made binding on the states through the Fourteenth Amendment. The free exercise clause was incorporated in *Cantwell v. Connecticut* (1940); the establishment clause was incorporated in *Everson v. Board of Education* (1947). Despite these developments, however, the Adventists' first strategy for change was not through the courts but was an attempt to negotiate solutions directly with employers.

Eventually, however, individual Adventists began to turn to the courts, and one of these cases (*Sherbert v. Verner*, 1963) resulted in a landmark Supreme Court decision. This case addressed the issue of an employee, fired for refusing to work on her Sabbath, who subsequently had been declared ineligible for unemployment benefits. The Court found that her disqualification from benefits because she had refused to accept employment that would have contravened her religious beliefs "imposed a burden on the free exercise of her religion." The decision propounded the first clear theory of the free exercise clause of the Constitution, which requires the state to demonstrate a compelling interest if a decision running counter to a religious belief is to withstand challenge. *Sherbert* consequently became an important precedent.

The number of court cases brought by Adventists has multiplied since *Sherbert*. The General Conference has sharply increased the size of its legal department and the number of cases litigated in house. These cases have recognized the right of Adventists to engage in door-to-door activity (*Tate v. Akers*, 1977; *Espinoza v. Rusk*, 1980); protected members with a conscientious objection to union membership (*Nottelson v. Smith*, 1981; *Tooley v. Martin-Marietta Corp.*, 1981); and extended the protection of unemployment benefits for those dismissed because of conflicts over the Sabbath to new converts (*Hobbie v. Unemployment Appeals Commission*, 1987). Most cases, however, have focused on attempts to preserve the jobs of Sabbatarians through application of the antidiscrimination clauses of Title VII of the Civil Rights Act of 1964, as amended in 1972. These cases have been relatively ineffective, however, because of a narrow interpretation given by the Supreme Court to the "escape" clause, which says that accommodation should not cause an employer "undue hardship." Adventism, then, has made the least legal progress in the area most important to it: Adventists still are frequently excluded from shifts that require work on Friday nights or Saturdays.

Adventist institutions, hospitals in particular, played a major role in accommodating Adventism to society. Hospitals were obliged to come under government regulation; they attracted patients from their communities; and their staffing needs encouraged members to seek higher levels of education. The participation of Adventist hospitals (and publishers) in the broader society, and especially in selling their products and services, led many of these institutions into disputes that had to be settled in the courts.

As members gained confidence in the court system and became more independent of church control, they were willing to initiate suits against their church and its institutions when they felt wronged by them and the problems seemed intractable. In some cases they were joined by government agencies seeking to enforce statutes outlawing discrimination on the basis of gender and race. The most important of these were a series of suits brought against the Pacific Press Publishing Association of Mountain View, California, in the 1970s. In these cases women charged discrimination in salaries and opportunities for promotion and—when they were fired as a result of their suits—retaliation *(Equal Employment Opportunity Commission and Silver v. Pacific Press Publishing Association,* 1976; *Equal Employment Opportunity Commission v. Pacific Press,* 1982). The church's defense, which was based principally on the free exercise clause of the Constitution, was based on a belief that its institutions, as religious organizations, were immune to antidiscrimination laws and a fear of state interference that was rooted in its apocalyptic expectations. The Court ruled that it was Congress's intent to prohibit religious organizations from discriminating among their employees and that applying the law to employees who did not fulfill the functions of a minister did not violate the First Amendment. This decision affected the rights of millions of employees of religious organizations and has since been cited widely in other cases.

Perhaps the most striking symbol of the Adventist Church's accommodation to its environment was its decision to trademark its name, an act that was completed in 1981. This church, whose apocalyptic vision had led it to expect persecution at the hands of the government, has made use of the government's legal system to attack schismatic Adventist groups *(General Conference Corporation of Seventh-day Adventist v. Seventh-day Adventist Congregational Church,* 1989) and disapproved organizations of church members, such as one representing gay and lesbian Adventists *(General Conference Corporation of Seventh-day Adventist v. Seventh-day Adventist Kinship, International, Inc.,* 1991). These cases mark a huge shift in its position.

Church-State Relations outside the United States

An important element of Adventism was sending missionaries to countries outside the United States. Adventists abroad modified the practices to fit the options open to them. Their primary goal was to avoid conflict with the state. During World War I, Adventists in Germany (which had the second largest concentration of Adventists), moved both by patriotism and the realization that the imperial government would not countenance a noncombatant position, reversed their earlier stance and chose to serve as combatants. This decision resulted in a bitter schism. The pacifist "two percent" who refused to compromise with the state created the schismatic Seventh Day Adventist Reform Movement.

A similar compromise was made in the Soviet Union when Joseph Stalin, the communist dictator, attacked religious freedom. In 1928 Russian Adventist leaders proclaimed that military service was a Christian duty and that anyone teaching otherwise must leave the church. They accepted new laws that proscribed proselytizing and charitable work. Although this capitulation allowed the Adventists to function openly, it caused another schism and brought persecution when the break-away members went underground. The schismatics called themselves the True and Free Adventists: "true" because they were faithful to the commandments to observe the Sabbath and refrain from killing and "free" because they refused to be registered by the government.

In Nazi Germany Adventists went out of their way to cooperate with authorities, fearing that their observance of the Sabbath and certain food prohibitions would result in their being confused with Jews. They expressed enthusiastic support for Hitler, most of their conscripts bore arms willingly even though they had been accorded the right to opt for medical duties, and some turned in pacifist Reformed Adventists to the authorities to distance themselves from the schismatics.

The major exception to this pattern of compromise occurred in South Korea during the Korean War in the 1950s. As a result of serving beside American troops, Korean Adventists trained for and sought positions in medical units, even though positions were not guaranteed. Two members who failed to secure noncombatant positions were executed when they refused to use their weapons; dozens of others faced long prison terms.

In recent decades, Adventists have sponsored several international congresses to highlight issues of religious liberty—though these congresses have not focused on the issue of separation of church and state. Indeed, the onetime policy of avoiding trouble abroad has been replaced by the pursuit of political advantages with various governments. Adventists were successful in establishing such relationships with authoritarian regimes, of both the left and the right, in Eastern Europe, Latin America, Africa, and Asia. The leaders of the General Conference frequently became actively involved in these relationships. Adventists sought liberties (freedom to evangelize, freedom to observe their Sabbath, protection of their institutions) and favors (accreditation of their schools). In return, they were willing to help legitimate or otherwise assist the regimes.

For example, Neil Wilson, president of the General Conference in the 1980s, intervened personally in the Soviet Union and Hungary, where schismatic Adventist groups, discontented with the church's history of making compromises with the state, were an irritant to political leaders. In both cases Wilson gave his blessing to the church, announcing that the official branch of the world church was the one recognized by the state. Both interventions resulted in favored treatment by the governments, and Adventists gained permission to establish a seminary outside Moscow.

In Chile the Adventist college was at a great disadvantage because it did not have accreditation. When Gen. Augusto Pinochet, the Chilean president, was invited to visit, he was greeted in a welcoming ceremony before television cameras, during which the college president offered a prayer thanking God for sending Pinochet to save the nation. This occurred at a time when the president was under attack from the Catholic cardinal for human rights violations. In return for this legitimation, the college received accreditation, and Adventists became known in Chile as "friends of Pinochet."

In Kenya Adventists fostered a close relationship with President Daniel Arap Moi, who in return arranged to provide them with land and a charter for their University of East Africa. In 1988, when the General Conference staged its annual council in Nairobi, its president's speech was reported under the headline, "SDA head lauds Kenya for upholding freedom." This public support was offered to Moi at a time when he was under attack from the National Council of Churches of Kenya for brutalizing opposition leaders and attempting to make constitutional changes designed to help him retain power.

Finally, Adventists have become a noticeable political presence in parts of the developing world. This is especially the case in Jamaica and in Papua New Guinea and other South Pacific island groups, where several Adventists have been cabinet members; in Micronesia, where the president of Palau is a church member; in Uganda, where the vice president (a former prime minister) is an active Adventist; and among the Aymara of Peru, in the highlands around Lake Titicaca. These developments took the leaders at church headquarters in the United States by surprise, for Adventists have rarely walked the corridors of political power in their home country.

See also *Constitution, U.S.; Freedom of religion; Millennialism; Morality; Pacifism; Prejudice; Revivalism; Separation of church and state.*

Ronald Lawson

BIBLIOGRAPHY

Blaich, Roland. "Religion under National Socialism: The Case of the German Adventist Church." *Central European History* 26 (1993): 255–280.

Bull, Malcolm, and Keith Lockhart. *Seeking a Sanctuary: Seventh-day Adventism and the American Dream.* San Francisco: Harper and Row, 1989.

Butler, Jonathan M. "Adventism and the American Experience." In *The Rise of Adventism: Religion and Society in Mid-Nineteenth-Century America,* edited by Edwin S. Gaustad. New York: Harper and Row, 1974.

Lawson, Ronald. "Church and State at Home and Abroad: The Evolution of Seventh-day Adventist Relations with Governments." *Journal of the American Academy of Religion* 64 (1996): 279–311.

———. "Onward Christian Soldiers? Seventh-day Adventists and the Issue of Military Service." *Review of Religious Research* 37 (1996): 97–122.

———. "Sect-State Relations: Accounting for the Differing Trajectories of Seventh-day Adventists and Jehovah's Witnesses." *Sociology of Religion* 56 (1995): 351–377.

Morgan, Douglas. *Adventism and the American Republic.* Bloomington: Indiana University Press, forthcoming.

Sapiets, Marite. *True Witness: The Story of Seventh Day Adventists in the Soviet Union.* Keston, England: Keston College, 1990.

Sicher, Erwin. "Seventh-day Adventist Publications and the Nazi Temptation." *Spectrum* 8 (March 1977): 11–24.

Syme, Eric. *A History of SDA Church-State Relations in the United States.* Mountain View, Calif.: Pacific Press, 1973.

Sexuality

Sexuality is the understanding, expression, and satisfaction of physical and affectional desires through bodily contact in the service of pleasure, intimacy, and procreation. Over the past thirty years no social issue has gained the attention of religious groups more often and more dramatically than two aspects of sexuality—abortion and homosexuality. Indeed, no issue has provided organized religion with a greater opportunity to be heard in the public arena and to influence civil legislation. In 1998, for example, the Christian Coalition, a national organization of evangelical Christians, organized a voter referendum in Maine that repealed the state law protecting lesbians and gay men from discrimination. Also in 1998 the Roman Catholic Church formed a political alliance with conservative Protestant groups to argue that New Jersey's policy of cutting off benefits to welfare recipients who give birth to additional children would encourage abortion.

Religious groups also have debated and adopted positions about the acceptability of homosexuality and the ordination of lesbians and gay men within their own systems of governance. Reputedly liberal bodies, such as the Unitarian Universalist Association, the United Church of Christ, and Reconstructionist Judaism, support a woman's right to a legal abortion and welcome lesbians and gay men as full members, while more conservative, evangelical, and fundamentalist bodies, such as the Catholic Church, the Southern Baptist Convention, and Orthodox Judaism, do not. In between these clear-cut positions are a range of semi-accepting, semi-rejecting, and unsettled positions held by such religious bodies as the Presbyterian Church (U.S.A.), which accepts homosexuals as members but not as ordained clergy, and Reform Judaism, which ordains gay clergy but does not perform gay marriages.

Denominational and Individual Views

Individual members of religious bodies do not always endorse the official positions and actions taken by those bodies. For example, surveys by Barry A. Kosmin and Seymour P. Lachman (1993), Edward O. Laumann et al. (1994), and John C. Green et al. (1996) show that only about half of Catholics in the United States agree with the Vatican's opposition to abortion, that less than half of evangelical Christians oppose gay civil rights, and that many local congregations within liberal religious bodies do not follow their national guidelines for ordaining and hiring gay clergy.

Several factors account for the discrepancy between official positions and members' attitudes. One factor is members' levels of commitment, indicated by frequency of church attendance and observance of religious rituals. Agreement with official positions is greater among those most highly committed than among those least committed. Geographical location is another factor. United Methodists in San Francisco, for example, may be very much more accepting of homosexual relationships than United Methodists in South Carolina. A third factor is the heightened striving of the baby boomer generation for individual fulfillment that questions institutional authority and undermines loyalty to a particular religious body. These people are less likely to adhere to denominational pronouncements than are their parents. Finally, socioeconomic change, such as the shift of many Catholics from working-class to middle-class and upper-middle-class status, has produced a laity that is to the right of the church's traditional support for the poor and to the left of its restrictions on sexual matters.

Not only do the positions taken by religious bodies not necessarily reflect the attitudes of their members, but also the focus of their positions on abortion and homosexuality ignores the other sexual issues and practices that concern their members more directly. For example, within some religious bodies efforts to discuss, study, and educate members about sexuality more broadly, such as the 1991 report of the Special Committee on Human Sexuality of the Presbyterian Church (U.S.A.), have been stopped by their national legislative bodies. The surveyed members of most religious bodies say they want such discussions but actually receive little to no guidance except to refrain from sex before and outside marriage.

In fact, more religious bodies have taken positions on homosexuality than on sexuality in general, and those on sexuality are mostly concerned with prohibiting premarital and extramarital sex. For example, the Southern Baptist Convention passed resolutions opposing homosexuality in 1976, 1977, 1980, and 1985, but only one resolution, in 1981, on heterosexuality that sought to strengthen "chastity before marriage and fidelity to marriage vows" by opposing the distribution of birth control devices to minors without parental consent. A few religious bodies have begun to place more emphasis on the relational and affectional dimensions of sexuality and less on abstract rules about when to or not to engage in sex. For example, in 1983 the Church of the Brethren issued a statement saying that sexuality "encompasses all that we are when we say 'I am female' or 'I am male.'" The statement went on to elaborate that sexuality is not just physical attributes, including genitals: it also includes "all thinking, feeling, acting and interacting" derived from maleness and femaleness.

Definition of Sexuality

In the early twentieth century, the founder of psychoanalysis, Sigmund Freud, observed that for most people sexual life consists of bringing one's own genitals into contact with those of someone of the opposite gender and of introductory and accompanying acts such as kissing, touching, and looking at other parts of the human body. He also found that for many people these accompanying acts or so-called foreplay were more desirable, primary, and important than the genital contact itself. Freud concluded that "sexual" and "genital" are not synonymous, and that sexual activities include more than, and often exclude, genital activity. Sexual life involves obtaining pleasure from various parts of the body and may or may not be brought into the service of reproduction. Sexuality includes not only a range of sexual activities but also how people regard their own bodies, how they express and satisfy their physical and affectional desires, and how they share their bodies with others. One's sexuality, therefore, may integrate or emphasize the procreational, relational, or recreational aspects of sexual activity.

The majority of Americans place more importance on one of these aspects of sexuality than on another. Laumann et al. (1994) found that almost one-third of the population attributes more importance to the procreative aspect and views reproduction as the primary purpose of sexual activity; almost one-half emphasizes the relational aspect and sees sexual activity as a natural part of a committed affectional relationship; and about one-quarter finds the recreational aspect more important and sees pleasure as the primary purpose of sexual activity.

Consistent with Freud's findings, James B. Nelson (1978) and Laumann et al. (1994) have traced the current prevalence of oral sex in the United States to a noticeable shift away from the traditional understanding of sex as brief foreplay that moves quickly to vaginal intercourse. Since the 1920s opposite-gender sex has involved more kissing, more caressing of the body, and more manual and oral stimulation of the genitals. Vaginal intercourse does remain overwhelmingly the sexual practice of choice and most people generally equate sex with this practice, but a significant minority of people do report sexual practices that do not involve vaginal intercourse, and a majority of people report supplementing vaginal intercourse with other sexual activities.

Sexual Practices and Religion

Recent studies provide information about the relationship of these sexual practices and religion. The 1994 study by Laumann et al. compares various groups of Christians and shows that evangelical/fundamentalist Protestants (61 percent) report less often than liberal/moderate Protestants and Catholics (each 78 percent) of having performed oral sex. So, too, do evangelical/fundamentalist Protestants (19 percent) report less often than liberal/moderate Protestants (21 percent) and Catholics (24 percent) having ever engaged in anal sex. Evangelical/fundamentalist Protestants (42 percent) also report less often than liberal/moderate Protestants (58 percent) and Catholics (54 percent) that they have masturbated. And slightly lower percentages of Catholics (less than 3 percent) and evangelical/fundamentalist Protestants (greater than 3 percent) than liberal/moderate Protestants (5 percent) report ever having engaged in same-gender sexual activities. Although involvement in various sexual activities other than vaginal intercourse is reported consistently less often by evangelical/fundamentalist Protestants, their rates are not always much less than those of other Christian groups, and reports do show that almost two-thirds of evangelical fundamentalists have engaged in oral sex, almost 20 percent have engaged in anal sex, more than 40 percent have masturbated, and nearly 4 percent have engaged in same-gender sex. Findings also show that people without formal religious affiliations and with other-than-Christian affiliations report having engaged in anal sex, masturbation, and same-gender sex, but not oral sex, more often than those within Christian groups.

As for sexual satisfaction and the frequency of sexual activity, significant differences are not found among religious groups or between people with and without formal religious affiliations. But the number of sexual contacts per month as reported by evangelical/fundamentalist Protestants (6.8) was slightly greater than that reported by people without religious affiliations (6.5), by Catholics (6.4), by liberal/moderate Protestants (6.0), and by those with other religious affiliations, such as Buddhists and Hindus (5.6). Also, evangelical/fundamentalist Protestants (45 percent) report extreme physical and emotional satisfaction with their current sexual partners somewhat more often than liberal/moderate Protestants (42 percent), those with other religious affiliations (41 percent), Catholics (40 percent), and those without formal religious affiliations (36 percent). However, sexual problems, such as pain during sex, sex without pleasure, inability to reach orgasm, lack of interest in sex, anxiety about performance, early climax, or inability to keep an erection or trouble with lubricating, also are reported slightly more often by evangelical/fundamentalist Protestants (18 percent) than by those without religious affiliations (17 percent), by Catholics (15 percent), by liberal/moderate Protestants (14 percent), and by those with other-than-Christian affiliations (less than 14 percent). And unwanted, coercive sex is reported more often by women without religious affiliations (31 percent) than by evangelical/fundamentalist Protestant women (25 percent), liberal/moderate Protestant women (21 percent), or Catholic women (17 percent). Although evangelical/fundamentalist Protestants report a slightly higher frequency of sex and rate of sexual satisfaction, they also report sexual problems more often.

A look at fertility reveals that evangelical/fundamentalist Protestants have notably more children than do liberal/moderate Protestants and Catholics. Even lower fertility rates are reported by those with no religious affiliation and by those with other-than-Christian affiliations such as Buddhists, Hindus, and Jews—with the exception of Orthodox Jews, whose rates resemble those of evangelical/fundamentalist Protestants. But about 50 percent of those in each Christian group, in other religious groups, and without religious affiliation report always using contraception with their primary sexual partners. Sterility-by-choice (vasectomy for men and tubal ligation for women) is reported more often by evangelical/fundamentalist Protestants (24 percent) and liberal/moderate Protestants (23 percent) than by those without religious affiliations (19 percent), Catholics (15 percent), and those with other-than-Christian affiliations (13 percent). Abortions are reported less often by members of each Christian group (about 10 percent) than by those without religious affiliations (14 percent) and those with other-than-Christian affiliations (22 percent). Among Christians, evangelical/fundamentalist Protestants (8 percent) report abortions slightly less often than Catholics (9 percent) and liberal/moderate Protestants (10 percent). Although evangelical/fundamentalist Protestants report the highest fertility rates, they do not appear to control fertility by artificial means less often than those within other religious groups and those without religious affiliations.

Sexual Practices and Social Policy

Social science data do not show any consistent or striking pattern in the sexual activities and interests of people across various religious groups. Evangelical/fundamentalist Protestants do appear to engage in nonprocreative sexual activities less often and to experience sexual satisfaction and to engage in sex more often than other groups, but they also report sexual problems more often and efforts to control fertility as often as other groups. Those in other-than-Christian groups appear to engage in sex less frequently than those in Christian groups, but they also report sexual problems less often than those in Christian groups and those without religious affiliations. And those without religious affiliations report nonprocreative sexual activities more often, but they also report sexual satisfaction less often and sexual coercion more often than those within religious groups.

These comparisons, then, reveal a patchwork of inconsistent, small differences in the sexual lives of Americans rather than the distinct divisions that characterize policy debates about sexual issues within civil and religious governing bodies. Even though evangelical Christians and the religiously unaffiliated are the fastest-growing groups in the United States, the differences between the sexual activities and views of each group are not well enough defined to align groups consistently with opposing positions. In fact, the religiously unaffiliated are not organized or mobilized. And although evangelical Christians have the highest level of commitment among religious groups and most often expect their leaders to be involved in social and political matters, they themselves have lower levels of actual public involvement than either mainline Protestants or Catholics. In general, the similarity with which most Americans approach sexual activities is not reflected in public and national debates. In addition, most religiously affiliated people feel that their respective religious bodies do not deal with the sexual issues that affect people most directly, and they cannot be relied on to deliver a predictable set of views on sexuality by virtue of the religious group of which they are a part.

The overlapping similarity of views across religious groups and diversity of views within groups can be grasped clearly by returning to the three primary ways—procreational, relational, recreational—in which people organize their sexual lives. Those in the population who emphasize procreation as the basis for their sexuality are united by their disapproval of premarital, extramarital, and same-gender sex and their adherence to orthodox religious doctrine, but they are divided on abortion. Half are as solidly in favor of a woman's right to obtain a legal abortion for any reason as the other half are against it.

Those in the population who emphasize relationship as the basis for their sexuality are united by their greater openness to premarital adult sex and their unwillingness to have sex with someone they do not love, but they do not share similar religious orientations. Some adhere to the views of mainstream moderate religious bodies that disapprove of premarital teenage sex, pornography, homosexuality, and abortion; others adhere to the views of liberal religious bodies and are more tolerant of those same issues. And still others are not influenced by any religious body but approve of those same issues with the exception of homosexuality.

Finally, those Americans who emphasize recreation as the basis for their sexuality are united by their acceptance of premarital sex and pornography, their greater tolerance for extramarital sex, their willingness to have sex with someone they do not love, and a lack of religious influence on their views, but many of them approve of abortion and homosexuality, and a corresponding large number of them do not.

Thus, when considering how people within, for example, the four largest religious groups in the United States view the currently most prominent sexual issues in the political arena, one finds small differences between the groups but different rank orders of groups in their approval for each issue: Catholics most often report support for gay civil rights (75 percent), followed by mainline Protestants (72 percent), black Protestants (71 percent), and evangelical Protestants (55 percent). Mainline Protestants most often report support for reproductive rights (68 percent), followed by black Protestants (56 percent), Catholics (54 percent), and evangelical Protestants (50 percent).

See also *Abortion; Feminism; Gender; Homosexuality.*

Gary David Comstock

BIBLIOGRAPHY

Comstock, Gary David. *Unrepentant, Self-Affirming, Practicing: Lesbian/Bisexual/Gay People Within Organized Religion.* New York: Continuum, 1996.

Green, John C., James L. Guth, Corwin E. Smidt, and Lyman A. Kellstedt, eds. *Religion and the Culture Wars.* Lanham, Md.: Rowman and Littlefield, 1996.

Kosmin, Barry A., and Seymour P. Lachman. *One Nation under God: Religion in Contemporary American Society.* New York: Harmony Books, 1993.

Laumann, Edward O., John H. Gagnon, Robert T. Michael, and Stuart Michaels. *The Social Organization of Sexuality: Sexual Practices in the United States.* Chicago: University of Chicago Press, 1994.

Melton, J. Gordon, and Nicholas Piediscalzi, eds. *The Churches Speak on Sex and Family Life: Official Statements from Religious Bodies and Ecumenical Organizations.* Detroit: Gale Research, 1991.

Nelson, James B. *Embodiment: An Approach to Sexuality and Christian Theology.* Minneapolis: Augsburg, 1978.

Pew Research Center for the People and the Press. "The Diminishing Divide . . . American Churches, American Politics." Washington, D.C., June 1996.

Presbyterian Church (U.S.A.). *Presbyterians and Human Sexuality 1991.* Louisville, Ky.: Office of the General Assembly, PCUSA, 1991.

Shiʿi Islam

See *Islam*

Shinto

Shinto, a collection of rites and beliefs concerning *kami*—a diverse group of mythological gods and goddesses, deified forces of nature and natural objects, and deified human beings—has at times received strong support from the Japanese government. The term *Shinto* literally translated means "the way of the *kami*."

From the beginning of its history, Shinto has been identified as an indigenous form of religion of the Japanese people, closely allied with Japan's other religious traditions (especially Buddhism) and with the Japanese state. Before ancient Japan entered into formal contact with the Asian continent in the first three centuries of the Christian era, no term existed to name the rites and beliefs of the Japanese people. It was only with the advent of Buddhism, formally introduced in the sixth century, that the word *Shinto* began to be used to distinguish indigenous thought and ritual from Buddhism. Through the medieval and early modern periods, Shinto theology developed in relation to Buddhism, in the sense that one of its central questions concerns the relation of Buddhas and *kami* to each other. Closely connected with that line of inquiry is another strand of philosophical thought seeking to clarify the relation between the *kami* and the imperial house, or to establish a theologically based rationale for its rule. In the modern period, much contention has surrounded the question of whether Shinto can be understood as a "religion," and this dispute has been linked to constitutional questions of religion and state, and of religious freedom.

For much of its history, Shinto existed not as a unified tradition but as the esoterically transmitted rituals and beliefs of the priests associated with particular shrines, without a sacred book or other generally recognized textual source. No central authority existed to ordain priests outside these separate priestly lineages before the advent of Shinto universities in the modern period, such as Kokugakuin University or Kogakkan University. No national association of Shinto priests was founded until 1900. There is no single leader of Shinto and no central institution to act as guide. The Association of Shinto Shrines is the most authoritative administrative body, and the Ise Shrines are regarded as most prestigious. There is a continuity in Shinto philosophy, heavily influenced by Confucian and Buddhist thought, but the influence of this philosophy over popular religiosity has been limited.

Shinto has been understood in popular religious practice to be complementary to Buddhism, with Shinto deities described as the phenomenal manifestations or earthly protectors of the universal, cosmic deities of Buddhism. Shinto has consistently sought a special connection to the imperial house, whose mythological ancestors (most especially Amaterasu Omikami, the sun goddess) are believed to be enshrined at the Ise Shrines. Shinto theology describes Japan as "the land of the gods," and the emperor has been regarded as a divine being, a belief that was codified in the Meiji Constitution of 1889. Although Emperor Hirohito, who reigned from 1926 to 1988, refuted the idea of his divinity as part of his announcement of Japan's surrender at the conclusion of World War II, this belief persists at a popular level.

Until Japan's modern period of imperialist expansion in the late nineteenth and early twentieth centuries, Shinto remained an entirely indigenous tradition. All the *kami* originate in Japan, and they are commonly understood to be restricted to the Japanese people. Some modern, sectarian types of Shinto regard the *kami* as universal deities, but this belief is rather rare. In the era of imperialist takeovers before 1945, however, worship of the *kami* was "exported" to Korea, Taiwan, and Japan's other colonies and forced upon colonial peoples as one expression of their submission to Japanese rule. Not surprisingly, shrines built in Korea and elsewhere were among the first Japanese buildings torn down by former colonials at the end of World War II.

Throughout its modern history, Shinto's theologians have argued that Shinto is less a religion than the rites and creed of the Japanese nation. This interpretation has made it possible to argue that, unlike religion, which is subject to individual conviction and therefore may be practiced or not, according to freedom of religion, Shinto is a suprareligious entity and falls within the duties of Japanese citizens, who thus can be compelled to support shrines, participate in their rites, and observe worship practices in the home. While this position is not frequently advanced today, ambiguity continues to surround the question of whether or not Shinto is properly considered a religion.

Shinto Mythology and the Early Japanese State

The Yamato clan achieved hegemony over other clans by the fourth century, marking the beginning of the ancient Japanese state. It commissioned the compilation of the myths and traditions of its own and other clans into a single mythic narrative that provided it with a rationale for its rule. According to myths compiled as the *Kojiki* (712) and the *Nihonshoki* (720), the Yamato are descendants of the sun goddess Amaterasu Omikami. She and other deities created the Japanese islands and the Japanese people, who thus share in the sacred origins of the imperial line. Amaterasu supposedly dispatched her grandson Ninigi to rule over Japan as its first emperor.

The Yamato clan's worship of its divine ancestors was centered at Ise, where the shrines date to the third century. Other clans followed a similar practice of enshrining ancestral deities in clan shrines, and deceased clan rulers as well as emperors were entombed in great tumuli, or mounds, called *kofun* until the mid-seventh century.

The advent of Buddhism allowed the Yamato clan to sponsor a universal religion with its own rationale for political rule transcending the old loyalties based on kinship and territory, but this did not mean that myths and rites of the *kami* were left behind. Instead, political rule came to be legitimated by these two lines of thought simultaneously. A new emperor underwent succession and accession ritual in both modes, so that not only was he united with his divine *kami* ancestors, receiving the three imperial regalia of mirror, sword, and sacred jewels, but also underwent Buddhist rites invoking Buddhism's ideal of the Wheel-Turning King, based on the model of the Indian king Asoka. From the seventh century, deceased emperors were given Buddhist funerals and memorial rites.

When a bureaucratic state based on the Chinese model was instituted in the seventh century, the imperial court began conducting an elaborate annual calendar of rites derived from Buddhism, Daoism, and Shinto, without declaring exclusive allegiance to a single tradition. In effect, all these traditions, as well as Confucianism, found a place in a multifaceted ritual, symbolic, and philosophical legitimation of the political order. Shinto's distinctive contribution to this assemblage lay in its ritual symbolism based on agriculture; the priestly order's emphasis on purity, purification, and the performance of abstinences; and on the priests' service to the *kami,* understood as one kind of divine protector of the state.

The Medieval Period

Medieval Shinto philosophy emphasized the theory elaborated in the fourteenth century by the statesman Kitabatake Chikafusa in his treatise *Jinnoshotoki* that Japan is and must always be ruled by an "unbroken line" of sovereigns. In this way, Japan would always be divinely guided, and imperial rule would always rest on a sacred foundation. Other Shinto theologians sought to establish a new preeminence for the *kami* by claiming that the *kami* were original divinities while the Buddhas were merely secondary. Their writings circulated mainly within shrine lineages and were submitted as memorials at court, but it is doubtful that they were widely known outside these circles.

Meanwhile, however, shrines originating as clan shrines expanded, generally in combination with Buddhist temples also originally sponsored by a clan. These temple-shrine complexes became large landowners in the medieval period, ruling with a free hand over their resident peasantry. Temple and shrine lands in the medieval period enjoyed a kind of "extraterritoriality" in that shogunal officials (military governors) were prohibited entry. The religious institutions exercised police, judicial, and taxation authority over their residents, without having to consult civil authority.

The Early Modern Period

This extraterritoriality was abolished in the succeeding Edo period (1600–1868), but both temples and shrines retained significant landholdings. The affairs of temples and shrines were put under a shogunal magistrate of temples and shrines, one of the highest offices in the shogunate. Shrine priests were placed under one of two shrine lineages, the Shirakawa (mainly associated with imperial ritual) and the Yoshida, which took in the great majority. By making payments to the Yoshida, provincial shrines and priests could advance in rank. Shinto philosophy during the Edo period was revitalized by the Shinto scholar Motoori Norinaga's great study of the *Kojiki,* titled *Kojikiden.* In this work, completed in 1798, Motoori mined the ancient myths to discover the life of the ancient Japanese before the advent of Buddhism. His assumption was that the spiritual life of the people and their original unity with the *kami* had been distorted by Buddhism, a foreign religion. Nativist philosophy stemming from Motoori's work was known as *kokugaku,* or National Learning. Although it began as a kind of historical-philological scholarship, during the nineteenth century, under the stimulus of the scholar Hirata Atsutane and his followers, it developed into a philosophy and a religious movement within the Shinto priesthood closely associated with xenophobia and the desire to rid shrines of all Buddhist elements. In truth, wherever Buddhism and Shinto were combined in one institution (a temple-shrine complex), the Buddhist clerics, because of their greater education and a higher level of state patronage, almost always had the advantage. The persistence of this situation through the Edo period meant that the Shinto priesthood had by its end built up a tremendous resentment against Buddhism.

Modern Japan (The Meiji Period to 1945)

This resentment was unleashed early in the Meiji period (1868–1912) in the "movement to destroy Buddhism," which closely followed a government order for the separation of Buddhism and Shinto in 1868. In effect, the official call for "separation" was taken as a tacit call for destruction, issued as it was by a faction within the early Meiji state that was closely associated with National Learning.

The term *State Shinto* is used to describe a systemic state support for Shinto in the modern period. It encompassed government support for and regulation of shrines and priests, the emperor's priestly roles, state creation of Shinto doctrine and ritual, construction of shrines in imperial Japan's colonies, compulsory participation in shrine rites, teaching Shinto myth as history, and suppression of other religions that contradicted some aspect of Shinto. Between 1870 and 1884, Shinto bureaucrats attempted to make a state religion out of Shinto, through the Great Promulgation Campaign. Bureaucrats composed an official creed loosely based on Shinto, and authorized Shinto priests to create a network of preachers to spread it to the populace. But because the creed had no basis whatever in popular religiosity, and because it mostly consisted of platitudinous injunctions to obey civil authority and revere the emperor (who previously had played no role in popular religious life), the people found it incomprehensible and the priests ludicrous. When the campaign failed, Shinto bureaucrats fell out of favor, and state support for Shinto declined. From about 1880 to 1905 the Shinto priests gradually organized themselves nationally to respond to what they saw as a deplorable lack of state support. A national association of priests was formed in 1900.

During the early Meiji period, shrines were drawn into a national hierarchy and into a unified annual ritual calendar centering on imperial ritual and observances on new, national holidays, with newly created national symbols, such as a flag and an anthem. This gave the shrines a national focus for the first time. The cult of the war dead was institutionalized with the construction of the Yasukuni Shrine (1879) in Tokyo and an associated network of provincial shrines for the war dead, the Nation-Protecting Shrines. The fate of dying in battle was upheld as the highest possible honor for a Japanese subject, since the emperor personally visited the Yasukuni Shrine to honor the spirits enshrined there.

Japan's victory in the Russo-Japanese War in 1905 stimulated a great expansion of Shinto's influence. The dead from this war were enshrined at Yasukuni (as those from the Sino-Japanese War of 1894–1895 had been), bringing many ordinary people to Tokyo to pay respect to their loved ones enshrined so splendidly in the nation's capital. The annexation of Korea in 1910 and the colonization of Manchuria led to a heightened mood of patriotism and to energetic shrine construction in the colonies. The state increased its support of Shinto and financed the training of shrine priests. Shrine priests of a certain rank became teachers in the public schools, where they promoted the teaching of mythology as history. Rites to revere the imperial portrait and ceremonial recitations of the Imperial Rescript on Education were established as regular school observances, along with pilgrimages to shrines for school pupils. Observance of shrine rites in local communities began to assume a semiobligatory character, and local administrations routinely assessed residents for the support of shrines.

Popular religious life was also influenced by state suppression and intimidation using Shinto elements. Most striking was the suppression in 1921 and again in 1935 of the rapidly growing new religion Omotokyo, which had been founded in 1892. Other religions were suppressed on charges of *lèse-majesté* if their doctrines conflicted with Shinto mythology. In 1932 Christian students of Sophia University refused to pay tribute at the Yasukuni Shrine, and a national outcry arose accusing Christianity as a whole of being unpatriotic.

In 1940 a Board of Rites was established within the state government, marking a further expansion of Shinto's influence. State appropriations for priests' training and for shrines continued at a high level. Shinto exerted great influence on popular religious life as more households enshrined talismans from the Ise Shrines in their homes. During World War II Shinto priests served as chaplains, and local shrine parishes were mobilized to support the war effort.

Contemporary Japan (1945 to Present)

State Shinto came to an end with the Shinto Directive of 1945. This administrative directive, which remained in force until the end of the Allied Occupation, prohibited all state support for and patronage of Shinto and directed that all Shinto influence be removed from the public schools. All bureaucratic mechanisms for the administration of shrines were dismantled, and many Shinto figures were purged. The priesthood as a whole suffered an immediate and seemingly irreversible loss of prestige. In the years since 1945, Shinto has, in addition, been dealt a heavy blow by the same demographic changes that have undermined the economic base of Buddhism.

Although all official relations between Shinto and the state were severed, various forms of covert support have quietly been reinstated, such as provision of official information about the death of combatants to the Yasukuni Shrine and denial of the same service to other religious groups that have requested it. It is notable that the state seeks to expand its connection only with Shinto religious bodies, not with Buddhist or other institutions. Meanwhile, the Supreme Court has gradually expanded the scope of religious activity deemed permissible to the state under the constitution.

The Yasukuni Shrine remains the center of much controversy, and the state has staked and lost much prestige on five failed efforts to reestablish state support for this shrine. So eager is the state to reappropriate Shinto symbolism in articulating a myth of cultural identity that it has supported several judicial decisions that seem to move toward a reestablishment of the former alliance of Shinto and the state, even when a curtailment of individual religious liberties is involved.

Shinto priests prepare to celebrate the new year at Tokyo's Meiji Shrine. The Japanese government in recent years has sought to revive Shinto symbolism in public life.

The general populace remains unaware of, and unconcerned with, these postwar developments for the most part. While some citizens, mainly Christians and members of those religious movements persecuted before 1945, closely monitor the state's actions in this area and protest vigorously, they are a minority. The academic community has consistently opposed all state efforts to revive Shinto symbolism, whether it be state support for the Yasukuni Shrine or the attempt to give legal status to the national flag, anthem, or names of reigns of the emperors as the official form of dating. Because of the postwar era's open and pluralistic political culture, the state must answer these vocal critics and is not free to reestablish its former patronage of Shinto without debate, although the priesthood overwhelmingly favors a return to the prewar situation.

See also *Buddha; Confucianism; Japan.*

Helen Hardacre

BIBLIOGRAPHY

Hardacre, Helen. *Shinto and the State, 1868–1988.* Princeton: Princeton University Press, 1989.

Holtom, Daniel Clarence. *Modern Japan and Shinto Nationalism: A Study of Present-day Trends in Japanese Religions.* New York: Paragon Book Reprint Corp., 1963.

Lokowandt, Ernst. *Die rechtliche Entwicklung des Staats-Shinto in der ersten Halfte der Meiji-Zeit (1868–1890).* Wiesbaden, Germany: Harrassowitz, 1978.

———. *Zum Verhaltnis von Staat und Shinto im heutigen Japan: Eine Materialsammlung.* Wiesbaden, Germany: Harrassowitz, 1981.

O'Brien, David M., with Yasuo Ohkoshi. *To Dream of Dreams: Religious Freedom and Constitutional Politics in Postwar Japan.* Honolulu: University of Hawaii Press, 1996.

Social Gospel

The Social Gospel was a theological and institutional reform movement in the United States among liberal Protestants, responding to changes in American culture in the late nineteenth century. Profound social change marked the decades at the turn of the twentieth century as industrialization and the growth of cities challenged American institutions and people in significant ways. A massive influx of immigrants altered the face of the population, and the rise of corporate capitalism changed the way Americans related to the economy. Labor unrest raised the specter of social chaos. Two notable events were the Haymarket affair of 1886, when a Chicago riot that killed both strikers and policemen was blamed on anarchists, and the Pullman strike of 1893, when workers for the Chicago-based railcar company shut down the nation's railroads.

These changes challenged the Protestant churches that had dominated American religion for more than two centuries. Immigration and secularization threatened the cultural authority of the churches, while industrialization and urbanization forced them to confront social disorder and injustice. In response, conservative churches formed rescue missions, and radical Protestants turned to socialism. The leaders of the evangelical liberal mainstream of Protestantism responded both to their challenged role and to social problems with the Social Gospel. This movement, strong from the 1880s until World War I (1914–1918), was both progressive and conservative. At its heart the Social Gospel movement was communitarian, trying to re-create the seventeenth-century Puritan commonwealth for an industrial age.

The Theological Movement

The Social Gospel was actually two movements—one theological, one institutional. The former has been better studied, while the latter was longer lasting. Theologically, the Social Gospel was rooted in Anglo-American liberal evangelical thought of the late nineteenth century, leavened with insights from the new fields of sociology and economics. This liberalism led to a faith in progress and the perfectibility of human society and a confidence that humans could bring about the Kingdom of God—a belief known as postmillennialism. (Conservative Christians, on the other hand, believed in premillennialism, the idea that only the bodily return of Jesus Christ could change the world.)

The best known of these thinkers were Washington Gladden, Robert Ely, and Walter Rauschenbusch. Gladden, a Congregationalist clergyman and advocate for labor, was also an early supporter of African American writer W. E. B. Du Bois. Ely, an economist who founded the American Economic Association (1885) and the American Institute of Christian Sociology (1893), wrote the *Social Aspects of Christianity* in 1889. Rauschenbusch, the dean of the movement, began his career as a pastor in New York City's Hell's Kitchen, a slum area of immigrants. His most important books were *Christianity and the Social Crisis* (1907), *Christianizing the Social Order* (1912), and the *Theology for the Social Gospel* (1917).

Progressivism lost legitimacy as the carnage of World War I shook liberals' faith in progress and human perfectibility, leading to the eclipse of Social Gospel theology. Later thinkers—such as the theologian Reinhold Niebuhr—criticized these writers for their naiveté about political power and for their patronizing attitude toward labor. Nevertheless, generations of American clergy—most prominently Martin Luther King Jr.—were influenced by the movement's social convictions.

The Institutional Movement

The institutional part of the movement had more long-term effect on American politics, as both clergymen and lay people responded to the massive changes in American society. Like the theologians, they were largely middle class; their work sought to bolster bourgeois society while moving beyond individual charity to social change. Most of this work was in northern cities. Clergymen in urban churches created organizations to address the needs of the city and recent immigrants. The most important were institutional churches, large facilities with classrooms, gymnasiums, and workshops, working to help slum residents integrate into the middle class—and make them less threatening to the social order. Most of the work in these organizations was done by laywomen, such as Jane Addams of Chicago's Hull House, who established settlement houses to improve life in the urban slums. These women, informed by their faith, idealism, and the new field of social science, involved themselves in urban and labor issues. The activists led a crusade to counteract the dominant materialism of the day.

Like much of the Progressive movement, the Social Gospel excelled in creating organizations and bureaucracies to direct and combine the energies evoked by these churches and individuals. The Young Men's Christian Association and the Student Volunteer Movement, student evangelical organizations born to bring about "the evangelization of the world in this generation," were soon influenced by the Social Gospel and encouraged their members to be active in changing the world as well as saving it.

These decades also saw the creation of activist offices and caucuses within denominations. This trend reached its peak in 1908, when the Methodist Church issued the Social Creed of the Churches. This statement of Social Gospel principles, including the abolition of child labor and the right of workers to earn a living wage, was later adopted by the Federal Council of Churches, which was founded to bring liberal evangelical agencies and energies under one Protestant umbrella. Once again, women did much of the

Walter Rauschenbusch

actual work of such organizations; they often found this work helpful in their quest to find a place in American public life. The most important example is the Women's Christian Temperance Union, led from 1879 to 1898 by Frances Willard.

Although much of the Social Gospel aimed at preserving Protestant hegemony, not all Social Gospelers were Protestant. Roman Catholic and (to a lesser extent) Jewish thinkers and institutions made important contributions. After years of suspicion of labor unions by the Catholic Church, Pope Leo XIII issued an encyclical, *Rerum Novarum* (1891), which was the first endorsement of labor's goals by the Catholic hierarchy. The leading Catholic Social Gospel thinker was John A. Ryan, professor of moral theology and industrial ethics at the Catholic University of America and author of *A Living Wage* (1906) and *Social Reconstruction* (1920). The encyclical and Ryan's work were some of the first contributions of the immigrant Catholic Church to American public theology. Rabbi Stephen Wise's work in New York paralleled much of the Social Gospel's convictions.

Although much of the Social Gospel, both theological and institutional, faded after World War I, the movement created the model for an activist church that still guides many Americans. This model continues to shape the political work of what are now called the mainline churches, as denominational and ecumenical agencies dedicated to social change and political action continue the movement's institutional work. Theologians and ethicists still echo the Social Gospel church's dedication to involvement in a changing and challenging society.

See also *Capitalism; Communitarianism; Evangelicalism; Justice, Social; King, Martin Luther, Jr.; Liberalism; Millennialism; Morality; Temperance movements.*

Daniel Sack

BIBLIOGRAPHY

Abell, Aaron I. *American Catholicism and Social Action: A Search for Social Justice, 1865–1950.* Notre Dame, Ind.: University of Notre Dame Press, 1963.

Curtis, Susan. *A Consuming Faith: The Social Gospel and Modern American Culture.* Baltimore: Johns Hopkins University Press, 1991.

Handy, Robert T. *A Christian America: Protestant Hopes and Historical Realities.* 2d ed. New York: Oxford University Press, 1984.

———, ed. *The Social Gospel in America, 1870–1920.* New York: Oxford University Press, 1966.

Hopkins, C. Howard. *The Rise of the Social Gospel in American Protestantism, 1865–1915.* New Haven: Yale University Press, 1940.

———, and Ronald C. White. *The Social Gospel: Religion and Reform in Changing America.* Philadelphia: Temple University Press, 1976.

Phillips, Paul T. *A Kingdom on Earth: Anglo-American Social Christianity, 1880–1940.* University Park: Pennsylvania State University Press, 1996.

White, Ronald C. *Liberty and Justice for All: Racial Reform and the Social Gospel.* San Francisco: Harper and Row, 1990.

Society of Jesus

See *Jesuits*

Solzhenitsyn, Aleksandr I.

Russian Nobel Prize-winning writer and historian. Solzhenitsyn (1918–) is probably best known in the West as a courageous dissident who for decades dared to oppose the Communist regime in the now defunct Soviet Union. But

Aleksandr Solzhenitsyn

concern for Christian values is a recurring theme in his writings, and he has been called a pioneer in the renaissance of religion in atheist nations. The reason communism took hold in Russia in the first place, he has said, is because men forgot God.

Solzhenitsyn was a follower of the Russian Orthodox Church until age fifteen, when he finally gave in to pressure to became first an atheist and eventually a Marxist. Educated in mathematics and literature, he taught briefly before serving as an artillery officer in the Red Army during World War II and might have returned to teaching had he not written letters criticizing Joseph Stalin, the Soviet dictator. That indiscretion cost him eight years in Siberian prison camps. The brutal conditions there failed to break his spirit; instead, he rediscovered his religious faith, concluding that the line separating good and evil passes not through states or other social or political divisions but through every human heart. Thereafter religion became a sustaining force for Solzhenitsyn, and Christian values became important in his life and work.

His first book, *One Day in the Life of Ivan Denisovich,* was published in the Soviet Union a few years after his release, during the period of liberalization that Soviet leader Nikita Khrushchev instituted. A frank exposé of prison camp life, the book was an immediate success when it appeared in 1962. Khrushchev's ouster in 1964 brought renewed tightening of controls in the Soviet Union, however, and Solzhenitsyn gradually fell out of official favor. He continued writing, publishing his works underground and outside his country, and produced such noted books as *The First Circle* (1968), *Cancer Ward* (1968), and *August 1914* (1971).

In 1970 Solzhenitsyn embarrassed the Soviet regime by winning the Nobel Prize for literature. But it was his explosive book about Stalin's vast system of prison camps, *The Gulag Archipelago* (1973), in which Solzhenitsyn estimated seventy million people perished, that finally provoked his ouster from the Soviet Union in early 1974. Solzhenitsyn spent eighteen years in the United States, writing and calling for an end to the Communist regime in the Soviet Union. He did not support the creation of a government based on Western-style democracy, which he considered materialistic and decadent. Instead, he wanted a benevolent, but authoritarian, government based on the old pre-Communist system in Russia, one that would incorporate Russia's traditional Christian values.

Returning to Russia in 1994, after the fall of the Soviet regime, Solzhenitsyn said he hoped for a spiritual revitalization of Russia. His ideas for political reform were largely dismissed as unrealistic and romantic by established political leaders.

Bruce Wetterau

South Africa

A former Dutch and British colony, South Africa officially adopted apartheid, the politics of racial separateness (later, separate development), in 1948. This policy led to strong organized opposition until the introduction of democracy in 1994.

Religion has been a significant social force in South Africa. More than two-thirds of the population claim to be Christians; nearly a third either choose not to reveal their religious preference or are members of African traditional religions. Hinduism, Islam, and Judaism account for less than 4 percent of the people. Of the Christians, about a third be-

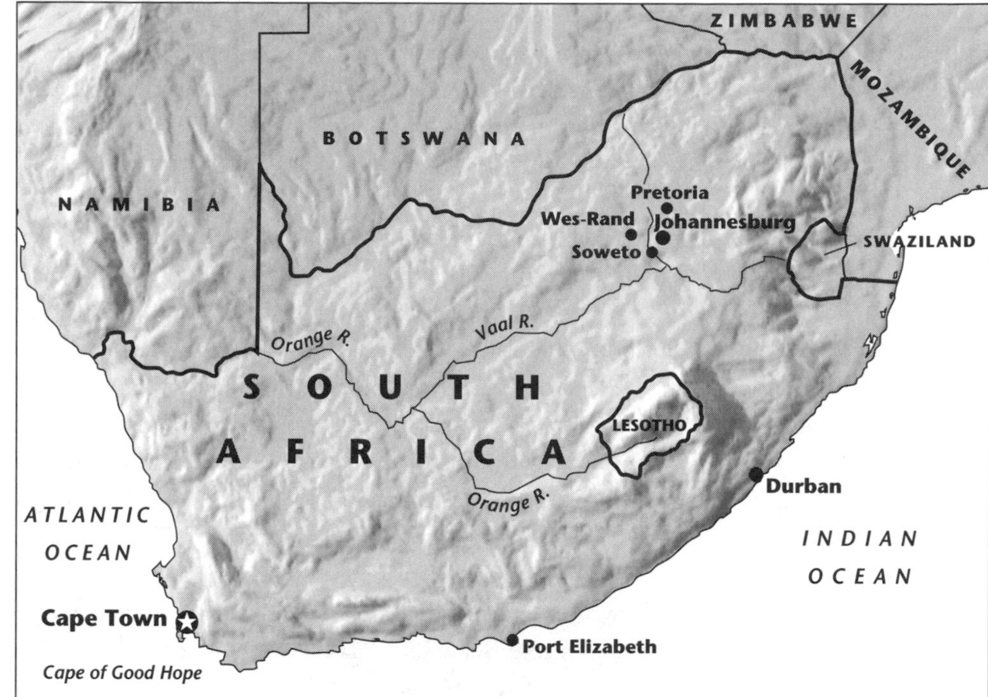

long to African Independent churches and a little more than half that number to the Dutch Reformed churches; another third are Roman Catholics, Methodists, Anglicans, Lutherans, and Presbyterians.

The relationship between politics and religion has a long history in South Africa. Three great migrations affected the religious scene and intricately wove religion into the political, economic, and social fabric of the country. For centuries, San and Khoikhoi people inhabited the land. Beginning about two thousand years ago, black people with traditional African religions migrated into the region, populating a major part of it. A second migration brought Europeans with their different forms of Christianity: the Dutch (1652), followed by French and German Protestants, and British settlers (especially since 1806). A third significant migration brought groups from Asia.

The Colonial Period

Dutch colonial control (1652–1795, 1803–1806) was not religiously motivated, but religious groups like the French Huguenots—Calvinist refugees—soon joined the colony (1688). The Dutch East India Company promoted Reformed Christianity, or Calvinism, as the public religion, and religious intolerance became official policy. Severe restrictions were placed on all non-Calvinists, including Muslims. The exile of Islamic leaders from the East Indies had brought Muslims to the colony, and for a variety of reasons many slaves had become Muslim. In 1804 the Dutch commissioner issued a proclamation separating state and (a subordinate) church and promoting religious toleration.

British rule (1806–1910) continued this policy of toleration. Many English-speaking Christians arrived as soldiers and civil servants, establishing settler churches reflecting their own denominational divisions. Although there was no official state church, many congregations received state support. Protestant missionaries became active.

British rule posed major difficulties for many Dutch colonists. During the mid-1830s many left in the migration to the north known as the Great Trek. The church-state relationship in the newly formed republics was complex. The British defeat of the Boer republics (the Orange Free State and Transvaal) in 1902, and the creation of the Union of South Africa from those republics, the Cape Province, and Natal in 1910 brought colonial conquest to a climax. The Voluntary Act (Cape law since 1875) in principle rendered all denominations and religious faiths equal. In practice, government policy during the twentieth century would publicly uphold Christian values.

Economic developments during the nineteenth century brought religious communities other than Christians. From

1860 to 1911 Indians arrived in Natal as laborers on sugarcane plantations and as independent merchants. Today, approximately 62 percent of the almost one million Indians in South Africa are Hindus. Jewish settlers increased during the nineteenth century, particularly those coming from Lithuania.

Racial tension reaches back to the beginning of colonization. It intensified when Britain, requiring a tightly controlled labor market, implemented laws limiting black ownership of land and imposed taxes, forcing blacks to sell their labor to white landowners. After the Anglo-Boer wars (1880–1881, 1899–1902), caused by the discovery of diamonds in 1867 and gold in 1886, British control led to stricter laws, including segregationist and discriminatory laws restricting the movement of black people, requiring them to carry passes, introducing job reservation (that is, reserving certain kinds of jobs for whites only), and controlling social practices. These laws served to provide cheap labor for the mining industry.

The story of segregation and discrimination also formed part of the story of Christianity. In 1829, when some frontier congregations asked for separate facilities for black converts, the Dutch Reformed Synod insisted that the Lord's Supper be administered to all baptized members, no matter what their color. In 1857 the synod revoked that decision, saying that "due to the weakness of some," blacks and whites could worship separately. What started as a concession became common practice and later determined the structure of the church. In 1881 a separate Dutch Reformed Mission Church was established for "coloured" people. This was followed by several other ethnic churches. Segregation was increasingly regarded as a divine mandate supported by biblical teaching. This church policy would later form the religious roots of the apartheid policy.

The English-speaking settler churches followed a similar practice of segregation. Observers increasingly criticized the missionaries, traditionally regarded as leading the liberal agitation during the nineteenth century, for their complicity, often indirect, in the imperial colonial enterprise.

Apartheid

In 1948 the Nationalist Party came to power, propagating a policy of apartheid based on a comprehensive set of racial laws. The Afrikaners' defeat in the Anglo-Boer War of 1899–1902 strengthened their desire to control their own destiny. The Nationalist Party was more a nationalist movement than a political organization. The Afrikaner Broederbond became a powerful secret society, furthering Afrikaner nationalism and Protestant Christianity in every social sphere, including education. During the 1930s this became a cultural movement promoting separate languages, identities, and public institutions.

Over the decades apartheid was legitimated as scriptural by white Reformed church leaders. The Dutch Reformed Church document *Human Relations and the South African Scene in the Light of Scripture* (1974) still effectively provided such a theological defense. In *Church and Society* (1986, revised 1990), the church, responding to criticism, rejected apartheid's implementation on ethical grounds.

The role of the English-speaking Christian churches was complex. They never offered theological justification for apartheid. The history of opposition against apartheid's religious roots and practices from within these churches has been described as "a church struggle." Other observers, however, find apartheid's roots in the policies of English-dominated capital. They regard the comprehensive political apartheid after 1948 as built upon already existing pillars, like the dispossession of land and its codification in law, the denial of majority vote, and systems of migratory labor and influx control (that is, the strict control of the movement of black people to "white" South Africa).

Resistance

Long before apartheid, religious groups were involved in many forms of resistance against racism and oppression: Muslims, Hindus, many individual Jews, and particularly African Christians, who played a leading role in the formation of the South African Native National Conference (later the African National Congress).

Even the establishment of African Independent churches (since 1884) can be seen in this way. The two major expressions of African Christianity, the Ethiopian and Zionist movements, are both radical departures from mission Christianity. Ethiopian churches broke away from mission control and the exclusion of Africans from positions of responsibility. Zionist churches rejected the exploitative colonial structures and attempted to serve the social and religious needs of the poor in the industrial cities.

During the 1950s blacks mobilized themselves increasingly against white domination. After the Sharpeville massacre, in which sixty-nine blacks were killed while protesting the pass laws (1960), the African National Congress and the Pan-

Africanist Congress were banned. Organized black political opposition was suppressed. Religious people and organizations became active as the voice of the voiceless.

The ecumenical movement became increasingly involved. The World Council of Churches (WCC) initiated the Cottesloe Consultation, held in December 1960, in reaction to Sharpeville and the political situation in the country. Some apartheid ideas were moderately rejected. Prime Minister Hendrik F. Verwoerd attacked the churches, and the Dutch Reformed member churches resigned from the WCC, reaffirming their theological justification of government policy.

The Christian Institute, formed by Beyers Naudé and others in 1963, became perhaps the country's most outspoken anti-apartheid body. Black South Africans, inspired by the black consciousness movement, took the initiative in their own struggle for freedom. In Christian circles black theology became influential. In 1977 Naudé and the institute were banned for seven years.

In 1968 the South African Council of Churches (SACC) published a "Message to the People of South Africa," condemning apartheid as a "pseudo-gospel." In 1970 the WCC established the Programme to Combat Racism. From 1978 to 1985 Desmond Tutu led the SACC as general-secretary. An Anglican priest and the archbishop of Cape Town, Tutu was known internationally for his leadership in the opposition against apartheid; he received the Nobel Peace Prize in 1984.

Many Christian churches rejected apartheid as a sin and its theological justification as a heresy. The World Alliance of Reformed Churches declared a state of confession and the Dutch Reformed Mission Church adopted the Belhar Confession, confessing God as the God of one church, of reconciliation, and of justice, thereby rejecting the theology of apartheid. Declarations such as the Kairos Document and the *Road to Damascus* offered radical challenges to the churches. The Kairos Document, attacking both a "state theology" with a national security ideology and a "church theology" of cheap reconciliation, and calling churches from protest to action, was extremely controversial. Similar declarations followed from evangelical and Pentecostal circles. Progressive Muslims were prominent in the anti-apartheid struggle. The transformation of Christianity from a white, European-dominated settler religion, openly supporting or trapped in apartheid, to a black-majority religion rooted in African culture and engaged in the struggle against white social, political, and ecclesial domination, has been called the most significant development of twentieth-century Christianity in South Africa.

Religion and the "New" South Africa

In 1990 restrictions were lifted from organizations that had been banned, and the African nationalist Nelson Mandela was released from prison, where he had been serving a life sentence. Apartheid laws were progressively repealed, multiparty negotiations were started, an interim constitution was accepted, and a constitutional court was established. Officially, apartheid ended with democratic elections in April 1994 and the implementation of a new democratic constitution in February 1997.

Religious communities were active in the changes. The most representative meeting of South African churches was one at Rustenburg in November 1990. The delegation from the Dutch Reformed Church endorsed a public confession of guilt. The conference issued a declaration calling for concrete restitution.

The constitution of 1997 describes South Africa as a democratic state founded on the values of human dignity, equality, nonracialism, and nonsexism. A bill of rights affirms a broad set of individual and social rights. Still controversial are sections on the freedom of religion, and on the rights of cultural, religious, and linguistic communities. They allow for religious observances at state-aided institutions, for legislation recognizing marriages and other practices according to different religious systems of personal and family law, and also for specific communities to maintain their own associations.

Many effects of apartheid continue to plague society. Dealing with them presents a major challenge to both state and society. A Truth and Reconciliation Commission was set up in 1996, with Tutu as chairperson. Its responsibilities are to conduct public hearings, in which victims tell their stories of suffering; consider amnesty applications for crimes committed; and deal with restitution claims. The commission has political and legal objectives but has looked for a spiritual and moral approach to issues of reconciliation and healing.

Apartheid prevented the country from facing the problem of poverty, and the gap between rich and poor has widened. Most religious communities support the government's Reconstruction and Development Programme, which attempts to meet the basic needs of the poor, abolish

Archbishop Desmond Tutu casts his vote in South Africa's first all-race democratic election, in 1994.

discrimination, redress policies of exploitation and repression, and reverse economic distortions.

South Africans still struggle to develop a common vision, a shared identity. Debates continue about the content and implementation of a multicultural society and a "rainbow nation." Particularly important for religious communities is the search for a common moral vision, for shared values, to resist a growing rate of crime and violence. Violence against women and children is alarmingly high. Appeals are made for a spirit of *ubuntu,* of humanness, based on traditional African moral and religious teachings, and for religious communities to strengthen this spirit of solidarity and humanity.

The religious communities themselves, however, sometimes need liberation from oppressive traditions, structures, convictions, and practices, and from inherited conflicts. Over decades, serious public conflicts concerning politics and religion have occurred, and many are still unresolved—for example, those concerning the acknowledgment of God in the constitution; religious education in schools; religion in the public media; moral issues, such as the death penalty and abortion; and the use of the Bible in politics.

See also *Colonialism; Human rights.*

Dirk J. Smit

BIBLIOGRAPHY

Alberts, Louw, and Frank Chikane, eds. *The Road to Rustenburg: The Church Looking Forward to a New South Africa.* Cape Town: Struik Christian Books, 1991.

Botman, H. Russel, and Robin Petersen, eds. *To Remember and to Heal: Theological and Psychological Reflections on Truth and Reconciliation.* Cape Town: Human and Rousseau, 1996.

Chidester, David. *Religions of South Africa.* New York: Routledge, 1992.

De Gruchy, John W. *The Church Struggle in South Africa.* 2d ed. Grand Rapids, Mich.: Eerdmans, 1986.

Elphrick, R., and T. Davenport. *Christianity in South Africa: A Political, Social, and Cultural History.* Cape Town: David Philip Publishers, 1997.

Esack, Farid. *Qur'an, Liberation, and Pluralism: An Islamic Perspective of Interreligious Solidarity against Oppression.* Oxford: Oneworld, 1997.

Prozesky, Martin, and John W. de Gruchy, eds. *Living Faiths in South Africa.* New York: St. Martin's, 1995.

Villa-Vicencio, Charles. *Trapped in Apartheid: A Socio-Theological History of the English-Speaking Churches.* Maryknoll, N.Y.: Orbis Books, 1988.

Soviet Union

See *Russia*

Spain

Located in the Iberian peninsula in southwestern Europe, Spain has been ruled from Madrid since the sixteenth century. It is divided into autonomous regions that generally correspond to the historic territories that emerged during the late medieval period, including the Basque provinces and Catalonia. A majority of the population identifies itself as Roman Catholic.

Politics and religion have been closely linked since the medieval period. The Islamic conquest of extensive areas of the Iberian peninsula, beginning in the eighth century, provoked centuries of warfare between Christians and Muslims. The conquest of Granada, the last Moorish stronghold, by Ferdinand and Isabella in 1492 and the expulsion of the Jews in the same year reflected the religious militancy of a triumphant Christian Spain. During the sixteenth and early seventeenth centuries, Spanish monarchs defended Catholicism in Europe against the Protestant Reformation. Their identification of Catholicism with the Spanish monarchy left a legacy that persisted well into the twentieth century.

The question of the church, the immense riches it had acquired over the centuries, and its religious monopoly became a source of intense controversy after 1800. The liberal

revolutions of the nineteenth century, beginning with the Cortes of Cádiz (1810–1813), Spain's first modern parliamentary assembly, undermined the elaborate organization and wealth of the eighteenth-century church, although the state remained officially Catholic until the Second Republic (1931–1939). Religious liberty was recognized for the first time in the 1869 constitution but was severely restricted by the more conservative 1876 constitution. The republic separated church and state, subjected the religious orders to severe controls in the midst of acrimonious debate with strong political repercussions, and introduced complete religious liberty.

The clergy and diverse right-wing parties supported a military rebellion of 1936 against the republic in a savage civil war that lasted until 1939. The dictatorship of Gen. Francisco Franco (1936–1975) reestablished Catholicism as the official state religion and bestowed significant privileges on the church. After Franco's death in 1975, the democratic constitution of 1978 officially separated church and state, although the government continues to provide generous financial assistance for clerical salaries and church schools.

Regalism

Philip—grandson of the Bourbon king of France, Louis XIV, and grandnephew of Spanish King Charles II, who died without issue—assumed the Spanish throne in 1700 as Philip V. The absolute monarchy of the eighteenth-century Bourbons exerted an unprecedented degree of control over ecclesiastical affairs. Through an aggressive policy of state intervention known as *regalism,* the royal administration appointed the bishops for all practical purposes, appropriated a generous portion of church revenues, and regulated the activities of the diocesan clergy and the religious orders. The alliance of throne and altar inclined heavily to the advantage of the crown, although for the most part a docile hierarchy accepted its decisive role without complaint.

This situation began to change during the reign of Charles IV (1788–1808), when the administration fell under the control of a royal favorite, Manuel Godoy. The government's arbitrary conduct toward the bishops, its appropriation of an ever larger share of ecclesiastical revenues to finance the wars unleashed by the French Revolution, its attempt to reduce papal jurisdiction, and its 1798 decision ordering the sale of the property of charitable institutions operating under church auspices to rescue the state's bankrupt finances generated resentment among the clergy. There was no direct challenge to the existing political order, but by 1807, when Napoleon I sent his armies into Spain, secular critics of absolute monarchy and a minority of progressive clergy, who later formed the first generation of Spanish liberals, began to demand political reform that would end capricious and arbitrary government.

Liberalism

Despite the limitations on royal authority imposed by the Cortes of Cádiz and the liberal revolution of 1820–1823, liberalism did not triumph over absolute monarchy until 1834. Except for periods of restored absolutist rule (1814–1819, 1823–1833) and the brief rule of the First Republic (1873–1874), liberalism dominated Spanish politics until 1923. Although the organization of the nineteenth-century liberal state took different forms, the question of the church, its resources, and its place within society was a constant source of political dissension. Although no government ever questioned the official relationship of the state to the Catholic Church, liberal politicians wished to end the vaguely theocratic character of civil-ecclesiastical relations identified with absolute monarchy in favor of a clearer separation of function between church and state. They viewed the vast landed holdings of the church as an obstacle to economic progress and wished to reform what they saw as an archaic and sprawling ecclesiastical organization.

In 1835 the Progressive Party government of Prime Minister Juan Álvarez Mendizábal ordered the suppression of the male religious orders and tried to ensure the gradual disappearance of female congregations by forbidding them to accept new entrants. The Progressives resented the support some religious orders gave to the cause of royal absolutism and saw the orders' substantial landholdings as a resource for saving the state from bankruptcy. As a result, the government ordered the sale of the property of suppressed religious communities to reduce the national debt. In 1841 the property of the diocesan clergy suffered the same fate.

These measures generated intense opposition from supporters of the reactionary pretender to the throne, Prince Carlos, who revolted against the regime between 1834 and 1839. The Carlist rebellion was in part a reaction against liberal ecclesiastical reforms and attracted the support of many clergy. But liberals gathered in the Moderate Party also objected to a policy that in their judgment had gone too far and too fast, although in principle they did not object to the sale of church property. Between 1840 and 1843, they objected strongly to the attempt of the regent, Gen. Baldomero Espartero, a practicing Catholic, to reduce the number of dioceses and parishes and the influence of the papacy over the Spanish church. In 1843 the Moderates took power and sought to reestablish good relations with the papacy and a church bruised and battered by the more radical liberalism of the Progressives. After prolonged negotiations, these efforts culminated in a diplomatic agreement with the papacy, the concordat of 1851.

The concordat governed civil-ecclesiastical relations until 1931 except for the revolutionary and republican period, 1868–1874. After the revolution of 1868, the Progressives and their parliamentary allies introduced religious liberty, expelled the Jesuits, and ordered the removal of male religious orders allowed to exist by earlier Moderate governments. These measures provoked the opposition of Carlists, who again rose in rebellion in 1872, and of the Moderates. In 1873 the short-lived First Republic contemplated establishing outright separation of church and state but failed to carry out its plan in the midst of political turmoil.

In 1874 a military revolt ended the republic and established a more flexible version of Moderate government under Prime Minister Antonio Cánovas del Castillo. The political system that he created, known as the Restoration, survived until 1923. Cánovas hoped to remove the issue of the church as a source of division among the liberal parties. Although he restored the 1851 concordat, recognized Catholicism as the official religion in the 1876 constitution, and permitted reintroduction of the male religious orders, he provided a restricted measure of religious liberty and insisted on retaining the state's episcopal patronage rights.

This policy of limited concessions to the church with regalist restraints was more or less accepted by the opposition Liberal Party until 1900. Thereafter, the remarkable growth of the religious orders occurring since the late 1870s stimulated a revival of the mild anticlericalism that always lay under the surface of the Liberal Party. The attempt of Liberal governments to restrict the orders' growth through the legislative device of a law of associations provoked serious conflicts with the Conservative Party. During the early twentieth century, a more radical and populist republicanism stressed attacks on the church's official privileges. With the growing popularity of socialism and anarchism, powerful anticlerical currents were also emerging outside parliament. By the end of the Restoration in 1923, the national consensus over the place of the church within the liberal political system envisaged by Cánovas had vanished.

The Republic and Franco

The church saw its position considerably improved during the dictatorship of Gen. Miguel Primo de Rivera (1923–1930), whom it backed unreservedly. But it paid a price for this support when the Second Republic was proclaimed in 1931. The republic worked aggressively to create a secular state. Church and state were separated, financial support for the clergy was eliminated, and the educational activities of the religious orders were curtailed. The hierarchy and Catholic activists fought against what they saw as the republic's antireligious policies by organizing politically. Some supported extreme right-wing parties. Others joined the only successful mass Catholic political party ever to exist in Spain, the Confederación Española de Derechas Autonomas (Spanish Confederation of the Autonomous Right, or CEDA), founded in 1933. Although the party's attitude toward the republic was ambiguous, it operated within the political system to achieve its goals through the electoral process.

The victory of the Popular Front, an alliance of the socialist and republican parties, in the February 1936 elections ended this illusion. Thereafter, authoritarian right-wing groups and many disgruntled members of CEDA supported conspiracies against the republic. A military uprising in July 1936 won the nearly unanimous support of the clergy and committed Catholics. Defense of religion provided the ideological glue that bound together the diverse and sometimes contradictory currents of Catholic opinion in support of the Nationalist cause headed by Franco. The clergy saw the Civil War (1936–1939) as a religious crusade. This militant ideology, known as National Catholicism, identified religion and nation more fully than at any time since the days of absolute monarchy. By the 1960s, however, the apparently monolithic facade of National Catholicism began to crack. The commitment of the Second Vatican Council (1962–1965) to human rights, including religious liberty, and the emergence of political dissent among the lower clergy, Catholic workers' associations, and clandestine Christian Democratic parties prepared the way for the hierarchy and the clergy to accept democracy after Franco's death.

Democratic Government

The introduction of a democratic system between 1976 and 1978 dramatically altered the church's constitutional position. In 1976 the state renounced its historic rights over ecclesiastical patronage. The 1978 constitution established full religious liberty and declared that "no religion will have an official character." But the constitution did not follow the model of absolute separation of church and state found in the republican charter of 1931. The 1978 text provided that "the public powers will maintain subsequent relations of cooperation with the Catholic church and other confessions." The specific mention of the Catholic Church in the constitution, the only religious group so recognized, as well as the educational and financial arrangements negotiated between the government and the Vatican in 1979, were severely criticized by the largest opposition party, the Socialists, as a means of introducing covert church influence into the new political order.

All things considered, the Catholic Church protected its interests remarkably well. The agreements with the Vatican, which enjoyed the status of international treaties binding future governments, assured the survival of the church's extensive school system and the public subsidies to maintain it. The government agreed to negotiate a financial formula that would provide for clerical salaries, and the church acquired complete liberty to administer its internal affairs, thereby ending a centuries-old regalist tradition.

The church did not fulfill all of its ambitions, however. It failed to halt the introduction of divorce in 1981 and the limited decriminalization of abortion introduced by the Socialist government following its massive electoral victory in 1982. Relations with the Socialists were marked by periodic crises. Although recognizing the right of church schools to official subsidies, the new government refused to fund such schools on the same basis as public institutions, and it required private schools receiving funding to meet contractual terms that Catholic educators found unacceptable. The hierarchy also objected to what it saw as the spread of moral permissiveness, which some bishops and priests believed was encouraged by the authorities. But in the end, the church received guaranteed financing for its schools, and the Socialist government punctually fulfilled its obligation to provide a significant subsidy for clerical salaries. Moreover, in spite of sometimes acute tension between church and state during the period of Socialist rule (1982–1996), neither side wished to burn bridges. Except for moral issues, most points of conflict were resolved through negotiation.

Introducing complete religious liberty did not mean, as generations of clerical apologists had predicted, that Spaniards would rush to join non-Catholic religious groups. By the early 1990s only 500,000 people in a population of 39 million belonged to religious minorities, the vast majority members of Protestant churches. Some, particularly the Anglican and various Reformed churches, dated back to the mid-nineteenth century. Others are of more recent origin, especially the Jehovah's Witnesses, who had limited success in recruiting new members in urban areas. Although the revolutionary parliament of 1869 had formally revoked the 1492 decree of expulsion, the Jewish population of Spain numbers only about 10,000. There is no significant Muslim population beyond small contingents of recent immigrants from North Africa.

The greatest challenge to Catholicism's historic dominance has come not from religious minorities but from the spread of indifference within a secularized society. Surveys have shown a steady decline in religious practice among Catholics since the 1960s to a level of observance of 20–25 percent. Although the rate of church attendance compares favorably with much lower levels for much of Catholic Western Europe, statistical surveys suggest that it will decline more in the future.

See also *Anticlericalism; Inquisition; Reformation.*

William Callahan

BIBLIOGRAPHY

Callahan, William J. "Church and State in Spain, 1976–1991." *Journal of Church and State* 34 (summer 1992): 503–519.

———. *Church, Politics, and Society in Spain, 1750–1874.* Cambridge: Harvard University Press, 1984.

Herr, Richard. *The Eighteenth-Century Revolution in Spain.* Princeton: Princeton University Press, 1958.

Lannon, Frances. *Privilege, Persecution, and Prophecy: The Catholic Church in Spain, 1875–1975.* Oxford: Oxford University Press, 1987.

Noel, Curtis C. "The Clerical Confrontation with the Enlightenment in Eighteenth-Century Spain." *European Studies Review* 5 (1975): 103–122.

Rosenblatt, Nancy. "The Spanish *Moderados* and the Church." *Catholic Historical Review* 57 (1971): 401–420.

Sánchez, José M. *The Spanish Civil War as a Religious Tragedy.* Notre Dame: Notre Dame University Press, 1987.

Spiritual healing

See *Medicine*

State churches

State churches are formed when a state system grants a privileged monopoly position to a specific religious institution, a church. In this arrangement the political system retains some control over the church, especially through the appointments made to higher offices and the granting of material resources. The church, in turn, provides legitimation to the political system by stressing mutual bonds of loyalty and solidarity and common obligations of obedience to the civic authorities.

Types of State Churches

State churches thus depict an extreme combination of political and religious authority. A state church may be regarded as an early modern extension of a tribal religion that venerates the awe of the ancestral charisma inherited by the chieftain or king. A modified version consists of established churches, in which special recognition is given to the religious affiliation of most of the population. Established churches thus maintain a higher degree of autonomy in relation to the state than do state churches. Another variation is the state cult, a legitimation of the political system that venerates the charisma invested in the political system by referring to an implicit "civil religion" that goes beyond specific denominations. A final type is the theocratic state, in which the political system is directed by a religious institution. Organization of religion in a church is a special feature of Western-Christian history, and state churches are thus based on that tradition.

Historical Background

Medieval Europe was characterized by a unique constellation of an emperor embodying the political power and a pope as head of the church. Some European countries (for example, England) were not subject to this formation. Instead, a corresponding constellation of political and sacred authority was formed between the king and the major bishops. The bishops could maintain a certain autonomy by referring to the papal see. It is especially in these countries that state churches were formed during the Protestant Reformation in the sixteenth century. The religious wars of the early sixteenth century were settled with the Augsburg Treaty of 1555, which established the principle that subjects should accept the religion of the head of state. Most Protestant countries were monarchies, and, accordingly, the king became the ruler and protector of the privileged church. With the advancement of absolutist monarchies in the seventeenth century, the national church became subjugated to the ruler as a part of the state apparatus. This development can be followed in both Protestant and Catholic countries. Concordats, or agreements between the Roman Catholic Church and secular rulers, have occasionally come close to the formation of state churches—for example, in France between 1801 and 1905, in Italy between 1848 and 1984, and in Spain from 1945 to 1978, especially under absolutist regimes.

In most Protestant nations the church became a department of the state apparatus. The secular power of the state was supposedly guided by a Protestant ethic that transpired in its laws. For example, the Danish-Norwegian laws under the absolutist monarchy followed the Old Testament Ten Commandments. The clergy, as members of a privileged estate, often had influence on political decisions. Since the religious wars, loyal citizens were obliged to be members of the state church or established church, and religious minorities were merely accepted by a special royal decree. Membership in the state church was a civil obligation in order to uphold absolute religious monism. In Sweden, for example, until 1860 it was impossible to withdraw from the church, and full religious freedom was not established by law until 1951. The state churches were involved in public administration, that is, public registry, in supervision of the educational system and social services, and as a major expression of the sacred position of the secular ruler.

Despite this historical background, state churches were not dissolved with the coming of modern nation-states. It is characteristic of a modern state to raise itself to a position of religious neutrality and to mediate in conflicts between religious interest groups. The democratic rights include a freedom of faith, which contradicts awarding privileges to a specific denomination. Furthermore, a pressure toward internal democratization can be found in most churches, and this development points toward autonomy from the political apparatus. The general tendency is therefore to change the status of state churches into established churches or—using the Scandinavian term—*folk churches.* A certain church thus acts as carrier of a national tradition and a vehicle for the religious affiliation among most of the population. This status simultaneously grants it certain privileges and some autonomy from the state. Similar changes can be seen in Roman Catholic countries.

The Nordic Countries

The Evangelical-Lutheran Church of Denmark is an example of a folk church that is still closely connected with the state. Since the institution of the democratic constitution of 1849, the Evangelical-Lutheran Church has been recognized as the church of the Danish people, and as such is supported by the state. Simultaneously, the constitution grants religious freedom. Formally, the monarch is head of the church. The legal affairs of the church are regulated by the government through a minister of the church. The official status of the folk church is demarcated by the obligation of its pastors to pray for the royal house and the government at Sunday services. The Danish church has no general council, or synod, even though local congregations elect councils, which employ pastors and bishops. The church has independent sources of income, although most of its resources come from church taxes collected from the membership by the municipal authorities. The church forms part of the state apparatus as the demographic bookkeeper and organizer of the common burial services. Formerly, the church had control over the public school system, but starting in 1933 this responsibility was gradually shifted to the state. More than 85 percent of Danish citizens are taxpaying members of the Danish folk church. Although attendance rates at normal services generally are low, the church is used by nearly all Danes for the rites of passage—baptism, confirmation, and burial—and a majority also are married in church. Because revivalist movements have remained within the state church, it has become a Protestant canopy institution that covers a wide range of theological views.

Norway, too, has what can be considered a state church. The constitution of 1814 awards the Evangelical-Lutheran Church a status as the official religion of the state. According to a verdict of the Norwegian supreme court of 1983, the government has to protect the Norwegian church and look after its interests, but this is not binding on legislation, for example, on abortion. Although the legal ruler of the Norwegian church is the Council of State, made up of ministers headed by the monarch, internal democratization developed gradually through the twentieth century. In 1984 the bishops' council and the church synod were granted legal status as representative organs for the Norwegian church, but government assent is still required. All Norwegians may participate at parish council elections. The official status of the church is highly visible at public festivities. The Norwegian church is administered by the Department of Church and Education, and financed by the public.

The role of public rituals in the Lutheran church of Sweden, a part of the state apparatus until the year 2000, has gradually been reduced. Still, nine out of ten Swedish citizens are members of the Swedish church. The monarch remains head of the church and is supposed to protect "the pure Evangelical faith." From the mid-twentieth century, when separation of the Swedish church from the state was put on the agenda, internal democracy has expanded. Since 1866 the Church of Sweden has had a representative body with veto power over parliamentary initiatives concerning the church. In 1982 this body was replaced by a general assembly elected through the parish councils. The authority of this synod has now expanded to such a degree that from the year 2000 the Swedish church has complete self-determination.

Finland represents a special variety of state church. According to the law of 1922 on religious freedom, the state is neutral in religious matters. Nevertheless, both the Lutheran Church and the Orthodox Church are awarded special protection by the state. The Lutheran Church is the most influential one, with a membership that includes nine out of ten Finns. The Orthodox Church is based on an Eastern Orthodox tradition and includes only one out of a hundred Finns. The Finnish Lutheran church is led by a synod and the bishops' assembly. The government and legal authorities formerly participated at synod meetings. Internal reforms have led to an internal democratization and self-determination. Still, the Finnish church retains a status as an official organ with the right of taxation, and the reform debates do not point to a separation of the ties between the state and the church.

Great Britain, Greece, and Germany

Great Britain has two established churches, namely, the Church of Scotland (Presbyterian) and the Church of England. The Church of Ireland was disestablished in 1871, and the Church in Wales in 1920. The Church of Scotland is self-governed, although the lord high commissioner is present at the General Assembly. The Church of England is "by law established," making the reigning monarch its supreme governor and "defender of the faith." Ecclesiastical law forms a part of the law of England. The general synod can propose to the Parliament legislation on church-related matters, and nearly all proposals are accepted without debate. The church is not funded by the state in any direct way. The status of the church is visible in public ceremonies. Being a part of the establishment did not bar spokesmen of the church from expressing a sharp critique of the social policy of the Conservative Party government in the 1980s. The Church of England is supposed to deliver religious services to all citizens. The 1970s saw an acceleration in the decline in active Church of England membership that had started earlier in the century.

Greece is exceptional in that it has an Orthodox Church as a state church. The 1833 constitution followed a German model, establishing the church under the directorship of the secular regent. The Orthodox Church thus became part of the state apparatus and independent of the Patriarch of Constantinople. The church is formally governed by a synod, although the secular rulers have interfered with nominations to the higher offices in the church, both during the era of monarchy, which lasted until 1975, and the present republican era. Every change in the political system has brought major changes in the administration of the church. This was especially noticeable after a coup ushered in a military dictatorship (1967–1974), which compromised the credibility of the church. Despite this, the constitution of 1975 upholds the religious articles with a few minor changes, and it still mentions the Holy Trinity in its preamble. The church is considered an important vehicle of Greek identity, and nine out of ten Greeks are members.

Germany does not have state churches in the proper sense, although church taxes for the established churches are collected by the municipal authorities, according to Article 137 of the Weimar constitution and Article 140 of the present constitution. The established churches are mainly the Evangelical-Lutheran Church and the Roman Catholic Church.

See also *Anglicanism; Civil religion; Great Britain; Orthodoxy, Greek; Scandinavia; Separation of church and state; Theocracy.*

Ole Riis

BIBLIOGRAPHY

Aarflot, Andreas, ed. *Kirke og stat i de nordiske land.* Oslo, Norway: Universitetsforlaget, 1971.

Badham, Paul, ed. *Religion, State, and Society in Modern Britain.* Lewiston, N.Y.: Edwin Mellen Press, 1989.

Casanova, Jose. *Public Religions in the Modern World.* Chicago: University of Chicago Press, 1994.
Champion, Françoise. "Les rapports église-état dans les pays européns de tradition protéstante et de tradition catholique." *Social Compass* 40 (1993).
Davie, Grace, and Dominique Hervieu-Léger, eds. *Identités religieuses en Europe.* Paris: Découverte, 1996.
Gustafsson, Göran. "Politicization of State Churches: A Welfare State Model." *Social Compass* 37 (1990).
Mol, Hans, ed. *Western Religion.* The Hague: Mouton, 1972.
Poulat, Émile. "Religione e sfera pubblica in Europa." In *La religione degli europei II.* Turin, Italy: Agnelli, 1993.

Sudan

The largest country in Africa, Sudan extends from Egypt along the Nile Valley to the Ethiopian Highlands and the rain forests of Central Africa. There is great ethnic and linguistic diversity, but the majority of Sudanese living in the northern two-thirds of the country are Muslims and speak Arabic. In the southern third of the country, the majority speak languages other than Arabic, and most continue to follow local African religious traditions or are Christians.

The territories now included in Sudan were brought together in a single unit during the nineteenth century. There were smaller states and ethnic communities including the Funj state in the Nile Valley, the Sultanate of Darfur to the west, and emerging sociopolitical systems in the south among the Dinka, Nuer, Shilluk, and Azande. Although inhabitants of the Nile Valley south of Egypt had been in contact with Muslims since the Muslim conquest of Egypt in the seventh century, it was not until the fifteenth and sixteenth centuries that many people in the northern Sudan became Muslim. The Funj and Darfur states were Islamic, but those in the southern regions were not. In the 1820s the Funj state was conquered by the newly modernized army of the Ottoman governor of Egypt, Muhammad Ali.

Under Ottoman-Egyptian rule, a central state structure was established and gradually extended its control, conquering Darfur by the 1870s and continually expanding in the south. This Turko-Egyptian state remained an institution of foreign rule, although efforts were made to develop the allegiance of Sudanese peoples. Muhammad Ali's army brought with it scholars from the old and prestigious Islamic university in Cairo, al-Azhar, who attempted to persuade Sudanese Muslims to accept Turko-Egyptian rule. Muslim institutional life in Sudan at the time was changing with the development of centralized Sufi (mystic) brotherhoods alongside the organizations of local teachers. The Turko-Egyptian rulers worked with one of these new brotherhoods, the Khatmiyyah led by the Mirghani family. This state established control over most of the territory now included in Sudan, and networks of trade and communication extended throughout the region. Little sense of a Sudanese cultural or national identity developed, however.

Opposition to Turko-Egyptian rule took many forms, including tribal revolts, military mutinies, and attacks by mercenary armies of slave traders. But the most successful opposition was assembled by a local Muslim teacher, Muhammad Ahmad, who became outraged by what he saw as the immorality of the rulers. In 1881 he proclaimed his mission as the *mahdi,* or the divinely guided leader who would establish justice and righteousness on Earth. He gathered large numbers of supporters from throughout northern Sudan and, in a series of military victories, succeeded in driving Turko-Egyptian forces out of virtually all of Sudan.

By the time of his death in 1885, the Mahdi had established the foundations for a state identified with Islam. His followers, called the *Ansar* ("companions"), maintained this state under his successor, the Khalifah Abdallahi. Although the Ansar were constantly at war with the Egyptians (and the British, who had occupied Egypt in 1882) and other neighboring states, the Mahdist state was an effectively functioning central state with financial and judicial institutions. Later Sudanese nationalists sometimes referred to the Mahdist state as the first Sudanese state, and Mahdist experiences established precedents that associated Muslim identities with political action.

Nationalism, Islam, and Party Politics

The Mahdist state came to an end in 1898 with the defeat of Sudanese forces at Omdurman and establishment of the Anglo-Egyptian condominium, in which Egypt and Britain formally shared sovereignty but Great Britain ruled Sudan. In the early years, British policy was influenced by memories of Mahdist successes, and the new rulers made special efforts to consult with Muslim leaders. The Khatmiyyah brotherhood and Sayyid Ali al-Mirghani, who had opposed the Mahdists and had close ties with Egypt, were especially influential. The Mahdist movement had not been destroyed, and a son of the Mahdi, Sayyid Abd al-Rahman al-Mahdi, reorganized the Ansar into a new style socioreligious and

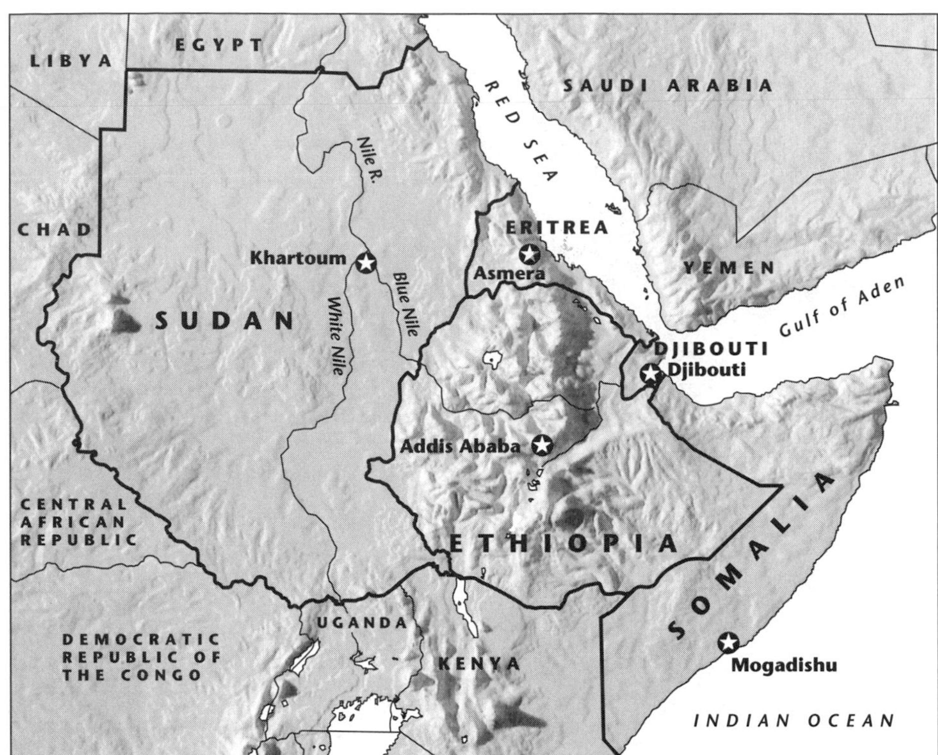

mass organization. Gradually the two Sayyids, Sayyid Ali al-Mirghani and Sayyid Abd al-Rahman, emerged as the most influential Sudanese in the condominium era.

Two branches of nationalism developed in Sudan because of the unusual form of imperial rule and local conditions. One opposed the British and allied with Egyptian nationalists to advocate the unity of the Nile Valley, and the other advocated a separate Sudan with the slogan "Sudan for the Sudanese." Sayyid Abd al-Rahman, in the Mahdist tradition, soon became the patron of nationalists seeking an independent Sudan, and Sayyid Ali supported the Unionists. Because it was the Sayyids and not the small modern-educated class who could mobilize mass support, when the first elections leading to self-government were held in 1953, the two major parties were based on the Sayyids' mass associations. The Ansar supported the Ummah Party and the Khatmiyyah supported the National Unionist Party. Although the Unionists won a majority, the parliament voted to create an independent Sudan in 1956.

Leaders from the southern third of the country were excluded from effective political participation, and southern resistance to northern control took many forms. A military mutiny in 1955 started the tradition of armed responses, and soon north-south civil war became a continuing feature of modern Sudanese history. Because the British excluded most northern Muslims from the south during the condominium, virtually all southern leadership was non-Muslim. Central government efforts to establish national unity after independence were viewed in the south as forced Arabization and Islamization. The north-south conflict was frequently viewed as a religious conflict between the Muslim north and the non-Muslim south.

Parliamentary politics did not provide effective national unity. Ismail al-Azhari, the leader of the National Union Party and the first prime minister, had been among the modern-educated intellectuals who had hoped to create nonsectarian parties. He soon clashed with the Sayyids, and the Khatmiyyah created a party of their own, the People's Democratic Party, which formed a coalition government with the Ummah. The first parliamentary era ended when the military under Ibrahim Abboud took control in 1958. Under Abboud the north-south conflict became a major war, and the economy deteriorated. Abboud was overthrown by a popular civilian revolution in 1964, and the parliamentary system was reestablished. The basic issues of north-south conflict and sectarian divisions were not resolved, however, and Jafar Numayri established a second military regime in 1969.

Military Regimes and Islamization

Numayri withstood revolts by the Ansar, the communists, and a national front of the old political parties. In 1972 he negotiated a settlement of the civil war by recognizing southern autonomy. The relatively pragmatic mode of Arab Socialism his regime represented began to change with the introduction of a so-called policy of national reconciliation in 1978. The major opposition leader to join Numayri at this time was Hasan al-Turabi, leader of the Sudanese Muslim Brotherhood, a new-style Islamist association that advocated Islamization of state and society. Numayri's policies became more formally Islamically oriented, culminating in the promulgation of the September Laws in 1983, which mandated adoption of Islamic law.

Fighting had already resumed in the south in 1981, but the September Laws reinforced the sense that the civil war was significantly a religious conflict. The Sudanese People's Liberation Army led by John Garang emerged as the major opposition group that advocated, among other things, the complete secularization of politics. The older parties and professional associations revived their opposition. Early in 1985 Mahmoud Mohammed Taha, an intellectual with a distinctive interpretation of Islam who had organized a small group called the Republican Brothers, was executed because of his opposition to the September Laws. Numayri was overthrown in 1985 by a military coup that opened the way for a third parliamentary era.

Sayyid-led parties again dominated the parliament. The Democratic Unionist Party was the product of the reunion of the National Union Party and Peoples' Democratic Party and was led by Sayyid Muhammad Uthman al-Mirghani. Sayyid Sadiq al-Mahdi, who had already been prime minister in the 1960s, led the Ummah. Turabi's National Islamic Front won almost 20 percent of the votes and emerged as a new force. But the Sudanese People's Liberation Army did not participate, military conflict intensified, and the politics of coalitions was not able to solve other major problems facing the country. Yet another military coup toppled the government in 1989, led by Umar al-Bashir, an Islamist leader who established close ties with the National Islamic Front.

During the 1990s the alliance of Bashir and Turabi worked to create a new style of political system that involved a hierarchy of popular councils, emphasizing the Islamic concepts of consultation *(shurah)* and consensus *(ijma)*. Although elections were held, political parties were not allowed, and supporters of the older political organizations were suppressed and imprisoned. The Ummah Party, Democratic Unionist Party, Sudanese People's Liberation Army, and other smaller groups formed an opposition coalition in exile that advocated a return to a multiparty, parliamentary system and a more secular separation of religion and politics. In 1997 this alliance organized an invasion of Sudan from Eritrea and Ethiopia, which, together with Sudanese People's Liberation Army actions in the south, posed a military threat to the central government. But the Sudanese Muslim Brotherhood provided the ideological foundations for a state system that, despite strong opposition and its own weaknesses, remained in power for longer than any other regime in Sudan except that of Numayri.

See also *Egypt; Islam; Mahdi.*

John O. Voll

BIBLIOGRAPHY

Beshir, M. O. *Revolution and Nationalism in the Sudan.* London: Rex Collings, 1974.

El-Affendi, Abdelwahab. *Turabi's Revolution: Islam and Power in Sudan.* London: Grey Seal, 1991.

Fluehr-Lobban, Carolyn, Richard A. Lobban Jr., and John O. Voll. *Historical Dictionary of Sudan.* 2d ed. Lanham, Md.: Scarecrow Press, 1992.

Hill, Richard. *Egypt in the Sudan, 1820–1881.* London: Oxford University Press, 1959.

Holt, P. M. *The Mahdist State in the Sudan, 1881–1898.* 2d ed. Oxford: Clarendon Press, 1970.

O'Fahey, R. S., and J. L. Spaulding. *Kingdoms of the Sudan.* London: Metheun, 1974.

Voll, John O., ed. *Sudan: State and Society in Crisis.* Bloomington: Indiana University Press, 1991.

Woodward, Peter. *Sudan, 1898–1989: The Unstable State.* Boulder, Colo.: Lynne Rienner, 1990.

Sufism

The mystical and ascetic tradition in the Islamic religious tradition is known in English as Sufism. More than half of the world's one billion Muslims interpret their religion in terms of Sufism, either through their devotion to the prophet Muhammad, his family, and the Sufi saints or through specialized religious practices beyond the minimum of Islamic observances. This prominent role of Sufism tends to be obscured, however, by a fundamentalist minority who claim a monopoly over Islamic religious authority that is uncritically accepted by Western media. Sufism is recognized as a powerful force by secular governments in Muslim countries because of its large following, though it is often rejected by modernists who identify it with medieval superstition.

Origins and Development

In the late seventh and eighth centuries pious Muslim critics of the worldliness of the early caliphs (the successors to Muhammad) included many who advocated cultivating the internal religious life. They formed circles of informal instruction, particularly in Baghdad in what is now Iraq and in eastern Iran, where Sufi masters and disciples experimented with asceticism and meditation. ("Sufi" comes from the Arabic word for wool, denoting the woolen garments of asceticism.)

In the eleventh and twelfth centuries noted Sufi masters established residential lodges for their followers. These were supported by new ruling dynasties, such as the Seljuk Turks in Iran and the Ayyubids in Egypt, who in their struggles against minority Shiʿa Islamic groups derived legitimation from their support of Sufis as well as from theologians of the majority Sunni Muslims. The Sufis provided direct access to God, ethical guidance, and miraculous support, while the Sunni scholars codified Islamic law and provided the officials to staff the courts. The legitimating role of Sufis became even more pronounced after the destruction of the caliphate by the Mongols in 1258. From that time until European conquest in Islamic lands began five centuries later, support of Sufism was an integral part of any regime that invoked the Islamic heritage. Despite an often strong linkage of Sufism with political power, Sufi groups also represented an alternative based on independent religious authority.

By the twelfth century Sufi orders began to be organized as societies based on teaching lineages, which were named after founders who codified and institutionalized distinctive teachings and meditative practices. Most orders were confined to particular regions, though a few such as the Qadiriyya and the Naqshbandiyya became widely distributed across many Muslim countries. The orders expanded as teaching networks in a chain descending from Muhammad. Some groups, such as the Chishtiyya in India, recommended avoiding formal ties with rulers and refused land endowments, while others sought to influence rulers to make decisions based on ethical and religious considerations.

The religious life of Sufis generally included the normal Islamic religious duties, to which were added numerous supplementary exercises of prayer, fasting, and meditation. Although full-time Sufis were precluded from following worldly occupations, many nobles and soldiers as well as people of the lower classes were followers of Sufi masters. Less conventional Sufis, known as Qalandars, pursued a radical form of asceticism that sometimes led to severe social conflicts, including attacks on established Sufis; they even led full-scale peasant revolts in the Ottoman Empire in the fifteenth and sixteenth centuries.

From Colonialism to the Present

The advent of European colonialism in the late eighteenth century, and the overthrow of nearly all Muslim governments by 1920, brought Sufi orders into new prominence. In a number of areas, Sufi orders were the strongest local institutions that remained when local rulers had been overthrown by European arms. Thus they were able to serve as centers of anticolonial resistance in a number of areas in the nineteenth century: notable were the Naqshbandiyya in the Caucasus and China, the Sammaniyya in Sudan, the Sanusiyya in Libya, and the Qadiriyya in Algeria. An uprising led by a Kurdish Naqshbandiyya leader prompted Kemal Atatürk, the founder and first president of the Republic of Turkey, to ban all Sufi orders in Turkey, in 1925. Sufi leaders have continued to play a role in political struggles in Afghanistan and in Chechnya in the 1980s and 1990s.

Once in control of Muslim countries, European colonial authorities viewed Sufi masters and their followers as a powerful social force to be tamed or co-opted into the political system. In the postindependence period after World War II, the governments of formerly colonized states made considerable efforts to appropriate the authority of Sufi shrines and orders into the program of the state. Official government organizations in countries like Egypt have attempted to regulate Sufi activities, although some of the largest orders remain beyond government control. The shrines of Sufi saints, which are the focus of large popular festivals, are subject to state oversight and even direct management in many Muslim countries.

Although Sufism played an important role in most premodern Muslim societies, several forces worked to weaken the religious credentials of Sufism. European Orientalists (scholars who studied the Islamic East during the colonial period) defined Sufism as a literary culture ultimately to be derived from non-Islamic sources. Nineteenth-century reformists and twentieth-century fundamentalists saw Sufism as un-Islamic, only slightly less threatening than Western secularism. This anti-Sufi attitude characterized reformers in Egypt such as Muhammad Abduh and the Salafiyya movement. Fundamentalist leaders raised in Sufi environments, such as Hasan al-Banna, founder of the Muslim Brethren in Egypt, and Sayyid Abu al-Ala Mawdudi, founder of the Jamaʿat-i Islami in India and Pakistan, rejected the practices of Sufism while claiming charismatic leadership similar to that of a Sufi shaykh. Secularized political elites in many Muslim countries viewed Sufism as a superstitious anachronism and an embarrassment. (Sufism in fact is banned in Saudi Arabia and is severely constrained in Iran.)

Sufi intellectuals have responded to these challenges, demonstrating the Islamic genealogies of Sufism and asserting that Sufism, contrary to what fundamentalists say, is the essence of Islam. With modernists, Sufis seize the rhetoric of science and present Sufism as the solution to the quest for truth. Still a significant force in Muslim countries, Sufism has also found a following in Europe and North America, both on the level of mystical literature and as an influence on popular culture through music.

See also *Atatürk, Kemal; Banna, Hasan-al; Colonialism; Islam; Mawdudi, Sayyid Abu al-Ala; Muslim encounters with the West.*

Carl W. Ernst

BIBLIOGRAPHY

Ernst, Carl W. *The Shambhala Guide to Sufism.* Boston: Shambhala Publications, 1997.

Hoffman, Valerie. *Sufism, Mystics, and Saints in Modern Egypt.* Columbia: University of South Carolina Press, 1995.

O'Fahey, R. S. *Enigmatic Saint: Ahmad Ibn Idris and the Idrisi Tradition.* Evanston, Ill.: Northwestern University Press, 1990.

Sukarno, Achmad

Leader of the Indonesian independence struggle and first president of the republic (1945–1967). Sukarno (1901–1970) formulated the basic tenets of Indonesian nationalism; however, he also left a legacy of bitter ideological discord. The son of a Balinese mother and a Javanese teacher (and Theosophist) in colonial schools, Sukarno was raised a nominal Muslim. After completing grade school, he continued his studies in the Dutch East Indies European school system, taking a degree in engineering in 1926 at the newly established Technical College in Bandung, West Java. After finishing his degree, Sukarno wrote the first of several tracts in which he sought to forge a uniquely Indonesian synthesis of Islam, Marxism, democratic socialism, and nationalism. The synthesis is often portrayed as a product of Javanese society's long tradition of cultural syncretism. But it was as much a desperate effort to unite modern Indonesia's fractious political groupings as it was the product of enduring civilizational influences. Although emphasizing unity and consensus, Sukarno's nation-building formula assumed secular nationalist domination of political life.

In the final months of the Japanese occupation during World War II, Sukarno led the committee involved in the preparation of a declaration of independence and provisional constitution. The committee split along ideological lines, with Christians, Hindus, and secular nationalists opposed to supporters of an Islamic state. To defuse the crisis, on June 1, 1945, Sukarno presented his doctrine of the "five principles" (Panca Sila), affirming the basis of the state as nationalism, humanitarianism, social justice, democracy, and belief in God. Muslims insisted that an additional clause (known as the Jakarta charter) be added to the fifth principle, emphasizing the "obligation for adherents of Islam to carry out Islamic law." Dropped at the last minute from the declaration of independence, the Jakarta charter remains a point of fierce disagreement to this day.

Disputes over religion and politics plagued Sukarno's presidency to the end. Having begun as a weak president in a system of parliamentary government, in 1959 Sukarno introduced a "guided democracy" with an authoritarian presidency. From this period on, a three-sided rivalry between Muslims, the Communist Party, and the military also intensified, exacerbated by Sukarno's tendency to play one rival against the other. What had begun as an idealistic effort to unite Indonesia's disparate political factions had, by the early 1960s, become little more than an exercise in authoritarian control. Drifting into closer alliance with the Communist Party, Sukarno displayed special hostility toward modernist

Achmad Sukarno (right) *reviews U.S. Air Force soldiers in 1956 with American vice president Richard M. Nixon* (left) *and an Air Force official.*

Muslims and liberal democrats. However, in the aftermath of a failed leftist officers' coup in September 1965, the Communist Party was destroyed and Sukarno's power crumbled. In 1967 he was stripped of all remaining authority; he died in 1970 under house arrest.

See also *Indonesia.*

Robert W. Hefner

Sultan

See *Islam*

Sunni Islam

See *Islam*

Survivalism

Primarily a phenomenon found in the United States, survivalism is the practice of preparing for an expected nationwide economic, political, or structural collapse. Survivalists stockpile weapons, medical supplies, and foodstuffs in anticipation of the predicted crisis. Central to survivalism is the idea that a generalized calamity is inevitable. Rather than preparing for a natural disaster or a time of civil disorder, survivalists predict a generalized collapse of society that will throw individuals or survivalist communities back on their own resources. They usually foresee such calamities as part of a larger political or religious worldview.

Survivalism is predominantly a rural phenomenon, with cities shunned as potential death traps. There is no evidence that survivalism attracts a disproportionate number of persons from a particular socioeconomic or educational background. The number of persons actively preparing singly or in groups for a crisis is small, numbering between several hundred and a few thousand. The number expressing an interest in survivalism, however, is much larger, perhaps in the hundreds of thousands. This larger population attends survivalist trade shows and seminars, purchases survivalist publications and products, and shares many of the survivalists' views. North American survivalists can be divided into two by no means exclusive categories: political and religious.

Political survivalism has several forms, drawing on ideas that include genetic deterioration, overpopulation, a coming "race war" between blacks and whites, the corruption of the United States, and the perceived tyranny of its government. The largest faction of political survivalists is associated with the self-described patriot or Christian patriot movement.

Patriots, who often combine political and religious views, believe that an elite conspiracy is consciously trying to destroy the "white, Christian republic" of the United States and replace it with a society of slaves to a global New World Order. The actions of the conspiracy—variously attributed to Jews, Masons, the United Nations, the Trilateral Commission (whose goal is to increase cooperation between the United States, Japan, and Western Europe), and dozens of other organizations—will, according to some patriots, lead to the collapse of American civilization. In response, some patriot leaders have instituted training programs to prepare others for the coming collapse and have founded independent communities.

Religiously motivated survivalists have garnered most of the media attention in the United States. This focus is due in large part to the dramatic and violent confrontations between religious survivalists Randy Weaver (1992) and David Koresh (1993) and the federal government. Weaver, an adherent of the white supremacist Aryan Nation sect, was involved in a months-long standoff with federal agents that culminated in the death of his wife and son. The best known case is probably that of Koresh and the Branch Davidians, which ended in the incineration of the Davidian compound in Waco, Texas, in April 1993. Koresh's death along with most of his followers had a widespread energizing effect on survivalist organizing. This incident confirmed patriots and other political survivalists in their opinions about the corruption of the U.S. government and the need to prepare for a coming crisis.

See also *Anti-Semitism; Cults; Freemasonry; Fundamentalism; Martyrdom; Millennialism.*

Steven L. Gardiner

BIBLIOGRAPHY

Aho, James A. *The Politics of Righteousness: Idaho Christian Patriotism.* Seattle: University of Washington Press, 1990.

Barkun, Michael. *Religion and the Racist Right: The Origins of the Christian Identity Movement.* Chapel Hill: University of North Carolina Press, 1994.

Bennett, David H. *The Party of Fear: From Nativist Movements to the New Right in American History.* Chapel Hill: University of North Carolina Press, 1988.

Stern, Ken. *A Force upon the Plain: The American Militia Movement and the Politics of Hate.* New York: Simon and Schuster, 1996.

Syria

The Syrian Arab Republic is bordered by Turkey, Iraq, Jordan, Israel, Lebanon, and the Mediterranean Sea. The Syrian lands passed from Christian to Muslim rule in 636 A.D. and shortly thereafter reached the peak of their power and prestige when Damascus became the capital, in 661, of the Umayyad empire, which extended from Spain to India. In 750 a new dynasty, the Abbasids, moved the capital of the Muslim world to Baghdad in what is today Iraq. After that time, Damascus served largely as a provincial capital for various imperial rulers, the last of whom were the Ottomans, who conquered the city in 1517 and remained for the next four hundred years. When the British destroyed the Ottoman Empire in 1918, an Arab government emerged in Damascus, but in 1920 France invaded and established a mandate over what became present-day Syria in the name of the League of Nations. Syria won its independence from France in 1946.

Syria is a country of great religious and social diversity, which has been a source of political weakness. The French governed through divide-and-rule tactics, splitting the countryside into three autonomous regions to win favor among the country's "compact minorities." The Alawis and Druze were given autonomous territories to administer. Both are heterodox Shiʿi Muslims who took refuge in Syria's mountain regions because of persecution by the Sunni Arab majority (who make up 61 percent of Syria's population) for being heretics. The Alawis (12 percent of the population) live in the western mountains; the Druze (3 percent) live in the southeast. The Jazira region in the northwest was also administered autonomously because it is home to most of Syria's Kurds and nomadic Arab tribes. The Kurds (9 percent of the population) are a non-Arab, Sunni Muslim peo-

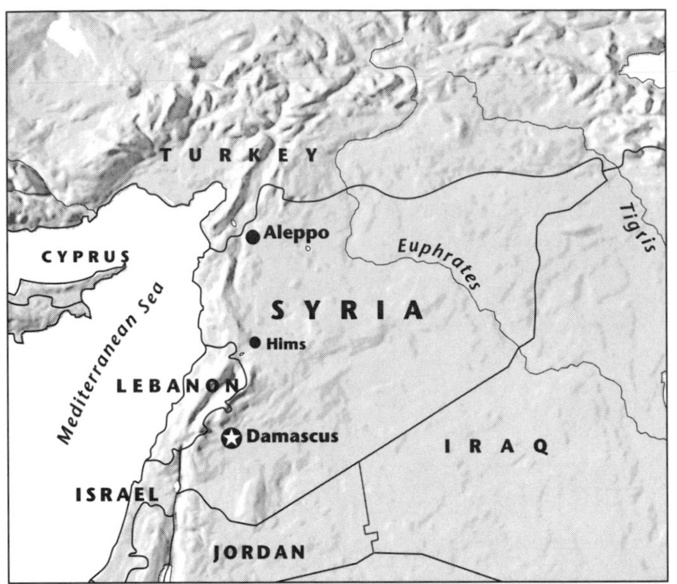

ple. The Sunni Arab population lived primarily in the cities of central Syria, which they shared with Syria's Christians (14 percent of the population). Other religious and ethnic minorities exist in Syria, such as the Isma'ilis, Turkomans, Circassians, and Jews. Not until independence were Syrians politically united as one people.

At independence, Syria inherited an inexperienced parliament, dominated by the Sunni elite, and an undisciplined army, dominated by the rural minorities. The French had favored recruitment of minorities in the army such that in 1954, for example, 60 percent of Syria's noncommissioned officers were Alawis. For thirteen years the army and civilian politicians traded control of government, beginning with a military coup in 1949 and ending in 1963, when the army swept the last freely elected government from power in the name of the Arab Socialist Renaissance Party, the Ba'th Party. The coups of the 1960s were guided by the Military Committee, established secretly by Alawi officers in 1960 to combat Sunni prejudice, which was pervasive in Syria when it was ruled by Egypt during the years of the United Arab Republic (1958–1961). By 1966 the Alawis had taken power directly, having purged competing officer groups from the highest ranks of the military. After a coup in 1970 Hafiz al-Asad became ruler of Syria, ushering in a period of unparalleled political stability. He remains president to this day.

The longevity of Asad's rule is due to his skillful manipulation of sectarian loyalties and kinship ties. To ensure against further coups, he has constructed the least representative regime in modern Syrian history. The uppermost echelons of many state institutions, in particular the power centers such as the independent security forces and the military, are dominated by members of the president's all-powerful Alawi faction. Sectarian discrimination at the apex of power, however, is contrasted by Asad's attempt to oppose religious discrimination in other aspects of political and social life. Government policy officially disavows sectarianism, and there is little evidence of societal discrimination or violence against religious minorities. Indeed, Asad has won the support of minority communities and secular nationalists by posing as a bulwark against Muslim fundamentalism and religious intolerance more generally.

The constitution of 1973 provides for freedom of religion; the government generally respects this right in practice. Islam is not prescribed as the state religion, but the president must be a Muslim and Islamic jurisprudence is the main source of legislation. Religious courts handle questions of personal and family law. Technically, all schools are government run and nonsectarian, although in practice some schools are run by Christian and Jewish minorities. Religious instruction is mandatory. The three branches of government are guided by the views of the Ba'th Party, whose primacy in state institutions is ensured by the constitution. Ba'th ideology endorses secularism, socialism, and pan-Arab nationalism. The most significant opposition to Asad has come from fundamentalist Sunni Muslims, who reject the Ba'th program and rule by Alawis, whom they consider heretical. In 1982 the army put down an uprising by the fundamentalist opposition in Hama, leveling parts of the city with artillery fire and killing many thousands of inhabitants. Since then, public manifestations of opposition to the regime have been limited.

See also *Druze; Kurds.*

Joshua M. Landis

BIBLIOGRAPHY

Dam, Nikolaos van. *The Struggle for Power in Syria: Politics and Society under Asad and the Ba'th Party.* London: I. B. Tauris, 1996.

Khoury, Philip S. *Syria and the French Mandate.* Princeton: Princeton University Press, 1986.

Seale, Patrick. *Asad of Syria: The Struggle for the Middle East.* London: I. B. Tauris, 1988.

———. *The Struggle for Syria.* London: Oxford University Press, 1965.

T

Taxation

Taxation, or the revenue raised by the state to be used for governing, has many political implications. The taxing authority, whether local or national, must, for example, determine what kinds of taxes to levy and on which part of the population the burden will fall. Religion and taxation have a long, complex relationship that varies tremendously over time and place. While this article focuses on taxation in the United States, it is important to recognize that practices are quite different in other countries.

Historically, in nations with an established church (for example, the Anglican Church in Great Britain) the privileged church clergy, property, and services were supported by general tax monies. In many Roman Catholic countries the church itself owned large tracts of land from which it earned income by taxing residents. In France and Italy the majority of these territories were eventually seized by national governments (as had happened earlier in England when Henry VIII dissolved the Church's monastic holdings in the late 1530s). Today church-state relations in these countries, including ownership of property and taxation, are governed by concordats—treaties between the Vatican and individual secular governments. As a general principle, religious property and donations are not taxed. ("The power to tax involves the power to destroy," as Chief Justice John Marshall declared in 1819.)

Germany has a unique arrangement. People who register with a church (and one must be registered to receive religious services) are assessed a 3 percent tax by the federal government. This tax is then distributed proportionately back to various church organizations. In Islamic countries major mosques and religious shrines are supported by the respective states. There are often private mosques supported by wealthy individuals and groups of the faithful. Depending on the country, minority religions may be prohibited from owning property or severely restricted in a variety of ways.

The United States has the most complex tax system in the world, yet it has been very successful in collecting taxes. A federal structure allows tax authorities to exist on national, state, and myriad local levels and gives each level the right to tax for more than one purpose. Tax policies are designed not only to raise revenue but to discourage certain activities, such as alcohol or tobacco consumption, and to encourage other activities, such as charitable giving or organizing for voluntary community services. It is within this context that religion and taxes must be understood. Four major levies that affect religious institutions are property, income, social security, and sales taxes. Of these, property taxes are the oldest and most deeply established.

Property Taxes

Property taxes in the United States are exclusively the domain of local governments and are a major source of funding for schools, police, and emergency services, as well as for maintaining public roads, water supplies, sewage systems, and other infrastructure. From the beginning of the American Republic in the late eighteenth century, every state in the union has exempted religious institutions from payment of property taxes. Most states provide a constitutional basis for these exemptions. Others have simply made statutory provisions. As other voluntary organizations, such as men's and women's clubs, schools, hospitals, settlement houses, libraries, museums, and the like, bought or were given property, they too were granted tax-exempt status.

Individual states have minor variations in their exemption laws, but all have certain common features. Groups must apply for tax-exempt status, specifying the charitable or religious purposes for which the property will be used. Property must actually be used for these purposes, not merely owned by an exempt group (although there is usually a grace period of a few years if a church buys land with plans to build a building). And, finally, if a property is used for commercial purposes (for example, rental of a parking lot), the church must pay both property and income taxes.

Reasons for granting these exemptions were rarely articulated. It was assumed that churches and other voluntary institutions provided valuable public services that otherwise might have to be provided at taxpayers' expense. Legal experts observed that the power to tax effectively meant the power to control and that the need to maintain separation of church and state precluded any taxing authority over religious institutions. A few religious scholars argued that the Bible, the free exercise clause in the First Amendment to the Constitution (which prevents Congress from "prohibiting the free exercise" of religion), or both, required property tax exemptions. Although some citizens objected to tax exemptions for religious institutions, it was not until 1970 that anyone successfully brought the issue before the Supreme Court. The case was *Walz v. Tax Commission.*

Frederick Walz, a New York attorney, bought a vacant lot on Staten Island about half the size of a tennis court. After paying property taxes, he filed for a partial refund. He argued that tax exemptions on property used for religious worship amounted to a subsidy of religion by taxpayers, including himself, in violation of the establishment clause of the First Amendment, which also prevents Congress from establishing any religion. Walz focused precisely on property used for worship to sidestep any counterargument based on the social services provided by religious organizations and to differentiate them from other nonprofit organizations. The tactic did not work.

Chief Justice Warren Burger, writing for an 8–1 majority, held that the tax exemption was constitutionally permissible on three grounds. First, churches are part of a larger class of nonprofit, voluntary organizations, all of which are given equal treatment under the tax code. Therefore churches are not advanced nor inhibited beyond what other nonreligious but similarly situated organizations are. Second, if states were to tax churches, civil servants would have to assess the value of the property, collect the taxes, negotiate disputes, and foreclose in the event of nonpayment. All of these activities could lead to an excessive entanglement between religious institutions and government. Finally, two centuries of allowing churches to remain exempt from taxation has shown that the practice does not lead to an established church.

The strongly worded opinion and large majority was a major setback for those who opposed religious tax exemptions. On the other hand, the *Walz* decision did not provide the constitutional protection many religious leaders had hoped to obtain. The chief justice's opinion simply stated that an exemption did not violate the establishment clause. It did not go the extra step and declare that exemptions are constitutionally mandated.

In the mid-1990s this distinction and a general antitax atmosphere led several groups to urge repeal of tax exemptions for all nonprofit organizations, including churches. Most significant was an initiative put on the ballot in Colorado. Despite, or perhaps because of, massive publicity and support of powerful lobbies, the initiative was soundly defeated at the polls. This defeat has led most observers to conclude that even if property tax exemptions are not constitutionally mandated, they are supported by a substantial majority of voters and are not likely to be removed any time soon.

Income Tax

In 1913 the Sixteenth Amendment to the U.S. Constitution became law. It allowed the federal government to create an income tax. (Before the amendment took effect, Article I, Sections 2 and 8, required all federal taxes to be proportional among states and population.) Federal tax law has developed into an extraordinarily complex set of statutes that provide a variety of exceptions and exclusions, often called loopholes, as well as different rates for different types of income. From its first draft legislation, however, Congress has consistently exempted religious organizations from paying income tax.

A series of changes culminated in the Internal Revenue Code passed in 1954. The relevant section, 501(c)(3), classifies charitable, religious, social, literary, and educational organizations that do not aspire to make a profit for the benefit of shareholders or owners as a single category for tax purposes. These groups are exempt from taxes if they meet certain requirements. Being recognized as a 501(c)(3) entity has two effects: it allows donors to give charitable contributions to the entity and take a deduction on their own income tax, and it allows the group to avoid paying any tax on its income. A 1969 amendment limited the latter effect so that religious organizations must pay tax on income from businesses not directly related to their charitable purposes.

No one has successfully challenged Congress's right to legislate income tax exemptions for charitable and religious organizations. What has caused confusion and some litigation are two limitations put on religious and charitable groups: they cannot make a "substantial attempt to influence legislation"—that is, to lobby political leaders—or participate in political campaigns for candidates running for public office.

It is unclear what a substantial part of one's activities might be. A rule of thumb has been 5 percent of one's total operations, but the Internal Revenue Service has never adequately clarified this figure. Groups that wish to lobby (Friends Committee on National Legislation, American Civil Liberties Union, NAACP, and Network, for example) will create companion 501(c)(4) corporations, often referred to as action organizations, to do the lobbying. These 501(c)(4) corporations pay no taxes, but contributions to them cannot be deducted from taxes. Americans United for Separation of Church and State is the most notable religious group to lose its tax-exempt status for excessive lobbying, but many religious scholars have complained about the chilling effect of this vague standard.

Neither the courts nor Congress has been sympathetic. In a 1973 appellate court case, *Christian Echoes National Ministry v. United States,* evangelist Billy Joe Hargis's organization was denied a tax exemption by the Internal Revenue Service because the group supported conservative political candidates and lobbied intensely for an amendment allowing prayer in public schools. The Supreme Court refused to review the decision. On the other hand, an effort by Abortion Rights Mobilization and a coalition of twenty other pro-choice groups to sue the United States Catholic Conference and National Conference of Catholic Bishops because of their antiabortion political activities fared no better, presumably because the latter carefully refrained from mentioning candidates by name.

How tenuous tax-exempt status can be is illustrated by *Bob Jones University v. United States* (1983). This fundamentalist Christian university had enjoyed 501(c)(3) status since its founding. In 1970 a federal district court issued an injunction prohibiting the IRS from according tax-exempt status to private schools that practice racial discrimination. In 1976 the IRS revoked Bob Jones University's tax-exempt status because, for religious reasons, it forbade interracial dating among its students. The Supreme Court, in hearing the case, reasoned that the government has a compelling interest in eradicating racial discrimination that substantially outweighs "whatever burden denial of tax benefits places on petitioners' exercise of their religious beliefs." The Court went further, noting that exempt organizations must provide some public benefit and that they may not violate established public policy. Clearly, designation as a 501(c)(3) tax-exempt entity is a legislatively mandated privilege, not a constitutional right, even for religious institutions.

Other Taxes

Several other tax issues may be treated more briefly. A 501(c)(3) organization may apply for exemption from state and federal sales taxes, although religious groups may not be singled out for either a tax benefit or a burden. Two Supreme Court cases have made this settled doctrine. In *Texas Monthly v. Bullock* (1989) the justices struck down a sales-tax exemption provided solely to religious publications, ruling that it violated the establishment clause. A year later, in *Swaggart Ministries v. California Board of Equalization* (1990), the same justices ruled that a tax on the sale of religious goods and services by a religious organization did not violate the free exercise clause if the tax was uniformly applied to all retail sales and did not single out religious goods or services.

Social Security (Federal Insurance Contribution Act, or FICA) and unemployment (Federal Unemployment Tax Act, or FUTA) taxes have presented slightly different problems. A 1965 federal law exempts self-employed Amish and members of similar groups from payment of FICA taxes if such payment is contrary to their religious beliefs and they decline benefits on the same grounds. *Self-employed* is the operative word. An Amish carpenter, Edwin Lee, hired fellow Old Order Amish and refused to file quarterly reports or pay the employer's half of the tax. A unanimous Supreme Court ruled in *United States v. Lee* (1982) that the government's interest in maintaining the integrity of the tax system outweighed any burden on Lee's religious convictions. Chief Justice Burger, writing for the Court, feared setting a precedent for other issues, for example, tax resistance by individuals opposed to war. Also, hiring other people borders on commercial activity, so the Court upheld the exemption but interpreted it quite narrowly.

Similarly, in a 1980 case the Court upheld an exemption from unemployment taxes that Congress had granted to churches and related organizations. In this case, *Evangelical Lutheran Church v. South Dakota,* a church school was permitted to decline to pay the unemployment tax. This decision also means that dismissed employees cannot collect unemployment compensation, though the Court held that legislative discretion would apply.

Finally, despite popular misconceptions, rabbis, ministers, and priests pay income and Social Security taxes just like other citizens. The only exceptions are members of religious orders such as Jesuits and Dominicans who take vows of poverty. If members of these orders work for a church organization or agency and their remuneration is under the control of the religious order, no taxes need be paid. If members work for a profit-making business, however, they must pay income and FICA taxes, although they may also claim a charitable deduction for the amount remitted to their religious order. In recent years, many religious orders have voluntarily paid the FICA tax for members who then qualify for Social Security benefits when they retire.

To summarize, taxation in the United States is complex and multilayered, leading to some litigation but overall quite successful. The same may be said for the relationships between taxing authorities and religious organizations.

See also *Constitution, U.S.; Freedom of religion; Separation of church and state.*

Paul J. Weber

BIBLIOGRAPHY

Bittker, Boris I. "Churches, Taxes, and the Constitution." *Yale Law Journal* 78 (1969): 1285–1310.

Kelley, Dean M. *Why Churches Should not Pay Taxes.* New York: Harper and Row, 1977.

Miller, Robert, and Ronald Flowers. *Toward Benevolent Neutrality: Church, State, and the Supreme Court.* 5th ed. Waco, Texas: Baylor University Press, 1997.

Monsma, Stephen V., and J. Christopher Soper. *The Challenge of Pluralism: Church and State in Five Democracies.* Lanham, Md.: Rowman and Littlefield, 1997.

Thomas, Oliver S. "The Power to Destroy: The Eroding Constitutional Arguments for Church Tax Exemption and the Practical Effect on Churches." *Cumberland Law Review* 22 (1992): 605–635.

Weber, Paul J., and Dennis Gilbert. *Private Churches and Public Money.* Westport, Conn.: Greenwood Press, 1981.

Technology

See *Science and technology*

Televangelism

See *Communication*

Temperance movements

Temperance movements, often motivated by religious belief or religiously based sensibilities, have arisen in many societies with the goal of reducing or eliminating consumption of alcoholic beverages. Believers' involvement in temperance movements sometimes flows from explicit scriptural injunctions against alcohol use or misuse. It can also derive from belief that alcohol use or abuse endangers the soul and causes physical damage or moral ruin to the drinker as well as injury to other members of the drinker's family, community, or society. Relationships between churches and believers on one hand and temperance movements on the other have been complex, however, because of the movements' proselytizing imperatives and frequent political involvement.

Temperance movements are a modern phenomenon, emerging since the early nineteenth century to accompany rapid economic change. They have appeared in societies characterized by various religious orientations, but they have been most durable and influential, as sociologist Harry Levine has pointed out, in cultures shaped by evangelical Protestantism. Both the contributions of evangelicalism to temperance and the complexities of their relationship can be seen in the United States, which has produced the world's most long-lasting and powerful series of temperance movements.

Nineteenth-century Temperance

Both religion and medicine influenced individual temperance advocacy and local societies during the late eighteenth and early nineteenth centuries. Temperance first became a mass movement during the 1820s, under the leadership of the American Temperance Society (founded in 1826). Its wide appeal was due in part to the influence of the religious revival of the Second Great Awakening (1800–1835), which, together with the stress on reason that came out of Enlightenment thought, envisioned the possibility of self-improvement for individuals and reform for society.

From the time they first began to attract large followings, temperance reformers faced a problem in justifying their evangelically inspired program in terms that would appeal to nonevangelicals and nonbelievers as well as evangelicals. As Protestant divisiveness and swelling tides of immigration made American society more diverse in religion and culture, their difficulties intensified. To sustain their cause, these earnest evangelicals came to present temperance more often as a road to individual health and social welfare than as a means of avoiding sin and finding salvation. Furthermore, they put forward a secular agency, the temperance society, as the best vehicle to travel that road. Temperance reformers thus inadvertently advanced the process of secularization.

The first major rift between temperance reformers and the churches appeared during the 1830s, after the temperance movement had shifted from its early program of abstinence from distilled spirits to teetotalism, or total abstinence from all intoxicating beverages. At this time, all Protestant churches holding a communion service used sacramental wine. In an effort to avoid alienating their religious supporters, teetotal activists tried either to claim that biblical use of wine was irrelevant to modern conditions or to reinterpret biblical references to wine as meaning unfermented grape juice. To Christians accustomed to regarding Scripture as a literal guide to action, the first argument was uncongenial, and the second, unpersuasive. As in Britain, the controversy over communion wine in the United States divided temperance reformers from their religious base. The sacramental function of wine continued to pose a problem for teetotalers and prohibitionists. Under national Prohibition (1920–1933), when sacramental wine was exempted from the scope of prohibitory legislation, the exemption created a loophole for nonsacramental uses.

The Women's Temperance Crusade of 1873–1874 and its product, the Woman's Christian Temperance Union (WCTU, founded in 1874), illustrate the tensions between temperance reformers and churches. The Women's Temperance Crusade, a nonviolent grassroots movement, featured mass marches against saloons and other retail liquor dealers in hundreds of northern communities, rescued temperance reform from its post–Civil War doldrums, and brought women to the forefront of temperance leadership. Many evangelical women took part in the marches and public prayers that constituted the crusade's principal tactics, churches often provided the crusaders' headquarters, and some evangelical ministers outspokenly supported the movement. But other clergymen, both nonevangelical and evangelical, held aloof or resisted the crusade, acting on fears that women's influence would increase or from anxiety that public prayer would be discredited.

By the 1890s, under the energetic and inspirational leadership of Frances E. Willard (1839–1898), the WCTU had grown to become the largest women's organization in the United States, and Willard became the period's most prominent woman evangelical. Yet evangelical churchmen were alienated when Willard endorsed radical causes such as woman suffrage, labor unionism, and Christian socialism. And Willard, an active lay Methodist, severely criticized the Methodist leadership for excluding her from the 1888 General Conference of the northern Methodist Episcopal Church because of her sex.

By the late nineteenth century most temperance reformers had become prohibitionists, advocating government action to ban the sale of alcoholic beverages, and prohibition became overtly political with the founding of the Prohibition Party in 1869. Despite their often impeccable evangelical credentials, some party prohibitionists voiced impatience with the evangelical churches because their institutional condemnations of the liquor trade were seldom backed up at the ballot box by evangelicals' votes for the Prohibition Party. A few such critics left the mainstream denominations to found "prohibition churches."

Although some party prohibitionists, like Willard, were radicalized by America's economic instability during the Gilded Age at the end of the century, conflict between labor and capital, and inequalities of wealth and power, the Protestant churches remained bastions of social and political conservatism. The party's relationship with the churches formed one of several divisive issues that eventually sundered the organization in 1896. As a result of the same conflicts, conservative prohibitionists organized the Anti-Saloon League of America in 1895 to compete with the Prohibition Party for the support of temperance voters. Central to its strategy was a radically different attitude toward the churches.

The Anti-Saloon League and National Prohibition

Looking for a political base among believers, the Anti-Saloon League labeled itself "the Church in Action Against the Saloon." To make prohibition politics less painful in a parti-

Law enforcement officials confiscate illegal liquor and a still during Prohibition. With the enactment of the Twenty-first Amendment repealing Prohibition, the states were granted power to regulate all aspects of alcohol control.

san age, the league asked voters to support only individual candidates who promised to vote for league-sponsored measures, not to abandon their political parties. To make its cause palatable to conservative middle-class voters, the league promised to confine its advocacy to prohibition. To present itself as successful, it accepted measures such as local option, which allowed districts to ban alcohol, as steps toward its eventual goal of national prohibition.

The Anti-Saloon League ensured church support by placing representatives of supporting denominations on its national and state boards of directors and giving them procedural control over its policy. These actions closed the rifts between the evangelical churches and the prohibition movement. Local churches began to designate one Sunday a year for an appeal from the pulpit by a league spokesperson, followed by a collection and pledge taking for the organization's support. The Prohibition Party had been led by businessmen, clergymen, and lawyers, but the Anti-Saloon League was staffed almost entirely by clergymen. National assemblies of the major evangelical churches supported the league's approach, and the Federal Council of Churches swung into action for prohibition. Most important, church-affiliated voters began to respond to the league's political endorsements and shift their votes accordingly.

As the Anti-Saloon League drew closer to the churches, changes within American religion made churchgoers more receptive to temperance reform. Within the Protestant churches, the progress of the Social Gospel—the churches' reform efforts to aid the poor—stemmed from dissatisfaction with the state of American society and justified political action to improve it. Prohibitionism appealed to this reformist mood by picturing itself as the key to reducing poverty and eliminating political corruption.

Within the Roman Catholic Church, the influence of Americanizers such as Archbishop John Ireland was used to promote temperance. American Catholic sympathy for temperance extended back at least as far as 1849, when the Irish priest Father Mathew followed his temperance triumphs in Ireland with a successful North American tour, during which he administered a temperance pledge to tens of thousands of immigrant Catholics. A successful similar campaign in Lower Canada by Father Charles Chiniquy about the same time demonstrated Catholic receptivity to the temperance message among a French-Canadian population. Irish immigrants and Irish-Americans were prominent in founding the Catholic Total Abstinence Union (1872). Catholic sympathy for temperance, however, rarely extended to prohibition, or even to support for non-Catholic temperance societies.

Having invested so heavily in the prohibition crusade, American Protestant churches seemed to have attained considerable influence when the Eighteenth Amendment to the Constitution, which enacted national Prohibition, went into effect in 1920. Prohibition held much popular support until the onset of the Great Depression in 1929, but the same could not be said for prohibition's leading advocates. For much of the decade of the 1920s the Anti-Saloon League maintained a rigid focus on law enforcement, refusing either to acknowledge the extent to which the law was flouted or to consider amending the law to allow consumption of light alcoholic beverages.

In the presidential campaign of 1928, "dry" southern evangelicals, led by Bishop James Cannon of the Methodist Episcopal Church South, mixed a stiff dose of anti-Catholicism with their opposition to the Democratic Party's "wet" standard-bearer, Al Smith. After the election, Cannon himself was discredited by allegations of corrupt and immoral activities. After the stock market crash of 1929, public opinion turned against national Prohibition, and the churches' political stock plunged accordingly.

Since Repeal

Since 1933, when the Twenty-first Amendment repealed national Prohibition, state governments have exercised greater authority over the conditions of liquor sale and consumption. Debates over liquor control have increasingly taken place among bureaucrats and academic experts, and America's long tradition of grassroots conflict over temperance has become attenuated. Religious belief has, however, figured prominently in the only significant grassroots temperance movement to appear in modern America.

The founders of Alcoholics Anonymous (AA), Bill Wilson (1895–1971) and Dr. Robert Smith (1879–1950), were influenced in their organization's early years (1935–1940) by the precepts of the Oxford Group, an organization founded in the United States that had branches in several countries. From the Oxford Group, Wilson and Smith took the practices of self-survey, confession, restitution to those one had harmed, and service to others. They added to their belief in the alcoholic's powerlessness against alcohol a conviction that recovery depended on surrender to a higher power (although the higher power could be the AA group as well as God).

Membership in AA expanded rapidly during the 1940s. During the same period the National Council on Alcoholism and the Yale Center for Alcohol Studies joined with AA to popularize a new view of habitual drunkenness, the disease concept of alcoholism. According to this view, most drinkers are not likely to misuse alcohol, but those who do act because they suffer from a physical malady that causes them to lose control over their drinking. Nevertheless, the disease of alcoholism is treatable. Original not in its view of alcohol as addictive but rather in the rigid distinction it drew between alcoholics and moderate drinkers, the identification of alcoholism as a disease rapidly gained currency during the 1940s and 1950s. Among its early supporters were the national assemblies of the major Protestant denominations and church federations.

Acceptance of alcoholism as a disease paved the way for increasing federal support for alcoholism research and treatment, especially after the establishment in 1970 of the National Institute on Alcohol Abuse and Alcoholism. It also fueled creation of a growing number of employee-assistance plans, through which corporations and government agencies could made provision for treatment of alcoholic workers. These changes subordinated religious perspectives to medical concerns and replaced religious activists with health care professionals and social workers. During the 1960s and 1970s, when rising consumption levels and increasing incidents of accidents involving drinking and driving led to consideration of new restrictions, churches played no significant role in the debates. Whether or not religion will reclaim its historically prominent place in the temperance cause, a role some researchers believe is necessary to lasting change in drinking habits, remains to be seen.

See also *Evangelicalism; Lobbying, Religious; Secularization*.

Jack S. Blocker Jr.

BIBLIOGRAPHY

Blocker, Jack S., Jr. *American Temperance Movements: Cycles of Reform.* Boston: Twayne, 1989.

———. *Retreat from Reform: The Prohibition Movement in the United States, 1890–1913.* Westport, Conn.: Greenwood Press, 1976.

Epstein, Barbara Leslie. *The Politics of Domesticity: Women, Evangelism, and Temperance in Nineteenth-Century America.* Middletown, Conn.: Wesleyan University Press, 1981.

Kurtz, Ernest R. *Not-God: A History of Alcoholics Anonymous.* Center City, Minn.: Hazelden Educational Services, 1979.

Levine, Harry G. "Temperance Cultures: Concern about Alcohol Problems in Nordic and English-Speaking Cultures." In *The Nature of Alcohol and Drug Related Problems,* edited by Malcolm Lader, Griffith Edwards, and D. Colin Drummond. New York: Oxford University Press, 1992.

Quinn, John F. "Father Mathew's Disciples: American Catholic Support for Temperance, 1840–1920." *Church History* 65 (December 1996): 624–640.

Tyrrell, Ian R. *Sobering Up: From Temperance to Prohibition in Antebellum America.* Westport, Conn.: Greenwood Press, 1979.

———. *Woman's World/Woman's Empire: The World's Woman's Christian Temperance Union in International Perspective, 1880–1930.* Chapel Hill: University of North Carolina Press, 1991.

Mother Teresa

Teresa, Mother

Roman Catholic nun, founder of the Missionaries of Charity, and winner of the 1979 Nobel Peace Prize. Mother Teresa (1910–1997) is considered by many to be a saint. She was born Agnes Gonxha Bojaxhiu in Skopje, Yugoslavia, the youngest of three children in a family of Albanian ethnicity. In 1928 she joined the Irish Sisters of Loreto, a religious community with a mission in Calcutta, India, and assumed the name Teresa. In 1929 she went to Calcutta, teaching at the prestigious St. Mary's High School. Eventually she became the school's principal. She served with distinction but felt her comfortable life and work becoming spiritually unfulfilling.

In 1946 she fell ill and was sent to recuperate in the mountain climate of Darjeeling. While on the train there, she felt a second call—to give up everything and follow Jesus to the slums of Calcutta. She left the convent and taught children in the slums. The children called her Mother Teresa.

In 1948 she found a woman lying in front of a Calcutta hospital, dying. Staying with the woman until she died, and comforting her, she found the vocation for which she is remembered. With a small group of like-minded women, she formed the Missionary Sisters of Charity, to serve the outcasts of Calcutta.

In 1952 she opened the Nirmal Hriday (Pure Heart) Home for the Dying in a former Hindu temple. Here destitute and dying people could be brought to end their lives with dignity in caring surroundings. From then until her death, Mother Teresa worked tirelessly for her cause. Her increasing fame became an important factor in her ministry's growth. At her death the organization had grown from 12 sisters in India to more than 3,000 in 517 missions in 100 countries. The order continues to provide food for the needy and operates hospitals, schools, orphanages, youth centers, and shelters for lepers and the dying poor. Personally vowed to poverty, Mother Teresa was a brilliant fund-raiser. Indeed, she was occasionally criticized as insufficiently sensitive to the origins of the money she was receiving. The most famous instance was a gift from the Duvalier family, then rulers of Haiti.

To understand how Mother Teresa's life relates to twentieth-century politics, it is important to note that for many

Christians the relationship with Jesus is a direct day-by-day encounter with a living person. They believe that they see Jesus in everyone they meet. And in helping the helpless they are not merely doing what Jesus would have done, they are in some sense helping Jesus himself. Mother Teresa's life is a good example of this tradition within Christianity.

A frequent consequence of this concern with helping individuals is a corresponding lack of emphasis on helping people as groups. Unlike Dorothy Day, another twentieth-century Roman Catholic regarded by many as a saint, Mother Teresa was not much involved with political activity on behalf of the poor and downtrodden.

She was an influential figure in the Catholic Church's life, and a friend of Pope John Paul II. A staunch defender of traditional Catholic positions, she put her prestige behind the church's stand against abortion, frequently saying that abortion was one of the greatest evils facing the world.

Mother Teresa received many honors, culminating with the 1979 Nobel Peace Prize. She insisted that the celebratory banquet be canceled in favor of a donation to help the destitute. The Indian government gave her a state funeral.

See also *Day, Dorothy; India.*

Tony Davies

BIBLIOGRAPHY

Hitchens, Christopher. *The Missionary Position: Mother Teresa in Theory and Practice.* New York: Verso Books, 1995.

Muggeridge, Malcolm. *Something Beautiful for God: Mother Teresa of Calcutta.* New York: Harper and Row, 1971.

Spink, Kathryn. *Mother Teresa: A Complete Authorized Biography.* San Francisco: Harper San Francisco, 1997.

Teresa, Mother. *My Life for the Poor: Mother Teresa of Calcutta.* San Francisco: Harper and Row, 1985.

Terrorism

See *Violence*

Theocracy

Theocracy, derived from two Greek words meaning "rule by the deity," is the name given to political regimes that claim to represent the Divine on earth both directly and immediately. The idea of direct and immediate representation is important for two reasons.

First, most governments throughout history and across cultures have claimed to be following their gods' designs or to be legitimated by a divine mandate. An example is the notion that kings rule by divine right. (This theory, which had been important in European politics in the sixteenth century, lost ground after the "Glorious Revolution" in England in 1688.) But governments in which the ruling and the priestly roles are separate are not considered to be theocracies. Second, the divine mandate must be interpreted by human beings in specific political contexts, such as wars or floods or famines. In theocracies the interpreters—who explain what these events mean—are the rulers. A number of ancient civilizations worshipped their kings as gods on earth, so the problem of interpretation was somewhat different. By definition, the king could not be wrong.

In theory, there is no reason why a theocracy and a democratic form of government are incompatible—*vox populi, vox dei* ("the voice of the people is the voice of God")—but historically those nations regarded as theocracies have been ruled by a theologically trained elite. This may be a council of clerics, or a charismatic leader may claim a special call from God and gain office by force of arms. The office might later become hereditary. The primary effort of government in a theocracy is to implement and enforce divine laws.

Variations on Theocratic Governments

As archeologists are slowly solving the mysteries of early civilizations it seems certain that the ancient Hebrews, Tibetans, and Egyptians lived in theocracies for some of their history. So did early American civilizations, including the Mayans, Toltecs, Aztecs, Natchez, and a still mysterious community that built the Teotihuacan pyramids north of Mexico City.

Generally, Christian nations have been inclined to keep church and state separate, although there have been frequent efforts by each to dominate the other. Among Christian societies the most notable attempts to create theocracies were the Papal States under various popes, Geneva under John Calvin's control in the sixteenth century, and the New England colonies under the Puritans in the seventeenth century. In the contemporary world only the Vatican might be considered a Christian theocracy—and that only in a technical sense. Vatican City, a one-hundred-acre-territory established in Rome by the Lateran Treaty of 1929, is the successor to

Banners depicting the former supreme religious leader of Iran, the late Ayatollah Ruholla Musavi Khomeini (left), and his successor, Ayatollah Sayed Ali Khameini, were unfurled in preparation for the eighth Islamic Summit, held in Tehran in December 1997. Khomeini led the 1979 religious revolution that toppled the shah and established a theocracy in Iran.

the Papal States. It is the headquarters of the Roman Catholic Church and the home of the pope. Final executive, legislative, and judicial powers are vested in the pope. The Vatican claims state sovereignty and maintains diplomatic relations with many nations. It has a small population and its primary purpose is to manage worldwide Catholicism.

In the latter part of the twentieth century numerous Muslim groups have attempted to establish Islamic theocracies. Some argue that theocracies are the natural form of government for Islam. Certainly, there is historic precedent. The community established by the prophet Muhammad in Medina in 622, and ruled by him until his death in 632, was a theocracy in which he served as both temporal and spiritual leader. The communities established by his father-in-law and successor, Abu Bakr, the first caliph, over the next ten years were organized as theocracies as well. These communities, which covered the territory that now encompasses Iraq, Syria, and Egypt, were regarded as an Islamic ideal for centuries to come.

There is also some theological basis for viewing theocracy as an Islamic ideal type of government. Muhammad established the *umma* (community of believers) as a holistic political community rooted in a faith that consciously sought to replace blood, geography, ethnicity, and language as the primary social bond. Yet there is no single model for how a contemporary Islamic theocracy should be organized. There is no certainty that people will voluntarily accept a theocratic form of government for long. There is even less agreement on whether theocracy is intrinsic to Islam or simply a historical phase. Some scholars argue that democracy is perfectly compatible with Islam, although this assertion is vigorously contested.

In the contemporary world, Iran and Afghanistan are considered theocracies because ultimate political authority in each is in the hands of religious leaders and a fundamentalist regime whose purpose is to organize society under religious law, the *shari'a*. There are significant political pressures from fundamentalist Muslims to move toward theocratic forms of government in Algeria, Pakistan, Egypt, Sudan, Turkey, and other Islamic countries. These efforts are resisted by various other groups within these nations, most notably by the armies in Turkey and Algeria, which prefer a more secular state. It is unclear which forces will eventually triumph.

It is also unclear exactly what these political pressures mean—whether they are efforts to establish a true theocratic form of government or, as some scholars claim, to use religious rhetoric, symbolism, and values for nationalistic purposes. Islamic ideals may be used to win popular support for liberation from foreign domination or from an autocratic ruling elite, to encourage economic renewal, and to revitalize Islamic cultural hegemony. There are historical examples to support these claims. Egyptian nationalists appealed to Islam to rally citizens in their struggle to win independence from Great Britain. Ayatollah Ruholla Khomeini smuggled religious sermons into Iran to turn Iranians against the corrupt regime of the shah. Saddam Husayn appealed to his people unsuccessfully to take up a *jihad,* or holy war, during the Persian Gulf War in 1991. Taliban imposition of *shariʿa* in Afghanistan is an effort to restore Islamic customs and culture.

In Israel as well there are political pressures to move in the direction of restoring the theocracy of ancient times. Several ultra-Orthodox parties advocate such a return but are not considered likely to succeed in the foreseeable future.

Internal and External Problems

When they do gain power theocracies tend to be short lived for a number of reasons, some internal to the regime and others external to it. Internally, clerics trained in religious dogma and jurisprudence are rarely skilled in economic matters and have difficulty maintaining a complex modern economy. When corruption occurs among government officials, ensuing scandals undermine religion as well as politics if those officials are also clerics. Resentment grows among the nonclerical populace when religious laws seem arbitrary or excessively strict and are enforced through civil power. Religious taxes imposed on top of other taxes, especially in times of economic hardship, cause added resentment. Finally, clerics who presume to speak in the name of the Divinity have difficulty engaging in normal compromises so essential for political effectiveness. Such compromises may even seem to them to be immoral or sinful. Finally, in states controlled by one party, which theocracies tend to be, police are often tempted to resort to brutality and other harsh measures that undermine the legitimacy of the regime.

Externally, rulers in other nations often fear the exportation of religious dogma backed by political power and move to isolate a theocratic regime. And because secular cultures from outside can exert a constant seductive influence on young people through music, arts, clothes, and movies, and infuse them with political ideas of freedom, democracy, and equality, a theocratic regime is inclined to limit contact with the outside world. Such actions increase isolation of the country but often lead to a fascination with the outside and an underground opposition to the regime. Such conditions are not conducive to longevity, and theocracies rarely outlive their founding generation.

See also *Calvinism; Separation of church and state; Vatican.*

Paul J. Weber

BIBLIOGRAPHY

Ajami, Fouad. "The Sorrows of Egypt." *Foreign Affairs* 74 (September–October 1995): 72–88.

Azar, Edward, and A. Chung-in Moon. "The Many Faces of Islamic Revivalism." In *Spirit Matters: The Worldwide Impact of Religion on Contemporary Politics,* edited by Richard L. Rubenstein. New York: Paragon House, 1987.

Mehr, Farhang. "The Impact of Religion on Contemporary Politics: The Case of Iran." In *Spirit Matters: The Worldwide Impact of Religion on Contemporary Politics,* edited by Richard L. Rubenstein. New York: Paragon House, 1987.

Schall, James V. "Theocracy." In *The Catholic Encyclopedia.* New York: McGraw-Hill, 1967.

Sprinzak, Ehud. *The Ascendance of Israel's Radical Right.* New York: Oxford University Press, 1991.

Teimourian, Hazhir. "Iran's Fifteen Years of Islam." *World Today,* April 1994, 67.

Tocqueville, Alexis de

Eminent European social thinker of the nineteenth century. Tocqueville (1805–1859) is regarded as an incomparable analyst of the prospects and pitfalls of modern democracy. He was the child of an aristocratic French family, some of whose members had suffered death and devastation at the hands of the French Revolution. As a consequence, Tocqueville was haunted all his life by the fear of revolutionary anarchy and of the ideological tyranny it brought in its wake. But such fears never led him to advocate the restoration of the prerevolutionary French social order. On the contrary, he was firmly convinced that the movement toward social equality represented an inescapable feature of the modern age, to which social or political analysis must accommodate itself. Although Tocqueville was a keen analyst of democracy's unlovely or dangerous features, he insisted that the most effective response to them was the development of a "new science of politics," designed to refine democracy's crudities and counter its pathologies.

A concern with the meaning of modern democracy is the pervasive theme of his *Democracy in America* (1835–1840), the work for which he is best known, and the one in which he dealt most explicitly with the relationship between religion and politics. A two-volume study based on his nine-month tour of the United States in 1831–1832, *Democracy* is one of the richest and most enduring studies of American society and culture ever written. Tocqueville envisioned the United States as a nation moving in the vanguard of history, a great republic with an extraordinary degree of social equality among its inhabitants. In America, he believed, one could see embodied, in exemplary or heightened form, the future

Alexis de Tocqueville

condition toward which the rest of the world was tending. In America one could gaze upon "the image of democracy itself, with its inclinations, its character, its prejudices, and its passions"—and, having so gazed, could proceed to deal more intelligently and effectively with the democratic changes coming to Europe.

Religion and Democracy

Although the two volumes of *Democracy in America* differed in significant ways, together they present a memorable image of American social and individual character. Tocqueville's America was a strikingly middle-class society: feverishly commercial and acquisitive, obsessively practical-minded, jealously egalitarian, and restlessly mobile. Chief among the dangers presented by this bumptious democracy were the linked phenomena of individualism and materialism: the tendency of citizens to withdraw from involvement in public life and instead regard themselves as autonomous and isolated actors, with no higher goal than the pursuit of material well-being. Tocqueville acknowledged that in a modern commercial democracy self-interest would inevitably come to be accepted as the chief engine of all human striving. So how had Americans of the 1830s prevented self-interest from overwhelming all considerations of the public good and undermining the sources of social cohesion?

Tocqueville found much of the answer in the pervasive influence of religion in American life. He was impressed by the persistence of Christianity in the American democracy and by the ways that American religion served to support democratic values and institutions. Such a development seemed particularly surprising, coming as it did at the very time when educated Europeans were abandoning religious faith and practice, in the mistaken belief that the "spirit of liberty" was incompatible with the authoritarian "spirit of religion." Tocqueville's visit to America convinced him that the opposite was true. In America religious beliefs and institutions restrained self-assertion in ways that made the exercise of freedom more stable and more effective than they otherwise would have been.

Although religion took no direct or official role in governance, Americans regarded it as indispensable to the maintenance of republican government. In a society that had clearly separated church and state, liberty and religion would actually reinforce one another. Liberty supported religion by making it voluntary, the democratic form of assent. But religion was also needed to support liberty, both as a source of independent support for the free will and as a way to strengthen the "moral tie" binding a society.

Materialism and Civil Religion

Tocqueville was always intensely concerned about materialism, a concern that connected acquisitive materialism—the desire to possess more and more things—with philosophical materialism—the belief that the soul is perishable and that only matter exists. As a social philosopher committed to the power of free will and the ideal of self-rule, Tocqueville found the deterministic implications of philosophical materialism intolerable and condemned it forcefully as a "dangerous disease of the mind." Fortunately, he believed, the Americans had so far proved resistant to its temptations. But without the countervailing force of religion and, in particular, without a belief in the moral responsibility of the immortal soul, democratic institutions could easily be overwhelmed by their tendency to beget an uncontrolled passion for physical gratification.

There are controversial points in Tocqueville's understanding of American religion. Many scholars complain that Tocqueville's generalizations about the American character miss the extraordinary social diversity that was already characteristic of the country. Some argue that, in dismissing American religion's disposition toward emotional revivalism as an expression of "fanatical spiritualism," Tocqueville underestimated one of the most vital forms of American Protestantism, one that played a crucial role in strengthening and stabilizing the democratic moral and political order. More generally speaking, Tocqueville's stance often makes it difficult to tell whether he believed that the power of American religion derived from its truth, its usefulness, or both. Nevertheless, Tocqueville remains a principal source for the influential idea that American democracy relies upon the moral support provided by a "civil religion," which legitimizes the political order by relating it to transcendent ideals and purposes. In this respect, as in many others, his work will continue to be at the center of debates over the relationship between religion and politics in a democratic society.

See also *Civil religion; Individualism; Public theology; Revivalism; Separation of church and state; Voluntarism.*

Wilfred M. McClay

BIBLIOGRAPHY

Boesche, Roger. *The Strange Liberalism of Alexis de Tocqueville.* Ithaca, N.Y.: Cornell University Press, 1987.

Eisenstadt, Abraham, ed. *Reconsidering Tocqueville's Democracy in America.* New Brunswick, N.J.: Rutgers University Press, 1988.

Goldstein, Doris S. *Trial of Faith: Religion and Politics in Tocqueville's Thought.* New York: Elsevier, 1975.

Jardin, André. *Tocqueville: A Biography.* Translated by Lydia Davis with Robert Hemenway. New York: Farrar, Straus, and Giroux, 1988.

Pierson, George Wilson. *Tocqueville and Beaumont in America.* New York: Oxford University Press, 1938.

Tocqueville, Alexis de. *Democracy in America.* 2 vols. Edited by Phillips Bradley. New York: Knopf, 1945.

Traditionalism

In simple terms, traditionalism may be defined as an adherence to the beliefs, values, and behaviors of previous generations; it implies a distrust of change and alternatives. It is a term that may refer either to the means by which truth or right belief is sought or to the nature of the ideological outcome. Traditionalism is not necessarily an orientation that excludes other dispositions, and many traditionalist ideas may coexist in a group or an individual with progressive ones. As a further obstacle to simple definition, traditionalism is a contextual phenomenon: a religious or political orientation is characterized as traditionalist in contrast to available alternatives. Thus a set of beliefs or practices may cease to be traditionalist when the context changes.

In one of its narrowest senses, for example, traditionalism is a philosophical system that arose in the Roman Catholic Church in Europe in the early nineteenth century according to which religious and moral truth is derived only from an original revelation mediated by traditional instruction. In this sense, it is the extreme form of anti-rationalism and is associated with French thinkers Joseph de Maistre (1753–1821), Louis de Bonald (1754–1840), and Félicité de Lamennais (1782–1854). In a broader sense, traditionalism represents a subscription to the authority of traditional doctrines and sources and may imply an excessive reverence for time-honored forms.

Both narrow and broad senses here refer to the process of belief rather than its product: they relate the believer or group of believers to a source of authority independent of the content of belief. From the work of de Lamennais, a priest who defended papal authority, is derived the idea that the authenticity of a religious system is tested by its antiquity, perpetuity, and universality.

Traditionalism is also used to signify the tendency to resist change: traditionalists are the opposite of progressives. It is widely associated with a view of history that the past is better than the present. In the Roman Catholic Church today, traditionalism normally signifies a reluctance to adopt the reformist spirit of the Second Vatican Council of the 1960s and its emphasis on renewal and rejuvenation. It implies a notion of human agency in degeneration such as that voiced by Old Testament prophets who called upon Israel to restore a right relationship with God (Yahweh). To talk of traditionalists in this way is to imply an overbearing disposition or personality that determines the wide agenda of religious belief and practice and of political orientation. There is substantial evidence against this view: the compartments of religious faith and practice are relatively independent of each other. A Christian may be traditionalist in liturgical preference yet radical in the preaching of a political gospel, and a religious organization like the Roman Catholic Church in Poland may deploy traditionalism in resistance of secularization yet endorse a progressive agenda on human rights (albeit prompted in part by an instinct for self-preservation).

Within the Western Christian churches—if not in the Eastern Orthodox churches, not in Islam, and not in academic usage—traditionalism has carried a sense of disapproval as though it represents an unrealistic, anti-intellectual stance and even a resistance to God's will. Some groups with a conservative agenda and traditionalist sense of church history are careful to avoid being thought of as traditionalist: for example, in the Church of England, the umbrella group that has continued to resist the ordination of women even after ordination was approved in 1992 uses the most modern of liturgies available and calls itself Forward in Faith.

Traditionalism and Change

Patterns of religious belief and behavior are most important to their adherents when they are threatened. It was during the Babylonian exile, beginning in 586 B.C., that the Jewish people introduced synagogue worship for the first time, made Hebrew their sacred language, introduced male circumcision as a sign of differentiation from gentiles, and imposed a taboo on intermarriage. Organized religion provided the Jews with a system that symbolized the social isolation of their subordinate community from that of the host society.

Similarly, communities have frequently celebrated their traditions in religious terms and withdrawn from the wider society to avoid various kinds of corruption. Such groups include the Amish in Pennsylvania, Illinois, and elsewhere in the United States; the Hutterite brethren now dispersed throughout the world; the communitarian Doukhobors, who were established mainly in Canada as refugees from Russia; and the American Shakers, now few in number but exerting a persistent cultural influence in the domain of values. Until late in the nineteenth century English Quakers, though not communitarian in their withdrawal, maintained a detachment from the dominant culture in their habits of speech and other forms of behavior called "peculiarities." Among American Quakers this kind of distancing persists in the Ohio (Conservative) Yearly Meeting. The Ohio meeting is the outstanding example of a tendency that is to be found in more moderate forms elsewhere. The behavioral manifestations include dress and peculiarities of speech formed in earlier centuries and a conservative position on moral issues.

Where a traditionalist community and the dominant society are compelled to confront each other, in such issues as military conscription or the payment of taxes, the conflict of ideologies may be expressed in political protest. Quakers have objected to national service on conscientious grounds and have withheld taxes for purposes unacceptable to them, be these defense or public education. In the period after the Second World War, Doukhobors in British Columbia protested against local government by removing their clothes and burning their own properties.

A particular aspect of sectarian detachment from state systems has been a resistance to the cosmopolitan educational curriculum in multicultural societies. Some faith communities have regarded the broad-based curriculum as a dilution of traditional forms and an erosion of received culture. In the United States, where neighborhoods have often been composed of single ethnic groups, there has been a tendency to use the language of the community in schools. In Britain, however, urban areas typically are multicultural and no one language or ethnic origin prevails. The minority communities, sensitive to the dilution of their cultures and religions, and especially to the elimination of mother tongues, look to their religious organizations to provide separate agencies to transmit the traditional culture and maintain the moral systems that are often seen to be more pure than those of the permissive Western society. In these circumstances, Muslims and other faith communities have widely organized their own "supplementary" weekend schools and campaigned for their own day schools.

Poland and Iran

In all of these cases the custodians of the traditions to be maintained constitute statistical minorities within their host societies. Similar issues and conflicts arise, however, when a secular or relatively secular state operates policies that are perceived to conflict with the inheritance of the majority. Two examples are Poland and Iran.

In the division of Eastern Europe among the victorious Allied forces at the end of the Second World War in 1945, Poland was assigned to Russia and accordingly given a Communist government. But "Mother Poland" is a cultural phenomenon that transcends political regimes: it exists as a spiritual identity even when it cannot be found on the map. Its history has been one of invasion, partition, and at times virtual extinction. The Polish Catholic Church had the capacity, after 1945, to connect with the country's historical identity, with national sentiment and emotion. It was, many believed, the Black Madonna of Czestochowa who had diverted German pilots sent to bomb the city. At Nowa Huta, the Communist model city near Krakow built to prove that man could live without God, there arose in the 1970s a magnificent and defiant church building. And Krakow's Cardinal Karol Wojtyla, a thorn in the flesh of the Communist government, went on to become Pope John Paul II, in 1978. Polish Catholicism had the capacity to inspire and legitimize political resistance. Its traditional power base was the Polish peasantry, which resisted land reform more effectively than any other peasantry in the Eastern bloc. In due course it came to address a modern agenda of human rights, issues of censorship, and the organization of independent trade unions like Solidarity. When a system such as the Communist becomes entrenched, the adherence to former values is seen as radical or progressive.

In Iran as in Poland the secular, or relatively secular, regime encountered economic problems, and a dormant religious opposition seized political opportunity. The last of the Pahlavi shahs, Muhammad Reza, introduced a "White Revolution," in 1963, which entailed a series of political and social reforms. Among the reforms were a literacy campaign, a program to pipe clean water to the villages, and measures to emancipate women. Resistance to this program from the mullahs, the religious intelligentsia, was aggravated by the shah's Western associations and evidence that modernization was being conceived in secular, Westernizing terms. Even the definition of "clean water" was disputed between medical and ritual specifications, and water pipes were sabotaged. Such was the extent of resistance to the shah's liberal reforms that he adopted extreme measures to see his White Revolution through, including the commissioning of a hated secret police, SAVAK. The benefits of Iran's oil wealth were not widely shared under the shah's rule, and the prospect of a traditionalist Islamic government seemed no worse than the Pahlavi dictatorship. So it was that in 1979 Muhammad Reza was forced to leave the country, and the leading religious dissident, Ruholla Khomeini, returned from exile in France and established a revolutionary Islamic government.

Both Iran and Poland illustrate the conditions conducive to the ascendancy of traditionalism. It is in the context of progressivism that traditionalism assumes a distinct identity. Indeed, the Roman Catholic Church in Poland adhered to values, such as the right to celebrate festivals, that were perceived as traditional and outmoded in the early years of its opposition. But those values were central to human rights claims that in time came to be seen as more modern than the ideology of the incumbent secular regime that disallowed them.

In both Poland and Iran religion provides the validating principle and system for the recovery of traditional values that are perceived to be jeopardized in the course of secularization. A secular state that is rejected as ungodly, whether it be the state of Israel in the estimation of Orthodox Jews or the American political system in the assessments of conservative churches, provides a focus for sectarian withdrawal and an independent quest for moral and spiritual purity. The steady growth enjoyed by all the major denominations in the United States from the early nineteenth century slowed and was reversed in the 1960s for all except the conservative churches.

Traditionalism as Religious Subculture

Within a religious culture there are likely to be conflicting tendencies toward opposite sets of beliefs and practices. These may be resolved by the forms of local or regional organization of churches and congregations that allow escape from an uncongenial climate and settlement in another. Alternatively, unacceptable belief and practice may provide the basis for a split and the establishment of a separate organization.

Significantly, traditionalist religious communities have tended to distinguish themselves in dress and other dimensions of behavior. Those that regard modernity as corrosive of the spiritual life have adopted the dress of a former age: among the most conspicuous of such groups are the Amish whose men and boys wear dark suits and brimmed hats and whose women wear bonnets and aprons.

As the principle of alignment, traditionalism has tended to prevail more in the smaller sects than in the mainstream churches. More recently, however, it has been a significant factor in the adjustment of identities within the churches of the Anglican Communion. The principal divide in the past has been that of churchmanship: those tending toward a "Catholic" sacramental type of theology and worship have occupied one end of the continuum (having some affinity with the church of Rome), and those of Protestant tendencies have occupied the other. These positions have been called respectively "high" and "low" church, and the ground between them has always been well populated.

In the late twentieth century, however, the principal basis for identifying positions within the Anglican Church has changed. Although affiliation at the local level continues to follow lines of churchmanship, individuals and local congregations have aligned themselves with camps in regard to a series of ecclesiastical and social issues. These issues have included divorce, the ordination of women, the modernization of the liturgy, and homosexuality in relation to the ordained ministry. Corresponding issues in the Roman Catholic Church have included the persistence of the traditional Latin Mass rather than the vernacular, teachings on abortion and birth control, and clerical celibacy and its formal alternative, the marriage of priests.

The effect of the debates and decisions in these matters has been to bring together factions of the high and low church in traditionalist organizations normally constituted around single issues. So in the United Kingdom, Australia, the United States, and other parts of the English-speaking world, the Prayer Book Society exists to maintain the use of the Book of Common Prayer of 1662 as a means of worship and a norm of doctrine. The Anglican ordination of women in Hong Kong in 1971, in Burma the following year, in Canada and New Zealand in 1975, and, in 1976, the formal acceptance of women illegally ordained in the United States culminated in a decision by the General Synod of the Church of England to allow women to be ordained in England, where the first ordinations of women were conducted in 1994. Like the Prayer Book Society, the Movement for the Ordination of Women and the organized resistance Forward in Faith brought together individuals and congregations representing the full range of churchmanship, from evangelical to Catholic.

For all this, it is not appropriate to talk of a "traditionalist camp" in modern Christianity, of which the case of the Church of England is discussed here. The traditionalist organizations have elements of common membership, but each relates to one issue alone. Members of the Prayer Book Society may be largely opposed to the ordination of women, but this opposition is not true of all and they look elsewhere for company and leadership on other issues.

Emerging Developments

Traditionalism commonly operates as a defensive and legitimizing ideology to maintain and transmit received culture, especially when it is endangered. In the late 1970s the Islamic governments of Gen. Mohammad Zia ul-Haq in Pakistan and Ayatolla Khomeini in Iran were established in the tension between a Western secular conception of modernization and the desires to conserve the traditional cultural inheritance. Traditionalism then is a function of particular social and political conditions. Where the dominance of an incompatible ideology threatens the survival of habits and values, the resort to traditionalism is a strategy of resistance. The introduction of secular programs of modernization provides the ideal condition for the ascendancy of traditionalism. Whether in ancient Babylon, modern Israel, Poland, Iran, or the United States, the resistance to corrosive values is ritually expressed in habits of traditional behavior and dress and is organized as political opposition with a sacred warrant.

One of the significant features of recent developments in the mainstream religious organizations has been the emergence of traditionalist subcultures as a reaction to the assimilation by churches of modern values dominant in the secular world and perhaps emanating from it: these include the admission of women to the ordained ministry and the increasing tolerance of alternatives in matters of sexual morality.

Traditionalist orientations may be found in a variety of religious dimensions, in liturgical preferences, in attitudes toward political systems, in morality, in issues of gender. These may coexist but they are essentially independent variables.

Within the religious domain, traditionalism may be typified at three levels of political engagement. First, many traditionalist religious movements are reclusive, withdrawing from a hostile world and seeking personal or communal purification in isolation. Seclusion offers the prospect of belief and lifestyle that are innocent of the tensions of the modern world to compete, to pursue material goals, and to assimilate undesired values and beliefs. Although frequently rationalized as a quest for lost values and the protection of the sacred community, insulation allows the exploration of sometimes radical modes of social organization. The American Amish provide a pure example of this type as do some—but by no means all—of the communal settlements *(kibbutzim)* in Israel. In Great Britain and other parts of the world the separatist movement among Muslims seeking ways to operate their own schools and administer an independent economy represents a current form of the reclusive mode.

Alternatively, traditionalist groups may enter the political sphere and elect or find themselves in a resistant, or opposition, mode. Such groups may participate in lobbying and crusading for moral causes. The conservative churches in the United States and the Noncomformist sects in Great Britain,

Jehovah's Witnesses the world over, Roman Catholic and Orthodox Churches in Eastern Europe, and minority Shi'ite Muslims in Iran have functioned, with various degrees of optimism, as dormant political opposition movements.

In recent years, however, religious traditionalists have increasingly been enfranchised or politically empowered. The establishment of governments with a religious base in Iran, Pakistan, and Poland is a phenomenon symptomatic of the fragility of secularism in the late twentieth century. Regimes that express themselves in material terms are compelled to deliver on those terms. As secular governments have either lost hold of the economy or lost touch with traditional and popular culture, the recovery of religious systems has been secured either by popular acclaim or by the strategy of religious leaders or by the dynamic connection of the two.

See also *Conservatism; Fundamentalism; Liberalism; Secularization.*

Roger Homan

BIBLIOGRAPHY

Haynes, Jeffrey. *Religion in Third World Politics.* Buckingham, England: Open University Press; Boulder, Colo.: Lynne Rienner, 1993.

Kelley, Dean M. *Why the Conservative Churches Are Growing: A Study in Sociology of Religion.* Macon, Ga.: Mercer University Press, 1977.

Martin, David, and Peter Mullen, eds. *No Alternative: The Prayer Book Controversy.* Oxford: Blackwell, 1981.

Michel, Patrick. *Politics and Religion in Eastern Europe: Catholicism in Hungary, Poland, and Czechoslovakia.* Translated by Alan Braley. London: Polity Press, 1991.

Wilson, Bryan R. *Religious Sects: A Sociological Study.* London: World University Library; New York: McGraw-Hill, 1970.

Tunisia

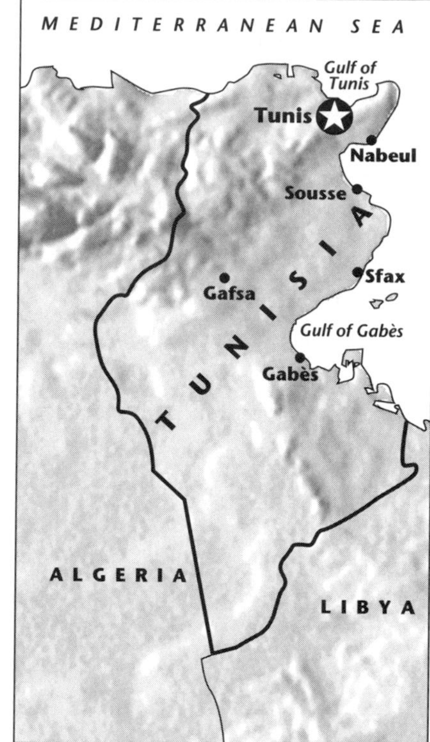

In the seventh century soldiers from Arabia introduced Islam into the area that is now Tunisia, a North African state with the Mediterranean Sea to the north and the Sahara to the south. For almost a millennium, a succession of Muslim rulers, some from North Africa, controlled this territory. The Ottoman Empire absorbed Tunisia in the sixteenth century and administered the province from Istanbul. By the eighteenth century these officials had become virtually independent of the sultan's authority. In 1882 France proclaimed a protectorate over Tunisia to secure the eastern borders of its Algerian colony and to deny control of Tunisia to its European rivals. A nationalist movement developed in the 1920s and, following World War II, demanded the termination of the protectorate.

After gaining independence from France in 1956, Tunisia embarked on an era of single-party rule under President Habib Bourguiba, who had led the nationalist movement since the 1930s, and Bourguiba's Neo-Dustur (New Constitution) Party. An early government priority was to improve Tunisians' quality of life through social and economic reform. Crucial to fulfilling this vision were the widespread availability of modern education and the enhancement of the status of women to enable them to engage actively in national development. The success of modernizing endeavors demanded state control over matters that previously had been within the purview of Muslim religious authorities.

A critical step in this process was the enactment in 1956 of a personal status code banning or altering many traditions sanctioned by Islamic law. Among other things the code, which was the most sweeping legislation of its kind in the Muslim world since Kemal Atatürk's reforms in Turkey three decades earlier, outlawed polygyny, set minimum ages for marriage, allowed either spouse to file for divorce, legitimized marriages between persons of different faiths, and increased the proportion of a widow's inheritance. Along with the government's incorporation of religious schools into the public education system and its abolition of Islamic courts, the code engendered animosity among those who disapproved of Tunisia's secular orientation. Lacking the wherewithal to confront the state, however, Islamist groups grudgingly acquiesced. Their smoldering resentment contributed to the emergence in the 1980s of a movement demanding a return to traditional Islamic practices.

By then Tunisia's economy had sustained a series of setbacks. After abandoning a controversial program of central planning and state intervention in the late 1960s, the government adopted a more liberal approach, only to see the trade deficit widen and consumer price increases outstrip wages in the decade that followed. A general strike in 1978 spawned the worst rioting since independence. Islamist groups took advantage of the generally deteriorating situation to mobilize large segments of the discontented populace.

The Islamists obsessed Bourguiba, who regarded them as mortal threats to the essentially secular society he had built. Despite mounting pressure for political liberalization, his fear of the Islamists' potential strength led him to reject any measure that might have amplified their influence. Bourguiba's insistence on severe punishment of Islamist leaders persuaded his associates that senility and ill health were preventing him from executing his duties responsibly. In accordance with a constitutional provision on the incapacity of the chief executive, Prime Minister Zine el-Abidine Ben Ali declared Bourguiba unable to govern and assumed the presidency on November 7, 1987.

Proclaiming his commitment to political pluralism and economic liberalism, Ben Ali legitimized many proscribed political organizations, eased restrictive press laws, granted amnesty to thousands of political prisoners, and opened negotiations with the Islamists, although he declined to recognize their party, al-Nahda (the Islamic Tendency Movement). The government's overwhelming electoral victory in 1989 convinced the Islamists that Ben Ali opposed their engagement in politics no less than Bourguiba had, prompting extremists to resort to violence. Supported by the many Tunisians who dreaded the prospect of their nation descending into sectarian strife, Ben Ali responded with vigorous repressive measures, which, by 1992, effectively crippled the public face of the Islamist movement. An underground opposition continued to operate.

See also *Bourguiba, Habib; Colonialism; Secularization.*

Kenneth J. Perkins

BIBLIOGRAPHY

Boulby, Marion. "The Islamic Challenge: Tunisia since Independence." *Third World Quarterly* 10 (1988): 590–614.

Burgat, François. *The Islamic Movement in North Africa.* Austin: University of Texas Press, 1993.

Dunn, Michael C. "The al-Nahda Movement in Tunisia: From Renaissance to Revolution." In *Islam and Secularism in North Africa,* edited by John Ruedy. New York: St. Martin's, 1994.

Tessler, Mark, Janet Rogers, and Daniel Schneider. "Women's Emancipation in Tunisia." In *Women in the Muslim World,* edited by Lois Beck and Nikki Keddie. Cambridge: Harvard University Press, 1978.

Zartman, I. William, ed. *Tunisia: The Political Economy of Reform.* Boulder, Colo.: Lynne Rienner, 1991.

Turkey

A predominantly Muslim country in southeastern Europe and southwestern Asia, the modern Republic of Turkey was founded in 1923 by Mustafa Kemal Atatürk from a portion of the Ottoman Empire (thirteenth to early twentieth centuries) when the empire broke up after World War I (1914–1918). Lying at the crossroads of Asia and Europe, the area has been politically strategic and religiously significant for millennia.

Modern Turkey inherited its pattern of religious and political interaction from the Ottoman Empire, which at its height extended into Asia, Europe, and Africa. Although the population of contemporary Turkey is 99 percent Muslim, it still encompasses interesting variations of religious organization and belief related to Ottoman history, to the politics of the republic, and to the twentieth-century revitalization of Islam in a number of areas outside Turkey.

Empire and Autonomy

A Muslim sultan ruled the Ottoman Empire, but the sultanate concerned itself primarily with expanding the empire and with fiscal, educational, and judicial matters, leaving subject peoples to carry out all other functions as they saw fit. For the most part, these groups governed themselves

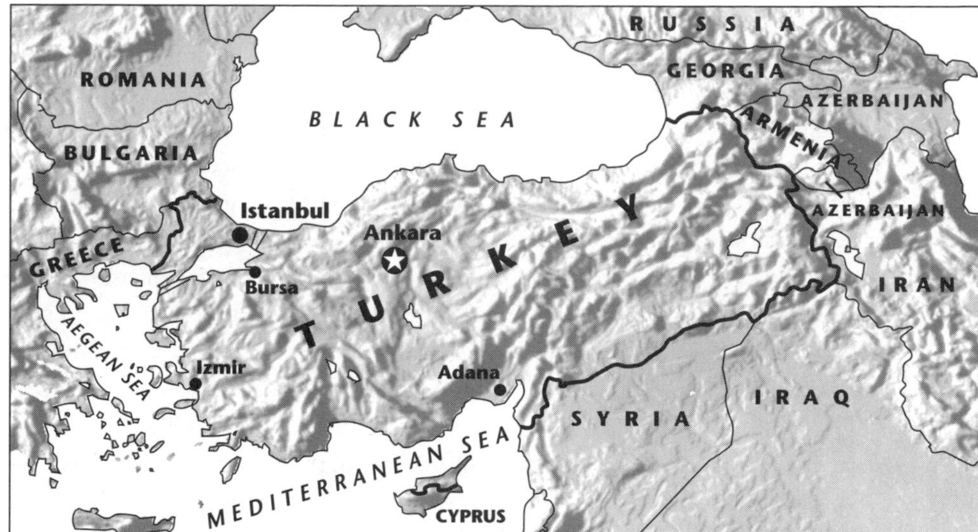

through religiously oriented communities called millets and through economic and social guilds. Jewish, Greek Orthodox, Armenian Gregorian, and Muslim millets—and later Roman Catholic, Protestant, and Bulgarian Orthodox millets—were allowed religious and cultural autonomy.

The Ottomans saw themselves as torch bearers of Islam, but the empire's founders also brought with them pre-Islamic beliefs and governmental traditions. Ottoman administration included a set of administrative-legal documents that were not derived from Islamic religious law. Nevertheless, the Ottomans did rely on an important hierarchy of doctors of Islamic law, the *ulama,* who were well integrated in administrative-military institutions. And Ottoman secular edicts and codes were always legitimated by formulas declaring their conformity with religious law. The chief interpreter of Islamic law, the Shaikh ul Islam, gained control of the entire corps of *ulama* in 1574. From then on he was drawn indirectly into political issues from which he had been previously insulated.

Islamic teaching and learning were also strictly organized. The complexes of mosques, seminaries, libraries, and hospitals created the foundation for cultural enrichment.

The institutionalization of mysticism, the *tarikat* or brotherhoods sometimes described as orders, was also important to Ottoman religious culture. Members of these brotherhoods were known as Sufis and sought close, direct, and personal experience of God. Among the preeminent mystical orders were the Halvetî, Melami-Bayrami, Bektashi, and Nakshibendi. Some of the Sufi brotherhoods were centers of heterodox and antinomian tendencies and were sometimes the focus for messianic movements. They also communicated the needs of the local population to the central administration. The state had a somewhat unsettled relation with these brotherhoods, although many among state personnel shared their ideas.

By the end of the seventeenth century Ottoman upper-class Islamic culture clashed with a group of populist preachers. The defeat of these so-called *kadizade* preachers by the Ottoman central state organization was part of a reform movement aimed at stopping what the ruling group saw as the undermining of its military, administrative, and fiscal control.

In the eighteenth century the gulf between the religious establishment and the state widened. Ottoman defeats in the 1690s and the Peace of Pasarowitz (1718) weakened Ottoman morale. Thereafter, officials focused on saving the state itself and relegated religion to the back burner.

Western-style Reform

In the nineteenth century Sultan Mahmud II (1784–1839) preceded the so-called *Tanzimat* reform by crushing the Janissary corps (1826), the military elite that had increasingly opposed modernization of the Ottoman army. By the time of his death the momentum of reform had been taken over by an emerging Ottoman bureaucracy.

The years between 1839 and 1865 were marked by the increasing influence of the reformist bureaucracy, which went on to westernize Ottoman administration, education, and justice. A group of intellectuals and liberals known as the Young Ottomans began to demand a limit to the power of the ruling class and the bureaucracy and a parliament to enforce the rights of the people. These intellectuals—who had been born out of the very reforms of the Tanzimat—accused earlier reformers both of never having taken the idea of freedom seriously and of having dismissed the possibility of using an Islamic foundation for their regime. They were severely repressed by Tanzimat leaders, and most fled to other countries.

In the late nineteenth century the Ottoman intelligentsia was divided between secularists, who were interested primarily in controlling the fate of the empire by using science as a philosophical guideline, and intellectuals, who were bent on retrieving Islam as a foundation for modernism. Muslim revivalist brotherhoods such as the Nakshibendi worked either underground or in the mountain regions of the Kurdish area of Asia Minor.

Sultan Abdulhamid II (1842–1918) promulgated a constitution and accepted a representative parliament, which convened in 1877 but was soon suspended because of war with Russia. In the face of continuing threats from Europe, Abdulhamid suspended the parliament again in 1878 and installed a highly autocratic government, centering power in the palace and suppressing all opposition. Political repression ultimately led to the rise of a new liberal opposition movement, the Young Turks, who forced the sultan to restore the constitution and parliament in what is known as the Young Turk revolution (1908).

Ottoman Decline

The Islamist modernist movement produced a number of important thinkers who began to publish after the Young Turks unseated Abdulhamid II. There were professed Muslims such as Mehmet Akif, who saw the decline of the Ottoman Empire as caused by its neglect of social problems. Intellectuals like Kurd Bediüzzaman Said Nursi, with links to the clerical establishment, saw solutions in a strengthening of faith. And there were those like Babanzâde Ismail Hakki who deplored the undermining of pan-Muslim sentiment through the incursions of Turkish nationalism.

The diversity of the empire, already compromised during the nineteenth century, essentially ended with its dissolution. The Treaty of Lausanne (January 30, 1923) required relocation of enormous populations—434,000 Muslims from Macedonia, Epirus, and Crete were exchanged for approximately 1.3 million Greeks from Asia Minor. During the First World War 600,000 Armenians perished under circumstances that are still debated, although a number of historians believe they died in Turkish reprisals against nationalist movements. Only small minorities of Orthodox Greeks, Armenian Uniats, Protestants, and Jews live in modern Turkey, and most are found in the commercial capital, Istanbul.

The defeat of the Ottoman Empire in the First World War united Turkish intellectual and religious leaders around a defense of Anatolia. In the wake of surrender, the Turkish government was placed under the authority of the Allied occupation powers led by the British. Especially after the occupation of Izmir by Greek forces (1919), a group for the Defense of the Rights of Anatolia and Rumelia was formed in which the military, religious leaders, and local notables figured.

The New Turkish State

The leader of the resistance movement, Mustafa Kemal Pasha (later known as Atatürk), was a general who had kept out of the bickering that characterized Ottoman politics after the fall of Sultan Abdulhamid II and remained aloof from the 1913–1918 Young Turk dictatorship. He united the disparate political forces in a fight for Turkish independence.

Atatürk was elected president of the assembly in 1920. A new constitution was adopted on January 20, 1921, and its preamble placed sovereignty firmly in the hands of the people. On November 1, 1922, the National Assembly abolished the sultanate. On March 3, 1924, the caliphate, which had been kept as a separate office, was itself abolished. In 1925 laws related to the obligatory wearing of the Western-style hat instead of the tassled fez, to the closing of brotherhood seats, and to the adoption of the Western calendar were passed. In 1926 the Swiss Civil Code was adopted. In 1928 Islam was struck out of the constitution of 1924 as the state religion of Turkey, and the Latin alphabet was adopted. In 1937 the constitution was amended to declare Turkey a republican, nationalist, populist, statist, secular, and revolutionary state.

By 1945 the secular radicalism of Atatürk and his political party had barely penetrated rural areas where Islam still functioned as a religion, an educational vehicle, a fountainhead of moral codes, a ladder for social mobility, and an instrument for community organization. As early as the 1930s there had been intellectuals such as the poet Necip Fazil Kisakürek who opposed Kemalism. The chasm between secularists and the provincial population who felt they had not had the advantages given to the urbanites created a provincial identity whose symbolic expression became Islamic.

Politics and the somewhat harsh limits on religious expression after 1925 were, however, only one root of the Islamist revival that has garnered growing influence since the multiparty elections of 1950. At one level politicians were simply using old local Islamic networks untouched by the republic. At another they were tapping a real need for ethical guidance, which, ironically, was the product not of backwardness but of the extent to which even provincial individuals had been able to integrate into Atatürk's modernization program. Interaction among Muslims throughout the world, promoted by the new Muslim nations such as Saudi Arabia since the 1930s, was also an element in Turkish Islamic revivalism after 1950.

Islamic Revivalism

The more direct politicization of Islam in Turkey was the consequence of an effort since the 1970s to create an Islamic political party. It is impossible to speak about Islam in modern Turkey without referring to the *cemaat,* a solidarity group established around Muslim principles and ideals. The history of the political force of Islam in contemporary Turkey is one in which the old brotherhood structure, although still alive, overlaps with a more fluid, less institutionalized type of social grouping. A number of these groups lent their support to the one significant party representing Islam in Turkey, the Refah (Welfare) Party.

A modern Nakshibendi leader, Mehmet Zahid Kotku (1897–1980), modernized the views of the brotherhood, placing among its aims elaborating a network of religious training centers to parallel the secular public education system, working to promote an Islamic industrial sector, and creating its own media. Muslim leader Bediüzzaman Said Nursi, whose newly formed religious association was more the *cemaat* type, had a similar agenda.

Kotku and Bediüzzaman spearheaded the two major trends of Islamicism in modern Turkey. Kotku's originality also consists in having promoted a serious ideological-Islamic periodical, *Islam,* with wide readership as well as having revived the religious foundation *Vakif,* which supports a number of educational and economic ventures.

The inheritance of Bediüzzaman, on the other hand, appears in the perpetuation of an Asian-oriented Islam with Ottoman roots led by Fethullah Gülen that proclaims its Turkishness in clear contrast to the Islam of Arabs and shows what may be termed an Ottoman respect for the modern Turkish state and its preservation even in its republican form.

In 1967 parliamentary representatives in the most powerful of the existing parties, the center-right Justice Party, began to look for the opportunity to form a party working for the creation of an Islamic society. Their leader was Nejmettim Erbakan, the representative of a growing group of provincial businessmen. In 1970 this group created the National Order Party. The Turkish Constitutional Court placed an interdiction on the party on May 20, 1971, a move which coincided with a prior military coup. The party reappeared under the new guise of the National Salvation Party on October 11, 1972. In the following national election (1973) the party obtained 11.8 percent of the vote. This victory was centered in the provinces where the Ottoman persecution of the Alevi—crypto-Shiʿis in the Ottoman view who were considered a fifth column of Persia, an Ottoman rival—had been perpetuated in the form of Alevi-Sunni conflicts.

The National Salvation Party thereafter entered into a coalition government with the secularist Republican People's Party. The National Salvation Party joined in various coalitions until the military coup of September 1980. Once again, the party reorganized and eventually emerged with 16.2 percent of the vote in the elections of 1991. In the municipal election of 1994 the party seized the municipalities of Istanbul, Ankara, and Izmir, as well as a large number of smaller municipalities. It finally emerged with a nationalist vote of 21.1 percent in the national elections of December 1995. Eventually, Erbakan was able to form a government in alliance with the center-right True Path Party in June 1996.

The response of the military-led secular establishment to this rise of Islamist fervor in Turkey has been one of dismay, and the rift between the secularists and the country's conservative Islamic movement has been growing. In January 1998 the Constitutional Court dissolved the Welfare Party for antisecular activities and banned Erbakan and five other party leaders from politics for five years. In early 1998 weeks of protests by Muslim students against the barring of Islamic-style headscarves for women and beards for men caused the government—which viewed the headscarves and beards as political as well as religious symbols—to back down from its policy against them. The challenge for Turkey is to maintain democracy in the face of such rifts.

See also *Atatürk, Kemal; Islam; Nationalism; Secularization.*

Şerif Mardin

BIBLIOGRAPHY

Allen, Henry Elisha. *The Turkish Transformation: A Study in Social and Religious Development.* Chicago: University of Chicago Press, 1935.

Berkes, Niyazi. *The Development of Secularism in Turkey.* Montreal: McGill University Press, 1964.

Zürcher, Erik J. *Turkey: A Modern History.* London and New York: I. B. Taurus, 1993.

U

Ulama

See *Islam*

Unification Church

The Unification Church was founded as the Holy Spirit Association for the Unification of World Christianity in 1954 in Korea by the Reverend Sun Myung Moon (1920–). Church members are popularly known as Moonies. Unification theology as found in the movement's scripture, *Divine Principle,* is an interpretation of the Bible influenced by Eastern thought. The eschatology promises the restoration of God's Kingdom of Heaven on Earth under the leadership of a messiah (whom his followers believe to be Moon).

For God's Kingdom to be restored, the church believes a Third World War is needed to overthrow atheistic socialism, the battle between North Korean communism and South Korean democracy epitomizing the battle between the anthropomorphically conceived God and Satan. It is, however, possible for the satanic world to be subjugated by a new, perfect, and absolute truth that reveals the falseness of other ideologies. A number of further revelations concerning the central role that Moon and his family are playing in establishing a theocratic world system are meant to be confined to Unificationists.

The mass wedding ceremony, or Blessing, is the church's most important ritual. Moon matches the marriage partners and performs the ceremony.

Church Politics

Moon's political career began when, as a student, he became involved in underground activities in support of Korean independence from the Japanese, who arrested him in 1944. Later he was imprisoned by the communists. Released by the Allies at the end of the Korean War, he gathered around him a band of devoted followers. During the 1960s he founded organizations such as the International Federation for Victory Over Communism and, in 1969, the Freedom Leadership Foundation was established in the West. In the early 1970s Moon moved his headquarters to the United States, where he supported President Richard Nixon with a nationwide campaign of advertisements, demonstrations, fasts, and candlelight vigils.

In 1978 a U.S. House of Representatives report concluded that an interagency task force should thoroughly investigate the interconnections between the political, financial, and other operations associated with Unificationism. But the sheer volume of interconnected Unification-related organizations made following Unification activities a daunting task, and the investigation seemed to lead nowhere. The movement continued to expand its activities. In 1980 another political organization, CAUSA, appeared, teaching the evils of communism and offering a version of Unification theology called Godism in its place; a more sophisticated operation was the Washington Institute for Values in Public Policy, a right-wing think tank that hosted political theorists, organized seminars, and published books on subjects of political moment. In 1984, however, Moon was convicted of tax evasion, fined $25,000, and sentenced to eighteen months' imprisonment.

Although individual Unificationists have been elected to political office (one was elected to the French parliament on Jean-Marie Le Pen's National Front ticket), Unification resources have more frequently been employed, either directly or indirectly, to support campaigns of right-wing non-Unificationist politicians and policies around the world. At one time, bright and attractive female Unificationists acted as assistants to U.S. senators and congressmen. The church-owned *Washington Times,* which operates at a hefty loss, is reputed to be one of the four newspapers that President Ronald Reagan regularly read; other Unification-owned papers include *Noticias del Mundo,* a Spanish-language daily for the New York and New Jersey Hispanic communities; the *Middle East Times,* a weekly covering the Middle East; *Sekai Nippo,* a daily published nationwide in Japan; and *Ultimas Noticias,* a Uruguayan national daily.

The movement also promotes its ideals through organizations such the American Freedom Coalition, the Collegiate Association for the Research of Principles, the Professors' World Peace Academy, the International Security Council, and the Global Economic Action Group. Then there is a plethora of conferences to which scientists, theologians, journalists, military personnel, and politicians are invited to exchange ideas in comfortable, sometimes luxurious, settings. Although few participants join the movement, those already of like mind are given the opportunity to network, and several independent or semi-independent liaisons have emerged as a consequence, with Unificationism facilitating such activities with money and personnel. Not all those wooed by Moon hold posts of political importance, but they may have the ear of more important personages; others, such as former U.S. president George Bush and former British prime minister Edward Heath, add a certain luster to Moon's campaigns and image, as do the well-publicized meetings with ruling heads of state including Mikhail Gorbachev in 1990, and, in 1991, Moon's erstwhile sworn enemy, the failing North Korean president, Kim Il Sung.

The Reverend Sun Myung Moon celebrates the launch in Argentina of a Unification Church newspaper. The church in the late 1990s invested heavily in Latin America.

International Activities

The collapse of the Berlin Wall in 1989 saw a radical increase in Unification activity in postcommunist societies. Potential leaders of the newly democratized states were invited to conferences and on visits to the West; English lessons were provided under the aegis of the movement; and books on moral education were distributed to numerous schools. The honeymoon did not last, however, and, like members of other foreign religions, Unificationist converts and missionaries came to be treated as an insidious threat from the West, undermining not only the cultural heritage but also the political security of the countries they were offering salvation.

Although the overall vision of Unificationism undoubtedly stems from Moon and his charismatic authority promotes the mobilization of willing collaborators, it could be argued that his genius has been not so much in what he has done as in facilitating others to engage in a wide variety of innovative enterprises. Despite the popular image of Moonies as brainwashed robots, the movement has succeeded, especially during the 1970s and 1980s, in attracting not vast numbers of brainless zombies but a relatively small number of intelligent, well-educated, and idealistic converts eager to further Unification ideals by whatever means they can muster.

The late 1990s were but one of several periods when Moon and his empire appeared to be on the verge of ruin. His one-time daughter-in-law was reportedly to publish a damaging exposé in 1998. Moon has been refused entry to several countries, and Unification missionaries have been refused the right to enter or proselytize elsewhere. But as one country dismisses him, another welcomes him. With growing problems in Asia, Europe, and North America, Latin America has been the recipient of what are said to be vast church investments. A township is being built on several thousand acres in southwest Brazil. As ever, interpretations of the significance of this move are diverse. Critics see it as a bolt hole into which Moon can escape should financial and political problems catch up with him. Unificationists see it as a new foundation for establishing God's Garden of Eden on Earth.

Eileen Barker

BIBLIOGRAPHY

Anderson, Scott, and Jon Lee Anderson. *Inside the League.* New York: Dodd, Mead and Co., 1986.

Barker, Eileen. *The Making of a Moonie: Brainwashing or Choice?* Oxford: Basil Blackwell, 1984; reprinted by Gregg Revivals, Aldershot, 1993.

Bromley, David G., and Anson D. Shupe. *"Moonies" in America: Cult, Church and Crusade.* Beverly Hills, Calif.: Sage, 1979.

Lofland, John. *Doomsday Cult.* 2d ed. New York: John Wiley, 1977.

Unitarians

Unitarians are a theologically liberal group of American Protestants characterized by an optimistic view of human nature, a rationalist approach to morality and history, and a belief in a nonhierarchical church, in which each congregation has autonomy. The Unitarians are so called because of their rejection of the Trinity, the fundamental Christian idea that God exists in three persons (the Father, Son, and Holy Spirit).

Unitarians were a significant religious force, as Protestantism's liberal wing, in late eighteenth and early twentieth century American religion. Since then their influence on American politics has diminished. The actual number of Unitarians was always small, its rationalist theology and rejection of traditional doctrine most at home among an upper-middle-class cultural elite on the New England seaboard. Also, the "modernist" impulse in American Protestantism moved the liberal wing of other denominations closer to Unitarian ideas, usurping much of their territory. Nonetheless, as a denomination, Unitarians had a significant effect on early national and pre–Civil War politics. As a cultural system, Unitarianism has affinities with progressivist themes in liberal political thought.

Unitarians as a Denomination

The American Protestants who were to become Unitarians had their beginnings in Congregationalist clergy who objected to the emotional revivalist religion and theological democracy of the Great Awakening, a movement in the 1740s that focused on individual experience. Led by Charles Chauncy, pastor of First Church Boston, "Old Light" Congregationalists increasingly emphasized a rationalist theology and the use of reason in creating moral individuals and a just society. Old Lights were concentrated around Boston and found their constituency among the educated merchant classes who were shaping colonial New England society. Over time, there was a greater emphasis on the human role in preparing for conversion and redemption. Trinitarian doctrine, literal interpretation of biblical Scripture, predestination, and other "supernatural" elements of Calvinist theology were gradually abandoned.

The theological controversy came to a head around the appointment of Henry Ware to a professorship at Harvard in 1805. Ware was a clergyman associated with the liberal, unitarian branch of Congregationalists. As Harvard became more unitarian in orientation, Andover Seminary was founded (1808) in response, and Yale countered with the revivalist "New England theology" of Timothy Dwight, a grandson of Jonathan Edwards (1703–1758), the most influential of the Puritan theologians. In 1809 William Ellery Channing of the Federal Street Church in Boston gave a sermon, "Unitarian Christianity," which established a formal name and clarified the religious fault lines. Finally, in 1825, the American Unitarian Association was formed, comprising approximately 125 churches, most in the Boston area. The schism marked the final blow to the Congregational religious establishment in Massachusetts, and the state church formally disestablished in 1833.

Migrating Yankees took Unitarianism west, particularly to Ohio and Illinois. Neither the congregationalist mind-set nor its polity, however, could enforce any orthodoxy, and western churches were more influenced by revivalist religion than were their eastern forebears. On Unitarianism's liberal side, a number of clergy began to push its humanist principles further from traditional Protestantism. Transcendentalism—and the Free Religious Association (1865; later to become the Society for Ethical Culture) that it spawned—was basically a Unitarian schism. The Transcendentalists, reacting to the rationalism of the Unitarians but unwilling to return to traditional Protestantism, focused on the spiritual and centered their faith in the divinity of nature.

Unitarian clergy were often active in abolitionist politics in the 1850s. Their commitment to human action and responsibility, and to individual rights, gave them a moral, religious, and humanist critique of slavery along with an impulse to activism. The clergy, however, on the issue of slavery were often well out-front of their parishioners, most of whom were more theologically than politically liberal. Clergy such as Samuel J. May, O. B. Frothingham, and Moncure Conway had to leave their pulpits as slavery became more contentious.

In the twentieth century Unitarian clergy were active in the pacificist movements before World Wars I and II and in other major political struggles. (For example, James Reeb, a Boston Unitarian pastor, was beaten to death after a march with Martin Luther King Jr. in 1965.) Finally, however, as other Protestants shifted to the left and the ideas of the Progressive Era's Social Gospel and the modernist movement became mainstream, Unitarians lost their pride of place as America's Protestant liberals. The Social Gospel's dedication to salvation through worldly action, and its optimistic view of history as progress, dovetailed with modernism's appreciation of reason and science. These themes had a strong affinity with Unitarianism.

In 1961 the American Unitarian Association formally merged with the Universalist Church of America to create the Unitarian-Universalist Association. The two groups had more social differences than theological ones: the Unitarians never expanded past their upper-middle-class, educated, cultural elite, while Universalists were less affluent, less rationalistic, and not as centered in New England.

Unitarianism as a Cultural System

Unitarianism's emphasis on rationality and human capacity was a legacy of the eighteenth-century Enlightenment that led to a certain "perfectionism"; this applied both to the individual's and to the nation's moral status. There was a self-confidence in human nature and ability but a dissatisfaction with the status quo and a desire for change. Boston was home to Unitarianism as well as to the American independence movement, the federalist system of government, and abolitionist politics. Unitarianism promoted the importance of written law as well, through its emphasis on rationalism and the education and status of its membership.

Theological liberalism, however, does not necessarily result in economic liberalism or in political and social activism. Although Unitarians' cultural sophistication often promoted social reformism, it also lent itself to a complacent civic concern, a polite humanitarian philanthropy.

When combined with its congregational organization, Unitarianism seems quintessentially American liberal: reasonable, optimistic, committed to the idea of progress, prizing individual autonomy, and stressing local control. The inherent universalism in this formulation has been a force for inclusion into American society, but it has always been reformist rather than revolutionary.

See also *Liberalism; Pacifism; Social Gospel; State churches.*

Rhys H. Williams

BIBLIOGRAPHY

Ahlstrom, Sydney E. *A Religious History of the American People.* New Haven: Yale University Press, 1972.

d'Entremont, John. *Southern Emancipator: Moncure Conway, the American Years, 1832–1865.* New York: Oxford University Press, 1987.

Gaustad, Edwin S., ed. *A Documentary History of Religion in America.* 2 vols. Grand Rapids, Mich.: Eerdmans, 1993.

Littell, Franklin Hamlin. *From State Church to Pluralism.* New York: Doubleday, 1962.

Queen, Edward L., II, Stephen R. Prothero, and Gardiner H. Shattuck Jr., eds. *The Encyclopedia of American Religious History.* New York: Facts on File, 1996.

Robinson, David M. *The Unitarians and the Universalists.* Westport, Conn.: Greenwood Press, 1985.

United States of America

The United States of America, a North American nation whose Constitution dates from 1787, is important for its experiment with a pattern in which politics and religion are legally distinct but in which religion prospers. Until its founders declared independence in 1776, the thirteen states that made up the original United States had been colonies of England. As such, most of them inherited British and European models in which politics and religion were linked because "church"—always a favored one and always Chris-

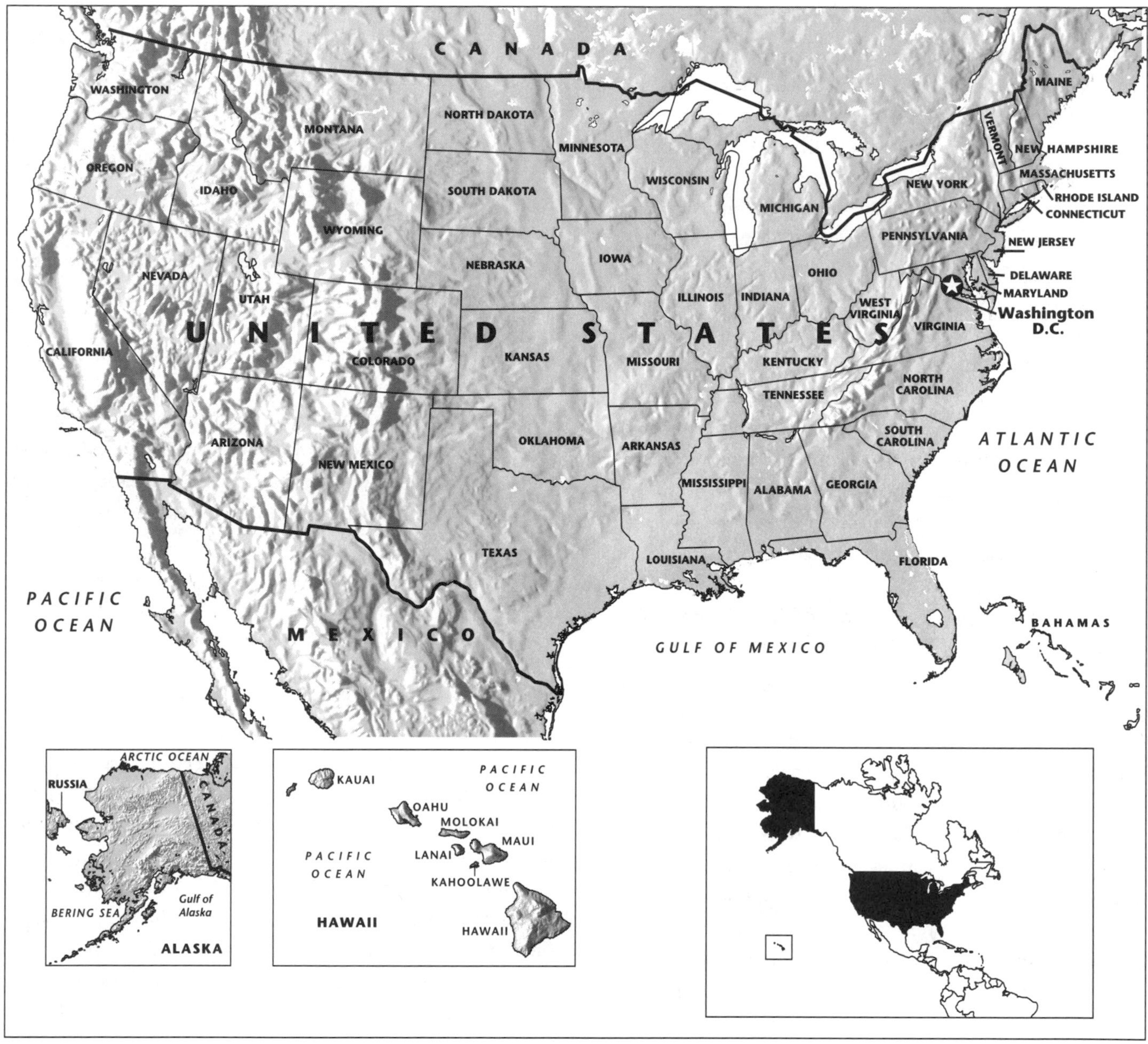

tian—and "state" were somehow united. In England, for example, the favored church was the Anglican Church. The result was an arrangement called "the establishment of religion." This meant that all taxpayers were forced to support the official religion, whether they practiced and favored it or not. Even colonists who opposed the establishment in England, groups of dissenters called Puritans, kept the old European ways and established their congregational churches in most of New England—Rhode Island was an exception—just as the Anglicans were reestablished in the southern colonies.

After struggles between established church leaders and dissenters in numerous colonies, the First Amendment to the U.S. Constitution, in 1789, forbade Congress from enacting laws "respecting an establishment of religion," but Congress could not interfere with practice in the states. All of them, however, by 1833 had rid themselves of establishment. Church and state were distinct. Leaders in politics and religion and their supporters had to find new ways to interrelate.

Necessary Interrelations and Experiments

Interrelate they did, and they have for more than two centuries. It was natural, perhaps inevitable, that citizens had to experiment with the various possible mixes of politics and religion. Everyone is born into and lives life in a political order, where laws can impinge on religion. Most people, certainly most Americans, also have been religious and have argued that they must give allegiance to God as well as to the state.

Although many traditional leaders feared that without tax support and legal favor religion would not prosper and that it therefore could not influence politics—thus leaving government and civic life deprived of moral influence since morality was seen to be connected with religion—religion did prosper. Revivalists on the frontier converted the new populations in the South and West, and churches in the original states also began to gain support of ever larger percentages of the population; this growth pattern prevailed into the late twentieth century.

Not all religion was in the hands of the churches. Following first president George Washington's precedent, voiced in his Farewell Address in 1796, political leaders found it in place to connect morality with religion—just as many gave evidence that they really believed that this connection was valuable for the public. How to connect them became the controversial point. The third president, Thomas Jefferson, in 1802 coined the concept of "the wall of separation of church and state." Many Americans ever since have spoken favorably of that wall as a barrier not only against politics invading religion but also against religious voices having power in the political realm. The clergy and other religious people were to keep their religion to themselves and not to meddle in politics. If individual citizens were made more moral because of religious beliefs about serving a just God and showing mercy to others, they were welcome to bring their beliefs into the political order. But the churches as churches should not turn political.

This Jeffersonian tradition has frequently been challenged in theory and in action by many in the religious world. After church and state were separated, "denominations" (churches that were on their own and operated on a legally level playing field) became active in promoting their causes, morality, and, where they found it necessary—and religious leaders almost always find areas where reform of society is in place—reform. In a few extreme cases, as in the example of a notable Philadelphia Presbyterian pastor, Ezra Stiles Ely, in 1827, there were efforts to invent what Ely called "a Christian party in politics." He preached on *The Duty of Christian Freemen to Elect Christian Rulers.* Ely and people of his outlook often called the main Protestant bodies to unite in forming such a party and voting for such rulers. That this kind of mixture would not serve partisan politics or churchly religion well became obvious to all but the few.

A second strategy for bringing politics under the influence of religion came from leaders of the clergy and the laity, across denominational lines early in the republic. They devised what historian Charles Foster called *An Errand of Mercy* and others have spoken of as a religious "voluntary association" network. The clergy preached sermons supporting these errands and associations to advance education, effect reform, and engage in charitable activity. The lay members, many of them prominent business people and other leaders in their community, held rallies, raised funds, and often "rolled up their sleeves" to engage not only in acts of mercy but in efforts to change the political order.

The leaders of this network found a zone of political issues on which they felt the religious should speak out. For example, they supported legislation to force the observance of Sunday, after Congress in 1810 passed legislation that permitted the Post Office to carry mail on Sundays. Gradually the advocates of Sabbath (or Sunday, in a largely Christian country) observance were thwarted, though a Lord's Day Alliance lived on through most of the twentieth century.

Some of the causes early in the life of the nation look trivial. There was considerable stir against dueling, for example. Some of it in retrospect looks ominous. The role of Catholics in politics was a volatile issue from 1787 until such events as the election of a Roman Catholic president, John F. Kennedy (in 1960), and the Second Vatican Council in Rome, which passed a Declaration on Religious Freedom (1965). The perceived threat of Catholicism served to unite all kinds of Protestants who disagreed with each other on almost everything else. They feared that the pope and his minions, the American clergy, would subvert American freedoms if large numbers of Catholic immigrants arrived and if they took an aggressive role in politics. Statements from the Vatican such as the *Syllabus of Errors,* in 1864, received much notice in the United States; in the *Syllabus* Pope Pius IX criticized republicanism and religious freedom.

Abolitionism and the Civil War

If Sabbatarian legislation suffered slow death, anti-dueling looked frivolous, and anti-Catholicism was often beside the point, if vicious, some causes that brought religion into politics related to the most profound and troubling issues of the day. Little attention was paid by the churches to the rights of Native Americans, though the white churches, Protestant and Catholic alike, carried on extensive missionary work among these people. But in South and North alike, religious leaders could not avoid the issue of black slavery.

Never before or since have there been such complex and jarring issues of politics and religion as there were in the case of support for slavery, on the one hand, or its abolition, on the other. These issues came to a head with the Civil War (1861–1865), when clergy on both the Union and Confederacy sides preached that keeping the Union or, conversely, breaking it up was what God had in mind for his people. But it was in the years between 1831 and 1865 that proslavery and antislavery forces were most explicit about the religious voice in politics.

After what was called the Cotton Kingdom matured in the South, about 1820, and when the political leaders after 1830 tried to extend slavery and the plantation system into territories west of the Mississippi River, most Southern clergy supported the moves, forcing antislavery people of conscience, usually with religious motivation, to make countermoves. For some, before the Cotton Kingdom was secure, this meant forming the American Colonization Society, in 1817. The goal was to buy freedom for slaves and remove them to Liberia in Africa. The society failed to attract much financial support from whites or much willingness on the part of blacks to be exported. Other strategies were necessary.

Abolition was the name given to the more extreme advocacy of slave liberation. Most of the abolitionists were Northern, the North largely having given up on slavery after the Revolution. Slavery was not economically feasible in the North, and new religious and humanitarian movements were forming there to regard slavery in new, utterly negative, ways. Most of the churches as churches were cautious about such a bold policy as abolition, and many abolitionists had to spend as much energy rousing churches as they did opposing slavery. Yet even the more critical of them tended to use religious motives and organization to effect political change.

Near the end of the Civil War, President Abraham Lincoln came to exemplify still another approach to religion and politics. The only president never to have been a church member, the biblically informed Lincoln spoke of his as a "political religion" and used elements of American political documents such as the Declaration of Independence in religious ways. He made many mentions of a transcendent God, a God beyond human political strivings as a judge of human injustice and an agent who would help reunite the two warring halves of the nation after the war.

Prohibition

Since Civil War days religion and politics have been mixed and leaders in both realms have related to each other in myriad ways. One of the best-known causes was Prohibition, an almost entirely religiously based movement. This time, unlike the situation in abolition days, the Protestant denominations and congregations, with the exception of some Reformed and Lutheran groups that were immigrating in increasing numbers from the European continent, worked to make illegal the production, sale, or consumption of alcoholic beverages. Without question, the abuse of alcohol was a social problem. Liquor interests took advantage of factory workers, miners, and others, and many families of addicted employed people were left destitute. In the course of time this social cause became fused with Protestant moral disdain for the individual drinker.

The Women's Christian Temperance Union, founded in 1874 and led after 1879 by Frances E. Willard, was the best-known religious organization agitating for Prohibition. The WCTU and other mainly Protestant organizations were successful in helping pass the Eighteenth Amendment to the Constitution (1919), which forbade the manufacture and sale of alcoholic beverages. Most of these Protestant agents continued to defend Prohibition, but it came to defeat when the Eighteenth Amendment was repealed in 1933 after a period of lawless rejection of the legislation.

Pluralism, Protest, and the Religious Right

By the Prohibition period, Roman Catholics, long edged out of the political mainstream, began to use their religion to effect legal and political change and to rule, especially in the large cities where Catholic immigrants had settled by the millions late in the nineteenth century. In 1919, for example, the Catholic leadership passed the Bishops' Program of Social Reconstruction. It opposed waste in the world of production and distribution, the low incomes of most wage earners, and the large incomes being made by the capitalist corporate leadership. Much of the American labor force was Catholic, and the administrators of the Bishops' Program characteristically took the side of labor in disputes—especially through the economic depression of the 1930s and the period of the New Deal under Franklin D. Roosevelt.

If two-thirds of America was Protestant in the middle of the twentieth century, and one-fourth was Catholic, this did not mean that only Christians had interests in bringing religion into politics. Jews represented only 2 or 3 percent of the population, but they had vital interests that could be protected only by law. Most of them made civil rights and civil liberties their causes, often because such support helped prevent the designation of the United States as an officially Christian society and also to block the passage of legislation unfavorable to Jewish and other non-Christian minorities.

When the nation of Israel was born in 1948, Jews made every effort to have the United States recognize it and then support it. Rabbinic and other Jewish groups formed lobbies and exercised considerable influence in legislation. More recently, the voice of Islam is being heard in the political realm, and a pluralist America finds itself coming to terms with ever more voices. That these often represent contradictory interests only adds to the intensity of religion-and-politics debates. Late in the century these centered on issues such as prayer in the public schools, religious opposition to abortion, and rights for homosexuals.

The most celebrated formal interaction of religious movements with political ones in the twentieth century has been the civil rights movement that prospered after the *Brown v. Board of Education* decision by the U.S. Supreme Court in 1954. The *Brown* decision, which outlawed racial segregation in public schools, went against the "separate but equal" notion that had governed educational policies in America. It inspired millions of Americans to use the moment in efforts to win an enlarged assurance of civil rights for all Americans.

African American churches represented the strongest black institutions and produced leadership for the movement. The Reverend Martin Luther King Jr., the acknowledged chief spokesperson, was by no means the only "reverend" in the company. When the movement came into its crisis stages about 1963–1965, King could appeal to Protestant ministers, Catholic priests and nuns, and Jewish rabbis who, with thousands in their flocks, engaged in demonstrations supporting blacks and lobbying for legislation to improve their situation. When major civil rights legislation passed in 1965, its opponents blamed the religious participants just as the advocates recognized the clergy and other religious support for change.

Another feature of politics has been the waging of war and the search for peace. Religious voices have often blessed the cannon, motivated the troops, and demonized the enemy—at least through the two World Wars that ended in 1918 and 1945, respectively. But the war in Vietnam, which involved the United States directly from the mid-1960s to the mid-1970s, found not only early support by some religious leaders but also telling and finally successful protest on the part of more in the course of a war they saw to be illegal, immoral, and unwinnable. Religion motivated much of the American interest in the cold war versus what President Ronald Reagan called "the evil empire" of the Soviet Union. Reagan used religious terminology to gather support for defense appropriations.

By the late twentieth century the old mainstream Protestant, Catholic, Jewish, and African American political forces were joined and outpaced by the mainly Protestant "new religious right." Its influence began to be reckoned with during Reagan's presidential campaign in 1980, and it has remained a considerable force. Now the most urgent voices of religion in politics belonged to anti-abortionists on the religious right, joined as they have been with Catholic forces. On economic and social policy issues, however, the Protestant majority on the right breaks ranks with the more left-leaning Catholic bishops and the Catholic Church's economic and welfare policies.

Theoretical Approaches

The politics-and-religion front has not been all action and no talk. Through the decades, numbers of theologians have reflected on the American experiment of separated church and state, voluntary church and associational life, pluralism and secularism, and practices such as lobbying for legislative change. Most of the time the reflecters were Protestants, like this century's most notable exemplar, Reinhold Niebuhr, who was in his prime from the Great Depression of the 1930s through the 1960s civil rights and Vietnam War days. But during those years he was matched by a Roman Catholic who led the ranks of his church on these issues, John Courtney Murray. Murray, a Jesuit, did more than anyone else to square Catholic thought with American political traditions and was instrumental in getting the Second Vatican Council's *Declaration on Religious Freedom* passed in 1965.

Whether on the specific issues labeled "church and state" or the general front called "religion and politics," it has become clear that the American experiment is just that—an experiment. In every generation, controversy accompanies the efforts of those who try various ways to bring together politics and religion or to keep them apart.

See also *Abolitionism; African American experience; Civil rights movement; Constitution, U.S.; Denominationalism; Freedom of religion; Jefferson, Thomas; King, Martin Luther, Jr.; Madison, James; Native Americans; Niebuhr, Reinhold; Pluralism; Presidents, American; Separation of church and state; Social Gospel; Temperance movements; Voluntarism.*

Martin E. Marty

BIBLIOGRAPHY

Curry, Thomas J. *The First Freedoms: Church and State in America to the Passage of the First Amendment.* New York: Oxford University Press, 1986.

Gaustad, Edwin S. *Faith of Our Fathers: Religion and the New Nation.* San Francisco: Harper and Row, 1987.

Greenawalt, Kent. *Religious Convictions and Political Choice.* New York: Oxford University Press, 1988.

Levy, Leonard W. *The Establishment Clause: Religion and the First Amendment.* 2d ed. Chapel Hill: University of North Carolina Press, 1994.

Lipset, Seymour Martin. "Religion and Politics in the American Past and Present." in *Religion and Social Conflict,* edited by Robert Lee and Martin E. Marty. New York: Oxford University Press, 1964.

Marty, Martin E. *Religion and Republic: The American Circumstances.* Boston: Beacon Press, 1987.

McBrien, Richard P. *Caesar's Coin: Religion and Politics in America.* New York: Macmillan, 1987.

Mead, Sidney E. *The Lively Experiment: The Shaping of Christianity in America.* New York: Harper and Row, 1963.

Noonan, John T., Jr. *The Believer and the Powers That Are: Cases, History, and Other Data Bearing on the Relation of Religion and Government.* New York: Macmillan, 1987.

Wald, Kenneth D. *Religion and Politics in the United States.* 3d ed. Washington, D.C.: CQ Press, 1996.

Utopianism

Utopianism posits a perfect world, proposing or advocating impracticably ideal social or political schemes. Utopia was invented by Sir Thomas More, an English Roman Catholic statesman and writer, in the book that gave name to the form—*Utopia* (1516)—as a description of an imagined land of total well-being and complete felicity. Utopia is nowhere (Greek *outopia),* and it is somewhere good *(eutopia).* The un-

Sir Thomas More

certainty as to whether it is realizable on earth, and whether authors of utopias have intended them as practicable political projects, has accompanied the genre for all of its nearly half-millennium of existence.

Utopias come generally in two forms. There are, following More, literary utopias, imaginative descriptions of fictitious lands stumbled on by travelers in remote parts of the Earth (and, later, in remote parts of the universe or through various kinds of time-travel). Of such are English philosopher Francis Bacon's *New Atlantis* (1627), American socialist Edward Bellamy's *Looking Backward* (1888), British poet and social reformer William Morris's *News from Nowhere* (1891), and British writer H. G. Wells's *A Modern Utopia* (1905). In this form utopias are essentially novels; they have tended to be absorbed by the newer genre of science fiction Wells pioneered.

There are also social and political works that deserve to be called utopian in the sense that they offer prescriptive accounts of social arrangements that will allegedly solve all of humanity's fundamental problems. These include Greek philosopher Plato's *Republic* (fourth century B.C.), English republican James Harrington's *Oceana* (1656), French philosopher Jean-Jacques Rousseau's *Social Contract* (1762), and a host of nineteenth-century socialistic writings, including several of the early works of German economist and revolutionary Karl Marx. Utopian social theory differs from the literary utopia in being more abstract, more concerned with the elaboration of general principles than with giving a detailed portrait of the ideal society. But there can be considerable overlap between the two types, especially when a literary utopia is offered as an illustration of a general social theory. Bellamy's *Looking Backward* and Morris's *News from Nowhere* are good examples of literary utopias that purport to show the fundamental principles of socialism in action. Despite their important differences, they can both be regarded as varieties of the socialist utopia, imaginative projections of what socialism would or could look like if put into practice.

One further distinction needs to be made. Utopia very early gave rise to anti-utopia, or dystopia. That is to say, writers employed the utopian form to cast doubt on or ridicule the hopeful or optimistic speculations of utopian writers. Irish-born satirist Jonathan Swift's *Gulliver's Travels* (1726), for instance, consists of a number of anti-utopian sketches of societies organized according to the utopian principles of science and reason. In the twentieth century, British writers Aldous Huxley's *Brave New World* (1932) and George Orwell's *Nineteen Eighty-Four* (1949) were similarly anti-utopian attacks on the utopias of science and socialism. The anti-utopia is utopia's ugly cousin, its dyspeptic alter ego. It turns utopia's heaven into a hell to be avoided at all costs. It imagines perfectly constructed societies to show their horror and to warn against attempts to realize them in practice.

Utopia is largely a form of the Western social imagination. Other parts of the world have golden ages, paradises, and Arcadias aplenty, but they do not have utopias. They do not, that is, have a tradition of thinking and writing that involves constructing ideal societies. Why that should be is not an easy question to answer. But part of the answer may lie in the peculiar inheritance of utopia, which is successor to the classical and the Christian traditions of the West. These lend it a distinctiveness that may explain why it is so rarely found in non-Western societies. They also partly account for the enduring popularity of the genre as well as its astonishing longevity and capacity for renewal.

Classical and Christian Roots

More's utopia, which is rational, almost utilitarian in character, seems to have set the pattern for most later utopias. Here utopia most clearly reflects its classical inheritance. A Renaissance humanist and admirer of Greek thought, More seems to have wished to continue Plato's speculations in the *Republic* and the *Laws*. Although with *Utopia* More invented a new literary genre, he was clearly indebted to the Greek tradition of reflection on the ideal city—the city of reason, the earthly embodiment of the Divine Reason that orders the cosmos. Renaissance utopias, inspired by Neoplatonic architectural ideas, often sought to realize the rational ideal in the physical structures of the city: as in Calabrian philosopher Tommaso Campanella's *City of the Sun* (1623), in which the walls dividing up the seven circles of the city are covered, in words and pictures, with the totality of human knowledge.

But if More gave utopia its predominantly rational, Platonic form, he also points, though more obliquely, to its religious roots. More was after all a profoundly religious man, a celebrated ascetic who had thought seriously about becoming a monk. His passionate Catholicism led him into martyrdom and, later, canonization. Is it really conceivable that he would have imagined an ideal society not shaped by religion?

More's Utopians are, admittedly, pagans and rationalists. But their rationalism leads them, as it were, into religion. They are sympathetic to the Christian doctrines expounded to them by the visitor, Raphael Hythloday. And more than one reader has been struck by the sense that the existence of the Utopians resembles nothing so much as monastic life. There is the same measured attitude toward work and leisure, the same thoroughness in planning the daily round; there is the devotion to contemplation as the highest pleasure of life; above all, there is the communism of property and communalism of daily life. It has plausibly been argued that one of the motives impelling More toward writing *Utopia* was to counterpose the religious order of the Middle Ages, with its sense of community and its compassion toward the poor, to the emerging individualism and commercialism of the sixteenth century.

The monastery's cloister was called "the gate of Paradise"; it opened to an order of timeless perfection. The monastery was meant to be in some sense an earthly simulacrum of the divine life to come. It is hardly surprising that it should prove so influential a utopian exemplar. The *City of the Sun,* whose author had been trained as a Dominican monk, is as much indebted to the monastery as More's *Utopia;* so too is another revered early modern utopia, German philosopher Johann Andreae's *Christianopolis* (1619). Even in Bacon's *New Atlantis,* an avowedly non-Christian rationalist and scientific utopia, the central institution of the House of Salomon is clearly modeled on the monastery. Partly through the great influence of Bacon's scientific utopia in the succeeding centuries, the monastery continued to supply utopian features throughout secular times. It turns up, for instance, in many hardheaded materialist and socialistic utopias of the nineteenth century, such as in the brotherhood of the Saint-Simonians—the followers of French philosopher Henri de Rouvroy (1675–1755), comte de Saint-Simon, who advocated a society led by scientists and industrialists and based on a scientific division of labor that would lead to social harmony—and the phalanstery of French socialist Charles Fourier (1772–1837), who proposed a communal society based on a phalanx of 1,620 people dividing work according to their natural inclinations.

The monastery gave the institutional and organizational form to utopia; the idea of the millennium provided the emotional and psychological drive. The millennial idea, fueled by such influential theories as those of the twelfth-century Calabrian monk Joachim of Fiore, held out the hope that a new earthly kingdom of Christ would be established, inaugurating the reign of justice, peace, freedom and love. Once again the relationship is complex. Thomas More was no millenarian, and the church—Catholic and established Protestant alike—remained formally opposed to millennial thinking. But it proved impossible to suppress millennial speculation or to prevent large-scale millennial movements from arising.

In most of the classical and early modern utopias, the utopian order is set up by some wise king or heroic legislator, such as King Utopus in More's *Utopia* or King Solamona in Bacon's *New Atlantis.* The utopia does not come into being as the result of some divinely ordained process of time or history, as in the case of the Christian millennium. But in later utopian thought, especially following the introduction of time and the future in eighteenth-century social and political theory, the utopian dispensation is the result of the more or less inevitable working out of human history. The idealist utopia of German philosopher Georg Wilhelm Friedrich Hegel, the positivist utopia of French mathematician and philosopher Auguste Comte, the socialist utopia of Marx, and the scientific, evolutionary utopias of English philosopher Winwood Reade (for example, *The Martyrdom of Man,* 1872) and Wells (for example, *A Short History of the World,* 1922) all come into being as the final consummatory wave of human development. All past suffering and struggle find their meaning and resolution in this culminating, redemptive stage of history.

It is in this form of utopianism that the influence of millenarianism is seen at its most powerful. Utopia cannot be equated with the millennium—in the final analysis the deliverance of the millennium is the result of divine intervention, whereas utopia remains a species of secularism. Utopia will come, or it will be constructed, as the result of specifically human history and action. But there can be no doubt that the millennial current in Western thought and Western social movements has contributed its characteristic dynamism to utopia. It has made utopia seem both possible and likely, if not absolutely certain. It may be too much to claim, as did the German philosopher Karl Löwith, that all significant Western social thought is but a footnote to the Christian philosophy of history, of which the messianic or millenarian idea is a central concept. But utopian social thought, with its concern with perfection and perfectibility, must surely have drawn much of its energy from such a powerful and long-lasting element of the Judeo-Christian inheritance. It is one reason some have argued that the decline of utopia in modern times is the result of the declining hold of religious ideas on Western societies. Both parts of that claim are questionable—neither utopia nor religion has declined as much as is often held—but the connection asserted in the claim certainly carries conviction.

One further connection between utopia and religion is worth mentioning. If, in the institution of the monastery and the idea of the millennium, Christianity made its contribution to utopia, so in a complex of other ideas it supplied powerful material for the anti-utopia as well. In the utopian tradition the perfected heaven of utopia is matched by the perfected hell of anti-utopia. So in Christianity Paradise is matched by the Fall; the horror of the Crucifixion by the Resurrection and the expectation of the joyful return of Christ to humanity; Christ by the supreme human antagonist, Antichrist, the agent of Satan who will oppose Christ's return in a final cataclysmic encounter. This whole dialectical pattern of Christian theology is echoed repeatedly in utopian and anti-utopian writing. The anti-utopia is replete with such themes as the false Messiah, the deceptive Antichrist, the blasphemous worship of the Golden Calf, the seductions of the flesh, and the temptations of the devil. Certain nineteenth-century treatment of these themes, as in the "Legend of the Grand Inquisitor" in Russian writer Fyodor Mikhailovich Dostoyevsky's novel *The Brothers Karamazov* (1880), had a particularly important influence on the modern anti-utopia. Both Huxley's *Brave New World* and Orwell's *Nineteen Eighty-Four* draw heavily on it and related religious ideas to convey their sense of the horror and emptiness of modern society.

Utopia, Community, and Religion

In addition to utopia and anti-utopia, there is, in some conceptions, a third form: the utopian community. Utopia can be sought in practice as well as in theory, in the imagination. This is somewhat paradoxical because utopia is, strictly speaking, nowhere. But all the way back to the ancient Greeks, there have been communities that have been deliberately set up so that their members can live what they conceive of as the life of perfection—or such perfection as is humanly attainable on Earth. Most of these communities have been religious, suggesting one more line of connection between religion and utopia.

In the period since the Protestant Reformation, the most important of these religious sects have been inspired by millennial ideas. For example, in Germany the radical, freethinking Anabaptists took over sixteenth-century Münster and ran it as though the millennium had arrived and they were freed from all earthly laws and constraints. The Diggers and the Fifth Monarchy Men of the seventeenth-century English Civil War believed in the imminent arrival of Christ and the onset of the millennium. And in nineteenth-century America, the Shakers, who looked on their leader Mother Ann Lee as the Messiah, and the Oneida community, who saw John Humphrey Noyes as preparing them for life in the millenarian community, both lived as though the millennium had arrived. In the belief that the second coming of Christ was imminent, or indeed that he had already returned, they anticipated in the pattern of their lives the free joyous order of the millennium.

There have also been more recent secular communities of perfection, many of them designed as practical demonstrations of utopian theory. These include the nineteenth-century Owenite (followers of British utopian theorist Robert Owen), Fourierist (adherents of Fourier), and Icarian (disciples of French Utopian socialist Etienne Cabet) communities in Britain, France, and America. In the 1960s and 1970s there was another wave of community building, many of them again inspired by utopian ideas: the anarchist ideas of French social theorist Pierre-Joseph Proudhon (1809–1865) and Russian anarchist Peter Kropotkin (1842–1921); the libertarian theories of American thinkers Paul Goodman and Ivan Illich; and the "behavioral engineering" of American psychologist B. F. Skinner's *Walden Two* (1948). Ecological ideas, stimulated in part by Morris's *News from Nowhere* and, more recently, American writer Ernest Callenbach's *Ecotopia* (1975), also gave rise to utopian communities.

It is significant that, of both the older and the newer communities, the religious communities have generally survived and prospered, while most of the secular communities have failed, often speedily. This suggests that the successful construction of a utopian community—as perhaps of any community—depends on the existence of "commitment mechanisms" of an essentially religious kind. Pragmatic and utilitarian, not to say purely hedonistic, motives for membership of a community are an insufficient basis; there must be the qualities of resilience, sacrifice, and dedication in the face of extreme difficulties that are generally evoked by religious commitment. This is not to say that only formal religions can underpin communities of perfection. Secular religions, such as Marxism or Zionism, may well prove an adequate basis. It is likely that in the late twentieth century ecology will prove the most vital and widespread of these secular religions. The ecological utopia, or *ecotopia,* may well turn out to be the most important stimulus to the construction of utopian communities in the coming years.

Utopia and religion, it is clear, are close though awkward bedfellows. They have accompanied each other since the birth of utopia in sixteenth-century England. In form, they are opposed to each other. Utopia is the construction, in imagination or in practical experiment, of the good society by the aid of reason and human will alone. It is a secular form of social thought. Characteristically, utopias are ruled by philosopher-kings of the Platonic sort; where more democratic and egalitarian forms of rule prevail, they are based on the assumption of the natural reason of humanity. Thomas More's preference for the pagan philosophy of antiquity over the Christian philosophy of his time has proved to be a decisive example.

But the matter has never been so simple. In a variety of ways, utopia has drawn on religious roots. It is even possible to argue that the entire utopian enterprise is religious in inspiration, that without some element of hope that is the common effect of religious faith, the imagination, let alone the attempted practice, of the good or ideal society is impossible. Certainly some kind of religious belief, such as that provided by millenarianism in Western societies, seems to have been a vital ingredient of utopian thought and practice. Religious forms too—the monastery, the embattled Protestant sect, at times even the church itself, in idealized expression—not infrequently seem to lie behind utopian schemes. It is hardly necessary to say that utopists themselves are generally unaware of this. Religion, it might be said on analogy with the Freudian view of the psyche, is the "unconscious" of utopia. It supplies the emotional energy and instinctual drive without which utopia shrivels up and may perhaps die. That this has not yet happened to utopia, and may never happen, is a testimony to religion's capacity to renew itself and to evolve into new forms.

See also *Millennialism*.

Krishan Kumar

BIBLIOGRAPHY

Buber, Martin. *Paths in Utopia.* Boston: Beacon Press, 1958.

Goodwin, Barbara, and Keith Taylor. *The Politics of Utopia: A Study in Theory and Practice.* London: Hutchinson, 1982.

Kateb, George. *Utopia and Its Enemies.* New York: Schocken Books, 1972.

Kanter, Rosabeth Moss. *Commitment and Community: Communes and Utopias in Sociological Perspective.* Cambridge: Harvard University Press, 1972.

Kumar, Krishan. *Utopia and Anti-Utopia in Modern Times.* Oxford: Blackwell, 1987.

Kumar, Krishan, and Stephen Bann, eds. *Utopias and the Millennium.* London: Reaktion Books, 1993.

Levitas, Ruth. *The Concept of Utopia.* New York: Philip Allan, 1990.

Mannheim, Karl. *Ideology and Utopia.* London: Routledge and Kegan Paul, 1960.

Manuel, Frank E., and Fritzie P. Manuel. *Utopian Thought in the Western World.* Cambridge: Harvard University Press, 1979.

Neville-Singleton, Pamela, and David Singleton. *Paradise Dreamed: How Utopian Thinkers Have Changed the Modern World.* London: Bloomsbury, 1993.

V

Vatican

In common usage "the Vatican" refers to the pope and the central administration of the Catholic Church, the Roman curia, which assists him in leading a community of nearly one billion believers, including members of some twenty-one Eastern Catholic churches and of the more numerous Western churches, or the Roman Catholic Church. In international relations, the proper term for the church as a sovereign entity is "the Holy See." It is the world's oldest diplomatic entity, predating the founding of modern nation-states, with formal diplomatic representation to most countries.

The Vatican's modern role dates from the loss of the Papal States to a united Italy in 1870 and the subsequent Lateran Treaty with Italy in 1929. That agreement recognized the Vatican City State and ended nearly fifty years of relative isolation of the popes as "prisoners of the Vatican." These events also marked the end of "the temporal power" of the papacy and opened a new phase of spiritual and moral leadership in international affairs for the pope and the Holy See.

Theological Rationale

The Second Vatican Council (1962–1965) in its "Declaration on Religious Liberty," also known by its Latin title *Dignitatis Humanae,* and its "Pastoral Constitution on the Church in the Modern World" *(Gaudium et Spes)* established the theological grounds for the church's contemporary involvement in politics.

Dignitatis Humanae abandoned the policy of securing special status for the church in concordats with Catholic countries. Instead it sought freedom of religion for all believers. One fruit of this doctrine was the 1994 Fundamental Agreement with the State of Israel, which was based on common commitment to United Nations documents guaranteeing freedom of religion and conscience. *Gaudium et Spes* went on to identify the church as serving the world in its defense of human rights and its promotion of unity in the human family.

Organization

The pope himself is the primary agent of Vatican international policy. Through his social encyclicals, public statements, communications with world leaders, and world travels, the pope exercises influence on world events. Commentators have associated visits by Pope John Paul II (1920–) with the demise of communism in Eastern Europe (1989). His travels may also be tied to the fall of the brutal Duvalier regime in Haiti (1986), moderating interreligious tensions in Lebanon (1997), and changes in U.S.-Cuban relations (1998).

Under the pope, primary responsibility for political affairs rests with the Secretariat of State. The secretary of state functions as the pope's prime minister. Under him, the secretary for relations with states holds immediate responsibility for the conduct of Vatican relations with governments outside Italy. Papal nuncios (or ambassadors) represent the Holy See to national governments and the Vatican to the local churches.

No single Vatican agency, however, exercises exclusive jurisdiction over political affairs. For example, the Congregation for the Oriental Churches, as well as the Secretariat of

Saint Peter's Basilica, in Vatican City.

State, deals with many issues in Eastern Europe, the Middle East, and Central Asia, and the Congregation for Christian Unity, with responsibility for ecumenical relations with Orthodox churches and religious relations with the Jews, attends to issues in traditionally Orthodox countries and in Israel. Likewise, offices handling specific issues, such as family life or migration, exercise influence in their respective fields. In addition, the Pontifical Council Cor Unum and Caritas Internationalis coordinate Catholic contributions in the field of relief and development.

Since 1968 the Pontifical Council for Justice and Peace has also played a major role in the Vatican's international policy. Pope Paul VI (1897–1978) founded the council in response to the Second Vatican Council's request that an agency of the church be set up for the promotion of justice for the poor throughout the world. A Vatican think tank on global issues, the council serves as a conduit for the concerns of churches in emerging nations to churches in Europe and North America.

Through its reports, conferences, and personal contacts, the council has helped shape the agenda for regional and national episcopal conferences, or conferences of bishops, and for the national justice and peace commissions established after the Second Vatican Council. In recent years it has focused attention on environmental concerns, the banning of antipersonnel land mines, limiting the arms trade, relief of the debt of poor nations, and land reform.

The Vatican and Local Churches

In an international environment marked by a decline in state sovereignty and a rise in "citizens' diplomacy," where many nongovernmental groups involve themselves in international affairs, regional and national episcopal conferences as well as other Catholic agencies relate to their own governments and international organizations on issues of human life, human rights, development, justice, and peace. Generally, the Vatican leaves local and regional problems to the respective episcopal conferences and justice and peace commissions. On occasion, however, the Holy See may also communicate its concerns directly to episcopal conferences, or, in turn, conferences may seek guidance from the Holy See. On some issues, such as debt relief, the ban on land mines, and abortion, the Holy See may also encourage the involvement of local episcopal conferences and Catholic agencies in broad social movements.

National justice and peace commissions, as well as diocesan human rights commissions, have played important roles in the defense of human rights, notably in Chile, El Salvador, and Chiapas (Mexico), but also in the Philippines, South Korea, East Timor, and some African countries. These agencies, often run by lay people, are usually semiautonomous, tied to the local episcopal conferences but not under their direct control. In recent years, moreover, the Vatican has also encouraged peace initiatives by Catholic lay groups, such as Rome's Community of San Egidio, notably in Mozambique and Kosovo (Yugoslavia).

Despite this general agreement on the implementation of social change, during the last years of the cold war the Vatican and popular church movements were sometimes at odds with some bishops, notably in Central America, over the bishops' support for social change and revolutionary movements, especially the Sandinista Party in Nicaragua. Also, the pope has intervened, in response to Jewish protests, with the hierarchy of his native Poland to persuade Carmelite nuns to leave a convent at the site of the Auschwitz concentration camp.

Religion and Politics

Even with this complex diplomatic and justice-and-peace apparatus, the church attempts to distinguish between involvement in the moral aspects of public policy and involvement in what it considers purely secular politics. One way the Vatican tries to sustain the distinction is to keep its comments on political matters at a level of ethical generality. This allows for various practical options in response to specified moral ends. Church teaching, moreover, opposes the politics of division and insists on maintaining a charitable attitude toward Catholics and others who have different views about how practically to achieve a designated goal.

Latitude is not encouraged, however, where human life is at stake. In the case of "intrinsically evil acts," church teaching insists on conforming civil law to the moral law. Pope John Paul II's 1995 encyclical letter *Evangelium Vitae* ("The Gospel of Life") declares that public officials are morally obligated to oppose legalizing abortion and active euthanasia. Where the law already permits these practices, public figures may compromise only in the interest of diminishing the harm done by the law and mitigating its impact on public morality.

In church teaching, direct involvement in politics is the proper province of lay people. Vatican practice discourages public engagement by clergy and members of religious orders in politics. This inhibition derives from the belief that symbolically and practically priests should foster the unity of the believing community and of the wider society.

An exception that proves the rule is the role of bishops as conciliators in the context of civil war, postconflict situations, and failed states (for example, Benin, Chiapas, Guatemala, Mozambique, Zaire). Such involvement, moreover, is temporary, and Vatican authorities expect that the ecclesiastic will withdraw once normal political life returns. As a diplomatic entity, however, the Holy See itself engages in negotiation over international agreements dealing with human life, development, disarmament, and human rights.

Catholic Social Teaching

A principal instrument of the Vatican's moral politics is Catholic social teaching, a body of statements on social, economic, and political questions meant to give guidance to Catholics and others in their attempts to realize greater justice in public affairs.

Modern Catholic social teaching began with Pope Leo XIII's encyclical letter *Rerum Novarum* (1891), which dealt with the rights of labor. Contemporary teaching may be traced to Pope John XXIII's *Pacem in Terris* ("Peace on Earth," 1963), which reconciled Catholic thought to the liberal concept of human rights and articulated an enduring view of international politics as a quest for order based on promoting and defending the rights of persons.

Economic Teaching

Recent teaching has dealt extensively with the question of development and a just economic order: John XXIII, *Mater et Magistra* ("Christianity and Social Progress," 1961); Vatican Council II, *Gaudium et Spes* (1965); Paul VI, *Populorum Progressio* ("On the Development of Peoples," 1968); the Synod of Bishops, *Justice in the World* (1971); John Paul II, *Laborem Exercens* ("On Human Work," 1983), *Sollicitudo Rei Socialis* ("On Social Concern," 1987), and *Centesimus Annus* ("On the Hundredth Anniversary of *Rerum Novarum*," 1991).

Proceeding from the biblical premise that the created world is given by God for the good of all humanity, as well as from a Gospel-inspired "preferential option for the poor," papal teaching on economic life has emphasized the right of peoples of the nonindustrial nations to development. Pope John Paul II's encyclical *Centesimus Annus,* for example, which is often cited for its support for a market economy, also called for "a concerted worldwide effort to promote development."

Catholic teaching on development underscores the insufficiency of economic growth alone to meet the needs of the human person. It upholds the demand of the common good for all sectors of society to enjoy the benefits of growth, and it insists on the responsibilities of industrial countries to aid developing nations out of solidarity with the one human family.

Historically, Catholic social teaching has been critical of both Marxism and capitalism. It regards both as forms of "economism," an implicit ideology that reduces human life to economic activity. While Marxism was explicitly atheist, church teaching regards capitalism as encouraging practical materialism, which accounts for its severe criticism of the consumerism and "superdevelopment" in the West.

With the emergence of free markets in Eastern Europe after 1989, however, Pope John Paul II praised the efficiency and productivity of the market economy and recognized a legitimate role for profits as an indicator of business's efficiency. At the same time, the pope noted that the market cannot satisfy many human needs, and he identified maldistributions of income and wealth, which prevent many people from entering the market economy. Accordingly, while affirming free enterprise, he also urged that the state and society exercise appropriate controls on the market to ensure that the basic needs of the whole society are satisfied.

Teaching on International Relations

Although the church participates in the existing network of international relations, its policies largely focus on realizing the rights of persons and the common good rather than narrowly on the interests of states (or of the church). It understands the end of government to be promotion of the common good, defined as securing and defending human rights, including the right to a sound environment. In support of the "universal common good," moreover, it favors the development of transnational bodies, including the United Nations, to address problems that exceed the capacity of individual states or traditional international arrangements to resolve.

Nonviolence and the Use of Force

While church social teaching demands active defense of the innocent against aggression, it nonetheless attempts to place stringent limits on the use of force by public authorities. The Second Vatican Council condemned total war and urged the banning of war; but the council also made realistic allowances for circumstances in which such a ban had not been reached.

Under Pope John Paul II, however, the Holy See has grown skeptical of the practicability of the church's traditional teaching on the justifiable use of force, or "just war." The pope was critical of the 1991 Persian Gulf War and has supported alternative dispute resolution mechanisms. *Centesimus Annus* praised nonviolent activists for their part in the events of 1989 in Eastern Europe. The pope himself played a key role in ensuring that the demise of communism in Eastern Europe came about nonviolently, and he has likewise actively opposed the death penalty. A significant exception to the Vatican's mistrust of the use of force in international affairs has been its calls for humanitarian intervention by the international community in Bosnia, Rwanda, and Kosovo.

See also *Catholicism, Roman; Human rights; Liberation theology; Papacy; Vatican Council, Second*. In Documents section, see *Roman Catholic readings*.

Drew Christiansen

BIBLIOGRAPHY

Hanson, Eric O. *The Catholic Church in World Politics*. Princeton: Princeton University Press, 1987.

O'Brien, David J., and Thomas A. Shannon, eds. *Catholic Social Thought: The Documentary Heritage*. Maryknoll, N.Y.: Orbis Books, 1992.

Reese, Thomas J. *Inside the Vatican: The Politics and Organization of the Catholic Church*. Cambridge: Harvard University Press, 1996.

Szulc, Tad. *Pope John Paul II*. New York: Scribner, 1995.

Weigel, George. *The Final Revolution: The Resistance Church and the Collapse of Communism*. New York: Oxford University Press, 1992.

Vatican Council, Second

The Second Vatican Council, also known as Vatican II, was a gathering of some twenty-three hundred Catholic bishops from seventy-nine countries that opened in St. Peter's Basilica, Vatican City, on October 11, 1962. It adjourned in December 1965 after producing in four momentous sessions sixteen documents that revolutionized Roman Catholicism. Convoked by Pope John XXIII, who died in June 1963 and was succeeded by Pope Paul VI (who served until 1978), Vatican II was the twenty-first general, or ecumenical, council of the church, but only the second held since the Reformation of the sixteenth century. In contrast to Vatican I (1869–1870), which set the church firmly against the modern world, the council fathers of Vatican II embraced Pope John's call for *aggiornamento* (updating) and thoroughly reshaped the church's relationship to modern society. They did so by turning back to the apostolic and subapostolic periods in church history (the era of Christ's apostles and their followers in the first Christian generation—considered a formative and doctrinally normative period for Christians) for theological, liturgical, and ecclesiastical models. In so doing they effected a paradigm shift in the church's understanding of its mission.

In the nineteenth century and the first half of the twentieth, the popes and their appointed guardians of orthodoxy became aware of the threatening intellectual trends of modernity—among them, the so-called higher criticism of the Bible (a method of examining the historical and literary character of the Bible as if it were just another book), the specter of godless evolutionism, and the rise of socialism and atheistic communism. In response, they sought refuge in the medieval system of thought known as scholasticism, presented most brilliantly in the theological treatises of St. Thomas Aquinas (1224–1274). Modern scholasticism (also known as neoscholasticism or neo-Thomism) preserved the supernatural character of the church, declared the compatibility of revealed truth and knowledge attained by reason, and reasserted the priority of the former over the latter. In the hands of ultramontanists (proponents of absolute papal authority), neoscholasticism eclipsed other traditional schools of Catholic theology and philosophy and lent itself to the building of a "fortress Catholicism" marked by dualism (the separation of the world into realms of absolute good and absolute evil) and triumphalism (the unambiguous identification of the church with goodness and truth and the church's enemies with evil and falsehood).

Pope John XXIII, in striking contrast, announced that it was time to throw open the windows of the church in order "to impress the modern world." The Second Vatican Council's goal, he proclaimed, was not to condemn errors or rehearse traditional doctrines, but to foster reconciliation among Christians and to promote the peace and unity of all humankind.

The pursuit of this vision, as it turned out, required a revolution within Catholicism itself. No longer could Catholics assume the existence of a Christianized and Europeanized culture as the framework for evangelization and apostolic work. The German theologian Karl Rahner (1904–1984),

Pope Paul VI

one of the chief intellectual architects of Vatican II, compared the postcolonial cultural and religious situation to the ancient pagan societies and the "diaspora Christianity" of the early church. To engage the diverse races, languages, class backgrounds, social experiences, and cultural forms present among the peoples of the twentieth century and beyond, Catholicism would have to disclose and retrieve its own internally plural theological and cultural resources.

Vatican II's dual emphasis on the need to plant Christianity anew in non-European and post-Christian European soil, and on the church's own historically diverse expression of the one apostolic faith, led to profound reforms in Catholic practices and institutional life. For decades preceding the council, for example, German and American Benedictine monks had been studying early Christian styles of worship and advocating a renewal of the liturgy, or public worship, based in part on that example. Vatican II officially blessed the liturgical movement and the new Mass, which emphasized greater levels of lay participation and was celebrated, accordingly, not in Latin but in the vernacular of the congregation.

The retrieval of apostolic models and practices paralleled a return to Scripture as the primary source of the Catholic religious imagination. Thus inclusive biblical terms such as "the Mystical Body of Christ" and "the People of God" displaced, at least temporarily, traditional descriptions of the church as an eternal, perfect society with unambiguous institutional boundaries and markers. This shift away from neoscholasticism to biblical theologies coincided with and reinforced Catholicism's "turn to the world"—the church's rejection of triumphalism and dualism and its corresponding affirmation of achievements in the non-Catholic and secular realms, including the sciences and political philosophy.

Renewing the Catholic Social Tradition

The most politically consequential aspect of the "turn to the world" was Vatican II's endorsement and development of Catholicism's seventy-year-old "tradition" of teachings on modern social and economic conditions, social justice, and human rights. For progressive Catholics dedicated to reversing the church's image as the last refuge of monarchists, theocrats, and reactionaries, the modern Catholic social tradition effectively began in 1891 with the appearance of Pope Leo XIII's encyclical *Rerum Novarum* ("The Condition of Labor"). By condemning atheistic socialism while providing a sustained economic as well as moral critique of the inhumane excesses of the unfettered market, *Rerum Novarum* set Catholics on a path-breaking, century-long intellectual journey which led ultimately to the affirmation of innate human dignity, rather than theological orthodoxy and Catholic Church membership, as the authentic source of civil rights and political self-determination.

Pope Leo XIII may have inaugurated the Catholic social tradition, but certain documents of Vatican II—especially *Gaudium et Spes* ("Pastoral Constitution on the Church in the Modern World")—placed it at the very center of Catholicism's understanding of its mission, doctrinal teaching, and pastoral practice. The relocation of fundamental human rights in the person rather than in the church or the state was articulated in Vatican II's *Dignitatis Humanae* ("Declaration on Religious Freedom") issued in December 1965. This historic document, its main ideas contributed by the American Jesuit John Courtney Murray (1904–1967), reversed Catholic teaching on church–state relations by accepting the fact of religious plurality and aligning the modern church unambiguously with democratic polities and against all forms of totalitarianism. In this declaration the church officially relinquished any ambition to grant full civil rights in a Catholic-majority state only to those who proclaimed "correct belief," or Catholic orthodoxy.

Thus in *Gaudium et Spes, Dignitatis Humanae,* and other seminal documents, the Second Vatican Council developed and extended a specifiable body of doctrines and principles governing Catholic participation in the social order. These basic principles and doctrines, which formed the foundation of postconciliar Catholic political philosophy and constitute the official frame of reference for every Catholic exercising his or her civil rights in the political order, include: (1) *the common good,* the notion that Catholics and other citizens should pursue policies and programs that serve the best interests of the public at large rather than a particular subgroup within society; (2) *solidarity,* the affirmation that all people at every level of society should work together in building a just society; (3) *subsidiarity,* the dictum (first articulated by Pope Pius XI, who served from 1846 to 1878) that greater and higher associations or governing bodies should not do what lesser and lower (more local) associations can do themselves (a sort of Catholic federalism); (4) *a preferential option for the poor,* a principle that carries concrete implications for a host of social welfare programs; (5) *the priority and inviolability of human rights,* especially the cornerstone right to life, but also the economic rights to own private property, to work for a just wage, and so forth; and (6) *a preferential option for the family* as the basic social unit.

In 1971 a synod of Catholic bishops meeting in Rome to reflect on the social and political legacy of Vatican II issued the document *Justice in the World,* which articulated the basic principle of the Catholic social tradition embraced by a generation of Catholic social activists and educators. Action on behalf of justice, they proclaimed, is a constitutive dimension of the Gospel and of the church's mission for the redemption of the human race and its liberation from every form of oppression.

Catholic Politics after Vatican II

The political legacy of Vatican II is complex and contested. In Latin America the council's unequivocal identification of the church's aspirations with those of the poor and oppressed led not only to the articulation of the "preferential option for the poor" by Catholic bishops meeting in Medellín, Colombia, in 1968, but also to a far more controversial development—the rise of liberation theology, a theology in which Christian Scripture and tradition are interpreted as calling first and foremost for the liberation of the oppressed from all forms of social and economic injustice. In the 1980s Pope John Paul II (who began his tenure in 1978) and Cardinal Joseph Ratzinger, prefect of the Vatican's Congregation for the Doctrine of the Faith, criticized liberation theology for its reliance on Marxist ideas and class analysis. Many theologians in North America and Latin America, however, rejected this criticism or deemed it misplaced.

The debate over liberation theology was part of a broader issue raised by the council: the respective roles of Catholic bishops, priests, religious, and laity in politics and political transformation. On the one hand, many Catholic bishops and priests played an active and historic role in resisting Chinese and Soviet totalitarianism; indeed, Pope John Paul II himself abetted the collapse of Soviet communism in 1991 by his support of Poland's Solidarity movement in particular and by his vigorous moral and spiritual leadership in general. On the other hand, the same pope forbade clergy to stand for elections and ordered priests in Nicaragua and the United States to resign from political offices they held.

Also controversial was the role of national episcopal conferences and their growing participation in shaping political discourse. In the United States, for example, the National Conference of Catholic Bishops, after consulting qualified lay Catholics (and non-Catholics) on the technical aspects of the topics in question, issued major pastoral letters on the nuclear arms race (*The Challenge of Peace,* 1983) and on the U.S. economy (*Economic Justice for All,* 1986). Conservative opponents within the church, however, claimed that the bishops misread or misstated various teachings of Vatican II. To complicate matters further for the conservatives, the American bishops advanced three concepts in the 1980s: a just war doctrine modified significantly by biblical pacifism (nonviolent nonresistance to evil), the "preferential option for the poor," and "a consistent ethic of life" (a moral stance demanding that Christians always choose the option that protects life—that is, that they oppose abortion, euthanasia, capital punishment, and so forth). These concepts were undeveloped or unknown in the classic, preconciliar Catholic social tradition.

Notwithstanding these and other areas of controversy, Catholics find themselves entering the twenty-first century positioned at the moral center of a vigorous public debate about the right ordering of society and the cultivation of those civic virtues essential to the renewal and extension of democratic institutions and practices. Perhaps to their surprise and certainly to their delight, Catholics today are cast by some independent observers as champions of democratic values and as protagonists in the contemporary struggle to build a universal regime of human rights, at the foundation of which is the right to religious freedom.

See also *Catholicism, Roman; Human rights; Liberation theology; Papacy; Vatican; War.* In Documents section, see *Roman Catholic readings.*

R. Scott Appleby

BIBLIOGRAPHY

Alberigo, Giuseppe, and Joseph Komonchak, eds. *History of Vatican II.* Vol. 1. *Announcing and Preparing Vatican Council II: Toward a New Era in Catholicism.* Maryknoll, N.Y., and Leuven, Belgium: Orbis/Peeters, 1995.

Burns, Gene. *The Frontiers of Catholicism: The Politics of Ideology in a Liberal World.* Berkeley: University of California Press, 1992.

Gremillion, Joseph, ed. *The Church and Culture since Vatican II: The Experience of North and Latin America.* Notre Dame, Ind.: University of Notre Dame Press, 1985.

———. *The Gospel of Peace and Justice: Catholic Social Teaching since Pope John.* Maryknoll, N.Y.: Orbis Books, 1976.

Gutiérrez, Gustavo. *Theology of Liberation.* Maryknoll, N.Y.: Orbis Books, 1976.

Himes, Michael J., and Kenneth R. Himes. *Fullness of Faith: The Public Significance of Theology.* Mahwah, N.J.: Paulist Press, 1993.

Novak, Michael. *The Catholic Ethic and the Spirit of Capitalism.* New York: Free Press, 1993.

Weigel, George. *Soul of the World: Notes on the Future of Public Catholicism.* Washington, D.C., and Grand Rapids, Mich.: William B. Eerdmans and the Ethics and Public Policy Center, 1996.

Vietnam

The Socialist Republic of Vietnam, created in 1976 following the defeat of the Republic of Vietnam (South Vietnam) by the Democratic Republic of Vietnam (North Vietnam), is a religiously diverse country. This diversity has contributed to the conflicts that have beset the country and they continue to generate tensions within the society. In a population of more than seventy-five million people, at least 15 percent follow religions that are quite different from Vietnamese traditional religion. Moreover, the Communist Party, which today still controls the government, has long adhered to a Marxist-Leninist ideology in which all religion is viewed with suspicion.

Confucianism, the Cult of National Heroes, and Popular Religion

The most important influence on religion in Vietnam until the nineteenth century was Chinese civilization. Vietnamese rulers, even after securing independence from the Chinese in the eleventh century, found in the teachings of

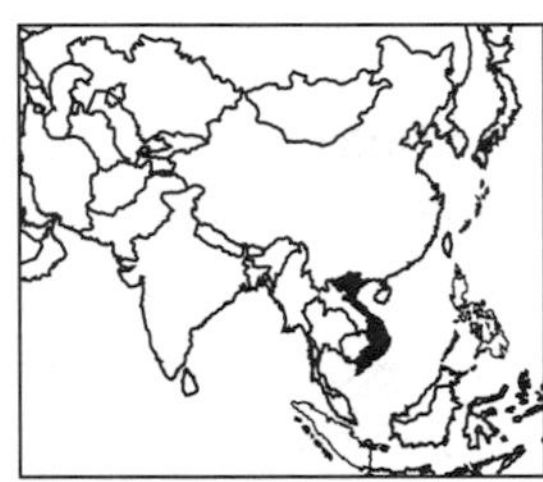

Confucius the cosmic basis for social order. Confucian ideals were also incorporated into popular practices relating to the family.

As in China, Confucianism in Vietnam did not provide the means to address all fundamental problems of meaning faced by Vietnamese and even proved inadequate for legitimating the Vietnamese political order. From at least the fourteenth century, Vietnamese rulers sought to justify the independence of their state from the Chinese empire by promoting cults of "national heroes" who had led Vietnamese resistance against the Chinese. The cult of the nationalist and Communist leader Ho Chi Minh (1890–1969), focused on the mausoleum in Hanoi that enshrines his body, can be seen as a continuation of this long-established cult of national heroes.

Confucianism was always only a subordinate part of the popular religion. Prior to modern times, and even today, villagers have worshiped a variety of local deities as well as Buddha and Confucius and have turned to sorcerers, mediums, astrologers, diviners, and practitioners of traditional medicine for help. And the popular religion in southern Vietnam, which was colonized by Vietnamese only after the fifteenth century, also showed influences of the Hindu and Buddhist religions that had once been dominant there.

Catholicism and the Cultural Crisis of the Colonial Period

In the seventeenth century Roman Catholicism was introduced into Vietnam. The Jesuit Alexandre de Rhodes not only began Catholic missionization but also devised a romanized orthography for Vietnamese that would, during the colonial period, totally supplant the Chinese-derived writing system. Rhodes's writing system would become *quoc ngu,* the "national language."

By the early eighteenth century, perhaps as much as 10 percent of the population of Vietnam were Catholic. The growth of Catholicism was perceived by the rulers of Vietnam as a fundamental threat to the Confucian-based order. The persecution of Catholics by Vietnamese rulers in the nineteenth century, while reducing the number of Catholics significantly, provided one of the major rationales for French intervention and conquest of Vietnam.

French rule (1858–1954) precipitated a cultural crisis that fostered significant religious fragmentation in Vietnamese society. Catholicism once again began to thrive, especially in northern Vietnam; by the end of the colonial period in 1954, about 7 percent of the population were Catholic. Protestant missionaries also succeeded in establishing a small number of churches among the upland minorities, mainly in the Central Highlands. In southern Vietnam a resurgent Buddhism attracted a large number of adherents, and Hoa Hao, a new Buddhist movement without a Buddhist clergy, also gained a wide following. Cao Dai, a religion known for its elaborate cosmology and iconography that subsume elements from all the major religions of the world and for a religious hierarchy modeled closely on that of the Catholic Church, was the most dramatic of the new movements.

Religion and the Wars in Vietnam

Those who ultimately succeeded in forcing the French to cede power drew their ideas of political order neither from Confucian teachings nor from one of the new religions but from Western nationalism and Marxist-Leninism. An international agreement reached at Geneva in 1954, however, allowed the Communist Party under Ho Chi Minh to take power only in northern Vietnam. Between 1954 and 1975 Vietnam was divided between South Vietnam and North Vietnam.

Many Catholics in North Vietnam, fearing that a Communist-led regime would be hostile, chose to resettle in South Vietnam. The government of the Democratic Republic of Vietnam did, in fact, institute new restrictive policies regarding religion. Buddhist and Catholic efforts to recruit clergy were made subject to the approval of the government, and prior to the 1980s very few Buddhist monks or Catholic priests were allowed to be ordained. The government also sought to stamp out "superstitions," a category that included most popular religious practices.

In South Vietnam Catholics were favored because the first president of the Republic of Vietnam from 1954 to 1963 was Ngo Dinh Diem (1901–1963), a staunch Catholic who relied strongly on the advice of one of his brothers, an archbishop. Diem first moved strongly against the Hoa Hao and Cao Dai and then attempted to suppress the resurgent Buddhist movement. The self-immolation of the elderly Vietnamese Buddhist monk, Thich Quang Duc, in Saigon on June 16, 1963, was interpreted at the time as indicating that Diem's regime had lost its moral authority. Within three months Diem himself lay dead, assassinated by those who felt their act would be widely accepted.

The immolation of Thich Quang Duc continues to the present day to be remembered as a powerful critique of the misuse of power. Although the government that established its control throughout the country in 1975, led by the Communist Party of Vietnam, sought to place all Buddhist monks under the firm control of a state-sponsored Buddhist organization, the act of Thich Quang Duc has not been forgotten. Enshrined at the Thien Mu pagoda in the central Vietnamese city of Hue are the car in which Thich Quang Duc was driven to his death and a picture of the immolation. Monks from Thien Mu have also been at the forefront of new protests in the 1980s and 1990s against the government's restrictions on the Buddhist organization.

The Buddhist movement that became politically visible in the 1960s, however, could count among its followers only a minority of the people of southern and central Vietnam. Although a majority of Vietnamese might be considered to have some relationship to Buddhism, only a small number actually practice Buddhism as their exclusive religion. Thus, while the Buddhists had radically undermined the moral authority of the Diem regime, their small number precluded their providing the moral authority for the creation of a viable political order. Instead, as the country became more intensely embroiled in the Vietnam War, the religious fragmentation of South Vietnam became more accentuated.

Communist Rule and Religious Resurgence

After the fall of South Vietnam in 1975 the Communist Party became the undisputed source of political authority throughout the country. The government of the Socialist Republic of Vietnam, as the country was now called, sharply restricted the autonomy of religious clergies. Many Buddhist monks and Catholic priests either fled the country or were placed in reeducation camps, and no new ordinations were permitted until the early 1980s. All remaining Buddhist monks and nuns had to join the state-sponsored organization known as the Vietnam Buddhist Sangha, and Catholic priests, the Association of Patriotic Catholics. While the Vietnamese government did not go as far as the Chinese in forcing the Catholic clergy to break with Rome, the state still insisted on approving all appointments in the hierarchy. Caodaists were considered to be beyond the limits of even the restricted tolerance shown to Buddhists and Catholics; many Cao Dai services were banned and its lands were confiscated.

By the early 1980s, however, the Communist Party recognized that the Marxist-Leninist vision was far from the reality of social life in the country. The party began to institute a radical shift in policy, culminating in the 1986 commitment to *doi moi,* "renovation." While *doi moi* has been understood primarily as a policy that opened the Vietnam economy to market forces, it was also associated with a shift in cultural policy. As early as 1982 the government began to allow new recruitment to the Buddhist and Catholic clergies, and by the mid-1980s restrictions on popular religious practices began to be eased.

The new openness has fostered a significant religious revival in Vietnam. Catholic masses attract large congregations that include many younger people. Many Buddhist pagodas not only have many worshipers on Buddhist holy days but also sponsor Buddhist study groups. Villagers now perform elaborate rituals, especially for funerals. Caodaists have reclaimed control of their holy see at Tay Ninh, and rites held there are very popular. Evangelical Protestantism has attracted thousands of followers, mainly among minority peoples living in the uplands. And new religious movements—for example, the cult of Quang-am, the Buddhist Bodhisattva of Compassion and Mercy, usually known in the West as Kuan-yin—have begun to attract followers, especially in southern Vietnam.

But the new openness has also brought conflict between religion and the state. Since the mid-1980s both Buddhist and Catholic clergies have pushed for increased autonomy; these pressures have been strongly resisted by the state. In 1988 the Catholic Church and the Vietnamese government engaged in a dramatic confrontation over the pope's recognition of 117 persons "martyred" in Vietnam as saints. No open split between the Vatican and Hanoi developed, however, and the Vietnamese Catholic church continues to press for greater autonomy.

Buddhists have fared less well. Some Buddhist monks, especially in Hue and Ho Chi Minh City, have sought to have the pre-1975 Unified Vietnamese Buddhist Congregation recognized as an alternative to the state-sponsored Vietnam Buddhist Sangha. Conflict with Buddhists became especially intense in 1993 when the government arrested several monks who had been leading demonstrations in Hue. In response to these arrests, at least two people immolated themselves. While these immolations did not inspire the outrage that the immolation of Thich Quang Duc did thirty years earlier, the government repression of the Buddhist movement has stimulated strong criticisms from Buddhist and human rights groups outside of Vietnam.

The reality is that Vietnam today is more religiously pluralistic than it has ever been in its history. The Communist Party finds itself caught between wishing to impose strong controls on all religious movements and feeling pressured to permit greater tolerance of religious activity. In such a situation, tensions and even conflicts between the state and religious organizations and movements are inevitable.

See also *Catholicism, Roman; China; Christianity in Asia; Confucianism; Confucius; Hinduism; Marxism; Nhat Hanh, Thich.*

Charles F. Keyes

BIBLIOGRAPHY

Condominas, Georges. "Vietnamese Religion." In *The Encyclopedia of Religion,* edited by Mircea Eliade. Vol. 15. New York: Collier Macmillan, 1987.

Ellwood, Robert S. "Cao Dai." In *The Encyclopedia of Religion,* edited by Mircea Eliade. Vol. 3. New York: Collier Macmillan, 1987.

Gheddo, Piero. *The Cross and the Bo-Tree: Catholics and Buddhists in Vietnam.* Translated from the Italian by Charles Underhill Quinn. New York: Sheed and Ward, 1970.

Marr, David G. "Church and State in Vietnam." *Indochina Issues* 74 (1987): 1–4.

Mularney, Shaun Kingsley. "The Limits of 'State Functionalism' and the Reconstruction of Funerary Ritual in Contemporary Northern Vietnam." *American Ethnologist* 23 (1996): 540–560.

Salemink, Oscar. "Buddhism on Fire: Buddhist Protests against Authoritarian Regimes in Vietnam." In *Casa Nova: Aspects of Asian Societies,* edited by Paul E. Baak. Amsterdam: Centre for Asian Studies, Thesis Publishers, 1995.

Tai, Hue-Tam Ho. *Millenarianism and Peasant Politics in Vietnam.* Cambridge: Harvard University Press, 1983.

———. "Monumental Ambiguity: The State Commemoration of Ho Chi Minh." In *Essays into Vietnamese Pasts,* edited by K. W. Taylor and John K. Whitmore. Ithaca, N.Y.: Cornell University, Southeast Asian Studies Program, 1995.

Violence

Violence is the use of physical force to injure or kill another being. It seems odd to conjoin religion to political murder, torture, and rape, but violence by its very nature resonates with religious energy. Dehusking religions of their theologies, ethical systems, vestments, and music leaves awefullness, God's terrifying wrath.

The primordial sacred is not only repellent, but it is also fascinating and wondrous. Its very horror is alluring, but this allure heightens its danger. The persons, objects, and events that occasion it must therefore be handled with utmost care, which is to say, religiously. They must be encumbered with ceremonies and set apart.

So it is with political violence, the instruments used to accomplish it, and those who deploy them. Like all sacred things, they are both accursed and intriguing. The booty of war, the Old Testament teaches, must pass through the fire before being redistributed. So too Yahweh's warriors: they are taboo. Like menstruating women or new mothers, they must be isolated for seven days and be cleansed before being readmitted into the community.

It is a mistake to imagine that this attitude is peculiar to Western civilization. The Hindu pantheon is replete with beguilingly violent deities. There is the erotically curvaceous, blood-lapping goddess Kali, adorned with a belt of human skulls; Shiva, the dancing lingam, otherwise known as Destroyer; the man-devouring Vishnu (Krishna) who announces, "I am death . . . who shatters worlds."

Furthermore, it is an error to view the union of religion with violence as a reflection of primitive psychology. Even in the most technologically advanced societies like our own, the soldier, his weapons, his actions, and victims are treated with a kind of reverence bordering on the cultic. When the first atom bomb illuminated the sky above the New Mexican desert in 1945, Robert Oppenheimer, an American physicist and government adviser who directed the development of the bomb, was not the only witness compelled to enframe the spectacle in religious poetry. One companion confessed to witnessing in the event the Second Coming of Christ. Another was reminded of a sixteenth-century painting by German artist Matthias Grünewald, *The Ascension of Christ to Heaven.*

How Religion Legitimizes Violence

Violence, then, is holy. But religions also routinely legitimize violence and contribute to it through their theologies, rituals, and organization. Religious beliefs also bear on the ways of violation, on the ethics of violence, the preferred manners by which killing, looting, and rape are to proceed. But religions are rarely the sole cause of violence. The strategic and economic milieu in which a faith operates must also be taken into consideration, as in three of the bloodiest encounters in European history: the Crusades (from the eleventh to the fourteenth centuries), the witch burnings (from 1400 to 1700, during which up to one million people died, mostly women), and the Nazi Holocaust (which resulted in an estimated eight million deaths). Although Christian exclusivity, misogyny, and anti-Semitism, respectively, can be implicated in these affairs, European political-economics were equally important.

When religions legitimize collective murder and pillage, they do so by mystifying it. That is, they take responsibility for violence out of human hands and attribute it to supernatural forces or beings. In this way it comes to be viewed as inevitable, necessary, reasonable—above all, as good. Why did the Taiping peasants of prerevolutionary China revolt (1850–1864)? Because, explains Confucianism, the Mandate of Heaven had been withdrawn from the Manchu emperor. The judgment of *T'ien* (the Heavens) is not understood to have caused the revolt as such. Rather, the unrest proves that the Heavens do not look upon the emperor with favor, and the revolt thus is predictable and proper.

That part of theology concerned with religious justifications for violence (or for other problematic events like slavery) is known as *theodicy* and is particularly pertinent in Western cultures wherein the godhead is believed to be all good, all knowing, and all powerful. How, it can be asked, can such a deity permit human beings to violate each other? There are four standard answers to this question: the arguments from ignorance, heroism, justice, and hope.

Mankind has no right to question God's will. It is enough to know that God has His reasons for permitting calamity, and that they are not ours. As the Qur'an (2: 216) says, humans cannot understand the ways of Allah.

Sixteenth-century French church reformer John Calvin once stated that God loves the well-tried wrestler. This is the person who, like Jacob, successfully struggles against temptations such as wanting to avoid the physical risks of battle or yearning to surrender to rage on witnessing the pain and terror of combat. This is to say nothing of the opportunities warfare routinely provides soldiers to sate their sexual appetites and to rob. True faith is evidenced, so to say, not by avoiding such temptations—by fleeing to the sanctity of a monastery, for example. Instead, faith is proven by being in the world but not of it. The hero is able to swallow qualms about the horrors.

The historical books of the Old Testament are a military history. In the frenzy of the berserks known as Nazarites who, like Samson, can slay a thousand men with the jawbone of an ass, Yahweh's presence to His people is truly felt and known. The same is true of the religions most indelibly imprinted with the Hebraic ethic, Islam and Christianity—in these confessions the faithful's rage at the world's injustice is God's. They are God's battle-ax and weapons of war.

The Old Testament war of Yahweh was not used to convert nonbelievers. Instead, it authorized the seizure of the land God promised Israel. Nevertheless, God's hatred of injustice is clearly evident in the Old Testament (for example,

Psalm 7: 9-13 or Ezekiel 7: 7-9). So, too, is the notion of God using His children as the means to administer divine punishment. When these notions were overlaid with Zoroastrian beliefs that the cosmos consists of diametrically opposed principles, good and evil, the product was the Islamic theory of *jihad* (righteous struggle).

The Islamic world is bifurcated into opposed realms: *Dar al-Islam* (the territory wherein Allah's word prevails) and *Dar al-Harb* (the territory of the enemy, where men are sexually immodest, drink wine, and gamble). The jihad is an instrument to cleanse the earth of *harbies.* It recompenses evil-doers for their sins. The ancient Assassins (the secret order of Muslims who terrorized Christian Crusaders and other enemies by clandestine murder committed under the influence of hashish and from whom comes the modern term), the Wahhabis, the Almoravids, and the Almohads of the early twentieth century as well as today's Hamas terrorists, the so-called Islamic Jihad, and fundamentalist Muslim rebels in Afghanistan, Algeria, and Egypt: all imagined themselves tools of Allah, protectors of the just, upholders of Law.

Violence and the Millennium

The end of the first Christian millennium saw an unprecedented interest in apocalyptic imagery and drama. One consequence during the following centuries was a series of armed pilgrimages to purify the Holy Land of Jews and Muslims in preparation for Christ's imminent arrival. As the second millennium drew to a close the idea of the apocalypse again seized the public imagination.

With its promise that worldly fortunes are soon to be reversed, millennialism—the belief in the future thousand-year reign of Christ—is a theodicy ideally suited for victims. The problem is that few people indeed do not view themselves as victims. When coupled with a theodicy of justice, millennialism is one of history's most compelling justifications for violence.

The Puritans metaphorically fancied themselves as Israelites fleeing slavery at the hands of Egypt (English and Dutch authorities). Following their respective exoduses to America and South Africa, Puritan exiles founded New Jerusalems (the new church foretold in the Book of Revelation) organized after the ancient covenant between God and His children. Among the commandments incumbent on them was Yahweh's terrifying admonition to smite the Canaanites (in this case, the American Indians and Bantu peoples). In manifesting their biblically decreed destiny, in other words, one-time victims became executioners. Hope for one people—the Puritans—meant damnation for another.

Millennialists see the existing world as a charnel house of corruption. It is an arena for ethical transformation, for efforts undertaken to remake it in a manner consonant with their utopian dreams. They alone presume to know God's heart. In whatever form the Antichrist-of-the-moment discloses itself—as a Freemason, a Mormon, a Catholic, or a Jew; as a member of the Hidden Hand or of the Order; as Force X or as communism, to mention just a few—millennialists are girded for battle. (The Hidden Hand, the Order, and Force X are right-wing code words for the so-called satanic Jewish conspiracy to rule the world.)

In Christianity millennialism has played a role in movements of popular dissent. The Waldenses and the Albigenses (who flourished around 1100) and the Lollards and the Taborites (from the fourteenth and fifteenth centuries) all saw themselves as the biblically decreed chosen remnant at war with the Babylonish Church (Roman Catholicism), laboring to establish a regime of peace, love, and equality.

In calling themselves Israelites, the League of the Elect, or the Sons of God, the Puritans spoke poetically. Christian Identity, a paramilitary sect that flourishes in the contemporary American West, takes such language literally. The European peoples, says Christian Identity, are actual descendants of the one-time Lost Tribes of Israel. The Bible is theirs alone, God theirs alone, along with His promise that in the coming millennium Israel shall rule the earth. Other contemporary groups like the Army of God, the Phinneas Priesthood, and the Covenant, Sword, and Arm of the Lord all are enacting their understanding of the War of Armageddon. Their fantasies culminate in murder.

Ways of Violence

Islam, Christianity, and ancient Judaism all posit etherealized deities, compared to which the earthly world is fallen. It is not just evil, but disenchanted, profane. Hence, in all three religions inordinate devotion to the things of this world is considered idolatry. Notable among these things is politics, the pursuit of power. Although political ends may be holy—for example, inflicting God's vengeance or establishing the promised millennium—the means used to achieve them are not. For this reason politics in Western religious cultures, and particularly political violence, is not typically circumscribed by ritual. Warriors are permitted any tack or tool that promises to provide them the greatest destructive power at the least cost. Hence, although the Old Testament Book of Numbers, the first Muslim Caliph Abu Bakr's "Ten Rules to Keep by Heart" (630), or the Protestant military leader Gustavus Adolphus's "Swedish Discipline" (1640) all have regulations on the division of booty, the treatment of protégés, pre-battle prayers, and camp behavior, ceremonial restrictions on fighting itself are absent.

To be sure, even in the Western world practical considerations may dictate that one act chivalrously toward opponents. But chivalry is not required by church, mosque, or synagogue. In the Old Testament Yahweh is entirely indifferent to how His champions subdue the enemy, as long as it is done effectively. The reader may recall that the conquest of the Promised Land is accomplished almost entirely by means of bald-faced treachery, the classic case being Gideon's defeat of the Midianites. His three-hundred-man contingent is handpicked for ferocity. For their part, *jihadists* are permitted to devastate enemy territory by smoke and fire, by surprise at day or night, or by pitched battle. They are even allowed to hold their own loyal subjects hostage.

Medieval Europe had an ethic of violence analogous to that of the Hindus when the church claimed authority over military affairs and ordained knights into service by means of a so-called eighth sacrament. After receiving the chrism from a priest, the knight was obliged to fight only on specific days, and then only with limited weaponry (crossbows and longbows being prohibited), as well as to respect the lives of noncombatants. To what degree these regulations were obeyed during the heat of battle is open to dispute. So, too, is the question of whether they derived from the doctrine of just war, which proposes that the means of violence must be balanced to the ends envisioned by fighting. And how did Christian pacifism affect the medieval art of war? One thing is certain, however. After the Reformation, military niceties of any sort were superseded by the science of mass destruction.

Martin Luther's beliefs were most influential in this transformation. Luther (1483–1546) maintained that the state should deal with matters of the world, period; the Church exclusively with those of the soul. "Holy war," he asserted, is an oxymoron. Juxtaposing the two words risks corrupting the Church with worldly cares while unnecessarily hamstringing the state in the pursuit of its own interests. After Luther, Protestant states were permanently liberated from the fetters of the church. One result was a series of revolutionary advances in military technology, including in the twentieth century the deployment of weaponry capable of exterminating all life. Equipped with this arsenal, Euro-America was positioned after 1500 to assume virtual hegemony over the planet.

Eastern Interpretations

Hinduism, Buddhism, and Confucianism are familiar with the terrifying, alluring paradox of the holy. But contrary to being pictured as a being residing wholly apart from the world, the great mystery is experienced as intimately bound up with mundane everydayness. The Divine may be invisible to the lazy, inattentive, or ignorant, but it is directly accessible to those who assiduously follow the Path *(dharma, -do, tao)* appropriate to their social status.

In times of war, the *ksthatriya* (members of the Hindu military caste) were forbidden—on pain of accumulating *karma* (the law of consequence of action) and thus of being reincarnated into a lower caste—to use barbed, poison, or fire weapons. Nor could they attack anyone but bonafide combatants. Furthermore, combatants were fair game only if not in distress or in some other way distracted (for example, by prayers or eating). Ideally, the foe would be permitted to shoot first and never be struck below the navel. The ancient Hindu Laws of Manu say that it is better to die fighting righteously than to win by sinful means. Like all laws, of course, these too were broken, probably with impunity. But clearly they evince an ethic of violence alien to Western religious culture.

A comparable ethic is found in the *Tso Chuan,* the commentaries to *The Spring and Autumn Annals* of ancient China. The Confucian doctor of martial arts, Sun Tzu, author of *The Art of War* (c. 403–221 B.C.), systematized them into an orientation—victory through skill or cunning rather than force—that informs military strategy throughout the Far East down to our era. (Today, this strategy is employed with tactical and technical innovations borrowed from Euro-America.)

Confucianism is fundamentally pacifistic. Better to be a dog and live in peace, goes an ancient adage, than a man in anarchy. Although it understands the necessity of force to quell disorder, Confucianism honors bloodless victory above all: victory obtained without the use of naked blades. Winning one hundred victories in one hundred battles is not the acme of skill, says Sun Tzu—to subdue the enemy without fighting is.

True, Sun Tzu advocates espionage, trickery, and feints to decrease destructive power, not increase it. In any case, more important than fakery is the general's cultivation of his own virtue (prudence, temperance, piety, and propriety). By being virtuous, he inspires the morale of his soldiers and thus forces foes to recognize the futility of fighting. He also renders himself invulnerable to the very deceits Sun Tzu himself advocates.

More than this, the general must learn to dance with the enemy. Instead of confronting its fury by facing it head on, he should be like water, which in yielding to all things overcomes them in the end. This strategy means moving where the opponent is not and turning the enemy's own force and momentum against him. Mao Zedong (1893–1976) would reiterate Sun Tzu's teachings. From this philosophy, teaches the sixth-century B.C. *Tao te Ching* (The Book of the Way and Its Power), comes the power of not contending. As France and the United States learned to their sorrow in Vietnam, this military wisdom is still practiced today in Asia.

During the period of enforced peace under the Tokugawa shoguns (1600 to 1867), Japanese Zen Buddhist monks refined the Confucian military ethic into *bushido* (the way of the warrior) and into the various combat arts familiar to modern readers: *kendo* (the way of the sword), *kyudo* (of the bow), and *karate-do* (of the hand). As in *judo* (the way of yielding [or wisdom]) and *aikido* (the way of harmony), reverently correct use of the means of violence paradoxically becomes a vehicle for illumination *(satori),* insight into That which Is. Violence itself is laden with the elemental sacred.

See also *Anti-Semitism; Calvinism; Confucianism; Confucius; Crusades; Hinduism; Holocaust; Jihad; Lutheranism; Millennialism; Pacifism; Utopianism; War.*

James Aho

BIBLIOGRAPHY

Aho, James. *Religious Mythology and the Art of War.* Westport, Conn.: Greenwood Press, 1981.

Chernus, Ira. *Dr. Strangegod: On The Symbolic Meaning of Nuclear Weapons.* Columbia: University of South Carolina Press, 1986.

Cohn, Norman. *The Pursuit of the Millennium.* New York: Oxford University Press, 1970.

Girard, Rene. *Violence and the Sacred.* Translated by Patrick Gregory. Baltimore, Md.: Johns Hopkins University Press, 1977.

Khadduri, Majid. *War and Peace in the Law of Islam.* Baltimore, Md.: Johns Hopkins University Press, 1955.

Murphy, Thomas, ed. *The Holy War.* Columbus: Ohio State University Press, 1976.

Ratti, Oscar, and Adele Westbrook. *Secrets of the Samurai.* Rutland, Vt.: Charles Tuttle, 1973.

Seward, Desmond. *The Monks of War.* London: Archon Press, 1972.

Smend, Rudof. *Yahweh War and Tribal Confederation.* Translated by Max Rogers. Nashville, Tenn.; Abingdon Press, 1970.

Walzer, Michael. *The Revolution of the Saints.* Cambridge: Harvard University Press, 1965.

Voluntarism

Voluntarism is the principle of acting out of one's own free will or relying on action taken without imposed obligation or constraint. In the United States voluntarism is a value deeply enmeshed in national culture as well as a principle supported by legal and institutional arrangements. It has roots deep in both American religious and political culture—and the centrality of each reinforces the other. Although voluntarism may not be unique to the United States, its cultural centrality and individualist interpretation there is probably more developed than anywhere else.

The relations between the American state and American religion are often described as a series of "disestablishments," in which the two institutional spheres become increasingly distant. The first disestablishment was the *legal* relationship of institutional separation embodied in the U.S. Constitution of 1787 and its First Amendment, which permits the free exercise of religion and prohibits the establishment of any official state religion. The second disestablishment was the *political* fracturing of Protestant dominance following World War II in the 1950s and 1960s as Roman Catholics, and then other religious minorities, began achieving political influence and cultural legitimacy. The third disestablishment—a more contested concept—is often understood as the *cultural* displacement of institutions from their positions as societal and cultural authorities. In this regard, people's religious sensibilities are decreasingly likely to be confined to or shaped by organized or institutionalized religion, and political loyalties are increasingly separated from political party identification and other established institutions.

Voluntarism in Religious Culture

The idea of voluntarism derives from the notion of the "community of the elect," a basic principle of Puritanism, an English Protestant reform movement in the sixteenth and seventeenth centuries. Briefly, God's people were understood as called individually to be his church. Blood and ethnicity, or the universal "Church," were no longer the basis for building the Kingdom of God on Earth; rather, the collection of individually called saints was charged with that task. Although the Puritans believed that the needs of the moral community clearly outweighed the personal preferences of individuals, their community of saints divorced religious status from either the circumstances of birth or from the established societal institutions of the state, the state church, and the patriarchal family.

In North America, where the Puritans established a colony in New England in 1620, the facts of frontier life made the highly institutionalized control of the integrated "covenant community"—the Puritan ideal—increasingly difficult to maintain. One result of the westward expansion of British colonial settlement was an increasingly individualized understanding of religious faith, salvation, and church membership. Revivalism, which became an important part of frontier religious life, promoted an ecstatic religious expression that accented the importance of individual piety and the direct experience of the spirit rather than such institutionalized credentials as formal education or ordination to the ministry.

By the early nineteenth century voluntarism had begun to emerge as an intellectual concept as well as a fact of American religious life. Lyman Beecher, a prominent New England Presbyterian clergyman, is often credited with first advancing the notion of voluntarism in the 1810s, to describe the necessity of lay involvement and support for newly disestablished churches. For Beecher, this was a strategy for maintaining the hegemony of the Reformed evangelical denominations that dominated New England and the parts of the west where emigrating New Englanders settled. Developing from the ideas of lay control and private associations was the dense network of voluntary civic and religious associations that so impressed Alexis de Tocqueville, the French political observer who wrote *Democracy in America* (1835–1840). Tocqueville called churches America's "first political institutions" as they supported dense social networks and gave common people practical experience in self-government.

In the South, however, the predominant and fast-growing religious groups such as Baptists and Methodists did not participate in this form of voluntarism. And yet their use of revivalism and itinerant preachers with little formal training also produced a distinct notion of voluntary religious action. The state of the individual's moral character, and the importance of the individual's voluntary acceptance of religious truth, became paramount. Over time, a focus on personal piety, emotion-based faith, and voluntary commitment spread to other forms of Protestantism, and even to American Catholics.

By the latter nineteenth century other forms of individualism, particularly involving economic life, became popular in American culture. One version of social Darwinism, which applied the ideas of biological evolution to social organization and societal inequality, emphasized individual motivation, mobility, and achievements. Individuals were seen as responsible for their own situation, for good or ill. In part, this was a handy justification used by business to resist workers' efforts to form trade unions; it also proved useful for both Protestant nativists and assimilationists trying to come to grips with the large numbers of Catholic and Jewish immigrants filling northern cities. Nativists opposed immigration and wanted to keep immigrants out; assimilationists encouraged immigration but thought it necessary to acculturate immigrants into the ways of Anglo-Saxon Protestant culture. For both groups social Darwinism justified the privileged status of the dominant classes, and individual motivation and change were regarded as the only acceptable means for social mobility. The American dream came to be symbolized by individual choice. The ability to change occupations, communities, and religions made all institutional affiliations that were not voluntarily chosen seem suspect.

The social and cultural changes of the 1960s and early 1970s further integrated individual choice and voluntary commitment into American culture. The primacy of individual self-expression and self-fulfillment brought an increasing sense of impermanence to all social commitments, emphasizing their transient nature and their inherent oppressive character unless they were voluntarily chosen. For many, the principles of free market economic theory were applied to other relationships, with the individual understood primarily as a "consumer." According to many observers these changes underscored a long-standing if implicit anti-institutionalism in American religion and accelerated a trend toward the "privatization" of religious belief, action, and identity.

Voluntarism in Political Life

The notion of voluntarism in political life is parallel in many ways to its religious forms. That is, there is both a cultural commitment to the idea that only voluntarily chosen political ideas and loyalties are legitimate, and there are a set of institutional arrangements that reinforce that belief.

In part, of course, the very notion of liberal democracy is based on the assumption that people choose their government without coercion and that government is answerable to the governed. Political participation takes the form of what Sidney Verba has called "civic voluntarism," participation in which individuals and interest groups get involved in the public sphere with the resources at their disposal to advance their own interests. This idea resonates with the notion of the social contract as the basic political relationship; that is, society is formed by the voluntary, rational relinquishing of some personal freedom in exchange for some societal security. Implied in this social contract is the right of the governed to rebel if the rulers do not uphold their contractual obligations. Thus the most basic political relationship is essentially voluntary.

Several institutional arrangements of the American state have reinforced the individual voluntarism in American culture. For example, the choice of single-member districts, in which each geographic area is represented in the national legislature by an individual, puts a premium on local interests and gives politicians a power base separate from the political party or the central capital. Also, the non-Constitutional status of political parties, and the well-known wariness of parties expressed by the Framers of the Constitution, have provided the rationale in which to channel anti-institutional sentiment that emphasizes personal interests over group interests. This inclination has become expressed as a personalized politics. Mass media–based appeals focus on personal characteristics of candidates, with marketing-based political strategies aimed at evermore specialized constituencies; and individualized campaign organizations, run by the candidates themselves, have further undercut the authority of political parties and other organizing institutions such as labor unions.

The separation of powers among the three branches of government—the executive, legislative, and judicial—has fostered both a suspicion of institutionalized power and inertia in policy making. Although such institutional arrangements need not necessarily lead to a voluntaristic political culture, they facilitated that already existing tendency. In any case, political parties and other regional and national interests play a decreasing role in organizing personal political identities and group-based partisan politics. There has been less realignment of parties than dealignment, and "independent" has become a common self-identifier for voters. The suspicion of political institutions represented by these trends has paralleled an increased reliance on personalized, voluntary accounts for political loyalties and decisions.

Voluntarism as a Religio-Political Issue

Two contemporary social issues highlight the importance of voluntarism as a cultural value in relating religion to politics. The first involves new religious movements and the charge of coercive conversions of recruits. The second involves the theme of voluntarism in American civil religion and its relation to government social welfare policy.

Controversy surrounding new religious movements, often pejoratively called cults, has frequently centered on whether their adherents are truly voluntary members or whether their intense religious commitments are irrational and hence not voluntary. For an action to be voluntary, an individual must have both "knowledge" and "capacity" when acting. Consequently, anticult activists argue that an individual must be making a knowledgeable choice in joining a cult and must have the capacity to make the choice. Those who charge new religious movements with "brainwashing" have generally held that recruits had the capacity to leave before they had full knowledge of the group's character; by the time they gained that knowledge, however, their capacity to leave was diminished. Because several "cures" for brainwashing by cults involve the coercive "deprogramming" of adult-aged children, this area of law is contested.

In political debates the notion of voluntarism as a valuable trait in American culture has been used to attack state initiatives in civil society, especially those that seek to regulate the market or redistribute wealth. Free enterprise, interpreted as unfettered individuals pursuing their own interests, is counterposed to "big government." These ideas became a mainstay of President Ronald Reagan's version of American civil religion in the 1980s. While Reagan generally favored reductions in government size and spending (with the exception of the military), the theme of voluntarism replacing "big government" was a pronounced goal regarding social welfare policies. Claiming that a "voluntary spirit" of neighborly care through churches, friends, and family had traditionally provided for America's unfortunate, Reagan contrasted that golden age with the "fallen" nature of the liberal welfare state. Thus a revival of voluntarism served as a form of salvation doctrine in Reagan's civil religion. That use of voluntarism, as a form of individualism that stands in contrast to socially determined or government-sponsored action, received a religious patina from Reagan. The fundamental view of the relationship between the individual and society, and the way in which that relationship should shape public policy, has decisively shaped welfare policy and attitudes toward the poor in recent years.

See also *Civil religion; Civil society; Communitarianism; Community organizing; Constitution, U.S.; Cults; Freedom of religion; Individualism; Nativism; Nongovernmental organizations; Philanthropy; Tocqueville, Alexis de.*

Rhys H. Williams

BIBLIOGRAPHY

Adams, David S. "Ronald Reagan's 'Revival': Voluntarism as a Theme in Reagan's Civil Religion." *Sociological Analysis* 48 (1987): 17–29.

Bellah, Robert N., Richard Madsen, William Sullivan, Ann Swidler, and Steven Tipton. *Habits of the Heart: Individualism and Commitment in American Life.* Berkeley: University of California Press, 1985.

Hall, Peter Dobkin. *Inventing the Nonprofit Sector: Essays on Philanthropy, Voluntarism, and Nonprofit Organization.* Baltimore: Johns Hopkins University Press, 1992.

Hammond, Phillip E. *Religion and Personal Autonomy: The Third Disestablishment in America.* Columbia: University of South Carolina Press, 1992.

Hatch, Nathan O. *The Democratization of American Christianity.* New Haven: Yale University Press, 1989.

Lewis, Michael. *The Culture of Inequality.* 2d ed. Amherst: University of Massachusetts Press, 1993.

Roof, W. Clark, and William McKinney. *American Mainline Religion: Its Changing Shape and Future.* New Brunswick, N.J.: Rutgers University Press, 1987.

Verba, Sidney, Kay Lehman Schlozman, and Henry E. Brady. *Voice and Equality: Civic Voluntarism in American Politics.* Cambridge: Harvard University Press, 1995.

Voting

Voting is the process by which citizens in democratic societies choose their public officials. Although most such societies treat the government as largely secular, in fact if not in law, religious factors have played a major role in the electoral processes of many countries. Recognizing that groups of voters often form cohesive blocs united by common religious identity, candidates for office may appeal to voters on the basis of shared religious convictions. In some nations, political parties claim to represent a particular religious vision and attempt to rally voters around that identity. This essay describes the extent of such linkages between religious affiliation and the vote. It then explores the historical bases of religious divisions and examines the future of religious differences in voting.

Linkages between Religion and Voting

When scholars first began to study voting behavior with scientific research methods in the late 1950s and early 1960s, they were often surprised to discover that religious factors played an extremely important role in vote choices. The results of opinion polls in many countries revealed two patterns. First, the electoral preferences of many voters were strongly related to their religious affiliation. Knowing that a voter had been raised a Roman Catholic or a member of a particular Protestant denomination often foretold with a high degree of accuracy which political party that voter would support. This pattern was particularly pronounced in countries that were religiously diverse. Second, the level of religious activity—what is sometimes called religious salience or religiosity—also exerted a significant effect upon political behavior. As a general rule, subject to considerable variation depending on the country being studied, voters who were deeply involved in a religious community tended to vote for political parties that were on the conservative end of the political spectrum and persons who were outside an organized religious culture disproportionately voted for liberal or left-wing parties. These two patterns usually reinforced each other. That is, the most religiously engaged members of a particular denomination were also more likely to behave in a politically distinctive manner than were those members of a denomination who were not so involved with denominational life.

The case of the Netherlands, a religiously diverse society, illustrates these patterns. In 1968, when asked which political party they supported, Dutch voters reacted according to their religious background and involvement. Among Roman Catholics, fully two-thirds supported the Catholic People's Party. A plurality of voters from the numerically dominant Dutch Reformed tradition supported either of two parties that were historically associated with Protestant supremacy in Holland. Voters from the various Orthodox Reformed churches, religious movements known for militant Protestantism, gave three-fourths of their support to the two historically pro-Protestant parties. More than four-fifths of Dutch voters who claimed to have no church affiliation endorsed either the major socialist party or a Liberal Party that had campaigned against religious influence in government. Strong as they were, these patterns became even more exaggerated when the analysis factored in levels of religious activity. Among Christians who had been in church the week of the survey, three-fourths of Catholics supported the Catholic party, more than 70 percent of the Dutch Reformed favored a Protestant party, and 82 percent of the Orthodox also claimed affiliation with the parties of Protestantism. By contrast, majorities of Christians who said they never attended church preferred the same secular parties that enjoyed such high levels of support from citizens who had no religious affiliation at all.

Such strong linkages between religion and politics emerged repeatedly in many if not most of the nations where voting behavior was analyzed scientifically. In one classic study from 1969, Richard Rose and Derek Urwin classified political parties in sixteen Western nations on the basis of whether their supporters were identified primarily by religious affiliation, socioeconomic traits, or some combination of these factors. They reported overall that religious differences, not social class, provided the major social base for Western political parties. Reviewing the broad sweep of scientific research on voting behavior, other studies (in Rose's *Electoral Behavior*, 1974) suggested that religious differences were one of the first places where analysts should look to explain voting patterns. In religiously diverse countries, like the Netherlands or Germany, each major religious denomination tended to support a particular party or set of parties. Where only one major religious tradition predominated, as in Catholic France or Lutheran Norway, the major electoral division seemed to run between people who practiced their religion and those who were religiously inactive. In the United States, with its system of separating church and state, the pattern was even more complex. Since the 1930s, it was found, Roman Catholics, Jews, black Protestants, and white evangelical Protestants had been part of the dominant Democratic Party coalition, while the Republican Party drew its most consistent support from white Protestants in mainline denominations, such as Methodist, Episcopal, and Presbyterian.

These tendencies were surprising for a number of reasons. In many of the countries where religious differences were observed—predominantly Western Europe and the Anglo-American nations—there seemed to be very little reason for them. In France, for example, few analysts could find any important political issues with obvious religious overtones to explain why practicing and nonpracticing Catholics voted so differently. Similarly, Canadian Catholics and Protestants also voted for competing parties, even though no major party in that country had embraced a Catholic or Protestant identity or appealed to voters on the basis of religious values. The voting differences between Anglicans (members of the state-backed Church of England) and other Protestants in England seemed to have outlasted by half a century any political disputes between the two groups.

If analysts were puzzled by the reasons religious differences were so strongly related to voting, they were also taken aback by the prevalence of such "primordial" political differences in advanced industrial societies during the last half of the twentieth century. For many scholars and journalists, the politics of the modern world are primarily about economic differences, and elections are sometimes described as the democratic expression of class conflict. With the increasing secularization of society, it was widely expected that religious differences would become less important generally and that political conflict would increasingly follow lines of occupation, wealth, and social class. To find powerful religious differences in voting seemed to contradict some basic assumptions about the evolution of society.

Sources of Religious Differences in Politics

Religious differences in voting, like other patterns of groups in the electorate, often originate in conflicts that arise when the nation is first created. As part of what is known as the process of political development, modern nation-states claim authority over practices and institutions that were formerly the preserve of religious organizations. If the new state is an ally of certain religious groups, providing continuing support for their public role and privileges, it may earn lasting political support. If, on the other hand, the emerging state infringes on the rights or liberties of a religious group, it may earn lasting opposition. Such tensions may produce durable alliances between particular churches and certain political movements.

In France, for example, the Revolution that began in 1789 attacked the Catholic Church along with the monarchy, aristocracy, and other social forces associated with French feudalism. The intense antireligious fervor of the revolutionary partisans made the church an implacable enemy of left-wing political forces. Nearly two centuries after the Revolution, practicing Catholics still voted disproportionately for conservative parties, and left-wing political parties, the heirs of the revolutionary tradition, still attracted substantial support from voters who were less rooted in Catholic tradition.

The case of England offers a variant of the pattern. After centuries of religious struggle between Royalists and Parliamentarians, the English state that emerged in the late 1600s was firmly associated with the Church of England. The Tory Party, which represented Anglican supremacy, was so strongly identified with the Church of England that one historian only half-jokingly described Anglican church services as "the Tory Party at prayers." More than three centuries later, these historical patterns still exerted an impact upon voting. Anglicans continued to give most of their vote to the Conservative Party, the heirs of the Tories, while Protestants who did not accept the authority of the state church and most Roman Catholics supported other political parties.

The persistence of such patterns long after the original causes had disappeared into the mists of history suggests that partisan alignments had somehow "frozen" in place and that many voters had "inherited" religious identities with distinctive political loyalties. Scholars have identified at least three mechanisms that seemingly perpetuate religious distinctiveness in voting: values, interests, and subcultures.

Values. Members of a religious group may behave as a cohesive force in politics because they share certain norms and values that have acquired political relevance. In the language of the nineteenth-century political observer Alexis de Tocqueville, there are "elective affinities" between religious values and certain political and social attitudes. For example, certain types of Christianity have been described as "other worldly," referring to the belief that life on earth is but preparation for the eternal bliss (or damnation) of an afterlife. For people who look at life in that manner, politics may seem irrelevant because it is concerned with the least important domain of human existence. On the other hand, the belief among some Christians that Jesus would not return to earth until human life had been purified or elevated stimulated all manner of political reform movements in nineteenth-century America.

Critics of this approach do not deny the possibility of an association between religious and political outlooks, but they doubt that religious ideas generally drive political positions. More likely, they argue, adherents of a political perspective can search among the diverse and complex tenets of religions until they find a religious basis for whatever political position they prefer on other grounds. It has been noted, for example, that white evangelical Protestants in the United States often opposed church involvement in the civil rights movement of the 1960s on the grounds that political activism would interfere with the priority of saving souls. By the 1970s, however, many of these same evangelicals found a doctrinal basis to justify their increasing political involvement in various moral crusades and political campaigns.

Interests. The links between religion and politics may also depend on interests. From this perspective, members of a religious group may rally around a single political party because that party will advance their cause. Parties devoted to religious "interests" often concentrate on securing state benefits for believers. The particular interests at work depend upon the nature of the political process in each country. In nations with an established church, one party may pledge to maintain the privileged role of the state church while its opponents press for religious equality. Where no single religion enjoys dominance, advocates of all religions may find one party that is more committed than its competitors to securing financial benefits for churches. In these two types of cases, the struggle may center on the continuing dominance of the state church in elementary education or general funding for religious education versus a more secular education system. Whatever the circumstances, it is not hard to understand why members of religious groups would find it advantageous to favor a party than served their tangible needs and interests.

Subcultures. The third explanation for the link between religion and voting treats religious groups as subcultures. Individuals may be born into a religious subculture by virtue of ancestry and acquire a distinctive set of political loyalties by virtue of tradition. Such loyalties may then be reinforced through education, socialization, and restricted patterns of social interaction. The most dramatic example of total integration would be a so-called religious cult in which members are tightly committed to a worldview and effectively cut off from outside sources of information. In some highly segmented, or "pillarized," societies, such as Belgium and the Netherlands, religion once provided the basis for a whole range of institutions that virtually surrounded the members with reminders of group identity—educational systems, newspapers, youth groups, labor unions, financial institutions, health care providers, and professional and business associations. Even a considerably looser form of religious involvement may help to promote political uniformity. Simply by attending church frequently, individuals are exposed to a common perspective that is communicated through formal religious education, reinforced by sermons and messages from religious leaders, and further promoted by regular social interaction with other members of the congregation. Through these influences, any tradition of support by a religious group for a certain party based on values or interests can be maintained and transmitted long after the causes of the tradition have passed.

Political Parties and Religion

Whatever the source of links between religion and politics, the relationship can take a variety of forms. In some societies, the association of religion and voting is expressed most clearly by the existence of religiously based political parties. These political parties that adhere to a particular tradition are tailored to the political circumstances of the countries where they exist. Some such parties exist to defend the interests and values of the largest or dominant religious traditions. This has been the case for the many Christian Democratic parties in Europe and Latin America that have attempted to present a distinctly Christian alternative to the dominant socialist and capitalist parties. There have been equivalent parties calling for a more militant Hinduism in India and a more assertive Buddhist presence in Japanese government.

In some places minority religions have been the driving force behind political parties. In Germany's democratic political system before the rise of Hitler's National Socialism in the 1930s, the country's Catholic minority supported a "Center" party that tried to preserve Catholic options in a predominantly Protestant society. In contemporary India, the minority Sikhs and Muslims have relied upon political parties to promote and protect their communities. Scholars have described such parties as "camp parties" because they tend to exist primarily to advance the interest of a specific and well-defined religious constituency. Elsewhere, religious minorities might decide their best hope would be to encourage policies that called for religious deregulation. Many of the liberal parties that emerged in nineteenth-century Europe enjoyed strong support from people in relatively small religious denominations. As an example, the British Liberal Party, which was not formally tied to any religious community, nonetheless emerged as the opponent of "religious coercion" by challenging legal disadvantages suffered by persons outside the state church.

Even in nations without overtly religious parties, political and religious elites play a crucial role in determining the electoral relevance of religious affiliation. In the religiously pluralistic United States, there have long been significant ties between certain religious groups and political parties, but these ties have shifted over time. In the early years of the Republic, religious groups entered into political debate on the question of whether the individual states that provided tax subsidies and support to established churches should continue the practice or promote religious neutrality by withholding government funding from all religious groups. As a rule, the pro-establishment Federalist Party drew support from members of the established churches, while Thomas Jefferson's Democratic Party appealed to Baptists, Methodists, and other religious groups who suffered at the hands of "official" state religions. With the gradual disappearance of that issue, as all states eventually chose to disestablish religion, the question of slavery engaged the various churches, and the parties began to bid for the support of different religious groups by offering religious grounds for their positions on slavery. Since the 1980s the Republican Party has attempted to become the political home of white evangelical Protestants and traditionalist Roman Catholics by endorsing conservative positions on such moral issues as abortion, gay rights, and pornography. The linkage between the party and moral conservatism is the joint product of efforts by Republican elites and sympathetic leaders of the targeted religious constituencies.

The Future

Will religion continue to play an important electoral role? The answer depends on the country where the question is asked. In many advanced Western societies, religious differences appear finally to be giving way in the manner predicted by other sources of differences in voting. Across Western Europe the period since the 1960s has been marked by a dramatic decline in formal religious adherence and devotion. Parties once defined principally by the religious character of their supporters have evolved into "catch-all" parties that now attempt to elicit support from voters across the religious and political spectrum. In the Netherlands, for example, the diverse denominational parties that were so powerful in the 1960s have merged into a single religious party (the Christian Democratic Appeal); as voting differences between believers and those with no religious affiliations have eroded over time, that party has lost the allegiance of a significant share of the electorate. This loss of allegiance has not eradicated religious influences in politics altogether, but it may have changed the form of partisan conflicts. Increasingly, it seems, partisan conflict is defined by differences of worldview in which cultural issues play an important role. Such issues may become one component of a larger worldview that becomes especially attractive to voters who remain involved in religious life.

The pattern appears to be quite different in the newly democratic states that have emerged in such large numbers since the 1980s. In Russia and Eastern Europe, a region emerging from the shadow of the Soviet Union, religion appears likely to be one of the principal political dividing lines in post-Soviet elections. During the nationalist uprisings against communist regimes, as in Poland, the church was often an important factor in mobilizing opposition to the state. Once independence was achieved, religious believers might naturally enough continue to rely on the church as a source of political information and inspiration.

Elsewhere, particularly in developing countries, religion often appears as an electoral force that may challenge governing parties with secular ideologies. The scenario in Iran, where opponents of "Westernization" turned to religious fundamentalism as a rallying point, seems to be repeating itself in nations like Algeria and Turkey. The striking electoral success of Islamist parties in those countries has prompted nervous secularists to turn to the military and other extralegal methods to "contain" the fundamentalist upsurge. We can thus safely anticipate that the electoral process across the globe will continue to bear the imprint of religious values, institutions, and cultures.

See also *Catholicism, Roman; Christian democracy; Denominationalism; Pluralism; Protestantism; Separation of church and state; State churches.*

Kenneth D. Wald

BIBLIOGRAPHY

Ayata, Sencer. "Patronage, Party, and State: The Politicization of Islam in Turkey." *Middle East Journal* 50 (winter 1996): 41–57.

Dogan, Mattei. "Erosion of Class Voting and of the Religious Vote in Western Europe." *International Social Science Journal* 47 (December 1995): 525–538.

Hammond, John L. *The Politics of Benevolence: Revival Religion and American Voting Behavior.* Norwood, N.J.: Ablex, 1979.

Hertzke, Allen D. *Echoes of Discontent: Jesse Jackson, Pat Robertson, and the Resurgence of Populism.* Washington, D.C.: CQ Press, 1993.

Kalyvas, Stathis N. *The Rise of Christian Democracy in Europe.* Ithaca, N.Y.: Cornell University Press, 1996.

Lipset, Seymour Martin, and Stein Rokkan. "Cleavage Structures, Party Systems, and Voter Alignments: An Introduction." in *Party Systems and Voter Alignments,* edited by Seymour Martin Lipset and Stein Rokkan. New York: Free Press, 1967.

Rose, Richard, ed. *Electoral Behavior: A Comparative Handbook.* New York: Free Press, 1974.

Rose, Richard, and Derek Urwin. "Social Cohesion, Political Parties, and Strains in Regimes." *Comparative Political Studies* 2 (1969): 7–67.

Veer, Peter van der. *Religious Nationalism: Hindus and Muslims in India.* Berkeley: University of California Press, 1994.

Wald, Kenneth D. *Crosses on the Ballot: Patterns of British Voter Alignment since 1885.* Princeton: Princeton University Press, 1983.

War

War is a state of hostility, conflict, or antagonism between peoples and is usually defined as armed conflict between two or more governments or states. Religion and warfare are ancient partners that remain inextricably bound. Virtually every war in human history was supported by at least one religious institution, as were movements of opposition to warfare. The widespread peace movements of the twentieth century were largely initiated and nurtured by the same religious institutions that promoted history's bloodiest wars.

Rarely if ever is religion the major cause of war, but it is often a critical factor. Faith serves primarily to legitimate, motivate, and increase intensities, whether it is promoting or protesting war. From earliest wars of conquest to colonial wars and contemporary ethnic conflicts, religion is at the core of war making. Although opposition to war comes from many sources, religious traditions provide the most potent and persistent antiwar movements.

Violence and the Sacred

The moral struggles religious people face in the nuclear age are not new; the ancient Hebrew prophets, the hero Prince Arjuna of the Bhagavad Gita, and early Christians, Muslims, Buddhists, and animists faced them as well. The world's scriptures are replete with stories and lessons about the ethics of force. In the modern world religious elements of the debate are even more significant because of the god-like powers given to those who control nuclear arsenals.

Violence and the sacred are intimately linked. Violence, in religious terms, can be a sacrificial act designed to appease the gods. The same act of violence is at some times considered criminal activity and at other times a sacred duty. Religious thought accounts for acts that are ordinarily forbidden. In societies without developed judicial systems religious institutions regulate problematic behaviors, especially through rituals that provide established scripts for determining when force is forbidden and when it is required. In this respect the modern global social order is similar to hunting-and-gathering societies in that it has no formally binding transnational system of sanctions.

The paradox of violence is that most people both condemn and condone it. Almost universally in modern society, the use of violence is considered taboo yet efficacious, creating a remarkable moral ambivalence. Violence is widely abhorred and yet frequently employed. Elaborate social mechanisms are thus institutionalized to distinguish between legitimate and illegitimate violence. The use of violence is a mechanism of social boundary maintenance, a profound expression of power that requires a rhetoric of justification, one found in the ancient warrior motifs of contemporary religious communities.

The Warrior Motif

The dominant theme in most religious traditions is the warrior motif that requires participation in warfare as a religious duty. Virtually every major tradition includes this concept, although it varies widely both within and between religions.

Hinduism and Buddhism, for example, contain nonviolent teachings but also have a long history of legitimating war. The Hindu Bhagavad Gita tells the story of Arjuna, who hesitates to fight against his relatives and is finally convinced to do so by Krishna, an incarnation of the god Vishnu. Krishna persuades Arjuna that it is his sacred duty—his *dharma*—to engage in battle because he was born a warrior. Moreover, he should not hesitate to kill, nor should he grieve for his victims because violence cannot destroy the soul but affects only the body, which one simply puts on and replaces like a garment. It is, therefore, not merely acceptable to engage in battle, it is obligatory. When the morally forbidden becomes required by the gods as sacrificial ritual, it is imbued with a cosmic justification that serves the purposes not only of the gods but also their alleged representatives.

This duty to fight coexists uneasily in contemporary Hinduism with norms of nonviolence but has driven Indians to war over the centuries and provides moral support for a large military budget and a nuclear weapons program in India, as well as ongoing conflicts between India and its neighbors.

The biblical exodus of the Hebrew slaves from bondage under the pharaoh of Egypt and their entry into a new homeland were eased by considerable violence believed to be perpetrated by God or carried out on God's behalf. The God of the Torah, the Jewish scripture, is perceived as the champion of the oppressed who wages war against the powerful; according to the Book of Joshua (24:8–13), the Lord told the Hebrews that "I brought you into the land of the Amorites who lived east of the Jordan; they fought against you, but I delivered them into your hands; you took possession of their country and I destroyed them for your sake." According to the tradition Yahweh later destroyed the Israelites because of their injustice. Yahweh was perceived as a God who used violence on behalf of justice.

Believers in the Hebrew God of war were, of course, also the inspiration for some of the most eloquent dreams of peace in the ancient world, such as the famous passage in Isaiah (2:4), "They shall beat their swords into plowshares and neither shall they learn war anymore." Indeed, for the ancient Hebrews, dreams of war and peace lived side by side, as they do in contemporary Judaism, in Israel and elsewhere. The ambivalent and often contradictory policies of the Israelis toward Palestinians and other Arab neighbors is, in a sense, an offspring of this ancient tradition; the contemporary rhetoric that justifies military campaigns echoes that in the Hebrew scriptures.

The Hebrew notion of God as warrior was greatly embellished by Christians waging the Crusades in medieval Europe. Although the early church was a pacifist community, the conversion of the Roman emperor Constantine in 312 transformed that institution and its teachings. He reportedly had a vision in which he saw the sign of a cross in the heavens accompanied by the words "In this sign conquer." The cross was painted on his troops' shields, and he won the decisive Battle of Molvena, consolidated his power, and became convinced that the Christian God was a great God of war.

By the eleventh century Christian ambivalence about warfare was nearly eradicated, and Rome aligned with European monarchies to free the Holy Land from the infidels (the Muslims). Armies swept across southern Europe in the name of Jesus, slaughtering many who opposed them. Guns were christened with apostles' names, and swords were engraved with religious scenes; men, women, and children were beheaded and stabbed in the name of Jesus.

The Crusade tradition became deeply engraved in Christian belief and practice in subsequent centuries, and the idea of loving one's enemies gave way to killing them under certain conditions. Early teachings against war gradually gave way as church elites aligned themselves with political and economic powers of Western civilization. The pacifism of the early church never fully disappeared but was marginalized, just as the emphasis on nonviolence was subordinated to the warrior dharma within Hinduism.

Nineteenth-century Europeans conquered most of the globe with guns and Bibles, twentieth-century troops are blessed by priests, and Christians around the world continue to pray for victory in battle. In a more subtle way the U.S. military's global policing efforts are embedded in the Crusade tradition, despite the secularization of official government policy. It is no accident that the most interventionist nation in the late twentieth century is a cultural heir of the Crusades.

Taboos

Religious institutions and leadership are not always rallying the troops to battle and justifying war campaigns. They also define the boundary lies drawn around both the decision to go to war and the conduct of war, promoting prohibitions against or limitations of spoils, establishing social boundaries around killing, and defining what constitutes a just war.

Legitimate war is allegedly conducted for selfless purposes, so limits are placed on ways in which soldiers can profit from their plunder. Efforts to draw taboo lines around warfare can diminish the carnage, at least initially, but can also lead to unanticipated consequences by providing the ultimate justification for the use of force: if it is not for political or military leaders who make the decision, but only for the glory of God, how could it be morally wrong? Rules against spoils can actually increase the violence of warfare; the ancient Hebrews, for example, were instructed to "destroy every living thing" in city after city, leaving no survivors to prevent the taking of slaves and other forms of booty (Jos. 10:39).

Taboo lines are sometimes created to protect the religious community from violence by its own members, so that warfare can be waged only against outsiders. The Islamic jihad, for example, is to be carried out within very strict guidelines and prohibits violating the rights of others or destroying their property. Originally developed as a way to minimize violence among warring Bedouin tribes, the rules of the jihad allow violence only against those who rebel against the *imam,* or head of the Muslim community, protected minorities who violate the conditions of protection, and hostile unbelievers. It cannot be conducted during the sacred month of Ramadan and must be undertaken within the bounds of rigorous criteria. Such boundaries are often redrawn and redefined, of course, to sacralize acts of violence and warfare, as they were in the Iran-Iraq war between two Muslim nations, the Iraqi invasion of Kuwait, the Euro-American allies' military actions in the Persian Gulf, Palestinian struggles with Israelis, Pakistan's quarrels with India, and so on.

Prohibitions against killing members of one's own religious group are found in many traditions but are often more complex then they originally appear, as one can see in the commandment against killing included in the Decalogue given to Moses on Mount Sinai. When Moses returns to the camp he finds the Hebrews engaged in forbidden worship practices. According to the Torah, he angrily shatters the tablets and instructs the Levites to "go through the camp from gate to gate and back again. Each of you kill his brother, his friend, his neighbor" in order to punish transgressors (Ex. 32:28).

Religious prohibitions thus include an exception clause that requires killing believed to be commanded by the deity. Thus even religious teachings that appear to prohibit war may be reinterpreted to legitimate it; such is the case with the Christian just war tradition.

Saint Ambrose (340–397), bishop of Milan, prayed for the victory of the Roman armies in the wake of Constantine's Christianization policies. He developed a Christian ethic of war later embellished by Saint Augustine (354–430), bishop of Hippo (in what is modern-day Algeria), that has become the cornerstone of Western debates about the morality of war, including an evaluation of the nuclear arms race in the 1980s and the Gulf War in 1991.

The U.S. Conference of Catholic Bishops reexamined the just war tradition during heated debates about nuclear war in the 1980s. They insisted that the doctrine begins with the presumption that Christians should do no harm to their neighbors and that how they treat their enemies is the true test of whether they love their neighbors. A just war thus has to meet two types of criteria: those relating to the decision to fight *(jus ad bellum)* and those regarding the conduct of the war *(jus ad bello).* A decision to wage war is just only when it meets the following conditions: just cause, competent authority, comparative justice, right intention, last resort, probability of success, and potential good. The decision to go to war must be decided primarily on the last principle: potential good from a battle must exceed its cost, a principle that must also apply to each act of war. The bishops conclude that these criteria call modern warfare into serious question because war does not discriminate between combatants and noncombatants and the harm caused would far outweigh any good accomplished even in the most optimistic scenarios of nuclear war.

Nuclear winter theories, moreover, suggest that even a relatively limited nuclear exchange could create fires that would block out the sun's rays to such an extent that plants could not undergo photosynthesis, and eventually the entire ecosphere could be destroyed, thus outweighing any possible objective gained by a nuclear confrontation. Ironically, the Pentagon used just war arguments in 1984 to promote new nuclear weapons programs following the bishops' condemnation. New smart bombs, it argued, are moral because they can be targeted more precisely at military targets rather than at civilians. Christianity traditionally included three approaches to the morality of war: the just war, the crusades, and pacifism. With the first two seriously challenged by many religious authorities in the modern world, many Christians are reconsidering the pacifist stance, relegated to a small minority for about fifteen hundred years.

The Pacifist Motif

All of the world's ethical systems raise questions about killing; some go so far as to forbid it under any circumstances, a position known as pacifism. The total rejection of warfare is relatively rare but is nonetheless significant in a number of traditions, notably the Buddhist and Christian.

The early Christian church was essentially a pacifist community that for four hundred years rejected killing humans for any reason. The early church fathers wrote about this problem extensively. Tertullian (160?–220?), the first important Christian ecclesiastical writer in Latin, for example, believed that killing and loving were incompatible with one another and that the injunction to love one's enemies was the most important test of one's relationship to God. He opposed the use of violence even in self-defense. Soldiers who converted to Christianity were allowed to remain in the military but under the strict condition that they were not to kill.

Contemporary Christian pacifism emerged from the biblical and early church traditions and from the historic peace churches, the Religious Society of Friends (Quakers), the Brethren, and the Mennonites. The nonviolence of these small groups has been embellished in the latter half of the twentieth century through the church itself but also through a burgeoning global peace movement and the inspiration of contemporary advocates of nonviolence such as Indian independence leader Mohandas K. Gandhi, U.S. civil rights activist Martin Luther King Jr., U.S. social reformer Dorothy Day, and American Trappist monk and religious writer Thomas Merton. King, Day, and Merton were influenced by Gandhi and the Eastern traditions; Gandhi himself was inspired by the teachings of Jesus, especially in the Sermon on the Mount.

As a result of pacifist convictions many Christians refuse to go into the military. In countries in which there is a legal provision for conscientious objectors to war, pacifists are allowed to work on approved community service projects rather than go into the armed forces. Where there is no such option—and sometimes out of a refusal to cooperate with the draft—pacifists are jailed for resisting the system. A number of pacifists are tax resistors, that is, they either refuse to pay the proportion of their taxes that would go to the military or they keep their total income under taxable levels. The amount of money that is withheld is usually donated to charities. Legislation in the U.S. Congress that would establish a peace tax fund allowing pacifists to earmark their tax monies for nonmilitary purposes has failed to gather sufficient support to be enacted.

Pacifism and nonviolence are not positions that come easily, especially in violent cultures in which people are routinely socialized into using violence to solve major problems. Martin Luther King Jr., for example, obtained a gun to protect his family after his house was bombed during the nonviolent Montgomery bus boycott and struggled mightily with the issue before deciding with the early Christians that it was not moral to use violence even in self-defense.

The Buddha was unequivocal in denouncing the use of violence in any form, although some of his subsequent followers managed to justify killing. The Noble Eightfold Path at the core of Buddhist ethics contains a set of Five Precepts for right behavior, the first of which prohibits killing in war, murder, and even the killing of animals either for food or for ritual sacrifice (although some branches of the tradition are not strictly vegetarian). Taking the life of any sentient being could result in negative consequences, or *karma,* and thus an inferior reincarnation. The Buddhist emphasis on compassion to all creatures thus leads naturally to an antiwar ethic.

This Buddhist ethic has its roots in the ancient Vedic doctrine of *ahimsa* (nonharmfulness) prominent in Jainism and Hinduism. A respect for all life and detachment from the world are the core of nonviolence in the Eastern traditions. Respect for sentient beings is a natural outcome of a pervasive belief in the unity of all beings. This idea is in turn related to the concept of reincarnation: all sentient beings have souls and are part of the same reality. To harm another being is thus ultimately to harm oneself and sets off a chain reaction of cause and effect (karma) that multiplies its negative consequences.

Conversely, acts of compassion create a positive karma that also multiplies, increasing happiness for all, including oneself. To escape endless cycles of rebirth into lives of suffering, most Eastern spiritual teachings promote various paths of detachment such as nonpossession and renunciation. Thus when one engages in war or other acts of violence, one may become more deeply enmeshed in the world, magnify one's own suffering, and further entrap oneself in its grasp. The practice of ahimsa, on the other hand, relieves suffering and helps one progress toward liberation (*moksha*) or enlightenment.

According to Gandhi, ahimsa forbids harming others but also requires active love toward all. For others, however, ahimsa is seen as a relative obligation. For example, a soldier might vow to do injury only in battle. The Buddhist monks of Hiei-zan reportedly covered their eyes when arming for battle. Thus, even in traditions that promote nonviolence and oppose warfare, the warrior tradition persists. Pacifism is very difficult to sustain when a religious tradition becomes allied with a powerful elite. Minority communities, however, sustain pacifist ideals within several spiritual traditions and are influential in modern peace movements.

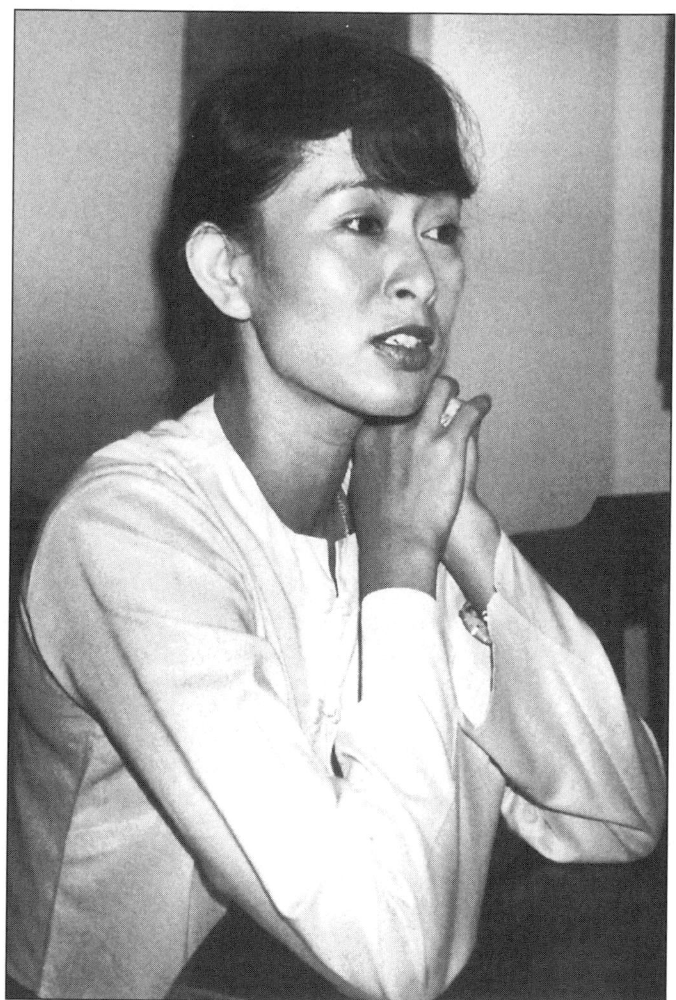

Aung San Suu Kyi

Nonviolence and Spirituality

Just as history's wars are legitimated by religious traditions, so too are the major movements for peace. A modern theory of nonviolence was developed first by Gandhi, who used nonviolent direct action to fight the colonial system and other systems of injustice by applying nonviolent philosophies from ancient teachings of Buddhism, Jainism, Christianity, and Hinduism and modern exemplars such as American philosopher and naturalist Henry David Thoreau and Russian novelist and social thinker Leo Tolstoy. The nonviolent Indian Freedom Movement that Gandhi led precipitated a worldwide diffusion of nonviolent movements, inspired by Day, King, Merton, American peace activist David Dellinger, Philippine president Corazon Aquino, South African activist and president Nelson Mandela, South African civil rights activist and Nobel laureate Archbishop Desmond Tutu, Burmese leader and Nobel laureate Aung San Suu Kyi, and many other lesser-known but highly influential people of faith. The peace movement of the nineteenth and twentieth centuries was precipitated and sustained (especially between wars) by countless people with deep spiritual faith who drew on various spiritual disciplines.

Within the sixteenth-century Protestant Reformation, the nonviolent Anabaptists gave the pacifist doctrine an institutional home in the post-Reformation Christian church. The peace churches generally opposed all war and violence as part of their effort to restore what they felt was the radical call of Jesus to discipleship. Members of these churches and other sympathetic Christians refused to participate in various wars and called on Christians to lay down their arms and follow Jesus to the cross, if necessary.

American abolitionist William Lloyd Garrison and others involved in the abolitionist movement in the nineteenth century denounced both slavery and war as antithetical to the teachings of Christ. They gathered in a peace conference and laid the groundwork for the modern antiwar movement. Tolstoy later praised the peace conference and insisted that Christians were morally obligated to resist participating in warfare.

In the twentieth century the Women's International League for Peace and Freedom and other antiwar groups, founded primarily by Christians and inspired by such leaders as American social reformer Jane Addams, developed a harsh critique of war systems and called on Christians to resist them. German and British Christians founded the Fellowship of Reconciliation during World War I, and at the war's end the disarmament movement spread rapidly as people reacted to the horrors of modern war. Public opposition to war was quickly crushed by Hitler's aggression, however, and as the world mobilized for another war, antiwar sentiment was rare outside of the peace churches.

In 1939 Dellinger founded an *ashram,* a spiritual community inspired by Gandhi's experiments in India and dedicated to nonviolence. Radical Christian pacifists affiliated with

Dellinger's community, the Fellowship of Reconciliation, the American Friends Service Committee, and the peace churches laid the groundwork for the Western antiwar movement, the American civil rights movement, and the elaboration of Gandhi's strategies of nonviolent direct action. In the post–World War II period antiwar sentiment was sustained primarily by these small communities of faith in the West and by some Buddhist and Gandhian movements in India, Japan, and elsewhere in the East.

Opposition to nuclear weapons grew in Japan and many parts of the West after World War II. Many of those involved in such groups as the Committee for a Sane Nuclear Policy and the peace churches formed the core of the movement opposing U.S. involvement in the war in Indochina in the 1960s and 1970s and the growing nuclear arms race in the 1970s and 1980s. Buddhist monks burned themselves to death protesting the Vietnam War, thousands of young Americans registered as conscientious objectors or refused to cooperate with the draft, and many were sent to jail or went into exile to avoid fighting in the war. Many Christians engaged in acts of civil disobedience in opposing war and nuclear weapons, protesting at the Pentagon and military installations and nonviolently invading nuclear weapons tests sites in an effort to bring the explosions to a halt.

In 1981 a group of women encircled the North Atlantic Treaty Organization military base in Greenham Common, England, to prevent nuclear-armed cruise missiles from being installed there, setting off a series of protests throughout Europe and the United States. Civil disobedience took many forms; in East Germany church groups broke the law and were sometimes harassed by police for simply wearing a symbol on their clothing with the words "Swords into Plowshares" from the biblical prophet Isaiah. Sit-ins and demonstrations at military installations, weapons factories, and embassies often resulted in arrests.

Although not all of the demonstrators were from religious communities, much of their leadership was, and religious groups around the world provided institutional resources for organizing and carrying out the protests. Although initiated primarily by radical pacifists, the peace movement eventually drew in mainstream religious leaders as well. Many religious leaders condemned the Vietnam War and urged their congregations to participate in antiwar protests. A 1982 rally cosponsored by a range of religious groups in New York City (for example, the American Friends Service Committee and the National Federation of Temple Youth) and demonstrating against cruise missiles drew the largest protest crowd in U.S. history.

In the 1980s the Netherlands Reformed Church declared that because multilateral arms negotiations had failed, Christians should support unilateral disarmament. Archbishop Raymond Hunthausen of Seattle called the nuclear submarine base in his diocese the "Auschwitz of Puget Sound" and advocated unilateral nuclear disarmament; the bishop of Amarillo, Texas, declared that the production of nuclear weapons was a sin that should be avoided by Christians, even though the Pantex plant that assembled nuclear weapons was one of the largest enterprises in his diocese.

Besides providing the core of institutional and ideological support for the modern antiwar movement and the central legitimation for warfare, religious institutions also provide the basis for traditional peace cultures. Many traditions offer rituals that sometimes limit and at other times provide what American pragmatist William James called a moral equivalent of war. Many traditional cultures sustain rituals of cooperation and mutual support that mitigate the possibilities of war and enable people to live in peace and to resolve conflict nonviolently, a phenomenon that is the subject of an ongoing investigation by UNESCO's peace cultures project.

Most of the world's spiritual traditions contain an element of universalism that affirms the kinship of all humanity and provide rituals that promote mutual affection and peace. Just as Gandhi used prayer meetings to mobilize people in nonviolent protest against British colonial rule, conflict between Hindus and Muslims, and injustices in Indian society, many people use traditional rituals to promote transnational and interfaith communication and cooperation.

In short, religious beliefs and institutions have promoted both the bloodiest conflicts and the most thorough opposition to war over the millennia and will no doubt greatly influence the path that human conflict follows in the future. Although humans have always faced the possibility of tremendous gains or losses through warfare, the stakes have never been higher, given the destructive capability of modern weapons. Martin Luther King Jr. insisted that the choice is no longer between violence and nonviolence but between nonviolence and nonexistence.

See also *Anabaptists; Civil disobedience; Crusades; Day, Dorothy; Friends, Society of; Hinduism; Gandhi, Mohandas Karamchand; Jihad; King, Martin Luther, Jr.; Merton, Thomas; Pacifism; Violence.*

Lester R. Kurtz

BIBLIOGRAPHY

Bainton, Roland. *Christian Attitudes toward War and Peace.* Nashville, Tenn.: Abingdon Press, 1960.

Boulding, Elise. *Building a Global Civic Culture: Education for an Interdependent World.* New York: Teachers College Press, Teachers College, Columbia University, 1988.

Ferguson, John. *War and Peace in the World's Religions.* New York: Oxford University Press, 1977.

Ghandi, Mohandas K. *All Men Are Brothers.* Edited by Krishna Kripalani. New York: Continuum, 1982.

Girard, Rene. *Violence and the Sacred.* Baltimore, Md.: Johns Hopkins University Press, 1977.

Johnson, James Turner. *Just War Tradition and the Restraint of War.* Princeton: Princeton University Press, 1981.

Juergensmeyer, Mark. *The New Cold War: Religious Nationalism Confronts the State.* Berkeley and Los Angeles: University of California Press, 1993.

Kurtz, Lester R. *Gods in the Global Village.* Thousand Oaks, Calif.: Pine Forge Press, 1995.

Weber, Max

German jurist, political economist, preeminent figure in sociology, and profound theorist of religion, capitalism, and democracy. Weber (1864–1920) has exerted wide influence on social thought. Empirical and theoretical claims he made have passed into the debates and conceptual vocabularies of diverse fields—economic history, law, politics, comparative religion, philosophy of social science, several specialized geographical area studies, and even applied policy studies of entrepreneurship, development, and modernization. Through widespread use, his originally technical concepts of "charisma" and "the Protestant ethic" have passed into everyday English.

Max Weber

Links between Political, Religious, and Economic Institutions

In Weber's theory of politics, *charisma* refers not to the mere magnetism of a public personality but to actual power. If, as he famously said, "the decisive means for politics is violence," nevertheless the stable footing of political order was not a material but a subjective one: the moral claim to uncoerced obedience—that is, to legitimate authority. Weber distinguished three types of justification for the fundamental inequality between rulers and ruled. As one of them, "charismatic authority" is a claim that points neither to custom and immemorial tradition nor to rational laws and constitutions but, instead, invokes extraordinary personal qualities. Weber's paradigmatic example of charismatic authority—Jesus' "It is written, but I say unto you"—dramatizes his point that matched beliefs and inner dispositions of rulers and ruled sustain power. Like religion, politics orients individual behavior within broad systems of meaning and culturally ratified values of right conduct and just deserts.

The subject of Weber's classic *The Protestant Ethic and the Spirit of Capitalism* (1904) is not simply the "work ethic" of everyday English but a complex of cultural and technical disciplines. Those embody the rationality peculiar to capitalism in its specifically modern form. While agreeing with Karl Marx that capitalism had material preconditions and produced new class antagonisms, Weber insisted that crucial to its emergence was an unprecedented human outlook: the "rational asceticism" of seventeenth-century Calvinist sectarians. Their goal of salvation rejected "the world," with its intermittent leisures and consoling traditions, to embrace methodical work in a calling with joy, as a pious end in itself. Thus, paradoxically, modern capitalism emerged as an unintended worldly consequence of other-worldly interests.

To test his theses about the relationships between religious interests and economic ethics, Weber studied the antecedents of modern capitalism in the West, while comparing the West with China, India, ancient Israel, and medieval Muslim societies. For example, *The Religion of China* presents Confucianism as the "status ethic" of rationalist bureaucrats, whose sober this-worldliness is fully at home with economic traditionalism. By contrast, his essay "Religious Rejections of the World and Their Directions" presents Christian other-worldliness in two radically different forms: "asceticism," with the active believer as instrument, and "mysticism," with the believer as passive vessel. The first opens worldly work to the pursuit of salvation, thus promoting rational rules of conduct held to please God. The second promotes contemplative withdrawal from a world deemed profane—and thus provides no bridge to economic ethics. Other conceptual contrasts that he developed for those purposes—such as prophet/priest, ethical prophecy/exemplary prophecy, and ultimate ends rationality/instrumental rationality—have proved applicable to many others.

In path-breaking essays on method, Weber elaborated a sociology suited to his chosen problems. That sociology does not seek explanations of group phenomena observed from the outside (like facts about nature) but instead starts with "individuals" as its conceptual units—these, however, are not actual persons but logically constructed "ideal types." He held that sociology should be able to reduce even collective concepts, such as "feudalism," "bureaucracy," and "state," to "understandable" action by individuals who, in pursuing purposes, attach meanings to their conduct. Weber's results are a theory of material power with the ideal element of legitimate authority, a theory of class that affiliates structural position with habits of mind and heart, and a theory of religion in which ideas, because they generate practical ethics, sometimes function as "switchmen of social progress."

Life and Career

Max Weber belonged to a generation for which the weakening of traditional religion, the rise of capitalism, and the emergence of mass democracy were current events. In the 1870s and 1880s Germany became a diplomatic and military giant in Europe, acquired African colonies, gave the vote to more of its citizens, and enacted protective social legislation. Its rapid industrial development and the resulting inequality led to religious and secular agitation for reform and to the rise of socialism with muscle at the polls. Growing up in Berlin, the burgeoning capital of Prussia (and of Germany as well after its unification by Chancellor Otto von Bismarck in 1871), Weber witnessed the human hubbub whose order he would later study. Some Germans embraced, some rebutted, but none ignored Marxist theory as an account of capitalism and of the new class system that displaced the old status hierarchy. Weber joined those debates. He rejected socialism but labored for reform; and he critically but carefully explored the implications of historical materialism.

Born April 21, 1864, in Erfurt, the town where Martin Luther once lived, Weber descended from well-to-do Protestants on both sides of his family. His father was a prominent jurist, and legislator; his mother, a well-educated, deeply religious woman of powerful social conscience. His elite milieu was conversant with the political, religious, and academic trends of his day. Weber's academic career began with the study of law and political economy, with a break for military service during which he earned a reserve officer's commission. A man of prodigious talent and capacity for work, he worked full time as a junior barrister while completing a doctoral thesis on the history of medieval trading associations and, two years later, a postdoctoral thesis on the history of agriculture in Roman antiquity.

Thereafter, he held several distinguished teaching appointments. In 1897, however, he experienced a depression that ended productive work for four years and precluded regular teaching for nearly twenty. During those years of mainly private scholarship, he worked on his monographs about the world religions and on his monumental *Economy and Society,* an outline of sociology and a seminal effort to grasp religion, politics, and economic life as interlocking institutional orders. In 1904 he toured widely in the United States, presenting a paper on Germany's social problems at the Congress of Arts and Sciences in St. Louis, participating in civil rights leader and author W. E. B. Du Bois's conference on crime at Atlanta University, visiting educator Booker T. Washington's Tuskegee Institute, attending many churches (including those of relatives in Virginia and North Carolina), and working on *The Protestant Ethic* in the library at Columbia University. In his essay "The Protestant Sects and the Spirit of Capitalism" and elsewhere, he commented on the links he saw in the United States between Protestant "believers' churches," the disciplined voluntary associations to which they gave rise, and the evolution of a secular political culture suited to modern democracies—developments he contrasted with the decadence he saw in German politics.

In its totality Weber's work is a vast investigation into the human significance of modernity. He argued that—for better and for worse—the trend of development in the West has been what he called "rationalization," the collective and objective output of individual reason. But to the Enlightenment's optimistic view that humans are most free when they are most rational, Weber responded with a paradox. If rationalization has meant the "disenchantment of the world" that enables scientific progress and limitless economic growth, it has also meant the dominance of bureaucracy in the coordination of everyday life, vocational specialization that narrows intelligence and experience, and the displacement of "substantive rationality" (reckoning with persons and customary expectations) by "formal rationality" (reliance on impersonal rules and cold calculation). Therefore his abiding question, as scientist and as citizen, was how to find ways to wrest human freedom from what he saw as its main antagonists in the modern world, capitalism and bureaucracy.

As a scientist, he advocated the posture of "ethical neutrality," a striving to separate fact from value, what is from what should be. That posture, controversial then and now, constituted his view of science as a vocation, as set forth in a 1919 lecture to activist students at the University of Munich. Science could clarify the likely outcomes of given policies and rationally relate means to ends, but the choice of ends lay outside its realm—and could accountably be made only through struggle in the public realm of political and moral choice. There, he insisted, a "polytheism" of values prevails. Struggle there was a citizen's duty. Accordingly, as citizen, he took strong public stands throughout his career: repeatedly denouncing authoritarian politics; initially supporting Germany's entry into World War I but later criticizing war policies; helping to found the Social Democratic Party; and serving on the commissions that drafted the German response to the charge of war guilt and the constitution of the Weimar Republic. In "Politics as a Vocation," a companion lecture that has resonated in social movements since, he contrasted the "ethic of responsibility," which foresees consequences, with the "ethic of ultimate ends," which sees pure intentions above all. Weber's young audience heard his prophetic warning that "a polar night of icy darkness" would intervene before their enthusiastic hopes had any chance of realization. He died June 14, 1920.

See also *Enlightenment; Germany; Marxism; Protestantism.*

Karen E. Fields

BIBLIOGRAPHY

Collins, Randall. *Weberian Social Theory.* Cambridge: Cambridge University Press, 1986.

Kalberg, Stephen. *Max Weber's Comparative and Historical Sociology.* Chicago: University of Chicago Press, 1994.

Mitzman, Arthur B. *The Iron Cage: An Historical Interpretation of Max Weber.* New York: Grossett and Dunlap, 1969.

Weber, Max. *From Max Weber: Essays in Sociology.* Translated and edited by H. H. Gerth and C. Wright Mills. New York: Oxford University Press, 1958.

———. *The Protestant Ethic and the Spirit of Capitalism.* Edited by Randall Collins. Los Angeles: Roxbury Publishing, 1996.

———. *The Sociology of Religion.* Translated by Ephraim Fischoff. Boston: Beacon Press, 1963.

Witchcraft

Witchcraft is the use of ritual power to influence events in the natural world. Often considered evil, and persecuted as such, witchcraft is practiced in cultures worldwide.

If all religion contains political elements, witchcraft is perhaps notable in the relative shamelessness of its relation to political power, and to power more generally. Whatever witchcraft is about—and it has been about many things in its long and controversial history—it is always about the manipulation of power for personal and political gain, however benign or even benevolent its goals might be.

The term *witchcraft* is notoriously difficult to define: it is a term of honor in some quarters and of horror in others; an identity that some proudly claim and that others accept only on pain of death. In spite of the growing presence of neopaganism, which has done much to rehabilitate witchcraft as a positive religious practice, in common parlance *witch* still carries nefarious connotations. Witches have been believed to be those who carry out bizarre rituals—drinking blood, boiling newts, and the like—with the intent of making the universe behave as they wish. And more often than not, they wish the universe to bring injury and disaster to those who have gained their disfavor. This is the lens through which

Europeans have interpreted witchcraft, and when in the course of their colonial incursions they encountered anything remotely similar to this practice in other cultures, they have called it witchcraft as well. Thus a whole host of individuals, practices, symbols, and cultural understandings have been packed uncomfortably under the umbrella label "witchcraft."

Elements of Witchcraft

What do these various types of witchcraft share in common? First, whether their power comes from God, Satan, the Goddess, lesser deities or spirits, or some amorphous universal energy source, witches are thought to be effective channels of unseen forces. The force they channel is not that of the gun, sword, or legislature—though it may involve the use of physical props, its magical action is invisible. Its practice is usually the province of the poor and powerless. This does not mean that the socially prominent may not also practice witchcraft, but elite individuals are far more likely to seek the witchcraft services of a more marginal individual than to engage directly in witchcraft themselves.

Those who are called witches are virtually always previously socially marked by gender, class, or individual idiosyncrasy. Although witches may be male or female, the predominant image of the witch is female, and unlike the vast majority of social roles, the witch is referred to in the female generic ("the witch . . . she"). Witchcraft is one way in which socially disenfranchised individuals seize power (at times, the only power available to them). More important, it is a way in which marginalized individuals—and through them, marginalized classes—can gain power that is often respected or even feared by their social superiors.

The phenomenon of witchcraft always has two markedly independent aspects—the practice of witchcraft and accusations of witchcraft. Both are intimately related to the disruptive interplay between invisible power and social location discussed above. The practice of witchcraft can embody the hope—or even the reality—of social power among the socially disempowered. But witchcraft accusations more often embody the fear generated among elites and authorities over the real or imagined discontent of the lower classes. Depending on whom the elites fear, witches may be personified as foreigners, slaves, transgressors of authoritative social categories (eunuchs, unmarried adults, widows—the possibilities are as endless as the particular social structures that give birth to them), and the perennial favorite, women.

Persecution

Over the long history of witchcraft, it is witchcraft accusations that have probably represented the stronger connection between witchcraft and political power. As many historians have shown, the great witch purges of sixteenth- and seventeenth-century Europe can be regarded only as a grotesque overreaction to whatever folk religious practices may or may not have been going on among women and the lower classes at the time. Thousands of individuals were executed as witches (estimates range from a conservative one hundred thousand to an outlandish eleven million) throughout continental Europe and Great Britain over many decades, with the witch fever spiking and receding periodically but never being soundly defeated until the mid-seventeenth century.

Historians differ as to what prompted the witch persecutions, but few believe—as did the witch hunters and indeed their entire cultural milieu—that they were aimed directly at eradicating the practice of witchcraft. Some scholars locate the primary source of the witch persecutions in power struggles between the Protestant and Catholic churches; others target deeply rooted psychological fantasies prevalent in the West from classical times; and others blame misogyny and male fears in relation to women's growing financial and personal independence. In sum, the witch persecutions had everything to do with the accusers and very little to do with the accused. And indeed, when the accusers and the accused approached one another too closely—that is, when an accuser's close family members were accused—the witch hunts had a way of dissipating, at least temporarily. The European witch persecutions were an essentially conservative political force, seeking to preserve an idealized status quo in which social classes were cleanly demarcated and those lacking social power did not seek to take it away from those who did.

The much smaller-scale witch trials in colonial New England both adhered to and departed from their European forbears. As in Europe, any actual practice of witchcraft was insignificant. Class issues and religious differences played a lesser role in Salem, however, and the Puritans did not subscribe to the prevailing European stereotype that women were inherently more evil than men and thus more likely to submit to the devil. In spite of official rhetoric, however, women were disproportionately accused and convicted of witchcraft, as they had been in Europe. Once accused, women confessed to witchcraft more often than men did.

Because women tended to see themselves as weak and sinful, they conflated ordinary sin (in Puritan theology, an implicit covenant with the devil) with an actual pact with the devil (the explicit writing of the individual's name in the devil's book).

Contemporary Practice

Accusations of witchcraft are still heard in the twentieth century, but because the legal structure of most countries is no longer conducive to witchcraft persecution, such accusations have lost the political strength they had in earlier centuries. For this reason, the practice of witchcraft itself is now more salient. Particularly in Europe and the English-speaking world, witchcraft is increasingly being adopted as a voluntary religious identity. Witches congregate in covens, occult bookstores, and at weekend seminars and retreats to teach one another the Craft. Some claim to have hereditary expertise at witchcraft, having been trained by older family members or other mentors, but many are happily creating their own versions of witchcraft out of bits and pieces of various religions and occult practices. These witches are predominantly women, and they frequently see their witchcraft as a political as well as a religious calling, serving to redefine female identity and give women an important source of power in their fight to liberate women from second-class status. For many contemporary witches, witchcraft is not an isolated practice, but the name given to a full religious worldview involving pantheism (which identifies God with the universe), goddess worship, environmentalism, and personal meditative and therapeutic practices.

Yet old tensions involving the term *witchcraft* persist. Many eagerly adopt the term in solidarity with the thousands persecuted for witchcraft in earlier centuries, yet just as many search for other terms that will not tie them to the traditional image of the malicious hag. This tension is particularly acute when neopagans and spiritual feminists discuss *hexing*—the use of magic for negative ends. Most contemporary witches insist that the magic they practice is positive—either the universe is designed such that only positive magic is efficacious, or karmic justice guarantees that the evil you send returns three times over. Yet others insist on their right to cause harm to those who have harmed them and say that this is what magic is for.

Clearly, both the practice of witchcraft and its persecution contain political aims. Witchcraft itself is typically politically radical, but accusations of witchcraft tend to be politically conservative. As to which is politically effective, the answer is probably both. Witchcraft is a complex phenomenon, and whether it emerges as politically radical or conservative at any given time has much to do with cultural specifics rather than with anything inherent in witchcraft itself.

See also *Feminism; Gender; Paganism.*

Cynthia Eller and Elizabeth Reis

BIBLIOGRAPHY

Adler, Margot. *Drawing Down the Moon: Witches, Druids, Goddess-Worshippers, and Other Pagans in America Today.* Boston: Beacon Press, 1997.

Barstow, Anne Llewellyn. *Witchcraze: A New History of the European Witch Hunts.* San Francisco: Harper San Francisco, 1994.

Eller, Cynthia. *Living in the Lap of the Goddess: The Feminist Spirituality Movement in America.* Boston: Beacon Press, 1995.

Reis, Elizabeth. *Damned Women: Sinners and Witches in Puritan New England.* Ithaca, N.Y.: Cornell University Press, 1997.

Roper, Lyndal. *Oedipus and the Devil: Witchcraft, Sexuality, and Religion in Early Modern Europe.* New York: Routledge, 1994.

Russell, Jeffrey B. *Witchcraft in the Middle Ages.* Ithaca, N.Y.: Cornell University Press, 1972.

Tambiah, Stanley Jeyaraja. *Magic, Science, Religion, and the Scope of Rationality.* Cambridge: Cambridge University Press, 1990.

Trevor-Roper, H. R. *The European Witch-Craze of the Sixteenth and Seventeenth Centuries and Other Essays.* New York: Harper and Row, 1956.

Women

See *Feminism*

World Council of Churches

The World Council of Churches, an international and interdenominational organization of Christian churches, founded in 1948, is dedicated to ecumenical dialogue and the promotion of mission, unity, justice, and peace throughout the world. It formally defines itself as "a fellowship of Churches which confess the Lord Jesus Christ as God and Savior according to the Scriptures and therefore seek to fulfill together their common calling."

With its permanent headquarters in Geneva, Switzerland, the WCC comprises some 332 members. These include Eastern Orthodox, Lutheran and Reformed, Methodist, Anglican, Old Catholic, Pentecostal, Baptist, United, and Independent churches. The Roman Catholic Church is not a member, having only official observer status, although in 1968 it joined the WCC's Faith and Order Commission. Nevertheless, the WCC remains the largest body of its type and has, over the years, been a significant moral force in the international community, espousing solidarity with the world's poor and oppressed and highlighting a wide range of major issues such as racism, the status of women, needy children, migrant workers, refugees, global warming, and the arms race. In recent years it has been subject to criticism for its alleged liberal political tendencies and has suffered a decline in financial support, budget, and staffing levels.

Formation

The WCC was the product of theological trends in Europe and North America that first arose in the eighteenth century as an evangelical revival known as the Great Awakening. In the nineteenth century, this movement stirred up within Protestant churches a renewed zeal for foreign missions. Throughout the century, missionary societies worked in India, the Middle East, and North America, often with several churches coming together in a common endeavor and thereby fostering interdenominational collaboration and ecumenical thinking. One notable offshoot was the promotion of missions among college youth; these became training arenas in ecumenism and cosmopolitanism for future WCC leaders. Among them was Willem Visser't Hooft (1900–1985), a Dutch clergyman who became the WCC's first general secretary. Through a series of world missionary conferences, starting in Edinburgh, Scotland, in 1910, and continuing with a second in Jerusalem in 1928, a vision of global Christian unity came into view, buttressed by practical organization building and providing a foundation for the WCC to develop.

The evangelical revival also promoted another of the WCC's roots, a renewed sense of social concern for human needs at home. Through Christian socialism in England, and the Social Gospel movement in the United States, cooperation was kindled among the churches to search for practical solutions to pressing social problems and issues of world peace. From this cooperative spirit came, in 1920, a Universal Christian Conference on Life and Work, which had delegates from ninety-one denominations and thirty-seven countries, mainly Western and Protestant or Orthodox. This conference became a permanent organization in 1928 and ultimately formed one of the two founding elements of the WCC.

Through the Conference on Life and Work the generally progressive political stance of the ecumenical movement was forged in the 1930s and influenced the orientation of the WCC a decade later. The leaders of the conference, notably W. A. Brown and William Temple, also warned the churches against Hitler and the authoritarian Nazi state. It threw its support to the "Confessing Church" as the true expression of Christianity in Germany. The Confessing Church arose as a movement to resist Hitler's incorporation of Christian churches into the Nazi state. Gradually, the confrontation with Nazism further focused and mobilized the ecumenical movement.

The other major organization that came together with Life and Work to form the WCC was the Faith and Order Movement. Also a product of the evangelical revival, Faith and Order was concerned with finding a common theological understanding of "the church" as an institution committed to active ministry in the world. A conference held in the United States in 1910 laid the groundwork for a World Conference on Faith and Order at Lausanne, Switzerland, in 1927. This, in turn, established a Continuing Committee to perpetuate its work. By 1933, under the leadership of Temple, Visser't Hooft, Brown, and others, there emerged a view that the two, Faith and Order and Life and Work, would be more effective if they worked together. This idea was endorsed at a Conference on Church, Community, and State held in Oxford, England, in 1937, in recognition of the darkening situation in Germany and the need for a common Christian voice to speak out. A subsequent committee agreed, and Samuel Cavert, a member, suggested the name World Council of Churches. An organizing committee met at Utrecht, Holland, in 1938 to set up the WCC as an interdenominational organization of churches dedicated to the proclamation of the spiritual unity of all nations and races in Christ and to affirm that the state is under God's judgment.

World War II strengthened this sense of unity and the churches' need for a permanent international Christian body. But the organizing committee was unable to meet again until 1946, when it chose 1948 as the date of foundation. Meanwhile, at the provisional headquarters in Geneva, agencies were created to deal with such issues as aid for prisoners of war and church rebuilding, refugees, international affairs, and youth. Finally, on August 22, 1948, the WCC was inaugurated by the assembling of 351 delegates in Amsterdam, principally from Western Europe and North America. Russian and East European Orthodox representatives were blocked by their governments from attending because the WCC was seen as "too political." For doctrinal reasons, the Roman Catholic Church also warned its members to stay away.

Organization and Program

The highest governing body of the WCC is the Assembly, which has the power to set policy and amend the WCC's constitution. All member churches are represented, sending delegates when the Assembly meets about every seven years. Eight assemblies have been held, the first in Amsterdam in 1948, followed by Evanston, Illinois (1954), New Delhi (1961), Uppsala (1968), Nairobi (1975), Vancouver (1983), and Canberra (1991). The eighth is scheduled for Harare, in Zimbabwe, in 1998. As the WCC has grown, so too has the size of the assemblies, from 350 delegates in 1948 to 950 in 1991. Equally, the WCC has become much more diverse. From its roots in Europe and North America, 116 countries now have members. The largest bloc remains Europe (81 members), but Africa (78), Asia (61), and Latin America (26) have shifted its center of gravity to the developing world. As a result, the institution has increasingly emphasized its concerns for justice, human rights, and solidarity with the poor and marginalized. The voicing of these concerns has made some of the assemblies controversial in the eyes of more conservative and Western churches. It has also raised questions about the authority of the WCC and the accountability of its programs, spokespersons, and agencies.

One set of particularly controversial issues surfaced in connection with the Program to Combat Racism and its associated Special Fund. This program was established in 1969 by the WCC's Central Committee, which meets annually to set policy between assemblies. Beginning in 1970, grants were disbursed to various organizations engaged in liberationist guerrilla struggles in southern Africa. Among the recipients were the South West Africa People's Organization (SWAPO) in Namibia; the National Union for the Total Independence of Angola (UNITA) and the Popular Movement for the Liberation of Angola (MPLA); the Zimbabwe African People's Union (ZAPU) and the Zimbabwe African National Union (ZANU); and the African National Congress (ANC) in South Africa. Though ostensibly for nonmilitary educational, health, and medical purposes, the grants led to criticism within church and governmental circles. For example, the Salvation Army, a founding member, objected to the funding of "groups espoused to violence." It suspended its membership in 1978 and withdrew completely in 1981. Despite such moves, the Special Fund to Combat Racism remains in place, although, following political changes in southern Africa, donations have dropped.

Controversy also erupted in the Seventh Assembly in early 1991. Meeting at the time of the Persian Gulf War, the assembly for called for the Western-led allies against Iraq to withdraw troops and initiate a cease-fire. This demand provoked renewed criticism from conservatives that the WCC's assembly was anti-Western and anti-American. The WCC was accused of overemphasizing political activism. In addition, old allegations that it had been infiltrated by the KGB, the Soviet police and intelligence service, in the past and had been unwilling to highlight religious persecution in communist states were raised. A leading Anglican called for urgent reform and more consultation with member churches. Subsequently, in 1993, the WCC bureaucracy was reorganized, although its commitment to activism on issues of justice, peace, the environment, and human needs remains.

Those commitments are currently carried out principally by Justice, Peace, and Creation, one of four WCC units. Its emphases include globalization; human rights; democracy and civil society; peace with justice; racial, economic, and ethnic discrimination; and environmental questions. Other units touch on issues to do with health and community development; women and children in need; the differently abled; the marginalized; and people uprooted or in situations of conflict or disaster. It is an agenda that brings the WCC into regular contact with governments, the United Nations, and international charitable agencies. Nevertheless, its ultimate authority is not to legislate for its member churches but to promote a unified and international Christian voice that commands the support of those churches.

The way the WCC has wrestled with these issues has provoked criticism, principally from conservatives who would prefer the WCC to focus primarily on less political questions of ecumenism and unity. Although this criticism seems to have led to some self-examination and institutional retrenchment, the WCC remains an important Christian voice in international policy making and diplomacy.

See also *Globalization; Human rights; Justice, Social; Missionaries; Nongovernmental organizations; Social Gospel.*

George Moyser

BIBLIOGRAPHY

"Commemorating Amsterdam 1948: Forty Years of the World Council of Churches." Special number of *Ecumenical Review* 40 (July–October 1988): 313–559.

Gaines, David P. *The World Council of Churches.* Peterborough, N.H.: Richard R. Smith, 1966.

Hudson, Darril. *The Ecumenical Movement in World Affairs.* Washington, D.C.: National Press, 1969.

Visser't Hooft, Willem A. *Memoirs.* Geneva: World Council of Churches, 1988.

World Council of Churches: Constitution, Rules, Regulations and By-laws. Geneva: WCC, 1996.

World Council of Churches: Resource Sharing Book. Geneva: WCC, 1996.

Y

Yugoslavia

A state on the Balkan peninsula in southeastern Europe, Yugoslavia existed from 1918 to 1991, when political and ethnic conflicts dissolved the state. It was first called the Kingdom of Serbs, Croats, and Slovenes but was renamed Yugoslavia in 1929. Yugoslavia emerged after the First World War when the South Slavs (Yugoslavia means South Slavia), who had until then lived in the Austro-Hungarian Empire, joined with the kingdom of Serbia in 1918. After the Second World War it became a federal republic comprising six federal units. It fell apart in 1991–1992, when four of them—Slovenia, Croatia, Bosnia and Herzegovina, and (Slavic) Macedonia proclaimed their independence. The name Yugoslavia has been used since that time by the union of Serbia and Montenegro.

History and Religions

Before Yugoslavia was established, its territory and peoples had never belonged to a single state except for a brief period under the rule of the Roman Empire. During Roman times there was already a border running across this territory between the Eastern and Western parts of the empire. This division was made more pronounced by the breach between Eastern (Greek, Byzantine) and Western (Latin, Roman) Christianity, which grew deeper after the Great Schism between the Orthodox and the Roman Catholic Churches in the eleventh century. This split also influenced the Slavic and other peoples who had in the sixth and seventh centuries settled in what would be Yugoslavia. Those in the east accepted Orthodox Christianity with the Byzantine cultural tradition, but those in the west and the north accepted Roman Catholicism.

In central areas (especially in the later Bosnia) borders changed and influences intermingled. The sway of the ninth-century Greek missionaries Saints Cyril and Methodius (the apostles of the Slavs), who created the Slavic liturgical language and writing (the Cyrillic alphabet), extended far north and west. After a brief independence the outermost northern and western territory of the future Slovenia had since the eighth century been included in Central European states, from the Frankish kingdom of Charlemagne to that of the Austrian Habsburgs. Croats, who likewise accepted Western Christianity, formed their own kingdom in 925 and remained independent until the twelfth century, when they recognized the supremacy of Hungary. In the east (in what would be Serbia, Montenegro, Macedonia), where the political, cultural, and church influence of Byzantium was predominant, various states were established that eventually gained their political and church independence from Byzantium. Serbian rulers were the first, establishing the independent Serbian Orthodox Church, headed by St. Sava, in 1174–1235. In the later fourteenth century an independent Bosnian state was formed where the widespread heresy of the Bogomils, members of a political and religious movement that resented Byzantine culture, was looked on sympathetically by individual rulers.

The Turkish invasion of the Balkans (the defeat of Serbs in Kosovo in 1389, the fall of the Bosnian kingdom in 1463, the occupation of Constantinople in 1453) changed the political, ethnic, and religious structure of the area. The Turks conquered the entire Orthodox area and at the height of their power penetrated deep into Catholic territory. Many Orthodox (Serbian) inhabitants fled the Turks and were settled by the Catholic Habsburg rulers in Croatian and Hungarian areas, where the Serbs were used to defend the borders. These Serbs were given special rights and granted the autonomy of their Orthodox Church. The deserted areas such as Kosovo were settled by ethnic Albanians, who became Muslims.

The Turks did not force the inhabitants of the Balkans to convert to Islam. Widespread conversion occurred only among the Albanians and in Bosnia as the westernmost border area of the Turkish empire. The former Bogomils accepted Islam.

In the occupied areas the Turks allowed the Orthodox churches autonomy. Under Turkish jurisdiction church rulers were also mediators between the Orthodox population and the Turkish and were in charge of certain secular affairs. In the nineteenth century Serbia and Montenegro gradually fought free of the Turks. In the first Balkan War (1912) they, together with Bulgaria and Greece, overthrew Turkish rule in the entire Balkan region and also occupied and divided up Macedonia. After anti-Turkish rebellions and unrest and the ruling of an international congress in Berlin in 1878, Austria-Hungary occupied and in 1908 annexed Bosnia Herzegovina.

The Modern Nations

In this politically, culturally, and religiously divided area were forged modern national identities. Serbs and Croats in the nineteenth century wanted to restore their respective former states, and in doing so both relied on their own religious and cultural traditions. Because they spoke the same language or related dialects, the most important criterion separating Serbs from Croats became their different religious affiliations and related cultural differences (for example, the use of Latin letters by Catholic Croats and Cyrillic letters by Orthodox Serbs and Montenegrins). For the Serbs, the Orthodox Church represented a link between former and restored Serbian statehood.

The primacy of religious affiliation and tradition as a criterion for the national identity made it impossible for Bosnians and other Muslims of Slavic origin and (Serbo-Croatian) language to define themselves as Serbs or Croats. Religious differences also prevented the inhabitants of Bosnia from feeling like members of a united Bosnian nation. Muslims were forced to take their Muslim identity as a basis for their special Muslim-Bošnjak cultural and national unity. Thus were included in the national identity and unity of the Serbs, Croats, and Muslim-Bošnjaks tensions and conflicts that had until then existed between Catholicism, Orthodoxy, and Islam.

The development of the Slovenes was different. Unlike the Croats, they did not have their own nobility, so the rather weak bourgeoisie and the Catholic clergy were most influential in the Slovene national awakening in the nineteenth century. National definition was not through affiliation with Catholicism, however, but with a special Slovene literary language that was (like the name Slovenes) created by Protestants who translated the entire Bible in 1584. Although linguistically close to Bulgaria, Slavic Macedonia, directed by its historical and political position between Serbia, Bulgaria, and Greece, sought independence in the local political and Orthodox Church tradition.

The Yugoslav Idea

In the nineteenth century the Yugoslav idea of joining all South Slavic peoples into one state emerged first among the South Slavs in the Habsburg empire. Unified into one state, they believed they could protect themselves from Germanic and Hungarian supremacy and from Italian interest in Slovene and Croatian territory. Among the most eminent advocates of the Yugoslav idea was the Croatian Catholic Bishop Josip Strossmayer (1815–1905).

Creation of Yugoslavia would bring all Serbs together in a single state. The Slovenes and the Croats believed that a common state would allow each people sufficient autonomy for independent development. Serbian politics, however, favored a state that would be unified and centralized enough to give the Serbs dominance. The fate of Yugoslavia was for a long time dependent on the balance between both viewpoints.

Church leaders, especially the Catholics, were very skeptical about the Yugoslav idea. But because of the danger that followed the end of World War I and the disintegration of Austria-Hungary (Italian territorial demands, the Bolshevik revolution), the Slovene and Croatian Catholic episcopacies supported unification under the throne of the Serbian king. Some, including the Serbian monarchy, nourished the illusion that a unified state would eventually lead to a unified nation with a single language and culture that would overcome existing religious and ethnic differences.

But the Catholic Church and the communists in the newly established Yugoslavia advocated the autonomy of individual nations and a federal system. The Serbian Orthodox Church also feared and resisted submerging Serbianness and Orthodoxy in a mixture of various traditions, which is why it favored the idea of a Greater Serbia that would encompass all the areas with Orthodox populations—including Montenegro and Macedonia—rather than a united and unifying Yugoslavia.

After Adolf Hitler's Germany and its allies defeated and occupied Yugoslavia in 1941, the so-called Independent State of Croatia (which comprised the territory of today's Croatia and Bosnia) was founded as a German and Italian protectorate. The Croatian Catholic episcopacy, headed by Alojzije Stepinac (1898–1960), supported the establishment of the new state, although Stepinac opposed the new government's way of solving the Serbian question through expulsions, massacres, and forced conversion of the Serbs from Orthodoxy to Catholicism. Slovenia, Serbia, Macedonia, and Montenegro were occupied and divided among Hitler's allies. To these actions of the Croatian state and the Croatian Fascist Ustasha, a nationalist terrorist organization, extreme nationalist Serbians responded with the massacres of the Catholic and especially Muslim populations in the areas they controlled. From these struggles the antifascist National Liberation Movement emerged. Led by the communists and Josip Broz Tito (1892–1980), the movement included members of all ethnic groups, although resistance to its revolutionary communist orientation made some Catholics in Slovenia collaborate with Italian and German invaders.

The victorious communists introduced a federal system after 1945 with five formally equal nations and six republics, out of which one—Bosnia and Herzegovina—was explicitly defined as a republic including Serbs, Croats, and Muslims living together. Albanians in the Serbian province Kosovo were gradually granted autonomy. The communist authority nationalized almost all church property; outlawed church political, cultural, educational, and charitable institutions; instituted a strict separation of the church from the state; and at first limited and controlled religious activities as well. The communist regime saw excluding religion from public life not only as necessary for its own unchallenged domination but also as a condition for a peaceful coexistence of various peoples in the Yugoslav federation and within every one of its units.

In the late 1980s the leaders and ideologists of all religious communities supported not only anticommunist and democratic movements but also nationalist tendencies among their respective peoples. After the otherwise peaceful abolishment of the communist system in 1990, the way was opened for the activity and influence of the church, and the concern for the special endangerment and suffering of particular peoples for the true religion was resuscitated.

Disintegration of Yugoslavia

The disintegration of Yugoslavia began in 1989, when the new nationalist Serbian movement, headed by Slobodan Miloševic, forced a change in the balance of Yugoslavia's confederate constitutional order and did away with the autonomy of the ethnic Albanians in Kosovo. This action fostered the fear among other groups of Serbian supremacy in a more centralized Yugoslavia and of reduced autonomy for their own republics. Without the Slovenes and other groups supporting a unified Yugoslavia as a place for autonomous existence and development of all nations, such a state could no longer exist. Serbian interest alone was not enough, especially because in Serbia, too, there was a growing radical nationalist belief that for the Serbs and Orthodoxy, a Greater Serbia—with the annexed and "ethnically cleansed" Serbian territories outside the then Republic of Serbia—would be better than a common state with other nations.

The war in Croatia and Bosnia that accompanied the disintegration of Yugoslavia was a war for power and territories but with religious overtones. In this war the sacredness of one's own people, for a long time cherished by the church, was also efficiently put to use. In the fighting, therefore, people to a large extent used their own religious symbols, and other religious symbols were systematically destroyed—mosques and Catholic and Orthodox Churches, for example. There have been occasional individual or joint appeals from the leaders of the Orthodox, Catholic, and Islamic religious communities—encouraged from abroad by the World Council of Churches, the Vatican, the Pax Christi organization, and so on—for peace, nonviolence, mutual respect, love in Christ and God, but these have had little significant effect. In the late 1990s the Muslim ethnic Albanians of Kosovo were still being persecuted by Serbia.

All the newly established states sprung from the former Yugoslavia have preserved a constitutional separation of church from the state. Churches are allowed to take part in civil society, and everywhere they are being given back their formerly confiscated property. Because particular churches are the majority in each of these states, each individual church in fact enjoys preferred status or strives to attain it.

See also *Balkan states; Ethnicity; Genocide; Nationalism; Nativism; Orthodoxy, Greek; Theocracy.*

Marko Kerševan

BIBLIOGRAPHY

Alexander, Stella. *Church and State in Yugoslavia since 1945.* Cambridge: Cambridge University Press, 1979.

Banac, Ivo. *The National Question in Yugoslavia.* Ithaca, N.Y.: Cornell University Press, 1984.

Lamie, John. *Yugoslavia as History.* Cambridge: Cambridge University Press, 1996.

Ramet, Pedro, ed. *Religion and Nationalism in Soviet and East European Politics.* Durham, N.C.: Duke University Press, 1989.

Ramet, Sabrina P. *Balkan Babel: The Disintegration of Yugoslavia from the Death of Tito to Ethnic War.* Boulder, Colo.: Westview Press, 1996.

Singleton, Fred. *Twentieth Century Yugoslavia.* New York: Columbia University Press, 1983.

van Dartel, Geert. "The Nations and Churches in Yugoslavia." *Religion, State, and Society* 20 (1992): 275–288.

Vrcan Srdjan. "The War in Former Yugoslavia." *Religion, State, and Society* 22 (1994): 367–378.

Z

Zimbabwe

Populated principally by the Shona and Ndebele peoples of southern Africa, Zimbabwe is located on a high plateau bounded by the Limpopo River and South Africa to the south, Mozambique to the east, the Zambezi River and Zambia to the north, and Botswana to the west. The Shona peoples, a modern designation for linguistically related groups such as the Zezuru, Manica, Karanga, Ndau, and Korekore, constitute about 70 percent of the population of about eleven million and are culturally dominant, while the Zulu-related Ndebele in the southwest constitute about 16 percent of the population; other African groups and a small number of whites make up the remainder. British colonial rule created the nation later to be known as Southern Rhodesia in 1890, and the borders of the modern nation were established shortly thereafter. The minority white settler population declared Southern Rhodesia independent from Britain in 1965, prompting a black guerrilla struggle that won majority rule for the new Republic of Zimbabwe in 1980.

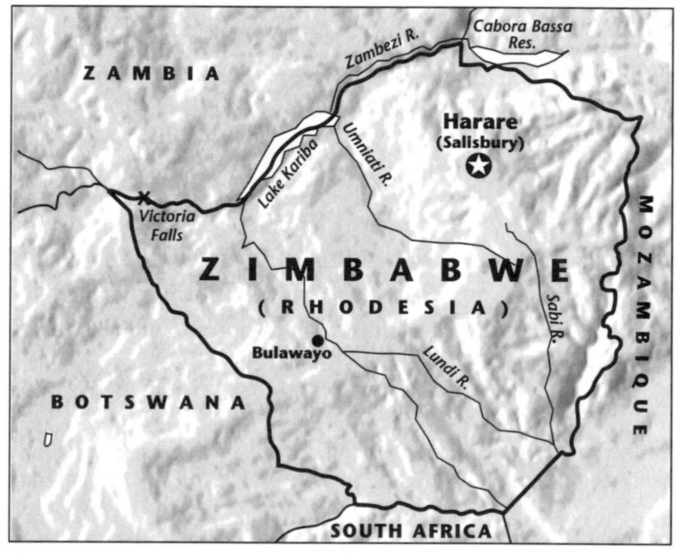

Religion and Politics in Traditional Society

The intertwining of political and religious authority in Zimbabwean society and history produced important permutations during the colonial period and a remarkable synthesis of divergent themes in the struggle for black-majority rule. In both Shona Spirit Religion and Ndebele Spirit Religion, the traditional religions of the two groups, deity is identified with the one High God (Mwari for the Shona, uNkulunkulu for the Ndebele), who created the world and who therefore owns the land. Consequently, human beings are accountable to the High God for their stewardship of the land and its inhabitants. Ancestral spirits mediate this divine authority so extensively that the communications of both ordinary people and spirit mediums with the supernatural realm focus mainly on such spirits rather than on the High God. Many living people feel they are accountable to the spirits of departed family members, clan elders, and ethnic leaders, who exercise authority over the geographical areas that correlate with these groups.

Political authority in Shona and Ndebele societies therefore has religious dimensions that have persisted through the colonial period and into the modern state, albeit with modifications. Ruling families claimed descent from community founders of the distant past and thereby justified their control of political, legal, and military affairs in the many local and regional chiefdoms of precolonial Zimbabwe. The continuing presence of such primordial founders (Shona: *mhondoro*) through their spirits made such claims fundamentally religious as well as juridical and political. A local chief (*ishe*) or king (*mambo*) claimed to exercise the ancestral ruler's oversight and even to embody his presence, a tradition that continues in the now largely ceremonial role of chiefs in the modern state. Ritual mediation of the ancestor's communication with the community, however, and authentication of the ancestor's choice of the chief are the province of the spirit medium. Pronouncements made from the mystical experience of possession identify the medium as the spirit's authoritative spokesperson in matters such as agricultural cultivation, land distribution, rain making, chiefly succession, and the living descendants' conduct. Both male and female mediums claim authority through a succession of antecedent mediums, whose spirits are invoked to authenticate the ancestors' utterances.

Prior to colonialism, chiefs and mediums derived power from ancient spirits in ways that were mutually inhibiting and enhancing. Mediums both authenticated chiefly rule and influenced it through denunciation; implementing power, however, lay with chiefs, who sometimes succeeded in displacing mediums who displeased them. The balancing tensions are apparent in the layout of Great Zimbabwe, the fourteenth-century city constructed by the Rozvi dynasty near present-day Masvingo in central Zimbabwe. The spirit medium's structures devoted to the Mwari cult on a high promontory overlook the ruler's large enclosure on the plain below. The Mwari cult was later transferred to Matonjeni in the Matopo Hills near Bulawayo, from where the cult was consulted by many southern and eastern Shona chiefdoms, as it continues to be today, and by the Ndebele from the establishment of their state in that region in the 1830s. Notably the medium warned the Ndebele chief Lobengula about European incursions during his negotiations with Cecil Rhodes's British South Africa Company (BSAC), which brought the first white settlers, known as the Pioneer Column, into his territories in 1890.

The Colonial Period

Estimates vary about the role of Ndebele and Shona spirit mediums in the major uprising against the Rhodesian settlers in 1896–1897, now commonly called the First Chimurenga ("rising"). It is clear that mediums were consulted and that some, including those at Matonjeni, offered approval and encouragement, while the mediums of some chiefdoms counseled support for the Europeans and encouraged their people to collaborate or, at least, to remain neutral. Two particular mediums, those of the Nehanda and Kaguvi *mhondoro* spirits, were widely credited with inspiring resistance and were later executed by the Rhodesian government. The settler victory introduced complexities for the traditional religio-political system, especially through mass conversions to Christianity early in the twentieth century. Yet spirit mediums continued to influence chiefdom politics; the great spirit hero Chaminuka, who had been in the First Chimurenga, continued to be invoked; and the Matonjeni shrine network occasionally encouraged nationalist resistance, responding, for instance, to Crown colony status in 1923 by urging people to hide their grain.

Although mining and agricultural opportunities, not religious zeal, motivated early European settlers, the BSAC shared a widespread European belief that Christianity would benefit Africans and reconcile them to European control. The company, therefore, granted large land concessions to missionary societies based in Britain, Europe, North America, and South Africa, ranging from the Roman Catholic and Anglican churches to the Salvation Army and Seventh-day Adventists. The density of such missions in the eastern highlands of Manicaland suggests a company objective to create a buffer along the initially contested border with the Portuguese in Mozambique. As the major institutions carrying out educational and medical work among rural Africans, the missions also served to mitigate the effects of Rhodesian land segregation. As early as 1894 blacks had begun to be assigned to poor quality "native reserves," later called "tribal trustlands," while the best land, 51 percent of the land mass according to the Land Apportionment Act of 1930, was reserved for whites. After Southern Rhodesia became a Crown colony in 1923, government grants to church schools and hospitals expanded greatly, creating a church-state partnership similar to that traditionally found in Britain, with a bias toward established churches in the Euro-American tradition. African-initiated churches founded by prophets—such as the Zion Christian Church, founded by Samuel Mutendi in the 1920s, and the African Apostolic Church, founded by Johane Maranke in 1932—were distrusted by the authorities as potentially subversive, as were Euro-American

Pentecostal churches. These groups were watched and often harassed until recognition began to be granted more routinely in the late 1930s, sometimes with permission to lease land for schools as well as churches.

On the land distribution issue that prompted the formation of black nationalist parties as early as 1936, church leaders frequently protested the small amount and poor quality of land granted to the African majority and sought to highlight the overcrowding and poverty caused by government policies. Missionaries condemned the first native reserves established after the Ndebele war of 1893, and in 1908 the Southern Rhodesian Missionary Conference pressed the BSAC to enlarge the reserves. Some missionaries were more radical in challenging the imperial premises of the colonial enterprise, among them the Methodist John White and the Anglican Arthur Shearley Cripps, as were some leaders of African-initiated churches, such as Matthew Zwimba of the Original Church of the White Bird, founded in 1915. Mission-founded churches generally worked within the Rhodesian colonial system, however, and thus were vulnerable to nationalist critiques of being complicit with or, at least, quiescent about injustice. While most African-initiated churches were not explicitly political in their public pronouncements, their African roots and leadership implicitly affirmed African initiative and, by extension, nationalism.

The Liberation War

Guerrillas of the Liberation War, or Second Chimurenga, that commenced in 1966 generally expressed hostility toward Christianity and the churches as allies of colonialism. This stance was prompted by the explicit championing of Christianity by the Rhodesia Front Party and its Unilateral Declaration of Independence from Britain in 1965. It was buttressed by the Marxist-Leninist training that guerrillas received through the Zimbabwe African National Union (ZANU) and the Zimbabwe African People's Union (ZAPU) and their military wings. The Mao-inspired mass mobilization that guerrillas initiated in the early 1970s took hold when they invoked the great spirits of the land—such as Chaminuka, Nehanda, and Kaguvi—for legitimation and formed alliances with local mediums in their operational areas. Not instigated by party hierarchies, this religious approach simply evolved among the guerrilla bands as they struggled to catalyze local support. The principal mobilization tool was the all-night vigil, called *pungwe,* which the guerrillas adapted from its ancestral roots in Shona Spirit Religion and the churches' all-night revivals. Although the guerrillas coerced participation in their *pungwe* rallies, their linking of the *mhondoro* spirits with the liberation struggle ignited a revival of ancestral religion whose flame continues to spread today.

Pragmatism guided the guerrillas' practical response to local religious institutions. Strategic divination was gratefully received from friendly mediums, whereas opponents and collaborators were executed as sorcerers. Leaders of African-initiated churches who used prophecy to guide guerrilla strategy and rally their congregations were supported, and opposing prophets and churches were harassed. Mission-founded churches were the most suspect on account of their white origins, but the quiet support of leaders, whether black or white, was reciprocated by the guerrillas; opposition or noninvolvement resulted in suppression of public worship and destruction of buildings in many areas. Public stances of mission-founded churches toward the struggle varied individually but were mediated by the Christian Council of Rhodesia, established in 1962, which initially criticized the Rhodesian Front government and then took an intermediate position between the moderate African National Council of Abel Muzorewa and the radicalism of ZANU and ZAPU. When implementation of the 1978–1979 Internal Settlement of Zimbabwe-Rhodesia was attempted, the council moved from conditional support to open criticism of the eventually unsuccessful agreement. The Commission for Peace and Justice, established by the Rhodesia Catholic Bishops Conference in 1972, was a major force in highlighting contradictions between Christianity and institutional injustice in Rhodesia and exposing the government forces' wartime atrocities to the international community. The government sought to buttress its position through such measures as taking over most church primary schools in 1971 and banning the Roman Catholic newspaper *Moto* in 1974.

The Independence Period

The constitution of independent Zimbabwe defines the nation as a secular state and recognizes individual religious liberty. At independence in 1980, 58 percent of Zimbabweans professed to be Christians, and about 41 percent identified themselves with traditional African religions; these percentages are predicted to be 69 and 29, respectively, at century's end, although many Zimbabweans participate in both Christianity and the ethnic spirit religions. The ruling party, ZANU, espouses "scientific socialism" along professedly

Marxist-Leninist. lines, emphasizing the importance of land redistribution and state-owned enterprises. While acknowledging the ideology's historic distrust of religion, President Robert Mugabe and other leaders affirm the positive role they believe religion plays in Zimbabwe's life and culture. The national policy of reconciliation rather than retribution, proclaimed upon independence, was viewed by many as profoundly religious in origin and intent. On the side of traditional religion, by invoking the spirits of Chaminuka, Nehanda, and Kaguvi, government officials defined Zimbabwe as a new spirit realm consonant with the prerogatives of the ancestors, especially at the reinterment rites for freedom fighters' remains at various "Heroes Acres." The ceremonial roles of chiefs receive public recognition, even as officially sanctioned prayers for rain are held under Christian auspices.

The government's call for the churches to be partners in the new nation's development reinforced their prominent role in education and public health, with continuing subsidies, and drew them further into community economic development and environmental renewal, often with international aid partners. The effective monitoring of the government's 1982–1986 repression of the Ndebele minority in Matabeleland by the Catholic Commission for Peace and Justice prompted official censure but emphasized the churches' critical role in public policy issues in the new republic as well as under colonialism. Similarly the government has extended recognition to some African-initiated churches in spite of their strictures against Western medicine and education.

See also *Africa, Christian; African traditional religions.*

Titus Leonard Presler

BIBLIOGRAPHY

Beach, David N. *War and Politics in Zimbabwe, 1840–1900.* Gweru: Mambo Press, 1986.

Daneel, Marthinus L. *The God of the Matopo Hills: An Essay on the Mwari Cult in Rhodesia.* The Hague: Mouton, 1970.

———. *Guerrilla Snuff: The Spirituality of a Bush War.* Harare: Baobab Books, 1996.

Hallencreutz, Carl F., and Ambrose M. Moyo, eds. *Church and State in Zimbabwe.* Gweru: Mambo Press, 1988.

Lan, David. *Guns and Rain: Guerrillas and Spirit Mediums in Zimbabwe.* Harare: Zimbabwe Publishing House, 1985.

Lapsley, Michael. *Neutrality or Co-option? Anglican Church and State from 1964 until the Independence of Zimbabwe.* Gweru: Mambo Press, 1986.

Presler, Titus Leonard. *Mission Nights: Transformed Culture in the Vigil Movement of Shona Christians in Zimbabwe.* Pretoria: University of South Africa Press, 1998.

Ranger, Terence O. *Peasant Consciousness and Guerrilla War in Zimbabwe: A Comparative Study.* Harare: Zimbabwe Publishing House, 1985.

Zionism

The modern movement of Jewish nationalism and political liberation, which emerged partly in response to the late nineteenth century rise of anti-Semitic parties in Europe and Russian anti-Jewish riots following the 1881 assassination of Tsar Alexander II, is called Zionism. Crystallized by the writings and activities of Theodor Herzl (1860–1904), Zionism was a nationalist movement that sought to answer anti-Semitism and end the persecution of Jews by providing them a sovereign homeland in the biblical patrimony. Zion is one of the Bible's names for Jerusalem. Although there were predecessors to Herzl, it was the publication of his manifesto *The Jewish State* (1896) and his organization of the first Zionist Congress a year later in Basel, Switzerland, that established the movement on the stage of world politics.

Herzl attempted to attain international recognition and legitimacy for Zionism, meeting with European leaders and the Ottoman sultan. This concern was at the heart of "political Zionism." Another variant, the "cultural Zionism" of Ahad Ha'Am (1856–1927), argued that the main goal of national awakening should be the cultural renaissance of Jewish identity and peoplehood. Less concerned with the "problem of Jews," Ahad Ha' Am was more concerned with the "problem of Judaism." The problem of Jews—protection from persecution and anti-Semitism—might be solved through a state of their own.

The problem of Judaism was different. Religion had defined the core of Jewish identity and peoplehood for millennia, but now traditional Judaism staggered under the affronts of such secular modernist ideologies as Marxism, socialism, or democratic liberalism. Zionism was itself a weakening of the traditional religious and communal ties that had preserved Jewish solidarity. What separated Zionism from some of the others is that it fundamentally rejected the assimilation of Jews into a majority community as a viable solution to the problems of Jews and Judaism. This rejection linked political to cultural Zionism, despite their differences. Political Zionism triumphed, first, with the 1917 Balfour Declaration, by which Great Britain viewed with favor "the establishment in Palestine of a National Home for the Jewish People," and with the advent of Israel in 1948. Perhaps the greatest triumph of cultural Zionism was the rebirth of biblical Hebrew into a modern vernacular, uniting diverse peoples as Israelis.

Zionism in the Yishuv and Early State Period

In addition to political and cultural Zionism, there was practical Zionism, concerned with the actual settlement of Palestine. In fact, a significant Zionist enterprise had already begun in Palestine fifteen years before the first Zionist Congress, with the arrival of the first of five major waves of mainly European Jews in 1882.

These immigrants did not encounter a Palestine devoid of inhabitants. Arabs, both Christian and Muslim, lived throughout the land in rural villages—especially in the Galilee region—and cities such as Jerusalem, Haifa, and Jaffa. As the Jewish population grew through immigration, Arab opposition to Jewish settlement intensified, leading to riots in 1929 and more serious disturbances in 1936. After Israel's independence in 1948, this opposition hardened into the fateful conflict between Israel, the Palestinians, and neighboring Arab countries.

Neither was Palestine devoid of Jewish inhabitants. About 25,00 Jews—the majority Sephardim, or Jews of Middle Eastern or North African descent—resided in Palestine in 1882. What differentiated the so-called Old Yishuv from the post-1882 New Yishuv (*yishuv* meaning the pre-state Jewish community of Palestine) was that the Jews of the Old Yishuv were religiously observant. The post-1882 immigrants were mostly secular and (if socialist) often antireligious.

Relations between Old and New Yishuv were hostile. The pious considered Zionism heretical since, from their standpoint, the secularists were "forcing" God's hand; only God could begin the ingathering of the Jewish people that marks the messianic age. The New Yishuv saw the pious as remnants of a medieval Jewry and Judaism as irrelevant to the nationalist dream of a sovereign state.

By the end of World War I, political, cultural, and practical Zionism had all but merged in a synthetic form, whose center of gravity increasingly was Palestine, not the Diaspora (the resettlement of Jews outside Israel that began with their exile to Babylonia in 586 B.C. and again by Rome after A.D. 70), and whose energies were devoted to building up the demographic and institutional infrastructures of the New Yishuv through immigration and settlement. But even synthetic Zionism contained several different strands which, although they cooperated against the British or the Arabs, saw themselves in opposition to one another. The branches were represented by political parties, but their organization went well beyond party to encompass distinct school systems, youth groups, militias, health and welfare organizations—even newspapers and publishing houses. There were four main Zionist groupings.

Socialist-Labor Zionism dominated Yishuv and Israeli politics until its defeat in 1977. It attempts to combine nationalism with class struggle, aiming to create a Jewish workers' state based on social justice and equality. Major figures include Nahman Syrkin, Ber Borochov, A. D. Gordon, and David Ben-Gurion (1886–1973).

Rejecting socialism, revisionist Zionism placed political and military matters—and dreams of a Greater Israel—in the forefront. Revisionist leaders were Ze'ev Vladimir Jabotinsky (1880–1940) and his successor Menachem Begin (1913–1992). Ironically, Revisionism was the most prescient about taking nascent Arab nationalism seriously as an eventual adversary of the Zionist undertaking. This form led to the Herut and then Likud Parties and, today, nationalist parties to the right of Likud.

The least ideological of all the trends was general Zionism. These were free-market capitalists—the bourgeoisie of the Yishuv. They were organized in the Progressive and Liberal Parties, which joined with Herut to form Gahal (1965) and Likud (1973).

Although traditional Judaism condemned the Zionist undertaking as heretical, there was an important exception: the so-called religious Zionists organized in the party Mizrahi (founded 1902). Supporters of Mizrahi saw in the Jewish resettlement of the land—even if by secularists—the hand of the Divine. The secular Zionists were thus—unconsciously and unintentionally—agents of God's will. Rabbis I. J. Reines and A. I. Kook (1864–1935) were among religious Zionist leaders. It was a Mizrahi official who cosigned the so-called status quo agreement in 1947 that effectively institutionalized Judaism in the political system of the new state. Mizrahi became the National Religious Party in 1956.

After 1967

Until the mid-1970s religious Zionists played a secondary role in the polity. In return for guarantees that maintained Judaism's role in the society—separate, state-funded schools, rabbinical control over matters of personal status, and so on—religious Zionist parties gave to secularists control over foreign affairs, state security, and finance. This began to change after the Six-Day War of June 1967 between Israel and the Arab nations of Egypt, Jordan, and Syria, when territories in the West Bank (the biblical Judea and Samaria), the Golan Heights, Gaza, and East Jerusalem (including the Old

City) were conquered by Israel. Some, including Rabbi A. I. Kook's son, Z. Y. Kook, saw in this the hand of God and the beginnings of the era of messianic redemption. By 1968 groups began to build settlements on the West Bank.

Labor governments of the time formally opposed this activity but did little to stop it. It was the 1973 Yom Kippur War, when Egypt and Syria attacked Israel on the Jewish holy day, that galvanized religious Zionism. The shock of the near loss of that war, and the heavy casualties suffered by Israel, convinced many that the war was a sign of God's displeasure with the desultory pace of Jewish settlement in the West Bank. By 1975 a group of young religious activists sprang from within the National Religious Party and, calling themselves Gush Emunim, the Bloc of the Faithful, made Jewish settlement of the West Bank the central issue of Israel's politics. They also claimed to have inherited the pioneering mantle of Labor Zionism and, indeed, Labor Zionism seemed to have been fading for decades—even many Labor Zionists sadly concurred.

In the 1977 elections that brought Begin's Likud to power, the inheritors of the Revisionist Zionist tradition, which favored a Greater Israel for nationalistic reasons, joined with a reconstituted religious Zionism that sought a Greater Israel for messianic ones. This alliance began to weaken by 1982—the death of Rabbi Z. Y. Kook, the disastrous invasion of Lebanon, and the withdrawal under Begin from the Sinai under the provisions of the Camp David accords (1979 Egyptian-Israeli peace treaty) contributed to the breakdown—with the result that religious nationalist parties to the right of the National Religious Party, and revisionist nationalist parties to the right of Likud, have appeared regularly since then. Today, the extreme religious nationalists are among the staunchest opponents of the peace process, and such a nationalist was the assassin of Prime Minister Yitzhak Rabin (1922–1995), whom some religious nationalists considered a traitor for his negotiations with Palestinian Liberation Organization leader Yasir Arafat (1929–), in November 1995.

Zionism and Religion

Zionism began in the nineteenth century as a modernist response to the problems of anti-Semitism and persecution—modernist because it held that human actors can be the agents of their own political redemption. In a sense it shed the old, passive religious "yearning for Jerusalem" and substituted for it political and ideological activism. Moreover, in its Labor-socialist form, focused on the ideals of equality and social justice, Zionism was universalistic in its outlook. Viewed solely as a nationalist movement, Zionism succeeded in bringing about the state of Israel. But after achieving its goal, it seemed to falter. Israel was established explicitly to be a Jewish state, and the universalistic interpreters of Zionism have never honestly confronted the relation of that state to its non-Jewish citizens. In this vacuum, the rise of religious nationalism produced what many Israelis called the New Zionism. In it, explicitly religious conceptions of Jewish fate, once shed, were reunited with Zionist doctrine. This Zionism focuses not on social justice and equality but on Jewish uniqueness. The results of the struggle between the universalist and the particularist faces of Jewish nationalism will prove fateful for Israel and all of its citizens in years to come.

See also *Gush Emunim; Herzl, Theodor; Israel; Judaism. In Documents section, see* Balfour Declaration.

Kevin Avruch

BIBLIOGRAPHY

Avineri, Shlomo. *The Making of Modern Zionism: The Intellectual Origins of the Jewish State.* New York: Basic Books, 1981.

Halpern, Ben. *The Idea of the Jewish State.* 2d ed. Cambridge: Harvard University Press, 1976.

Hertzberg, Arthur. *The Zionist Idea: A Historical Analysis and Reader.* New York: Atheneum, 1969.

Leibowitz, Yeshayahu. *Judaism, Human Values, and the Jewish State.* Cambridge: Harvard University Press, 1992.

Liebman, Charles, and Eliezer Don-Yehiya. *Civil Religion in Israel.* Berkeley and Los Angeles: University of California Press, 1983.

Vital, David. *The Origins of Zionism.* Oxford: Oxford University Press, 1975.

APPENDIX

Documents on Politics and Religion

Selected Readings

Reference Materials

Ninety-Five Theses (1517)

Martin Luther (1483–1546), German theologian and noted translator of the Bible, initiated the doctrinal revolution that led to the Protestant Reformation. Luther's Ninety-Five Theses, which he posted on the door of the castle church at Wittenberg, were to be a polite challenge to the selling of "indulgences" (remission of punishment for sins committed) by the Roman Catholic Church. Although the sale of indulgences, also known as pardons, had been criticized by many Catholic theologians, it nevertheless provided the church with a steady source of income and therefore was allowed to continue. The Theses were intended to open a peaceful line of communication with Catholic officials; their effect was much more dynamic. This and other challenges initiated one of the most important religious movements in history: the Protestant Reformation.

Throughout the Ninety-Five Theses, which is translated here from the German, Luther chastised the greed found in the Catholic Church. He began with his thoughts on repentance, pointing out that the pope, according to canon law, cannot remit any penalties to souls in purgatory. He attacked the false teaching that anyone could buy admission to heaven. Luther ended the Theses by claiming that only Christ can grant salvation and that individuals must rely upon faith in him alone. Luther's writings from 1517 to 1523 inspired several groups to deny the universal authority of the pope and reaffirm the principle of justification by faith alone.

The Theses produced a lasting schism between the Catholic Church and the followers of Luther. At a meeting with papal authorities at Augsburg in 1518, Luther, viewed as a heretic by his opponents, refused to renounce his ideas. In following years he continued to challenge church doctrine and in 1521 was formally excommunicated. Eluding an attempt later in the year by the Diet of Worms to seize him, he escaped to Wartburg, where he began translating the Bible into German, a ten-year process. The dominant position of the Catholic Church was subsequently imperiled by the rise of Protestantism.

Ninety-Five Theses

Out of love for the truth and the desire to bring it to light, the following propositions will be discussed at Wittenberg, under the presidency of the Reverend Father Martin Luther, Master of Arts and of Sacred Theology, and Lecturer in Ordinary on the same at that place. Wherefore he requests that those who are unable to be present and debate orally with us, may do so by letter.

In the Name our Lord Jesus Christ. Amen.

1. Our Lord and Master Jesus Christ, when He said *"Poenitentiam agite,"* he willed that the whole life of believers should be repentance.

2. This word cannot be understood to mean sacramental penance, i.e., confession and satisfaction, which is administered by the priests.

3. Yet it means not inward repentance only; nay, there is no inward repentance which does not outwardly produce mortifications of the flesh.

4. The penalty [of sin], therefore, continues so long as hatred of self continues; for this is the true inward repentance, and continues until our entrance into the kingdom of heaven.

5. The pope does not intend to remit, and cannot remit any penalties other than those which he has imposed either by his own authority or by that of the Canons.

6. The pope cannot remit any guilt, except by declaring that it has been remitted by God and by assenting to God's remission; though, to be sure, he may grant remission in cases reserved to his judgment. If his right to grant remission in such cases were despised, the guilt would remain entirely unforgiven.

7. God remits guilt to no one whom He does not, at the same time, humble in all things and bring into subjection to His vicar, the priest.

8. The penitential canons are imposed only on the living, and, according to them, nothing should be imposed on the dying.

9. Therefore the Holy Spirit in the pope is kind to us, because in his decrees he always makes exception of the article of death and of necessity.

10. Ignorant and wicked are the doings of those priests who, in the case of the dying, reserve canonical penances for purgatory.

11. This changing of the canonical penalty to the penalty of purgatory is quite evidently one of the tares that were sown while the bishops slept.

12. In former times the canonical penalties were imposed not after, but before absolution, as tests of true contrition.

13. The dying are freed by death from all penalties; they are already dead to canonical rules, and have a right to be released from them.

14. The imperfect health [of soul], that is to say, the imperfect love, of the dying brings with it, of necessity, great fear; and the smaller the love, the greater is the fear.

15. This fear and horror is sufficient of itself alone (to say nothing of other things) to constitute the penalty of purgatory, since it is very near to the horror of despair.

16. Hell, purgatory, and heaven seem to differ as do despair, almost-despair, and the assurance of safety.

17. With souls in purgatory it seems necessary that horror should grow less and love increase.

18. It seems unproved, either by reason or Scripture, that they are outside the state of merit, that is to say, of increasing love.

19. Again, it seems unproved that they, or at least that all of them, are certain or assured of their own blessedness, though we may be quite certain of it.

20. Therefore by "full remission of all penalties" the pope means not actually "of all," but only of those imposed by himself.

21. Therefore those preachers of indulgences are in error, who say that by the pope's indulgences a man is freed from every penalty, and saved.

22. Whereas he remits to souls in purgatory no penalty which, according to the canons, they would have had to pay in this life.

23. If it is at all possible to grant to any one the remission of all penalties whatsoever, it is certain that this remission can be granted only to the most perfect, that is, to the very fewest.

24. It must needs be, therefore, that the greater part of the people are deceived by that indiscriminate and high-sounding promise of release from penalty.

25. The power which the pope has, in a general way, over purgatory, is just like the power which any bishop or curate has, in a special way, within his own diocese or parish.

26. The pope does well when he grants remission to souls [in purgatory], not by the power of the keys (which he does not possess), but by way of intercession.

27. They preach doctrines that say that as soon as the penny jingles into the money-box, the soul flies out [of purgatory].

28. It is certain that when the penny jingles into the money-box, gain and avarice can be increased, but the result of the intercession of the Church is in the power of God alone.

29. Who knows whether all the souls in purgatory wish to be bought out of it, as in the legend of Sts. Severinus and Paschal.

30. No one is sure that his own contrition is sincere; much less that he has attained full remission.

31. Rare as is the man that is truly penitent, so rare is also the man who truly buys indulgences, i.e., such men are most rare.

32. They will be condemned eternally, together with their teachers, who believe themselves sure of their salvation because they have letters of pardon.

33. Men must be on their guard against those who say that the pope's pardons are that inestimable gift of God by which man is reconciled to Him.

34. For these "graces of pardon" concern only the penalties of sacramental satisfaction, and these are appointed by man.

35. They preach no Christian doctrine who teach that contrition is not necessary in those who intend to buy souls out of purgatory or to buy confessional privileges.

36. Every truly repentant Christian has a right to full remission of penalty and guilt, even without letters of pardon.

37. Every true Christian, whether living or dead, has part in all the blessings of Christ and the Church; and this is granted him by God, even without letters of pardon.

38. Nevertheless, the remission and participation [in the blessings of the Church] which are granted by the pope are in no way to be despised, for they are, as I have said, the declaration of divine remission.

39. It is most difficult, even for the very keenest theologians, at one and the same time to commend to the people the abundance of pardons and [the need of] true contrition.

40. True contrition seeks and loves penalties, but liberal pardons only relax penalties and cause them to be hated, or at least, furnish an occasion [for hating them].

41. Apostolic pardons are to be preached with caution, lest the people may falsely think them preferable to other good works of love.

42. Christians are to be taught that the pope does not intend the buying of pardons to be compared in any way to works of mercy.

43. Christians are to be taught that he who gives to the poor or lends to the needy does a better work than buying pardons.

44. Because love grows by works of love, and man becomes better; but by pardons man does not grow better, only more free from penalty.

45. Christians are to be taught that he who sees a man in need, and passes him by, and gives [his money] for pardons, purchases not the indulgences of the pope, but the indignation of God.

46. Christians are to be taught that unless they have more than they need, they are bound to keep back what is necessary for their own families, and by no means to squander it on pardons.

47. Christians are to be taught that the buying of pardons is a matter of free will, and not of commandment.

48. Christians are to be taught that the pope, in granting pardons, needs, and therefore desires, their devout prayer for him more than the money they bring.

49. Christians are to be taught that the pope's pardons are useful, if they do not put their trust in them; but altogether harmful, if through them they lose their fear of God.

50. Christians are to be taught that if the pope knew the exactions of the pardon-preachers, he would rather that St. Peter's church should go to ashes, than that it should be built up with the skin, flesh and bones of his sheep.

51. Christians are to be taught that it would be the pope's wish, as it is his duty, to give of his own money to very many of those

from whom certain hawkers of pardons cajole money, even though the church of St. Peter might have to be sold.

52. The assurance of salvation by letters of pardon is vain, even though the commissary, nay, even though the pope himself, were to stake his soul upon it.

53. They are enemies of Christ and of the pope, who bid the Word of God be altogether silent in some Churches, in order that pardons may be preached in others.

54. Injury is done the Word of God when, in the same sermon, an equal or a longer time is spent on pardons than on this Word.

55. It must be the intention of the pope that if pardons, which are a very small thing, are celebrated with one bell, with single processions and ceremonies, then the Gospel, which is the very greatest thing, should be preached with a hundred bells, a hundred processions, a hundred ceremonies.

56. The "treasures of the Church," out of which the pope grants indulgences, are not sufficiently named or known among the people of Christ.

57. That they are not temporal treasures is certainly evident, for many of the vendors do not pour out such treasures so easily, but only gather them.

58. Nor are they the merits of Christ and the Saints, for even without the pope, these always work grace for the inner man, and the cross, death, and hell for the outward man.

59. St. Lawrence said that the treasures of the Church were the Church's poor, but he spoke according to the usage of the word in his own time.

60. Without rashness we say that the keys of the Church, given by Christ's merit, are that treasure.

61. For it is clear that for the remission of penalties and of reserved cases, the power of the pope is of itself sufficient.

62. The true treasure of the Church is the Most Holy Gospel of the glory and the grace of God.

63. But this treasure is naturally most odious, for it makes the first to be last.

64. On the other hand, the treasure of indulgences is naturally most acceptable, for it makes the last to be first.

65. Therefore the treasures of the Gospel are nets with which they formerly were wont to fish for men of riches.

66. The treasures of the indulgences are nets with which they now fish for the riches of men.

67. The indulgences which the preachers cry as the "greatest graces" are known to be truly such, in so far as they promote gain.

68. Yet they are in truth the very smallest graces compared with the grace of God and the piety of the Cross.

69. Bishops and curates are bound to admit the commissaries of apostolic pardons, with all reverence.

70. But still more are they bound to strain all their eyes and attend with all their ears, lest these men preach their own dreams instead of the commission of the pope.

71. He who speaks against the truth of apostolic pardons, let him be anathema and accursed!

72. But he who guards against the lust and license of the pardon-preachers, let him be blessed!

73. The pope justly thunders against those who, by any art, contrive the injury of the traffic in pardons.

74. But much more does he intend to thunder against those who use the pretext of pardons to contrive the injury of holy love and truth.

75. To think the papal pardons so great that they could absolve a man even if he had committed an impossible sin and violated the Mother of God—this is madness.

76. We say, on the contrary, that the papal pardons are not able to remove the very least of venial sins, so far as its guilt is concerned.

77. It is said that even St. Peter, if he were now Pope, could not bestow greater graces; this is blasphemy against St. Peter and against the pope.

78. We say, on the contrary, that even the present pope, and any pope at all, has greater graces at his disposal; to wit, the Gospel, powers, gifts of healing, etc., as it is written in I. Corinthians xii.

79. To say that the cross, emblazoned with the papal arms, which is set up [by the preachers of indulgences], is of equal worth with the Cross of Christ, is blasphemy.

80. The bishops, curates and theologians who allow such talk to be spread among the people, will have an account to render.

81. This unbridled preaching of pardons makes it no easy matter, even for learned men, to rescue the reverence due to the pope from slander, or even from the shrewd questionings of the laity.

82. To wit:—"Why does not the pope empty purgatory, for the sake of holy love and of the dire need of the souls that are there, if he redeems an infinite number of souls for the sake of miserable money with which to build a Church? The former reasons would be most just; the latter is most trivial."

83. Again:—"Why are mortuary and anniversary masses for the dead continued, and why does he not return or permit the withdrawal of the endowments founded on their behalf, since it is wrong to pray for the redeemed?"

84. Again:—"What is this new piety of God and the pope, that for money they allow a man who is impious and their enemy, to buy out of purgatory the pious soul of a friend of God, and do not rather, because of that pious and beloved soul's own need, free it for pure love's sake?"

85. Again:—"Why are the penitential canons long since in actual fact and through disuse abrogated and dead, now satisfied by the granting of indulgences, as though they were still alive and in force?"

86. Again:—"Why does not the pope, whose wealth is to-day greater than the riches of the richest, build just this one church of St. Peter with his own money, rather than with the money of poor believers?"

87. Again:—"What is it that the pope remits, and what participation does he grant to those who, by perfect contrition, have a right to full remission and participation?"

88. Again:—"What greater blessing could come to the Church than if the pope were to do a hundred times a day what he now does once, and bestow on every believer these remissions and participations?"

89. "Since the pope, by his pardons, seeks the salvation of souls rather than money, why does he suspend the indulgences and pardons granted heretofore, since these have equal efficacy?"

90. To repress these arguments and scruples of the laity by force alone, and not to resolve them by giving reasons, is to expose the Church and the pope to the ridicule of their enemies, and to make Christians unhappy.

91. If, therefore, pardons were preached according to the spirit and mind of the pope, all these doubts would be readily resolved; nay, they would not exist.

92. Away, then, with all those prophets who say to the people of Christ, "Peace, peace," and there is no peace!

93. Blessed be all those prophets who say to the people of Christ, "Cross, cross," and there is no cross!

94. Christians are to be exhorted that they be diligent in following Christ, their Head, through penalties, deaths, and hell.

95. And thus be confident of entering into heaven rather through many tribulations, than through the assurance of peace.

Memorial and Remonstrance against Religious Assessments (1785)

American statesman James Madison (1751–1836) is often referred to as the "father of the U.S. Constitution." A member of the Virginia aristocracy and an able scholar at the College of New Jersey (now Princeton University), Madison continued to study law and religion upon his return to Virginia after graduation. An influential political thinker and product of the Enlightenment, Madison served as secretary of state for President Thomas Jefferson for two terms before becoming the fourth president of the United States (1809–1817).

Madison, himself an Episcopalian, shared with Jefferson a lifelong passion for religious freedom and distrust of clericalism. He believed that the exercise of religion should be completely separated from the government so that all people would be free to worship—or not to worship—whenever and wherever they pleased. He believed that there should be a large number of religions, as this would prevent one from dominating others.

In 1785 the Virginia legislature attempted to impose a tax for the support of "teachers of the Christian religion." Madison viewed this attempt as an assault on religious freedom by the Virginia Anglicans, who though a minority in the state enjoyed social and economic prominence and held a majority in the General Assembly. General assessment taxes were to be collected and distributed to the denomination designated by the taxpayer; if no designation had been specified, the assessment would be used for education. The bill before the 1784 legislature passed preliminary votes in the assembly, but Madison prevented the final consideration of the bill until late 1785. He led the successful attack against the bill, writing *Memorial and Remonstrance against Religious Assessments,* which was addressed to the General Assembly of the Commonwealth of Virginia and widely distributed during the summer of 1785. This classic statement of religious freedom is regarded as a major factor in the defeat of the bill and a testament to the power of Madison's belief that the connection between church and state must be severed to prevent religious injustice and promote a system of checks and balances.

Memorial and Remonstrance against Religious Assessments

We, the subscribers, citizens of the said Commonwealth, having taken into serious consideration, a Bill printed by order of the last Session of General Assembly, entitled "A Bill establishing a provision for Teachers of the Christian Religion," and conceiving that the same, if finally armed with the sanctions of a law, will be a dangerous abuse of power, are bound as faithful members of a free State to remonstrate against it, and to declare the reasons by which we are determined. We remonstrate against the said Bill,

1. Because we hold it for a fundamental and undeniable truth "that Religion or the duty which we owe to our Creator, and the manner of discharging it, can be directed only by reason and conviction, not by force or violence." The Religion then of every man must be left to the conviction and conscience of every man; and it is the right of every man to exercise it as these may dictate.

This right is in its nature an unalienable right. It is unalienable, because the opinions of men, depending only on the evidence contemplated by their own minds, cannot follow the dictates of other men: It is unalienable also, because what is here a right towards men, is a duty towards the Creator.

It is the duty of every man to render to the Creator such homage and such only as he believes to be acceptable to him. This duty is precedent, both in order of time and in degree of obligation, to the claims of Civil Society. Before any man can be considered as a member of Civil Society, he must be considered as a subject of the Governor of the Universe: And if a member of Civil Society, who enters into any subordinate Association, must always do it with a reservation of his duty to the general authority; much more must every man who becomes a member of any particular Civil Society, do it with a saving of his allegiance to the Universal Sovereign.

We maintain therefore that in matters of Religion, no man's right is abridged by the institution of Civil Society, and that Religion is wholly exempt from its cognizance. True it is, that no other rule exists, by which any question which may divide a Society, can be ultimately determined, but the will of the majority; but it is also true that the majority may trespass on the rights of the minority.

2. Because Religion be exempt from the authority of the Society at large, still less can it be subject to that of the Legislative Body. The latter are but the creatures and vicegerents of the former. Their jurisdiction is both derivative and limited: it is limited with regard

to the co-ordinate departments, more necessarily is it limited with regard to the constituents.

The preservation of a free Government requires not merely, that the metes and bounds which separate each department of power be invariably maintained; but more especially that neither of them be suffered to overleap the great Barrier which defends the rights of the people. The Rulers who are guilty of such an encroachment, exceed the commission from which they derive their authority, and are Tyrants. The People who submit to it are governed by laws made neither by themselves nor by an authority derived from them, and are slaves.

3. Because it is proper to take alarm at the first experiment on our liberties. We hold this prudent jealousy to be the first duty of Citizens, and one of the noblest characteristics of the late Revolution. The free men of America did not wait till usurped power had strengthened itself by exercise, and entangled the question in precedents. They saw all the consequences in the principle, and they avoided the consequences by denying the principle. We revere this lesson too much soon to forget it.

Who does not see that the same authority which can establish Christianity, in exclusion of all other Religions, may establish with the same ease any particular sect of Christians, in exclusion of all other Sects? That the same authority which can force a citizen to contribute three pence only of his property for the support of any one establishment, may force him to conform to any other establishment in all cases whatsoever?

4. Because the Bill violates the equality which ought to be the basis of every law, and which is more indispensable, in proportion as the validity or expediency of any law is more liable to be impeached. If "all men are by nature equally free and independent," all men are to be considered as entering into Society on equal conditions; as relinquishing no more, and therefore retaining no less, one than another, of their natural rights.

Above all are they to be considered as retaining an "equal title to the free exercise of Religion according to the dictates of Conscience." Whilst we assert for ourselves a freedom to embrace, to profess and to observe the Religion which we believe to be of divine origin, we cannot deny an equal freedom to those whose minds have not yet yielded to the evidence which has convinced us.

If this freedom be abused, it is an offence against God, not against man: To God, therefore, not to man, must an account of it be rendered. As the Bill violates equality by subjecting some to peculiar burdens, so it violates the same principle, by granting to others peculiar exemptions. Are the Quakers and Menonists the only sects who think a compulsive support of their Religions unnecessary and unwarrantable? Can their piety alone be entrusted with the care of public worship? Ought their Religions to be endowed above all others with extraordinary privileges by which proselytes may be enticed from all others?

We think too favorably of the justice and good sense of these denominations to believe that they either covet pre-eminences over their fellow citizens or that they will be seduced by them from the common opposition to the measure.

5. Because the Bill implies either that the Civil Magistrate is a competent Judge of Religious Truth; or that he may employ Religion as an engine of Civil policy. The first is an arrogant pretension falsified by the contradictory opinions of Rulers in all ages, and throughout the world: the second an unhallowed perversion of the means of salvation.

6. Because the establishment proposed by the Bill is not requisite for the support of the Christian Religion. To say that it is, is a contradiction to the Christian Religion itself; for every page of it disavows a dependence on the powers of this world: it is a contradiction to fact; for it is known that this Religion both existed and flourished, not only without the support of human laws, but in spite of every opposition from them, and not only during the period of miraculous aid, but long after it had been left to its own evidence and the ordinary care of Providence.

Nay, it is a contradiction in terms; for a Religion not invented by human policy, must have pre-existed and been supported, before it was established by human policy. It is moreover to weaken in those who profess this Religion a pious confidence in its innate excellence and the patronage of its Author; and to foster in those who still reject it, a suspicion that its friends are too conscious of its fallacies to trust it to its own merits.

7. Because experience witnesseth that ecclesiastical establishments, instead of maintaining the purity and efficacy of Religion, have had a contrary operation.

During almost fifteen centuries has the legal establishment of Christianity been on trial. What have been its fruits? More or less in all places, pride and indolence in the Clergy; ignorance and servility in the laity; in both, superstition, bigotry and persecution. Enquire of the Teachers of Christianity for the ages in which it appeared in its greatest luster; those of every sect, point to the ages prior to its incorporation with Civil policy.

Propose a restoration of this primitive State in which its Teachers depended on the voluntary rewards of their flocks; many of them predict its downfall. On which Side ought their testimony to have greatest weight, when for or when against their interest?

8. Because the establishment in question is not necessary for the support of Civil Government. If it be urged as necessary for the support of Civil Government only as it is a means of supporting Religion, and it be not necessary for the latter purpose, it cannot be necessary for the former. If Religion be not within the cognizance of Civil Government, how can its legal establishment be necessary to Civil Government? What influence in fact have ecclesiastical establishments had on Civil Society?

In some instances they have been seen to erect a spiritual tyranny on the ruins of the Civil authority; in many instances they have been seen upholding the thrones of political tyranny: in no instance have they been seen the guardians of the liberties of the people. Rulers who wished to subvert the public liberty, may have found an established Clergy convenient auxiliaries.

A just Government instituted to secure & perpetuate it needs them not. Such a Government will be best supported by protecting every Citizen in the enjoyment of his Religion with the same equal hand which protects his person and his property; by neither invading the equal rights of any Sect, nor suffering any Sect to invade those of another.

9. Because the proposed establishment is a departure from the generous policy, which, offering an Asylum to the persecuted and oppressed of every Nation and Religion, promised a luster to our country, and an accession to the number of its citizens. What a melancholy mark is the Bill of sudden degeneracy? Instead of holding forth an Asylum to the persecuted, it is itself a signal of persecution.

It degrades from the equal rank of Citizens all those whose opinions in Religion do not bend to those of the Legislative authority. Distant as it may be in its present form from the Inquisition, it differs from it only in degree. The one is the first step, the other the last in the career of intolerance. The magnanimous sufferer under this cruel scourge in foreign Regions, must view the Bill as a Beacon on our Coast, warning him to seek some other haven, where liberty and philanthropy in their due extent, may offer a more certain repose from his Troubles.

10. Because it will have a like tendency to banish our Citizens. The allurements presented by other situations are every day thinning their number. To superadd a fresh motive to emigration by revoking the liberty which they now enjoy, would be the same species of folly which has dishonored and depopulated flourishing kingdoms.

11. Because it will destroy that moderation and harmony which the forbearance of our laws to intermeddle with Religion has produced among its several sects. Torrents of blood have been split in the old world, by vain attempts of the secular arm, to extinguish Religious discord, by proscribing all difference in Religious opinion. Time has at length revealed the true remedy. Every relaxation of narrow and rigorous policy, wherever it has been tried, has been found to assuage the disease.

The American Theater has exhibited proofs that equal and complete liberty, if it does not wholly eradicate it, sufficiently destroys its malignant influence on the health and prosperity of the State. If with the salutary effects of this system under our own eyes, we begin to contract the bounds of Religious freedom, we know no name that will too severely reproach our folly. At least let warning be taken at the first fruits of the threatened innovation.

The very appearance of the Bill has transformed "that Christian forbearance, love and charity," which of late mutually prevailed, into animosities and jealousies, which may not soon be appeased. What mischiefs may not be dreaded, should this enemy to the public quiet be armed with the force of a law?

12. Because the policy of the Bill is adverse to the diffusion of the light of Christianity. The first wish of those who enjoy this precious gift ought to be that it may be imparted to the whole race of mankind. Compare the number of those who have as yet received it with the number still remaining under the dominion of false Religions; and how small is the former! Does the policy of the Bill tend to lessen the disproportion?

No; it at once discourages those who are strangers to the light of revelation from coming into the Region of it; and countenances by example the nations who continue in darkness, in shutting out those who might convey it to them. Instead of Leveling as far as possible, every obstacle to the victorious progress of Truth, the Bill with an ignoble and unchristian timidity would circumscribe it with a wall of defense against the encroachments of error.

13. Because attempts to enforce by legal sanctions, acts obnoxious to so great a proportion of Citizens, tend to enervate the laws in general, and to slacken the bands of Society. If it be difficult to execute any law which is not generally deemed necessary or salutary, what must be the case, where it is deemed invalid and dangerous? And what may be the effect of so striking an example of impotency in the Government, on its general authority?

14. Because a measure of such singular magnitude and delicacy ought not to be imposed, without the clearest evidence that it is called for by a majority of citizens, and no satisfactory method is yet proposed by which the voice of the majority in this case may be determined, or its influence secured.

"The people of the respective counties are indeed requested to signify their opinion respecting the adoption of the Bill to the next Session of Assembly." But the representation must be made equal, before the voice either of the Representatives or of the Counties will be that of the people. Our hope is that neither of the former will, after due consideration, espouse the dangerous principle of the Bill. Should the event disappoint us, it will still leave us in full confidence, that a fair appeal to the latter will reverse the sentence against our liberties.

15. Because finally, "the equal right of every citizen to the free exercise of his Religion according to the dictates of conscience" is held by the same tenure with all our other rights.

If we recur to its origin, it is equally the gift of nature; if we weigh its importance, it cannot be less dear to us; if we consult the Declaration of those rights which pertain to the good people of Virginia, as the "basis and foundation of Government," it is enumerated with equal solemnity, or rather studied emphasis.

Either then, we must say, that the Will of the Legislature is the only measure of their authority; and that in the plenitude of this authority, they may sweep away all our fundamental rights; or, that they are bound to leave this particular right untouched and sacred:

Either we must say, that they may control the freedom of the press, may abolish the Trial by Jury, may swallow up the Executive and Judiciary Powers of the State; nay that they may despoil us of our very right of suffrage, and erect themselves into an independent and hereditary Assembly or, we must say, that they have no authority to enact into the law the Bill under consideration.

We, the Subscribers, say that the General Assembly of this Commonwealth have no such authority. And in order that no effort may be omitted on our part against so dangerous an usurpation, we oppose to it, this remonstrance; earnestly praying, as we are in duty bound, that the Supreme Lawgiver of the Universe, by illuminating those to whom it is addressed, may on the one hand, turn their Councils from every act which would affront his holy prerogative, or violate the trust committed to them: and on the other, guide them into every measure which may be worthy of his blessing, may rebound to their own praise, and may establish more firmly the liberties, the prosperity, and the happiness of the Commonwealth.

Thomas Jefferson on Religious Freedom (1786, 1802)

Although Thomas Jefferson is most often remembered as the principal author of the Declaration of Independence (1776), in his own view his advocacy of religious freedom and the separation of an individual's religious beliefs from the intrusion of the state was equally important. On his tombstone he quotes as a life's accomplishment the authorship of a statute establishing religious freedom in his home state of Virginia.

Following are the text of the Virginia statute and of the famous Danbury Letter—two documents that stand as monuments to Jefferson's position on religion and the state. The letter is a reply to an address by an association of Baptists in Danbury, Connecticut, congratulating him on his election to the presidency. No doubt expecting it would have wide circulation Jefferson uses words that have been part of the constitutional debate ever since. Such is Jefferson's prestige that the phrase "a wall of separation between church and state" has been debated, until the present day, as though it were part of the constitution itself.

The Virginia Act For Establishing Religious Freedom (1786)

Well aware that Almighty God hath created the mind free; that all attempts to influence it by temporal punishments or burdens, or by civil incapacitations, tend only to beget habits of hypocrisy and meanness, and are a departure from the plan of the Holy Author of our religion, who being Lord both of body and mind, yet chose not to propagate it by coercions on either, as was in his Almighty power to do; that the impious presumption of legislators and rulers, civil as well as ecclesiastical, who, being themselves but fallible and uninspired men, have assumed dominion over the faith of others, setting up their own opinions and modes of thinking as the only true and infallible, and as such endeavoring to impose them on others, hath established and maintained false religions over the greatest part of the world, and through all time; that to compel a man to furnish contributions of money for the propagation of opinions which he disbelieves, is sinful and tyrannical; that even the forcing him to support this or that teacher of his own religious persuasion, is depriving him of the comfortable liberty of giving his contributions to the particular pastor whose morals he would make his pattern, and whose powers he feels most persuasive to righteousness, and is withdrawing from the ministry those temporal rewards, which proceeding from an approbation of their personal conduct, are an additional incitement to earnest and unremitting labors for the instruction of mankind; that our civil rights have no dependence on our religious opinions, more than our opinions in physics or geometry; that, therefore, the proscribing any citizen as unworthy the public confidence by laying upon him an incapacity of being called to the offices of trust and emolument, unless he profess or renounce this or that religious opinion, is depriving him injuriously of those privileges and advantages to which in common with his fellow citizens he has a natural right; that it tends also to corrupt the principles of that very religion it is meant to encourage, by bribing, with a monopoly of worldly honors and emoluments, those who will externally profess and conform to it; that though indeed these are criminal who do not withstand such temptation, yet neither are those innocent who lay the bait in their way; that to suffer the civil magistrate to intrude his powers into the field of opinion and to restrain the profession or propagation of principles, on the supposition of their ill tendency, is a dangerous fallacy, which at once destroys all religious liberty, because he being of course judge of that tendency, will make his opinions the rule of judgment, and approve or condemn the sentiments of others only as they shall square with or differ from his own; that it is time enough for the rightful purposes of civil government, for its officers to interfere when principles break out into overt acts against peace and good order; and finally, that truth is great and will prevail if left to herself, that she is the proper and sufficient antagonist to error, and has nothing to fear from the conflict, unless by human interposition disarmed of her natural weapons, free argument and debate, errors ceasing to be dangerous when it is permitted freely to contradict them.

Be it therefore enacted by the General Assembly, That no man shall be compelled to frequent or support any religious worship, place, or ministry whatsoever, nor shall be enforced, restrained, molested, or burdened in his body or goods, nor shall otherwise suffer on account of his religious opinions or belief; but that all men shall be free to profess, and by argument to maintain, their opinions in matters of religion, and that the same shall in nowise diminish, enlarge, or affect their civil capacities.

And though we well know this Assembly, elected by the people for the ordinary purposes of legislation only, have no powers equal to our own and that therefore to declare this act irrevocable would be of no effect in law, yet we are free to declare, and do declare, that the rights hereby asserted are of the natural rights of mankind, and that if any act shall be hereafter passed to repeal the present or to narrow its operation, such act will be an infringement of natural right.

Letter to the Danbury Baptists (1802)

To messers. Nehemiah Dodge, Ephraim Robbins, and Stephen S. Nelson, a committee of the Danbury Baptist association in the state of Connecticut.

Gentlemen:

Believing with you that religion is a matter which lies solely between man and his God, that he owes account to none other for his faith or his worship, that the legitimate powers of government reach actions only, and not opinions, I contemplate with sovereign reverence that act of the whole American people which declared that their legislature should "make no law respecting an establishment of religion, or prohibiting the free exercise thereof," thus building a wall of separation between Church and State. Adhering to this expression of the supreme will of the nation in behalf of the rights of conscience, I shall see with sincere satisfaction the progress of those sentiments which tend to restore to man all his natural rights, convinced he has no natural right in opposition to his social duties.

I reciprocate your kind prayers for the protection and blessing of the common father and creator of man, and tender for you for yourselves and your religious association, assurances of my high respect and esteem.

Th. Jefferson
Jan. 1, 1802

Federalist No. 10 (1787)

In addition to promoting religious freedom (see *Memorial and Remonstrance against Religious Assessments,* p. 813), American statesman James Madison (1751–1836) was one of the driving forces behind the enactment of the U.S. Constitution and the American Bill of Rights.

In 1780 Madison was selected to serve in the Continental Congress, where he worked to bring greater organization to the federal government under the new Articles of Confederation. He believed the Articles had to be strengthened if the government was to survive. Madison's extensive knowledge of political theory came to great use at the Constitutional Convention in the summer of 1787, as his "Virginia Plan," which stressed the creation of a three-branch government by the people rather than the states, served as the basis for the Constitution.

After the Constitutional Convention, Madison, along with fellow statesmen Alexander Hamilton (1755–1804) and John Jay (1745–1829), wrote a series of eighty-five articles that appeared under the pseudonym "Publius" in several New York newspapers (Hamilton wrote fifty-one, Madison twenty-six, Jay five, and Hamilton and Madison jointly wrote three). These articles explained and defended the new Constitution, which had to be ratified by the states before becoming law. They were later gathered into a book called *The Federalist Papers,* which is regarded as one of the greatest books ever written on U.S. political philosophy.

Federalist No. 10 proposed that the government should be able to check and limit the excesses of parties but not abolish them. Madison believed that separate, competing interests were inevitable in a free society; snuffing out competition would curb free thought and action. He stressed that the only satisfactory method of "curing the mischiefs of faction" was to control their effects. To attempt to silence factions by eliminating competing interests would be to destroy liberty.

In *Federalist No. 10* Madison recognized the "class" divisions in society, which led to and explained his belief that there also existed an inescapable division of opinions. He advocated openly recognizing and accepting the existence of human diversity, in both opinion and property. According to Madison, the primary object of government was to prevent one group or party from invading the rights of the others. The government must be neutral, with clear definitions of its powers and separation of functions.

In 1789, as a member of the first U.S. Congress, Madison spearheaded the movement for passage of the Bill of Rights, which guaranteed basic liberties, including religious freedom, for all Americans. He had proposed nine amendments to the Constitution, which became the basis for the Bill of Rights.

Federalist No. 10

To the People of the State of New York:

AMONG the numerous advantages promised by a well-constructed Union, none deserves to be more accurately developed than its tendency to break and control the violence of faction. The friend of popular governments never finds himself so much alarmed for their character and fate, as when he contemplates their propensity to this dangerous vice. He will not fail, therefore, to set a due value on any plan which, without violating the principles to which he is attached, provides a proper cure for it. The instability, injustice, and confusion introduced into the public councils, have, in truth, been the mortal diseases under which popular governments have everywhere perished; as they continue to be the favorite and fruitful topics from which the adversaries to liberty derive their most specious declamations. The valuable improvements made by the American constitutions on the popular models, both ancient and modern, cannot certainly be too much admired; but it would be an unwarrantable partiality, to contend that they have as effectually obviated the danger on this side, as was wished and expected. Complaints are everywhere heard from our most considerate and virtuous citizens, equally the friends of public and private faith, and of public and personal liberty, that our governments are too unstable, that the public good is disregarded in the conflicts of rival parties, and that measures are too often decided, not according to the rules of justice and the rights of the minor party, but by the superior force of an interested and overbearing majority. However anxiously we may wish that these complaints had no foundation, the evidence, of known facts will not permit us to deny that they are in some degree true. It will be found, indeed, on a candid review of our situation, that some of the distresses under which we labor have been erroneously charged on the operation of our governments; but it will be found, at the same time, that other causes will not alone account for many of our heaviest misfortunes; and, particularly, for that prevailing and increasing distrust of public engagements, and alarm for private rights, which are echoed from one end of the continent to the other. These must be chiefly, if not wholly, effects of the unsteadiness and injustice with which a factious spirit has tainted our public administrations.

By a faction, I understand a number of citizens, whether amounting to a majority or a minority of the whole, who are united and actuated by some common impulse of passion, or of interest, adversed to the rights of other citizens, or to the permanent and aggregate interests of the community.

There are two methods of curing the mischiefs of faction: the one, by removing its causes; the other, by controlling its effects.

There are again two methods of removing the causes of faction: the one, by destroying the liberty which is essential to its existence; the other, by giving to every citizen the same opinions, the same passions, and the same interests.

It could never be more truly said than of the first remedy, that it was worse than the disease. Liberty is to faction what air is to fire, an aliment without which it instantly expires. But it could not be less folly to abolish liberty, which is essential to political life, because it nourishes faction, than it would be to wish the annihilation of air, which is essential to animal life, because it imparts to fire its destructive agency.

The second expedient is as impracticable as the first would be unwise. As long as the reason of man continues fallible, and he is at liberty to exercise it, different opinions will be formed. As long as the connection subsists between his reason and his self-love, his opinions and his passions will have a reciprocal influence on each other; and the former will be objects to which the latter will attach themselves. The diversity in the faculties of men, from which the rights of property originate, is not less an insuperable obstacle to a uniformity of interests. The protection of these faculties is the first object of government. From the protection of different and unequal faculties of acquiring property, the possession of different degrees and kinds of property immediately results; and from the influence of these on the sentiments and views of the respective proprietors, ensues a division of the society into different interests and parties.

The latent causes of faction are thus sown in the nature of man; and we see them everywhere brought into different degrees of activity, according to the different circumstances of civil society. A zeal for different opinions concerning religion, concerning government, and many other points, as well of speculation as of practice; an attachment to different leaders ambitiously contending for pre-eminence and power; or to persons of other descriptions whose fortunes have been interesting to the human passions, have, in turn, divided mankind into parties, inflamed them with mutual animosity, and rendered them much more disposed to vex and oppress each other than to co-operate for their common good. So strong is this propensity of mankind to fall into mutual animosities, that where no substantial occasion presents itself, the most frivolous and fanciful distinctions have been sufficient to kindle their unfriendly passions and excite their most violent conflicts. But the most common and durable source of factions has been the various and unequal distribution of property. Those who hold and those who are without property have ever formed distinct interests in society. Those who are creditors, and those who are debtors, fall under a like discrimination. A landed interest, a manufacturing interest, a mercantile interest, a moneyed interest, with many lesser interests, grow up of necessity in civilized nations, and divide them into different classes, actuated by different sentiments and views. The regulation of these various and interfering interests forms the principal task of modern legislation, and involves the spirit of party and faction in the necessary and ordinary operations of the government.

No man is allowed to be a judge in his own cause, because his interest would certainly bias his judgment, and, not improbably, corrupt his integrity. With equal, nay with greater reason, a body of men are unfit to be both judges and parties at the same time; yet what are many of the most important acts of legislation, but so many judicial determinations, not indeed concerning the rights of single persons, but concerning the rights of large bodies of citizens? And what are the different classes of legislators but advocates and parties to the causes which they determine? Is a law proposed concerning private debts? It is a question to which the creditors are parties on one side and the debtors on the other. Justice ought to hold the balance between them. Yet the parties are, and must be, themselves the judges; and the most numerous party, or, in other words, the most powerful faction must be expected to prevail. Shall domestic manufactures be encouraged, and in what degree, by restrictions on foreign manufactures? are questions which would be differently decided by the landed and the manufacturing classes, and probably by neither with a sole regard to justice and the public good. The apportionment of taxes on the various descriptions of property is an act which seems to require the most exact impartiality; yet there is, perhaps, no legislative act in which greater opportunity and temptation are given to a predominant party to trample on the rules of justice. Every shilling with which they overburden the inferior number, is a shilling saved to their own pockets.

It is in vain to say that enlightened statesmen will be able to adjust these clashing interests, and render them all subservient to the public good. Enlightened statesmen will not always be at the helm. Nor, in many cases, can such an adjustment be made at all without taking into view indirect and remote considerations, which will rarely prevail over the immediate interest which one party may find in disregarding the rights of another or the good of the whole.

The inference to which we are brought is, that the CAUSES of faction cannot be removed, and that relief is only to be sought in the means of controlling its EFFECTS.

If a faction consists of less than a majority, relief is supplied by the republican principle, which enables the majority to defeat its sinister views by regular vote. It may clog the administration, it may convulse the society; but it will be unable to execute and mask its violence under the forms of the Constitution. When a majority is included in a faction, the form of popular government, on the other hand, enables it to sacrifice to its ruling passion or interest both the public good and the rights of other citizens. To secure the public good and private rights against the danger of such a faction, and at the same time to preserve the spirit and the form of popular government, is then the great object to which our inquiries are directed. Let me add that it is the great desideratum by which this form of government can be rescued from the opprobrium under which it has so long labored, and be recommended to the esteem and adoption of mankind.

By what means is this object attainable? Evidently by one of two only. Either the existence of the same passion or interest in a majority at the same time must be prevented, or the majority, having such coexistent passion or interest, must be rendered, by their number and local situation, unable to concert and carry into effect schemes of oppression. If the impulse and the opportunity be suffered to coincide, we well know that neither moral nor religious motives can be relied on as an adequate control. They are not found to be such on the injustice and violence of individuals, and lose their efficacy in proportion to the number combined together, that is, in proportion as their efficacy becomes needful.

From this view of the subject it may be concluded that a pure democracy, by which I mean a society consisting of a small number of citizens, who assemble and administer the government in person, can admit of no cure for the mischiefs of faction. A common passion or interest will, in almost every case, be felt by a majority of the whole; a communication and concert result from the form of government itself; and there is nothing to check the inducements to sacrifice the weaker party or an obnoxious individual. Hence it is that such democracies have ever been spectacles of turbulence and contention; have ever been found incompatible with personal security or the rights of property; and have in general been as short in their lives as they have been violent in their deaths. Theoretic politicians, who have patronized this species of government, have erroneously supposed that by reducing mankind to a perfect equality in their political rights, they would, at the same time, be perfectly equalized and assimilated in their possessions, their opinions, and their passions.

A republic, by which I mean a government in which the scheme of representation takes place, opens a different prospect, and promises the cure for which we are seeking. Let us examine the points in which it varies from pure democracy, and we shall comprehend both the nature of the cure and the efficacy which it must derive from the Union.

The two great points of difference between a democracy and a republic are: first, the delegation of the government, in the latter, to a small number of citizens elected by the rest; secondly, the greater number of citizens, and greater sphere of country, over which the latter may be extended. The effect of the first difference is, on the one hand, to refine and enlarge the public views, by passing them through the medium of a chosen body of citizens, whose wisdom may best discern the true interest of their country, and whose patriotism and love of justice will be least likely to sacrifice it to temporary or partial considerations. Under such a regulation, it may well happen that the public voice, pronounced by the representatives of the people, will be more consonant to the public good than if pronounced by the people themselves, convened for the purpose. On the other hand, the effect may be inverted. Men of factious tempers, of local prejudices, or of sinister designs, may, by intrigue, by corruption, or by other means, first obtain the suffrages, and then betray the interests, of the people. The question resulting is, whether small or extensive republics are more favorable to the election of proper guardians of the public weal; and it is clearly decided in favor of the latter by two obvious considerations:

In the first place, it is to be remarked that, however small the republic may be, the representatives must be raised to a certain number, in order to guard against the cabals of a few; and that, however large it may be, they must be limited to a certain number, in order to guard against the confusion of a multitude. Hence, the number of representatives in the two cases not being in proportion to that of the two constituents, and being proportionally greater in the small republic, it follows that, if the proportion of fit characters be not less in the large than in the small republic, the former will present a greater option, and consequently a greater probability of a fit choice.

In the next place, as each representative will be chosen by a greater number of citizens in the large than in the small republic, it will be more difficult for unworthy candidates to practice with success the vicious arts by which elections are too often carried; and the suffrages of the people being more free, will be more likely to centre in men who possess the most attractive merit and the most diffusive and established characters.

It must be confessed that in this, as in most other cases, there is a mean, on both sides of which inconveniences will be found to lie. By enlarging too much the number of electors, you render the representatives too little acquainted with all their local circumstances and lesser interests; as by reducing it too much, you render him unduly attached to these, and too little fit to comprehend and pursue great and national objects. The federal Constitution forms a happy combination in this respect; the great and aggregate interests being referred to the national, the local and particular to the State legislatures.

The other point of difference is, the greater number of citizens and extent of territory which may be brought within the compass of republican than of democratic government; and it is this circumstance principally which renders factious combinations less to be dreaded in the former than in the latter. The smaller the society, the fewer probably will be the distinct parties and interests composing it; the fewer the distinct parties and interests, the more frequently will a majority be found of the same party; and the smaller the number of individuals composing a majority, and the smaller the compass within which they are placed, the more easily will they concert and execute their plans of oppression. Extend the sphere, and you take in a greater variety of parties and interests; you make it less probable that a majority of the whole will have a common motive to invade the rights of other citizens; or if such a common motive exists, it will be more difficult for all who feel it to discover their own strength, and to act in unison with each other. Besides other impediments, it may be remarked that, where there is a consciousness of unjust or dishonorable purposes, communication is always checked by distrust in proportion to the number whose concurrence is necessary.

Hence, it clearly appears, that the same advantage which a republic has over a democracy, in controlling the effects of faction, is enjoyed by a large over a small republic,—is enjoyed by the Union over the States composing it. Does the advantage consist in the substitution of representatives whose enlightened views and virtuous sentiments render them superior to local prejudices and schemes of injustice? It will not be denied that the representation of the Union will be most likely to possess these requisite endowments. Does it consist in the greater security afforded by a greater variety of parties, against the event of any one party being able to outnumber and oppress the rest? In an equal degree does the increased variety of parties comprised within the Union, increase this security. Does it, in fine, consist in the greater obstacles opposed to the concert and accomplishment of the secret wishes of an unjust and interested majority? Here, again, the extent of the Union gives it the most palpable advantage.

The influence of factious leaders may kindle a flame within their particular States, but will be unable to spread a general conflagration through the other States. A religious sect may degenerate into a political faction in a part of the Confederacy; but the variety of sects dispersed over the entire face of it must secure the national councils against any danger from that source. A rage for paper money, for an abolition of debts, for an equal division of property, or for any other improper or wicked project, will be less apt to pervade the whole body of the Union than a particular member of it; in the same proportion as such a malady is more likely to taint a particular county or district, than an entire State.

In the extent and proper structure of the Union, therefore, we behold a republican remedy for the diseases most incident to republican government. And according to the degree of pleasure and pride we feel in being republicans, ought to be our zeal in cherishing the spirit and supporting the character of Federalists.

PUBLIUS.

Balfour Declaration (1917)

On November 2, 1917, Arthur James Balfour, the British foreign secretary, wrote what has become known as the Balfour Declaration. Addressed to Jewish leader Lord Rothschild, the declaration stated that the British government supported the establishment in Palestine of a homeland for the Jews. During World War I (1914–1918) the British army had moved into Palestine, replacing the occupying Turkish forces. Seeking to retain an interest in the area, in particular, the Suez Canal, the British cabinet felt its interests would be best served if the area was controlled by a friendly Jewish population.

This declaration marked the first time that Zionist aims were recognized by a world power. Zionism, a political program dedicated to the establishment of a national Jewish homeland, had been championed twenty years earlier by Theodor Herzl at the first Zionist Congress, in Basel, Switzerland. In the intervening years, Zionists of many persuasions—some seeking social and cultural goals, others political aims—competed for influence within the movement, but they were united in their insistence that the Jewish people were entitled to a homeland. With the drafting of the Balfour Declaration, their cause was furthered considerably, though the document was met with strong opposition by some British cabinet members and received a cool response from the governments of allies Italy and France. Thirty-one years would pass before the Zionists would witness the creation of the State of Israel, on May 14, 1948.

The Balfour Declaration was thought to be a means to generate goodwill among Jews worldwide, who would, in turn, pressure their respective governments to support British policy. It was hoped that American Jews would support U.S. entry into the war and that Jews who had participated in the Bolshevik Revolution would press to keep Russia in the war.

The overriding impact of the Balfour Declaration was to begin the process of reparation to the Jewish people. The letter, as reproduced here, was published a week after its drafting in *The Times* of London.

The Balfour Declaration

Foreign Office
November 2nd, 1917

Dear Lord Rothschild,

I have much pleasure in conveying to you, on behalf of His Majesty's Government, the following declaration of sympathy with Jewish Zionist aspirations which has been submitted to, and approved by, the Cabinet.

> "His Majesty's Government view with favour the establishment in Palestine of a national home for the Jewish people, and will use their best endeavours to facilitate the achievement of this object, it being clearly understood that nothing shall be done which may prejudice the civil and religious rights of existing non-Jewish communities in Palestine, or the rights and political status enjoyed by Jews in any other country."

I should be grateful if you would bring this declaration to the knowledge of the Zionist Federation.

Yours sincerely,
Arthur James Balfour

Barmen Declaration (1934)

Following the seizure of power by the Nazis in 1933, Protestant Christians in Germany faced pressure to "Aryanize" their churches. The government attempted to force religious authorities to sign an oath of loyalty to Adolf Hitler.

In many cases the churches gave in to the pressure, but others—especially Lutheran churches—vigorously opposed the Nazi encroachment on their beliefs. The Barmen Declaration, named for the German city in which it was drafted, was a statement of resistance against the theological claims of the Nazi state.

In defense of the Lutheran leadership and in response to Hitler's incorporation of German churches into the Nazi Party, a resistance movement was formed. This emerging "Confessing Church" (a church that confesses itself to be for its Lord and against its enemies) actively opposed the incorporation process, which it viewed as an attempt to destroy German Protestantism. Composed of pastors from United, Lutheran, and Reformed Churches, including the Lutheran theologian Dietrich Bonhoeffer, who later would be imprisoned and executed for serving as its spokesperson, the Confessing Church convened a synod at Barmen in May 1934 to formulate a response to Nazi aggression. It adopted a declaration drafted by theologians Karl Barth and Hans Asmussen that dismissed the claim that any power other than Christ could be the source of God's revelation. The German Evangelical Church proclaimed its right to determine its own constitution, despite the harassment and persecution of its members. For his open opposition to the Hitler regime, widely considered the high point of his political life, Barth was expelled from Germany in 1935 and spent much of the remainder of his career in Basel, Switzerland. Many other Christians who resisted the regime were arrested and executed in concentration camps.

The Barmen Declaration was a source of hope for many in Germany during the dark days of the Hitler regime. It was a source of strength for those who aimed to drive violence and heresy from their church and the world.

The Barmen Declaration

In view of the errors of the "German Christians" and of the present Reich Church Administration, which are ravaging the Church and at the same time also shattering the unity of the German Evangelical Church, we confess the following evangelical truths:

1. "I am the Way and the Truth and the Life; no one comes to the Father except through me." *(Jn. 14:6)*

"Truly, truly I say to you, he who does not enter the sheepfold through the door but climbs in somewhere else, he is a thief and a robber. I am the Door; if anyone enters through me, he will be saved." *(Jn. 10:1,9)*

Jesus Christ, as he is attested to us in Holy Scripture, is the one Word of God which we have to hear, and which we have to trust and obey in life and in death.

We reject the false doctrine that the Church could and should recognize as a source of its proclamation, beyond and besides this one Word of God, yet other events, powers, historic figures, and truths as God's revelation.

2. "Jesus Christ has been made wisdom and righteousness and sanctification and redemption for us by God." *(I Cor. 1:30)*

As Jesus Christ is God's comforting pronouncement of the forgiveness of all our sins, so, and with equal seriousness, he is also God's vigorous announcement of his claim upon our whole life. Through him there comes to us joyful liberation from the godless ties of this world for free, grateful service to his creatures.

We reject the false doctrine that there could be areas of our life in which we would belong not to Jesus Christ but to other lords, areas in which we would not need justification and sanctification through him.

3. "Let us, however, speak the truth in love, and in every respect grow into him who is the head, into Christ, from whom the whole body is joined together." *(Eph. 4:15-16)*

The Christian Church is the community of brethren in which, in Word and sacrament, through the Holy Spirit, Jesus Christ acts in the present as Lord. With both its faith and its obedience, with both its message and its order, it has to testify in the midst of the sinful world, as the Church of pardoned sinners, that it belongs to him alone and lives and may live by his comfort and under his direction alone, in expectation of his appearing.

We reject the false doctrine that the Church could have permission to hand over the form of its message and of its order to whatever it itself might wish or to the vicissitudes of the prevailing ideological and political convictions of the day.

4. "You know that the rulers of the Gentiles exercise authority over them and those in high position lord it over them. So shall it not be among you; but if anyone would have authority over you, let him be your servant." *(Matt. 20:25-26)*

The various offices in the Church do not provide a basis for some to exercise authority over others but for the ministry with which the whole community has been entrusted and charged to be carried out.

We reject the false doctrine that, apart from this ministry, the Church could, and could have permission to, give itself or allow itself to be given special leaders—*(Führer)*—vested with ruling authority.

5. "Fear God, honour the King." *(I Pet. 2:17)*

Scripture tells us that by divine appointment the State, in this still unredeemed world in which also the Church is situated, has the task of maintaining justice and peace, so far as human discernment and human ability make this possible, by means of the threat and use of force. The Church acknowledges with gratitude and reverence toward God the benefit of this, his appointment. It draws attention to God's Kingdom *(Reich)*, God's commandment and justice, and with these the responsibility of those who rule and those who are ruled. It trusts and obeys the power of the Word, by which God upholds all things.

We reject the false doctrine that beyond its special commission the State should and could become the sole and total order of human life and so fulfil the vocation of the Church as well.

We reject the false doctrine that beyond its special commission the Church should and could take on the nature, tasks, and dignity which belong to the State and thus become itself an organ of the State.

6. "See, I am with you always, to the end of the age." *(Matt. 28:20)*. "God's Word is not fettered." *(II Tim. 2:9)*

The Church's commission, which is the foundation of its freedom, consists in this: in Christ's stead, and so in the service of his own Word and work, to deliver to all people, through preaching and sacrament, the message of the free grace of God.

We reject the false doctrine that with human vainglory the Church could place the Word and work of the Lord in the service of self-chosen desires, purposes, and plans. The Confessional Synod of the German Evangelical Church declares that it sees in the acknowledgment of these truths and in the rejection of these errors the indispensable theological basis of the German Evangelical Church as a confederation of Confessional Churches. It calls upon all who can stand in solidarity with its Declaration to be mindful of these theological findings in all their decisions concerning Church and State. It appeals to all concerned to return to unity in faith, hope, and love.

Verbum Dei manet in aeternum.
The Word of God will last for ever.

Universal Declaration of Human Rights (1948)

The rights of individuals became a concern of the international community only in the twentieth century. Before World War I (1914–1918), the political, civil, and human rights of citizens, including the right to free exercise of religion, were considered properly to be the internal concerns of sovereign states. In the peace treaties concluded at the end of the war, some limited attempts were made for the first time to provide for the political and civil rights of certain minority groups. After the widespread horrors of World War II (1939–1945), the international community, as embodied in the United Nations, placed the extension and protection of individual rights at the forefront of the world agenda.

When the United Nations Charter was drafted in 1944–1945, a decision was made to defer a statement of fundamental human rights because of the cultural, political, and ideological difficulties involved in drafting such a document. In 1947 the UN Commission on Human Rights began working toward an international bill of human rights that would be acceptable to all member states: the long established and the newly independent; the industrially developed and the underdeveloped; communist and noncommunist; colonial powers and noncolonial powers. The resolution was adopted by a vote of 48–0 with eight abstentions by the UN General Assembly on December 10, 1948. (The six states of the Soviet bloc, Saudi Arabia, and the Union of South Africa abstained.)

The UN declaration includes the political and civil rights common to Western democratic constitutions: the rights to life, liberty, and equality; freedom of conscience and religion; freedom from arbitrary arrest and the right to a public hearing by an impartial jury; and freedom of assembly and association. It also addresses economic, social, and cultural issues not normally considered fundamental rights in the Western democratic tradition.

The Universal Declaration of Human Rights does not have the force of international law and hence places no obligations or restrictions on its signatory states. The declaration, however, provided the moral and intellectual underpinnings for subsequent covenants and conventions that do have the force of law. Among them are the International Covenant on Civil and Political Rights and the International Covenant on Economic, Social, and Cultural Rights, both of which were adopted in 1966 and entered into force in 1976.

Preamble

Whereas recognition of the inherent dignity and of the equal and inalienable rights of all members of the human family is the foundation of freedom, justice and peace in the world,

Whereas disregard and contempt for human rights have resulted in barbarous acts which have outraged the conscience of mankind, and the advent of a world in which human beings shall enjoy freedom of speech and belief and freedom from fear and want has been proclaimed as the highest aspiration of the common people,

Whereas it is essential, if man is not to be compelled to have recourse, as a last resort, to rebellion against tyranny and oppression, that human rights should be protected by the rule of law,

Whereas it is essential to promote the development of friendly relations between nations,

Whereas the peoples of the United Nations have in the Charter reaffirmed their faith in fundamental human rights, in the dignity and worth of the human person and in the equal rights of men and women and have determined to promote social progress and better standards of life in larger freedom,

Whereas Member States have pledged themselves to achieve, in co-operation with the United Nations, the promotion of universal respect for and observance of human rights and fundamental freedoms,

Whereas a common understanding of these rights and freedoms is of the greatest importance for the full realization of this pledge,

Now, therefore,

The General Assembly

Proclaims this Universal Declaration of Human Rights as a common standard of achievement for all peoples and all nations, to the end that every individual and every organ of society, keeping this Declaration constantly in mind, shall strive by teaching and education to promote respect for these rights and freedoms and by progressive measures, national and international, to secure their universal and effective recognition and observance, both among the peoples of Member States themselves and among the peoples of territories under their jurisdiction.

Article 1

All human beings are born free and equal in dignity and rights. They are endowed with reason and conscience and should act towards one another in a spirit of brotherhood.

Article 2

Everyone is entitled to all the rights and freedoms set forth in this Declaration, without distinction of any kind, such as race, colour, sex, language, religion, political or other opinion, national or social origin, property, birth or other status.

Furthermore, no distinction shall be made on the basis of the political, jurisdictional or international status of the country or territory to which a person belongs, whether it be independent, trust, non-self-governing or under any other limitation of sovereignty.

Article 3

Everyone has the right to life, liberty and security of person.

Article 4

No one shall be held in slavery or servitude; slavery and the slave trade shall be prohibited in all their forms.

Article 5

No one shall be subjected to torture or to cruel, inhuman or degrading treatment or punishment.

Article 6

Everyone has the right to recognition everywhere as a person before the law.

Article 7

All are equal before the law and are entitled without any discrimination to equal protection of the law. All are entitled to equal protection against any discrimination in violation of this Declaration and against any incitement to such discrimination.

Article 8

Everyone has the right to an effective remedy by the competent national tribunals for acts violating the fundamental rights granted him by the constitution or by law.

Article 9

No one shall be subjected to arbitrary arrest, detention or exile.

Article 10

Everyone is entitled in full equality to a fair and public hearing by an independent and impartial tribunal, in the determination of his rights and obligations and of any criminal charge against him.

Article 11

(1) Everyone charged with a penal offence has the right to be presumed innocent until proved guilty according to law in a public trial at which he has had all the guarantees necessary for his defence.

(2) No one shall be held guilty of any penal offence on account of any act or omission which did not constitute a penal offence, under national or international law, at the time when it was committed. Nor shall a heavier penalty be imposed than the one that was applicable at the time the penal offence was committed.

Article 12

No one shall be subjected to arbitrary interference with his privacy, family, home or correspondence, nor to attacks upon his honour and reputation. Everyone has the right to the protection of the law against such interference or attacks.

Article 13

(1) Everyone has the right to freedom of movement and residence within the borders of each State.

(2) Everyone has the right to leave any country, including his own, and to return to his country.

Article 14

(1) Everyone has the right to seek and to enjoy in other countries asylum from persecution.

(2) This right may not be invoked in the case of prosecutions genuinely arising from non-political crimes or from acts contrary to the purposes and principles of the United Nations.

Article 15

(1) Everyone has the right to a nationality.

(2) No one shall be arbitrarily deprived of his nationality nor denied the right to change his nationality.

Article 16

(1) Men and women of full age, without any limitation due to race, nationality or religion, have the right to marry and to found a

family. They are entitled to equal rights as to marriage, during marriage and at its dissolution.

(2) Marriage shall be entered into only with the free and full consent of the intending spouses.

(3) The family is the natural and fundamental group unit of society and is entitled to protection by society and the State.

Article 17

(1) Everyone has the right to own property alone as well as in association with others.

(2) No one shall be arbitrarily deprived of his property.

Article 18

Everyone has the right to freedom of thought, conscience and religion; this right includes freedom to change his religion or belief, and freedom, either alone or in community with others and in public or private, to manifest his religion or belief in teaching, practice, worship and observance.

Article 19

Everyone has the right to freedom of opinion and expression; this right includes freedom to hold opinions without interference and to seek, receive and impart information and ideas through any media and regardless of frontiers.

Article 20

(1) Everyone has the right to freedom of peaceful assembly and association.

(2) No one may be compelled to belong to an association.

Article 21

(1) Everyone has the right to take part in the government of his country, directly or through freely chosen representatives.

(2) Everyone has the right of equal access to public service in his country.

(3) The will of the people shall be the basis of the authority of the government; this will shall be expressed in periodic and genuine elections which shall be by universal and equal suffrage and shall be held by secret vote or by equivalent free voting procedures.

Article 22

Everyone, as a member of society, has the right to social security and is entitled to realization, through national effort and international co-operation and in accordance with the organization and resources of each State, of the economic, social and cultural rights indispensable for his dignity and the free development of his personality.

Article 23

(1) Everyone has the right to work, to free choice of employment, to just and favourable conditions of work and to protection against unemployment.

(2) Everyone, without any discrimination, has the right to equal pay for equal work.

(3) Everyone who works has the right to just and favourable remuneration ensuring for himself and his family an existence worthy of human dignity, and supplemented, if necessary, by other means of social protection.

(4) Everyone has the right to form and to join trade unions for the protection of his interests.

Article 24

Everyone has the right to rest and leisure, including reasonable limitation of working hours and periodic holidays with pay.

Article 25

(1) Everyone has the right to a standard of living adequate for the health and well-being of himself and of his family, including food, clothing, housing, and medical care and necessary social services, and the right to security in the event of unemployment, sickness, disability, widowhood, old age or other lack of livelihood in circumstances beyond his control.

(2) Motherhood and childhood are entitled to special care and assistance. All children, whether born in or out of wedlock, shall enjoy the same social protection.

Article 26

(1) Everyone has the right to education. Education shall be free, at least in the elementary and fundamental stages. Elementary education shall be compulsory. Technical and professional education shall be made generally available and higher education shall be equally accessible to all on the basis of merit.

(2) Education shall be directed to the full development of the human personality and to the strengthening of respect for human rights and fundamental freedoms. It shall promote understanding, tolerance and friendship among all nations, racial or religious groups, and shall further the activities of the United Nations for the maintenance of peace.

(3) Parents have a prior right to choose the kind of education that shall be given to their children.

Article 27

(1) Everyone has the right freely to participate in the cultural life of the community, to enjoy the arts and to share in scientific advancement and its benefits.

(2) Everyone has the right to the protection of the moral and material interests resulting from any scientific, literary or artistic production of which he is the author.

Article 28

Everyone is entitled to a social and international order in which the rights and freedoms set forth in this Declaration can be fully realized.

Article 29

(1) Everyone has duties to the community in which alone the free and full development of his personality is possible.

(2) In the exercise of his rights and freedoms, everyone shall be subject only to such limitations as are determined by law solely for the purpose of securing due recognition and respect for the rights and freedoms of others and of meeting the just requirements of morality, public order and the general welfare in a democratic society.

(3) These rights and freedoms may in no case be exercised contrary to the purposes and principles of the United Nations.

Article 30

Nothing in this Declaration may be interpreted as implying for any State, group or person any right to engage in any activity or to perform any act aimed at the destruction of any of the rights and freedoms set forth herein.

The Irish Peace Accord (1998)

After nearly thirty years of sectarian conflict between the Roman Catholics and Protestants of Northern Ireland a peace accord was agreed upon in Belfast on April 10, 1998—Good Friday. More than thirty-two hundred people have been killed since "the troubles," as the strife is known, began. In actuality, the dispute has been more political than religious; the Protestants are predominantly "unionists," preferring to retain links to Great Britain, and the Catholics are primarily "nationalists," wishing instead to reunite Northern Ireland with the Republic of Ireland.

Eight political parties and the governments of Britain and Ireland took part in the negotiations, which continued for nearly two years. The British prime minister, Tony Blair, and his Irish counterpart, Bertie Ahern, were influential in gaining the agreement, as was U.S. president Bill Clinton, whose last-minute telephone calls to participants in the final negotiations were the culmination of several years of working toward the agreement. George Mitchell, the former U.S. Senate majority leader, won wide praise for his efforts as mediator of the talks. Other important players were David Trimble, leader of the Ulster Unionist Party; John Hume, head of the Social Democratic and Labour Party, Northern Ireland's largest Catholic party; and Gerry Adams, president of Sinn Féin, the political section of the Irish Republican Army. The leader of the Democratic Unionists, Ian Paisley, a fundamentalist Presbyterian preacher, refused to take part in the talks. Two militant Protestant groups, including Trimble's Ulster Unionist Party, the largest Protestant faction, walked out of the negotiations. Trimble, nevertheless, endorsed the agreement. Sinn Féin failed to endorse it but took part in negotiations.

Concessions were made on both sides. Although Northern Ireland is to remain part of Britain and the Republic of Ireland is to give up its territorial claims to Northern Ireland, the two entities are to work together in both the political and the economic realms. And the way has been left open for Northern Ireland to unite with the Republic of Ireland and cut its ties with Britain if the people of Northern Ireland, by majority vote, so choose. A 108-member Northern Ireland Assembly is to replace direct rule by Britain and is to be "inclusive in its membership," thus giving the residents of Northern Ireland the power to govern themselves for the first time since 1972 and assuring the Catholic minority of a greater voice in governing Northern Ireland.

A majority of voters in Northern Ireland and the Republic of Ireland approved the agreement in a referendum on May 22, 1998. Almost 95 percent of the voters in the Republic of Ireland and slightly more than 71 percent in Northern Ireland voted yes. How the vote was split between Catholics and Protestants was impossible to know because all votes were counted at one place, but an exit poll reported majority support from both groups.

The conflict now has shifted from one between Catholics and Protestants to one between those who support the agreement and those who do not. The elections held on June 25, 1998, for the Northern Ireland Assembly resulted in clear support for the agreement, with the nonsupporters winning not quite enough votes to block the peace process. Catholics and Protestants of the new assembly joined together to elect the Protestant David Trimble as first minister and the Catholic Seamus Mallon as deputy first minister. As noted by Clinton and others, the agreement represents the promise, but not the guarantee, of peace. Excerpts of the agreement follow.

Declaration of Support

1. We, the participants in the multi-party negotiations, believe that the agreement we have negotiated offers a truly historic opportunity for a new beginning.

2. The tragedies of the past have left a deep and profoundly regrettable legacy of suffering. We must never forget those who have died or been injured, and their families. But we can best honour them through a fresh start, in which we firmly dedicate ourselves to the achievement of reconciliation, tolerance, and mutual trust, and to the protection and vindication of the human rights of all.

3. We are committed to partnership, equality and mutual respect as the basis of relationships within Northern Ireland, between North and South, and between these islands.

4. We reaffirm our total and absolute commitment to exclusively democratic and peaceful means of resolving differences on political issues, and our opposition to any use or threat of force by others for any political purpose, whether in regard to this agreement or otherwise.

5. We acknowledge the substantial differences between our continuing, and equally legitimate, political aspirations. However, we will endeavour to strive in every practical way towards reconciliation and rapprochement within the framework of democratic and agreed arrangements. . . .

Constitutional Issues

1. The participants endorse the commitment made by the British and Irish Governments that, in a new British-Irish Agreement replacing the Anglo-Irish Agreement, they will:

(i) recognise the legitimacy of whatever choice is freely exercised by a majority of the people of Northern Ireland with regard to its status, whether they prefer to continue to support the Union with Great Britain or a sovereign united Ireland;

(ii) recognise that it is for the people of the island of Ireland alone, by agreement between the two parts respectively and without external impediment, to exercise their right of self-determination on the basis of consent, freely and concurrently given, North and South, to bring about a united Ireland, if that is their wish, accepting that this right must be achieved and exercised with and subject to the agreement and consent of a majority of the people of Northern Ireland;

(iii) acknowledge that while a substantial section of the people in Northern Ireland share the legitimate wish of a majority of the people of the island of Ireland for a united Ireland, the present wish of a majority of the people of Northern Ireland, freely exercised and legitimate, is to maintain the Union and, accordingly, that Northern Ireland's status as part of the United Kingdom reflects and relies upon that wish; and that it would be wrong to make any change in the status of Northern Ireland save with the consent of a majority of its people;

(iv) affirm that if, in the future, the people of the island of Ireland exercise their right of self-determination . . . to bring about a united Ireland, it will be a binding obligation on both Governments to introduce and support in their respective Parliaments legislation to give effect to that wish;

(v) affirm that whatever choice is freely exercised by a majority of the people of Northern Ireland, the power of the sovereign government with jurisdiction there shall be exercised with rigorous impartiality on behalf of all the people in the diversity of their identities and traditions and shall be founded on the principles of full respect for, and equality of, civil, political, social and cultural rights, of freedom from discrimination for all citizens, and of parity of esteem and of just and equal treatment for the identity, ethos, and aspirations of both communities;

(vi) recognise the birthright of all the people of Northern Ireland to identify themselves and be accepted as Irish or British, or both, as they may so choose, and accordingly confirm that their right to hold both British and Irish citizenship is accepted by both Governments and would not be affected by any future change in the status of Northern Ireland.

2. The participants also note that the two Governments have accordingly undertaken in the context of this comprehensive political agreement, to propose and support changes in, respectively, the Constitution of Ireland and in British legislation relating to the constitutional status of Northern Ireland. . . .

Strand One

Democratic Institutions in Northern Ireland

1. This agreement provides for a democratically elected Assembly in Northern Ireland which is inclusive in its membership, capable of exercising executive and legislative authority, and subject to safeguards to protect the rights and interests of all sides of the community. . . .

3. The Assembly will exercise full legislative and executive authority in respect of those matters currently within the responsibility of the six Northern Ireland Government Departments, with the possibility of taking on responsibility for other matters as detailed elsewhere in this agreement.

4. The Assembly—operating where appropriate on a cross-community basis—will be the prime source of authority in respect of all devolved responsibilities. . . .

34. A consultative Civic Forum will be established. It will comprise representatives of the business, trade union and voluntary sectors, and such other sectors as agreed by the First Minister and the Deputy First Minister. It will act as a consultative mechanism on social, economic and cultural issues. . . .

Strand Two

North/South Ministerial Council

1. . . . a North/South Ministerial Council to be established to bring together those with executive responsibilities in Northern Ireland and the Irish Government, to develop consultation, co-operation and action within the island of Ireland. . . .

13. It is understood that the North/South Ministerial Council and the Northern Ireland Assembly are mutually inter-dependent, and that one cannot successfully function without the other. . . .

Annex

Areas for North-South co-operation and implementation may include the following:

1. Agriculture—animal and plant health.
2. Education—teacher qualifications and exchanges.
3. Transport—strategic transport planning.
4. Environment—environmental protection, pollution, water quality, and waste management.
5. Waterways—inland waterways.

6. Social Security/Social Welfare—entitlements of cross-border workers and fraud control.

7. Tourism—promotion, marketing, research, and product development.

8. Relevant EU [European Union] Programmes. . . .

9. Inland Fisheries.

10. Aquaculture and marine matters.

11. Health: accident and emergency services and other related cross-border issues.

12. Urban and rural development.

Strand Three

British-Irish Council

1. A British-Irish Council (BIC) will be established . . . to promote the harmonious and mutually beneficial development of the totality of relationships among the peoples of these islands. . . .

5. The BIC will exchange information, discuss, consult and use best endeavours to reach agreement on co-operation on matters of mutual interest within the competence of the relevant Administrations. Suitable issues for early discussion in the BIC could include transport links, agricultural issues, environmental issues, cultural issues, health issues, education issues and approaches to EU issues. Suitable arrangements to be made for practical co-operation on agreed policies.

British-Irish Intergovernmental Conference

1. . . . a new British-Irish Agreement . . . will establish a standing British-Irish Intergovernmental Conference, which will subsume both the Anglo-Irish Intergovernmental Council and the Intergovernmental Conference established under the 1985 Agreement.

2. The Conference will bring together the British and Irish Governments to promote bilateral co-operation at all levels on all matters of mutual interest within the competence of both Governments. . . .

Rights, Safeguards and Equality of Opportunity

Human Rights

1. The parties affirm their commitment to the mutual respect, the civil rights and the religious liberties of everyone in the community. Against the background of the recent history of communal conflict, the parties affirm in particular:

the right of free political thought;

the right to freedom and expression of religion;

the right to pursue democratically national and political aspirations;

the right to seek constitutional change by peaceful and legitimate means;

the right to freely choose one's place of residence;

the right to equal opportunity in all social and economic activity, regardless of class, creed, disability, gender or ethnicity;

the right to freedom from sectarian harassment; and

the right of women to full and equal political participation. . . .

3. . . . the British Government intends, as a particular priority, to create a statutory obligation on public authorities in Northern Ireland to carry out all their functions with due regard to the need to promote equality of opportunity in relation to religion and political opinion; gender; race; disability; age; marital status; dependants; and sexual orientation. . . .

5. A new Northern Ireland Human Rights Commission, with membership from Northern Ireland reflecting the community balance, will be established . . . , independent of Government, with an extended and enhanced role beyond that currently exercised by the Standing Advisory Commission on Human Rights. . . .

9. The Irish Government will also take steps to further strengthen the protection of human rights in its jurisdiction. . . . In addition, the Irish Government will:

establish a Human Rights Commission with a mandate and remit equivalent to that within Northern Ireland;

. . . ratify the Council of Europe Framework Convention on National Minorities (already ratified by the UK);

implement enhanced employment equality legislation;

introduce equal status legislation. . . .

10. It is envisaged that there would be a joint committee of representatives of the two Human Rights Commissions, North and South, as a forum for consideration of human rights issues in the island of Ireland. . . .

12. It is recognised that victims have a right to remember as well as to contribute to a changed society. The achievement of a peaceful and just society would be the true memorial to the victims of violence. The participants particularly recognise that young people from areas affected by the troubles face particular difficulties and will support the development of special community-based initiatives based on international best practice. The provision of services that are supportive and sensitive to the needs of victims will also be a critical element and that support will need to be channelled through both statutory and community-based voluntary organisations facilitating locally-based self-help and support networks. This will require the allocation of sufficient resources, including statutory funding as necessary, to meet the needs of victims and to provide for community-based support programmes.

13. The participants recognise and value the work being done by many organisations to develop reconciliation and mutual understanding and respect between and within communities and traditions, in Northern Ireland and between North and South, and they see such work as having a vital role in consolidating peace and political agreement.

Accordingly, they pledge their continuing support to such organisations. . . . An essential aspect of the reconciliation process is the promotion of a culture of tolerance at every level of society, including initiatives to facilitate and encourage integrated education and mixed housing.

Economic, Social and Cultural Issues

1. Pending the devolution of powers to a new Northern Ireland Assembly, the British Government will pursue broad policies for sustained economic growth and stability in Northern Ireland and for promoting social inclusion, including in particular community development and the advancement of women in public life.

2. Subject to the public consultation currently under way, the British Government will make rapid progress with:

(i) a new regional development strategy for Northern Ireland. . . .

(ii) a new economic development strategy for Northern Ireland. . . .

(iii) measures on employment equality. . . .

3. All participants recognise the importance of respect, understanding and tolerance in relation to linguistic diversity, including in Northern Ireland, the Irish language, Ulster-Scots and the languages of the various ethnic communities, all of which are part of the cultural wealth of the island of Ireland.

4. In the context of active consideration currently being given to the UK signing the Council of Europe Charter for Regional or Minority Languages, the British Government will in particular in relation to the Irish language, where appropriate and where people so desire it:

take resolute action to promote the language;

facilitate and encourage the use of the language in speech and writing in public and private life where there is appropriate demand. . . .

explore urgently with the relevant British authorities, and in co-operation with the Irish broadcasting authorities, the scope for achieving more widespread availability of Teilifis na Gaeilige in Northern Ireland;

seek more effective ways to encourage and provide financial support for Irish language film and television production in Northern Ireland. . . .

5. All participants acknowledge the sensitivity of the use of symbols and emblems for public purposes, and the need in particular in creating the new institutions to ensure that such symbols and emblems are used in a manner which promotes mutual respect rather than division. . . .

Decommissioning

1. Participants recall their agreement in the Procedural Motion adopted on 24 September 1997 "that the resolution of the decommissioning issue is an indispensable part of the process of negotiation.". . .

2. They note the progress made by the Independent International Commission on Decommissioning and the Governments in developing schemes which can represent a workable basis for achieving the decommissioning of illegally-held arms in the possession of paramilitary groups. . . .

3. All participants . . . reaffirm their commitment to the total disarmament of all paramilitary organisations. They also confirm their intention to continue to work constructively . . . to achieve the decommissioning of all paramilitary arms within two years following endorsement in referendums North and South of the agreement. . . .

Security

1. The participants note that the development of a peaceful environment on the basis of this agreement can and should mean a normalisation of security arrangements and practices.

2. The British Government will make progress towards the objective of as early a return as possible to normal security arrangements in Northern Ireland, consistent with the level of threat. . . .

5. The Irish Government will initiate a wide-ranging review of the Offences Against the State Acts 1939-85 with a view to both reform and dispensing with those elements no longer required as circumstances permit.

Policing and Justice

1. The participants . . . believe that the agreement provides the opportunity for a new beginning to policing in Northern Ireland with a police service capable of attracting and sustaining support from the community as a whole. They also believe that this agreement offers a unique opportunity to bring about a new political dispensation which will recognise the full and equal legitimacy and worth of the identities, senses of allegiance and ethos of all sections of the community in Northern Ireland. They consider that this opportunity should inform and underpin the development of a police service representative in terms of the make-up of the community as a whole and which, in a peaceful environment, should be routinely unarmed. . . .

3. An independent Commission will be established to make recommendations for future policing arrangements in Northern Ireland. . . .

4. The participants believe that the aims of the criminal justice system are to:

deliver a fair and impartial system of justice to the community;

be responsive to the community's concerns, and encouraging community involvement where appropriate;

have the confidence of all parts of the community; and

deliver justice efficiently and effectively. . . .

Prisoners

1. Both Governments will put in place mechanisms to provide for an accelerated programme for the release of prisoners, including transferred prisoners, convicted of scheduled offences in Northern Ireland or, in the case of those sentenced outside Northern Ireland, similar offences (referred to hereafter as qualifying prisoners). Any such arrangements will protect the rights of individual prisoners under national and international law.

2. Prisoners affiliated to organisations which have not established or are not maintaining a complete and unequivocal ceasefire will not benefit from the arrangements. The situation in this regard will be kept under review.

3. Both Governments will complete a review process within a fixed time frame and set prospective release dates for all qualifying prisoners. The review process would provide for the advance of the release dates of qualifying prisoners while allowing account to be taken of the seriousness of the offences for which the person was convicted and the need to protect the community. In addition, the intention would be that should the circumstances allow it, any qualifying prisoners who remained in custody two years after the commencement of the scheme would be released at that point.

4. The Governments will seek to enact the appropriate legislation to give effect to these arrangements by the end of June 1998.

5. The Governments continue to recognise the importance of measures to facilitate the reintegration of prisoners into the community. . . .

Validation, Implementation and Review

Validation and Implementation

1. The two Governments will as soon as possible sign a new British-Irish Agreement replacing the 1985 Anglo-Irish Agreement, embodying understandings on constitutional issues and affirming their solemn commitment to support and, where appropriate, implement the agreement reached by the participants in the negotiations which shall be annexed to the British-Irish Agreement.

2. Each Government will organise a referendum on 22 May 1998. Subject to Parliamentary approval, a consultative referendum in Northern Ireland, organised under the terms of the Northern Ireland (Entry to Negotiations, etc.) Act 1996, will address the question: "Do you support the agreement reached in the multi-party talks on Northern Ireland and set out in Command Paper 3883?". The Irish Government will introduce and support in the Oireachtas a Bill to amend the Constitution . . . to permit the Government to ratify the new British-Irish Agreement. On passage by the Oireachtas, the Bill will be put to referendum.

3. If majorities of those voting in each of the referendums support this agreement, the Governments will then introduce and support, in their respective Parliaments, such legislation as may be necessary to give effect to all aspects of this agreement, and will take whatever ancillary steps as may be required including the holding of elections on 25 June, subject to parliamentary approval, to the Assembly, which would meet initially in a "shadow" mode. The establishment of the North-South Ministerial Council, implementation bodies, the British-Irish Council and the British-Irish Intergovernmental Conference and the assumption by the Assembly of its legislative and executive powers will take place at the same time on the entry into force of the British-Irish Agreement. . . .

Islam: Selected Readings on Religion and Politics

Islam frequently is characterized as a way of life rather than a divinely ordained religion that exists apart from politics and other aspects of society. Indeed, Islam requires that believers submit to its prescriptions for personal faith and piety, the organization of the community (*umma*) of believers, ethics, culture, a system of laws, and the function of the state.

Followers of Islam, or Muslims, are guided in all dimensions of their personal, social, and political behavior by two sources of teaching. The first, and most important, is the Qur'an, the Muslim record of Allah's (God's) revelations to the prophet Muhammad (570–632). Qur'anic rules and jurisprudential details, along with accounts of the statements and behavior of Muhammad known as the *hadith*—the second source of guidance for Muslims—are the basis for Muslim recognition of divine law (*shari'a,* or the way) and the foundation for the sociopolitical organization of Muslim societies. Militant groups and opposition parties in many Muslim countries draw on both the legal and linguistic aspects of the Qur'an as a means of legitimating their calls for social and political reform. Among its many political injunctions, the Qur'an includes rules about the obligation of rulers to consult with the people (*shura*), and by extension to set up parliamentary bodies—today known as *Majlis al-Shura*.

Islam achieved early political success, even in the time of the prophet Muhammad, and this set the pattern for the new religion being concerned with both this world and the world to come. The ideal was that Muslims formed a single community led by a caliphate (or successor to the prophet Muhammad). The reality was necessarily different with many different ruling dynasties as well as sectarian splits, the most important being that dividing the majority Sunni from the Shi'a. Most Muslims during most of the fourteen plus centuries of Islamic history have lived under at least nominally Muslim political rule. Major dynasties include the early Umayyads (661–750) followed by the Abbasids (749–1258). Early modern and modern times witnessed the long-lived Ottomans (ruling most of the Middle East and North Africa plus much of Southeast Europe from 1517 to 1924), the Safavids (1499–1722) in Iran and the Moguls (1526–1857) in the Indian subcontinent.

Beginning in the late eighteenth century Muslim political self-sufficiency began to crumble before the onslaught of an increasingly powerful Europe. By the beginning of the nineteenth century the British East India Company was consolidating its control of India, Europeans were the dominant political actors in the East Indies, the Ottomans, defeated in war, were conceding territories and privileges, and Napoleon's bold invasion of Egypt in 1798 brought an infidel army into the Muslim heartland. Since that time Muslim thinkers and political leaders have wrestled with the problem of regaining Muslim autonomy. Westernizers and fundamentalists, reformers and revolutionaries have contended for the body and soul of the Muslim *umma* (or some part thereof) over the past two centuries as illustrated by the names of such diverse individuals as Muhammad Ali, Jamal al-Din al-Afghani, Muhammad Abduh, Sir Sayyid Ahmad Khan, Kemal Atatürk, Hasan al-Banna, Sayyid Abu al-Ala Mawdudi, and Ruholla Musavi Khomeini. Many of these individuals are represented in the following readings, excerpted from sources that have been important in shaping political and religious beliefs in Islamic society.

Political Consultation, Political Authority, and Community in Islamic Society

What is with God is better and more lasting for those who believe and place their trust in their Lord . . . whose affairs are settled by mutual consultation.

Qur'an 42: 36–38

O ye who believe! Obey Allah, and obey the messenger and those of you who are in authority.

Qur'an 4: 59

"Shouldn't we fight against them [evil rulers]?" Muhammad, "No, not so long as they say their prayers."

Hadith from Sahih Muslim

"There will be leaders who will not be led by my guidance and who will not adopt my ways. There will be among them men who will have the heart of devils in bodies of human beings." When asked what one should do, Muhammad replied, "You will listen to the amir and carry out his orders, even if your back is flogged and your wealth is snatched you should listen and obey."

Hadith from Sahih Muslim

"If he [the ruler] oppresses you, be patient; if he dispossesses you, be patient."

Hadith attributed to Umar, the second caliph

"If one avenges himself after he has been wronged, there is no way of blaming him. Blame lies on those who oppress, and terrorise the land unjustly."

Qur'an 42: 41–42

If we compare the circumstances under which the Prophet of Islam appeared with those under which other prophets appeared—whether true or false—such as Jesus, Abraham, Moses, Zoroaster, Confucius, Buddha and so forth, we reach the following remarkable conclusion: all the prophets, with the exception of those of Abrahamic line, turn immediately to the existing secular power and seek association with it, hoping to propagate their religion and message in society by means of that power. By contrast, all the prophets of the Abrahamic line, from Abraham down to the Prophet of Islam, proclaim their missions in the form of rebellion against the existing secular power.

Ali Shariati, *On the Sociology of Islam*

This *Umma* of yours is a single *umma,* and I [Allah] am your Lord so worship me.

Qur'an 21: 92

And hold fast, all of you together, to the rope of Allah.

Hadith from Sahih Muslim

The hand of Allah is with the community. He who stands alone stands alone in hell.

Hadith from Mishkat al-Masabih

The believer is to the believer like [the several stones] of a building. Each supports the other.

Hadith from Sunan al-Tirmidhi

Reasons for Abolishing the Caliphate

It is easy to understand that the real intention of those who claimed that the substance of the Caliphate is temporal power was to make the people believe that the Caliphate is State and the Caliph the head of the state and, hence, in reality, the Caliph should be the head of the Turkish state. . . . I explained to the nation that for the sake of the utopia of establishing a world-wide Islamic state, the Turkish state and its handful of people cannot be subjugated to the service of a Caliph.

Kemal Atatürk, as quoted in Niyazi Berkes, *The Development of Secularism in Modern Turkey*

The Sublime Ottoman Sultanate, which possesses the Supreme Islamic Caliphate, will appertain to the eldest of the descendants of the house.

Article 3, 1876 Ottoman Constitution

His Majesty, the Sultan, as Caliph, is the protector of the Muslim religion.

Article 4, 1876 Ottoman Constitution

Observations before Abolishing the Islamic Brotherhoods in Turkey

To seek help from the dead is a disgrace to a civilized community. . . . What can be the objects of the existing brotherhoods (*tarikat*) other than to secure the well-being, in worldly and moral life, of those who follow them? I flatly refuse to believe that today, in the luminous presence of science, knowledge, and civilization in all its aspects, there exist, in the civilized community of Turkey, men so primitive as to seek their material and moral well-being from the guidance of one or another *seyh.* Gentlemen, you and the whole nation must know, and know well, that the Republic of Turkey cannot be the land of *seyhs,* dervishes, disciples and lay brothers. The straightest, truth Way (*tarikat*) is the way of civilization. To be a man, it is enough to do what civilization requires. The heads of the brotherhoods will understand this truth that I have uttered in all its clarity, and will of their own accord at once close their convents, and accept the fact that their disciples have at last come of age.

Kemal Atatürk, *Collected Speeches*

Islamic Solidarity

When men recognize the existence of the Supreme Judge . . . they will leave it entirely to the possessor of sacred power to safeguard good and repel evil. No longer will they have any need for an ethnic sentiment which has lost its purpose and whose memory has been erased from their souls; judgment belongs to Allah, the Sublime, the Magnificent.

That is the secret of the aversion which the Muslims have for manifestations of ethnic origin in every country where they live. That is why they reject all clan loyalty with the exception of Islamic sentiment and religious solidarity. The believers in Islam are preoccupied neither with their ethnic origins nor with the people of which they are a part because they are loyal to their faith; they have given up a narrow bond in favor of a universal bond: the bond of faith.

Actually, the principles of the Islamic religion are not restricted to calling man to the truth or to considering the soul only in a spiritual context which is concerned with the relationship between this world and the one to come. . . . There is more besides: Islamic principles are concerned with relationships among the believers, they explain the law in general and in detail, they define the executive power which administers the law, they determine sentences and limit their conditions; also, they are concerned with the unique goal that the holder of power ought to be the most submissive of men to the rules regulating that power which he gains neither by heritage, nor inheritance, nor by virtue of his race, tribe, material strength, or wealth. On the contrary, he acquires it only if he submits to the stipulations of the sacred law, if he has the strength to apply it, and if he judges with the concurrence of the community.

Thus, in truth, the ruler of the Muslims will be their religious, holy, and divine law which makes no distinction among peoples. This will also be the summary of the ideas of the nation. A Muslim ruler has no other privilege than that of being the most ardent of all in safeguarding the sacred law and defending it.

Jamal al-Din al-Afghani, as quoted in
The Emergence of the Modern Middle East,
edited by Robert G. Landon

The Form of Islamic Government

The fundamental difference between Islamic government, on the one hand, and constitutional monarchies and republics, on the other, is this: whereas the representatives of the people or the monarch in such regimes engage in legislation, in Islam the legislative power and competence to establish laws belongs exclusively to God Almighty. The Sacred Legislator of Islam is the sole legislative power. No one has the right to legislate and no law may be executed except the law of the Divine Legislator. It is for this reason that in an Islamic government, a simple planning body takes the place of the legislative assembly that is one of the three branches of government. This body draws up programs for the different ministries in the light of the ordinances of Islam and thereby determines how public services are to be provided across the country. . . .

Since Islamic government is a government of law, knowledge of the law is necessary for the ruler, as has been laid down in tradition. Indeed such knowledge is necessary not only for the ruler, but also for anyone holding a post or exercising some government function. The ruler, however, must surpass all others in knowledge. . . .

If the ruler is unacquainted with the contents of the law, he is not fit to rule; for if he follows the legal pronouncements of others, his power to govern will be impaired, but if, on the other hand, he does not follow such guidance, he will be unable to rule correctly and implement the laws of Islam. It is an established principle that "the *faqih* has authority over the ruler." If the ruler adheres to Islam, he must necessarily submit to the *faqih,* asking him about the laws and ordinances of Islam in order to implement them. This being the case, the true rulers are the *fuqaha* themselves, and rulership ought officially to be theirs, to apply to them, not to those who are obliged to follow the guidance of the *fuqaha* on account of their own ignorance of the law. . . .

When we say that after the Occultation, the just *faqih* has the same authority that the Most Noble Messenger and the Imams had, do not imagine that the status of the *faqih* is identical to that of the Imams and the Prophet. For here we are not speaking of status, but rather of function. By "authority" we mean government, the administration of the country, and the implementation of the sacred laws of the *shari'a.* These constitute a serious, difficult duty but do not earn anyone extraordinary status or raise him above the level of common humanity. In other words, authority here has the meaning of government, administration, and execution of law; contrary to what many people believe, it is not a privilege but a grave responsibility. The governance of the *faqih* is a rational and extrinsic matter; it exists only as a type of appointment, like the appointment of a guardian for a minor. With respect to duty and position, there is indeed no difference between the guardian of a nation and the guardian of a minor.

Islam and Revolution: Writings and Declarations of Iman Khomeini, translated and annotated by Hamid Algar (1981)

WORKS CITED

Jamal al-Din al-Afghani and Muhammad Abduh, *Al-'urwah al-Wuthga* ("The Indissolvable Bond"), in *The Emergence of the Modern Middle East,* edited by Robert G. Landon (New York: Van Nostrand and Reinhold, 1970), 105–110; Kemal Atatürk, *Collected Speeches,* trans. Bernard Lewis, in *The Emergence of Modern Turkey,* 2d ed. (New York: Oxford University Press, 1968), 410–411; Kemal Atatürk, *Nutuk,* in *The Development of Secularism in Modern Turkey,* edited by Niyazi Berkes (Toronto: McGill University Press, 1964), 459; *Islam and Revolution: Writings and Declarations of Imam Khomeini,* trans. and ann. Hamid Algar (Berkeley, Calif.: Mizan Press, 1981), 55–56, 59, 60, 62–63; Ali Shariati, *On the Sociology of Islam* (Berkeley, Calif.: Mizan Press, 1980), 66.

Roman Catholicism: Selected Readings (1891–1986)

For progressive Roman Catholics dedicated to reversing the church's image as the last refuge of monarchists, theocrats, and reactionaries, the modern Catholic social tradition effectively began in 1891 with the appearance of Pope Leo XIII's encyclical letter *Rerum Novarum* ("On the Condition of the Working Classes"), the first official statement of modern Catholic social doctrine. By systematically addressing the pressing social and economic questions of the day, such as the strengths and weaknesses of capitalist and socialist economic systems, the desirability of labor unions, and the plight of the industrial worker, *Rerum Novarum* set Catholics on a path-breaking, century-long intellectual journey that prepared them to articulate and espouse not only the rights of workers but also the desire of all peoples to be liberated from every form of oppression and discrimination based on race, religion, or class.

The church's desire to continue its heightened involvement in political and social issues played a role in the convocation, over seventy years later, of the Second Vatican Council (also known as Vatican II) on October 11, 1962. The gathering of some twenty-three hundred Catholic bishops from seventy-nine countries in Vatican City adjourned in December 1965 after producing in four momentous sessions sixteen documents that revolutionized Catholicism. Convoked by Pope John XXIII, who died in June 1963 and was succeeded by Pope Paul VI (who served until 1978), Vatican II was the twenty-first general, or ecumenical, council of the church, but only the second held since the Reformation of the sixteenth century. In contrast to Vatican I (1869–1870), which set the church firmly against the modern world, Vatican II embraced Pope John's call for *aggiornamento* (updating) and thoroughly reshaped the church's relationship to modern society.

In this vein Pope Paul VI promulgated on November 21, 1964, *Lumen Gentium* ("Light of Humanity"), which described the church as the "People of God" and introduced what some called the concept of inculturation. Informed by a sophisticated awareness of the diverse social forms Christianity has taken over the two millennia of its history, inculturation is a process by which the Gospel is adapted to a particular culture. Rome recognized that a monolithic European model was ill-suited to a culturally diverse church thriving on five continents. Catholics began to rethink their methods and purposes in preaching the Gospel to people inside and outside the church's visible institutional borders.

A second document, *Gaudium et Spes,* promulgated by Pope Paul VI on December 7, 1965, declared the church's openness to and respect for all human cultures. Indeed, it aligned the church with the social, political, and economic aspirations of all people seeking equality and opportunity for self-improvement. After the concept was discussed in *Gaudium et Spes,* the pastoral constitution of the Second Vatican Council, popes, bishops, theologians, and missionaries gradually worked out the pastoral and ecclesiological implications of inculturation. Pope Leo XIII may have inaugurated the Catholic social tradition, but certain documents of Vatican II—especially *Gaudium et Spes*—placed it at the very center of Catholicism's understanding of its mission, doctrinal teaching, and pastoral practice.

The political legacy of Vatican II has been complex and contested. In Latin America the council's unequivocal identification of the church's aspirations with those of the poor and oppressed led not only to the articulation of the "preferential option for the poor" by Catholic bishops meeting in Medellín, Colombia, in 1968, but also to a far more controversial development—the rise of liberation theology, in which Christian Scripture and tradition are interpreted as calling first and foremost for the liberation of the oppressed from all forms of social and economic injustice. Two documents were issued by the conference. The document entitled *Justice* called for changing the structures producing injustice in Latin American countries—families, the economy, organizations of workers, the conditions of rural life, and industrialization. It also called for political reform leading to greater citizen participation in political processes. And, no less important, the document expressed the hope that social conscience would arise in various sectors of society, bring about a new emphasis on religious values, and spark social harmony among the peoples of Latin America. The document entitled *Peace* focused on the unjust situations that promote tensions inhibiting the development of peace. Tensions were evident in the friction between social classes, in the relationship between international complications and external neocolonialism, and in the relationships among the Latin American countries themselves. In the 1980s Pope John Paul II (who began his tenure in 1978) and Cardinal Joseph Ratzinger, prefect of the Vatican's Congregation for the Doctrine of the Faith, criticized liberation theology for its reliance on Marxist ideas and class analysis. Many theologians in North America and Latin America, however, rejected this criticism or deemed it misplaced.

In 1971 a synod of Catholic bishops meeting in Rome to reflect on the legacy of Vatican II issued *Justice in the World,* expressing Catholicism's commitment to political and social change. The document, praised for its realistic, substantive nature in contrast to that of some earlier papal proclamations, lent new credence to the Vatican's stance on political and social issues. As a result, it provided strong support for those working within the church to strengthen its involvement in the problems of world peace and justice.

The controversy stemming from the 1968 Medellín conference was matched in later years by that surrounding the role of national episcopal conferences and their growing participation in shaping political discourse. In the United States, for example, the National Conference of Catholic Bishops, after consulting qualified lay Catholics (and non-Catholics) on the technical aspects of the topics in question, issued major pastoral letters on the nuclear arms race (*The Challenge of Peace,* 1983) and on the U.S. economy (*Economic Justice for All,* 1986). *Economic Justice for All* was drafted over five years by an ad hoc committee of bishops, based on extensive research and public hearings. The document rests on three premises: first, human dignity is the measure against which every economic and policy decision and institution must be judged; second, because human dignity can be realized only in a community, every person has the right to participate in the economic life of society; and, third, all members of society have a special obligation to the poor and disadvantaged.

Rerum Novarum *("On the Condition of the Working Classes")*

(Encyclical Letter of Pope Leo XIII, Issued May 15, 1891)

1. Once the passion for revolutionary change was aroused—a passion long disturbing governments—it was bound to follow sooner or later that eagerness for change would pass from the political sphere over into the related field of economics. In fact, new developments in industry, new techniques striking out on new paths, changed relations of employer and employee, abounding wealth among a very small number and destitution among the masses, increased self-reliance on the part of workers as well as a closer bond of union with one another, and, in addition to all this, a decline in morals have caused conflict to break forth. . . .

6. After the old trade guilds had been destroyed in the last century, and no protection was substituted in their place, and when public institutions and legislation had cast off traditional religious teaching, it gradually came about that the present age handed over the workers, each alone and defenseless, to the inhumanity of employers and the unbridled greed of competitors. A devouring usury, although often condemned by the Church, but practiced nevertheless under another form by avaricious and grasping men, has increased the evil; and in addition the whole process of production as well as trade in every kind of goods has been brought almost entirely under the power of a few, so that a very few rich and exceedingly rich men have laid a yoke almost of slavery on the unnumbered masses of non-owning workers.

7. To cure this evil, the Socialists, exciting the envy of the poor toward the rich, contend that it is necessary to do away with private possession of goods and in its place to make the goods of individuals common to all, and that the men who preside over a municipality or who direct the entire State should act as administrators of these goods. They hold that, by such a transfer of private goods from private individuals to the community, they can cure the present evil through dividing wealth and benefits equally among the citizens.

8. But their program is so unsuited for terminating the conflict that it actually injures the workers themselves. Moreover, it is highly unjust, because it violates the rights of lawful owners, perverts the function of the State, and throws governments into utter confusion.

9. Clearly the essential reason why those who engage in any gainful occupation undertake labor, and at the same time the end to which workers immediately look, is to procure property for themselves and to retain it by individual right as theirs and as their very own. When the worker places his energy and his labor at the disposal of another, he does so for the purpose of getting the means necessary for livelihood. He seeks in return for the work done, accordingly, a true and full right not only to demand his wage but to dispose of it as he sees fit. Therefore, if he saves something by restricting expenditures and invests his savings in a piece of land in order to keep the fruit of his thrift more safe, a holding of this kind is certainly nothing else than his wage under a different form; and on this account land which the worker thus buys is necessarily under his full control as much as the wage which he earned by his labor. But, as is obvious, it is clearly in this that the ownership of movable and immovable goods consists. Therefore, inasmuch as the Socialists seek to transfer the goods of private persons to the community at large, they make the lot of all wage earners worse, because in abolishing the freedom to dispose of wages

they take away from them by this very act the hope and the opportunity of increasing their property and of securing advantages for themselves. . . .

10. But, what is of more vital concern, they propose a remedy openly in conflict with justice, inasmuch as nature confers on man the right to possess things privately as his own.

28. It is a capital evil with respect to the question We are discussing to take for granted that the one class of society is of itself hostile to the other, as if nature had set rich and poor against each other to fight fiercely in implacable war. This is so abhorrent to reason and truth that the exact opposite is true; for just as in the human body the different members harmonize with one another, whence arises that disposition of parts and proportion in the human figure rightly called symmetry, so likewise nature has commanded in the case of the State that the two classes mentioned should agree harmoniously and should properly form equally balanced counterparts to each other. Each needs the other completely: neither capital can do without labor, nor labor without capital. Concord begets beauty and order in things. Conversely, from perpetual strife there must arise disorder accompanied by bestial cruelty. But for putting an end to conflict and for cutting away its very roots, there is wondrous and multiple power in Christian institutions.

29. And first and foremost, the entire body of religious teaching and practice, of which the Church is interpreter and guardian, can pre-eminently bring together and unite the rich and the poor by recalling the two classes of society to their mutual duties, and in particular to those duties which derive from justice.

30. Among these duties the following concern the poor and the workers: To perform entirely and conscientiously whatever work has been voluntarily and equitably agreed upon; not in any way to injure the property or to harm the person of employers; in protecting their own interests, to refrain from violence and never to engage in rioting; not to associate with vicious men who craftily hold out exaggerated hopes and make huge promises, a course usually ending in vain regrets and in the destruction of wealth.

31. The following duties, on the other hand, concern rich men and employers: Workers are not to be treated as slaves; justice demands that the dignity of human personality be respected in them, ennobled as it has been through what we call the Christian character. If we hearken to natural reason and to Christian philosophy, gainful occupations are not a mark of shame to man, but rather of respect, as they provide him with an honorable means of supporting life. It is shameful and inhuman, however, to use men as things for gain and to put no more value on them than what they are worth in muscle and energy. Likewise it is enjoined that the religious interests and the spiritual well-being of the workers receive proper consideration. Wherefore, it is the duty of employers to see that the worker is free for adequate periods to attend to his religious obligations; not to expose anyone to corrupting influences or the enticements of sin, and in no way to alienate him from care for his family and the practice of thrift. Likewise, more work is not to be imposed than strength can endure, nor that kind of work which is unsuited to a worker's age or sex.

32. Among the most important duties of employers the principal one is to give every worker what is justly due him. Assuredly, to establish a rule of pay in accord with justice, many factors must be taken into account. But, in general, the rich and employers must remember that no laws, either human or divine, permit them for their own profit to oppress the needy and the wretched or to seek gain from another's want. . . .

48. [T]hose governing the State ought primarily to devote themselves to the service of individual groups and of the whole commonwealth, and through the entire scheme of laws and institutions to cause both public and individual well-being to develop spontaneously out of the very structure and administration of the State. For this is the duty of wise statesmanship and the essential office of those in charge of the State. Now, States are made prosperous especially by wholesome morality, properly ordered family life, protection of religion and justice, moderate imposition and equitable distribution of public burdens, progressive development of industry and trade, thriving agriculture, and by all other things of this nature, which the more actively they are promoted, the better and happier the life of the citizens is destined to be. Therefore, by virtue of these things, it is within the competence of the rulers of the State that, as they benefit other groups, they also improve in particular the condition of the workers. Furthermore, they do this with full right and without laying themselves open to any charge of unwarranted interference. For the State is bound by the very law of its office to serve the common interest. And the richer the benefits which come from this general providence on the part of the State, the less necessary it will be to experiment with other measures for the well-being of workers.

49. This ought to be considered, as it touches the question more deeply, namely, that the State has one basic purpose for existence, which embraces in common the highest and the lowest of its members. Non-owning workers are unquestionably citizens by nature in virtue of the same right as the rich, that is, true and vital parts whence, through the medium of families, the body of the State is constituted; and it hardly need be added that they are by far the greatest number in every urban area. Since it would be quite absurd to look out for one portion of the citizens and to neglect another, it follows that public authority ought to exercise due care in safe-guarding the well-being and the interests of non-owning workers. . . .

If, therefore, any injury has been done to or threatens either the common good or the interests of individual groups, which injury cannot in any other way be repaired or prevented, it is necessary for public authority to intervene.

53. It is vitally important to public as well as to private welfare that there be peace and good order; likewise, that the whole regime of family life be directed according to the ordinances of God and

the principles of nature, that religion be observed and cultivated, that sound morals flourish in private and public life, that justice be kept sacred and that no one be wronged with impunity by another, and that strong citizens grow up, capable of supporting, and, if necessary, of protecting the State. Wherefore, if at any time disorder should threaten because of strikes or concerted stoppages of work, if the natural bonds of family life should be relaxed among the poor, if religion among the workers should be outraged by failure to provide sufficient opportunity for performing religious duties, if in factories danger should assail the integrity of morals through the mixing of the sexes or other pernicious incitements to sin, or if the employer class should oppress the working class with unjust burdens or should degrade them with conditions inimical to human personality or to human dignity, if health should be injured by immoderate work and such as is not suited to sex or age—in all these cases, the power and authority of the law, but of course within certain limits, manifestly ought to be employed. And these limits are determined by the same reason which demands the aid of the law, that is, the law ought not to undertake more, nor it go farther, than the remedy of evils or the removal of danger requires.

54. Rights indeed, by whomsoever possessed, must be religiously protected; and public authority, in warding off injuries and punishing wrongs, ought to see to it that individuals may have and hold what belongs to them. In protecting the rights of private individuals, however, special consideration must be given to the weak and the poor. For the nation, as it were, of the rich, is guarded by its own defenses and is in less need of governmental protection, whereas the suffering multitude, without the means to protect itself, relies especially on the protection of the State. Wherefore, since wage workers are numbered among the great mass of the needy, the State must include them under its special care and foresight.

55. But it will be well to touch here expressly on certain matters of special importance. The capital point is this, that private property ought to be safeguarded by the sovereign power of the State and through the bulwark of its laws. And especially, in view of such a great flaming up of passion at the present time, the masses ought to be kept within the bounds of their moral obligations. For while justice does not oppose our striving for better things, on the other hand, it does forbid anyone to take from another what is his and, in the name of a certain absurd equality, to seize forcibly the property of others; nor does the interest of the common good itself permit this. Certainly, the great majority of working people prefer to secure better conditions by honest toil, without doing wrong to anyone. Nevertheless, not a few individuals are found who, imbued with evil ideas and eager for revolution, use every means to stir up disorder and incite to violence. The authority of the State, therefore, should intervene and, by putting restraint upon such disturbers, protect the morals of workers from their corrupting arts and lawful owners from the danger of spoliation.

56. Labor which is too long and too hard and the belief that pay is inadequate not infrequently give workers cause to strike and become voluntarily idle. This evil, which is frequent and serious, ought to be remedied by public authority, because such interruption of work inflicts damage not only upon employers and upon the workers themselves, but also injures trade and commerce and the general interests of the State; and, since it is usually not far removed from violence and rioting, it very frequently jeopardizes public peace. In this matter it is more effective and salutary that the authority of the law anticipate and completely prevent the evil from breaking out by removing early the causes from which it would seem that conflict between employers and workers is bound to arise. . . .

59. Now as concerns the protection of corporeal and physical goods, the oppressed workers, above all, ought to be liberated from the savagery of greedy men, who inordinately use human beings as things for gain. Assuredly, neither justice nor humanity can countenance the exaction of so much work that the spirit is dulled from excessive toil and that along with it the body sinks crushed from exhaustion. The working energy of a man, like his entire nature, is circumscribed by definite limits beyond which it cannot go. . . . With respect to daily work, therefore, care ought to be taken not to extend it beyond the hours that human strength warrants. . . .

60. Finally, it is not right to demand of a woman or a child what a strong adult man is capable of doing or would be willing to do. Nay, as regards children, special care ought to be taken that the factory does not get hold of them before age has sufficiently matured their physical, intellectual, and moral powers. . . . Certain occupations, likewise, are less fitted for women. . . .

61. We shall now touch upon a matter of very great importance. . . . We are told that free consent fixes the amount of a wage; that therefore the employer, after paying the wage agreed to would seem to have discharged his obligation and not to owe anything more; that only then would injustice be done if either the employer should refuse to pay the whole amount of the wage, or the worker should refuse to perform all the work to which he had committed himself; and that in those cases, but in no others, is it proper for the public authority to safeguard the rights of each party.

62. An impartial judge would not assent readily or without reservation to this reasoning, because it is not complete in all respects; one factor to be considered, and one of the greatest importance, is missing. To work is to expend one's energy for the purpose of securing the things necessary for the various needs of life and especially for its preservation. . . . Accordingly, in man sweat labor has two marks, as it were, implanted by nature, so that it is truly personal, because work energy inheres in the person and belongs completely to him by whom it is expended, and for whose use it is destined by nature; and secondly, that it is necessary, because man has need of the fruit of his labors to preserve his life, and nature itself, which must be most strictly obeyed, commands him to preserve it. If labor should be considered only under the aspect that it is personal, there is no doubt that it would be entirely in the worker's power to set the amount of the agreed wage at too low a figure. For inasmuch as he performs work by his own free will, he can also by his own free will be satisfied with either a paltry wage for his work or even with none at all. But this matter must be judged

far differently, if with the factor of personality we combine the factor of necessity, from which indeed the former is separable in thought but not in reality. In fact, to preserve one's life is a duty common to all individuals, and to neglect this duty is a crime. Hence arises necessarily the right of securing things to sustain life, and only a wage earned by his labor gives a poor man the means to acquire these things.

63. Let it be granted then that worker and employer may enter freely into agreements and, in particular, concerning the amount of the wage; yet there is always underlying such agreements an element of natural justice, and one greater and more ancient than the free consent of contracting parties, namely, that the wage shall not be less than enough to support a worker who is thrifty and upright. . . .

68. Finally, employers and workers themselves can accomplish much in this matter, manifestly through those institutions by the help of which the poor are opportunely assisted and the two classes of society are brought closer to each other. Under this category come associations for giving mutual aid; various agencies established by the foresight of private persons to care for the worker and likewise for his dependent wife and children in the event that an accident, sickness, or death befalls him; and foundations to care for boys and girls, for adolescents, and for the aged.

69. But associations of workers occupy first place, and they include within their circle clearly all the rest. The beneficent achievements of the guilds of artisans among our ancestors have long been well known. Truly, they yielded noteworthy advantages not only to artisans, but, as many monuments bear witness, brought glory and progress to the arts themselves. In our present age of greater culture, with its new customs and ways of living, and with the increased number of things required by daily life, it is most clearly necessary that workers' associations be adapted to meet the present need. It is gratifying that societies of this kind composed either of workers alone or of workers and employers together are being formed everywhere, and it is truly to be desired that they grow in number and in active vigor. . . .

Lumen Gentium ("Light of Humanity"), Dogmatic Constitution on the Church

(Proclaimed by Pope Paul VI, November 21, 1964)

Chapter II: The People of God

9. At all times and in every race, anyone who fears God and does what is right has been acceptable to him *(cf. Acts 10:35)*. He has, however, willed to make men holy and save them, not as individuals without any bond or link between them, but rather to make them into a people who might acknowledge him and serve him in holiness. He therefore chose the Israelite race to be his own people and established a covenant with it. He gradually instructed this people—in its history manifesting both himself and the decree of his will—and made it holy unto himself. All these things, however, happened as a preparation and figure of that new and perfect covenant which was to be ratified in Christ, and of the fuller revelation which was to be given through the Word of God made flesh. "Behold the days are coming, says the Lord, when I will make a new covenant with the house of Israel and the house of Judah . . . I will put my law within them, and I will write it upon their hearts, and they shall be my people . . . For they shall all know me from the least of them to the greatest, says the Lord" *(Jer. 31:31–34)*. Christ instituted this new covenant, namely the new covenant in his blood *(cf. 1 Cor. 11: 25)*; he called a race made up of Jews and Gentiles which would be one, not according to the flesh, but in the Spirit, and this race would be the new People of God. . . .

13. All men are called to belong to the new People of God. This People therefore, whilst remaining one and only one, is to be spread throughout the whole world and to all ages in order that the design of God's will may be fulfilled: he made human nature one in the beginning and has decreed that all his children who were scattered should be finally gathered together as one *(cf. John 11:52)*. It was for this purpose that God sent his Son, whom he appointed heir of all things *(cf. Heb. 1:2)*, that he might be teacher, king and priest of all, the head of the new and universal People of God's sons. This, too, is why God sent the Spirit of his Son, the Lord and Giver of Life. The Spirit is, for the Church and for each and every believer, the principle of their union and unity in the teaching of the apostles and fellowship, in the breaking of bread and prayer *(cf. Acts 2:42 Gk.)*.

The one People of God is accordingly present in all the nations of the earth, since its citizens, who are taken from all nations, are of a kingdom whose nature is not earthly but heavenly. All the faithful scattered throughout the world are in communion with each other in the Holy Spirit so that "he who dwells in Rome knows those in most distant parts to be his members". . . . Since the kingdom of Christ is not of this world *(cf. Jn. 18:36)*, the Church or People of God which establishes this kingdom does not take away anything from the temporal welfare of any people. Rather she fosters and takes to herself, in so far as they are good, the abilities, the resources and customs of peoples. In so taking them to herself she purifies, strengthens and elevates them. The Church indeed is mindful that she must work with that king to whom the nations were given for an inheritance (cf. Ps. 2:8) and to whose city gifts are brought *(cf. Ps. 71[72]: 10; Is. 60:4–7; Apoc. 21:24)*. This character of universality which adorns the People of God is a gift from the Lord himself whereby the Catholic ceaselessly and efficaciously seeks for the return of all humanity and all its goods under Christ the Head in the unity of his Spirit. . . . In virtue of this catholicity each part contributes its own gifts to other parts and to the whole Church, so that the whole and each of the parts are strengthened by the common sharing of all things and by the common effort to attain to fullness in unity. Hence it is that the People of God is not only an assembly of various peoples, but in itself is made up of different ranks. This diversity among its members is either by reason of their duties—some exercise the sacred ministry for the good of their brethren—or it is due to their condition and manner of life—many enter the religious state and, intending to sanctity by the narrower way, stimulate their brethren by their example. Holding a rightful place in the communion of the Church there are also particular Churches that retain their own traditions, without prejudice to the Chair of Peter which presides over the whole assembly of charity, . . . and protects their legitimate variety while at the same time taking care that these differences do not hinder unity, but rather contribute to it. Finally, between all the various parts of the Church there is a bond of close communion whereby spiritual riches, apostolic workers and temporal resources are shared. For the members of the People of God are called upon to share their goods, and the words of the apostle apply also to each of the Churches, "according to the gift that each has received, administer it to one another as good stewards of the manifold grace of God" *(1 Pet. 5:10)*.

All men are called to this catholic unity which prefigures and promotes universal peace. And in different ways to it belong, or are related: the Catholic faithful, others who believe in Christ, and finally all mankind, called by God's grace to salvation.

14. This holy Council first of all turns its attention to the Catholic faithful. Basing itself on scripture and tradition, it teaches that the Church, a pilgrim now on earth, is necessary for salvation: the one Christ is mediator and the way of salvation; he is present to us in his body which is the Church. He himself explicitly asserted the necessity of faith and baptism *(cf. Mk. 16:16; Jn. 3:5)*, and thereby affirmed at the same time the necessity of the Church which men enter through baptism as through a door. Hence they could not be saved who, knowing that the Catholic Church was founded as necessary by God through Christ, would refuse either to enter it, or to remain in it.

Fully incorporated into the Church are those who, possessing the Spirit of Christ, accept all the means of salvation given to the Church together with her entire organization, and who—by the bonds constituted by the profession of faith, the sacraments, ecclesiastical government, and communion—are joined in the visible structure of the Church of Christ, who rules her through the Supreme Pontiff and the bishops. Even though incorporated into the Church, one who does not however persevere in charity is not saved. He remains indeed in the bosom of the Church, but "in body" not "in heart." . . . All children of the Church should nevertheless remember that their exalted condition results, not from their own merits, but from the grace of Christ. If they fail to respond in thought, word and deed to that grace, not only shall they not be saved, but they shall be the more severely judged. . . .

Catechumens who, moved by the Holy Spirit, desire with an explicit intention to be incorporated into the Church, are by that very intention joined to her. With love and solicitude mother Church already embraces them as her own.

15. The Church knows that she is joined in many ways to the baptized who are honored by the name of Christian, but who do not however profess the Catholic faith in its entirety or have not preserved unity or communion under the successor of Peter. . . . For there are many who hold sacred scripture in honor as a rule of faith and of life, who have a sincere religious zeal, who lovingly believe in God the Father Almighty and in Christ, the Son of God and the Saviour, . . . who are sealed by baptism which unites them to Christ, and who indeed recognize and receive other sacraments in their own Churches or ecclesiastical communities. Many of them possess the episcopate, celebrate the holy Eucharist and cultivate devotion of the Virgin Mother of God. . . . There is furthermore a sharing in prayer and spiritual benefits; these Christians are indeed in some real way joined to us in the Holy Spirit for, by his gifts and graces, his sanctifying power is also active in them and he has strengthened some of them even to the shedding of their blood. And so the Spirit stirs up desires and actions in all of Christ's disciples in order that all may be peaceably united, as Christ ordained, in one flock under one shepherd. . . . Mother Church never ceases to pray, hope and work that this may be achieved, and she exhorts her children to purification and renewal so that the sign of Christ may shine more brightly over the face of the Church.

16. Finally, those who have not yet received the Gospel are related to the People of God in various ways. . . . There is, first, that people to which the covenants and promises were made, and from which Christ was born according to the flesh *(cf. Rom. 9:4–5)*: in view of the divine choice, they are a people most dear for the sake of the fathers, for the gifts of God are without repentance *(cf. Rom. 11:29)*. But the plan of salvation also includes those who acknowledge the Creator, in the first place amongst whom are the Moslems: these profess to hold the faith of Abraham, and together with us they adore the one, merciful God, mankind's judge on the last day. Nor is God remote from those who in shadows and images seek the unknown God, since he gives to all men life and breath and all things *(cf. Acts 17:25–28)*, and since the Savior wills all men to be saved *(cf. 1 Tim. 2:4)*. Those who, through no fault of their own, do not know the Gospel of Christ or his Church, but who nevertheless seek God with a sincere heart, and, moved by grace, try in their actions to do his will as they know it through the dictates of their conscience—those too may achieve eternal salvation. . . . Nor shall divine providence deny the assistance necessary for salvation to those who, without any fault of theirs, have not yet arrived at an explicit knowledge of God, and who, not without grace, strive to lead a good life. Whatever good or truth is found amongst them is considered by the Church to be a preparation for the Gospel . . . and given by him who enlightens all men that they may at length have life. But very often, deceived by the Evil One, men have become vain in their reasonings, have exchanged the truth of God for a lie and served the world rather than the Creator *(cf. Rom. 1:21 and 25)*. Or else, living and dying in this world without God, they are exposed to ultimate despair. Hence to procure the glory of God and the salvation of all these, the Church, mindful of the Lord's command, "preach the Gospel to every creature" *(Mk. 16:16)* takes zealous care to foster the missions.

17. As he had been sent by the Father, the Son himself sent the apostles *(cf. Jn. 20:21)* saying, "go, therefore, and make disciples of all nations, baptizing them in the name of the Father, and of the Son, and of the Holy Spirit, teaching them to observe all that I have commanded you; and behold I am with you all days even unto the

consummation of the world" *(Mt. 28:18–20)*. The Church has received this solemn command of Christ from the apostles, and she must fulfill it to the very ends of the earth *(cf. Acts 1:8)*. Therefore, she makes the words of the apostle her own, "Woe to me if I do not preach the Gospel" *(1 Cor. 9:16)*, and accordingly never ceases to send heralds of the Gospel until each time as the infant Churches are fully established, and can themselves continue the work of evangelization. For the Church is driven by the Holy Spirit to do her part for the full realization of the plan of God, who has constituted Christ as the source of salvation for the whole world. By her proclamation of the Gospel, she draws her hearers to receive and profess the faith, she prepares them for baptism, snatches them from the slavery of error, and she incorporates them into Christ so that in love for him they grow to full maturity. The effect of her work is that whatever good is found sown in the minds and hearts of men or in the rites and customs of peoples, these not only are preserved from destruction, but are purified, raised up, and perfected for the glory of God, the confusion of the devil, and the happiness of man. Each disciple of Christ has the obligation of spreading the faith to the best of his ability. . . . But if any believer can baptize, it is for the priests to complete the building up of the body in the eucharistic sacrifice, thus fulfilling the words of the prophet, "From the rising of the sun, even to going down, my name is great among the gentiles. And in every place there is a sacrifice, and there is offered to my name a clean offering" *(Mal. 1:11)*. . . . Thus the Church prays and likewise labors so that into the People of God, the Body of the Lord and the Temple of the Holy Spirit, may pass the fullness of the whole world, and that in Christ, the head of all things, all honor and glory may be rendered to the Creator, the Father of the universe. . . .

Gaudium et Spes (Joys and Hopes), Pastoral Constitution on the Church in the Modern World

(Promulgated by Pope Paul VI, December 7, 1965)

Preface

1. The joys and the hopes, the griefs and the anxieties of the men of this age, especially those who are poor or in any way afflicted, these are the joys and hopes, the griefs and anxieties of the followers of Christ. Indeed, nothing genuinely human fails to raise an echo in their hearts. For theirs is a community composed of men. . . .

2. Hence this Second Vatican Council, having probed more profoundly into the mystery of the Church, now addresses itself without hesitation, not only to the sons of the Church and to all who invoke the name of Christ, but to the whole of humanity. For the council yearns to explain to everyone how it conceives of the presence and activity of the Church in the world of today.

Therefore, the council focuses its attention on the world of men, the whole human family along with the sum of those realities in the midst of which it lives. . . .

3. Though mankind is stricken with wonder at its own discoveries and its power, it often raises anxious questions about the current trend of the world, about the place and role of man in the universe, about the meaning of its individual and collective strivings, and about the ultimate destiny of reality and of humanity. . . . The council brings to mankind light kindled from the Gospel, and puts at its disposal those saving resources which the Church herself, under the guidance of the Holy Spirit, receives from her Founder. For the human person deserves to be preserved; human society deserves to be renewed. Hence the focal point of our total presentation will be man himself, whole and entire, body and soul, heart and conscience, mind and will. . . .

Introductory Statement: The Situation of Men in The Modern World

4. To carry out such a task, the Church has always had the duty of scrutinizing the signs of the times and of interpreting them in the light of the Gospel. Thus, in language intelligible to each generation, she can respond to the perennial questions which men ask about this present life and the life to come, and about the relationship of the one to the other. We must therefore recognize and understand the world in which we live, its explanations, its longings, and its often dramatic characteristics. Some of the main features of the modern world can be sketched as follows. Today, the human race is involved in a new stage of history. Profound and rapid changes are spreading by degrees around the whole world. Triggered by the intelligence and creative energies of man, these changes recoil upon him, upon his decisions and desires, both individual and collective, and upon his manner of thinking and acting with respect to things and to people. Hence we can already speak of a true cultural and social transformation, one which has repercussions on man's religious life as well. As happens in any crisis of growth, this transformation has brought serious difficulties in its wake. Thus while man extends his power in every direction, he does not always succeed in subjecting it to his own welfare. Striving to probe more profoundly into the deeper recesses of his own mind, he frequently appears more unsure of himself. Gradually and more precisely he lays bare the laws of society, only to be paralyzed by uncertainty about the direction to give it. Never has the human race enjoyed such an abundance of wealth, resources and economic power, and yet a huge proportion of the world's citizens are still tormented by hunger and poverty, while countless numbers suffer from total illiteracy. Never before has man had so keen an understanding of freedom, yet at the same time new forms of social and psychological slavery make their appearance. Although the world of today has a very vivid awareness of its unity and of how one man depends on another in needful solidarity, it is most grievously turned into opposing camps by conflicting forces. For political, social, economic, racial and ideological disputes still continue bitterly, and with them the peril of a war which would reduce everything to ashes. True, there is a growing exchange of ideas, but the very words by which key concepts are expressed take on quite different meanings in diverse ideological systems. Finally, man painstakingly searches for a better world, without a corresponding spiritual advancement. Influenced by such a variety of complexities, many of our contemporaries are kept from accurately identifying perma-

nent values and adjusting them properly to fresh discoveries. As a result, buffeted between hope and anxiety and pressing one another with questions about the present course of events, they are burdened down with uneasiness. This same course of events leads men to look for answers; indeed, it forces them to do so. . . .

Chapter I: The Dignity of the Human Person

12. According to the almost unanimous opinion of believers and unbelievers alike, all things on earth should be related to man as their center and crown. But what is man? About himself he has expressed, and continues to express, many divergent and even contradictory opinions. In these he often exalts himself as the absolute measure of all things or debases himself to the point of despair. The result is doubt and anxiety. The Church certainly understands these problems. Endowed with light from God, she can offer solutions to them, so that man's true situation can be portrayed and his defects explained, while at the same time his dignity and destiny are justly acknowledged. . . .

Section II: Setting Up an International Community

83. In order to build up peace above all, the causes of discord among men, especially injustice, which foment wars, must be rooted out. Not a few of these causes come from excessive economic inequalities and from putting off the steps needed to remedy them. Other causes of discord, however, have their source in the desire to dominate and in a contempt for persons. And, if we look for deeper causes, we find them in human envy, distrust, pride, and other egotistical passions. Man cannot bear so many ruptures in the harmony of things. Consequently, the world is constantly beset by strife and violence between men, even when no war is being waged. Besides, since these same evils are present in the relations between various nations as well, in order to overcome or forestall them and to keep violence once unleashed within limits it is absolutely necessary for countries to cooperate more advantageously and more closely together and to organize together international bodies and to work tirelessly for the creation of organizations which will foster peace.

84. In view of the increasingly close ties of mutual dependence today between all the inhabitants and peoples of the earth, the apt pursuit and efficacious attainment of the universal common good now require of the community of nations that it organize itself in a manner suited to its present responsibilities, especially toward the many parts of the world which are still suffering from unbearable want. To reach this goal, organizations of the international community, for their part, must make provision for men's different needs, both in the fields of social life—such as food supplies, health, education, labor—and also in certain special circumstances which can crop up here and there, e.g., the need to promote the general improvement of developing countries, or to alleviate the distressing conditions in which refugees dispersed throughout the world find themselves, or also to assist migrants and their families. Already existing international and regional organizations are certainly well-deserving of the human race. These are the first efforts at laying the foundations on an international level for a community of all men to work for the solution to the serious problems of our times, to encourage progress everywhere, and to obviate wars of whatever kind. In all of these activities the Church takes joy in the spirit of true brotherhood flourishing between Christians and non-Christians as it strives to make ever more strenuous efforts to relieve abundant misery.

85. The present solidarity of mankind also calls for a revival of greater international cooperation in the economic field. Although nearly all peoples have become autonomous, they are far from being free of every form of undue dependence, and far from escaping all danger of serious internal difficulties. The development of a nation depends on human and financial aids. The citizens of each country must be prepared by education and professional training to discharge the various tasks of economic and social life. But this in turn requires the aid of foreign specialists who, when they give aid, will not act as overlords, but as helpers and fellow-workers. Developing nations will not be able to procure material assistance unless radical changes are made in the established procedures of modern world commerce. Other aid should be provided as well by advanced nations in the form of gifts, loans or financial investments. Such help should be accorded with generosity and without greed on the one side, and received with complete honesty on the other side. If an authentic economic order is to be established on a world-wide basis, an end will have to be put to profiteering, to national ambitions, to the appetite for political supremacy, to militaristic calculations, and to machinations for the sake of spreading and imposing ideologies.

86. The following norms seem useful for such cooperation:

a) Developing nations should take great pains to seek as the object for progress to express and secure the total human fulfillment of their citizens. They should bear in mind that progress arises and grows above all out of the labor and genius of the nations themselves because it has to be based, not only on foreign aid, but especially on the full utilization of their own resources, and on the development of their own culture and traditions. Those who exert the greatest influence on others should be outstanding in this respect.

b) On the other hand, it is a very important duty of the advanced nations to help the developing nations in discharging their above-mentioned responsibilities. They should therefore gladly carry out on their own home front those spiritual and material readjustments that are required for the realization of this universal cooperation. Consequently, in business dealings with weaker and poorer nations, they should be careful to respect their profit, for these countries need the income they receive on the sale of their homemade products to support themselves.

c) It is the role of the international community to coordinate and promote development, but in such a way that the resources earmarked for this purpose will be allocated as effectively as possible, and with complete equity. It is likewise this community's duty, with due regard for the principle of subsidiarity, so to regulate economic relations throughout the world that these will be carried out in accordance with the norms of justice. Suitable organizations should be set up to foster and regulate international business affairs, particularly with the underdeveloped countries, and to compensate for losses resulting from an excessive inequality of power among the various nations. This type of organization, in unison with technical, cultural and financial aid, should provide the help which developing nations need so that they can advantageously pursue their own economic advancement.

d) In many cases there is an urgent need to revamp economic and social structures. But one must guard against proposals of technical solutions that are untimely. This is particularly true of those solutions providing man with material conveniences, but nevertheless contrary to man's spiritual nature and advancement. For "not by bread alone does man live, but by every word which proceeds from the mouth of God" *(Matt. 4:4)*. Every sector of the family of man carries within itself and in its best traditions some portion of the spiritual treasure entrusted by God to humanity, even though many may not be aware of the source from which it comes.

87. International cooperation is needed today especially for those peoples who, besides facing so many other difficulties, likewise undergo pressures due to a rapid increase in population. There is an urgent need to explore, with the full and intense cooperation of all, and especially of the wealthier nations, ways whereby the human necessities of food and a suitable education can be furnished and shared with the entire human community. But some peoples could greatly improve upon the conditions of their life if they would change over from antiquated methods of farming to the new technical methods, applying them with needed prudence according to their own circumstances. Their life would likewise be improved by the establishment of a better social order and by a fairer system for the distribution of land ownership. Governments undoubtedly have rights and duties, within the limits of their proper competency, regarding the population problem in their respective countries, for instance, in the line of social and family life legislation, or regarding the migration of country-dwellers to the cities, or with respect to information concerning the condition and needs of the country. Since men today are giving thought to this problem and are so greatly disturbed over it, it is desirable in addition that Catholic specialists, especially in the universities, skillfully pursue and develop studies and projects on all these matters. But there are many today who maintain that the increase in world population, or at least the population increase in some countries, must be radically curbed by every means possible and by any kind of intervention on the part of public authority. In view of this contention, the council urges everyone to guard against solutions, whether publicly or privately supported, or at times even imposed, which are contrary to the moral law. For in keeping with man's inalienable right to marry and generate children, a decision concerning the number of children they will have depends on the right judgment of the parents and it cannot in any way be left to the judgment of public authority. But since the judgment of the parents presupposes a rightly formed conscience, it is of the utmost importance that the way be open for everyone to develop a correct and genuinely human responsibility which respects the divine law and takes into consideration the circumstances of the situation and the time. But sometimes this requires an improvement in educational and social conditions, and, above all, formation in religion or at least a complete moral training. Men should discreetly be informed, furthermore, of scientific advances in exploring methods whereby spouses can be helped in regulating the number of their children and whose safeness has been well proven and whose harmony with the moral order has been ascertained.

88. Christians should cooperate willingly and wholeheartedly in establishing an international order that includes a genuine respect for all freedoms and amicable brotherhood between all. This is all the more pressing since the greater part of the world is still suffering from so much poverty that it is as if Christ Himself were crying out in these poor to beg the charity of the disciples. Do not let men, then, be scandalized because some countries with a majority of citizens who are counted as Christians have an abundance of wealth, whereas others are deprived of the necessities of life and are tormented with hunger, disease, and every kind of misery. The spirit of poverty and charity are the glory and witness of the Church of Christ. Those Christians are to be praised and supported, therefore, who volunteer their services to help other men and nations. Indeed, it is the duty of the whole People of God, following the word and example of the bishops, to alleviate as far as they are able the sufferings of the modern age. They should do this too, as was the ancient custom in the Church, out of the substance of their goods, and not only out of what is superfluous. The procedure of collecting and distributing aids, without being inflexible and completely uniform, should nevertheless be carried on in an orderly fashion in dioceses, nations, and throughout the entire world. Wherever it seems convenient, this activity of Catholics should be carried on in unison with other Christian brothers. For the spirit of charity does not forbid, but on the contrary commands that charitable activity be carried out in a careful and orderly manner. Therefore, it is essential for those who intend to dedicate themselves to the services of the developing nations to be properly trained in appropriate institutes.

89. Since, in virtue of her mission received from God, the Church preaches the Gospel to all men and dispenses the treasures of grace, she contributes to the ensuring of peace everywhere on earth and to the placing of the fraternal exchange between men on solid ground by imparting knowledge of the divine and natural law. Therefore, to encourage and stimulate cooperation among men, the Church must be clearly present in the midst of the community of nations both through her official channels and through the full and sincere collaboration of all Christians—a collaboration motivated solely by the desire to be of service to all. This will come about more effectively if the faithful themselves, conscious of their responsibility as men and as Christians, will exert their influence in their own milieu to arouse a ready willingness to cooperate with the international community. Special care must be given, in both religious and civil education, to the formation of youth in this regard.

90. An outstanding form of international activity on the part of

Christians is found in the joint efforts which, both as individuals and in groups, they contribute to institutes already established or to be established for the encouragement of cooperation among nations. There are also various Catholic associations on an international level which can contribute in many ways to the building up of a peaceful and fraternal community of nations. These should be strengthened by augmenting in them the number of well-qualified collaborators, by increasing needed resources, and by advantageously fortifying the coordination of their energies. For today both effective action and the need for dialogue demand joint projects. Moreover, such associations contribute much to the development of a universal outlook—something certainly appropriate for Catholics. They also help to form an awareness of genuine universal solidarity and responsibility. Finally, it is very much to be desired that Catholics, in order to fulfill their role properly in the international community, will seek to cooperate actively and in a positive manner both with their separated brothers who together with them profess the Gospel of charity and with all men thirsting for true peace. The council, considering the immensity of the hardships which still afflict the greater part of mankind today, regards it as most opportune that an organism of the universal Church be set up in order that both the justice and love of Christ toward the poor might be developed everywhere. The role of such an organism would be to stimulate the Catholic community to promote progress in needy regions and international social justice.

Medellín Conference Documents, Justice and Peace

(Promulgated September 6, 1968)

Justice

I. Pertinent Facts

1. There are in existence many studies of the Latin American people. . . . The misery that besets large masses of human beings in all of our countries is described in all of these studies. That misery, as a collective fact, expresses itself as injustice which cries to the heavens. . . .

But what perhaps has not been sufficiently said is that in general the efforts which have been made have not been capable of assuring that justice be honored and realized in every sector of the respective national communities. . . .

2. The lack of socio-cultural integration, in the majority of our countries, has given rise to the superimposition of cultures. In the economic sphere systems flourished which consider solely the potential of groups with great earning power. This lack of adaptation to the characteristics and to the potentials of all our people, in turn, gives rise to frequent political instability and the consolidation of purely formal institutions. To all of this must be added the lack of solidarity which, on the individual and social levels, leads to the committing of serious sins, evident in the unjust structures which characterize the Latin American situation. . . .

III. Projections for Social Pastoral Planning

6. Our pastoral mission is essentially a service of encouraging and educating the conscience of believers, to help them to perceive the responsibilities of their faith in their personal life and in their social life. This Second Episcopal Conference wishes to point out the most important demands, taking into account the value judgment which the latest Documents of the Magisterium of the Church have already made concerning the economic and social situation of the world today and which applies fully to the Latin American continent.

Direction of Social Change

7. The Latin American Church encourages the formation of national communities that reflect a global organization, where all of the peoples but more especially the lower classes have, by means of territorial and functional structures, an active and receptive, creative and decisive participation in the construction of a new society. Those intermediary structures—between the person and the state—should be freely organized, without any unwarranted interference from authority or from dominant groups, in view of their development and concrete participation in the accomplishment of the total common good. They constitute the vital network of society. They are also the true expression of the citizens' liberty and unity. . . .

Political Reform

16. Faced with the need for a total change of Latin American structures, we believe that change has political reform as its prerequisite.

The exercise of political authority and its decisions have as their only end the common good. In Latin America such authority and decision-making frequently seem to support systems which militate against the common good or which favor privileged groups. By means of legal norms, authority ought effectively and permanently to assure the rights and inalienable liberties of the citizens and the free functioning of intermediary structures.

Public authority has the duty of facilitating and supporting the creation of means of participation and legitimate representation of the people, or if necessary the creation of new ways to achieve it. We want to insist on the necessity of vitalizing and strengthening the municipal and communal organization, as a beginning of organizational efforts at the departmental, provincial, regional and national levels.

The lack of political consciousness in our countries makes the educational activity of the Church absolutely essential, for the purpose of bringing Christians to consider their participation in the political life of the nation as a matter of conscience and as the practice of charity in its most noble and meaningful sense for the life of the community.

Information and "Concientización"

17. We wish to affirm that it is indispensable to form a social conscience and a realistic perception of the problems of the com-

munity and of social structures. We must awaken the social conscience and communal customs in all strata of society and professional groups regarding such values as dialogue and community living within the same group and relations with wider social groups (workers, peasants, professionals, clergy, religious, administrators, etc.)

This task of *"concientización"* and social education ought to be integrated into joint pastoral action at various levels.

18. The sense of service and realism demands of today's hierarchy a greater social sensitivity and objective. In that regard there is a need for direct contact with the different social-professional groups in meetings which provide all with a more complete vision of social dynamics. Such encounters are to be regarded as instruments which can facilitate a collegial action on the part of the bishops, guaranteeing harmony of thought and activities in the midst of a changing society.

Peace

I. The Latin American Situation and Peace

1. "If development is the new name for peace," . . . Latin American underdevelopment with its own characteristics in the different countries is an unjust situation which promotes tensions that conspire against peace.

We can divide these tensions into three major groups, selecting, in each of these, those variables which constitute a positive menace to the peace of our countries by manifesting an unjust situation.

When speaking of injustice, we refer to those realities that constitute a sinful situation; this does not mean, however, that we are overlooking the fact that at times the misery in our countries can have natural causes which are difficult to overcome.

In making this analysis, we do not ignore or fail to give credit to the positive efforts made at every level to build a more just society. We do not include this here because our purpose is to call attention to those aspects which constitute a menace or negation of peace. . . .

II. Doctrinal Reflexion: Christian View of Peace

14. The above mentioned Christian viewpoint on peace adds up to a negation of peace such as Christian tradition understands it.

Three factors characterize the Christian concept of peace:

a) Peace is, above all, a work of justice. . . . It presupposes and requires the establishment of a just order . . . in which men can fulfill themselves as men, where their dignity is respected, their legitimate aspirations satisfied, their access to truth recognized, their personal freedom guaranteed; an order where man is not an object, but an agent of his own history. Therefore, there will be attempts against peace where unjust inequalities among men and nations prevail.

Peace in Latin America, therefore, is not the simple absence of violence and bloodshed. Oppression by the power groups may give the impression of maintaining peace and order, but in truth it is nothing but the "continuous and inevitable seed of rebellion and war." . . .

"Peace can only be obtained by creating a new order which carries with it a more perfect justice among men." . . . It is in this sense that the integral development of a man, the path to more human conditions, becomes the symbol of peace.

b) Secondly, peace is a permanent task. . . . A community becomes a reality in time and is subject to a movement that implies constant change in structures, transformation of attitudes, and conversion of hearts.

The "tranquillity of order," according to the Augustinian definition of peace, is neither passivity nor conformity. It is not something that is acquired once and for all. It is the result of continuous effort and adaptation to new circumstances, to new demands and challenges of a changing history. A static and apparent peace may be obtained with the use of force; an authentic peace implies struggle, creative abilities and permanent conquest. . . .

Peace is not found, it is built. The Christian man is the artisan of peace. . . . This task, given the above circumstances, has a special character in our continent; thus, the People of God in Latin America, following the example of Christ, must resist personal and collective injustice with unselfish courage and fearlessness.

c) Finally, peace is the fruit of love. . . . It is the expression of true fraternity among men, a fraternity given by Christ, Prince of Peace, in reconciling all men with the Father. Human solidarity cannot truly take effect unless it is done in Christ, who gives Peace that the world cannot give. . . . Love is the soul of justice. The Christian who works for social justice should always cultivate peace and love in his heart.

Peace with God is the basic foundation of internal and social peace. Therefore, where this social peace does not exist there will we find social, political, economic and cultural inequalities, there will we find the rejection of the peace of the Lord, and a rejection of the Lord Himself. . . .

The Problem of Violence in Latin America

15. Violence constitutes one of the gravest problems in Latin America. A decision on which the future of the countries of the continent will depend should not be left to the impulses of emotion and passion. We would be failing in our pastoral duty if we were not to remind the conscience, caught in this dramatic dilemma, of the criteria derived from the Christian doctrine of evangelical love.

No one should be surprised if we forcefully re-affirm our faith in the productiveness of peace. This is our Christian ideal. "Violence is neither Christian nor evangelical." . . . The Christian man is peaceful and not ashamed of it. He is not simply a pacifist, for he can fight, . . . but he prefers peace to war. He knows that "violent changes in structures would be fallacious, ineffectual in themselves and not conforming to the dignity of man, which demands that the necessary changes take place from within, that is to say, through a fitting awakening of conscience, adequate preparation and effective participation of all, which the ignorance and often inhuman conditions of life make it impossible to assure at this time." . . .

16. As the Christian believes in the productiveness of peace in order to achieve justice, he also believes that justice is a prerequisite

for peace. He recognizes that in many instances Latin America finds itself faced with a situation of injustice that can be called institutionalized violence, when, because of a structural deficiency of industry and agriculture, of national and international economy, of cultural and political life, "whole towns lack necessities, live in such dependence as hinders all initiative and responsibility as well as every possibility for cultural promotion and participation in social and political life,"... thus violating fundamental rights. This situation demands all-embracing, courageous, urgent and profoundly renovating transformations. We should not be surprised, therefore, that the "temptation to violence" is surfacing in Latin America. One should not abuse the patience of a people that for years has borne a situation that would not be acceptable to anyone with any degree of awareness of human rights.

Facing a situation which works so seriously against the dignity of man and against peace, we address ourselves, as pastors, to all the members of the Christian community, asking them to assume their responsibility in the promotion of peace in Latin America.

17. We would like to direct our call in the first place to those who have a greater share of wealth, culture and power. We know that there are leaders in Latin America who are sensitive to the needs of the people and try to remedy them. They recognize that the privileged many times join together, and with all the means at their disposal pressure those who govern, thus obstructing necessary changes. In some instances, this pressure takes on drastic proportions which result in the destruction of life and property.

Therefore, we urge them not to take advantage of the pacifist position of the Church in order to oppose, either actively or passively, the profound transformations that are so necessary. If they jealously retain their privileges and defend them through violence they are responsible to history for provoking "explosive revolutions of despair."... The peaceful future of the countries of Latin America depends to a large extent on their attitude.

18. Also responsible for injustice are those who remain passive for fear of the sacrifice and personal risk implied by any courageous and effective action. Justice, and therefore peace, conquer by means of a dynamic action of awakening (*concientización*) and organization of the popular sectors, which are capable of pressing public officials who are often impotent in their social projects without popular support.

19. We address ourselves finally to those who, in the face of injustice and illegitimate resistance to change, put their hopes in violence. With Paul VI we realize that their attitude "frequently finds its ultimate motivation in noble impulses of justice and solidarity." ... Let us not speak here of empty words which do not imply personal responsibility and which isolate from the fruitful non-violent actions that are immediately possible.

If it is true that revolutionary insurrection can be legitimate in the case of evident and prolonged "tyranny that seriously works against the fundamental rights of man, and which damages the common good of the country,"... whether it proceeds from one person or from clearly unjust structures, it is also certain that violence or "armed revolution" generally "generates new injustices, introduces new imbalances and causes new disasters; one cannot combat a real evil at the price of a greater evil."...

If we consider then, the totality of the circumstances of our countries, and if we take into account the Christian preference for peace, the enormous difficulty of a civil war, the logic of violence, the atrocities it engenders, the risk of provoking foreign intervention, illegitimate as it may be, the difficulty of building a regime of justice and freedom while participating in a process of violence, we earnestly desire that the dynamism of the awakened and organized community be put to the service of justice and peace.

Finally, we would like to make ours the words of our Holy Father to the newly ordained priests and deacons in Bogota, when he referred to all the suffering and said to them: "We will be able to understand their afflictions and change them, not into hate and violence, but into the strong and peaceful energy' of constructive works."...

III. Pastoral Conclusions

20. In the face of the tensions which conspire against peace, and even present the temptation of violence; in the face of the Christian concept of peace which has been described, we believe that the Latin American Episcopate cannot avoid assuming very concrete responsibilities; because to create a just social order, without which peace is illusory, is an eminently Christian task.

To us, the Pastors of the Church, belongs the duty to educate the Christian conscience, to inspire, stimulate and help orient all of the initiatives that contribute to the formation of man. It is also up to us to denounce everything which, opposing justice, destroys peace.

In this spirit we feel it opportune to bring up the following pastoral points:

21. To awaken in individuals and communities, principally through mass media, a living awareness of justice, infusing in them a dynamic sense of responsibility and solidarity.

22. To defend the rights of the poor and oppressed according to the Gospel commandment, urging our governments and upper classes to eliminate anything which might destroy social peace: injustice, inertia, venality, insensibility.

23. To favor integration, energetically denouncing the abuses and unjust consequences of the excessive inequalities between poor and rich, weak and powerful.

24. To be certain that our preaching, liturgy and catechesis take into account the social and community dimensions of Christianity, forming men committed to world peace.

25. To achieve in our schools, seminaries and universities a healthy critical sense of the social situation and foster the vocation of service. We also consider very efficacious the diocesan and national campaigns that mobilize the faithful and social organizations, leading them to a similar reflection.

26. To invite various Christian and non-Christian communities to collaborate in this fundamental task of our times.

27. To encourage and favor the efforts of the people to create

and develop their own grass-roots organizations for the redress and consolidation of their rights and the search for true justice.

28. To request the perfecting of the administration of justice, whose deficiencies often cause serious ills.

29. To urge a halt and revision in many of our countries of the arms race that at times constitutes a burden excessively disproportionate to the legitimate demands of the common good, to the detriment of desperate social necessities. The struggle against misery is the true war that our nations should face.

30. To invite the bishops, the leaders of different churches and all men of good will of the developed nations to promote in their respective spheres of influence, especially among the political and financial leaders, a consciousness of greater solidarity facing our underdeveloped nations, obtaining among other things, just prices for our raw materials.

31. On the occasion of the twentieth anniversary of the solemn declaration of Human Rights, to interest universities in Latin America to undertake investigations to verify the degree of its implementation in our countries.

32. To denounce the unjust action of world powers that works against self-determination of weaker nations who must suffer the bloody consequences of war and invasion, and to ask competent international organizations for effective and decisive procedures.

33. To encourage and praise the initiatives and works of all those who in the diverse areas of action contribute to the creation of a new order which will assure peace in our midst.

Justice in the World

(Synod of Bishops, November 6, 1971)

Introduction

Gathered from the whole world, in communion with all who believe in Christ and with the entire human family, and opening our hearts to the Spirit who is making the whole of creation new, we have questioned ourselves about the mission of the People of God to further justice in the world.

Scrutinizing the "signs of the times" and seeking to detect the meaning of emerging history, while at the same time sharing the aspirations and questionings of all those who want to build a more human world, we have listened to the Word of God that we might be converted to the fulfilling of the divine plan for the salvation of the world.

Even though it is not for us to elaborate a very profound analysis of the situation of the world, we have nevertheless been able to perceive the serious injustices which are building around the world of men a network of domination, oppression and abuses which stifle freedom and which keep the greater part of humanity from sharing in the building up and enjoyment of a more just and more fraternal world.

At the same time we have noted the inmost stirring moving the world in its depths. There are facts constituting a contribution to the furthering of justice. In associations of men and among peoples themselves there is arising a new awareness which shakes them out of any fatalistic resignation and which spurs them on to liberate themselves and to be responsible for their own destiny. Movements among men are seen which express hope in a better world and a will to change whatever has become intolerable. . . .

Action on behalf of justice and participation in the transformation of the world fully appear to us as a constitutive dimension of the preaching of the Gospel, or, in other words, of the Church's mission for the redemption of the human race and its liberation from every oppressive situation.

Chapter I: Justice and World Society

Crisis of Universal Solidarity

The world in which the Church lives and acts is held captive by a tremendous paradox. Never before have the forces working for bringing about a unified world society appeared so powerful and dynamic. . . .

The new technological possibilities are based upon the unity of science, on the global and simultaneous character of communications, and on the birth of an absolutely interdependent economic world. Moreover, men are beginning to grasp a new and more radical dimension of unity; for they perceive that their resources, as well as the precious treasures of air and water—without which there cannot be life—and the small delicate biosphere of the whole complex of all life on earth, are not infinite, but on the contrary must be saved and preserved as a unique patrimony belonging to all mankind.

The paradox lies in the fact that within this perspective of unity the forces of division and antagonism seem today to be increasing in strength. Ancient divisions between nations and empires, between races and classes, today possess new technological instruments of destruction. . . . At the same time new divisions are being born to separate man from his neighbor. Unless combatted and overcome by social and political action, the influence of the new industrial and technological order favours the concentration of wealth, power and decision-making in the hands of a small public or private controlling group. Economic injustice and lack of social participation keep a man from attaining his basic human and civil rights. . . .

The strong drive towards global unity, the unequal distribution which places decisions concerning three quarters of income, investment and trade in the hands of one third of the human race, namely the more highly developed part, the insufficiency of a merely economic progress, and the new recognition of the material limits of the biosphere—all this makes us aware of the fact that in today's world new modes of understanding human dignity are arising.

The Right to Development

In the face of international systems of domination, the bringing about of justice depends more and more on the determined will for development.

In the developing nations and in the so-called socialist world, that determined will asserts itself especially in a struggle for forms of claiming one's rights and self-expression, a struggle caused by the evolution of the economic system itself.

This aspiring to justice asserts itself in advancing beyond the threshold at which begins a consciousness of enhancement of personal worth . . . with regard both to the whole man and the whole of mankind. This is expressed in an awareness of the right to development. The right to development must be seen as a dynamic interpenetration of all those fundamental human rights upon which the aspirations of individuals and nations are based. . . .

This desire, however, will not satisfy the expectations of our time if it ignores the objective obstacles which social structures place in the way of conversion of hearts, or even of the realization of the ideal of charity. It demands on the contrary that the general condition of being marginal in society be overcome, so that an end will be put to the systematic barriers and vicious circles which oppose the collective advance towards enjoyment of adequate remuneration of the factors of production, and which strengthen the situation of discrimination with regard to access to opportunities and collective services from which a great part of the people are now excluded. . . .

By taking their future into their own hands through a determined will for progress, the developing peoples—even if they do not achieve the final goal—will authentically manifest their own personalization. And in order that they may cope with the unequal relationships within the present world complex, a certain responsible nationalism gives them the impetus needed to acquire an identity of their own. From this basic self-determination can come attempts at putting together new political groupings allowing full development to these peoples; there can also come measures necessary for overcoming the inertia which could render fruitless such an effort—as in some cases population pressure; there can also come new sacrifices which the growth of planning demands of a generation which wants to build its own future.

On the other hand, it is impossible to conceive true progress without recognizing the necessity—within the political system chosen—of a development composed both of economic growth and participation; and the necessity too of an increase in wealth implying as well social progress by the entire community as it overcomes regional imbalance and islands of prosperity. Participation constitutes a right which is to be applied both in the economic and in the social and political field. . . .

By his action and teaching Christ united in an indivisible way the relationship of man to God and the relationship of man to other men. . . .

According to the Christian message, therefore, man's relationship to his neighbour is bound up with his relationship to God; his response to the love of God, saving us through Christ, is shown to be effective in his love and service of men. Christian love of neighbour and justice cannot be separated. For love implies an absolute demand for justice, namely a recognition of the dignity and rights of one's neighbor. Justice attains its inner fullness only in love. Because every man is truly a visible image of the invisible God and a brother of Christ, the Christian finds in every man God himself and God's absolute demand for justice and love. . . .

Of itself it does not belong to the Church, insofar as she is a religious and hierarchical community, to offer concrete solutions in the social, economic and political spheres for justice in the world. Her mission involves defending and promoting the dignity and fundamental rights of the human person.

The members of the Church, as members of society, have the same right and duty to promote the common good as do other citizens. . . .

Economic Justice for All

(A Pastoral Letter on Catholic Social Teaching and the U.S. Economy, November 13, 1986)

. . . This letter is a personal invitation to Catholics to use the resources of our faith, the strength of our economy, and the opportunities of our democracy to shape a society that better protects the dignity and basic rights of our sisters and brothers, both in this land and around the world. . . .

6. Economic life raises important social and moral questions for each of us and for the society as a whole. Like family life, economic life is one of the chief areas where we live out our faith, love our neighbor, confront temptation, fulfill God's creative design, and achieve holiness. Our economic activity in factory, field, office, or shop feeds our families—or feeds our anxieties. It exercises our talents—or wastes them. It raises our hopes—or crushes them. It brings us into cooperation with others—or sets us at odds. The Second Vatican Council instructs us "to preach the message of Christ in such a way that the light of the Gospel will shine on all activities of the faithful" (Pastoral Constitution, no. 43). In this case, we are trying to look at economic life through the eyes of faith, applying traditional church teaching to the U.S. economy.

7. In our letter, we write as pastors, not public officials. We speak as moral teachers, not economic technicians. We seek not to make some political or ideological point but to lift up the human and ethical dimensions of economic life, aspects too often neglected in public discussion. We bring to this task a dual heritage of Catholic social teaching and traditional American values. . . .

Principal Themes of the Pastoral Letter

12. The pastoral letter is not a blueprint for the American economy. It does not embrace any particular theory of how the economy works, nor does it attempt to resolve disputes between different schools of economic thought. Instead, our letter turns to Scripture and to the social teaching of the Church. There, we discover what

our economic life must serve, what standards it must meet. Let us examine some of these basic moral principles.

13. Every economic decision and institution must be judged in light of whether it protects or undermines the dignity of the human person. The pastoral letter begins with the human person. We believe the person is sacred—the clearest reflection of God among us. Human dignity comes from God, not from nationality, race, sex, economic status, or any human accomplishment. We judge any economic system by what it does *for* and *to* people and by how it permits all to *participate* in it. The economy should serve people, not the other way around.

14. Human dignity can be realized and protected only in community. In our teaching, the human person is not only sacred but social. How we organize our society—in economics and politics, in law and policy—directly affects human dignity and the capacity of individuals to grow in community. The obligation to "love our neighbor" has an individual dimension, but it also requires a broader social commitment to the common good. We have many partial ways to measure and debate the health of our economy: Gross National Product, per capita income, stock market prices, and so forth. The Christian vision of economic life looks beyond them all and asks, Does economic life enhance or threaten our life together as a community?

15. All people have a right to participate in the economic life of society. Basic justice demands that people be assured a minimum level of participation in the economy. It is wrong for a person or a group to be excluded unfairly or to be unable to participate or contribute to the economy. For example, people who are both able and willing, but cannot get a job are deprived of the participation that is so vital to human development. For, it is through employment that most individuals and families meet their material needs, exercise their talents, and have an opportunity to contribute to the larger community. Such participation has a special significance in our tradition because we believe that it is a means by which we join in carrying forward God's creative activity.

16. All members of society have a special obligation to the poor and vulnerable. From the Scriptures and church teaching, we learn that the justice of a society is tested by the treatment of the poor. . . . As Christians, we are called to respond to the needs of *all* our brothers and sisters, but those with the greatest needs require the greatest response.

17. Human rights are the minimum conditions for life in community. In Catholic teaching, human rights include not only civil and political rights but also economic rights. . . . This means that when people are without a chance to earn a living, and must go hungry and homeless, they are being denied basic rights. Society must ensure that these rights are protected. . . .

18. Society as a whole, acting through public and private institutions, has the moral responsibility to enhance human dignity and protect human rights. In addition to the clear responsibility of private institutions, government has an essential responsibility in this area. This does not mean that government has the primary or exclusive role, but it does have a positive moral responsibility in safeguarding human rights and ensuring that the minimum conditions of human dignity are met for all. In a democracy, government is a means by which we can act together to protect what is important to us and to promote our common values.

19. These six moral principles are not the only ones presented in the pastoral letter, but they give an overview of the moral vision that we are trying to share. This vision of economic life cannot exist in a vacuum; it must be translated into concrete measures. Our pastoral letter spells out some specific applications of Catholic moral principles. We call for a new national commitment to full employment. We say it is a social and moral scandal that one of every seven Americans is poor, and we call for concerted efforts to eradicate poverty. The fulfillment of the basic needs of the poor is of the highest priority. We urge that all economic policies be evaluated in light of their impact on the life and stability of the family. We support measures to halt the loss of family farms and to resist the growing concentration in the ownership of agricultural resources. We specify ways in which the United States can do far more to relieve the plight of poor nations and assist in their development. We also reaffirm church teaching on the rights of workers, collective bargaining, private property, subsidiarity, and equal opportunity.

20. We believe that the recommendations in our letter are reasonable and balanced. In analyzing the economy, we reject ideological extremes and start from the fact that ours is a "mixed" economy, the product of a long history of reform and adjustment. We know that some of our specific recommendations are controversial. As bishops, we do not claim to make these prudential judgments with the same kind of authority that marks our declarations of principle. But, we feel obliged to teach by example how Christians can undertake concrete analysis and make specific judgments on economic issues. The Church's teachings cannot be left at the level of appealing generalities.

21. In the pastoral letter, we suggest that the time has come for a "New American Experiment"—to implement economic rights, to broaden the sharing of economic power, and to make economic decisions more accountable to the common good. This experiment can create new structures of economic partnership and participation within firms at the regional level, for the whole nation, and across borders. . . .

25. The challenge of this pastoral letter is not merely to think differently, but also to act differently. A renewal of economic life depends on the conscious choices and commitments of individual believers who practice their faith in the world. The road to holiness for most of us lies in our secular vocations. We need a spirituality that calls forth and supports lay initiative and witness not just in our churches but also in business, in the labor movement, in the professions, in education, and in public life. Our faith is not just a weekend obligation, a mystery to be celebrated around the altar on Sunday. It is a pervasive reality to be practiced every day in homes, offices, factories, schools, and businesses across our land. We cannot

separate what we believe from how we act in the marketplace and the broader community, for this is where we make our primary contribution to the pursuit of economic justice. . . .

~

27. The pursuit of economic justice takes believers into the public arena, testing the policies of government by the principles of our teaching. We ask you to become more informed and active citizens, using your voices and votes to speak for the voiceless, to defend the poor and the vulnerable and to advance the common good. We are called to shape a constituency of conscience, measuring every policy by how it touches the least, the lost, and the left-out among us. This letter calls us to conversion and common action, to new forms of stewardship, service, and citizenship.

Constitutions of the World

Following are excerpts from several world constitutions that include provisions on religion or religious practice. The selections, by no means exhaustive, are intended to provide a representative look at how some countries have sought to codify national policies on separation of church and state, state establishment of religion, freedom of conscience, and religious toleration. The Internet address of each constitution is listed after each country name. For further information, including the full text of most world constitutions, see the Web site administered by International Constitutional Law *(http://www.uni-wuerzburg.de/law)*.

Cambodia (1993)

(http://www.uni-wuerzburg.de/law/cb00000_.html)

Article 4 [Motto]

The motto of the Kingdom of Cambodia is: "Nation, Religion, King."

Article 31 [Human Rights, Equality, Restrictions]

(2) Every Khmer citizen is equal before the law, enjoying the same rights and freedom and fulfilling the same obligations regardless of race, colour, sex, language, religious belief, political tendency, birth origin, social status, wealth or other status. . . .

Article 43 [Religion]

(1) Khmer citizens of either sex enjoy the freedom of belief.

(2) Freedom of religious belief and worship is guaranteed by the State on the condition that such freedom does not affect other religious beliefs or violate public order and security.

(3) Buddhism is the State religion.

China (1982)

(http://www.uni-wuerzburg.de/law/ch00000_.html)

Article 34 [Electoral Rights and Equality]

All citizens of the People's Republic of China who have reached the age of 18 have the right to vote and stand for election, regardless of nationality, race, sex, occupation, family background, religious belief, education, property status, or length of residence, except persons deprived of political rights according to law.

Article 36 [Religion]

(1) Citizens of the People's Republic of China enjoy freedom of religious belief.

(2) No state organ, public organization, or individual may compel citizens to believe in, or not to believe in, any religion; nor may they discriminate against citizens who believe in, or do not believe in, any religion.

(3) The state protects normal religious activities. No one may make use of religion to engage in activities that disrupt public order, impair the health of citizens or interfere with the educational system of the state.

(4) Religious bodies and religious affairs are not subject to any foreign domination.

France (1958)

(http://www.uni-wuerzburg.de/law/fr00000_.html)

Article 2 [State Form and Symbols]

(1) France is an indivisible, secular, democratic, and social Republic. It ensures the equality of all citizens before the law, without distinction as to origin, race, or religion. It respects all beliefs. . . .

Article 77 [Autonomy]

(3) All citizens shall be equal before the law, regardless of their origin, race or religion. They shall have the same duties.

Germany (1949)

(http://www.uni-wuerzburg.de/law/gm00000_.html)

Article 3 [Equality]

(3) No one may be disadvantaged or favored because of his sex, his parentage, his race, his language, his homeland and origin, his faith, or his religious or political opinions. No one may be disadvantaged because of his handicap.

Article 4 [Freedom of Faith, of Conscience, and of Creed]

(1) Freedom of creed, of conscience, and freedom to profess a religious or non-religious faith are inviolable.

(2) The undisturbed practice of religion is guaranteed.

(3) No one may be compelled against his conscience to render war service involving the use of arms. Details are regulated by a federal statute.

Article 7 [Education]

(3) Religion classes form part of the ordinary curriculum in state schools, except for secular schools. Without prejudice to the state's right of supervision, religious instruction is given in accordance with the tenets of the religious communities. No teacher may be obliged against his will to give religious instruction.

Article 12a [Liability to Military and Other Service]

(2) A person who refuses, on grounds of conscience, to render war service involving the use of arms can be required to render a substitute service. The duration of such substitute service may not exceed the duration of military service. Details are regulated by a statute which may not interfere with freedom to take a decision based on conscience and which must also provide for the possibility of a substitute service not connected with units of the Armed Forces or of the Federal Border Guard.

Greece (1975)

(http: //www.uni-wuerzburg.de/law/gr00000_.html)

Article 3 [Relations of Church and State]

(1) The prevailing religion in Greece is that of the Eastern Orthodox Church of Christ. The Orthodox Church of Greece acknowledging as its head Our Lord Jesus Christ is indissolubly united in doctrine with the Great Church of Constantinople and every other Church of Christ of the same doctrine. It observes steadfastly, as they do, the holy apostolic and synodical canons and the holy tradition. It is autocephalous, exercising its sovereign rights independently of any other church, and is administered by the Holy Synod of Bishops and the Parliament Holy Synod which emanates from the former and is constituted in accordance with the Constitutional Chart of the Church and the provisions of the Patriarchal Document of 29 June 1850 and the Synodal Deed of 4 September 1928.

(2) The religious status prevailing in certain parts of the State is not contrary to the provisions of the aforegoing paragraph.

(3) The text of the Holy Scriptures shall be maintained unaltered. The official translation thereof into any other linguistic form, without the sanction of the Autocephalous Church of Greece and the Great Church of Christ in Constantinople, is prohibited.

Article 13 [Religion]

(1) The freedom of religious conscience is inviolable. The enjoyment of civil and individual rights does not depend on the religious conviction of each individual.

(2) Every known religion is free and the forms of worship thereof shall be practiced without any hindrance by the State and under protection of the law. The exercise of worship shall not contravene public order or offend morals. Proselytizing is prohibited.

(3) The ministers of all religions are subject to the same obligations towards the State and to the same state supervision as the ministers of the established religion.

(4) No person shall, by reason of his religious convictions, be exempt from discharging his obligations to the State, or refuse to comply with the laws.

(5) No oath shall be imposed without a law specifying the form thereof.

Article 59 [Oath]

(1) Before entering upon their duties the deputies shall take the following oath in the House of Parliament in public session: "I swear in the name of the Holy, Consubstantial, and Indivisible Trinity to be loyal to the Motherland and the democratic form of government, obey the Constitution and the laws and discharge my duties conscientiously."

(2) Deputies of other religions or dogmas shall give the same oath in the manner of their own religion or dogma.

(3) Deputies who enter upon their duties during the recess of Parliament shall take the oath before a Department thereof which is in session.

Hong Kong (1990)

(http: //www.uni-wuerzburg.de/law/hk00000_.html)

Article 1 Entitlement to rights without distinction

(1) The rights recognized in this Bill of Rights shall be enjoyed without distinction of any kind, such as race, colour, sex, language, religion, political or other opinion, national or social origin, property, birth or other status.

Article 15 Freedom of thought, conscience and religion

(1) Everyone shall have the right to freedom of thought, conscience and religion. This right shall include freedom to have or to adopt a religion or belief of his choice, and freedom, either individually or in community with others and in public or private, to manifest his religion or belief in worship, observance, practice and teaching.

(2) No one shall be subject to coercion which would impair his freedom to have or to adopt a religion or belief of his choice.

(3) Freedom to manifest one's religion or beliefs may be subject only to such limitations as are prescribed by law and are necessary to protect public safety, order, health, or morals or the fundamental rights and freedoms of others.

(4) The liberty of parents and, when applicable, legal guardians to ensure the religious and moral education of their children in conformity with their own convictions shall be respected.

Article 20 Rights of children

(1) Every child shall have, without any discrimination as to race, colour, sex, language, religion, national or social origin, property or birth, the right to such measures of protection as are required by his status as a minor, on the part of his family, society and the State.

Article 22 Equality before and equal protection of law

All persons are equal before the law and are entitled without any discrimination to the equal protection of the law. In this respect, the law shall prohibit any discrimination and guarantee to all persons equal and effective protection against discrimination on any ground such as race, colour, sex, language, religion, political or other opinion, national or social origin, property, birth or other status.

Article 23 Rights of minorities

Persons belonging to ethnic, religious or linguistic minorities shall not be denied the right, in community with the other members of their group, to enjoy their own culture, to profess and practise their own religion, or to use their own language.

Article 32 [Religion]

(1) Hong Kong residents shall have freedom of conscience.

(2) Hong Kong residents shall have freedom of religious belief and freedom to preach and to conduct and participate in religious activities in public.

Article 141

(1) The Government of the Hong Kong Special Administrative Region shall not restrict the freedom of religious belief, interfere in the internal affairs of religious organizations or restrict religious activities which do not contravene the laws of the Region.

(2) Religious organizations shall, in accordance with law, enjoy the rights to acquire, use, dispose of and inherit property and the right to receive financial assistance. Their previous property rights and interests shall be maintained and protected.

(3) Religious organizations may, according to their previous practice, continue to run seminaries and other schools, hospitals and welfare institutions and to provide other social services.

(4) Religious organizations and believers in the Hong Kong Special Administrative Region may maintain and develop their relations with religious organizations and believers elsewhere.

Section 5 Public emergencies

(1) In time of public emergency which threatens the life of the nation and the existence of which is officially proclaimed, measures may be taken derogating from the Bill of Rights to the extent strictly required by the exigencies of the situation, but these measures shall be taken in accordance with law.

(2) No measure shall be taken under Subsection (1) that —

(b) involves discrimination solely on the ground of race, colour, sex, language, religion or social origin. . . .

India (1950)

(http: //www.uni-wuerzburg.de/law/in00000_.html)

Article 15 Prohibition of discrimination on grounds of religion, race, caste, sex or place of birth

(1) The State shall not discriminate against any citizen on grounds only of religion, race, caste, sex, place of birth or any of them.

(2) No citizen shall, on ground only of religion, race, caste, sex, place of birth or any of them, be subject to any disability, liability, restriction or condition with regard to -

(a) access to shops, public restaurants, hotels and places of public entertainment; or

(b) the use of wells, tanks, bathing ghats, roads and places of public resort maintained whole or partly out of State funds or dedicated to the use of the general public. . . .

Article 16 Equality of opportunity in matters of public employment

(2) No citizen shall, on grounds only of religion, race, caste, sex, descent, place of birth, residence or any of them, be ineligible for, or discriminated against in respect of, any employment or office under the State. . . .

(5) Nothing in this article shall affect the operation of any law which provides that the incumbent of an office in connection with the affairs of any religious or denominational institution or any member of the governing body thereof shall be a person professing a particular religion or belonging to a particular denomination.

Article 17 Abolition of Untouchability

"Untouchability" is abolished and its practice in any form is forbidden. The enforcement of any disability arising out of "Untouchability" shall be an offence punishable in accordance with law.

Article 23 Prohibition of traffic in human beings and forced labour

(2) Nothing in this article shall prevent the State from imposing compulsory service for public purposes, and in imposing such service the State shall not make any discrimination on ground only of religion, race, caste or class or any of them.

Article 25 Freedom of conscience and free profession, practice and propagation of religion

(1) Subject to public order, morality and health and to the other provisions of this Part, all persons are equally entitled to freedom of conscience and the right freely to profess, practice and propagate religion.

(2) Nothing in this article shall affect the operation of any existing law or prevent the State from making any law

(a) regulating or restricting any economic, financial, political or other secular activity which may be associated with religious practice;

(b) providing for social welfare and reform or the throwing open of Hindu religious institutions of a public character to all classes and sections of Hindus.

Explanation I: The wearing and carrying of kirpans shall be deemed to be included in the profession of the Sikh religion.

Explanation II: In sub-Clause (b) of clause (2), the reference to Hindus shall be construed as including a reference to persons professing the Sikh, Jaina or Buddhist religion, and the reference to Hindu religious institutions shall be construed accordingly.

Article 26 Freedom to manage religious affairs

Subject to public order, morality and health, every religious denomination or any section thereof shall have the right

(a) to establish and maintain institutions for religious and charitable purposes;

(b) to manage its own affairs in matters of religion;

(c) to own and acquire movable and immovable property; and

(d) to administer such property in accordance with law.

Article 27 Freedom as to payment of taxes for promotion of any particular religion

No person shall be compelled to pay any taxes, the proceeds of which are specifically appropriated in payment of expenses for the promotion or maintenance of any particular religion or religious denomination.

Article 28 Freedom as to attendance at religious instruction or religious worship in certain educational institutions

(1) No religious instruction shall be provided in any educational institution wholly maintained out of State funds.

(2) Nothing in clause (1) shall apply to an educational institution which is administered by the State but has been established under any endowment or trust which requires that religious instruction shall be imparted in such institution.

(3) No person attending any educational institution recognised by the State or receiving aid out of State funds shall be required to take part in any religious instruction that may be imparted in such institution or to attend any religious worship that may be conducted in such institution or in any premises attached thereto unless such person or, if such person is minor, his guardian has given his consent thereto.

Article 29 Protection of interests of minorities

(2) No citizen shall be denied admission into any educational institution maintained by the State or receiving aid out of State funds on grounds only of religion, race, caste, language or any of them.

Article 30 Right of minorities to establish and administer educational institutions

(1) All minorities, whether based on religion or language, shall have the right to establish and administer educational institutions of their choice. . . .

(2) The State shall not, in granting aid to educational institutions, discriminate against any educational institution on the ground that it is under the management of a minority, whether based on religion or language.

Iran (1979)

(http: //www.uni-wuerzburg.de/law/ir00000_.html)

Article 1 [Form of Government]

The form of government of Iran is that of an Islamic Republic, endorsed by the people of Iran on the basis of their longstanding belief in the sovereignty of truth and Koranic justice, in the referendum of 29 and 30 March 1979, through the affirmative vote of a majority of 98.2% of eligible voters, held after the victorious Islamic Revolution led by Imam Khumayni.

Article 2 [Foundational Principles]

The Islamic Republic is a system based on belief in: 1) the One God (as stated in the phrase "There is no god except Allah"), His exclusive sovereignty and right to legislate, and the necessity of submission to His commands; 2) Divine revelation and its fundamental role in setting forth the laws; 3) the return to God in the Hereafter, and the constructive role of this belief in the course of man's ascent towards God; 4) the justice of God in creation and legislation; 5) continuous leadership and perpetual guidance, and its fundamental role in ensuring the uninterrupted process of the revolution of Islam; 6) the exalted dignity and value of man, and his freedom coupled with responsibility before God; in which equity, justice, political, economic, social, and cultural independence, and national solidarity are secured by recourse to: a) continuous leadership of the holy persons, possessing necessary qualifications, exercised on the basis of the Koran and the Sunnah, upon all of whom be peace; b) sciences and arts and the most advanced results of human experience, together with the effort to advance them further; c) negation of all forms of oppression, both the infliction of and the submission to it, and of dominance, both its imposition and its acceptance.

Article 12 [Official Religion]

The official religion of Iran is Islam and the Twelver Ja'fari school, and this principle will remain eternally immutable. Other Islamic schools are to be accorded full respect, and their followers are free to act in accordance with their own jurisprudence in performing their religious rites. These schools enjoy official status in matters pertaining to religious education, affairs of personal status (marriage, divorce, inheritance, and wills) and related litigation in courts of law. In regions of the country where Muslims following any one of these schools constitute the majority, local regulations, within the bounds of the jurisdiction of local councils, are to be in accordance with the respective school, without infringing upon the rights of the followers of other schools.

Article 13 [Recognized Religious Minorities]

Zoroastrian, Jewish, and Christian Iranians are the only recognized religious minorities, who, within the limits of the law, are free to perform their religious rites and ceremonies, and to act according to their own canon in matters of personal affairs and religious education.

Article 14 [Non-Muslims' Rights]

In accordance with the sacred verse "God does not forbid you to deal kindly and justly with those who have not fought against you because of your religion and who have not expelled you from your homes" [60:8], the government of the Islamic Republic of Iran and all Muslims are duty-bound to treat non-Muslims in conformity with ethical norms and the principles of Islamic justice and equity, and to respect their human rights. This principle applies to all who refrain from engaging in conspiracy or activity against Islam and the Islamic Republic of Iran.

Article 64 [270 Members, Religious Representatives]

(1) There are to be two hundred seventy members of the Islamic Consultative Assembly which, keeping in view the human, political, geographic, and other similar factors, may increase by not more than twenty for each ten-year period from the date of the national referendum of the year 1368 of the solar Islamic calendar.

(2) The Zoroastrians and Jews will each elect one representative; Assyrian and Chaldean Christians will jointly elect one representative; and Armenian Christians in the north and those in the south of the country will each elect one representative.

(3) The delimitation of the election constituencies and the number of representatives will be determined by law.

Article 67 [Oath]

(1) Members of the Assembly must take the following oath at the first session of the Assembly and affix their signatures to its text: "In the Name of God, the Compassionate, the Merciful. In the presence of the Glorious Koran, I swear by God, the Exalted and Almighty, and undertake, swearing by my own honor as a human being, to protect the sanctity of Islam and guard the accomplishments of the Islamic Revolution of the Iranian people and the foundations of the Islamic Republic; to protect, as a just trustee, the honor bestowed upon me by the people, to observe piety in fulfilling my duties as people's representative; to remain always committed to the independence and honor of the country; to fulfil my duties towards the nation and the service of the people; to defend the Constitution; and to bear in mind, both in speech and writing and in the expression of my views, the independence of the country, the freedom of the people, and the security of their interests."

(2) Members belonging to the religious minorities will swear by their own sacred books while taking this oath.

(3) Members not attending the first session will perform the ceremony of taking the oath at the first session they attend.

Article 121 [Oath]

The President must take the following oath and affix his signature to it at a session of the Islamic Consultative Assembly in the presence of the head of the judicial power and the members of the Guardian Council: "In the Name of God, the Compassionate, the Merciful, I, as President, swear, in the presence of the noble members of parliament and the people of Iran, by God, the Exalted and Almighty, that I will guard the official religion of the country, the order of the Islamic Republic, and the Constitution of the country; that I will devote all my capacities and abilities to the fulfillment of the responsibilities that I have assumed; that I will dedicate myself to the service of the people, the honor of the country, the propagation of religion and morality, and the support of truth and justice, refraining from every kind of arbitrary behavior; that I will protect the freedom and dignity of all citizens and the rights that the Constitution has accorded the people; that in guarding the frontiers and the political, economic, and cultural independence of the country I will not avoid any necessary measure; that, seeking help from God and following the Prophet of Islam and the infallible Imams (peace be upon them), I will guard, as a pious and selfless trustee, the authority vested in me by the people as a sacred trust, and transfer it to whomever the people may elect after me."

Israel (Declaration of Independence, 1948)

(http://www.yale.edu/lawweb/avalon/israel.htm)

The Land of Israel was the birthplace of the Jewish people. Here their spiritual, religious and national identity was formed. Here they achieved independence and created a culture of national and universal significance. Here they wrote and gave the Bible to the world.

Exiled from Palestine, the Jewish people remained faithful to it in all the countries of their dispersion, never ceasing to pray and hope for their return and the restoration of their national freedom. . . .

The State of Israel will be open to the immigration of Jews from all countries of their dispersion; will promote the development of the country for the benefit of all its inhabitants; will be based on the precepts of liberty, justice and peace taught by the Hebrew Prophets; will uphold the full social and political equality of all its citizens, without distinction of race, creed or sex; will guarantee full freedom of conscience, worship, education and culture; will safeguard the sanctity and inviolability of the shrines and Holy Places of all religions; and will dedicate itself to the principles of the Charter of the United Nations.

Luxembourg (1868)

(http://www.uni-wuerzburg.de/law/lu00000_.html)

Article 19 [Freedom of Religion]

Freedom of religion and of public worship as well as freedom to express one's religious opinions are guaranteed, subject to the repression of offenses committed in the exercise of such freedoms.

Article 20 [No Forced Religion]

No one may be forced to take part in any way whatsoever in the acts and ceremonies of a religion or to observe its days of rest.

Article 22 [State and Church]

The State's intervention in the appointment and installation of heads of religions, the mode of appointing and dismissing other ministers of religion, the right of any of them to correspond with their superiors and to publish their acts and decisions, as well as the Church's relations with the State shall be made the subject of conventions to be submitted to the Chamber of Deputies for the provisions governing its intervention.

Article 25 [Assembly]

Luxembourgers have the right to assemble peaceably and unarmed in compliance with the laws governing the exercise of this right which may not require prior authorization. This provision does not apply to open-air political, religious, or other meetings which are fully governed by laws and police regulations.

Article 106 [Salaries of Priests]

The salaries and pensions of ministers of religion shall be borne by the State and regulated by the law.

Malta (1964)

(http: //www.uni-wuerzburg.de/law/mt00000_.html)

Section 2 [State Religion]

(1) The religion of Malta is the Roman Catholic Apostolic Religion.

(2) The authorities of the Roman Catholic Apostolic Church have the duty and the right to teach which principles are right and which are wrong.

(3) Religious teaching of the Roman Catholic Apostolic Faith shall be provided in all State schools as part of compulsory education.

Section 40 [Religion, Belief]

(1) All persons in Malta shall have full freedom of conscience and enjoy the free exercise of their respective mode of religious worship.

(2) No person shall be required to receive instruction in religion or to show knowledge or proficiency in religion if, in the case of a person who has not attained the age of sixteen years, objection to such requirement is made by the person who according to law has authority over him and, in any other case, if the person so required objects thereto: Provided that no such requirement shall be held to be inconsistent with or in contravention of this section to the extent that the knowledge of, or the proficiency or instruction in, religion is required for the teaching of such religion, or for admission to the priesthood or to a religious order, or for other religious purposes and except so far as that requirement is shown not to be reasonably justifiable in a democratic society. . . .

(3) Nothing contained in or done under the authority of any law shall be held to be inconsistent with or in contravention of subsection (1), to the extent that the law in question makes provision that is reasonably required in the interests of public safety, public order, public morality or decency, public health, or the protection of the rights and freedoms of others, and except so far as that provision or, as the case may be, the thing done under the authority thereof, is shown not to be reasonably justifiable in a democratic society.

Section 45 [Discrimination]

(1) Subject to the provisions of subsections (4), (5) and (7) of this section, no law shall make any provision that is discriminatory either of itself or in its effect.

(2) Subject to the provisions of subsections (6), (7) and (8) of this section, no person shall be treated in a discriminatory manner by any person acting by virtue of any written law or in the performance of the functions of any public office or any public authority.

(3) In this section, the expression "discriminatory" means affording different treatment to different persons attributable wholly or mainly to their respective descriptions by race, place of origin, political opinions, colour, creed or sex whereby persons of one such description are subjected to disabilities or restrictions to which persons of another such description are not made subject or are accorded privileges or advantages which are not accorded to persons of another such description. . . .

(9) A requirement, however made, that the Roman Catholic Apostolic Religion shall be taught by a person professing that religion shall not be held to be inconsistent with or in contravention of this section. . . .

Mauritania (1991)

(http: //www.uni-wuerzburg.de/law/mr00000_.html)

Article 1 [State Integrity, Equal Protection]

(1) Mauritania is an indivisible, democratic, and social Islamic Republic.

(2) The Republic guarantees equality before the law to all of its citizens without distinction as to origin, race, sex, or social condition.

(3) All particularist propaganda of racial or ethnic character shall be punished by the law.

Article 5 [State Religion]

Islam shall be the religion of the people and of the State.

Nepal (1990)

(http: //www.uni-wuerzburg.de/law/np00000_.html)

Article 11 Right to Equality

(2) No discrimination shall be made against any citizen in the application of general laws on grounds of religion (dharma). . . .

(3) The State shall not discriminate among citizens on grounds

of religion, race, sex, caste, tribe, or ideological conviction or any of these. Provided that special provisions may be made by law for the protection and advancement of the interests of women, children, the aged or those who are physically or mentally incapacitated or those who belong to a class which is economically, socially or educationally backward.

(4) No person shall, on the basis of caste, be discriminated against as untouchable, be denied access to any public place, or be deprived of the use of public utilities. Any contravention of this provision shall be punishable by law.

Article 19 Right to Religion

(1) Every person shall have the freedom to profess and practise his own religion as handed down to him from ancient times having due regard to traditional practices; provided that no person shall be entitled to convert another person from one religion to another.

(2) Every religious denomination shall have the right to maintain its independent existence and for this purpose to manage and protect its religious places and trusts.

Article 27 His Majesty

(1) In this Constitution, the words "His Majesty" mean His Majesty the King for the time being reigning, being a descendant of the Great King Prithvi Narayan Shah and an adherent of Aryan Culture and the Hindu Religion.

Nigeria (1989)

(http://star.hsrc.ac.za/constitutions/constnigcont.html)

Article 11

The Government of the Federation or of a State, shall not adopt any religion as State Religion.

Article 37

(1) Every person shall be entitled to freedom of thought, conscience and religion, including freedom to change his religion or belief, and freedom (either alone or in community with others, and in public or in private) to manifest and propagate his religion or belief in worship, teaching, practice and observance.

(2) No person attending any place of education shall be required to receive religious instruction or to take part in or attend any religious ceremony or observance if such instruction, ceremony or observance relates to a religion other than his own, or a religion not approved by his parent or guardian.

(3) No religious community or denomination shall be prevented from providing religious instruction for pupils of that community or denomination in any place of education maintained wholly by that community or denomination. . . .

Article 236

(1) There shall be a Court of Appeal.

(2) The Court of Appeal shall consist of

(a) a President of the Court of Appeal; and

(b) such number of Justices of the Court or Appeal, not less than 15, of which not less than 3 shall be learned in Islamic law, and not less than 3 shall be learned in Customary law, as may be prescribed by an Act of the National Assembly.

Norway (1814)

Sec. 2.

All inhabitants of the Kingdom shall have the right to free exercise of their religion.

The Evangelical-Lutheran religion shall remain the official religion of the State. The inhabitants professing it shall be bound to bring up their children in the same.

Sec. 4.

The King shall at all times profess the Evangelical-Lutheran religion, and uphold and protect the same.

Sec. 12.

. . .More than half the number of Members of the Council of State shall profess the official religion of the State. . . .

Sec. 16.

The King shall give directions for all public church services and public worship, all meetings and assemblies dealing with religious matters, and shall ensure that the public teachers of religion follow the rules prescribed for them.

Sec. 27.

. . .Members of the Council of State who do not profess the official religion of the State shall not take part in proceedings on matters which concern the State Church.

Sec. 100.

There shall be liberty of the Press. No person may be punished for any writing, whatever its contents, which he has caused to be printed or published, unless he willfully and manifestly has either himself shown or incited others to disobedience to the laws, contempt of religion or morality or the constitutional powers, or resistance to their orders, or has advanced false and defamatory accusations against anyone. Everyone shall be free to speak his mind frankly on the administration of the State and on any other subject whatsoever.

Paraguay (1992)

(http://www.uni-wuerzburg.de/law/pa00000_.html)

Article 24 Religious and Ideological Freedom

(1) Freedom of religion, worship, and ideology is hereby recognized without any restrictions other than those established in this Constitution and the law. The State has no official religion.

(2) Relations between the State and the Catholic Church are based on independence, cooperation, and autonomy.

(3) The independence and autonomy of all churches and religious denominations, without restrictions other than those imposed by this Constitution and the law, are hereby guaranteed.

(4) No one may be disturbed, questioned, or forced to give testimony by reason of his beliefs or ideology.

Article 37 The Right to Conscientious Objection

The right to conscientious objection for ethical or religious reasons is hereby recognized for those cases in which this Constitution and the law permits.

Article 74 The Right to Learn and the Freedom to Teach

The right to learn and to have equal access opportunities to the benefits of humanistic culture, science, and technology, without any discrimination, is hereby guaranteed. Freedom to teach, without any requirement other than having ethical integrity and being competent for the job, as well as the right to have a religious education and ideological pluralism are also guaranteed.

Article 82 Recognition of the Catholic Church

The role played by the Catholic Church in the historical and cultural formation of the Republic is hereby recognized.

Article 88 Nondiscrimination

No discrimination will be permitted against workers for reasons of race, sex, age, religion, social status, political, or union preference. Special protection will be given to the work of physically or mentally handicapped individuals.

Article 197 Causes of Ineligibility

The following cannot be candidates for deputies or senators: . . .

(5) Ministers or clergymen of any religion . . . .

Article 235 Causes for Ineligibility

The following are ineligible to run as candidates for president or vice president of the Republic: . . .

5) Ministers or clergymen of any religion . . .

Portugal (1976)

(http: //www.uni-wuerzburg.de/law/po00000_.html)

Article 13 Principle of Equality

(2) No one is privileged, favored, injured, deprived of any right, or exempt from any duty because of his ancestry, sex, race, language, territory of origin, religion, political or ideological convictions, education, economic situation, or social condition.

Article 35 Use of Data Processing . . .

(3) Data processing may not be used in regard to information concerning a person's philosophical or political convictions, party or trade union affiliations, religious beliefs, or private life, except in the case of non-identifiable data for statistical purposes. . . .

Article 41 Freedom of Conscience, Religion, and Worship

(1) Freedom of conscience, religion, and worship are inviolable.

(2) No one may be persecuted, deprived of rights, or exempted from civil obligations or duties because of his convictions or religious practices.

(3) No one may be questioned by any authority about his or her convictions or religious practices, except for gathering of statistical data that cannot be identified individually, nor shall anyone be prejudiced by his or her refusal to reply.

(4) The churches and religious communities are separate from the State and free to organize and exercise their own ceremonies and worship.

(5) The freedom to teach any religion within its own denomination and the use of its own means of public information for the pursuit of its activities, are safeguarded.

(6) The right to be a conscientious objector is safeguarded in accordance with the law.

Article 43 Freedom to Learn and Teach

(2) The State may not arrogate to itself the right to plan education and culture in accordance with any philosophical, aesthetic, political, ideological, or religious guidelines.

(3) Public education is non-denominational.

Article 51 Political Associations and Parties

(3) Without prejudice to the philosophy or ideology inspiring their programs, political parties may not use names that contain terms directly related to any religion or church or use emblems which may be mistaken for national or religious symbols. . . .

Russia (1993)

(http: //www.uni-wuerzburg.de/law/rs00000_.html)

Article 14

(1) The Russian Federation shall be a secular state. No religion may be instituted as state-sponsored or mandatory religion.

(2) Religious associations shall be separated from the state, and shall be equal before the law.

Article 19

(2) The state shall guarantee the equality of rights and liberties regardless of sex, race, nationality, language, origin, property or employment status, residence, attitude to religion, convictions, membership of public associations or any other circumstance. Any restrictions of the rights of citizens on social, racial, national, linguistic or religious grounds shall be forbidden.

Article 28

Everyone shall be guaranteed the right to freedom of conscience, to freedom of religious worship, including the right to profess, individually or jointly with others, any religion, or to profess no religion, to freely choose, possess and disseminate religious or other beliefs, and to act in conformity with them.

Article 29

(2) Propaganda or campaigning inciting social, racial, national or religious hatred and strife is impermissible. The propaganda of social, racial, national, religious or language superiority is forbidden.

(3) No one may be coerced into expressing one's views and convictions or into renouncing them.

Saudi Arabia (Basic Law of Government, 1992)

(http: //www.uni-wuerzburg.de/law/sa00000_.html)

Article 1

The Kingdom of Saudi Arabia is a sovereign Arab Islamic state with Islam as its religion; God's Book and the Sunnah of His Prophet, God's prayers and peace be upon him, are its constitution, Arabic is its language and Riyadh is its capital.

Article 6

Citizens are to pay allegiance to the King in accordance with the holy Koran and the tradition of the Prophet, in submission and obedience, in times of ease and difficulty, fortune and adversity.

Article 7

Government in Saudi Arabia derives power from the Holy Koran and the Prophet's tradition.

Article 8 [Government Principles]

Government in the Kingdom of Saudi Arabia is based on the premise of justice, consultation, and equality in accordance with the Islamic Shari'ah.

Article 23 [Islam]

The state protects Islam; it implements its Shari'ah; it orders people to do right and shun evil; it fulfills the duty regarding God's call.

Article 24 [Holy Places]

The state works to construct and serve the Holy Places; it provides security and care for those who come to perform the pilgrimage and minor pilgrimage in them through the provision of facilities and peace.

Singapore (1963)

(http: //www.uni-wuerzburg.de/law/sn00000_.html)

Article 12 Equality

(2) Except as expressly authorized by this Constitution, there shall be no discrimination against citizens of Singapore on the ground only of religion, race, descent or place of birth in any law or in the appointment to any office or employment under a public authority or in the administration of any law relating to the acquisition, holding, or disposition of property or the establishing or carrying on of any trade, business, profession, vocation or employment.

(3) This article does not invalidate or prohibit

(a) any provision regulating personal law; or

(b) any provision or practice restricting office or employment connected with the affairs of any religion, or of an institution managed by a group professing any religion, to persons professing that religion.

Article 15 Freedom of Religion

(1) Every person has the right to profess and practice his religion and to propagate it.

(2) No person shall be compelled to pay any tax the proceeds of which are specially allocated in whole or in part for the purposes of a religion other than his own.

(3) Every religious group has the right

(a) to manage its own religious affairs;

(b) to establish and maintain institutions for religious or charitable purposes; and

(c) to acquire and own property and hold and administer it in accordance with law.

(4) This article does not authorize any act contrary to any general law relating to public order, public health or morality.

Article 16 Rights in Respect of Education

(1) Without prejudice to the generality of Article 12, there shall be no discrimination against any citizens of Singapore on the grounds only of religion, race, descent or place of birth

(a) in the administration of any educational institution maintained by a public authority, and, in particular, the admission of pupils or students or the payment of fees; or

(b) in providing out of the funds of a public authority financial aid for the maintenance or education of pupils or students in any educational institution (whether or not maintained by a public authority and whether within or outside Singapore).

(2) Every religious group has the right to establish and maintain institutions for the education of children and provide therein instruction in its own religion, and there shall be no discrimination on the ground only of religion in any law relating to such institutions or in the administration of any such law.

(3) No person shall be required to receive instruction in or to take part in any ceremony or act of worship of a religion other than his own.

(4) For the purposes of clause (3), the religion of a person under the age of 18 years shall be decided by his parent or guardian.

Slovakia (1993)

(http: //www.uni-wuerzburg.de/law/lo0000_.html)

Article 12 [Equality]

(2) Basic rights and liberties on the territory of the Slovak Republic are guaranteed to everyone regardless of sex, race, color of skin, language, creed and religion, political or other beliefs, national or social origin, affiliation to a nation or ethnic group, property, descent, or another status. No one must be harmed, preferred, or discriminated against on these grounds. . . .

Article 24 [Freedom of Religion]

(1) The freedoms of thought, conscience, religion, and faith are guaranteed. This right also comprises the possibility to change one's religious belief or faith. Everyone has the right to be without religious belief. Everyone has the right to publicly express his opinion.

(2) Everyone has the right to freely express his religion or faith on his own or together with others, privately or publicly, by means of divine and religious services, by observing religious rites, or by participating in the teaching of religion.

(3) Churches and religious communities administer their own affairs. In particular, they constitute their own bodies, inaugurate their clergymen, organize the teaching of religion, and establish religious orders and other church institutions independently of state bodies. . . .

Article 25

(2) No one must be forced to perform military service if this runs counter to his conscience or religious belief. The details will be specified in a law.

South Korea (1948)

(http: //www.uni-wuerzburg.de/law/ks00000_.html)

Article 11 [Equality]

(1) All citizens are equal before the law, and there may be no discrimination in political, economic, social, or cultural life on account of sex, religion, or social status.

(2) No privileged caste is recognized or ever established in any form. . . .

Article 19 [Conscience]

All citizens enjoy the freedom of conscience.

Article 20 [Religion, Church]

(1) All citizens enjoy the freedom of religion.

(2) No state religion may be recognized, and church and state are to be separated.

Spain (1978)

(http: //www.uni-wuerzburg.de/law/sp00000_.html)

Article 14 [Equality]

Spaniards are equal before the law, without any discrimination for reasons of birth, race, sex, religion, opinion, or any other personal or social condition or circumstance.

Article 16 [Religion, Belief, No State Church]

(1) Freedom of ideology, religion, and cult of individuals and communities is guaranteed without any limitation in their demonstrations other than that which is necessary for the maintenance of public order protected by law.

(2) No one may be obliged to make a declaration on his ideology, religion, or beliefs.

(3) No religion shall have a state character. The public powers shall take into account the religious beliefs of Spanish society and maintain the appropriate relations of cooperation, with the Catholic Church and other denominations.

Syria (1973)

(http: //www.uni-wuerzburg.de/law/sy00000_.html)

Article 3 [Islam]

(1) The religion of the President of the Republic has to be Islam.

(2) Islamic jurisprudence is a main source of legislation.

Article 7 [Oath]

The constitutional oath is as follows: "I swear by God the Almighty to sincerely preserve the republican, democratic, and popular system, respect the constitution and the laws, watch over the interests of the people and the security of the homeland, and work and struggle for the realization of the Arab nation's aims of unity, freedom, and socialism."

Tibet (Charter of the Tibetans In-Exile, 1991)

(http: //www.uni-wuerzburg.de/law/t100000_.html)

Article 9 Equality before the Law

All Tibetan citizens shall be equal before the law and shall enjoy the rights and freedoms set forth in this Chapter without discrimination on grounds of birth, sex, race, religion, language, lay or ordained, social origin, rich or poor, elected position or other status.

Article 10 Religious Freedom

All religious denominations are equal before the law. Every Tibetan shall have the right to freedom of thought, conscience and religion. These religious rights include the freedom to manifest one's belief, to receive initiation into religious traditions, practice with matters relating to religious commitment, such as preaching and worship of any religion, either alone or in community with others.

Article 12 Other Fundamental Rights and Freedoms

Subject to any law imposing restrictions in the immediate and ultimate interest of the Tibetan people and for the benefit of the public, and subject to legal restrictions imposed by the Tibetan Assembly during the tenureship of a civil servant, all Tibetans shall be entitled to the following rights and freedoms: . . .

(g) right to form, and become a member of any religious, cultural, economic, corporate, union or other association. . . .

Tunisia (1991)

(http: //www.uni-wuerzburg.de/law/ts00000_.html)

Article 1 [State]

Tunisia is a free State, independent and sovereign; its religion is Islam, its language is Arabic, and its form is the Republic.

Article 5 [Personal Integrity, Conscience, Belief]

The Tunisian Republic guarantees the inviolability of the human person and freedom of conscience, and protects the free exercise of beliefs, with reservation that they do not disturb the public order.

Article 38 [Head of State]

The President of the Republic is the Head of the State. His religion is Islam.

Article 40 [Eligibility]

(1) Any Tunisian who does not carry another nationality, who is of Moslem religion, and whose father, mother, and paternal and maternal grandfather have been of Tunisian nationality without interruption, may present himself as a candidate for the Presidency of the Republic. . . .

Article 42 [Oath]

The elected President of the Republic gives the following oath before the National Parliament: "I swear by God Almighty to safeguard the national independence and the integrity of the territory, to respect the Constitution and the law, and to watch meticulously over the interests of the Nation."

United States (1789)

(http: //www.uni-wuerzburg.de/law/us00000_.html)

Article VI [Religious Tests]

The Senators and Representatives . . . , and the Members of the several State Legislatures, and all executive and judicial Officers, both of the United States and of the several States, shall be bound by Oath or Affirmation, to support this Constitution; but no religious Test shall ever be required as a Qualification to any Office or public Trust under the United States.

Amendment 1 [Religion, Speech, Press, Assembly, Petition]

Congress shall make no law respecting an establishment of religion or prohibiting the free exercise thereof; or abridging the freedom of speech, or of the press; or the right of the people peaceably to assemble, and to petition the Government for a redress of grievances.

Zambia (1991)

(http: //www.uni-wuerzburg.de/law/za00000_.html)

Article 19 [Freedom of Conscience]

(1) Except with his own consent, no person shall be hindered in the enjoyment of his freedom of conscience, and for the purposes of this Article the said freedom includes freedom of thought and religion, freedom to change his religion or belief, and freedom, either alone or in community with others, and both in public and in private, to manifest and propagate his religion or belief in worship, teaching, practice and observance.

(2) Except with his own consent, or, if he is a minor, the consent of his guardian, no person attending any place of education shall be required to receive religious instruction or to take part in or attend any religious ceremony or observance if that instruction, ceremony or observance relates to a religion other than his own.

(3) No religious community or denomination shall be prevented from providing religious instruction for persons of that community or denomination in the course of any education provided by the community or denomination or from establishing and maintaining institutions to provide social services for such persons.

(4) No person shall be compelled to take any oath which is contrary to his religion or belief or to take any oath in a manner which is contrary to his religion or belief.

(5) Nothing contained in or done under the authority of any law shall be held to be inconsistent with or in contravention of this Article to the extent that it is shown that the law in question makes provision which is reasonably required

(a) in the interests of defence, public safety, public order, public morality or public health; or

(b) for the purpose of protecting the rights and freedoms of other persons, including the right to observe and practice any religion without the unsolicited intervention of members of any other religion; and except so far as that provision or, the thing done under the authority thereof as the case may be, is shown not to be reasonably justified in a democratic society.

Politics and Religion on the Internet

Scholars examining the interrelationship of politics and religion are increasingly turning to the Internet for both primary and secondary research materials. Thousands of Web sites offer an ever growing array of resources, ranging from recent U.S. Supreme Court decisions about the separation of church and state to position papers from advocacy organizations to information about individual denominations.

To assist in the search for useful information, the editors have compiled the following list of sites relevant to the study of politics and religion. The list was current at the time of the book's publication in October 1998. The editors attempted to choose sites that showed some degree of stability, but site addresses may change or sites may disappear altogether.

The list is by no means comprehensive, and many other excellent sites can be identified using a search engine such as AltaVista *(http://altavista.digital.com)* or a directory such as Yahoo! *(http://www.yahoo.com)*. The list is divided into three sections:

1. Politics and Religion: Sites that provide specific information about the topic.
2. Meta-Indexes: Sites that offer multiple links to other religion-oriented Internet sites.
3. Individual Denominations and Organizations: Sites about specific religious denominations or sites operated by religious organizations. Unless otherwise noted, the sites are officially sponsored by their respective churches or groups.

Politics and Religion

American Civil Liberties Union

http://www.aclu.org

The ACLU site provides updates about religion cases in the courts, news about religion-related bills before Congress, and briefing papers about such issues as the separation of church and state, the proposed constitutional amendment on school prayer, and the establishment clause and public schools. The site also has materials about cyber liberties, the death penalty, lesbian and gay rights, and reproductive rights, among other issues.

Americans United for Separation of Church and State

http://www.au.org

This site's highlight is its summaries of church-state legislation introduced in state legislatures around the country. It also has news about recent court cases, updates about congressional actions, articles from the magazine *Church and State,* and pamphlets about such topics as prayer in public schools and education vouchers.

Catholics for a Free Choice

http://www.cath4choice.org

The highlight of this site is a publication titled *Everything You Always Wanted to Know About the Catholic Vote.* Some of the individual article titles include "What do Catholics do in the voting booth?" "Where do Catholics live and vote?" "What's a Catholic politician to do about abortion?" and "How much politicking can churches do?"

Christian Coalition

http://www.cc.org

The Christian Coalition site offers news reports about religious rights, information about state and international affiliates, and selected articles from the magazine *Christian American.* It also has contact information for members of Congress and state legislatures around the country, calendars of daily activities in the U.S. House and Senate, and weekly lists of congressional committee hearings.

Free!

http://www.freedomforum.org/religion/welcome.asp

A strong collection of news stories about religious freedom issues around the country is the highlight of the Free! site. It also has reports and brochures about religion and public schools, religion and the news media, religious liberty in America, and religion among prisoners, among other topics. The site is operated by the Freedom Forum, a foundation that focuses on free press and free speech issues.

Legal Information Institute

http://supct.law.cornell.edu/supct

All U.S. Supreme Court decisions from May 1990 to the present are available at this site, in addition to nearly six hundred historic decisions from before May 1990. The site also provides the Court calendar for the current term and the schedule of oral arguments. It is operated by Cornell University's Legal Information Institute.

National Conference of Catholic Bishops/ United States Catholic Conference

http://www.nccbuscc.org

A variety of church documents, congressional testimony, fact sheets, and press releases about such topics as abortion, cloning, the death penalty, euthanasia, the federal budget, immigration, landmines, refugees, and school vouchers are provided at this site.

National Council of Churches

http://www.ncccusa.org

This site, which is operated by the National Council of Churches, features congressional testimony, legislative analyses, and other resources about religious freedom and persecution around the world. It also has resolutions about antipersonnel landmines, organ and tissue donations, and other issues.

People for the American Way Foundation

http://www.pfaw.org

This site features numerous reports about what it terms the "religious right." Some of the available titles include "Parental Rights: The Trojan Horse of the Religious Right Attack on Public Education," "Attacks on the Freedom to Learn," "Artistic Freedom Under Attack," "The Republicans and the Religious Right," "Teaching Fear: The Religious Right's Campaign Against Sexuality Education," "Buying a Movement: Right-Wing Foundations and American Politics," and "How to Win: Fighting the Religious Right in Your Community." The site also has a set of fact sheets titled "Who's Who on the Religious Right" and updates about religious liberty issues being considered by Congress.

Religion and the Founding of the American Republic

http://lcweb.loc.gov/exhibits/religion

The Library of Congress produced this site, which is an online companion to an exhibit at the library about religion's role in the early days of the United States. The online version has images of more than two hundred objects, including early American books, manuscripts, letters, prints, paintings, and artifacts, in addition to text. The exhibit is divided into seven sections: America as a Religious Refuge: The Seventeenth Century, Religion in Eighteenth-Century America, Religion and the American Revolution, Religion and the Congress of the Confederation, Religion and the State Governments, Religion and the Federal Government, and Religion and the New Republic.

THOMAS

http://thomas.loc.gov

THOMAS, which is named for Thomas Jefferson and operated by the Library of Congress, offers a wealth of congressional information. THOMAS's highlight is its databases containing the full text of all bills introduced in Congress since 1989, the full text of the *Congressional Record* since 1989, and status and summary information for all bills introduced since 1973. THOMAS also offers special links to bills that have received or are expected to receive floor action during the current week and to newsworthy bills that are pending or that have recently been approved. Finally, THOMAS has selected committee reports, answers to frequently asked questions about accessing congressional information, publications titled *How Our Laws Are Made* and *Enactment of a Law*, and links to many other congressional Web sites.

Meta-Indexes

Academic Info—Religious Studies

http://www.academicinfo.net/Religion.html

Internet resources about comparative religion are featured at this site, which is operated by Academic Info. The listings cover such topics as world scriptures, women and religion, studying religion in the electronic age, online publications, religious tolerance and dialogue, religion in the ancient world, Eastern religions, Islam, Zoroastrianism, and new religious movements, among others. Some of the listings are annotated.

APS Guide to Resources in Theology

http://www.utoronto.ca/stmikes/theobook.htm

The annotated links at this site are divided by subject: Anglican/Episcopalian resources, Catholic resources, Orthodox resources, evangelical resources, Protestant resources, ecumenical resources, manuscripts/papyri, textual resources, and miscellaneous resources. It is operated by the University of St. Michael's College, which is affiliated with the University of Toronto.

Berkeley Buddhist Research Center

http://ishi.lib.berkeley.edu/buddhist/bbrc

Translations of Buddhist manuscripts, publications in the Berkeley Buddhist Studies Series, and links to more than two dozen related Internet sites are featured at this site. It is maintained by the Group in Buddhist Studies at the University of California at Berkeley and the Berkeley Buddhist Research Center.

Catholic Online

http://www.catholic.org

Catholic Online provides links to dozens of Catholic-oriented sites, ranging from the Catholic News Service to the Catholic League for Religious and Civil Rights to the Pro-Life Council.

The Center for Middle Eastern Studies

http://menic.utexas.edu/menic

A highlight of this site is its links to Internet sites about specific countries of the Middle East. It also offers hundreds of links to Web sites around the world about such topics as ancient history and archaeology, arts and culture, business and economics, travel, news, religion, and oil and natural resources. The site is operated by the University of Texas at Austin.

Christianity Online

http://www.christianity.net

A searchable database containing links to more than eight thousand Christian Web sites around the world is the highlight of Christianity Online. The links also can be browsed by more than a dozen subjects, including Bible and reference, churches and denominations, ministries and organizations, newsstand, and spiritual growth. Another database contains links to more than sixty-nine hundred church Web sites. The site is operated by *Christianity Today* and also offers daily religious news stories.

Church Internet Assistance
http://www.711.net

Christian-related Internet sites are the focus of Church Internet Assistance, which provides links to hundreds of sites that can be searched or browsed by subject. Dozens of subjects are covered, including abortion alternatives, campus ministries, denominations, ethics, health and medical services, marriage, missions, reference and research, relief and social services, witnessing, and world relief.

Finding God in Cyberspace: A Guide to Religious Studies Resources on the Internet
http://gabriel.franuniv.edu/jp2/fgic.htm

The annotated links at this site are divided into dozens of subjects, ranging from religion in cyberspace to Internet tools for finding religious studies print sources. The site is operated by a librarian at Franciscan University of Steubenville.

Interfaith Working Group
http://www.libertynet.org/iwg/other.html

The hundreds of links at this site are divided by political topic. Some of the subjects covered include homosexuality and religion, religion and sexual orientation, equal treatment for sexual minorities, reproductive freedom, the separation of church and state, religious diversity, and the radical religious right. The site is operated by the Interfaith Working Group, a Philadelphia organization that supports gay rights, reproductive freedom, and the separation of church and state.

Political Science and Public Policy Resources
http://www.lib.msu.edu/harris23/govdocs/pol_sci.htm

This site has links to Internet sites operated by political science journals, think tanks, U.S. political parties and groups, and political science associations. It also provides links to sites that provide information about public policy issues, campaigns, international relations, and area studies. It is operated by a librarian at Michigan State University.

Politics and Religion Academic Network (PARAN)
http://www.linacre.ox.ac.uk/research/PARAN

PARAN provides links to research centers and groups, documents, and conferences. The Politics and Religion Specialist Group of the Political Studies Association of the United Kingdom operates the site.

Religion Religions Religious Studies
http://www.clas.ufl.edu/users/gthursby/rel

This superb site has hundreds of annotated links to some of the best religion resources on the Internet. The listings are divided by a dozen major topics, including Afro-European traditions, Asian traditions, guides to Internet sites, new or alternative religions, relations among religions, Internet and religion, and mysticism resources, among others. The site is maintained by an associate professor at the University of Florida.

Virtual Religion Index
http://religion.rutgers.edu/links/vrindex.html

The detailed site annotations provided by the Virtual Religion Index make it an excellent place to start a search for religion information on the Internet. The links are divided into more than a dozen topics, including academia, American religions, ancient Near Eastern studies, anthropology and sociology of religion, archaeology and religious art, biblical studies, Buddhist tradition, Christian tradition, comparative religion, confessional agencies, East Asian studies, ethics and moral values, Greco-Roman studies, Hindu tradition, Islam, Jewish studies, philosophy and theology, and psychology of religion. The site is operated by a professor in the Religion Department at Rutgers University.

World Council of Churches
http://www.wcc-coe.org

The highlight of this site is its links to more than one hundred Internet sites operated by religious denominations around the world. It also offers links to sites that provide religious news from various denominations and religious publications, in addition to sites operated by aid, development, and relief organizations, many of which are church affiliated.

Worldwide Faith News
http://www.wfn.org/wfn

A database containing thousands of official press releases and other documents issued by religious organizations around the world is the highlight of this site. The documents can be searched in English, French, German, and Spanish. Users also can browse the headlines of all releases posted in the last thirty days and subscribe to a mailing list to receive all documents as they are posted.

Yahoo!
http://www.yahoo.com/Society_and_Culture/Religion

The religion section of the Yahoo! directory offers links to more than ten thousand Internet sites. The links, which are divided by subject, cover church-state issues, creation vs. evolution, faiths and practices, organizations, science and religion, and women, among many other topics.

Individual Denominations and Organizations

All About Mormons (unofficial)
http://www.mormons.org

American Baptist Churches in the USA
http://www.abc-usa.org

Anglicans Online
http://anglican.org/online

The Assemblies of God Online
http://www.ag.org

The Baha'i World
http://www.bahai.org

Billy Graham Evangelistic Association
http://www.graham-assn.org

The Canadian Council of Churches
http://www.web.net/~ccchurch

Catholic Information Center on Internet (unofficial)
http://www.catholic.net

Christian Church (Disciples of Christ)
http://www.disciples.org

The Church of Christ, Scientist
http://www.tfccs.com

The Church of England
http://www.church-of-england.org

The Church of Jesus Christ of Latter-day Saints
http://www.lds.org

Church of the Nazarene
http://www.nazarene.org

Church of the Province of Southern Africa (Anglican)
http://www.cpsa.org.za

The Church of Scotland
http://www.cofs.org.uk

The Churches of Christ
http://church-of-christ.org

DharmaNet International (Buddhism—unofficial)
http://dharmanet.org

Ecumenical Patriarchate of Constantinople
http://www.patriarchate.org

The Episcopal Church
http://ecusa.anglican.org

Evangelical Lutheran Church in America
http://elca.org

Friends United Meeting (Quaker)
http://www.fum.org

General Board of Church and Society, United Methodist Church
http://www.umc-gbcs.org

Greek Orthodox Church of America
http://www.goarch.org

The Hindu Universe (unofficial)
http://www.hindunet.org/home.shtml

Hong Kong Christian Council
http://www.hk.super.net/~hkcc

International Pentecostal Holiness Church
http://www.iphc.org

Islamic Affairs Department at the Royal Embassy of Saudi Arabia (unofficial)
http://www.iad.org

Islamic Foundation of America (unofficial)
http://www.islamic-foundation.org

Islamic Texts and Resources MetaPage (unofficial)
http://wings.buffalo.edu/student-life/sa/muslim/isl/isl.html

Jewishnet (unofficial)
http://jewishnet.net

The Lutheran Church Missouri Synod
http://www.lcms.org

The Lutheran World Federation
http://www.lutheranworld.org

The Moravian Church
http://www.moravian.org

National Council of Churches in Korea
http://www.peacenet.or.kr/ncck

Orthodox Church in America
http://www.oca.org

The Orthodox Presbyterian Church
http://opc.org

Presbyterian Church (U.S.A.)
http://www.pcusa.org

Presbyterian Church in America
http://www.pcanet.org

Presbyterian Church of Brazil
http://www.ipb.org.br

Project Genesis: Torah on the Information Superhighway (unofficial)
http://www.torah.org

Protestant Church in Germany
http://www.ekd.de

The Religious Society of Friends (Quaker)
http://www.quaker.org

Russian Orthodox Church
http://www.russian-orthodox-church.org.ru

SBCNet (Southern Baptist Convention)
http://www.sbcnet.org

Seventh-day Adventist Church
http://www.adventist.org

South African Council of Churches
http://www.sacc.org.za

Syrian Orthodox Church of Antioch
http://syrianorthodoxchurch.org

Unitarian Universalist Association
http://uua.org

United Church of Christ
http://www.ucc.org

United Methodist Information
http://www.umc.org

United Pentecostal Church International
http://www.upci.org

The Vatican
http://www.vatican.va

The Worldwide Anglican Communion
http://www.aco.org

Glossary

Following is a selection of terms that arise frequently in discussions about politics and religion. Far from comprehensive, the glossary nevertheless covers many of the concepts, sacred texts, movements, and phrases that may be unfamiliar to readers and do not appear as separate entries in the encyclopedia.

Act of Settlement. British act of 1701 requiring that the monarch be a member of the Church of England.

Act of Supremacy. British act of 1534 recognizing Henry VIII and succeeding monarchs as "the only supreme head on earth of the Church of England." The act of 1559 established the monarch, then Elizabeth I, as "Supreme Governor" of the Church of England.

Act of Toleration. British act of 1689 that granted limited religious liberty to all Protestant sects. *See also* Dissenting churches.

Act of Uniformity. English law of 1662 that required the use of the Book of Common Prayer and made absence from church punishable by a fine. The act was directed against Roman Catholics and Protestant dissenters from the policies of the Church of England.

Aggiornamento. The goal of "updating" pursued by liberal Roman Catholic leaders of the Second Vatican Council (1962–1965). In seeking to synthesize ancient faith and modern thought, these leaders, including Pope John XXIII, encouraged *ressourcement,* the selective retrieval of neglected Catholic theological and spiritual traditions.

Allah. The one true God in Islam.

Antinomianism. The Christian belief that according to the Gospel the moral law is irrelevant because faith alone is necessary for salvation.

Apostolic succession. The notion that the power for ministry conferred on the apostles by Christ has been passed along to their successors (the bishops, in Roman Catholicism, Anglicanism, and Eastern Orthodoxy).

Augsburg, Peace of. Law of 1555 allowing princes within the Holy Roman Empire to decide whether Roman Catholicism or Lutheranism would prevail in their lands.

Autocephalous. Having its own bishop; independent of external authority. The term describes those national Eastern Orthodox churches that operate independently of the ecumenical patriarchate. *See also* Patriarch.

Autochthonous. Term referring to a church that has local membership, origin, and financial resources. It distinguishes churches that originate in the community from those initiated by outsiders.

Ayatollah. "Sign of God"; the title for the highest-ranking legal scholar in Twelver Shi'ism. *See also* Twelver Shi'ism.

Blue laws. American laws regulating private and public behavior. The first blue laws, printed on blue paper, were enacted in the seventeenth century in the theocratic colony of New Haven and prohibited drunkenness and the breaking of the Sabbath, among other activities deemed offensive. In the nineteenth and early twentieth centuries the prohibition movement gave rise to similar laws outlawing the sale of cigarettes and work on Sunday.

Bodhisattva. In general, one committed to attaining the status of a Buddha; one who vows to attain perfect awakening for the sake of all living creatures.

Book of Common Prayer. Liturgical book of the Anglican Church.

Book of Mormon. Scriptures of the Church of Jesus Christ of Latter-day Saints. Church members, known as Mormons, believe that the book was revealed on gold tablets to Joseph Smith, the church's founder.

Brahma. The supreme being in Hinduism.

Broad Church movement. Nineteenth-century movement within the Church of England advocating liberal stands on theology and Bible study. The movement challenged Low Church proponents, who emphasized the Bible and preaching. *See also* High Church; Low Church; Oxford movement.

Caesaropapism. Form of government in which the lay head of state exercises authority over the church and seeks to influence doctrinal or liturgical affairs. A form of caesaropapism existed under Charlemagne and in czarist Russia, the Holy Roman Empire, and Gallican France. *See also* Augsburg, Peace of; *Cuius regio, eius religio;* Gallicanism.

Caliph. The successor of Muhammad and the supreme leader of the unified Muslim community. The rulership of the caliph is the caliphate.

Canon law. The codified body of regulations governing, individually, the Roman Catholic, Orthodox, and Anglican Churches.

Charismatics. Christian individuals, groups, or churches that place special emphasis on the activity of the Holy Spirit in religious life. Charismatic persons practice ecstatic forms of worship and believe in the "gifts of the Holy Spirit," including speaking in tongues *(glossolalia).*

Concordats. Public treaties between the Vatican and individual secular governments.

Confessing Church. The church movement led by theologians Karl Barth and Dietrich Bonhoeffer that resisted Adolf Hitler's incorporation of German churches into the Nazi Party during World

War II. The Confessing Church in 1934 issued the Barmen Declaration opposing Nazi aggression and proclaiming the independence of the German Evangelical Church. *See also* Barmen Declaration in Documents section.

Consistory. A collegial body comprising both pastors and lay elders; in Roman Catholicism, a formal meeting of cardinals convoked and presided over by the pope.

Coptic Church. The independent Christian church in Egypt and Ethiopia. The Coptic Church is believed to have been founded by Mark the Evangelist, the first bishop of Alexandria.

Cuius regio, eius religio. "In a ruler's country, the ruler's religion"; the guiding principle of the Peace of Augsburg (1555), permitting rulers of the Holy Roman Empire to choose the religion of their realm. *See also* Augsburg, Peace of.

Curia. The Roman Catholic Church's central administrative offices.

Dar al-Harb. *See* Dar al-Islam.

Dar al-Islam. The land of Islam, where Islamic law applies; one of the two spheres into which Islamic legal scholars divide the world, the other sphere being *Dar al-Harb,* the land of war, where the absence of Islamic law fosters anarchy and immorality. It is the duty of the Islamic state to reduce *Dar al-Harb*—through peaceful means if possible, through war if necessary—until it has been incorporated into *Dar al-Islam.*

Deism. The system of belief asserting that God created the world but does not exercise control over it.

Dhimmis. Non-Muslim religious groups exercising communal autonomy within the Islamic state in return for tax payments.

Diaconia theology. The policy of accommodation followed by some East European churches and world church bodies in response to the advance of communist atheism in the 1940s and 1950s.

Dispensationalism. The Christian belief that history is divided into several periods, or dispensations, the last of which will be the reign of Christ. A version of dispensationalism, termed premillennial, is professed by some evangelical Protestant groups and the Jehovah's Witnesses. It holds that Christ will reign one thousand years in Jerusalem before the final judgment.

Dissenting churches. Churches that object to the requirements of established state churches; also known as nonconforming churches. The term was first used to describe Protestant churches that dissented from the policies of the Church of England not long after the Reformation.

Dissolution of monasteries. Occurred in Great Britain in the 1530s under the supervision of Thomas Cromwell, minister to King Henry VIII. Following the king's break with the Roman Catholic Church over his decision to divorce his wife, Katharine, Catholic clergy were persecuted, monasteries were seized by the crown, and some of their property was given to the landed gentry.

Divine right of kings. A monarch's claim to absolute authority based on the belief that the right to rule has been granted by God and comes from birth alone.

Eastern rite churches. Catholic churches that originated in Eastern Europe, Asia, or Africa, possess their own distinctive liturgical traditions, and are distinguished by their national or ethnic character. Eastern rite churches are outnumbered within the Catholic Church by those that practice the Latin rite.

Ecclesiastical. Concerning the laws, jurisdiction, or official organization of the church.

Edict of Nantes. Decree of 1598 that defined the rights of the persecuted French Protestants, or Huguenots, in the wake of the Wars of Religion. Among the rights established by the decree were freedom of conscience and worship and the right to hold public office.

Encyclical. In Roman Catholicism, a papal letter directed to a group of bishops with the intent of informing the entire church on a matter of moral importance. Many encyclicals had wide-ranging influence; for example, *Rerum Novarum* (1891) prepared the way for the involvement of the modern church in social and economic issues around the world.

Episcopal. Governed by bishops (from the Latin *episcopus).*

Erastian government. A unitary form of government in which religion is subject to the state. The term is derived from the name of Thomas Erastus, a Swiss Protestant theologian who feared the encroachment of the church upon civil authority. *See also* Theocracy.

Establishment clause. *See* Free exercise clause.

Fatwa. A religious edict concerning law, morals, or doctrine issued by a recognized authority on Islamic jurisprudence.

Fifth Monarchists. British religious group spun off from the Particular Baptists and active from the 1640s to the 1660s. Its members believed that the reign of Jesus Christ on Earth might be ushered in by apocalyptic violence. Consequently, they were involved in several insurrections in the late 1650s and early 1660s. *See also* Particular Baptists.

First Great Awakening. Revival movement based largely on Calvinist theology that occurred in the American colonies during the 1730s and 1740s. The movement helped to unify colonists and prepare them for their break with England. *See also* Second Great Awakening.

Five pillars of Islam. The five duties required of all Muslims: (1) the statement of faith ("There is no God but God, and Muhammad is the Prophet of God"); (2) almsgiving; (3) prayer performed five times daily; (4) fasting from dawn to sunset during the month of Ramadan, the ninth month of the Islamic year; and (5) the pilgrimage to Mecca, or *hajj.*

Free exercise clause. The provision in the First Amendment to the U.S. Constitution granting freedom of religion and prohibiting state establishment of religion.

Gallicanism. A movement originated by the French Roman Catholic Church in 1682 that advocated administrative independence from papal control for the Roman Catholic churches of each nation. *See also* Ultramontanism.

Glorious Revolution of 1688. The events culminating in the ouster of the English king James II, who was believed to want to restore Roman Catholicism in place of the Anglican Church, and the succession of Protestants William of Orange and his wife Mary (daughter of James) at the invitation of parliamentary leaders. The revolution guaranteed the supremacy of Parliament over the king and assured the Protestant succession.

Hadith. The sayings and actions attributed to Muhammad that do not appear in the Qur'an. *See also* Qur'an.

Hajj. The pilgrimage to Mecca, to be made if at all possible at least once in the life of every Muslim. *See also* Five pillars of Islam.

High Church. The liturgical tradition within the Church of England that emphasizes "Catholic" ritual and sacramental theology, as opposed to the more Protestant Low Church tradition. *See also* Broad Church movement; Low Church; Oxford movement.

Holy See. The Diocese of Rome, the chief diocese of the Roman Catholic Church; the Vatican.

Huguenots. Calvinist Protestants who suffered persecution in France from the sixteenth to the eighteenth centuries. *See also* Edict of Nantes.

Imam. In Sunni Islam, a prayer leader. In Shi'ite Islam, the term refers to a historical leader of the Shi'ite community. Sunnis and Shi'ites differ over the imam's selection, status, and role in the Muslim community.

Inculturation. In the Roman Catholic Church, the process by which the Gospel is adapted to a particular culture.

Indulgence. The remission of temporal punishment for sins committed. The selling of indulgences by the Roman Catholic Church came under attack in the late Middle Ages and was one of the principal causes of the Protestant Reformation.

Intifada. The Arab uprising initiated in 1987 against Israel's occupation of the West Bank and Gaza Strip.

Jahiliyya. The period of "pre-Islamic ignorance" before knowledge of God brought civilization to the world.

Jihad. Islamic term for struggle, especially that of believers against persecution and idolatry. This struggle may take the form of war in certain circumstances.

Just wage and just price. The idea that the determination of wages and prices should depend not only on market forces but also on the responsibility of society to ensure that work is rewarded according to the reasonable needs of workers.

Ka'ba. The cubic, black-draped stone structure located within the Grand Mosque in Mecca and regarded by Muslims as the holiest place on earth.

Karma. The doctrine held by Buddhists and Hindus that the force generated by a person's actions, whether positive or negative, has consequences that determine the cycle of birth and death.

Koran. *See* Qur'an.

Lateran Treaty. The concordat signed in 1929 by Italian dictator Benito Mussolini and the papal secretary of state. In establishing Vatican City, recognizing it as an independent state, and making Roman Catholicism the official religion of Italy, the agreement resolved the "Roman Question," or the problems that arose from Italy's restriction in 1871 of papal sovereignty. *See also* Roman Question.

"Lemon test." The judicial test formulated by the U.S. Supreme Court to determine whether laws violate the establishment clause of the First Amendment to the U.S. Constitution. Introduced in *Lemon v. Kurtzman* (1971), the test holds that a statute must meet three criteria to be constitutionally permissible: (1) it must have a secular legislative purpose, (2) its principal effect must be one that neither advances nor inhibits religion, and (3) it must not foster excessive government entanglement with religion.

Low Church. The liturgical tradition within the Church of England that emphasizes evangelism, preaching, and the Bible, as opposed to the High Church, or Anglo-Catholic, tradition. *See also* Broad Church movement; High Church; Oxford movement.

Marabout. In West Africa, a Muslim spiritual leader who is influential in national politics. Marabouts are religious specialists trained in the knowledge of the Qur'an, as well as in traditional medicine, the making of amulets, and occult science.

Maronites. Lebanese Christians whose religious practice incorporates features of Roman Catholic and Eastern rites.

Monophysitism. The belief, present among churches in Armenia, Syria, Egypt, and Ethiopia, that Jesus Christ had only one nature, wholly divine. It opposes the notion that Christ was both fully God and fully human.

Mujahedin. Muslim activists who seek to resanctify Muslim society, sometimes by waging war. The name was used by Muslim rebels fighting the Soviet-backed Marxist regime in Afghanistan throughout the 1980s.

Nonconforming churches. *See* Dissenting churches.

Oxford movement. The nineteenth-century movement within the Church of England that emphasized ritual and reinvigorated the High Church tradition. The movement challenged Low Church proponents, who stressed the Bible and preaching. *See also* Broad Church movement; Low Church.

Panca Sila. In Indonesia, the "five principles" accepted as the ideological basis of the state by most Muslim leaders, who believe that Islam does not require an Islamic state. The Panca Sila rejects formal separation of religion and state, affirms that religion is a public good, and directs the state to promote religious life.

Papal States. Independent territory in central Italy under the temporal rule of the popes until 1870, when Italy was unified. *See also* Roman Question.

Particular Baptists. A sect of Puritans who renounced infant baptism and sought Spirit-led preaching rather than ministry by designated clerics.

Pastoral letter. In Roman Catholicism, a letter on church instruction or activity from a bishop or bishops to his people.

Patriarch. Title for a bishop with authority over other bishops in the Roman Catholic, Orthodox, or Oriental Orthodox Churches.

Peace churches. Churches opposed to war on ethical grounds, including Mennonites, Amish, and Quakers.

Petrine Commission. Foundation of the Roman Catholic doctrine of papal primacy, which recognizes the direct authority of the pope, the successor of St. Peter, over the whole church. The commission is expressed in Christ's words to Peter: "And so I say to you, you are Peter, and upon this rock I will build my church, and the gates of the netherworld shall not prevail against it. I give you the keys to the kingdom. Whatever you bind on earth shall be bound in heaven; and whatever you loose on earth shall be loosed in heaven."

Pillarization. The division of society on the basis of religion or ideology, which has been institutionalized in the Low Countries (Belgium and the Netherlands).

Primus interpares. "First among equals." The term describes the authority of the chief bishop in Anglican and Orthodox churches in relation to other bishops. Unlike the authority of the pope, which is absolute and extends over the entire Roman Catholic Church, this authority is considered honorary, conferring prestige and an elevated platform from which to speak on church matters but lacking in enforcement power.

Qur'an (also Koran). The sacred book of Islam containing the word of God as revealed to the prophet Muhammad. *See also* Hadith.

Rapture. In the New Testament, the event during which the elect on earth, at the end of the world, will be "raised into the air" with Christ. The rapture figures prominently in millennialist theology.

Reformed churches. Churches that hold to the system of doctrine and polity as set out by John Calvin in the sixteenth century and expressed in various "Reformed" confessions.

Roman Question. The complications arising from the 1871 annexation by Italy of the Papal States, the independent territory under temporal papal authority. Italy awarded the Roman Catholic Church an annual indemnity as compensation for the loss of the Papal States, but the church refused to accept it. The Roman Question was resolved by the Lateran Treaty (1929). *See also* Lateran Treaty.

Sayyid. Islamic term for prince or lord.

Second Great Awakening (1800–1835). A religious revival movement based on the Enlightenment principle of confidence in human reason. It envisioned the possibility of self-improvement for individuals and reform for society as it strove to abolish slavery, reduce drunkenness, improve education, and help the indigent. *See also* First Great Awakening.

Shari'a. Islamic law based on the Qur'an and the *sunna. See also* Qur'an; Sunna.

Shaykh. An elder, chief, teacher, or honored person of Islam.

Shi'a. One of the two major branches of Islam, the other being the larger Sunni branch. Shi'a Muslims believe that Ali ibn Abi Talib and his heirs are the rightful inheritors of Muhammad's political and religious authority. *See also* Sunni; Twelver Shi'ism.

Social Darwinism. The application of scientist Charles Darwin's theories of biological evolution—"natural selection" and "survival of the fittest"—to human social and economic systems.

Subsidiarity. A concept established by Pope Pius XI in the 1931 encyclical *Quadragesimo Anno.* Warning against the encroachments of the modern state, subsidiarity holds that a community of a higher order should not interfere in the internal life of a community of a lower order, depriving the latter of its appropriate functions.

Sufism. The mystical tradition of Islam.

Sunna. The written record of the prophet Muhammad's words and actions. Binding on all Muslims, the *sunna,* together with the Qur'an, forms the Shari'a, or Islamic law. *See also* Qur'an; Shari'a.

Sunni. One of the two major branches of Islam, the other being the smaller Shi'a branch. Sunni Muslims accept the *sunna* and the historic succession of the caliph, the leader chosen by elders as Muhammad's successor. *See also* Caliph; Shi'a; Sunna.

Sura. A collection of verses contained in a single chapter or literary division of the Qur'an.

Syncretism. The intermingling of different beliefs and practices. The term is frequently applied to the religions of developing nations.

Synod. A gathering of church officials and representatives with policy-making authority.

Ta'if accord. Agreement of 1989 that provided the blueprint for ending the Lebanese civil war (1975–1990). The accord retained Lebanon's confessional system of government, in which parliamentary seats are allocated by religious affiliation, but reshuffled the political privileges between religious sects. Parliament was split evenly between Christians and Muslims, the prerogatives of the Maronite president were reduced by the power of the Sunni prime minister, and the power of the Shi'i speaker of the parliament was enhanced.

Talmud. The collection of authoritative writings that constitutes Jewish civil and religious law.

Theocracy. A unitary form of government in which the state is subordinate to religion; the opposite of an Erastian form of government. *See also* Erastian government; Unitary government.

Theodicy. An attempt to reconcile the existence of evil and suffering in the world with a belief in a God who is just, all powerful, and all knowing.

Torah. Specifically, the five books of Moses, or the Pentateuch. More broadly, the term refers to all of the Hebrew scriptures that make up the Old Testament.

Tories. British political party. The first Tories were supporters of the duke of York, the future James II, whose succession to the throne was opposed because of his Roman Catholicism. Led by the first earl of Shaftesbury, those who opposed succession came to be known as Whigs. Tories were supporters of divine right, tradition, and ecclesiastical uniformity.

Trent, Council of. Roman Catholic ecumenical council held between 1545 and 1563 in Trent, Italy, that sought to reform the church and respond to the challenges of the Protestant Reformation.

Twelver Shi'ism. The largest movement within Shi'a Islam. Twelver Shi'ites believe that twelve imams, or authoritative leaders of the community and interpreters of religion, existed on earth, the last one having left the world in 874. Since then, Twelver Shi'ites have looked for guidance in religious and political matters to their scholars, called *mujtahids* or *ayatollahs.*

Ulama. Scholars of Islamic law.

Ultramontanism. A movement that called for greater papal supremacy over the national churches. Ultramontanism backed the universal supremacy of the pope and culminated in the decree of papal infallibility at the First Vatican Council (1869–1870). *See also* Gallicanism.

Umma. The Muslim community of believers.

Unitary government. Form of government in which church and state are not separate but unified. *See also* Erastian government; Theocracy.

"Urbi et orbi." "To the city [Rome] and the world"; the designation given certain papal blessings.

Vedas. The wide-ranging collection of Hindu sacred texts.

Westminster Confession. The Calvinist statement of belief drafted in 1643 and adopted by the Scottish Parliament in 1649. It is the creed of English-speaking Presbyterians.

Whigs. *See* Tories.

Yeshiva. A Jewish academy that instructs its all-male student body in talmudic literature; also a Jewish primary or secondary school offering secular as well as religious courses. *See also* Talmud.

Yishuv. The Jewish community in Israel.

Credits for Photographs and Other Images

A
Abortion / *Michael Jenkins, Congressional Quarterly*
African American experience / *NAACP*
Anabaptists / *Reuters*
Anglicanism / *Reuters*
Anti-Semitism / *U.S. Holocaust Memorial Museum*
Atatürk, Kemal / *Library of Congress*

B
Baptists / *Library of Congress*
Barth, Karl / *Bettmann*
Bonhoeffer, Dietrich / *Christian Kaiser Verlag*
Bourguiba, Habib / *Library of Congress*
Buddha / *Bettmann*
Buddhism / *Reuters*
Burke, Edmund / *Library of Congress*

C
Calvinism / *Library of Congress*
Catholicism, Roman / *Catholic News Service*
Censorship / *Reuters/Bettmann*
Christian Science / *Church of Christ, Scientist*
Christianity / *The Metropolitan Museum of Art*
Civil disobedience / *UPI/Bettmann*
Civil religion / *Library of Congress*
Civil rights movement / *Tommy Giles*
Communism / *Reuters*
Confucius / *National Archives*
Constitution, U.S. / *Bettmann*
Cults / *Reuters*

D
Dalai Lama / *Bettmann*
Day, Dorothy / *Marquette University Archives*
Douglass, Frederick / *Bettmann*
Druze / *Reuters*
Durkheim, Emile / *Bettmann*

E
English revolution / *The Bettmann Archive*

F
Fascism / *Library of Congress*
Friends, Society of / *Library of Congress*
Fundamentalism / *Michael Jenkins, Congressional Quarterly*

G
Gandhi, Mohandas Karamchand / *Library of Congress*
Genocide / *U.S. Holocaust Memorial Museum*
Graham, Billy / *Reuters*

H
Havel, Václav / *Michael Jenkins, Congressional Quarterly*
Herzl, Theodor / *Library of Congress*
Heschel, Abraham Joshua / *Bettmann*
Hinduism / *India Tourism Office*
Hobbes, Thomas / *Library of Congress*
Holocaust / *U.S. Holocaust Memorial Museum*

I
Iqbal, Muhammad / *Bettmann*
Islam / *Saudi Arabian Embassy*

J
James, William / *Houghton Library, Harvard University*
Jefferson, Thomas / *Library of Congress*
Jehovah's Witnesses / *Library of Congress*
Jerusalem / *Courtesy of the Embassy of Israel*
Jesus / *Canadian Press*
Jinnah, Muhammad Ali / *Pakistani Embassy*
Judaism / *Reuters*

K
Khomeini, Ruholla Musavi / *Reuters/Bettmann*
King, Martin Luther, Jr./ *Bettmann*

L
Latter-day Saints, Church of Jesus Christ of / *Church of Jesus Christ of Latter-day Saints*
Lobbying, Religious / *Reuters*
Lutheranism / *© Austrian Archives/Corbis*

M
Madison, James / *Library of Congress*
Maritain, Jacques / *French Embassy*
Marxism / *Library of Congress*
Mecca / *Saudi Arabian Embassy*
Merton, Thomas / *Thomas Merton Center, Bellarmine College*
Methodism / *Library of Congress*
Millennialism / *Reuters*
Muhammad / *The British Library*
Muslim encounters with the West / *Library of Congress*

N
Nasser, Gamal Abdel / *© Hulton-Deutsch Collection/Corbis*
Nation of Islam/ *Library of Congress*
Native Americans / *Library of Congress*
Nhat Hanh, Thich / *Parallax Press*
Niebuhr, Reinhold / *Bettmann*
Nietzsche, Friedrich / *Library of Congress*

P
Paganism / *Harper San Francisco*
Papacy / *Archive Photos*
Pentecostalism / *Flower Pentecostal Heritage Center*
Presbyterians / *Library of Congress*
Protestantism / *Archive Photos*

Q

Qaddafi, Muammar al- / *Bettmann*

R

Reformation / *Library of Congress*
Romero, Oscar A./ *Bettmann*

S

Sacred places / *Library of Congress*
Sadat, Anwar / *Library of Congress*
Shinto / *Reuters*
Social Gospel / *Library of Congress*
Solzhenitsyn, Aleksandr I. / *Bettmann*

South Africa / *Reuters*
Sukarno, Achmad / *National Archives*

T

Temperance movements / *Library of Congress*
Teresa, Mother / *Ronald Reagan Library*
Theocracy / *Reuters*
Tocqueville, Alexis de / *The Bettmann Archive*

U

Unification Church / *Reuters*
Utopianism / *The Frick Collection*

V

Vatican / *Catholic News Service*
Vatican Council, Second / *Catholic News Service*

W

War / *Reuters* / *Bettmann*
Weber, Max / *Library of Congress*

Index

M

O

P